AUTOCAD® 2010 AND AUTOCAD LT® 2010

NO EXPERIENCE REQUIRED™

AUTOCAD® 2010 AND AUTOCAD LT® 2010
NO EXPERIENCE REQUIRED™

Jon McFarland

Wiley Publishing, Inc.

Senior Acquisitions Editor: Willem Knibbe
Development Editor: Gary Schwartz
Technical Editor: John Evansco
Production Editor: Christine O'Connor
Copy Editor: Liz Welch
Production Manager: Tim Tate
Vice President and Executive Group Publisher: Richard Swadley
Vice President and Publisher: Neil Edde
Book Designer and Compositor: Franz Baumhackl
Proofreader: Jen Larsen, Word One New York
Indexer: Robert Swanson
Project Coordinator, Cover: Lynsey Stanford
Cover Designer: Ryan Sneed
Cover Image: Dieter Spannknebel / Digital Vision / Getty Images, Inc.

Library of Congress Cataloging-in-Publication Data

McFarland, Jon.

  AutoCAD 2010 and AutoCAD LT 2010 : no experience required / Jon McFarland.

    p. cm.

  ISBN 978-0-470-43868-8 (paper/website)

  1. Computer graphics. 2. AutoCAD. I. Title.

  T385.M3783 2009

  620'.00420285536—dc22

                              2009009717

Dear Reader,

Thank you for choosing *AutoCAD 2010 and AutoCAD LT 2010: No Experienced Required.* This book is part of a family of premium-quality Sybex books, all of which are written by outstanding authors who combine practical experience with a gift for teaching.

Sybex was founded in 1976. More than thirty years later, we're still committed to producing consistently exceptional books. With each of our titles we're working hard to set a new standard for the industry. From the paper we print on, to the authors we work with, our goal is to bring you the best books available.

I hope you see all that reflected in these pages. I'd be very interested to hear your comments and get your feedback on how we're doing. Feel free to let me know what you think about this or any other Sybex book by sending me an email at nedde@wiley.com, or if you think you've found a technical error in this book, please visit **http://sybex.custhelp.com**. Customer feedback is critical to our efforts at Sybex.

Best regards,

NEIL EDDE
Vice President and Publisher
Sybex, an Imprint of Wiley

To my lovely wife, Lucy,
and our two sons,
Zach and Jacob

ACKNOWLEDGMENTS

I am grateful to the many people who contributed to the publication of this update of the book. For those involved in this project at Sybex and Wiley, I extend my thanks.

Sandy Jaffe clarified the nuances of the contract, and helped with the logistics around the signing. Thanks to Senior Acquisitions Editor Willem Knibbe who brought me into this project and has served as acquisitions editor for this and previous updates. He has continued to rally support for its publication, and he has maintained a constructive relationship with Jim Quanci and Denis Cadu of the Autodesk Developer Network. Thanks to Shaan Hurley and Nate Bartley from Autodesk, who provided me with access to the software in development and answered many of my questions.

Thanks to John Evansco, who provided his expertise to do the technical editing. I very much appreciate his lending his teaching and engineering expertise in checking the text and figures for technical accuracy. Gary Schwartz served well as developmental editor and quickly responded to issues that arose. The production editor was Christine O'Connor; she kept track of the submissions and all the changes and, thanks to her, the work progressed at a rate to meet the schedule. Liz Welch served as copy editor and, in doing so, helped update the language and syntax to keep the book very readable, and she was also an asset in this project. Thanks to Andre Evans for providing the excellent hand-drawn graphics in Chapter 16.

Finally, I want to thank the production team at Wiley. Franz Baumhackl has again served skillfully as compositor and designer. Jen Larsen took on the arduous task of proofreader, and Jack Lewis served as indexer. They have all performed very well. Everyone involved has been successful in maintaining standards of high quality, and I appreciate their work on this book.

About the Author

Jon McFarland manages the CAD department for a company that owns, develops, and manages retail, office and, residential properties. He has written and contributed to several books on AutoCAD and 3ds Max and teaches AutoCAD and 3ds Max at the college level.

CONTENTS AT A GLANCE

CONTENTS

CHAPTER 9   Using Dynamic Blocks and Tables   409

CHAPTER 10   Generating Elevations   463

CHAPTER 11   Working with Hatches, Gradients, and Tool Palettes   509

CHAPTER 12   Dimensioning a Drawing   545

CHAPTER 13   Managing External References   601

CHAPTER 14   Using Layouts to Set Up a Print   637

CHAPTER 17   Rendering and Materials   791

INTRODUCTION

This book was born of the need for a simple, yet engaging tutorial that would help beginners step into the world of AutoCAD or AutoCAD LT without feeling intimidated. That tutorial has evolved over the years into a full introduction to the ways in which architects and civil and structural engineers use AutoCAD to increase their efficiency and ability to produce state-of-the-art computerized production drawings and designs.

Because AutoCAD and AutoCAD LT are so similar, it makes sense to cover the basics of both programs in one book. For most of the book, the word *AutoCAD* stands for both AutoCAD and AutoCAD LT.

When you come to a section of a chapter that applies to AutoCAD only, the icon shown here is displayed in the margin to alert you. When appropriate, extra information for AutoCAD LT users is provided to give you a workaround or otherwise keep you in step with the tutorial.

The last two chapters, which are an introduction to drawing in 3D, apply only to AutoCAD, because AutoCAD LT doesn't have AutoCAD's 3D commands and features. But LT users can be assured that LT is very much the same program as AutoCAD, with only minor differences. You'll be prompted when those differences, most of which are 3D features, come along.

This book is directed toward AutoCAD and AutoCAD LT novices—users who know how to use a computer and perform basic file-managing tasks, such as creating new folders and saving and moving files, but who know nothing or little about AutoCAD or LT (as I'll call AutoCAD LT throughout the book). If you're new to the construction and design professions, this book will be an excellent companion as you learn AutoCAD. If you're already practicing in those fields, you'll immediately be able to apply the skills you'll pick up from this book to real-world projects. The exercises have been successfully used to train architects, engineers, and contractors, as well as college and high school students, in the basics of AutoCAD.

For those of you in other trades and professions, the project that runs through the book—drawing a small cabin—has been kept simple so that it doesn't require special training in architecture or construction. Also, most chapters have additional information and exercises specifically designed for non-AEC users. Anyone wanting to learn AutoCAD will find this book helpful.

What Will You Learn from This Book?

Learning AutoCAD, like learning any complex computer program, requires a significant commitment of time and attention and, to some extent, a tolerance for repetition. You must understand new concepts to operate the program and to appreciate its potential as a drafting and design tool. However, to become proficient at AutoCAD, you must also use the commands enough times to gain an intuitive sense of how they work and how parts of a drawing are constructed.

At the end of most chapters, you'll find one or more additional exercises and a checklist of the tools you have learned (or should have learned). The steps in the tutorial have a degree of repetition built into them that allows you to work through new commands several times and build up confidence before you move on to the next chapter.

Progressing through the book, the chapters fall into five general areas of study:

▶ Chapters 1 through 3 familiarize you with the organization of the AutoCAD user interface, cover a few of the basic commands, and equip you with the tools necessary to set up a new drawing.

▶ Chapters 4 and 5 introduce the basic drawing commands and develop drawing strategies that will help you use commands efficiently.

▶ Chapters 6 through 11 work with AutoCAD's major features.

▶ Chapters 12 through 15 examine intermediate and advanced Auto-CAD features.

▶ Chapters 16 and 17 cover the 3D modeling tools and the methods for applying materials in AutoCAD.

In the process of exploring these elements, you'll follow the steps involved in laying out the floor plan of a small cabin. You'll then learn how to generate elevations from the floor plan and, eventually, how to set up a title block and layouts to print your drawing. Along the way, you'll also learn how to do the following:

▶ Use the basic drawing and modify commands in a strategic manner

▶ Set up layers

▶ Assign colors to your drawing

▶ Define and insert blocks

▶ Generate elevation views

▶ Place hatch patterns and fills on building components

▶ Use text in your drawing

Chapters in the latter part of the book touch on more advanced features of AutoCAD, including:

- ▶ Dimensioning the floor plan

- ▶ Drawing a site plan

- ▶ Using external references

- ▶ Setting up a drawing for printing with layouts

- ▶ Making a print of your drawing

- ▶ Working in 3D (for AutoCAD users)

All these features are taught using the cabin as a continuing project. As a result, you'll build a set of drawings that document your progress throughout the project. You can use these drawings later as reference material if you need to refresh your memory with material covering a specific skill.

At the end of the book is a glossary of terms that are used in the book and are related to AutoCAD and building design. This is followed by an index.

Files on the Website

If you're already somewhat familiar with AutoCAD and you're reading only some of the chapters, or if you want to check your work on the cabin against the book at different stages, you can pull accompanying files from this book's page on Wiley's website at www.sybex.com/go/autocad2010ner. Click the Resources & Downloads button on that page.

Hints for Success

Because this book is essentially a step-by-step tutorial, it has a common side effect with tutorials of this type. After you finish a chapter and see that you have progressed further through the cabin project, you may wonder exactly what you just did and whether you could do it again without the help of the step-by-step instructions.

This feeling is a natural result of this type of learning tool, and you can do a couple of things to get beyond it:

- ▶ You can work through the chapter again. Doing so may seem tedious, but it will help you draw faster. You'll be able to accomplish the same task in half the time it took you to do it the first time. If you do a chapter a third time, you'll halve your time again. Each time you repeat a chapter, you can skip more and more of the explicit instructions, and eventually you'll be able to execute the commands and finish the chapter by just looking at the figures and glancing at the text. In many ways, this process is like learning a musical instrument. You must go slowly at first, but over time and through practice, your pace will pick up.

▶ Another suggestion for honing your skills is to follow the course of the book but apply the steps to a different project. You might draw your own living space or design a new one. If you have a real-life design project that isn't too complex, that's even better. Your chances for success in learning AutoCAD, or any computer program, are greatly increased when you're highly motivated, and a real project of an appropriate size can be the perfect motivator.

Ready, Set...

When I started learning AutoCAD about 19 years ago, I experienced a level of frustration that I never thought I was capable of feeling. When I finally got over the hump and began feeling that I could successfully draw with this program after all, I told myself that I would someday figure out a way to help others get past their initial frustration. That was the primary motivating force for my writing this book. I hope it works for you and that you too get some enjoyment while learning AutoCAD. As the title says, there is "no experience required"—only an interest in the subject and a willingness to learn!

CHAPTER 1

Getting to Know AutoCAD

▶ Opening a new drawing

▶ Getting familiar with the AutoCAD and AutoCAD LT graphics windows

▶ Modifying the display

▶ Displaying and arranging AutoCAD tools

Your introduction to AutoCAD and AutoCAD LT begins with a tour of the user interfaces of the two programs. In this chapter, you'll also learn how to use some tools that help you control their appearance and how to find and start commands. For the material covered in this chapter, the two applications are almost identical in appearance. Therefore, as you tour AutoCAD, I'll point out any differences between AutoCAD and AutoCAD LT. In general, LT is a 2D program, so it doesn't have most of the 3D features that come with Auto-CAD, such as solids modeling and rendering. The AutoLISP programming language found in AutoCAD is also absent from LT, as is the Action Recorder. The other differences are minor. As mentioned in this book's introduction, when I say AutoCAD, I mean both AutoCAD and AutoCAD LT. I'll also specifically refer to AutoCAD LT as LT throughout this chapter and the rest of the book. Starting AutoCAD is the first task at hand.

Starting AutoCAD

If you installed AutoCAD using the default settings for the location of the program files, start the program by choosing Start ➤ Programs ➤ Autodesk ➤ AutoCAD 2010 ➤ AutoCAD 2010 or by choosing Start ➤ Programs ➤ Autodesk ➤ AutoCAD LT 2010 ➤ AutoCAD LT 2010, depending on your program. (This command path might vary depending on the Windows operating system and scheme you are using.) You can also find and double-click the AutoCAD 2010 icon or the AutoCAD LT 2010 icon on your desktop.

The Initial Setup Dialog Box

When you first start AutoCAD, you may encounter the Initial Setup dialog box shown in Figure 1.1. In this dialog box, you can select the field most closely associated with the type of drawings you create. AutoCAD then displays the Ribbon panels and palettes usually associated with that field.

If you encounter this dialog box, click the Skip button. AutoCAD has several available configurations, and clicking Skip will be more likely to result in your setup looking like the one in this book. You'll next encounter the Initial Setup dialog box shown in Figure 1.2. Be sure the Remind Me The Next Time AutoCAD 2010 Starts option is checked, and then click the Start AutoCAD 2010 button.

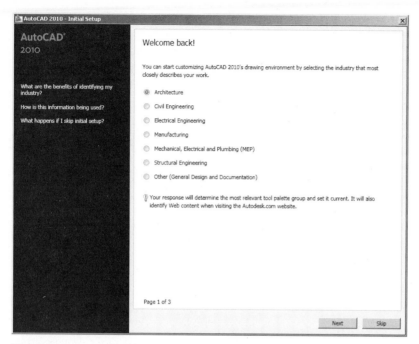

FIGURE 1.1: The first Initial Setup dialog box

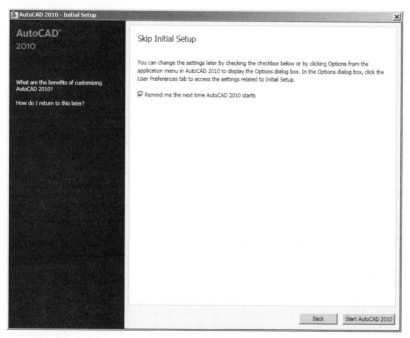

FIGURE 1.2: The second Initial Setup dialog box

ACCESSING THE INITIAL SETUP DIALOG BOXES

To access the Initial Setup dialog boxes after the program has started, enter
op⏎ to open the Options dialog box, click the User Preferences tab, and
then click the Initial Setup button.

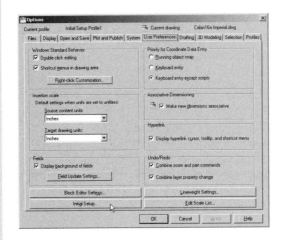

Exploring the New Features Workshop

The New Features Workshop welcome screen opens when you first start
AutoCAD and leads to several animated demonstrations and explanations
of the new features included in the latest release of AutoCAD (see Figure 1.3).
This is a quick and easy way to see how AutoCAD 2010 has improved over Auto-
CAD 2009 and which tools you can use to augment any skills you already have.
Choosing Maybe Later on the left side causes the dialog box to reappear every
time you start AutoCAD. Choosing the No, Don't Show This To Me Again option
dismisses the dialog box indefinitely. If you choose that option, you must then
access the New Features Workshop through the Help button on the right end of
the AutoCAD title bar.

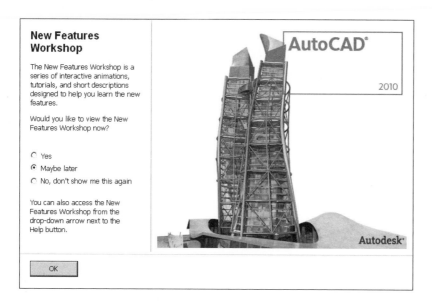

FIGURE 1.3: The AutoCAD welcome screen provides access to the New Features Workshop.

Selecting the Yes radio button on the left side of the dialog box opens the New Features Workshop dialog box (see Figure 1.4). Here you navigate to and select the feature you want to investigate in the left pane and observe the selection in the right pane. The drop-down list in the upper-left corner provides access to the New Features Workshops for other Autodesk products installed on your system.

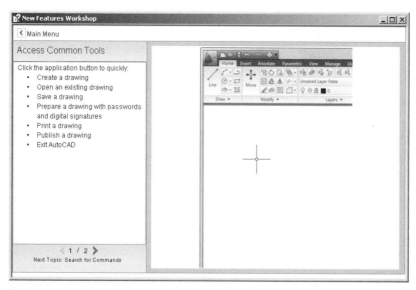

FIGURE 1.4: The New Features Workshop dialog box

The Customer Involvement Program

Nearly all the recent releases of Autodesk products include the opportunity to participate in a customer involvement program (CIP). The CIP is designed to collect nonpersonal information about your Autodesk products and computer system to help the product programmers and developers design software that best meets your needs. If you haven't yet agreed or declined to participate, when you first start AutoCAD the Customer Involvement Program dialog box (Figure 1.5) might prompt you to join.

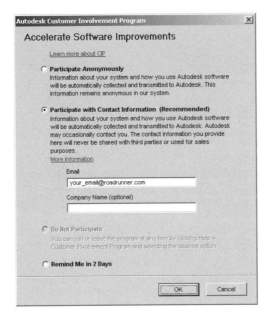

FIGURE 1.5: The Customer Involvement Program dialog box

Participation is strictly voluntary and, if you choose to participate, AutoCAD will periodically send a small file to Autodesk containing information such as your software name and version, the commands you use, and your system configuration information. An Internet connection is required, and you must ensure that your firewall settings don't prevent the information from being transmitted.

Exploring the AutoCAD User Interface

After bypassing the initial dialog boxes that AutoCAD provides, the program opens to display the AutoCAD user interface, also called the *graphics window*. AutoCAD provides many methods for creating and editing objects, changing the view of a drawing, or executing AutoCAD file maintenance or other utilities. In LT, your screen looks similar to Figure 1.6. For AutoCAD, your monitor displays one of three *workspaces*:

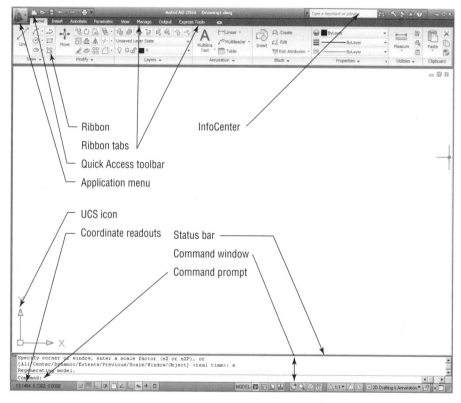

Ribbon

Ribbon tabs

Quick Access toolbar

Application menu

InfoCenter

UCS icon

Coordinate readouts

Status bar

Command window

Command prompt

F I G U R E   1 . 6 : The AutoCAD graphics window using the 2D Drafting & Annotation workspace

AutoCAD and LT offer numerous dialog boxes with various combinations of buttons and text boxes. You'll learn many of their functions as you progress throughout the book.

▶ The 2D Drafting & Annotation workspace (shown in Figure 1.6)

▶ The AutoCAD Classic workspace

▶ For AutoCAD users only, the 3D Modeling workspace (see Figure 1.7)

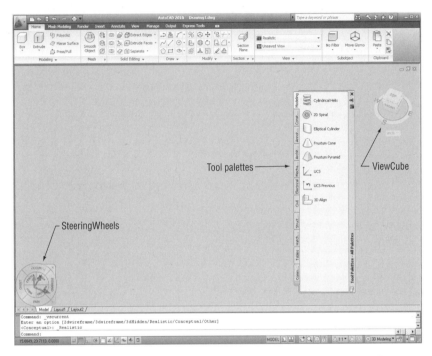

FIGURE 1.7: The AutoCAD graphics window using the 3D Modeling workspace

You'll be using the 2D Drafting & Annotation workspace for the first 15 chapters in this book. In the final two chapters, you'll switch to the 3D Modeling workspace. For now, however, you need to get your AutoCAD user interface to look like Figure 1.6.

N O T E   The figures and graphics in this book show the drawing area of the AutoCAD user interface with a white background, but the default, and preferred, method is to use a black background to reduce eyestrain. The color choice in the book is simply for readability.

If your screen looks like Figure 1.7, or isn't at all like Figure 1.6, you need to make a few changes:

1. Click the Workspace Switching button in the status bar, and choose 2D Drafting & Annotation, as shown in Figure 1.8. Alternately, you can enter wscurrent↵ 2d drafting & annotation↵.

FIGURE 1.8: Selecting the 2D Drafting & Annotation workspace

2. The 2D Drafting & Annotation workspace may display the tool *palettes* on the screen. If the palettes are displayed, you need to turn them off for now by clicking the X in the upper-right corner. Your workspace might have different palettes displayed than those shown in Figure 1.9. If other palettes are still visible, click the X in the upper-right or upper-left corner of each palette to close them.

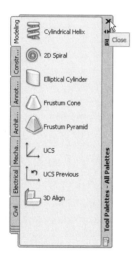

FIGURE 1.9: The tool palettes

3. The large area in the middle of the screen is called the *drawing area*. It might need adjusting. Enter **visualstyles**↵ to open the Visual Styles Manager, and then click the 2D Wireframe option (see Figure 1.10). Close the Visual Styles Manager.

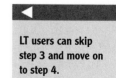

LT users can skip step 3 and move on to step 4.

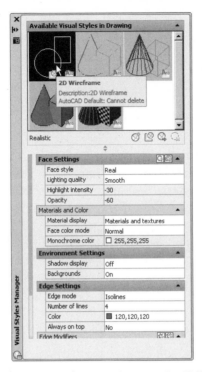

FIGURE 1.10: Selecting the 2D Wireframe visual style

4. Enter **plan**↵ and then **world**↵, or click the World option in the pop-up menu if it appears, as shown in Figure 1.11. This procedure ensures that your view is perpendicular to the drawing area. It should be as though you were looking straight down at a piece of paper on a drawing table.

FIGURE 1.11: Selecting the World option from the pop-up menu

If dots appear in the drawing area, the grid, a drawing aid that we'll look at later, is turned on.

5. Move the cursor to the left side of the status bar at the bottom of the screen, and click the Grid Display button so it's in the Off (unpushed) position and the dots disappear. Be sure all the other readout buttons except Dynamic Input are in their Off (unpushed) positions. You can pause your cursor over each button to reveal its name in a tooltip.

Your screen should now look similar to Figure 1.6.

Introducing the AutoCAD Graphics Window

At the top of the graphics window (see Figure 1.12) sit the Ribbon, the Quick Access toolbar to the left, and the InfoCenter and related tools on the right.

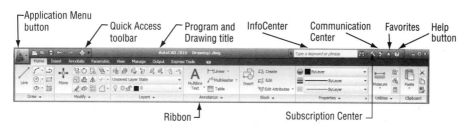

FIGURE 1.12: The Ribbon, Quick Access toolbar, and InfoCenter

The *title bar* is analogous to the title bar in any Windows program. It contains the program name (*AutoCAD* or *AutoCAD LT*) and the title of the current drawing with its *path*, as long as any drawing other than the default Drawing*n*.dwg is open. Below the title bar is the *Ribbon*, where you'll find most of the AutoCAD commands and tools needed to complete any drawing task. Related tasks are found under the different tabs, which are further segmented into panels containing similar tools.

To the far right of the title bar is the InfoCenter containing the Search, Subscription Center, Communication Center, Favorites, and Help buttons. You can enter a question in the field to the left of the Search button to access information from the Help system quickly through the drop-down panel. With the Communication Center, you can determine what type of information, such as software updates, product support, or Really Simple Syndication (RSS) feeds, Autodesk sends directly to your system. With the Favorites tool, you can define a list of help or informational topics that can be quickly accessed whenever you need them. The Help button is a direct link to the AutoCAD help system.

The title bar and menu bar at the top of the LT screen are identical to those in AutoCAD except that *AutoCAD LT* appears in the title bar rather than AutoCAD.

The blank middle section of the screen is called the *drawing area*. Notice the movable *crosshair cursor* (see Figure 1.13). The crosshairs on your cursor might extend completely across the screen. Later in this chapter, I will show you how to modify the length of the crosshairs as well as make a few other changes.

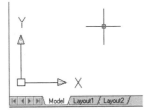

FIGURE 1.13: The crosshair cursor placed near the UCS icon

Notice the little box at the intersection of the two crosshair lines. This is one of several forms of the AutoCAD cursor. When you move the cursor off the drawing area, it changes to the standard Windows pointing arrow. As you begin using commands, it will take on other forms, depending on which step of a command you're performing.

The icon with a double arrow in the lower-left corner of the drawing area is the *UCS icon* (UCS stands for *user coordinate system*). It indicates the positive direction for the x- and y-axes. You won't need it for most of the chapters in this book, so you'll learn how to turn it off in Chapter 3, "Setting Up a Drawing."

Below the drawing area is the *Command window,* shown in Figure 1.14.

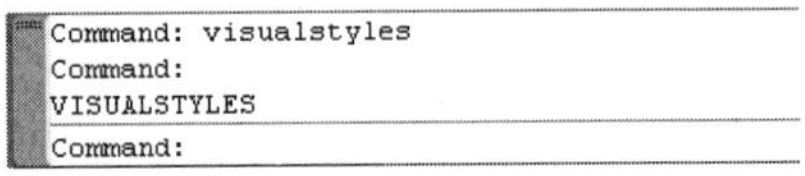

```
Command: visualstyles
Command:
VISUALSTYLES
Command:
```

FIGURE 1.14: The Command window

When you enter commands in addition to using the Ribbon or pop-up menus, the Command window is where you tell the program what to do and where the program tells you what's happening. It's an important feature, and you'll need to learn how it works in detail. Four lines of text should be visible. You'll learn how to increase the number of visible lines later in this chapter in the section "Working in the Command Window." When the Dynamic Input feature is active, much of the Command window information is displayed at the cursor as well.

Below the Command window is the *status bar* (see Figure 1.15).

FIGURE 1.15: The left side of the status bar (top) and the right side of the status bar (bottom)

On the left end of the status bar, you'll see a coordinate readout window. In the middle are 10 buttons (LT has only 9) that activate various drawing modes. It's important to learn about the coordinate system and most of these drawing aids (Snap Mode, Grid Display, Ortho Mode, Object Snap, and so on) early on as you learn to draw in AutoCAD. They will help you create neat and accurate drawings. Polar Tracking and Object Snap Tracking are advanced drawing tools and will be introduced in Chapter 5, "Developing Drawing Strategies: Part 2." Dynamic UCS stands for *Dynamic User Coordinate System*; it's used in 3D drawings and is not available in LT. The Dynamic Input button is an On/Off toggle that activates or suppresses the dynamic display of information next to the crosshair cursor when it's in the drawing area. For now, keep it in the On (pushed) mode. The Show/Hide Lineweight button toggles the display of *line weights (*discussed in Chapter 14, "Using Layouts to Set Up a Print") in the drawing area. When active, the Quick Properties tool displays the most common properties for the selected object(s) in a dialog box where they can be edited. If you prefer text-based buttons rather than icons, you can right-click on any of the tools mentioned here and uncheck the Use Icons option.

 At the right side of the status bar are tools for controlling the appearance of annotation objects in AutoCAD, tools for navigating in the drawing area and controlling the display, and tools to control access to other drawings or features within the current drawing. The padlock icon controls which types of toolbars and windows are locked in their current positions on the screen. Leave it in the unlocked mode for now.

To conclude this quick introduction to the various parts of the graphics window, I need to mention a couple of items that might be visible on your screen. You might have scroll bars below and to the right of the drawing area; although they can be useful, they can take up precious space in the drawing area. They won't be of any use while working your way through this book, so I suggest you remove them for now.

To remove these features temporarily, follow these steps:

1. Click the Application menu button in the upper-left corner of the AutoCAD window, and then click the Options button at the bottom of the menu (see Figure1.16), or enter **options**↵.

FIGURE 1.16: Click the Options button in the Application menu.

The Options dialog box (shown in Figure 1.17) opens. It has 10 tabs (LT has only 8) across the top that act like tabs on file folders.

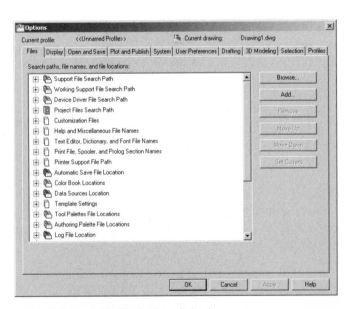

FIGURE 1.17: The Options dialog box

2. Click the Display tab, which is shown in Figure 1.18. Focus on the Window Elements section. If scroll bars are visible on the lower and right edges of the drawing area, the Display Scroll Bars In Drawing Window check box will be selected.

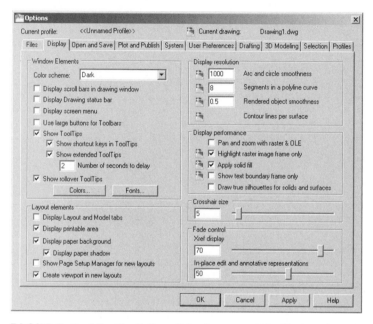

FIGURE 1.18: The Options dialog box open at the Display tab

3. Click the check box to turn off the scroll bars. Also be sure the check boxes for Display Screen Menu and, in the Layout Elements section, Display Layout And Model Tabs are not selected. Don't click the OK button yet.

LT doesn't have the screen menu, so the option to turn it off isn't on LT's Display tab.

Another display setting that you might want to change at this point controls the color of the cursor and the drawing area background. If you want to change the colors, follow these steps:

1. In the Window Elements area of the Display tab, click the Colors button to open the Drawing Window Colors dialog box (see Figure 1.19). In the upper-left corner of the dialog box, in the Context list box, 2D Model Space should be selected. If it's not, select it.

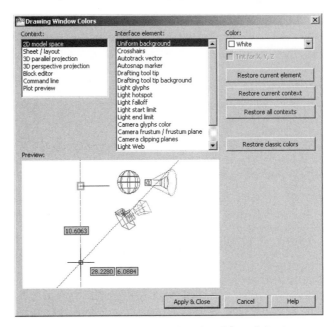

FIGURE 1.19: The Drawing Window Colors dialog box

 N O T E   The screen-captured images in this book are taken from AutoCAD sessions using the Dark Color scheme. You can set the color scheme at the top of the Window Elements area and choose either the Light or Dark scheme.

2. Move to the Color drop-down list, which is in the upper-right corner. If your drawing area background is currently white, a square followed by the word *White* is displayed. Open the Color drop-down list and select Black (or the background color you want). The drawing area will now be that color, and the cursor color will change to white, as shown in the Preview window in Figure 1.19.

3. Click the Apply & Close button to close the Drawing Window Colors dialog box. The background and cursor colors change.

4. If you want to change the length of the lines of your crosshair cursor, go to the lower-right corner of the Display tab (the middle of the right side for LT), and move the slider to change the Crosshair Size setting. The crosshair length changes as a percentage of the drawing area.

5. Click OK to apply any remaining changes, and close the Options dialog box.

T I P   If you choose a color other than black as the drawing area background color, the color of the crosshair cursor remains the same as it was. To change the crosshair color, go to the Interface Element list box in the Drawing Window Colors dialog box and select Crosshairs. Then select a color from the Color drop-down list.

Working in the Command Window

Just below the drawing area is the Command window. This window is separate from the drawing area and behaves like a Windows window—that is, you can drag it to a different place on the screen and resize it, although I don't recommend you do this at first. If you currently have fewer than four lines of text in the window, you should increase the window's vertical size. To do so, move the cursor to the horizontal boundary between the drawing area and the Command window until it changes to an up-and-down arrow broken by two parallel horizontal lines.

Hold down the left mouse button, drag the cursor up by approximately the same amount that one or two lines of text would take up, and then release the mouse button (see Figure 1.20). You should see more lines of text, but you might have to try this a few times to display exactly four lines. A horizontal line will separate the top two lines of text from the bottom line of text. When you close the program, AutoCAD will save the new settings. The next time you start AutoCAD, the Command window will display four lines of text.

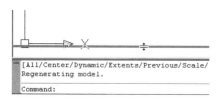

FIGURE 1.20: Resizing the Command window

The Command window is where you give information to AutoCAD and where AutoCAD prompts you for the next step in executing a command. It's a good practice to keep an eye on the Command window as you work on your drawing. Many errors can occur when you don't check it frequently. If the Dynamic Input button on the status bar is in the On position, some of the information in the Command window will appear in the drawing area next to the cursor. I'll cover this feature when you start drawing.

Before you begin to draw in the next chapter, take a close look at the Ribbon, Application menu, toolbars, and keyboard controls.

N O T E   Often, you can start AutoCAD commands in a number of ways: from the Ribbon, the Application menu, the Command window, and the menus that appear when you right-click. When you get used to drawing with Auto-CAD, you'll learn some shortcuts that start commands quickly, and you'll find the way that best suits you.

Using the Ribbon

The Ribbon is a consolidated location for nearly all the AutoCAD tools in the form of easily recognizable buttons or drop-down lists. A set of tabs delineates the different collections of tools by their purposes: creating and editing objects, adding notes and dimensions, sending the drawing to a printer or plotter, and so on.

Displaying the Ribbon Tools

The Ribbon self-adjusts according to the width of the AutoCAD window. The panels have the most commonly used command as a button, larger than the others, centered on the left side (see the top of Figure 1.21). Often, this button has a down arrow below it that opens a menu displaying additional, similar commands. When the width is too narrow to display each panel fully, the panels will begin to collapse first by replacing the large buttons with smaller buttons and then by replacing the panels with a single button bearing the name of the panel. The collapsed panel's tools are displayed by clicking this single button, as shown at the bottom of Figure 1.21.

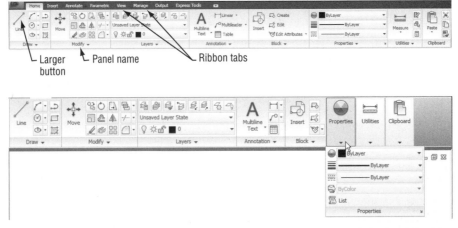

F I G U R E   1 . 2 1 : The Ribbon fully displaying all panels (top) and with partially and completely collapsed panels (bottom)

Coilapsing, Moving, and Hiding the Ribbon

 Available drawing area is always at a premium, and you can regain some of it by collapsing the Ribbon. When you click the Minimize button to the right of the Ribbon tabs once, the panels are collapsed vertically and only show their titles. Clicking it a second time collapses the Ribbon further until only the tabs show. When the Ribbon is in either of these states, you can expand any panel or tab by clicking its visible panel or tab name. Clicking the Minimize button a third time returns the Ribbon to its default state.

The Ribbon's default location is at the top of the screen, but it can be undocked, or floating over the drawing area; or it can be moved to a second monitor, or docked on either side of the drawing area. To undock the Ribbon, right-click to the right of the tab names and choose Undock from the pop-up menu, as shown in Figure 1.22.

FIGURE 1.22: Undocking the ribbon

The Ribbon detaches from the top of the drawing area and floats on the screen, as shown in Figure 1.23. To dock it, click the title bar on the side of the floating Ribbon and drag it to the side or the top of the drawing area. Experiment with detaching the Ribbon, but when you are finished, dock it back at the top so that you can follow the graphics in this book more easily.

FIGURE 1.23: The Ribbon after undocking it from the top of the drawing area

If you don't want the Ribbon at all, you can turn it off by right-clicking to the right of the Ribbon tabs and choosing Close. To turn it on, enter **ribbon**↵. You'll use the Ribbon throughout this book.

Using the Ribbon Tools

Each panel contains tools from a related family of functions. For example, all the common tools for editing objects in the drawing area are consolidated in the Modify panel. When more tools are available than will fit on the panel, an arrow is displayed on the panel's title bar. Clicking the title bar expands the panel and exposes the additional tools. Follow these steps to learn how the Ribbon tools work and how they display information.

1. Click the Home tab on the Ribbon to expose the Home tab's panels (see the top of Figure 1.21 shown earlier).

2. Move the cursor over the Modify panel. The panel and panel title bar change from light gray to white to indicate that that panel has the program's focus, while the tool or feature directly beneath the cursor turns blue.

3. Pause the cursor over the Bring To Front button to expose the button's tooltip, as shown at the top of Figure 1.24. This tooltip displays the name of the tool, a brief description of its function, the command-line equivalent of clicking the tool, and instructions to click the F1 key to open the AutoCAD Help file to the current tool's Help page.

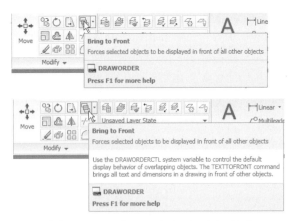

F I G U R E 1 . 2 4 : The tooltip for the Bring To Front command (top) and the extended tooltip (bottom)

4. After a few seconds of hovering over the Bring To Front button, the tooltip expands to display the extended tooltip (see the bottom of Figure 1.24) with a more complete description.

5. Pause the cursor over the Copy button in the Modify panel. This time, after a few seconds, the tooltip is replaced with a cue card, as shown in Figure 1.25, instead of an extended tooltip. Cue cards show the step-by-step implementation of the tool.

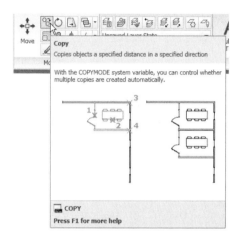

FIGURE 1.25: The cue card for the Copy tool

6. Click the Modify panel's title bar to expand the panel and expose all of the Modify tools.

7. Often, you may find yourself returning to the same tool on an expanded Ribbon panel. When that happens, you can pin the panel open by clicking the pushpin-shaped button in the bottom-left corner. When the panel is pinned open, it remains open even when the cursor is not hovering over it (see Figure 1.26).

FIGURE 1.26: The Modify panel pinned to stay open

8. Click the button again to unpin the panel, and then move the cursor off the panel to collapse it.

Customizing the Ribbon

You can customize each panel of the Ribbon, and you can build your own custom tabs and panels to display only the buttons you use frequently. You can even design your own buttons for commands that aren't already represented by buttons on the toolbars. These activities are for more advanced users, however, and aren't covered in this book. To find out more about how to customize toolbars, see *Mastering AutoCAD 2010 and AutoCAD LT 2010* by George Omura (Wiley, 2009).

Using the Application Menu

The Application menu contains the tools for opening, saving, and printing your drawings, similar to the options found under the File pull-down menu in Auto-CAD and many other programs. The tools menus now project from the upper-left corner of the AutoCAD window and cover the drawing area and any open dialog boxes, but only when the Application Menu is open.

1. Click the Application menu button, the large, red A button in the top-left corner of the AutoCAD window, to open the Application menu.

2. The left pane of the Application menu displays the different commands. Clicking or hovering over a menu displays the command options in the right pane, as shown in Figure 1.27.

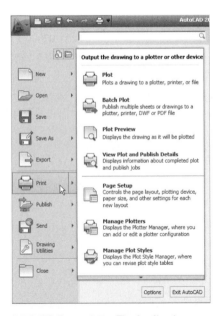

FIGURE 1.27: The Application menu showing the Print command options

A bar with an up or down arrow at the top or bottom of the right pane indicates that additional tools are available. You can display these tools by placing your cursor over either bar.

Opening a Drawing with the Application Menu

The Application Menu offers a quick method for opening drawings. You can even see a thumbnail preview of the drawings and arrange drawings that you frequently edit so that they are easily accessible. Here's how:

1. To open a new AutoCAD file from the Application menu, click New ➤ Drawing, as shown in Figure 1.28.

FIGURE 1.28: Opening a new drawing from the Application menu

This opens the Select Template dialog box, where you select a template on which to base the new drawing. Opening a file with a template is covered in Chapter 2, "Learning Basic Commands to Get Started."

2. To open an existing file from the Application menu, click Open ➤ Drawing as shown in Figure 1.29.

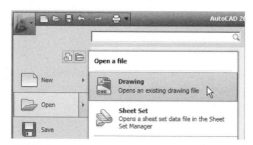

FIGURE 1.29: Opening an existing drawing from the Application menu

This opens the Select File dialog box, where you can navigate to the desired drawing file and select it.

OPENING NEW FILES

You can open new or existing files using the QNew or Open button in the Quick Access toolbar. Existing drawings can also be opened by dragging them from a Windows Explorer window to the AutoCAD title bar.

 3. To open a file that you've worked on recently, click the Recent Documents button at the top of the Application menu's left pane. This displays the most recent files opened in AutoCAD in the right pane, as shown in Figure 1.30.

F I G U R E   1 . 3 0 : Displaying the recent documents in the Application menu

The Recent Documents list is updated whenever a new drawing is opened. Clicking the pushpin icon next to a drawing name in the right pane pins that drawing to its current location in the list. Pinned documents don't scroll off the list when newer files are opened.

4. Hover over a filename in the right pane to display a thumbnail preview of the drawing and additional information, including the drawing location and AutoCAD drawing format (see Figure 1.31).

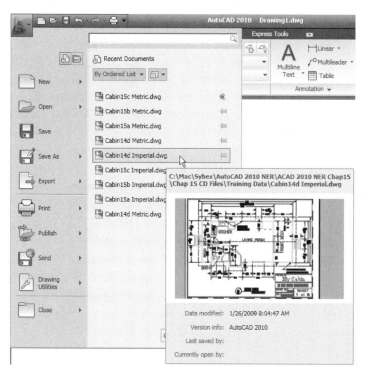

FIGURE 1.31: Displaying a thumbnail of the selected file

N O T E   AutoCAD 2010 drawing files do not use the same drawing format as prior AutoCAD versions. This means that the files created in AutoCAD 2010 are not compatible with any previous versions without requiring conversion. To convert a 2010 drawing to a prior version, open the Application menu and then click Save As ➢ AutoCAD Drawing and choose version you want from the Files Of Type drop-down list at the bottom of the Save Drawing As dialog box.

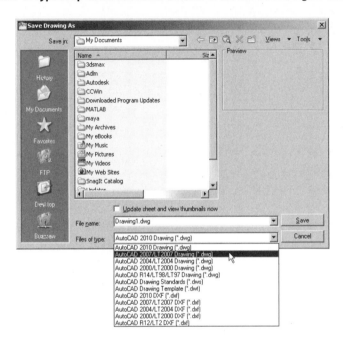

Switching Between Open Drawings

As in many programs, you can have multiple drawing files open in the same session of AutoCAD. Each drawing is stacked behind the drawings in front of it. There are several ways to switch between the open files, including using the Application menu, as shown next.

1. Start or open two or more AutoCAD files.

2. Open the Application menu, and then click the Open Documents option at the top of the left pane. The open drawings are displayed in the right pane, as shown in Figure 1.32.

3. Click on any drawing to bring it to the front of the AutoCAD window.

4. You can change the way AutoCAD displays the list of open drawings by clicking the icon near the top of the right pane and choosing one of four sizes of icons or thumbnail images to represent the open drawings.

FIGURE 1.32: Displaying the open drawings in the Application menu

5. Another option for switching between open drawings is to click the Quick View Drawings button in the status bar. This displays thumbnails for the open drawings, and you can click any thumbnail to make that drawing active. Hovering over a thumbnail displays that drawing's layouts (see Figure 1.33). Layouts are designated views of the drawing with scaled viewports looking into the drawing model. Viewports are covered in Chapter 14, "Using Layouts to Set Up a Print."

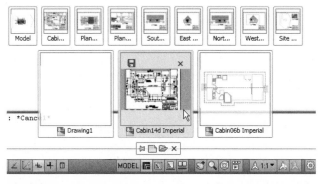

FIGURE 1.33: Displaying the open drawings with the Quick View Drawings tool

Using the Drop-Down Menus

If you prefer to use drop-down menus, they're still available in AutoCAD 2010, although they are turned off by default in the 2D Drafting & Annotation and 3D Modeling workspaces. You can display them by switching to the AutoCAD Classic workspace, by clicking the down arrow at the right end of the Quick Access toolbar and choosing Show Menu Bar (see Figure 1.34), or by entering **menubar**⏎ **1**⏎. The menu bar isn't used in the first few exercises in this book, but I'll cover the menus here so that you'll be familiar when you use them in the future.

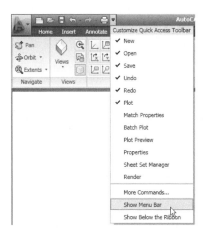

FIGURE 1.34: Turning on the menu bar

The left end of the menu bar, just below the title bar (see Figure 1.35), consists of an icon and 13 (11 if you don't have the Express Tools installed or are using LT) menus. Click any of these to display a drop-down menu. The icon and the File and Edit menus are included with all Windows-compliant applications, although they are somewhat customized to work with AutoCAD. The drop-down menu associated with the icon contains commands to control the appearance and position of the drawing area.

FIGURE 1.35: The AutoCAD user interface showing the menu bar

Commands in the File menu are for opening and saving new and existing drawing files, printing, exporting files to another application, choosing basic utility options, and exiting the application. The Edit menu contains the Undo and Redo commands, the Cut and Paste tools, and options for creating links between AutoCAD files and other files. The Help menu works like most Windows Help menus and contains a couple of AutoCAD-specific entries as well, including some online resources and a link to the New Features Workshop.

The other eight (or ten) menus contain the most frequently used AutoCAD commands. You'll find that if you master the logic of how the commands are organized by menu, you can quickly find the command you want. Here are short descriptions of the other AutoCAD drop-down menus:

View   Contains tools for controlling the display of your drawing file.

Insert   Contains commands for placing drawings and images or parts of them inside other drawings.

Format   Contains commands for setting up the general parameters for a new drawing or changing the entities in a current drawing.

Tools   Contains special tools for use while you're working on the current drawing, such as those used for finding the length of a line or for running a special macro.

Draw   Contains commands for creating new objects (such as lines or circles) on the screen.

Dimension   Contains commands for dimensioning and annotating a drawing.

Modify   Contains commands for changing existing objects in the drawing.

Parametric   Contains commands for constraining objects or dimensions to specific values or parameters.

Window   Contains commands for displaying currently open drawing windows and lists currently open drawing files.

Express   Contains a library of productivity tools that cover a wide range of Auto-CAD functions. Express Tools are widely used but unsupported directly by Autodesk. They might or might not be installed on your computer.

You can turn off the menu bar by clicking the down arrow on the right end of the Quick Access toolbar and choosing Hide Menu Bar, or by entering **menubar↵ 0↵**.

Using the Toolbars

The AutoCAD toolbars have essentially been replaced by the Ribbon or other features, so I'll only touch on them briefly here. Toolbars, like the Ribbon panels, are collections of tools grouped by similar tasks. Like the Ribbon itself, any toolbar can be displayed or hidden without affecting the others, and they can all be docked to a side or the top of the drawing area or float freely. To display a toolbar, first display the menu bar; then choose Tools ➤ Toolbars, click a toolbar category, and click the toolbar that you want to open (see Figure 1.36).

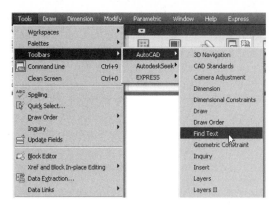

FIGURE 1.36: Selecting a toolbar to display

Take a few minutes to explore the available toolbars, and then close them and hide the display of the menu bar. You'll touch on a few of the toolbars throughout the course of this book, but most of the tools used will be accessed from the Ribbon.

Workspaces

You haven't been directed to make any significant changes to the workspace, but when you do, you can save this setup as a new workspace. Using this feature, you can always return to your preferred layout by activating the saved layout. Follow these steps:

 1. Click the Workspace Switching button on the right side of the status bar, and choose Save Current As from the pop-up menu. This opens the Save Workspace dialog box, shown in Figure 1.37.

FIGURE 1.37: The Save Workspace dialog box

2. Enter a name for the workspace and click Save. The dialog box closes, and you are returned you to your workspace. Until you change it or select a different workspace, the new workspace setup will remain as it is now.

When you make changes to the new workspace by adding a toolbar or changing the background color of the drawing area, you can easily update the current workspace to accommodate those changes. Follow steps 1 and 2, naming the workspace again with the same name. You'll get a warning window telling you that a workspace by that name already exists and asking you whether you want the new arrangement to replace the old one. Click Yes.

Using the Keyboard

The keyboard is an important tool for entering data and commands. If you're a good typist, you can gain speed in working with AutoCAD by learning how to enter commands from the keyboard. AutoCAD provides what are called *alias* commands—single keys or key combinations that start any of several frequently used commands. You can add more or change the existing aliases as you become more familiar with the program.

In addition to the alias commands, you can use several of the F keys (function keys) on the top row of the keyboard as two-way or three-way toggles to turn AutoCAD functions on and off. Although buttons on the screen duplicate these functions (Snap, Grid, and so on), it's sometimes faster to use the F keys.

While working in AutoCAD, you'll need to enter a lot of data, such as dimensions and construction notes; answer questions with "yes" or "no," and use the arrow keys. You'll use the keyboard constantly. It might help to get into the habit of keeping your left hand on the keyboard and your right hand on the mouse if you're right-handed, or the other way around if you're left-handed.

Using the Mouse

Your mouse most likely has two buttons and a scroll wheel. So far in this chapter, you have used the left mouse button to choose menus, commands, and options, and you've held it down to drag the Ribbon. The left mouse button is the one you'll be using most often, but you'll also use the right mouse button.

While drawing, you'll use the right mouse button for the following three operations:

▶ To display a menu containing options relevant to the particular step you're in at the moment

▶ To use in combination with the Shift or Ctrl key to display a menu containing special drawing aids called *object snaps*

▶ To display a menu of toolbars when the pointer is on any icon of a toolbar that is currently open

If you have a three-button mouse, the middle button is usually programmed to display the Object Snap menu, instead of using the right button with the Shift key. If you have a mouse with a scroll wheel, you can use the wheel in several ways to control the view of your drawing. I'll cover those methods in subsequent chapters.

AutoCAD makes extensive use of toolbars and the right-click menu feature. This makes your mouse an important input tool. The keyboard is necessary for inputting numeric data and text, and it has hot keys and aliases that can speed up your work; however, the mouse is the primary tool for selecting options and controlling toolbars.

The next chapter will familiarize you with a few basic commands that will enable you to draw a small diagram. If want to take a break and close AutoCAD, choose File ➣ Exit, and choose not to save the drawing.

Are You Experienced?

Now you can. . .

- ☑ **recognize the elements of the AutoCAD graphics window**

- ☑ **understand how the Command window works and why it's important**

- ☑ **start commands from the Ribbon**

- ☑ **start commands from the command line**

- ☑ **use the Application menu**

- ☑ **display the drop-down menus**

- ☑ **open and control the positioning of toolbars**

- ☑ **save a workspace of your screen setup in AutoCAD**

CHAPTER 2

Learning Basic Commands to Get Started

- ▶ Understanding coordinate systems
- ▶ Drawing your first object
- ▶ Erasing, offsetting, filleting, extending, and trimming objects in a drawing

Now that you've taken a quick tour of the AutoCAD and LT screens, you're ready to begin drawing. In this chapter, you'll be introduced to a few basic commands used in drawing with AutoCAD and AutoCAD LT. To get you started, I'll guide you through the process of drawing a simple shape (see Figure 2.1).

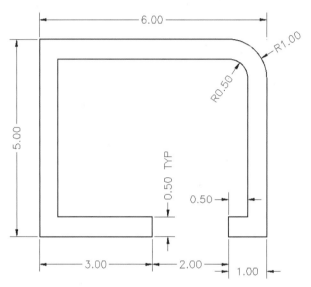

FIGURE 2.1: The shape you'll draw

You will need to use only five or six commands to draw the box. First you'll become familiar with the Line command and how to make lines a specific length. Then I'll go over the strategy for completing the form.

Using the Line Command

In traditional architectural drafting, lines were often drawn to extend slightly past their endpoints (see Figure 2.2). This is rarely done in CAD nowadays except as a special effect.

The *Line command* draws a straight line segment between locations on existing objects, geometric features, or two points that you can choose anywhere within the drawing area. You can designate these points by left-clicking them on the screen, by entering the x- and y-coordinates for each point, or by entering distances and angles from an existing point. After you draw the first segment of a line, you can end the command or draw another line segment beginning from the end of the previous one. You can continue to draw adjoining line segments for as long as you like. Let's see how this works.

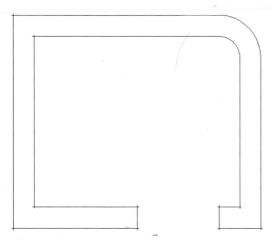

FIGURE 2.2: The shape drawn with overlapping lines

To be sure that you start with your drawing area set up the way it's set up for this book, expand the Application menu (the red A button in the top-left corner of the AutoCAD user interface) and then choose Close ➤ All Drawings to close any open drawings. The Application menu is shown in Figure 2.3.

FIGURE 2.3: Use the Application menu to close any open drawings.

If multiple drawings are open, and you want to close each one individually, choose Close ➤ Current Drawing and then repeat the command for each drawing until you no longer have any drawings open. Your drawing area will be a gradient gray and blank with no crosshair cursor; the Ribbon will disappear and only three buttons will remain in the Quick Access toolbar area on the left side of the title bar (along with the three informational buttons in the Quick Access toolbar). Now follow these steps:

1. Click the New button at the left end of the Quick Access toolbar. In the Select Template dialog box, select the acad.dwt file, if it's not already selected, and click Open, as shown in Figure 2.4. The menus, crosshair cursor, and toolbars return, and you now have a blank drawing in the drawing area.

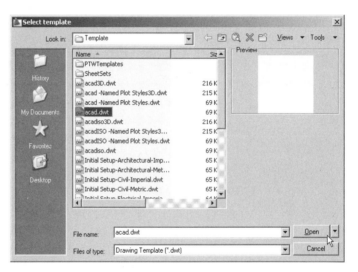

FIGURE 2.4: Choose the acad.dwt template in the Select Template dialog box.

N O T E   DWT files are drawing templates with several parameters, such as dimension styles, layers, and plotting settings, already set.

2. Glance at the status bar at the bottom of your screen. On the right side, all buttons except Model should be off—that is, in an unpushed state. If any of the others appear to be pushed, click on them to turn them off.

3. On the left side, some of the tools, such as Object Snap and Dynamic Input, are turned on while others remain off. Make sure that Polar Tracking, Object Snap, Object Snap Tracking, Allow/Disallow Dynamic UCS, and Dynamic Input are turned on and all the others are turned off. You can identify the buttons by pausing over each and exposing its tooltip. Your AutoCAD window should look similar to Figure 2.5.

FIGURE 2.5: The AutoCAD window as it has been set up

4. Click the Line button in the Draw panel of the Ribbon. Look at the bottom of the Command window and see how the command prompt has changed, as shown in Figure 2.6.

FIGURE 2.6: The command prompt changes to reflect the current command.

T I P   You can also start the Line command by typing **line** or **l** and pressing the Enter key or the right mouse button.

The prompt now tells you that the Line command is started (Command: _line) and that AutoCAD is waiting for you to designate the first point of the line (Specify first point:).

5. Move the cursor onto the drawing area and notice that the small box at the intersection of the crosshairs is not there.

When the cursor is used to select objects, the default condition, the pickbox appears in the cursor. When the cursor is used to designate a point, the pickbox is not visible. Using the left mouse button, click a random point in the drawing area to start a line.

6. Move the cursor away from the point you clicked and notice how a line segment appears that stretches like a rubber band from the point you just picked to the cursor. The line changes length and direction as you move the cursor, and these values are shown as input boxes in the drawing area.

7. Look at the Command window again and notice that the prompt has changed (see Figure 2.7).

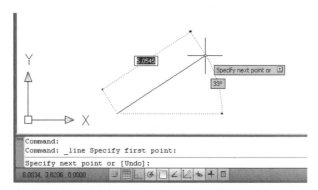

F I G U R E 2 . 7 : The command prompt changes for the next point, and the line's length and direction are shown in the drawing area.

It's now telling you that AutoCAD is waiting for you to designate the next point (Specify next point or [Undo]:).

8. Continue picking points and adding lines as you move the cursor around the screen (see Figure 2.8). After you draw the second segment, the Command window repeats the Specify next point or

[Close/Undo] : prompt each time you pick another point. The
Dynamic Input fields and command prompt appear near the cursor,
showing the angle and distance from the last point selected.

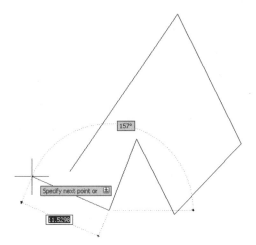

FIGURE 2.8: Drawing several line segments

9. When you've drawn six or seven line segments, press Enter to end the
   Line command. The cursor separates from the last drawn line segment.

   The command prompt has returned to the bottom line. This tells you
   that no command is currently running.

T I P   The Enter key exits the Line command and several others. Another
option is to right-click and choose Enter from the context menu. This may
require an extra step, but it may still be faster because your eyes never leave
the screen. When you're not entering data, the spacebar also acts like the
Enter key and executes a command.

   In this exercise, you used the left mouse button to click the Line button on the
Ribbon and also to pick several points in the drawing area to make the line segments. You then pressed Enter (↵) on the keyboard to end the Line command.

N O T E   In the exercises that follow, the Enter symbol (↵) will be used.
When I say to "type" or "enter" something, it means to type the data that follows the word *type* or *enter* and then to press the Enter key (↵). For example,
rather than writing "type I and press the Enter key," I'll write "enter I↵."

Using Coordinates

A coordinate system consists of numbered scales that identify an initial, or base, point and the direction for measuring subsequent points on a graph. The Cartesian Coordinate System, named after the philosopher René Descartes, who defined the x,y-coordinate system in the 1600s, consists of three numbered scales, called the x-axis, y-axis, and z-axis, that are perpendicular to each other and extend infinitely in each direction. Each pair of axes (xy, xz, yz) forms a flat plane. Most of your time using AutoCAD will be spent drawing in the xy plane.

The point where the scales intersect is called the *origin*. For each axis, all values on one side of the origin are positive, all values on the other side are negative, and values that fall in line with the origin have a value of 0 (zero). The divisions along the scales may be any size, but each division must be equal. The axes divide the coordinate system into four regions called quadrants. Quadrant I is the region above the x-axis and to the right of the y-axis. Quadrant II is the region above the x-axis and to the left of the y-axis. Quadrant III is the region below the x-axis and to the left of the y-axis. Quadrant IV is the region below the x-axis and to the right of the y-axis. Most of your work in AutoCAD will be done in Quadrant I, and this is the area shown when you first open a drawing.

Any point on a graph can be specified by giving its coordinates relative to the origin given as a combination of the X value and the Y value delineated with a comma. For example, a coordinate of 5,7 means a point on the coordinate system that is 5 units in the positive X direction and 7 units is the positive Y direction. Figure 2.9 shows a typical Cartesian coordinate system and the default region used as the drawing area in a new AutoCAD file.

N O T E   In AutoCAD, you see a readout for the z-coordinate as well, but you can ignore it for now because you'll be working in only two dimensions for the majority of this book. The z-coordinate always reads 0 until you work in three dimensions. (This will be covered in the later chapters.) AutoCAD LT doesn't have the readout for the z-coordinate because it doesn't have 3D capabilities.

You can also start the Erase command by entering e↵.

In this next exercise, you'll try using the Line command again, but instead of picking points in the drawing area with the mouse as you did before, this time enter x- and y-coordinates for each point from the keyboard. To see how to do this, follow these steps:

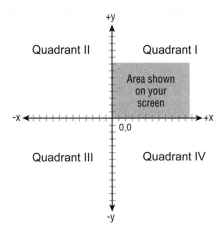

FIGURE 2.9: The x- and y-coordinates of the drawing area

1. Click the Erase button on the Modify panel of the Ribbon.

2. Enter all↵. The objects in the drawing become dashed to indicate that they are selected.

3. Press ↵ to clear the screen.

4. Click the Dynamic Input button in the command line to turn off this feature.

Now begin drawing lines again by following these steps:

1. Start the Line command by clicking the Line button on the Draw panel of the Ribbon.

2. Enter 2,2↵ to start the first line segment at a location 2 units above and 2 units to the right of the drawing's origin point.

3. Enter 6,3↵ to determine the endpoint of the line.

4. Enter 4,6↵.

5. Enter 1,3↵.

6. Enter 10,6↵.

7. Enter 10,1↵.

8. Enter 2,7↵.

9. Press ↵ again to end the command.

The lines are similar to those you drew previously, but this time you know where each point is located relative to the 0,0 point. In the drawing area, every point has an absolute x- and y-coordinate. In steps 2 through 8, you entered the x- and y-coordinates for each point. For a new drawing such as this one, the origin (0,0 coordinate) is in the lower-left corner of the drawing area and all points in the drawing area have positive x- and y-coordinates.

Let's explore how the cursor is related to the coordinates in the drawing.

1. At the command prompt, enter **zoom**↵ **e**↵ to adjust your view to show the extents of the drawing area.

2. Move the cursor around, and notice the left end of the status bar at the bottom of the screen. This is the coordinate readout, and it displays the coordinates of the cursor's position, as shown in Figure 2.10.

FIGURE 2.10: The x- and y-coordinates of the cursor are shown at the bottom of the AutoCAD window.

3. Move the cursor as close to the lower-left corner of the drawing area as you can without it changing into an arrow. The coordinate readout should be close to 0.0000, 0.0000, 0.0000.

4. Move the cursor to the top-left corner of the drawing area. The readout changes to something close to 0.0000, 7.0000, 0.0000, indicating that the top of the screen is 7 units from the bottom.

5. Move the cursor one more time to the upper-right corner of the drawing area. The readout still has a y-coordinate of approximately 7.0000. The x-coordinate now has a value around 10.5.

The drawing area of a new drawing is preset with the lower-left corner of the drawing at the coordinates 0,0.

N O T E   For the moment, it doesn't matter what measure of distance these units represent. I'll address that topic in Chapter 3, "Setting Up a Drawing." Don't worry about the four decimal places in the coordinate readout; the number of places is controlled by a setting you'll learn about soon.

Using Relative Coordinates

Once you understand the coordinate system used by AutoCAD, you can draw lines to any length and in any direction. Look at the shape shown earlier in Figure 2.1. Because you know the dimensions, you can calculate, by adding and subtracting, the absolute coordinates for each *vertex*—the connecting point between two line segments—and then use the Line command to draw the shape by entering these coordinates from the keyboard. However, AutoCAD offers you several tools for drawing this box much more easily. Two of these tools are the relative Cartesian and the relative polar coordinate systems.

When you're drawing lines, these coordinate systems use a set of new points based on the last point designated, rather than on the 0,0 point of the drawing area. They're called *relative* systems because the coordinates used are relative to the last point specified. If the first point of a line is located at the coordinate 4,6, and you want the line to extend 8 units to the right, the coordinate that is relative to the first point is 8,0 (8 units in the positive x direction and 0 units in the positive y direction), whereas the actual—or *absolute*—coordinate of the second point is 12,6.

The *relative Cartesian coordinate system* uses relative x- and y-coordinates in the manner shown, and the *relative polar coordinate system* relies on a distance and an angle relative to the last point specified. You'll probably favor one system over the other, but you need to know both systems because you'll sometimes find that, given the information you have at hand, one will work better than the other. A limitation of this nature will be illustrated in Chapter 4, "Developing Drawing Strategies: Part 1."

When entering relative coordinates, with the Dynamic Input tool turned off, you need to enter an "at" symbol (@) before the coordinates. In the previous example, you would enter the relative Cartesian coordinates as @8,0. The @ lets AutoCAD know that the numbers following it represent coordinates that are relative to the last point designated. When the Dynamic Input tool is turned on, relative coordinates are employed and the @ symbol is not required.

Relative Cartesian Coordinates

The Cartesian system of coordinates uses a horizontal (x) component and a vertical (y) component to locate a point relative to the 0,0 point. The relative Cartesian system uses the same components to locate the point relative to the last point picked, so it's a way of telling AutoCAD how far left or right and up or down to extend a line or to move an object from the last point picked (see Figure 2.11). If the direction is to the left, the x-coordinate will be negative. Similarly, if the direction is down, the y-coordinate will be negative. Use this system when you know the horizontal and vertical distances from point 1 to point 2. To enter data using this system, use this form: @x,y.

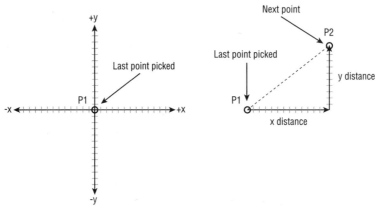

FIGURE 2.11: The relative Cartesian coordinate system

Relative Polar Coordinates

This system requires a known distance and direction from one point to the next. Calculating the distance is straightforward: it's always positive and represents the distance away from the first point that the second point will be placed. The direction requires a convention for determining an angle. AutoCAD defines right (toward three o'clock) as the default direction of the 0° angle. All other directions are determined from a counterclockwise rotation (see Figure 2.12). On your screen, up is 90°, left is 180°, down is 270°, and a full circle is 360°. To let AutoCAD know that you're entering an angle and not a relative y-coordinate, use the less-than symbol (<) before the angle and after the distance. Thus in the previous example, to designate a point 8 units to the right of the first point, you would enter @8<0 or simply 8<0 when the Dynamic Input tool is active.

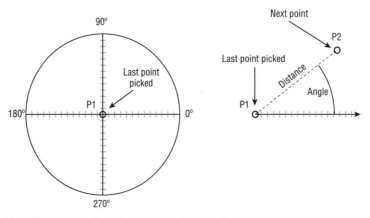

FIGURE 2.12: The relative polar coordinate system

N O T E   Remember, use the relative polar coordinates method to draw a line from the first point when you know the distance and direction to its next point. Enter data using this form: *@distance<angle*.

Using the Direct Distance Method

You can also draw lines by placing the cursor at any angle relative to the last point and entering a distance value at the command prompt. The line is drawn from the last point toward or through the cursor location at the length specified. The Direct Distance method is often used when either Ortho mode or polar tracking is turned on.

 N O T E   When in a drawing command, Ortho mode restricts the cursor to horizontal or vertical movements. Lines, for example, can only be drawn at 0°, 90°, 180°, and 270°. Ortho mode is toggled on using the Ortho Mode button at the bottom of the user interface (UI) or by pressing the F8 key.

Drawing the Shape

Now that you have the basics, the following exercises will take you through the steps to draw the four lines that form the outline of the shape using both relative coordinate systems.

Using Relative Cartesian Coordinates

To begin drawing the box, use the same drawing:

1. If your drawing is already blank, jump to step 2. If you still have lines on your drawing, start the Erase command, enter **all**↵, and then press ↵ again to delete them.

2. Start the Line command.

3. At the Specify first point: prompt in the Command window, enter 3,3↵. This is an absolute Cartesian coordinate and will be the first point.

4. Enter @6,0↵.

5. Enter @0,5↵.

6. Turn on the Dynamic Input tool in the status bar and, if necessary, scroll the mouse wheel to zoom out to see the extents of the lines.

7. Enter -6,0↵. Notice that the @ symbol is no longer required to input relative coordinates.

8. Look at the command prompt. It reads: Specify next point or [Close/Undo]:. Items enclosed in brackets are additional available options at that particular point of the command that can be entered at the command prompt. Only the capitalized letters are required to execute an option.

9. Enter c↵ to execute the Close option. Entering this letter after drawing two or more lines closes the shape by extending the next line segment from the last point specified to the first point (see Figure 2.13). It also ends the Line command. Notice that in the Command window the prompt is Command:. This signifies that AutoCAD is ready for a new command.

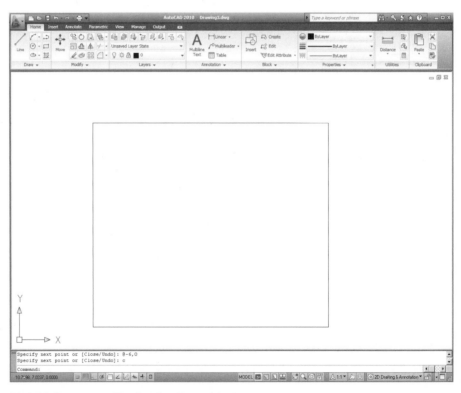

FIGURE 2.13: The first four lines of the box

Erasing Lines

To prepare to draw the box again, use the *Erase* command to erase the four lines you just drew:

1. Start the Erase command. Notice how the cursor changes from the crosshair to a little square. This is called the *pickbox*. When you see it on the screen, it's a sign that AutoCAD is ready for you to select objects on the screen. Also notice the Command window; it's prompting you to select objects.

2. Place the pickbox on one of the lines, and click it when it highlights. The line changes to a dashed line to indicate that it is selected.

3. Repeat step 2 with the rest of the lines.

4. Press ↵. The objects are erased, and the Erase command ends.

N O T E   You've been introduced to two methods of selecting lines to be erased: typing all↵ and using the pickbox to select them. Throughout the book, you'll learn other ways to select objects. The selection process is important in AutoCAD because you need to be able to select objects quickly and precisely.

Controlling How the Selection Tools Are Displayed

When you move the cursor over an object, AutoCAD highlights the object. This is called *rollover highlighting*. It tells you that clicking while the object is highlighted selects that object. You have some choices as to how this highlighting appears:

1. In the Application menu, click the Options button at the bottom to open the Options dialog box.

2. Click the Selection tab. Notice the Selection preview area in the middle of the left side (see Figure 2.14, top). Here you can activate or deactivate the check boxes to control whether rollover highlighting occurs when a command is running or when no command is running. If both check boxes are checked, the feature works all the time.

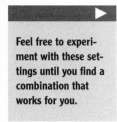

Feel free to experiment with these settings until you find a combination that works for you.

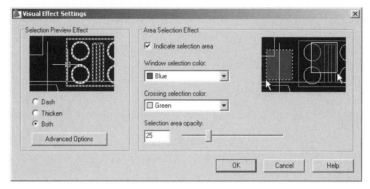

FIGURE 2.14: The Selection Preview area of the Selection tab in the Options dialog box (top), and the Visual Effect Settings dialog box (bottom)

3. Click the Visual Effect Settings button below the check boxes to open the Visual Effect Settings dialog box (see Figure 2.14, bottom). There are two areas: Selection Preview Effect and Area Selection Effect. The Selection Preview Effect area controls how the rollover highlighting feature is displayed. Lines dash, lines thicken, and lines both dash and thicken, depending on which radio button is selected.

4. Make any changes you want, and then click OK. Back in the Options dialog box, click OK to return to your drawing.

Using Relative Polar Coordinates

Now draw the shape again using the relative polar method by following these steps:

1. Start the Line command.

2. Enter 3,3↵ to start the box at the same point.

3. Enter 6<0↵. Because the Dynamic Input tool is turned on, the @ symbol is not required.

4. Enter 5<90↵.

5. Enter 6<180↵.

6. Enter c↵ to close the box and end the Line command. Your box once again resembles the box shown earlier in Figure 2.13.

You can see from this exercise that you can use either method to draw a simple shape. When the shapes you're drawing get more complex and the amount of available information about the shapes varies from segment to segment, one of the two relative coordinate systems will turn out to be more appropriate. As you start drawing the floor plan of the cabin in Chapters 3 and 4, you'll get more practice using these systems.

Using Direct Input

Now draw the box once more, this time using the direct input method by following these steps:

1. Erase the lines in your drawing as you did in a prior exercise.

2. Make sure Polar Tracking is turned on; then start the Line command.

3. Enter 3,3↵ to start the box at the same point.

4. Place the cursor so that it is directly to the right of the first point. When the cursor is nearly perpendicular, it will snap to a perfectly horizontal orientation. The Dynamic Input field shows a value of 0° and the distance from the first point, as shown in Figure 2.15.

FIGURE 2.15: Drawing a line using Direct Input

5. Enter 6↵. The first line is created extending from the initial point to a point 6 units away at an angle of 0°. Notice that the @ symbol is not required when using direct input.

6. Move the cursor so that it is directly above the last point until the angle field reads 90°; then enter 5↵. A 5-unit-long vertical line is drawn from the previous point.

7. Move the cursor so that it is directly to the left of the end of the last line drawn and then enter 6↵. A 6-unit-long horizontal line is drawn from the previous point. Even though the line is drawn in the negative X direction, the minus sign (negative indicator) is not required when using direct input.

8. Enter c↵ to close the box and end the Line command. Your box once again resembles the box shown earlier in Figure 2.13.

You can see from these exercises that you can use multiple methods to draw a simple shape. When the shapes you're drawing get more complex and the amount of available information about the shapes varies from segment to segment, one method or another will turn out to be more appropriate. As you start drawing the floor plan of the cabin in Chapters 3 and 4, you'll get more practice using these systems.

Some additional tools make the process of drawing simple, *orthogonal* lines like these much easier. I'll introduce these tools in the following three chapters.

Using the Offset Command

The next task is to create the lines that represent the inside walls of the box. Because they're all equidistant from the lines you've already drawn, the *Offset* command is the appropriate command to use. You'll offset the existing lines 0.5 units to the inside.

The Offset command involves three steps:

1. Setting the offset distance

2. Selecting the object to offset

3. Indicating the offset direction

Here's how it works:

You can also start the Offset command by typing o↵.

1. Be sure the prompt line in the Command window reads Command:. If it doesn't, press the Esc key until it does. Then click the Offset button in the Modify panel of the Ribbon. The prompt changes to Specify offset distance or [Through/Erase/Layer] <Through>:. This is a confusing prompt, but it will become clear soon. For now, let's specify an offset distance through the keyboard.

> **WARNING** As important as it is to keep an eye on the Command window, some prompts may not make sense to you until you get used to them. When using the Dynamic Input option, notice that the command prompt also appears at the cursor.

2. Enter 0.5↵ for a distance to offset the lines ½ unit. Now you move to the second stage of the command. Note that the cursor changes to a pickbox, and the prompt changes to Select object to offset or [Exit/Undo] <Exit>:.

3. Place the pickbox on one of the lines, and click it when it highlights. The selected line appears dashed to indicate that it is selected (see Figure 2.16), the cursor changes back to the crosshair, and the prompt changes to `Specify point on side to offset or [Exit/Multiple/ Undo] <Exit>:`. AutoCAD is telling you that to determine the direction of the offset, you must specify a point on one side of the line or the other. You make the choice by selecting anywhere in the drawing area on the side of the line where you want the offset to occur.

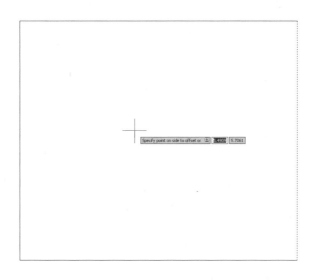

FIGURE 2.16: The first line to be offset is selected.

4. Click a point somewhere inside the box. The offset takes place, and the new line is exactly 0.5 units to the inside of the chosen line (see Figure 2.17). Notice that the pickbox comes back on. The Offset command is still running, and you can offset more lines the same distance.

FIGURE 2.17: The first line is offset.

You have three more lines to offset.

5. Click another line; then click inside the box again. The second line is offset.

6. Click a third line, click inside the box; click the fourth line, and then click again inside the box (see Figure 2.18).

> ► You can cancel a command at any time by pressing Esc or by right-clicking and choosing Cancel from the context menu.

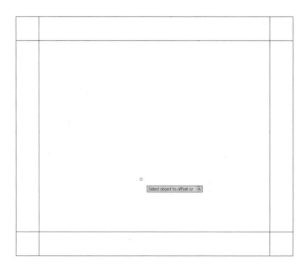

FIGURE 2.18: Four lines have been offset.

N O T E   The offset distance stays set at the last distance you specify—0.5, in this case—until you change it.

7. Press ↵ to end the Offset command.

This command is similar to the Line command in that it keeps running until it's stopped. With Offset, after the first offset, the prompts switch between `Select object to offset or [Exit/Undo] <Exit>:` and `Specify point on side to offset or [Exit/Multiple/Undo] <Exit>:` until you press ↵ or the spacebar to end the command.

The inside lines are now drawn, but to complete the box, you need to clean up the intersecting corners. To handle this task efficiently, you'll use a tool called the Fillet command.

SPECIFYING DISTANCES FOR THE OFFSET COMMAND

The prompt you see in the Command window after starting the Offset command is

`Specify offset distance or [Through/Erase/Layer] <Through>:`

This prompt describes several options for setting the offset distance:

▶ Enter a distance from the keyboard.

▶ Select two points on the screen to establish the offset distance as the distance between those two points.

▶ Press ↵ to accept the offset distance or option that is displayed in the prompt in the angle brackets.

▶ Enter **t**↵ to use the Through option. When you select this option, you're prompted to select the line to offset. You're then prompted to pick a point. The line will be offset to that point. When you pick the next line to offset, you then pick a new point to locate the position of the new line. The Through option allows each line to be offset a different distance.

▶ Enter **e**↵, and then enter **y**↵ to tell AutoCAD to erase the original line that was offset. (After doing this, however, AutoCAD continues erasing offset lines until you reset it by typing **e**↵ **n**↵ at the beginning of the Offset command.)

▶ Enter **l**↵ to use the Layer option. (I'll discuss this option in Chapter 6, "Using Layers to Organize Your Drawing.")

As you become accustomed to using Offset, you'll find uses for each of these options.

Using the Fillet Command

The *Fillet* command lets you round off a corner formed by two lines. You control the radius of the curve, so if you set the curve's radius to zero, the lines form a sharp corner. In this way, you can clean up corners such as the ones formed by the lines inside the box. You must pick points on the filleted lines on portions that will remain after the fillet is implemented; otherwise the wrong portion of the line may be retained.

 1. When the command line just reads Command:, click the Fillet button in the Modify panel of the Ribbon. Notice how the Command window changes after you've clicked the Fillet button (see Figure 2.19).

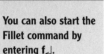
You can also start the Fillet command by entering **f↵**.

```
Command: _fillet
Current settings: Mode = TRIM, Radius = 0.0000
Select first object or [Undo/Polyline/Radius/Trim/Multiple]:
```

FIGURE 2.19: The command prompt after initiating the Fillet command

The default fillet radius should be 0.0000 units. Like the Offset distance, the Fillet radius remains set at whatever value you specify until you change it.

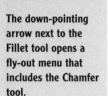
The down-pointing arrow next to the Fillet tool opens a fly-out menu that includes the Chamfer tool.

2. If your Command window displays a radius of 0.0000, go on to step 3. Otherwise, enter **r↵**, and then enter **0↵** to change the radius to zero.

 T I P   When the radius value is set higher than 0, you can temporarily override this by holding the Shift key down while picking the two objects to be filleted. They will be filleted with a radius of 0 while the value set in the Fillet command remains unchanged.

3. Move the cursor—now a pickbox—to the shape, and click two intersecting lines, as shown in Figure 2.20. The intersecting lines are both trimmed to make a sharp corner (see Figure 2.21). The Fillet command automatically ends.

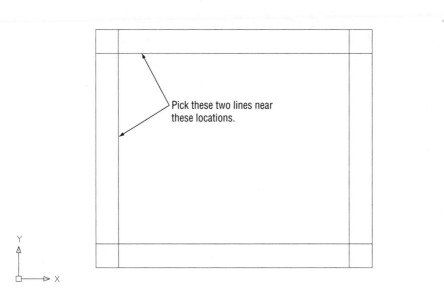

FIGURE 2.20: Pick two lines to execute the Fillet command.

FIGURE 2.21: The first cleaned-up corner

4. Press ↵ to restart the command, and this time enter **m**↵ to activate the Multiple option. Multiple repeats the Fillet command until another option is initiated at the command prompt or the command is terminated with the Enter or Esc keys or the spacebar.

Once a command has
ended, you can
restart it by pressing
either ↵ or the
spacebar or by right-
clicking and choosing
Repeat from the con-
text menu.

5. Fillet the lower-left and lower-right crossing lines to clean up those corners (see Figure 2.22) and press ↵.

FIGURE 2.22: The box with three corners cleaned up

T I P   In most cases, you'll get the same effect by pressing the spacebar as you get by pressing ↵. The exception is when you're entering data in a text box in a dialog box or a palette; in those cases, pressing the spacebar inserts a space.

N O T E   If you make a mistake and pick the wrong part of a line or the wrong line, press Esc to end the command and then enter u↵. This will undo the effect of the last command.

6. Press ↵ to restart the Fillet command. This time, enter r↵ 0.5↵ to set the fillet radius to 0.5, and then click the two lines that make up the interior upper-right corner.

7. Restart the command, set the radius to 1.0, and then fillet the outer upper-right corner. Your box should look like Figure 2.23.

FIGURE 2.23: The box with the curved radii in the upper-right corner

Used together like this, the Offset and Fillet commands are a powerful combination of tools to lay out walls on a floor plan drawing. Because these commands are so important, let's take a closer look at them to see how they work. Both commands are in the Modify panel of the Ribbon and in the Modify menu of the Menu bar, both have the option to enter a numeric value or accept the current value—for offset distance and fillet radius—and both hold that value as the default until it's changed. However, the Offset command keeps running until you stop it, and the Fillet command stops after each use unless the Multiple option is invoked. These commands are two of the most frequently used tools in AutoCAD. You'll learn about more of their uses in later chapters.

The Fillet command has a sister command, *Chamfer*, which is used to bevel corners with straight lines. When the distances for the Chamfer command are set to 0, you can use the command to clean up corners the same way that you use the Fillet command. Some users prefer to use Chamfer rather than Fillet because they don't bevel corners, but they may at times use Fillet to round off corners. If you use Chamfer to clean up corners, Fillet can have any radius and won't have to be overridden or reset constantly to 0. You'll develop your own preference.

Completing the Shape

The final step in completing the box (see Figure 2.1 at the beginning of this chapter) is to make an opening in the bottom wall. From the diagram, you can see that the opening is 2 units wide and set off from the right inside corner by 0.5 units. To make this opening, you'll use the Offset command twice, changing the offset distance for each offset, to create marks for the opening.

Offsetting Lines to Mark an Opening

Follow these steps to establish the precise position of the opening:

1. At the command prompt, start the Offset command. Notice the Command window. The default distance is now set at 0.5, the offset distance you previously set to offset the outside lines of the box to make the inside lines. If the distance is different, enter 0.5↵. You'll want to use this distance again. Press ↵ to accept this preset distance.

2. Pick the inside vertical line on the right, and then pick a point to the left of this line. The line is offset to make a new line 0.5 units to its left (see Figure 2.24).

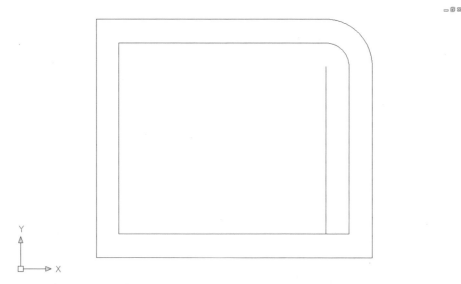

FIGURE 2.24: Offsetting the first line of the opening

3. Press ↵ to end the Offset command, and then press it again to restart the command. This will allow you to reset the offset distance.

4. Enter 2 as the new offset distance, and press ↵.

5. Click the new line, and then pick a point to the left. Press ↵ to end the Offset command (see Figure 2.25).

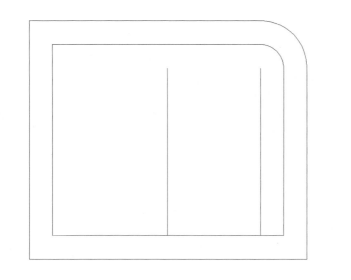

FIGURE 2.25: Offsetting the second line of the opening

You now have two new lines indicating where the opening will be. You can use these lines to form the opening using the Extend and Trim commands.

T I P   The buttons you've been clicking in this chapter are also referred to as *icons* and *tools*. When they're in dialog boxes or on the status bar, they have icons (little pictures) on them and look like buttons to push. When they're on the Ribbon or toolbars, they look like icons. But when you move the pointer arrow cursor onto one, it takes on the appearance of a button with an icon on it. I'll use all three terms—*button*, *icon*, and *tool*—interchangeably in this book.

Extending Lines

You can also start the Extend command by entering ex↵.

You use the *Extend* command to lengthen (extend) lines to meet other lines or geometric figures (called *boundary edges*). Executing the Extend command may be a little tricky at first until you see how it works. Once you understand it, however, it will become automatic. The command has two steps: first, you pick the boundary edge or edges; second, you pick the lines you want to extend to meet those boundary edges. After selecting the boundary edges, you must press ↵ before you begin selecting lines to extend.

1. To begin the Extend command, click the Extend button in the Modify panel of the Ribbon. If you don't see it, click the down arrow next to the Trim icon and then choose Extend from the flyout menu.

2. Notice in the Command window that the bottom line says `Select objects or <select all>:`, but in this case you need to observe the bottom two lines of text in order to know that AutoCAD is prompting you to select boundary edges (see Figure 2.26).

```
Current settings: Projection=UCS, Edge=None
Select boundary edges ...
Select objects or <select all>:
```

F I G U R E   2 . 2 6 : The Command window while using the Extend command

3. Pick the very bottom horizontal line (see Figure 2.27), and press ↵.

 T I P   The `Select Objects:` **prompt would be more useful if it said "Select objects and press Enter when finished selecting objects." But it doesn't. You have to train yourself to press** ↵ **when you finish selecting objects in order to get out of selection mode and move on to the next step in the command.**

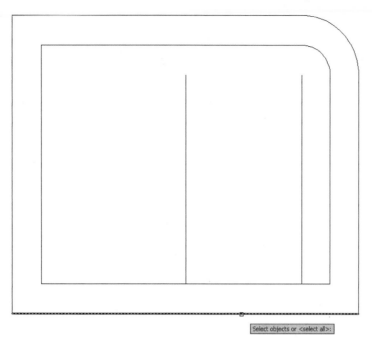

Select objects or <select all>:

F I G U R E 2 . 2 7 : Selecting a line to be a boundary edge

4. Pick the two new vertical lines created by the Offset command. Be sure to place the pickbox somewhere on the lower halves of these lines or AutoCAD will attempt to extend the opposite ends of the lines. Because there are no boundary edges that could intersect with extensions from the top end of the lines, AutoCAD will apparently ignore your picks if you select the wrong ends. The lines are extended to the boundary edge line.

5. Press ↵ to end the Extend command (see Figure 2.28).

You can also start the Trim command by entering **tr**↵.

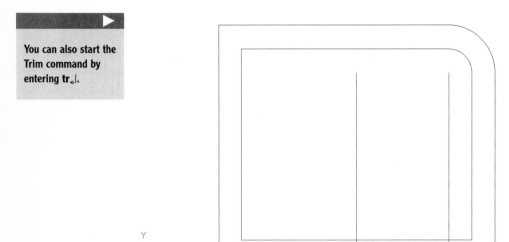

FIGURE 2.28: The lines are extended to the boundary edge.

Trimming Lines

The final step is to trim away the horizontal lines to complete the opening and the unneeded portions of the two most recent vertical lines that you offset. To do this, you use the *Trim command*. As with the Extend command, there are two steps. The first is to select reference lines. In this case, they're called *cutting edges* because they determine the edge or edges to which a line is trimmed. The second step is to pick the lines that are to be trimmed.

1. Click the down arrow next to the Extend button, and then choose Trim from the fly-out menu to start the Trim command. Notice the Command window. Similar to the Extend command, the bottom line prompts you to select objects or select everything in the drawing, but the second line up tells you to select cutting edges.

2. Pick the two vertical offset lines that were just extended as your cutting edges, and then press ↵ (see Figure 2.29).

3. Pick the two horizontal lines across the opening somewhere between the cutting edge lines (see Figure 2.30).

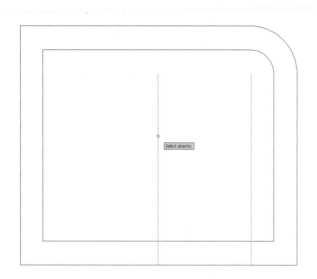

FIGURE 2.29: Lines selected to be cutting edges

 N O T E If you trim the wrong line, or the wrong part of a line, you can click the Undo button on the Quick Access toolbar on the left side of the Auto-CAD title bar. This undoes the last trim without canceling the Trim command, and you can try again.

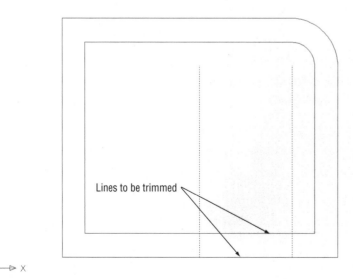

FIGURE 2.30: Lines selected to be trimmed

The opening is trimmed away (see Figure 2.31).

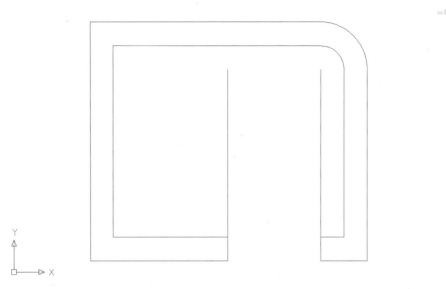

FIGURE 2.31: Lines are trimmed to make the opening.

Now let's remove the extra part of the trimming guidelines.

1. Press ↵ twice—once to end the Trim command and again to restart it. This will let you pick new cutting edges for another trim operation.

2. Pick the two upper horizontal lines next to the opening as your cutting edges, shown in Figure 2.32, and press ↵.

3. Pick the two vertical lines that extend above the new opening. Be sure to pick them above the opening (see Figure 2.33). The lines are trimmed away, and the opening is complete. Press ↵ to end the Trim command (see Figure 2.34).

Congratulations! You've just completed the first drawing project in this book and covered all the tools in this chapter. These skills will be useful as you learn how to work on drawings for actual projects.

A valuable exercise at this time would be to draw this box two or three more times, until you can do it without the instructions. This will be a confidence-builder to get you ready to take on new information in the next chapter, in which you'll set up a drawing for a building

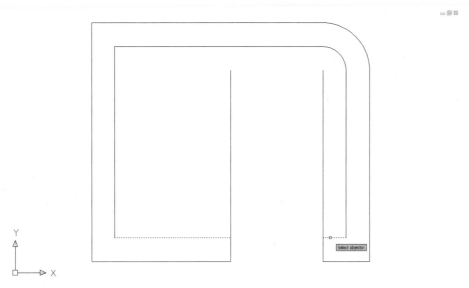

FIGURE 2.32: Lines picked to be cutting edges

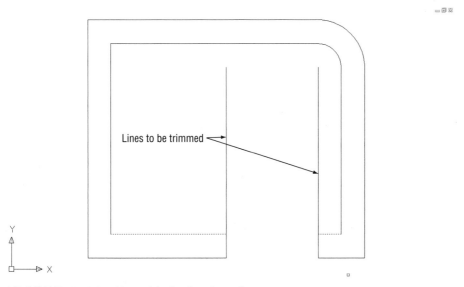

FIGURE 2.33: Lines picked to be trimmed

The box you drew was 6 units by 5 units, but how big was it? You really don't know at this time because the units could represent any actual distance: inches, feet, meters, miles, and so on. Also, the box was positioned conveniently on the screen so you didn't have any problem viewing it. What if you were drawing a building that was 200′ (60.96 meters) long and 60′ (18.29 meters) wide or a portion of a microchip circuit that was only a few thousandths of an inch or millimeters long? In the next chapter, you'll learn how to set up a drawing for a project of a specific size.

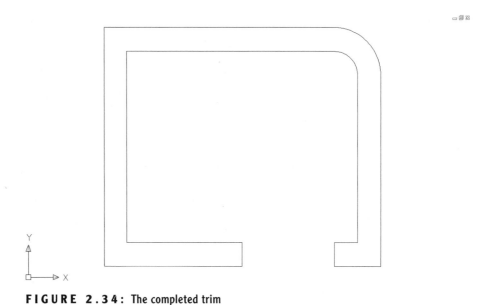

FIGURE 2.34: The completed trim

A completed version of this exercise can be found in this book's web page, `www.sybex.com/go/autocad2010ner`, as `Chapter02 Shape Completed.dwg`.

You can save the file by clicking the Save button on the Quick Access toolbar or exit AutoCAD now without saving this drawing. To do the latter, expand the Application menu, and then click the Exit AutoCAD button in the lower-right corner. When the dialog box asks if you want to save changes, click No. Alternatively, you can leave AutoCAD open and go on to the following practice section or the next chapter.

If You Would Like More Practice...

Draw the object shown in Figure 2.35.

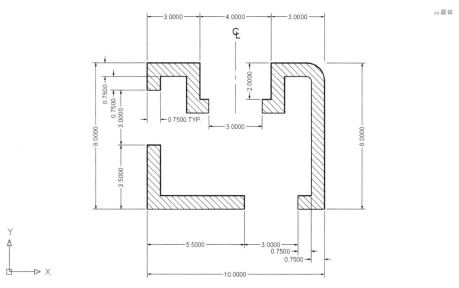

FIGURE 2.35: Practice drawing

You can use the same tools and strategy used to draw the shape. Choose New from the Application menu to start a new drawing, and then use the acad.dwt template file. Here's a summary of the steps to follow:

1. Ignore the three openings at first.

2. Draw the outside edge of the shape using one of the relative coordinate systems. To make sure the shape fits on your screen, start the outline of the box in the lower-left corner at the absolute coordinate of 1,0.5.

3. Offset the outside lines to create the inside wall.

4. Fillet the corners to clean them up. (Lines that aren't touching can be filleted just like lines that intersect.)

5. Use the Offset, Extend, and Trim commands to create the three openings.

Feel free to check your work against Chapter02 More Practice Completed.dwg on this book's web page. Don't worry about trying to put in the dimensions, center line, or hatch lines. You'll learn how to create those objects later in the book.

Are You Experienced?

Now you can...

- ☑ understand the basics of coordinates

- ☑ distinguish between absolute and the two relative coordinate systems used by AutoCAD

- ☑ input coordinates using the Direct Input method

- ☑ use the Line, Erase, Offset, Fillet, Extend, and Trim commands to create a drawing

CHAPTER 3

Setting Up
a Drawing

▶ Setting up drawing units

▶ Using AutoCAD's grid

▶ Zooming in and out of a drawing

▶ Naming and saving a file

I n Chapter 2, "Learning Basic Commands to Get Started," we explored the default drawing area that is set up when you open a new drawing. You drew a box within the drawing area. If you drew the additional diagram offered as a supplemental exercise, the drawing area was set up the same way.

From this point forward, I'll provide the metric equivalents in parentheses for those readers who do not work in Imperial units. For most of the rest of this book, you'll be developing drawings for a cabin with outside wall dimensions of 28′×18′ (8550 mm×5490mm), but the tools you'll use and the skills you'll learn will enable you to draw objects of any size and in any discipline. In this chapter, you'll learn how to set up the drawing area to lay out the floor plan for a building of a specific size. The Decimal units with which you have been drawing until now will be changed to feet and inches, and the drawing area will be transformed so that it can represent an area large enough to display the floor plan of the cabin you'll be drawing.

You'll be introduced to some new tools that will help you visualize the area your screen represents and allow you to draw lines to a specified incremental distance, such as to the nearest foot. Finally, you'll save this drawing to a special folder on your hard drive. At the end of the chapter is a general summary of the various kinds of units that AutoCAD supports.

Setting Up the Drawing Units

When you draw lines of a precise length in AutoCAD, you use one of five kinds of linear units. Angular units can also be any of five types. You can select the type of units to use, or you can accept the default Decimal units that you used in the previous chapter.

When you start a new drawing, AutoCAD displays a blank drawing called Draw-ingn.dwg with the linear and angular units set to decimal numbers. The units and other basic setup parameters applied to this new drawing are based on a prototype drawing with default settings—including those for the units. This chapter covers some of the tools for changing the basic parameters of a new drawing so that you can tailor it to the cabin project or for your own project. Begin by setting up new units:

 1. With AutoCAD running, close all drawings and then click the New button (on the Quick Access toolbar) to start a new drawing. In the Select Template dialog box, click the arrow to the right of the Open button and select Open With No Template—Imperial (see Figure 3.1) or Open With No Template—Metric, depending on your preference.

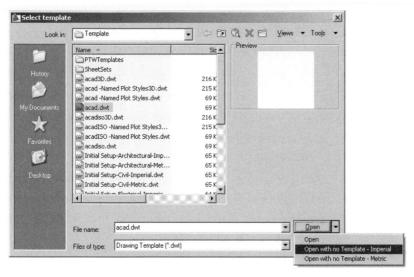

FIGURE 3.1: The Select Template dialog box

To get started with the steps in this chapter, check to be sure that, for now, all the status bar buttons, except Dynamic Input on the left side of the status bar and Model on the right, are clicked to the off position—that is, they appear unpushed. When we get to later chapters, you'll learn how to use the other tools, and in Chapter 10, "Generating Elevations," you'll see how to use templates to set up drawings.

2. Choose Application menu ➢ Drawing ➢ Units to open the Drawing Units dialog box (see Figure 3.2). In the Length area, Decimal is currently selected. Similarly, in the Angle area, Decimal Degrees is the default.

You can also open the Drawing Units dialog box by typing **un↵** or by clicking the Tools tab of the Ribbon (if it's displayed) and then clicking the Units button in the Drawing Utilities panel.

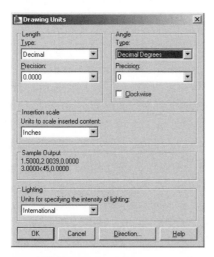

FIGURE 3.2: The Drawing Units dialog box

N O T E   You may notice that the Drawing option listed in the Application menu is followed by an ellipsis (...). The ellipsis indicates that the options open a dialog box rather than executing a command. The same convention applies to buttons with ellipses included in their labels.

3. In the Length area, click the arrow in the Type drop-down list and select Architectural (metric users can leave this set to Decimal). These units are feet and inches, which you'll use for the cabin project.

Notice the two Precision drop-down lists at the bottom of the Length and Angle areas. When you changed the linear units specification from Decimal to Architectural, the number in the Precision drop-down list on the left changed from 0.0000 to 0'-0 1/16". At this level of precision, linear distances are displayed to the nearest 1/16". Metric users should set this to 0 because we won't be using units smaller than a millimeter.

4. Select some of the other Length unit types from the list, and notice the way the units appear in the Sample Output area at the bottom of the dialog box. Then select Architectural again or leave it set to Decimal for metric users.

N O T E   Drop-down lists are lists of options with only the selected choice displayed when the list is closed. When you click the arrow, the list opens. When you make another selection, the list closes and your new choice is displayed. When an item on the list is selected and the focus of the program (indicated by a blue highlight), you can change the available options using the scroll wheel on a mouse or the up and down arrows on the keyboard. You can choose only one item at a time from the list.

5. Click the down arrow in the Precision drop-down list in the Length area to display the choices of precision for Architectural units (see Figure 3.3). This setting controls the degree of precision to which AutoCAD displays a linear distance. If it's set to 1/16", any line that is drawn more precisely—such as a line 6'-3 1/32" long—when queried, displays a length value to the nearest 1/16" or, in the example, as 6'-3 1/16". But the line is still 6'-3 1/32" long.

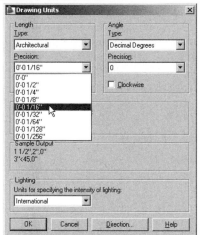
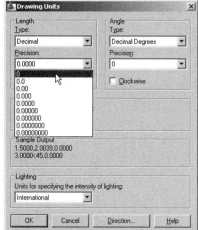

FIGURE 3.3: The Precision drop-down list for Architectural units (left) and Decimal units (right)

6. Click 0'-1/16" to maintain the precision for display of linear units at 1/16".

If you open the Type drop-down list in the Angle area, you'll see a choice, among others, between Decimal Degrees and Deg/Min/Sec. Most AutoCAD users find the Decimal angular units the most practical, but the default precision setting is to the nearest degree. This may not be accurate enough, so you should change it to the nearest hundredth of a degree:

1. Click the arrow in the Precision drop-down list in the Angle area.

N O T E   When using metric units, 1 unit = 1 millimeter.

2. Click 0.00. The Drawing Units dialog box will now indicate that, in your drawing, you plan to use Architectural or Decimal length units with a precision of 1/16" or 0 units and Decimal angular units with a precision of 0.00° (see Figure 3.4). This doesn't restrict the precision at which you draw, just the values that AutoCAD reports.

FIGURE 3.4: The Drawing Units dialog box after changes

Clicking the Direction button at the bottom of the Drawing Units dialog box opens the Direction Control dialog box, which has settings to control the direction of 0°. By default, 0° is to the right (east), and positive angular displacement goes in the counterclockwise direction. (See Figure 2.11 in Chapter 2 for an explanation.) These are the standard settings for most users of CAD. There is no need to change them from the defaults. If you want to take a look, open the Direction Control dialog box, note the choices, and then click Cancel. You won't have occasion in the course of this book to change any of those settings.

N O T E   You'll have a chance to work with the Surveyor's angular units later in this book, in Chapter 12, "Dimensioning a Drawing," when you develop a site plan for the cabin.

3. Click OK in the Drawing Units dialog box to accept the changes and close the dialog box. Notice the coordinate readout in the lower-left corner of the screen: it now reads out in feet and inches.

This tour of the Drawing Units dialog box has introduced you to the choices you have for the types of units and the degree of precision for linear and angular measurement. The next step in setting up a drawing is to determine its size.

N O T E If you accidentally click the mouse when the cursor is on a blank part of the drawing area, AutoCAD starts a rectangular window. I'll talk about these windows soon, but for now just press the Esc key to close the window.

Setting Up the Drawing Size

Now that you have changed the units to Architectural, the drawing area is approximately 12″ to 16″ (500 mm) wide and 9″ (300 mm) high. You can check this by moving the crosshair cursor around on the drawing area and looking at the coordinate readout, as you did in the previous chapter.

T I P When you change Decimal units to Architectural units, one Decimal unit translates to one inch. Some industries, such as civil engineering, often use Decimal units to represent feet instead of inches. If the units in their drawings are switched to Architectural, a distance that was a foot now measures as an inch. To correct this, the entire drawing must be scaled up by a factor of 12.

The drawing area is defined as the part of the screen in which you draw. You can make the distance across the drawing area larger or smaller through a process known as *zooming in or out*. To see how this works, you'll learn about a tool called the *grid* that helps you to draw and to visualize the size of your drawing.

The Grid

The *AutoCAD grid* is a pattern of regularly spaced dots used as an aid to drawing. You can set the grid to be visible or invisible. The area covered by the grid depends on a setting called Drawing Limits, explained in the section "Setting Up Drawing Limits," later in this chapter. To learn how to manipulate the grid size, you'll make the grid visible, use the Zoom In and Zoom Out commands to vary the view of the grid, and then change the area over which the grid extends by resetting the drawing limits. Before doing this, however, let's turn off the User Coordinate System (UCS) icon that currently sits in the lower-left corner of the drawing area. You'll display it again and learn how to use it in Chapter 10.

1. Click the View tab on the Ribbon, and then click the small arrow at the bottom-right corner of the Coordinates panel to open the UCS dialog box. If you pause the cursor over the arrow, you'll see a tooltip that identifies the command that the button initiates, as shown in Figure 3.5.

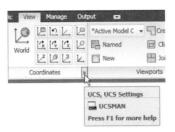

FIGURE 3.5: Opening the UCS dialog box

You can also control the visibility of the UCS icon by entering ucsicon↵, and then enter off↵ at the command prompt.

2. In the UCS Icon Settings area, uncheck the On option, as shown in Figure 3.6, and then click OK. The dialog box closes and the UCS icon disappears.

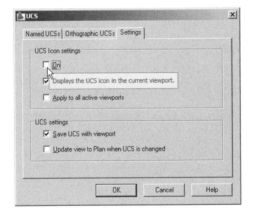

FIGURE 3.6: Turning off the UCS icon

3. Move the crosshair cursor to the status bar at the bottom of the screen, and click the Grid Display button. The button changes from the off to the on state, and dots appear in the drawing area. These dots are the grid. They are preset by default to be ½″ (10 mm) apart, and they extend from the 0,0 point (the origin) out to the right and up to the coordinate point 1′-0″,0′-9″ (490 mm, 290 mm). In the drawing area, the grid points may measure a greater distance apart, especially if you zoom out in the drawing. This is because, at the relatively large drawing area, dots spaced ½″ (10 mm) apart would be very dense and difficult to work with. AutoCAD automatically reduces the density of the displayed grid points to maintain a reasonable appearance in the drawing area.

4. To open the Drafting Settings dialog box, right-click on the Grid Display button and then choose Settings from the context menu that appears (see Figure 3.7).

FIGURE 3.7: Displaying the Drafting Settings dialog box

 T I P   **Right-clicking on any of the buttons (except Allow/Disallow Dynamic UCS and Ortho Mode) on the left side of the status bar and choosing Settings opens the Drafting Settings dialog box (or other appropriate dialog box for defining the tool's parameters) to the tab with the parameters that relate to that specific button. You can also open the Drafting Settings dialog box by entering ds↵.**

5. The Snap And Grid tab should be active (see Figure 3.8). If it's not, click the tab. In the Grid Behavior area, be sure Adaptive Grid and Display Grid Beyond Limits are checked. Then click OK. The grid now not only covers the area from the origin to 12",9" (490 mm, 290 mm), the area defined by the limits of the drawing, but extends to the extents of the drawing area. This will be evident after step 6.

Limits are discussed in the next section. The Adaptive Grid option causes AutoCAD to reduce the number of the grid's columns and rows proportionally whenever the zoom factor would cause the grid to become too dense to be effective.

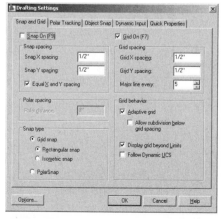

FIGURE 3.8: The Snap And Grid tab of the Drafting Settings dialog box

6. To display a larger area within the drawing area, scroll the mouse wheel by dragging it toward you or use the Zoom Out command by clicking the drop-down arrow next to the Zoom tool in the Navigate panel under the View tab.

The view changes and there are more grid dots in a denser configuration. (See Figure 3.9.) You may need to zoom twice to see the effect. Move the crosshair cursor to the lower-left corner of the grid, and then move it to the upper-right corner. Notice the coordinate readout in the lower left of your screen now shows a large negative number for the lower-left corner and a larger positive number for the upper-right corner. You're displaying a greater amount of space in the drawing area.

FIGURE 3.9: The grid after zooming out

 7. On the status bar next to the Grid Display button, click the Snap Mode button, and then move the cursor back onto the grid and look at the coordinate readout again. The cursor stops at each grid point, even those that are no longer displayed due to the zoom factor, and the readout is to the nearest half inch. The Snap tool locks the cursor onto the grid dots; even when the cursor isn't on the visible grid but somewhere outside it on the drawing area, the cursor maintains the grid spacing and jumps from one location to another.

8. Use the Zoom Out command a few more times or scroll the mouse wheel.

 9. From the Navigate panel, choose Zoom ➤ Zoom In or roll the scroll wheel on your mouse enough times to bring the view of the grid back to the way it appeared when it was first displayed. You aren't changing the size of the grid, just the view of it. It's like switching from a normal to a telephoto lens on a camera.

The grid is more of a guide than an actual boundary of your drawing. You can change a setting to force lines to be drawn only in the area covered by the grid, but this isn't ordinarily done. For most purposes, you can draw anywhere on the screen. The grid merely serves as a tool for visualizing how your drawing will be laid out.

Because it serves as a layout tool for this project, you need to increase the area covered by the grid from its present size to 60′×40′ (18,000 mm×12,000 mm). Because the Drawing Limits setting controls the size of the grid, you need to change it.

Setting Up Drawing Limits

The Drawing Limits setting defines two properties in a drawing: it records the coordinates of the lower-left and upper-right corners of the grid and identifies what is displayed when the user executes a Zoom ➤ All command with only a small portion of the drawing area in use. The coordinates for the lower-left corner are 0,0 by default and are usually left at that setting. You need to change only the coordinates for the upper-right corner and change the settings so that the grid is only displayed within the limits:

1. Be sure the Command window displays the Command: prompt; then enter **limits**↵. Notice how the Command window has changed, as shown in Figure 3.10.

```
Command:
Command: '_limits
Reset Model space limits:

Specify lower left corner or [ON/OFF] <0'-0",0'-0">:
```

FIGURE 3.10: The Command window after starting the Limits command

The bottom command line tells you that the first step is to decide whether to change the default x- and y-coordinates for the lower-left limits, both of which are currently set at 0',0" (0,0). There is no need to change these.

2. Press ↵ to accept the 0',0" (0,0) coordinates for this corner. The bottom command line changes and now displays the coordinates for the upper-right corner of the limits. This is the setting you want to change.

3. Enter 60',40' (18000,12000)↵. Be sure to include the foot sign (').

N O T E   AutoCAD requires that, when using Architectural units, you always indicate that a distance is measured in feet by using the foot sign ('). You don't have to use the inch sign (") to indicate inches.

4. To bring the entire area defined by the drawing limits onto the screen, use the Zoom command again, but this time use the All option: click the down arrow next to the Zoom tool in the Navigate panel, and then click the All option or enter z↵ a↵. The All option zooms the view to display all the objects in the drawing or, in a blank drawing, zooms to the limits. The drawing area expands to display the drawing limits, and the grid changes appearance to accommodate the new view.

5. Right-click on the Grid Display button and click Settings to open the Drafting Settings dialog box.

6. Uncheck the Display Grid Beyond Limits option and click OK. The grid no longer fills the screen, and there are blank areas on either side of the drawing area. (See Figure 3.11.)

7. Move the cursor from one dot to another and watch the coordinate readout. The coordinates are still displayed to the nearest half inch (10 mm), but the dots are much more than half an inch (10 mm) apart.

FIGURE 3.11: The drawing with the grid extending to the 60′×40′ (18,000 mm × 12,000 mm) limits

By default, when you zoom in or out, AutoCAD adjusts the grid spacing to keep the dots from getting too close together or too far apart. In this case, remember that you found the grid spacing to be ½″ (10 mm) by default. If the drawing area is giving you a view of a 60′×40′ (18,000 mm×12,000 mm) grid with dots at ½″ (10 mm), the grid is 1440 (1800) dots wide and 960 (1200) dots high. If the whole grid were to be shown on the screen, the dots would be so close together that they would only be about one pixel in size and would solidly fill the drawing area. So AutoCAD adjusts the spacing of the dots to keep the grid readable. You need to change that spacing to a more usable value.

For the drawing task ahead, it will be more useful to have the spacing set differently. Remember how you turned on Snap mode, and the cursor stopped at each dot? If you set the dot spacing to 2′ (1000 mm) and the Snap Spacing to 6″ (50 mm), you can use Grid and Snap modes to help you draw the outline of the cabin, because the dimensions of the outside wall line are in whole feet (millimeters) and divisible by 2: 28′×16′ (8550 mm×4850 mm) and the exterior walls are 6″ (150 mm) thick. Here's how:

1. Right-click the Grid Display button and click Settings to open the Drafting Settings dialog box one more time. The Drafting Settings dialog box opens and the Snap And Grid tab is active. The settings in both the Grid and Snap areas include X and Y Spacing settings. Notice that they're all set for a spacing of ½″ (10).

2. In the Grid Spacing area, click in the Grid X Spacing text box and change ½″ (10) to 2′ (1000). Then click in the Grid Y Spacing text box. It automatically changes to match the Grid X Spacing text box. If you want different Grid X and Grid Y Spacing values, you must uncheck the Equal X and Y Spacing option in the Snap Spacing area.

3. In the Snap section, change the Snap X Spacing setting to 6 (50). The inch sign isn't required. Then click the Snap Y Spacing input box or press the Tab key. The Snap Y spacing automatically changes to match the Snap X Spacing setting.

4. In the Snap Type area, be sure Grid Snap and Rectangular Snap are selected.

5. In the Grid Behavior area, only Adaptive Grid should be checked. With the grid set this way, AutoCAD will adjust the number of dots displayed as you zoom in and out but won't add dots between the lowest grid spacing.

6. The Snap On and Grid On check boxes at the top of the dialog box should be selected. If they aren't, click them. Your Snap And Grid tab should look like Figure 3.12.

> If you set the Grid Spacing to 0, the grid takes on whatever spacing you set for the Snap X Spacing and Snap Y Spacing text boxes. This is how you lock the snap and grid together.

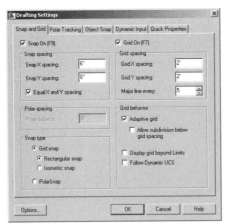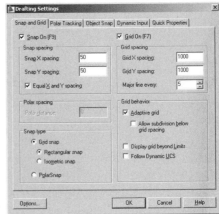

FIGURE 3.12: New settings on the Snap And Grid tab of the Drafting Settings dialog box using Imperial units (left) and Metric (right)

7. Click OK. The new 2′ (1000 mm) grid is now visible. Move the cursor around on the grid—be sure Snap is on. (Check the Snap Mode button on the status bar; it's pressed when Snap is on.) Notice the coordinate readout. It's displaying coordinates to the nearest 6″ (50 mm)

to conform to the new 6″ (50) snap spacing. The cursor stops at several snap points between each grid dot.

8. Move the crosshair cursor to the upper-right corner of the grid and check the coordinate readout. It should display 60′-0″, 40′-0″, 0′-0″ (18000.0000, 12000.0000, 0). (In AutoCAD LT, you won't have the third coordinate.)

Drawing with Grid and Snap

Your drawing area now has the proper settings and is zoomed to a convenient magnification. You're ready to draw the first lines of the cabin:

1. When the Command window displays the Command: prompt, start the Line command. Click the Line button on the Draw panel of the Ribbon's Home tab or enter l↵. Enter 8′,8′↵ (2500,2500↵), or move the cursor until the dynamic input fields indicate the cursor is over the 8′,8′ (2500,2500) point and then click to define the starting point of the line.

2. Hold the crosshair cursor above and to the right of the point you just picked. AutoCAD shows ghosted linear and angular dimensions that dynamically display the length and angle of the first line segment as the cursor moves, and a tooltip window displays the current prompt for the Line command (see Figure 3.13).

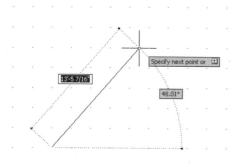

FIGURE 3.13: One point picked on the grid

3. Don't click yet. Hold the crosshair cursor directly out to the right of the first point picked and note how the linear dimension displays a distance in 6″ (50 mm) increments. The angular dimension should have an angle of 0.00°, as shown in Figure 3.14.

FIGURE 3.14: Setting the angle for the first line

4. Continue moving the crosshair cursor left or right until the dashed linear dimension displays 28′ (8550). At this point, click the left mouse button to draw the first line of the cabin wall (see Figure 3.15).

FIGURE 3.15: The first line of the cabin wall is drawn.

5. Move the crosshair cursor directly above the last point picked to a position such that the dashed linear dimension displays 18′ (5490) and the dashed angular dimension displays 90.00°, and then pick that point.

6. Move the crosshair cursor directly left of the last point picked until the dashed linear dimension displays 28′ (8550) and the dashed angular dimension displays 180.00°, and then pick that point (see Figure 3.16).

7. Finally, enter c↵ to close the box. This tells AutoCAD to draw a line from the last point picked to the first point picked and, in effect, closes the box. AutoCAD then automatically ends the Line command (see Figure 3.17).

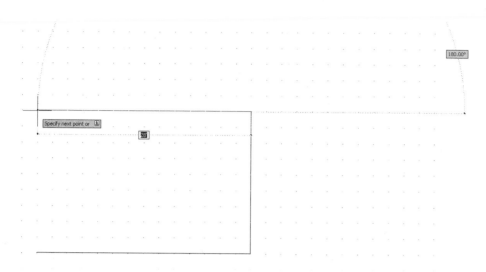

FIGURE 3.16: Drawing the second and third wall lines

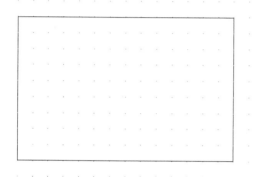

FIGURE 3.17: The completed outside wall lines

This method for laying out building lines by using Snap and Grid and the dynamic input is useful if the dimensions all conform to a convenient rounded-off number, such as the nearest six inches. The key advantage to this method over just typing the relative coordinates, as you did with the box in Chapter 2, is that you avoid having to enter the numbers. You should, however, assess whether the layout you need to draw has characteristics that lend themselves to using Grid, Snap, and dynamic input or whether typing the relative coordinates would be more efficient. As you get more comfortable with AutoCAD, you'll see that this sort of question comes up often: which way is the most efficient? This happy dilemma is inevitable in an application with enough tools to give you many strategic choices. In Chapters 4 and 5, you'll learn other techniques for drawing rectangles.

A Closer Look at Dynamic Input

The kind of information shown in dynamic display is similar to that shown in the Command window, and the intent of this feature is to keep your eyes on the screen as much as possible. Like the information on the command line, it depends on what you're doing at the time and on several settings that you access by right-clicking the Dynamic Input button on the status bar and selecting Settings from the context menu. This opens the Drafting Settings dialog box with the Dynamic Input tab activated (see Figure 3.18).

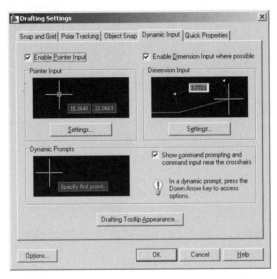

FIGURE 3.18: The Dynamic Input tab of the Drafting Settings dialog box

This tab has three check boxes; two at the top and one near the middle on the right, and three buttons to open three feature-specific Settings dialog boxes. To make the dynamic input conform to what is shown in the book, do the following:

1. Be sure all three check boxes are selected.

2. In the Pointer Input area, click the Settings button to open the Pointer Input Settings dialog box (see Figure 3.19). In the Format area, the Polar Format and Relative Coordinates radio buttons should be selected. Click OK.

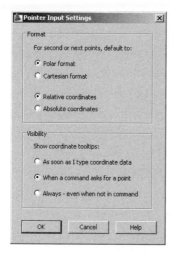

FIGURE 3.19: The Pointer Input Settings dialog box

3. In the Dimension Input area, click the Settings button to open the Dimension Input Settings dialog box (see Figure 3.20).

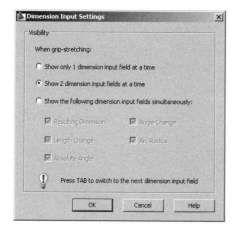

FIGURE 3.20: The Dimension Input Settings dialog box

4. Be sure the Show 2 Dimension Input Fields At A Time radio button is selected and then click OK.

5. Below the Dynamic Prompts area of the Drafting Settings dialog box, click the Drafting Tooltip Appearance button to open the Tooltip Appearance dialog box (see Figure 3.21). In the Apply To area at the bottom of the box, be sure the Use Settings Only For Dynamic Input

Tooltips radio button is selected. Vary the Colors, Size, and Transparency settings according to your preference. (I used a setting of 1 for Size and 0% for Transparency.) Don't worry about Layout Color for now. The Model Color you choose depends on whether your drawing area has a light or dark background. Experiment. When you're finished, click OK.

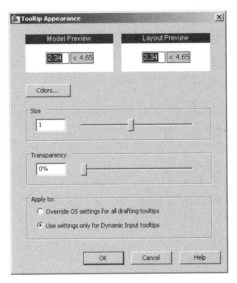

FIGURE 3.21: The Tooltip Appearance dialog box

6. Click OK again to close the Drafting Settings dialog box.

If you decide to disable dynamic input, you can easily do so by clicking its button in the status bar so that it's in unpushed mode.

Saving Your Work

As with all Windows-compliant applications, when you save a file for the first time by choosing Save, you can designate a name for the file and a folder in which to store it. I recommend that you create a special folder, called something like Training Data, for storing the files you'll generate as you work your way through this book. This will keep them separate from project work already on your computer, and you'll always know where to save or find a training drawing. To save your drawing, follow these steps:

1. In AutoCAD, click the Save button on the Quick Access toolbar or choose Save from the Application menu. Because you haven't named this file yet, the Save Drawing As dialog box, opens as shown in Figure 3.22.

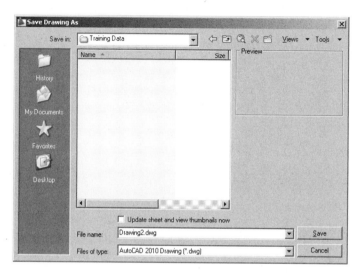

FIGURE 3.22: The Save Drawing As dialog box

The Save button in the Quick Access toolbar, the Application menu ➤ Save option, and the Ctrl+S key combination actually invoke the QSave (Quick Save) command in AutoCAD.

QSave only asks for a filename when the drawing has not yet been saved for the first time, after which it simply overwrites the existing file without prompting. Entering the Save command at the command line (**save↵**) always opens the Save Drawing As dialog where the filename and path are modified.

N O T E   The actual folders and files may be different on your computer.

2. In the Save In drop-down list, designate the drive and folder where you want to save the drawing. If you're saving it on the hard drive or server, navigate to the folder in which you want to place the new Training Data folder.

3. Click the Create New Folder button near the top-right corner of the dialog box. The folder appears in the list of folders and is highlighted. It's called New Folder, and a cursor flashes just to the right of the highlighting rectangle.

4. Enter **Training Data↵** (or whatever name you want to give the new folder).

5. Double-click the new folder to open it.

6. In the File Name box, change the name to Cabin03. You're not required to enter the .dwg extension.

N O T E From now on, when you're directed to save the drawing, save it as Cabinx, with x indicating the number of the chapter. This way, you'll know where in the book to look for review, if necessary. Name multiple saves within a chapter Cabinxa, Cabinxb, and so on. To save the current drawing under a different name, used the Save As command (Application menu ➤ Save As or saveas↵).

7. Click Save. Notice that the AutoCAD title bar displays the new name of the file along with its path. It's now safe to exit AutoCAD.

8. If you want to shut down AutoCAD at this time, choose Application Menu ➤ Exit AutoCAD or click the X button in the top-right corner of the AutoCAD window. Otherwise, keep your drawing up and read on.

The tools covered in this chapter are your key to starting a new drawing from scratch and getting it ready for a specific project.

A Summary of AutoCAD's Units

The following is a brief description of each of the linear and angular unit types that AutoCAD offers and how they are used. The example distance is 2'-6½". The example angle is 126°35'10".

Linear Units

The linear unit types that AutoCAD uses are as follows:

Architectural This unit type uses feet and inches with fractions. You must use the foot sign ('): for example, 2'-6½". For this distance, enter **2'6-1/2** or **2'6.5**. For the most part, these are the units that you'll use in this book.

Decimal This unit type uses Decimal units that can represent any linear unit of measurement. You don't use the foot sign, the inch sign, or fractions. For example, if each Decimal unit equals 1 inch, then to specify a line to be 2'-6½" long, you must convert feet to inches and enter a length of **30.5**. But if each Decimal unit equals 1 foot, you must convert the inches to the decimal equivalent of a foot and enter **2.5417**.

Engineering   This unit is equivalent to Architectural units except that inches are displayed as decimals rather than fractions. For a distance of 2'-6½", enter **2'6.5** or **2.5417'**. In either method, the resulting distance is displayed as 2'-6.5".

Fractional   These units are just like Architectural units except there is no use of feet. Everything is expressed in inches and fractions. If you enter **30-1/2** or **30.5**, the resulting distance displays as 30½.

Scientific   This unit system is similar to the Decimal unit system except for the way in which distances are displayed. If you enter **3.05E+01**, that is what is displayed. The notation always uses an expression that indicates a number from 1 to 10 that is to be multiplied by a power of 10. In this case, the power is 1, so the notation means 3.05×10, or 30.5 in Decimal units.

Angular Units

The angular unit types that AutoCAD uses are as follows:

Decimal   This type uses 360° in a circle in decimal form, with no minutes and no seconds. All angles are expressed as decimal degrees. For example, an angle of 126°35'10"is entered as **126.586** or **126d35'10"** and displays as 126.5861. Auto-CAD uses the letter *d* instead of the traditional degree symbol (°).

Deg/Min/Sec   This is the traditional system for measuring angles. In AutoCAD's notation, degrees are indicated by the lowercase *d*, the minutes use the traditional ', and the seconds use the traditional ". The system is clumsy. Most users now use decimal angles instead of this system and choose their preference for precision.

Grads   This unit is based on a circle being divided into 400 grads, so 90° equals 100 grads. One degree equals 1.11 grads, and 1 grad equals 0.90 degrees. Auto-CAD uses *g* as the symbol for grads.

Radians   The radian is the angle from the center of a circle made by the radius of the circle being laid along the circumference of the circle.

One radian equals 57.3 degrees, and 360° equals 6.28 radians, or 2π radians. AutoCAD uses *r* as the symbol for radians.

Surveyor   These units use bearings from the north and south directions toward the east or west direction and are expressed in degrees, minutes, and seconds. They're discussed in Chapter 12. In this example, 126° 35'10" translates to N 36d35'10" W in bearings, or Surveyor units.

The next chapter will focus on adding to the drawing, modifying commands you learned as part of Chapter 2, and creating strategies for solving problems that occur in the development of a floor plan.

Are You Experienced?

Now you can...

- ☑ **set up linear and angular units for a new drawing**
- ☑ **make the grid visible and modify its coverage**
- ☑ **use the Zoom In and Zoom Out commands**
- ☑ **activate the Snap mode and change the Snap and Grid spacings**
- ☑ **use the Zoom All function to fit the grid on the drawing area**
- ☑ **draw lines using Grid, Snap, and the Dynamic Input feature**
- ☑ **create a new folder on your hard drive from within AutoCAD**
- ☑ **name and save your file**

CHAPTER 4

Developing Drawing Strategies: Part 1

▶ Making interior walls

▶ Zooming in on an area using various zoom tools

▶ Making doors and swings

▶ Using object snaps

▶ Using the Copy and Mirror commands

Assuming that you have worked your way through the first three chapters, you have now successfully drawn a shape (Chapter 2) as well as the outer wall lines of a cabin (Chapter 3). From here on, you'll develop a floor plan for the cabin. In Chapter 10, you'll work on *elevations* (views of the front, back, and sides of the building that show how the building will look if you're facing it). The focus in this chapter is on gaining a feel for the strategy of drawing in AutoCAD and on how to solve drawing problems that come up in the course of laying out the floor plan. As you work your way through this chapter, the activities will include making the walls, cutting doorway openings, and drawing the doors (see Figure 4.1). In Chapter 5, you'll add steps and two decks and you'll place fixtures and appliances in the bathroom and kitchen.

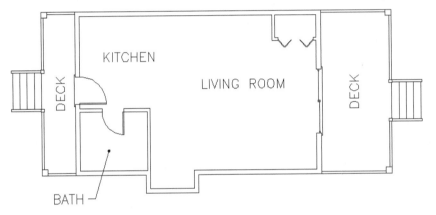

FIGURE 4.1: The basic floor plan of the cabin

Each exercise in this chapter presents opportunities to practice using commands you already know from earlier chapters and also to learn a few new ones. The most important goal is to begin to use strategic thinking as you develop methods for creating new elements of the floor plan.

T I P   Because you'll be doing quite a bit of drawing in this and the next chapter, this is a good opportunity to activate the Dynamic Input feature introduced in Chapter 3 if you've turned it off. Turn it off and on as you work through the exercises, and notice how the information displayed in the drawing area changes as you move from one command to another. Commands that you enter only appear at the cursor, and not at the command line, while dynamic input is active. The feature is designed to help you avoid having continually to glance down at the Command window as you work through the steps of a command. Sometimes, however, the information you need is displayed only in the Command window, so you still have to glance down at it. By the time you finish Chapter 5, you'll know whether or not you want the feature to be active.

Laying Out the Walls

For most floor plans, the walls come first. The first lesson in this chapter is to understand that you won't be drawing many new lines in the floor plan, at least not as many as you might expect. You'll create most new objects in this chapter from items already in your drawing. In fact, you'll only draw a few new lines to make walls. You'll generate most of the new walls from the four exterior wall lines you drew in the previous chapter.

You'll need to create an inside wall line for the exterior walls (because the wall has thickness) and then make the three new interior walls (see Figure 4.2). The thickness will be 4″ (100 mm) for interior walls and 6″ (150 mm) for exterior walls because exterior walls are sturdier and load bearing and have an additional layer or two of weather protection, such as siding or stucco. Finally, you'll need to cut four openings in these walls (interior and exterior) for the doorways.

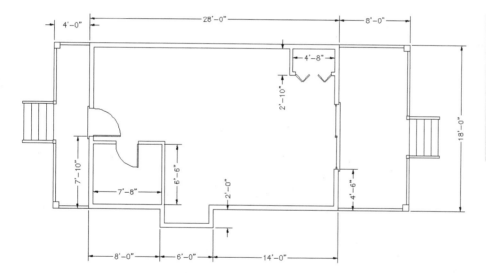

◀ Most of the commands used for this exercise were presented in Chapters 2 and 3. If you need a refresher, glance back at those chapters.

FIGURE 4.2: The wall dimensions

Creating a Polyline

Using the tools you've already learned, you would first offset the existing four wall lines to the inside to make the inside wall lines for the exterior walls. Then you would fillet them to clean up their corners, just as you did for the box in Chapter 2. In this chapter, you'll instead begin to use the polyline object. While a line is a single, straight object with no measurable width, polylines are composed of several straight or curved segments that can also maintain a user-defined width. When a polyline is offset, all segments are offset equally and the corners are left sharp without the need to use the Fillet command to clean them up. Any polyline can be disassembled into its component lines and arcs using the Explode command. Using the Pedit command, several lines and arcs can be converted into a single polyline as long as the endpoints of the various segments terminate in exactly the same location.

1. With AutoCAD running, choose Application menu ➢ Open ➢ Drawing. In the Select File dialog box, navigate to the folder you designated as your training folder and select your cabin drawing. (You named it Cabin03.dwg at the end of Chapter 3.) Click Open to display the cabin drawing as shown in Figure 4.3.

FIGURE 4.3: The cabin as you left it in Chapter 3

2. On the status bar, click the Grid Display and Snap Mode buttons to turn them off.

3. Expand the Modify Ribbon panel and click Edit Polyline, as shown in Figure 4.4, or enter **pe↵** to start the Pedit command.

FIGURE 4.4: Starting the Edit Polyline command

4. Select one of the exterior wall lines. The line ghosts, and because it is not a polyline yet, the command line prompts you to turn it into one, as shown in Figure 4.5.

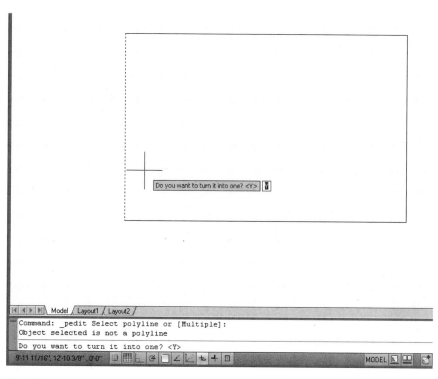

Do you want to turn it into one? <Y>

Command: _pedit Select polyline or [Multiple]:
Object selected is not a polyline
Do you want to turn it into one? <Y>

9'-11 11/16", 12'-10 3/8", 0'-0"   MODEL

F I G U R E   4 . 5 : The command line when a nonpolyline object is selected

5. Press the ⏎ key to accept the default Yes option.

6. The command line now shows all of the possible polyline editing options: Enter an option [Close/Join/Width/Edit vertex/Fit/ Spline/Decurve/Ltype gen/Reverse/Undo]:.

To choose the Join option, enter j⏎ or click the Join option at the Dynamic Input prompt that appears near the cursor (see Figure 4.6). The intent here is to join the four lines into a single four-segment closed polyline.

FIGURE 4.6: Select the Join option at the Dynamic Input prompt.

7. Select all the lines in the drawing, including the original line you selected at the beginning of this exercise. Press the ↵ key when you are done.

8. The second line in the Command window shows 3 `segments added to polyline`—indicating that the three subsequent lines selected have been added to the original line that was converted to a polyline in step 5. The bottom line indicates that you're still in the Pedit command (see Figure 4.7).

FIGURE 4.7: The Command window after converting the lines to a single polyline

9. Press the ↵ key again or choose the Exit option to exit the Pedit command.

   Select one segment of the polyline that forms the perimeter of the box in the drawing area. All four polyline segments are selected, indicating that they exist as a single object, and blue boxes appear at the corners. The blue boxes, called *grips,* appear because you selected the object outside of a command and are not exclusive to polylines. Grips are explained in Chapter 8, "Controlling Text in a Drawing."

Editing a Polyline

Polylines are composed of segments, which may be straight or curved lines, and vertices that terminate the segments. Each segment must have a vertex at each end, but several segments can share a single vertex. The perimeter that you drew follows the major length and width dimensions of the cabin but doesn't account for the small pop-out on the south side of the structure. In this exercise, you will add the pop-out, trim the original polyline, and then join the two polylines into a single entity.

1. Click the Polyline button in the Draw panel of the Ribbon to start the polyline command.

2. At the Specify start point: prompt, enter 16′,8′↵ (4850,2500↵). With the Dynamic Input feature turned on, the comma not only designates the X and Y locations for the start point, but also instructs AutoCAD to switch the current input field from the X field to the Y field.

    When Dynamic Input is turned off, the values that are types are shown in the Command window at the bottom of the AutoCAD window.

    A rubber-banding line, similar to the one you saw when you used the Line command, is attached to the point you designated in step 2 and to the cursor.

3. Enter 0,-2′↵ (0,-610↵) 6′,0↵ (1830,0↵) 0,2′↵↵ (0,610↵↵). Your screen should look like Figure 4.8.

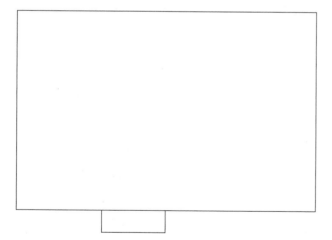

FIGURE 4.8: The pop-out added to the cabin

4. Start the Trim command.

5. At the Select Objects or <select all>: prompt, pick the pop-out that you just drew and press ↵. All segments of the pop-out are ghosted to indicate that the entire polyline is designated as a cutting edge.

6. Place the pickbox over the portion of the long, lower horizontal line of the cabin between the two short, vertical pop-out lines, as shown in Figure 4.9, and click to trim this line.

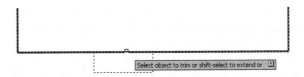

FIGURE 4.9: Selecting the polyline segment to trim away

7. Press ↵ to end the Trim command.

8. From the expanded Modify panel, choose Edit Polyline and then pick either of the two polylines.

9. Select Join from the context menu that appears.

10. Pick the other polyline and press ↵ twice—first to join them and then to end the command. Your drawing now consists of a single polyline made up of eight segments, as shown in Figure 4.10.

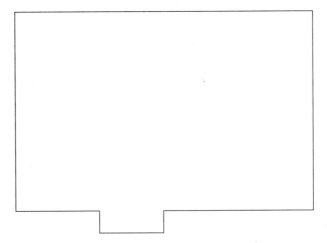

FIGURE 4.10: The polyline after trimming the original and then joining the remaining entities

Creating the Exterior Wall Lines

Here you will use the Offset command to create all the interior lines for the exterior walls at one time.

1. Start the Offset command by clicking the Offset button on the Modify panel.

2. At the `Specify offset distance or:` Dynamic Input prompt, enter 6↵ (150↵).

N O T E You don't have to enter the inch sign ("), but you're required to enter the foot sign (') when appropriate.

3. At the `Select object to offset or:` prompt, select the polyline.

4. Click in a blank area inside the cabin's perimeter. All segments of the pline are offset 6″ (150 mm) to the inside (see Figure 4.11). The Offset command is still running; press ↵ to terminate it.

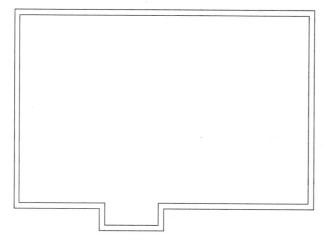

FIGURE 4.11: All line segments are now offset 6″ (150 mm) to the inside.

> You can restart the most recently used command by pressing the spacebar or ↵ at the command prompt or by right-clicking and choosing the Repeat option from the context menu.

As you can see, there is no need to fillet the corners, and using polylines can lessen the number of steps and picks required to draw the inside lines. I'll diverge from the cabin exercise briefly to examine the capabilities of the Fillet command when used in conjunction with polylines.

5. Start the Fillet command by clicking the Fillet button on the Modify panel.

6. Enter r↵ to select the Radius option; then set the radius to 12' (3600).

7. Select any two polyline segments that share a corner of the inner box. The two segments are shortened and a curved segment with a 12" (3600 mm) radius is inserted. The polyline now has nine contiguous segments (see Figure 4.12). The Fillet command automatically ends after each fillet.

FIGURE 4.12: The first corner is filleted.

8. Press ↵ or the spacebar to restart the Fillet command.

9. Enter p↵ to instruct AutoCAD that the fillet is to be performed on all intersections of a polyline. At the Select 2D polyline: prompt, select the inner box. All corners are now filleted (see Figure 4.13).

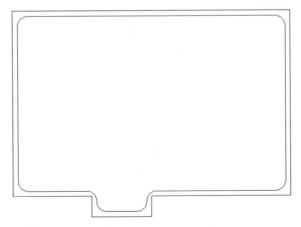

FIGURE 4.13: The polyline's corners are filleted.

10. You can see how the Fillet command, when used with a polyline, can save time. You don't want the objects to remain as polylines for this project, so click the Undo button on the Quick Access toolbar or enter **u↵** until all of the filleted edges are square again.

You can also use the Windows standard Ctrl+Z keyboard combination to undo AutoCAD actions.

 11. Click the Explode button in the Modify panel, or enter **explode↵** to start the Explode command. Select both of the polylines and then press the ↵ key. The two polylines are now 16 separate line objects. You will be using the Offset command to create the interior wall from the lines that make up the exterior walls. Exploding the polylines into individual line objects allows you to offset single, straight objects rather than the closed polylines that would require trimming to clean up.

OFFSET VS. FILLET

These are the characteristics that Offset and Fillet have in common:

- ▶ Both are on the Modify panel.
- ▶ Both have a default setting—offset distance and fillet radius—that you can accept or change.

These are the characteristics that are different in Offset and Fillet.

- ▶ You select one object with Offset and two objects or polyline segments with Fillet.
- ▶ Offset keeps running until you stop it. Fillet ends after each fillet operation, so you need to restart Fillet to use it again unless you use the Multiple option.

You'll find several uses for Offset and Fillet in the subsequent sections of this chapter and throughout the book.

Creating the Interior Walls

You will create the cabin's interior wall lines by offsetting the exterior wall lines:

1. Start the Offset command.

2. At the Specify Offset distance or: prompt, enter 7'8↵ (2350↵). Leave no space between the foot sign (') and the 8.

N O T E AutoCAD requires that you enter a distance containing feet and inches in a particular format: no space between the foot sign (') and the inches value, and a hyphen (-) between the inches and a fraction. For example, if you're entering a distance of 6'-4³/₄", you enter 6'4-3/4. The measurement is displayed in the normal way, 6'-4³/₄", but you must enter it in the format that has no spaces because the spacebar acts the same as the ↵ in most cases.

3. Click the inside line of the left exterior wall (see Figure 4.14).

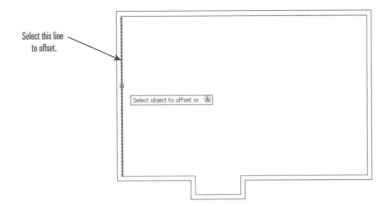

Select this line to offset.

Select object to offset or

FIGURE 4.14: Selecting the wall line to offset

4. Click in a blank area to the right of the selected line. The line is offset 7'-8" (2250 mm) to the right.

5. Press ↵ twice, or press the spacebar twice. The Offset command is terminated and then restarted, and you can reset the offset distance.

T I P In the Offset command, your opportunity to change the offset distance comes right after you start the command. So, if the Offset command is already running and you need to change the offset distance, you must stop and then restart the command. To do so, press ↵ or the spacebar twice.

6. Enter 4↵ (100↵) to reset the offset distance to 4" (100 mm).

7. Click the new line that was just offset, and then click in a blank area to the right of that line. You have created a vertical interior wall (see Figure 4.15). Press ↵ twice to stop and restart the Offset command.

FIGURE 4.15: The first interior wall

8. Enter 6.5′↵ (1980↵) to set the distance for offsetting the next wall.

N O T E With Architectural units set, you can still enter distances in decimal form for feet and inches, and AutoCAD will translate them into their appropriate form. For example, you can enter 6′-6″ as 6.5′, and you can enter 4 ½″ as 4.5 without the inch sign.

9. Pick a point on the inside, lower-left exterior wall line (see Figure 4.16).

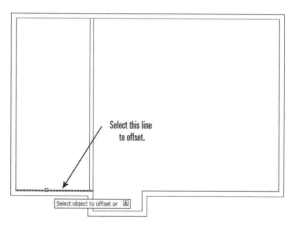

FIGURE 4.16: Selecting another wall line to offset

10. Click in a blank area above the line selected. The inside exterior wall line is offset to make a new interior wall line. Press the spacebar twice to stop and restart the Offset command.

11. Enter 4↵ (100↵). Click the new line, and click again above it. A second wall line is made, and you now have two interior walls. Press the spacebar to end the Offset command.

These interior wall lines form the boundary of the bathroom. You need to clean up their intersections with each other and with the exterior walls. If you take the time to do this properly, it will be easier to make changes in the future. Refer to Figures 4.1 and 4.2 earlier in this chapter to see where we're headed.

Cleaning Up Wall Lines

Earlier in the book, you used the Fillet command to clean up the corners of intersecting lines. You can use that command again to clean up some of the interior walls, but you'll have to use the Trim command to do the rest of them. You'll see why as you progress through the next set of steps:

1. It will be easier to pick the wall lines if you make the drawing larger on the screen. Switch to the Ribbon's View tab, and then click the down arrow next to the current Zoom tool in the Navigate panel to expose all the Zoom options; then click Extents to zoom to display all the objects in your drawing within the boundaries of the drawing area.

2. Expand the Zoom menu again, click Scale, and then enter 0.75x↵. The drawing zooms out a bit. You've just used two options of the Zoom command. First, you zoomed to Extents to display all the objects in your drawing. You then zoomed to a scale (0.75x) to make the drawing 75 percent the size it was after zooming to Extents. This is a change in magnification on the view only; the building is still 28′ (8550 mm) long and 18′ (5490 mm) wide.

3. Start the Fillet command and set the radius to 0; click the two interior wall lines, as shown in the top of Figure 4.17. The lines are filleted, and the results will look like the bottom of Figure 4.17.

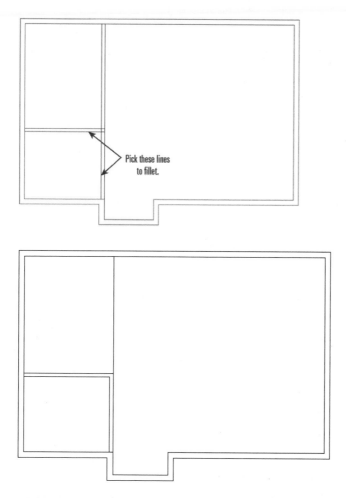

FIGURE 4.17: Selecting the first two lines to fillet (top) and the result of the fillet (bottom)

4. Press the spacebar to restart the Fillet command. Select the two lines, as shown in the top of Figure 4.18. The results are shown in the bottom of Figure 4.18.

> Here's the best rule for choosing between Fillet and Trim: if you need to clean up a single intersection between two lines, use the Fillet command. For other cases, use the Trim command.

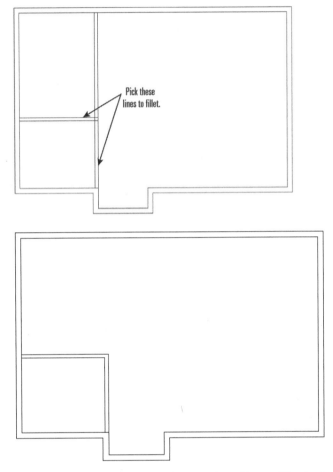

Pick these lines to fillet.

FIGURE 4.18: Selecting the second two lines to fillet (top) and the result of the second fillet (bottom)

The two new interior walls are now the correct length, but you'll have to clean up the areas where they form T-intersections with the exterior walls. The Fillet command won't work in T-intersections because too much of one of the wall lines gets deleted. You need to use the Trim command in T-intersection cases. The Fillet command does a specific kind of trim and is easy and quick to execute, but its uses are limited (for the most part) to single intersections between two lines or multiple intersections on a polyline.

Using the Zoom Command

To do this trim efficiently, you need a closer view of the T-intersections. Use the Zoom command to get a better look:

1. Enter z↵. Then move the crosshair cursor to a point slightly above and to the left of the upper T-intersection (see Figure 4.19), and click in a blank area outside the floor plan.

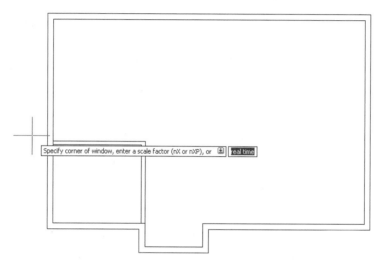

Specify corner of window, enter a scale factor (nX or nXP), or 🔲 real time

F I G U R E   4 . 1 9 : Positioning the cursor for the first click of the Zoom command

2. Move the cursor down and to the right, and notice a rectangle with solid lines being drawn. Keep moving the cursor down and to the right until the rectangle encloses the upper T-intersection (see the top of Figure 4.20). When the rectangle fully encloses the T-intersection, click again. The view changes to a closer view of the intersection of the interior and exterior walls (see the bottom of Figure 4.20).

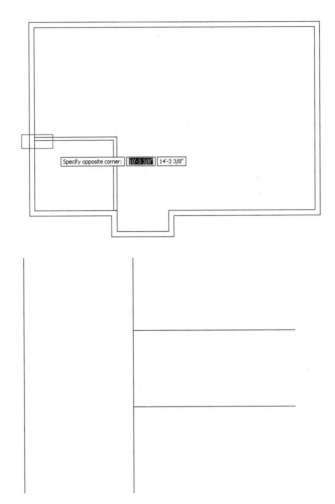

When you start the
Zoom command by
entering z↵ and then
picking a point on
the screen, a zoom
window begins.

FIGURE 4.20: Using the Zoom Window option: positioning the rectangle (top) and the new view after the Zoom command (bottom)

The rectangle you've just specified is called a *zoom window*. The area of the drawing enclosed by the zoom window becomes the view on the screen. This is one of several zoom options for changing the magnification of the view. Other zoom options are introduced later in this chapter and throughout the book.

3. Switch back to the Home tab; then on the Modify panel, click the Trim button. In the Command window, notice the second and third lines of text. You're being prompted to select *cutting edges* (objects to use as limits for the lines you want to trim).

4. Select the two horizontal interior wall lines, and press the spacebar or ↵. The prompt changes and asks you to select the objects to be trimmed.

5. Select the inside exterior wall line at the T-intersection, between the two intersections with the interior wall lines that you have just picked as cutting edges (see the top of Figure 4.21). The exterior wall line is trimmed at the T-intersection (see the bottom of Figure 4.21). Press the spacebar to end the Trim command.

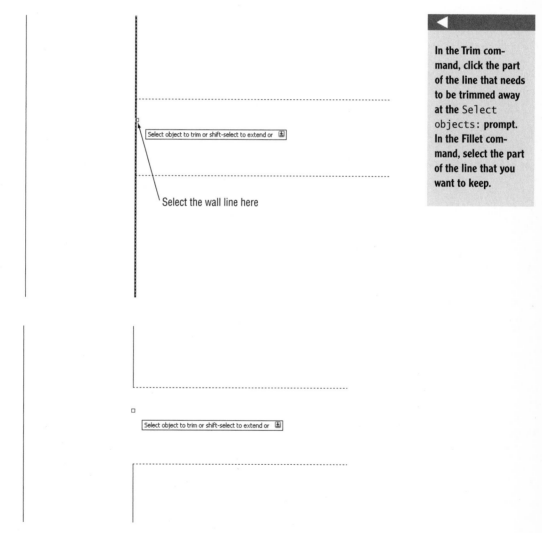

In the Trim command, click the part of the line that needs to be trimmed away at the `Select objects:` prompt. In the Fillet command, select the part of the line that you want to keep.

FIGURE 4.21: Selecting a line to be trimmed (top), and the result of the Trim command (bottom)

6. Return to a view of the whole drawing by entering z⏎ and then p⏎. This is the Zoom command's Previous option, which restores the view that was active before the last use of the Zoom command (see Figure 4.22). This command is also available from the Zoom fly-out menu on the View tab's Navigate panel.

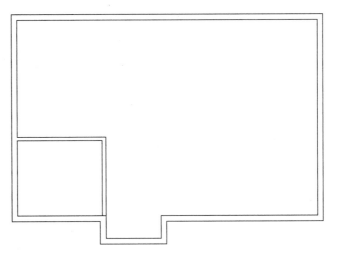

FIGURE 4.22: The result of the Zoom Previous command

Repeat the procedure to trim the lower T-intersection. Follow these steps:

1. Enter z⏎, and click two points to make a rectangular zoom window around the intersection.

2. Start the Trim command again, select the interior walls as cutting edges, and press the spacebar.

3. Select the inside exterior wall line between the cutting edges.

4. Press the spacebar or ⏎ to end the Trim command.

5. Zoom Previous by entering z⏎ p⏎.

Figure 4.23 shows the results.

You need to create one more set of interior walls to represent the closet in the upper-right corner of the cabin.

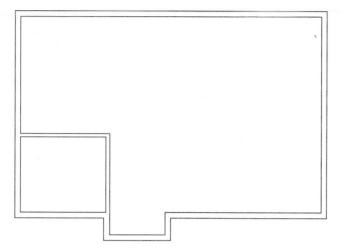

FIGURE 4.23: The second trim is completed.

Finishing the Interior Walls

You'll use the same method to create the closet walls that you used to make the first two interior walls. Briefly, this is how it's done:

1. Offset the inside line of the upper exterior wall 2'-6" (762 mm) downward; then offset this new line 4"(100 mm) downward (see Figure 4.24).

FIGURE 4.24: Offsetting the lines for the first wall

2. Offset the inside line of the right exterior wall 4'-8" (1420 mm) to the left; then offset this new line 4" (100 mm) to the left (see Figure 4.25).

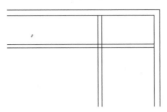

FIGURE 4.25: Offsetting the lines for the second wall

3. Use a zoom window to zoom into the closet area.

T I P   Make a zoom window just large enough to enclose the closet. The resulting view should be large enough to allow you to fillet the corners and trim the T-intersections without zooming again.

4. Use the Fillet command to clean up the interior and exterior wall line intersections, as shown in Figure 4.26.

FIGURE 4.26: Fillet the two corners.

5. Use the Trim command to trim away the short portions of the intersecting wall lines between the two new interior walls. This can be accomplished in one use of the Trim command. Once you select all four of the new wall lines as cutting edges, you can trim both lines that run across the ends of the selected lines to those same cutting edges.

6. Use Zoom Previous to restore the previous view.

The results should look like Figure 4.27.

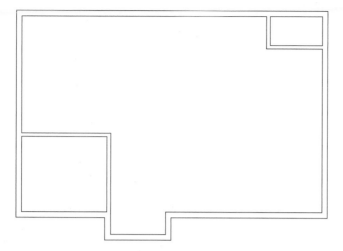

FIGURE 4.27: The completed interior walls

You used Offset, Fillet, Trim, and a couple of zooms to create the interior walls. The next task is to create four doorway openings in these walls. If you need to end the drawing session before completing the chapter, choose Application menu ➤ Save As ➤ AutoCAD Drawing and then change the name of this drawing to Cabin04a.dwg and click Save. You can then exit AutoCAD. To continue, do the same Save As operation and move on to the next section.

 T I P   Check your work against the online project files. Throughout the book, you will be directed to save your cabin project in progress at major stages. Files corresponding to each stage where you save your files are available on this book's web page: www.sybex.com/go/autocad2010ner.

Cutting Openings in the Walls

Of the four doorway openings needed, two are on interior and two are on exterior walls (see Figure 4.28). Two of them are for swinging doors, one is for a sliding glass door, and one is a set of bi-fold doors. You won't be doing the hatchings and dimensions shown in the figure—those features will be covered in future chapters.

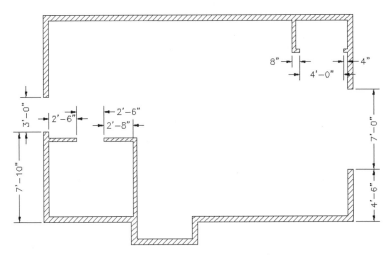

FIGURE 4.28: The drawing with doorway openings

The procedure used to make each doorway opening is the same one that you used to create the opening for the box in Chapter 2. First you establish the location of the *jambs*, or sides, of an opening. Once the location of one jamb is located, the line defining that side is offset by the width of the door opening. When the jambs are established, you'll trim away the wall lines between the edges. The commands used in this exercise are Offset, Extend, and Trim. You'll make openings for the 3'-0" (915 mm) exterior doorway first.

Creating the 3'-0" (915 mm) Exterior Opening

This opening is on the back wall of the cabin and has one side set in 7'-10" (2388 mm) from the outside corner:

1. Start the Offset command, and then enter 7'10↵ (2388↵) to set the distance to 7'-10" (2388 mm).

2. Click the lower outside line indicated in Figure 4.29, and then click in a blank area above the line you selected. You have to offset one line at a time because of the way the Offset command works.

3. End and restart the Offset command by pressing the spacebar or ↵ twice; then enter 3' ↵ (915↵) to set a new offset distance, and offset the new line up (see Figure 4.30).

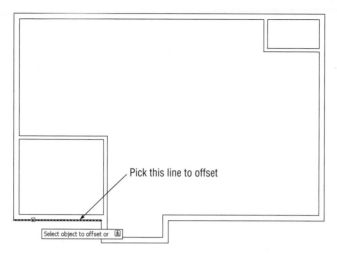

FIGURE 4.29: Select this line to offset.

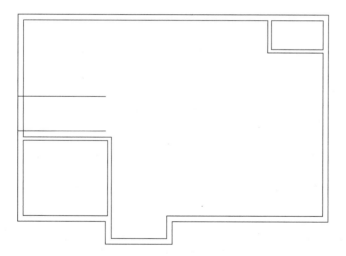

FIGURE 4.30: The offset line for the 3'-0″ (915 mm) opening

4. Start the Trim command, and then trim the new lines created with the Offset command and the 3′ (915 mm)-long line segments between the jambs. The result should look like Figure 4.31.

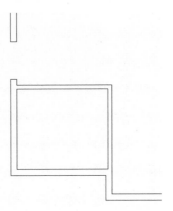

FIGURE 4.31: The doorway after trimming away the unneeded lines.

Creating the 7'-0" (2134 mm) Opening

Take another look at Figure 4.28 and notice that the opening on the right side of the building has one jamb set in 4'-6" (1372 mm) from the outside corner. This opening is for the sliding glass door.

You've done this procedure before, so here's a quick summary of the steps:

1. Offset the lower exterior wall line 4'-6" (1372 mm).

2. Offset the new line 7'-0" (2134 mm).

3. Trim the new lines and the wall lines to complete the opening. Your cabin should look like Figure 4.32.

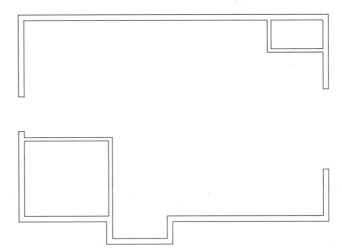

FIGURE 4.32: The cabin with the 7'-0" (2134 mm) sliding door opening

Creating the 2'-6" (762 mm)
Interior Opening

The 2'-6" (762 mm) opening to the bathroom starts 30" (762 mm) from the inside of the left exterior wall. You can't simply offset the wall and trim the excess, because the offset lines would not cross both the interior wall lines. So instead you will use the Extend command exactly as you used it in Chapter 2.

1. Start the Offset command and offset the interior line of the lower, left exterior wall 2'-6" (762 mm) to the right; then offset the new line another 2'-6" (762 mm) to the right.

2. Start the Extend command, and then select the upper horizontal bathroom wall line as the boundary edge (see Figure 4.33), and press the spacebar or ↵.

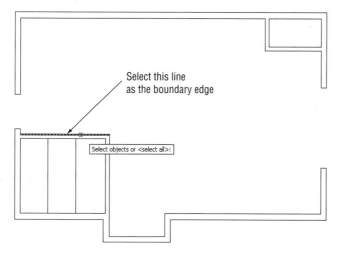

Select this line
as the boundary edge

Select objects or <select all>:

FIGURE 4.33: Select the boundary edge.

 T I P   If you start a new command by entering letters on the keyboard, you must first make sure that the previous command has ended by pressing the Esc key at least twice. On the other hand, if you start a new command by clicking its icon on the Ribbon, it doesn't matter if the previous command is still running. AutoCAD will cancel it.

3. Click the two jamb lines to extend them. Be sure to pick points on the lines that are near the boundary edges, as shown in Figure 4.34, or

the lines will be extended in the opposite direction if a boundary edge exists. The lines are extended through the interior walls to make the jambs (see Figure 4.34). End the Extend command by pressing the spacebar or ↵.

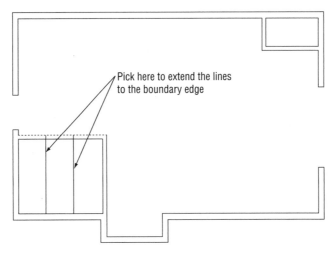

Pick here to extend the lines
to the boundary edge

FIGURE 4.34: The lines after being extended through the bathroom walls

 T I P The Trim command has the same functionality as the Extend command. While using Trim, select the cutting edges and then hold the Shift key down at the `Select object to trim or shift-select to extend or:` prompt. The cutting edges act as boundary edges, and the object is extended rather than trimmed.

To complete the openings, continue with steps 4 and 5. First you'll trim away the excess part of the jamb lines, and then you'll trim away the wall lines between the jamb lines. You'll use the Trim command the same way you used it in Chapter 2, but this time you'll access the command from the context menu. A *context menu,* also called a pop-up menu or right-click menu, appears when you click the right mouse button and contains common commands and options specific to the actions being performed when the menu was opened.

4. To start the Trim command, right-click and choose Recent Input ➤ TRIM from the context menu (see Figure 4.35).

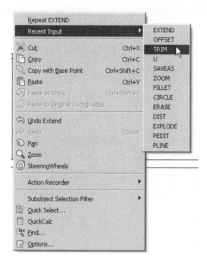

FIGURE 4.35: The context menu allows you to choose recently used commands.

5. Select the four lines that make up the upper bathroom wall and the jambs. Then press the spacebar or ↵ to tell AutoCAD you're finished selecting objects to serve as cutting edges.

6. Pick the two wall lines between the jamb lines, and then pick the jamb lines—the lines you just extended to the outside exterior walls. Your cabin should appear as shown in Figure 4.36.

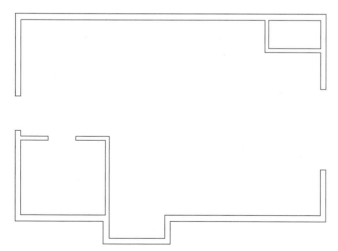

FIGURE 4.36: The cabin after creating the opening for the bathroom door

> **T I P**   When picking lines to be trimmed, remember to pick the lines on the portion to be trimmed away.

You can construct the closet opening using the same procedure.

The Closet Opening

This doorway is 4'-0" (1220 mm) wide and has one jamb set in 4" (100 mm) from the inside of the exterior wall. Figure 4.37 shows the three stages of fabricating this opening. Refer to the previous section on making openings for step-by-step instructions.

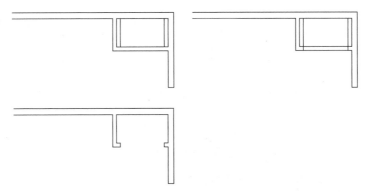

FIGURE 4.37: Creating the interior openings: the offset lines that locate the jamb lines (top left), the extended lines that form the jamb lines (top right), and the completed openings after trimming (bottom)

When you are finished, save this drawing as Cabin04b.dwg. This completes the openings. The results should look like Figure 4.38.

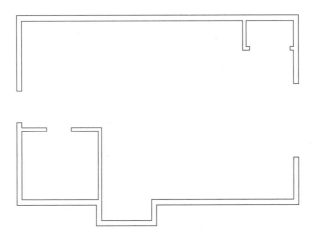

FIGURE 4.38: The completed doorway openings

As you gain more control over the commands you used here, you'll be able to anticipate how much of a task can be accomplished with each use of a command. Each opening required offsetting, extending, and trimming. It's possible to do all the openings using each command only once. In this way, you do all the offsetting, then all the extending, and finally all the trimming. In cutting these openings, however, the arrangement of the offset lines determined how many cycles of the Trim command were most efficient to use. If lines being trimmed and used as cutting edges cross each other, the trimming gets complicated. For these four openings, the most efficient procedure is to use each command twice. In Chapter 8, you'll get a chance to work with more complex, multiple trims when you draw the elevations.

Now that the openings are complete, you can place doors and door swings in their appropriate doorways. In doing this, you'll be introduced to two new objects and a few new commands, and you'll have an opportunity to use the Offset and Trim commands in new, strategic ways.

WHAT TO DO WHEN YOU MAKE A MISTAKE

When you're offsetting, trimming, and extending lines, it's easy to pick the wrong line, especially in a congested drawing. Here are some tips on how to correct these errors and get back on track:

▶ You can always cancel any command by pressing the Esc key until you see the Command: prompt in the Command window. Then click the Undo button on the Quick Access toolbar to undo the results of the last command. If you undo too much, click the Redo button. You can click it more than once to redo several undone commands. Redos must be performed immediately following an undo.

▶ Errors possible with the Offset command include setting the wrong distance, picking the wrong line to offset, and picking the wrong side to offset toward. If the distance is correct, you can continue offsetting, end the command when you have the results you want, and then erase the lines that were offset wrong. Otherwise, press Esc and undo your previous offset.

▶ Errors made with the Trim and Extend commands can sometimes be corrected on the fly, so you don't have to end the command because each of these commands has an Undo option. If you pick a line and it doesn't trim or extend the right way, you can undo that last action without stopping the command and then continue trimming or extending. You can activate the Undo option used while the command

Continued

WHAT TO DO WHEN YOU MAKE A MISTAKE *(Continued)*

is running in two ways: enter **u⤶**, or right-click and choose Undo from the context menu. Either of these actions undoes the last trim or extend, and you can try again without having to restart the command. Each time you activate the Undo option *from within the command*, another trim or extend is undone.

▶ The Line command also has the same Undo option as the Trim and Extend commands. You can undo the last segment drawn (or the last several segments) and redraw them without stopping the command.

Creating Doors

In a floor plan, a rectangle or a line for the door and an arc showing the path of the door swing usually indicates a pivot door. The door's position varies, but it's most often shown at 90° from the closed position (see Figure 4.39). The best rule I have come across is to display the door in such a way that others working with your floor plan will be able to see how far, and in what direction, the door will swing open.

FIGURE 4.39: Possible ways to illustrate pivot doors

The cabin has four openings. Two of them need swinging doors, which open 90°. The main entry is a sliding glass door and the closet is accessed by a pair of bi-fold doors. Drawing each type of door will require a different approach.

Drawing Swinging Doors

The swinging doors are of two widths: 3' (915 mm) for exterior and 2'-6" (762 mm) for interior (refer to Figure 4.1 earlier in this chapter). In general, doorway openings leading to the outside are wider than interior doors, with bathroom and bedroom doors usually being the narrowest. For the cabin, you'll use two sizes of swinging doors. If multiple doors of the same width existed in this design, you could draw one door of each size and then copy them to the other openings as required. Start with the back door on the left side of the floor plan. To get a closer view of the front door opening, use the Zoom Window command. Follow these steps:

1. Before you start drawing, check the status bar at the bottom of the screen and make sure only the Model button at the far right and the Dynamic Input on the far left are pressed. All other buttons should be in the off position. If any are pressed, click them once to toggle them off.

 2. Right-click the Object Snap button on the status bar, and choose Settings from the context menu to open the Drafting Settings dialog box. The Object Snap tab is activated (Figure 4.40).

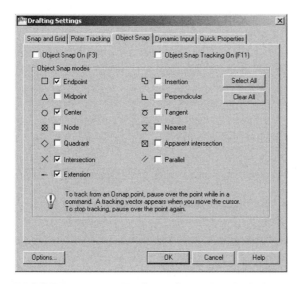

FIGURE 4.40: The Object Snap tab of the Drafting Settings dialog box

3. Be sure all check boxes are unchecked. If any boxes have check marks in them, click the Clear All button to uncheck them. Then click OK to close the dialog box. This step isn't essential, as long as the Object Snap button is turned off, but it's best to be sure in this case. Object snaps are covered in depth in Chapter 5 and used throughout the remainder of the book.

4. When the Command: prompt is displayed in the Command window, click the View tab on the Ribbon, move the cursor to the Navigate Ribbon panel, expand the Zoom drop-down menu, and click the Zoom Window button. This has the same result as typing z↵, with the addition of prompts for the two points.

5. Pick two points to form a window around the back doorway opening, as shown in Figure 4.41 (left). The view changes, and you now have a close-up view of the opening (see Figure 4.41, right). You'll draw the door in a closed position and then rotate it open.

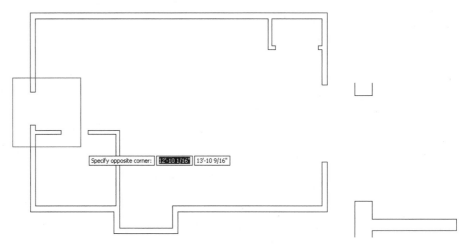

F I G U R E 4 . 4 1 : Forming a zoom window at the back door opening (left) and the result (right)

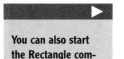
You can also start the Rectangle command by entering rec↵ at the Command: prompt.

 6. To draw the door, switch back to the Home tab and then click the Rectangle button on the Draw panel of the Ribbon.

Notice the Command: prompt in the Command window. Several options are in brackets, but the option Specify first corner point (before the brackets) is the default and it is the one you want. You can also expose these options (see Figure 4.42) at the cursor by pressing the down arrow on the main keyboard (not the down arrow in the numeric keypad).

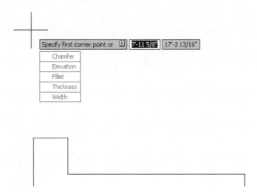

FIGURE 4.42: The Rectangle command options exposed at the cursor

You form the rectangle in the same way that you form the Zoom window—by picking two points to represent opposite corners of the rectangle. In its closed position, the door will fit exactly between the jambs, with its two right corners coinciding with the rightmost endpoints of the jambs. To make the first corner of the rectangle coincide with the upper endpoint of the right jamb exactly, you'll use an object snap to assist you. *Object snaps* (or *osnaps*) allow you to pick specific points on objects such as endpoints, midpoints, the center of a circle, and so on. When the Osnap button is active, the cursor will snap to any of the options selected in the Object Snap tab of the Drafting Settings dialog box. These are called *running osnaps*.

Osnap **is short for** *object snap.* **The two terms are used interchangeably.**

7. Enter **end**↵. This activates the Endpoint osnap for one pick and will snap the cursor to the nearest endpoint of any line, arc, or polyline that you select.

8. Move the cursor near the right side of the upper jamb line. When the cursor gets very close to a line, a colored square, called a *marker*, appears at the nearest endpoint along with a tooltip that indicates which osnap is active, as shown in Figure 4.43. This shows you which endpoint in the drawing is closest to the position of the crosshair cursor at that moment.

FIGURE 4.43: The Endpoint osnap marker

> Because of the way AutoCAD displays the crosshair cursor, both the lines and the crosshair disappear when its lines coincide with lines in the drawing. This makes it difficult to see the rectangle being formed.

9. Move the cursor until the square is positioned on the right end of the upper jamb line as shown, and then click that point. The first corner of the rectangle now is located at that point. Move the cursor to the right and slightly down to see the rectangle being formed (see Figure 4.44, left). To locate the opposite corner, let's use the relative Cartesian coordinates discussed in Chapter 2.

10. When the command prompt shows the `Specify other corner point or [Area/Dimensions/Rotation]:` prompt, enter **-1.5,-3′↵↵** (-40,-915↵↵). The rectangle is drawn across the opening, creating a door in a closed position (see Figure 4.44, right). The door now needs to be rotated around its hinge point to an opened position.

    When you used the Rectangle command to draw the swinging doors, you had to use relative Cartesian coordinates because relative polar coordinates would have required you to know the diagonal distance across the plan of the door and the angle of that distance as well.

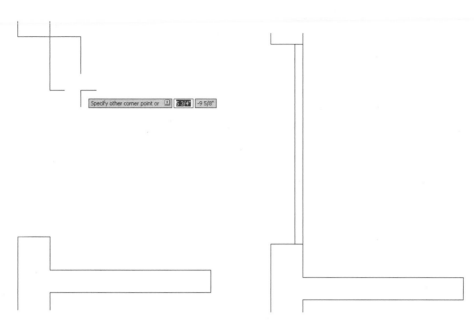

FIGURE 4.44: The rectangle after picking the first corner (left) and the completed door in a closed position (right)

Rotating the Door

This rotation will be through an arc of 90° in the clockwise direction, making it a rotation of –90°. By default, counterclockwise rotations are positive, while clockwise rotations are negative. You'll use the Rotate command to rotate the door.

1. Click the Rotate button on the Modify panel or enter **ro↵**. You'll see a prompt to select objects. Click the door and press ↵.

    You're prompted for a base point—a point around which the door will be rotated. To keep the door placed correctly, pick the hinge point for the base point. The hinge point for this opening is the right endpoint of the bottom jamb line.

2. Enter **end↵** to activate the Endpoint snap.

3. Move the cursor near the lower-right corner of the door. When the marker is displayed at that corner, left-click to locate the base point.

4. Check the status bar to be sure the Ortho Mode button isn't pressed. If it is, click it to turn off Ortho. When the Ortho Mode button is on, the cursor is forced to move in a vertical or horizontal direction. This is useful at times, but in this instance such a restriction would keep you from being able to see the door rotate.

5. Move the cursor away from the hinge point, and see how the door rotates as the cursor moves (see the left image in Figure 4.45). If the door swings properly, you're reassured that you correctly selected the base point. The prompt in the Command window reads Specify rotation angle or [Copy/Reference]<0.00>:, asking you to enter an angle.

6. Enter -90↵. The door is rotated 90° to an open position (see the right image in Figure 4.45).

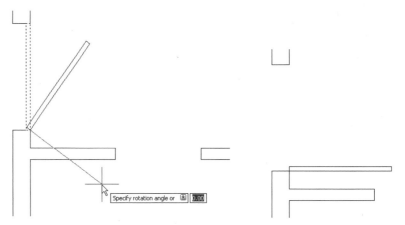

FIGURE 4.45: The door rotating with movement of the cursor (left), and the door after the 90° rotation (right)

To finish this door, you need to add the door's swing. You'll use the Arc command for this.

Drawing the Door Swing

The *swing* shows the path that the outer edge of a door takes when it swings from closed to fully open. Including a swing with the door in a floor plan helps to identify the rectangle as a door and resolve clearance issues. You draw the swings using the Arc command, in this case using the Endpoint osnap. This command has many options, most of which are based on knowing three aspects of the arc, as you'll see.

 1. Click the down arrow next to the Arc button in the Draw panel.

The menu expands to show the 11 different methods for creating an arc. On the menu, 10 of the 11 options have combinations of three aspects that define an arc. The arc for this door swing needs to be drawn from the right end of the upper jamb line through a rotation of 90°. You know the start point of the arc, the center of rotation (the hinge point), and the angle through which the rotation occurs, so you can use the Start, Center, Angle option on the Arc menu.

THE OPTIONS OF THE ARC COMMAND

The position and size of an arc can be specified by a combination of its components, some of which are start point, endpoint, angle, center point, and radius. The Arc command gives you 11 options, 10 of which use three components to define the arc. With a little study of the geometric information available to you about your drawing, you can choose the option that best fits the situation.

When you start the Arc command by entering **a**↵, you get an abbreviated form of the command in the command prompt. You can access all 11 options of the command through this prompt, but you have to select the various components along the way.

2. From the expanded Arc menu, choose Start, Center, Angle as shown in Figure 4.46. The command prompt now reads Specify start point of arc:; this is the default option. You could also start with the center point, but you would have to enter c↵ before picking a point to be the center point.

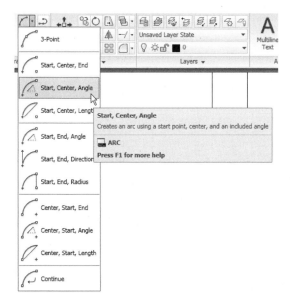

FIGURE 4.46: The expanded Arc menu

3. Activate the Endpoint osnap (enter **end**↵), and pick the right end-point of the upper jamb line, as shown in Figure 4.47.

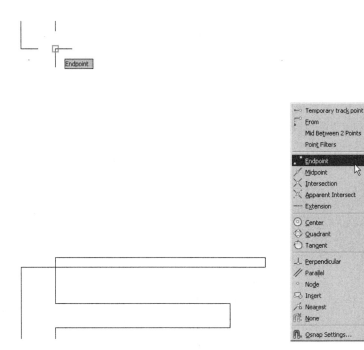

FIGURE 4.47: Specifying the start point for the Arc command

FIGURE 4.48: Select the End-point osnap from the Object Snap context menu.

The prompt changes to read: Specify second point of arc:. Because you previously chose the Start, Center, Angle option, AutoCAD automatically chooses Center for you as the second point. That is the last part of the prompt. You'll need the Endpoint osnap again, but this time you will pick it from a menu.

4. Hold the Shift key down, and right-click in the drawing area to open a context menu containing all the available osnaps. Click on the Endpoint option, as shown in Figure 4.48, to activate the endpoint osnap.

5. Select the hinge point. The arc is now visible, and its endpoint follows the cursor's movement, but the arc is extending in the wrong direction (see the top image in Figure 4.49). The prompt displays the Specify Included Angle option.

6. Enter -90↵. The arc is completed, and the Arc command ends (see the bottom image in Figure 4.49).

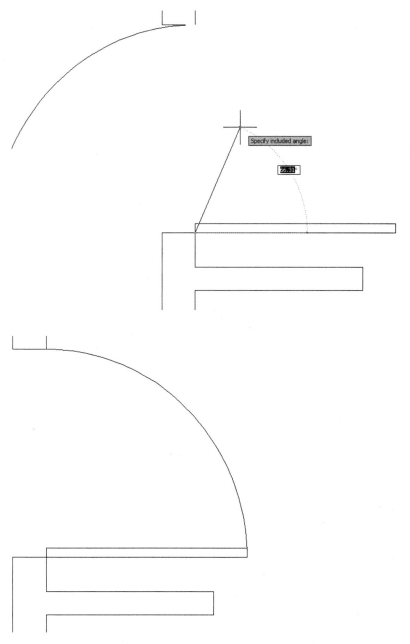

FIGURE 4.49: Drawing the arc: the ending point of the arc follows the cursor's movements (top), and the completed arc (bottom)

W A R N I N G In this situation, the arc must be created by selecting the jamb end first and the door end later. Arcs are made in a counterclockwise fashion, so selecting the door end first and the jamb end later would result in a 270° arc that extends behind the door and through the external wall.

The back door is completed. Next you'll copy and then modify the back door to form the bathroom door.

Copying Objects

As you would expect, the Copy command makes a copy of the objects you select. You can locate this copy either by picking a point or by entering relative coordinates from the keyboard. For AutoCAD to position these copied objects, you must designate two points: a base point, which serves as a point of reference for where the copy move starts, and then a second point, which serves as the ending point for the Copy command. The copy is moved the same distance and direction from its original position that the second point is located from the first point. When you know the actual distance and direction to move the copy, the base point isn't critical because you specify the second point with relative polar or relative Cartesian coordinates. But in this situation, you don't know the exact distance or angle to move a copy of the back door to the bathroom door opening, so you need to choose a base point for the copy carefully.

In copying this new door and its swing to the back door opening of the cabin, you must find a point somewhere on the existing door or swing that can be located precisely on a point at the back door opening. You can choose from two points: the hinge point and the start point of the door swing. Let's use the hinge point. You usually know where the hinge point of the new door belongs, so this is easier to locate than the start point of the arc.

 1. Click the Copy button on the Modify panel of the Ribbon or enter co↵. The prompt asks you to select objects to copy. Pick the door and swing and then press ↵. The prompt in the Command window reads Specify base point or [Displacement/mOde]<Displacement>:.

Activate the Endpoint osnap, and pick the hinge point. A copy of the door and swing is attached to the crosshair cursor at the hinge point (see Figure 4.50). The prompt changes to Specify second point or <use first point of displacement>:. You need to pick where the hinge point of the copied door will be located at the bathroom door opening.

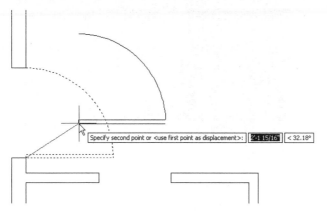

FIGURE 4.50: The copy of the door and swing attached to the crosshair cursor

The Copy command keeps running until you end it. This allows you to make multiple copies of the same object. You'll do that in Chapter 5 when you draw the stove top.

2. Activate the Endpoint osnap, and pick the lower end of the right jamb line on the bathroom door opening. The copy of the door and swing is placed in the opening (see Figure 4.51) and, by looking at the command prompt, you can see that the Copy command is still running. Notice that a copy of the door and swing remains attached to the cursor. Press ↵ to end the command.

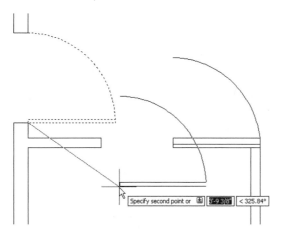

FIGURE 4.51: The door is copied to the bathroom door opening.

You can use the Zoom command while you are in the middle of using the Copy command. You can use most of the display commands (Zoom, Pan, and so on) in this way. This is called using a command *transparently*.

The door is oriented the wrong way, but you'll fix that next.

When you copy doors from one opening to another, often the orientation doesn't match. The best strategy is to use the hinge point as a point of reference and place the door where it needs to go, as you just did. Then flip or rotate the door so that it sits and swings the right way. The flipping of an object is known as *mirroring*.

Mirroring Objects

You have located the door in the opening, but it needs to be rotated 90° to be perpendicular to the wall and then flipped so that it swings to the inside of the bathroom. To do this, you'll use the Rotate command that you used earlier, and then the *Mirror command*.

The Mirror command allows you to flip objects around an axis called the *mirror line*. You define this imaginary line by designating two points on the line. Strategic selection of the mirror line ensures the accuracy of the mirroring action, so it's critical to visualize where the proper line lies. Sometimes you'll have to draw a guideline in order to designate one or both of the endpoints.

1. Click the Rotate button, select the door and swing for the bathroom door, and press ↵.

2. At the Specify base point: prompt, enter **end**↵ to activate the Endpoint osnap; then pick the hinge point.

3. At the Specify rotation angle: prompt, enter **90**↵. The door is rotated 90° but its orientation is incorrect, as shown in Figure 4.52.

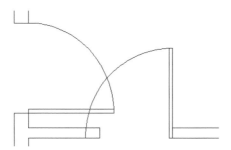

FIGURE 4.52: The door after rotating it 90°

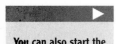

You can also start the Mirror command by entering mi↵.

4. On the Modify Ribbon panel, click the Mirror button. Select the bathroom door and swing and press ↵. The prompt line changes to read Specify first point of mirror line:.

5. Activate the Endpoint osnap, and then pick the hinge point of the door. The prompt changes to read Specify second point of mirror line:, and you'll see the mirrored image of the door and the swing moving as you move the cursor around the drawing area. You're rotating the mirror line about the hinge point as you move the cursor. As the mirror line rotates, the orientation of the mirrored image changes (see Figure 4.53).

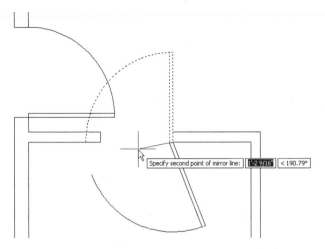

Specify second point of mirror line: 1'-2 9/16" < 190.79°

FIGURE 4.53: The mirror image changes as the mirror line rotates.

6. Activate the Endpoint osnap again, and pick the lower end of the left jamb line. The mirror image disappears, and the prompt changes to read `Erase source objects? [Yes/No] <N>:`. You have two choices. You can keep both doors by pressing ↵ and accepting the default (No). Or you can discard the original one by entering y (for Yes) in the command line and pressing ↵.

7. Enter y↵. The flipped door is displayed, and the original one is deleted (see Figure 4.54). The Mirror command ends.

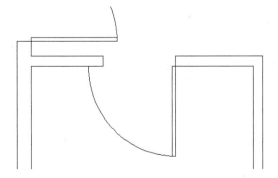

FIGURE 4.54: The mirrored door and swing

It may take some practice to become proficient at visualizing and designating the mirror line, but once you're used to it, you'll have learned how to use a powerful tool. Because many objects—including building layouts, mechanical parts, steel beams, road cross sections, and so on—have some symmetry to them, wise use of the Mirror command can save you a lot of drawing time.

Now let's change the scale of the interior to match the available opening.

Scaling the Bathroom Door

You could have used the Stretch command to make the door narrower, but that's an advanced Modify command and won't be introduced until Chapter 11, "Working with Hatches and Gradients." Besides, the arc would have to be modified to a smaller radius. It's easier to scale the objects and the slightly thinner door can be attributed to interior doors being thinner than exterior doors. In Chapter 9, "Using Dynamic Blocks and Tables," I'll demonstrate a *dynamic block* that can serve as a door block for several door sizes. For this exercise, you will use the Scale command to resize the bathroom door to fit the existing opening. The Scale command changes the size of all the selected objects by an equal amount based on keyboard input or the location of the cursor. The objects scale up or down in relation to their position relative to a base point you've defined. Objects scaled up will appear to get farther away from the base point while objects scaled down will appear to get closer.

The 30″ (762 mm) bathroom door opening is 5/6 the size of the 36″ (915 mm) back door opening; therefore, 5/6, or its decimal equivalent of 0.8333, can be used as the scale factor. Because fractions are inherently more accurate than rounded-off decimal values, we'll use the fractional scale factor.

> ►
>
> A 762 mm door isn't exactly 5/6 the size of a 915 mm door, and using the method that follows results in a door that is approximately $^{1}/_{2}$ mm too long, but that is close enough for our purposes here. If you prefer to be more accurate, substitute 0.832787 for 5/6 in step 5.

1. Click the Zoom Window button on the Zoom fly-out menu to zoom in to the interior door opening (see Figure 4.55).

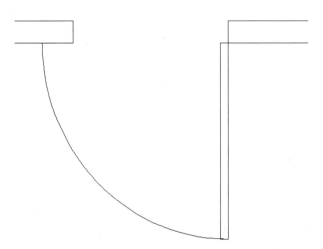

FIGURE 4.55: A close-up view of the bathroom door

2. Click the Scale button in the Modify panel or enter **sc**↵ to start the Scale command.

3. At the Select objects: prompt, select the bathroom door and swing and press ↵.

4. At the Specify base point: prompt, enter **end**↵ and pick the hinge point. As you move the cursor, you can see the scaled version of the door change size depending on how far the cursor is located from the base point (see Figure 4.56).

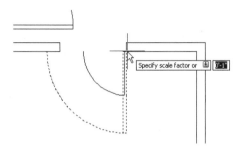

FIGURE 4.56: Using the Scale tool to resize the bathroom door

5. Enter **5/6**↵ to scale the 36″ (915 mm) door down to 30″ (762 mm). The rescaled door should look like Figure 4.57.

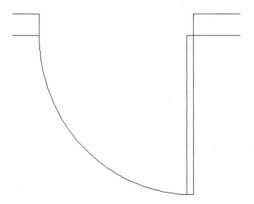

FIGURE 4.57: The rescaled bathroom door

As you can see, as long as you know the scale factor, it's easy to use the Scale command to resize objects in your drawing. The next door to draw is the sliding glass door. This kind of door requires an entirely different strategy, but you'll use commands familiar to you by now.

Drawing a Sliding Glass Door

You will need to use the Endpoint osnap a lot while creating, copying, rotating, and mirroring objects; it's probably the most frequently used of the osnaps. Rather than activating it as needed, you will turn on Endpoint as a running osnap—an osnap that is permanently turned on.

1. Right-click on the Object Snap button in the status bar, and then select the Settings option in the context menu.

2. In the Object Snap tab of the Drafting Settings dialog box, check the Endpoint option. While the cursor is near the selection, a tooltip appears describing the features to which the osnap moves the cursor. Take a moment to investigate what each of the osnap options does before clicking the OK button (see Figure 4.58).

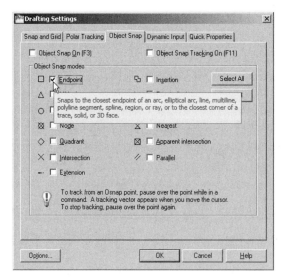

FIGURE 4.58: The Object Snap tab of the Drafting Settings dialog box

3. The osnap is active, but the running osnaps are not turned on. Click the Object Snap button to turn on running osnaps. Now whenever you are prompted to pick a point, a marker will appear over the nearest endpoint of the object the cursor is over.

Sliding glass doors are usually drawn to show their glass panels within the door frames, as shown in Figure 4.59.

FIGURE 4.59: A common appearance for a sliding glass door

To draw the sliding door, you'll apply the Line, Offset, and Trim commands to the 7′ (2134 mm) opening you made earlier. It's a complicated exercise, but it will teach you a lot about the power of using these three commands in combination:

1. Zoom out by rolling the mouse wheel toward you or by using the Zoom Extents command. Zooming with the mouse wheel zooms the drawing toward or away from the location of the cursor.

2. Zoom closely around the 7′ (2134 mm) opening. If you make a zoom window, pick one point just above and to the left of the upper door-jamb and another below and to the right of the lower jamb. Try zooming with the scroll wheel by placing the cursor in the center of the opening and rolling the scroll wheel away from you. Make the opening as large as possible while including everything you'll need in the view (see Figure 4.60).

You can control how quickly rolling the mouse wheel zooms in your drawing using the Zoomfactor variable. Enter zoomfactor↵ and then, when prompted, enter a value between 3 and 100. Lower values perform slower zoom and higher values perform faster zooms.

FIGURE 4.60: The view when zoomed in as closely as possible to the 7′ (2134 mm) opening

You'll be using several osnaps for this procedure. Rather than entering each osnap, you can activate any object snap by holding down the Shift key and right-clicking in the drawing area. This opens a context menu with all the object snap options shown earlier in Figure 4.48. Selecting any of these options activates the osnap for a single pick.

You probably noticed the list of osnaps that appeared when you right-clicked the Object Snap button in the status bar. These do not activate an osnap for a single pick; rather they are a quick method for activating or deactivating a running osnap.

3. Offset each jamb line 2″ (51 mm) into the doorway opening (see Figure 4.61).

FIGURE 4.61: Jamb lines offset 2″ (51 mm) into the doorway opening

4. Start the Line command. Choose the Midpoint osnap from the Shift+right-click context menu, and then place the cursor near the midpoint of the upper doorjamb line. Notice that the marker, now a triangle, appears when your cursor is in the vicinity of the midpoint (see Figure 4.62). A symbol with a distinctive shape is associated with each osnap. When the triangle appears at the midpoint of the jamb line, left-click.

F I G U R E 4 . 6 2 : Using the Midpoint osnap to select the start point of the line

5. Move the cursor over the bottom jamb line and you'll notice the Endpoint markers appear. The Endpoint running osnap is still active, but
typing in the first three letters of an osnap or clicking an osnap
option from the context menu overrides it. Click the Midpoint Osnap
option again, move the cursor to the bottom jamb line. When the triangle appears at that midpoint, click again. Press ↵ to end the Line
command.

6. Start the Offset command, and enter **1.5**↵ (**38**↵) to set the offset distance. Pick the newly drawn line, and then pick a point anywhere to
the right side. Then, while the Offset command is still running, pick
the original line again and pick another point in a blank area somewhere to the left side of the doorway opening (see Figure 4.63). Press
↵ to end the Offset command.

FIGURE 4.63: The offset vertical lines between the jambs

7. In the status bar, click the Ortho Mode button to turn it on. Ortho mode restricts the cursor to vertical and horizontal movements only. Start the Line command, choose the Midpoint osnap option, and then move the cursor near the midpoint of the left vertical line. When the marker appears at the midpoint, click to set the endpoint of the line. Hold the cursor out directly to the right of the point you just selected to draw a horizontal line through the three vertical lines. When the cursor is about 2′ to the right of the three vertical lines, pick a point to set the endpoint of this guideline (see Figure 4.64). Press ↵ to end the Line command. Click Ortho mode off.

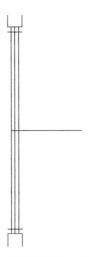

FIGURE 4.64: The horizontal guideline drawn through vertical lines

8. Enter o↵ or click Offset on the Modify panel to start the Offset command, and then enter 1↵ (25↵) to set the offset distance to 1" (25 mm). Select this new line, and then pick a point in a blank area anywhere above the line. Pick the first horizontal line again, and then pick anywhere below it. The new line has been offset 1" (25 mm) above and below itself (see Figure 4.65). Now you have placed all the lines necessary to create the sliding glass door frames in the opening. You still need to trim back some of these lines and erase others. Press ↵ to end the Offset command.

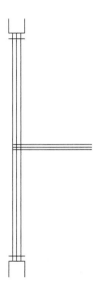

FIGURE 4.65: The offset horizontal guideline

9. Start the Trim command. When you're prompted to select cutting edges, pick the two horizontal lines that were just created with the Offset command and press ↵.

10. Trim the two outside vertical lines by selecting them, as shown on the left of Figure 4.66. The result is shown on the right.

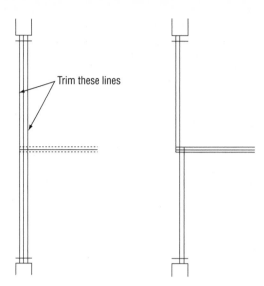

FIGURE 4.66: Picking the vertical lines to trim (left), and the result (right)

11. Press ↵ twice to stop and restart the Trim command. When you're prompted to select cutting edges, use a special window called a *crossing window* to select all the lines visible in the drawing. A crossing window selects everything within the window or crossing it. See the sidebar titled "Understanding Selection Windows," later in this chapter, for additional information about this feature. Here's how to do it:

   a. Pick a point above and to the right of the opening.

   b. Move the cursor to a point below and to the left of the opening, forming a semitransparent green-colored window with dashed boundary lines (see Figure 4.67).

   c. Pick that point. Everything inside the rectangle or crossing an edge of it is selected.

   d. Press ↵.

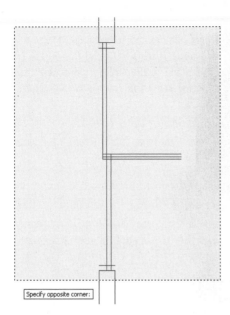

FIGURE 4.67: The crossing window for selecting cutting edges

12. To trim the lines, pick them at the points noted on the left of Figure 4.68. When you finish trimming, the opening should look like the right side of Figure 4.68. Be sure to press ↵ to end the Trim command.

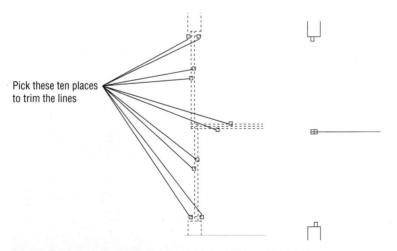

FIGURE 4.68: Lines to trim (left), and the result (right)

N O T E   If all the lines don't trim as you would expect, you may have to change the setting for the Edgemode system variable. Cancel the trim operation, and undo any trims you've made to the sliding glass door. Enter **edge-mode↵**, and then enter **0↵**. Now start the Trim command and continue trimming.

13. Start the Erase command, and erase the remaining horizontal guideline.

To finish the sliding glass doors, you need to draw two lines to represent the glass panes for each door panel. Each pane of glass is centered inside its frame, so the line representing the pane will run between the midpoints of the inside edge of each frame section.

14. Start the Line command, hold down the Shift key, and right-click; then select the Midpoint osnap option from the context menu.

15. For each of the two sliding door frames, put the cursor near the midpoint of the inside line of the frame section nearest the jamb. When the colored triangle appears there, click. Enter **per↵** or click the Perpendicular osnap from the Object Snap context menu, and move the cursor to the other frame section of that door panel. When you get near the horizontal line that represents both the inside edge of one frame section and the back edge of the frame section next to it, the colored Perpendicular osnap marker will appear on that line, as shown in Figure 4.69. When it does, select that point.

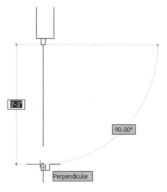

F I G U R E 4 . 6 9 : Using the Perpendicular osnap to set the endpoint of the line

16. Press ↵ to end the Line command.

17. Press ↵ to restart the Line command and repeat the procedure described in steps 14 through 16 for the other door panel, being sure to start the line at the frame section nearest the other jamb. The finished opening should look like Figure 4.70.

F I G U R E 4 . 7 0 : The finished sliding glass doors

Drawing the Bi-fold Doors

Bi-fold doors are generally shown with each door in a half-open position to indicate their distinctive design. Although there are four door panels on the cabin's closet door, you will only need to draw one, rotate it into place, and then create copies with the Mirror command. To begin the exercise, you will use the Pan command to shift the view of your drawing to see the closet area without changing the zoom factor. Here is how you do it:

1. Click the View tab then, from the Navigate panel, click the Pan button or enter p↵. The cursor changes appearance to look like an open hand.

2. Place the cursor near the upper jamb of the sliding glass door, and then click and drag the mouse downward until the drawing area shifts to display the closet area (see Figure 4.71).

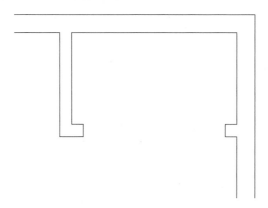

FIGURE 4.71: Pan the view to show the closet area.

3. Press the Esc key to end the Pan command, or right-click and choose Exit from the context menu.

4. The closet opening is 4′ (1220 mm) wide, so you will need to make four 1′ (305 mm)-wide door panels. Start the Rectangle command and specify the lower corner of the right closet jamb as the first corner point. The running Endpoint osnap ensures that the corner point is selected precisely.

5. Enter -1,-12↵ (-25,-305↵) to create a rectangle 1″ (25 mm) wide and 12″ (305 mm) long oriented toward the bottom of the cabin, as shown in Figure 4.72.

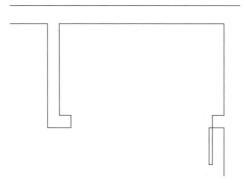

FIGURE 4.72: The first closet door panel is drawn.

6. Start the Rotate command and select the door panel. At the Specify base point: prompt, select the intersection of the jamb and the door panel.

7. Enter -45↵. The door rotates 45° (see Figure 4.73), and the Rotate command ends.

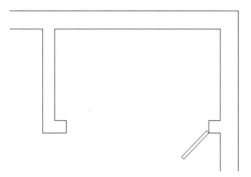

FIGURE 4.73: The first closet door panel is rotated.

8. Start the Mirror command from the Modify panel, and then select the closet door panel.

9. Click the Ortho Mode button or press the F8 shortcut key to turn on Ortho mode.

10. At the Specify first point of mirror line: prompt, click the far-left corner point of the selected panel.

11. Move the cursor either up or down until you see the mirror door panel directly to the left of the first panel (see Figure 4.74); then click to specify the second point of the mirror line.

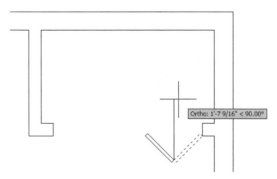

FIGURE 4.74: Mirroring the first closet door panel

12. Press ↵ to accept the default No option when prompted to erase the source object.

13. Start the Mirror command again, and this time select both of the door panels.

14. Choose the midpoint of the back wall of the closet as the first point of the mirror line. Then move the cursor downward to mirror the existing panels directly to the left, as shown in Figure 4.75. Click to set the second point, and then press ↵ to retain the source objects.

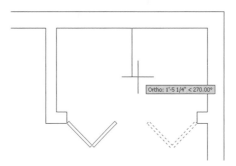

FIGURE 4.75: The closet door is complete.

15. Click the Zoom Extents button to see the full floor plan with all doors (see Figure 4.76).

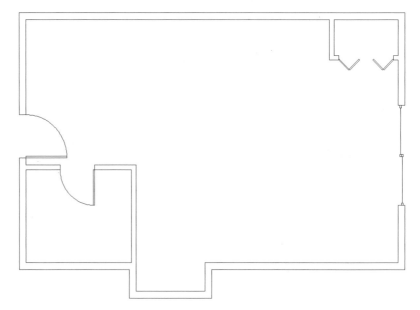

FIGURE 4.76: The cabin with the walls and doors completed

16. Save this drawing as Cabin04c.dwg.

UNDERSTANDING SELECTION WINDOWS

In addition to selecting objects using a direct pick, you can select objects using a rectangular selection window. To use a selection window at any Select objects: prompt, pick a point at a blank spot in the drawing area to define one corner of the window and then a second point to define the opposite corner.

Selection windows come in two styles: windows and crossing windows. When you use a window selection, all objects must be entirely inside the boundary of the window to be selected. When you use a crossing window, all objects entirely within the boundary as well as any objects that cross the boundary are selected. AutoCAD distinguishes the two types of selection windows visually. Window selection areas are transparent blue and have solid boundary lines, and crossing windows are transparent green with dashed boundary lines.

By default, window selections are used when the boundary is created from left to right, and crossing selections are used when the boundary is created from right to left. By entering **w**↵ or **c**↵ at the Select objects: prompt, you can override the direction default or create a selection window even when the mouse is clicked when the cursor is over an object.

Selection windows can even be used to select objects to be trimmed or extended. For instance, visualize a horizontal line with dozens of vertical lines crossing it, and each of those lines must be trimmed back to the horizontal line. After designating the horizontal line as the cutting edge, use a crossing selection window to select all of the vertical lines on the trim side. All the lines are trimmed with two picks instead of many.

Options   To change settings that control the appearance of the crossing and regular selection windows, open the Application menu and click the Options button in the lower-right corner, or enter **op**↵.

Click the Selection tab of the Options dialog box and then, in the Selection Preview area, click the Visual Effect Settings button, as shown in Figure 4.77.

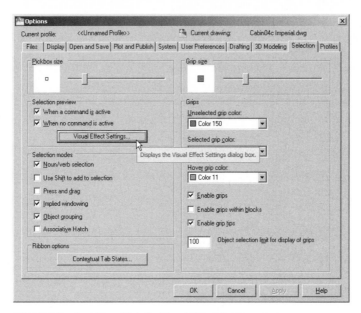

FIGURE 4.77: Click the Visual Effect Settings button.

In the Visual Effect Settings dialog box that opens (see Figure 4.78), in the Area Selection Effect area are settings for controlling whether the selection windows have color in them, which color will be in each window, and the percentage of transparency of the colors. The left side of the dialog box controls the appearance of an object's highlighting when the cursor hovers over it. Experiment with different settings. Click OK twice to return to your drawing, and test the windows to see how they look. This completes the doors for the floor plan. The focus here has been on walls and doors and the strategies for drawing them. As a result, you now have a basic floor plan for the cabin, and you'll continue to develop this plan in the next chapter.

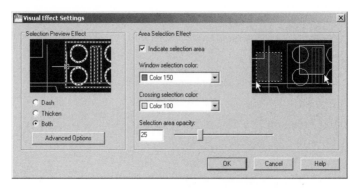

FIGURE 4.78: The Visual Effect Settings dialog box

The overall drawing strategy emphasized in this chapter uses objects already in the drawing to create new ones. You started with several lines that constituted the outside wall lines. By offsetting, filleting, extending, and trimming, you drew all the walls and openings without drawing any new lines. For the swinging doors, you made a rectangle and an arc. Then by copying, rotating, and mirroring, you formed the other swinging door. For the sliding glass door, you drew two new lines; then, you used Offset, Trim, and Erase to finish the door. Thus you used four lines and created six new objects to complete the walls and doors. This is a good start in learning to use AutoCAD efficiently.

Throughout this chapter, I have indicated several instances when you can press the spacebar instead of the ↵ key. This can be handy if you keep one hand resting on the keyboard while the other hand controls the mouse. For brevity, I'll continue to instruct you to use ↵ and not mention the spacebar, but as you get better at drawing in AutoCAD, you may find the spacebar a useful substitute for ↵ in many cases. You'll determine your preference. You can substitute the spacebar for 96 when handling the following tasks:

- ▶ Restarting the previous command

- ▶ Ending a command

- ▶ Moving from one step in a command to the next step

- ▶ Entering a new offset distance or accepting the current offset distance

- ▶ Entering relative or absolute coordinates

- ▶ Entering an angle of rotation

By working with the tools and strategies in this chapter, you now should have an idea of an approach to drawing many objects. In the next chapter, you'll continue in the same vein, learning a few new commands and strategies as you add steps, a balcony, a kitchen, and a bathroom to the floor plan.

If You Would Like More Practice...

If you would like to practice the skills you have learned so far, here are some extra exercises.

An Alternative Sliding Glass Door

Here is a simplified version of the sliding glass door of the cabin as shown in Figure 4.79. It doesn't include any representation of the panes of glass and their frames.

FIGURE 4.79: An alternative to the sliding glass door

To draw it, use a technique similar to the one described in the previous section. Copy the jambs for the 7′ (2134 mm) opening to the right, and draw this door between them.

An Addition to the Cabin

This addition is connected to the cabin by a sidewalk and consists of a remodeled two-car garage in which one car slot has been converted into a storage area and an office (see Figure 4.80). Use the same commands and strategies you have been using up to now to draw this layout adjacent to the cabin. Save this exercise as Cabin04c-addon.dwg.

Refer to this chapter and the preceding one for specific commands. Here is the general procedure:

1. Draw the outside exterior wall lines.

2. Use Offset, Fillet, and Trim to create the rest of the walls and wall lines.

3. Use Offset, Extend, and Trim to create the openings.

4. Use Rectangle and Arc to create a swinging door.

5. Use Copy, Rotate, and Mirror to put in the rest of the doors.

6. Use Offset, Line, and Copy to draw the storage partitions.

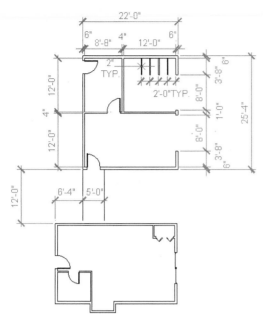

FIGURE 4.80: The garage addition

Draw Three Views of a Block

Use the tools you have learned in the last few chapters to draw the top, right side, and front views of the block shown in Figure 4.81.

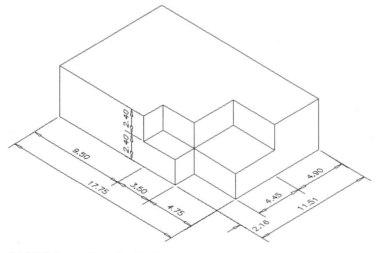

FIGURE 4.81: The block

Figure 4.82 gives you a graphic representation of the 12 steps necessary to complete the exercise.

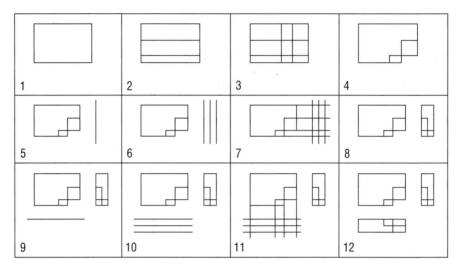

FIGURE 4.82: The 12 steps for creating the block

Here are the 12 steps in summary that correspond to the 12 drawings. Start with the top view:

1. Start a new drawing. Leave all settings at the defaults. Use relative polar or relative Cartesian coordinates and the Line command to draw a rectangle 17.75 wide and 11.51 high. Zoom out if necessary.

2. Offset the bottom horizontal line up 2.16 and the new line up 4.45.

3. Offset the right vertical line 4.75 to the left and the new line 3.50 to the left.

4. Use the Trim command to trim back lines and complete the view.

Next, do the right side view:

5. Draw a vertical line to the right of the top view. Make it longer than the top view is deep.

6. Offset the vertical line 2.4 to the right, and then offset the new line 2.4 to the right also.

7. Use the Endpoint osnap to draw lines from the corner points of the top view across the three vertical lines.

8. Trim the lines back to complete the side view.

Finally, draw the front view:

9. Draw a horizontal line below the top view. Make it longer than the top view is wide.

10. Offset this line 2.4 down, and then offset the new line 2.4 down.

11. Use the Endpoint osnap to draw lines from the corner points of the top view, down across the three horizontal lines.

12. Trim the lines back to complete the view.

This ends the exercise. You can rotate and move each view relative to the other views in several ways. We'll look at those commands later in the book and then draw more views in Chapter 8.

Are You Experienced?

Now you can...

☑ **create polylines**

☑ **offset exterior walls to make interior walls**

☑ **zoom in on an area with the Zoom Window command and zoom back out with the Zoom Previous command**

☑ **use the Rectangle and Arc commands to make a door**

☑ use the Endpoint, Midpoint, and Perpendicular object snap modes

☑ use the Crossing Window selection tool

☑ use the Copy and Mirror commands to place an existing door and swing in another opening

☑ use the Offset and Trim commands to make a complex assembly

☑ begin drawing 2D representations of 3D shapes

CHAPTER 5

Developing Drawing Strategies: Part 2

▶ Using running object snaps

▶ Using polar tracking

▶ Using the Stretch command

▶ Using point filters

▶ Zooming and panning with the Realtime commands

▶ Copying and moving objects

▶ Using direct entry of distances

▶ Creating circles and ellipses

▶ Drawing using parametric constraints

The preceding chapter emphasized using existing geometry (or objects) in a drawing to create new geometry. In this chapter, you'll look at new tools for forming an efficient drawing strategy. Before getting back to the cabin, I'll give you a brief overview of the tools available for starting and running commands.

Developing a drawing strategy begins with determining the best way to start a command or determining when to start it. AutoCAD provides several ways to start most of the commands you'll be using. You have seen that you can start the Offset, Fillet, Trim, and Extend commands from either the Ribbon's Modify panel or by typing the first letter or two of the command and then pressing ↵. You can also display the menu bar and access the commands from a pull-down menu or expose the Modify toolbar and choose the tools from it.

T I P   Here's a quick recap. To start the Offset command from the keyboard, enter o↵. To start the Fillet command, enter f↵. To start the Trim command, enter tr↵; and to start the Extend command, enter ex↵. You can also start almost all AutoCAD commands by entering the full name of the command; for example, to start the Extend command, enter extend↵. If you have the AutoCAD classic workspace open, you can access menus and menu items by pressing the Alt key and then the hot key—the letter that is underlined in the menu or menu item name when you press the Alt key. For example, to open the Modify menu, press Alt+M.

You'll determine which method to use, to an extent, by what you're doing at the time as well as by your preference in using the Ribbon, menu bar, toolbars, or the keyboard. The purpose of the Ribbon is to make the most frequently used tools readily available, but when using the command aliases, keyboard entry can also be a fast method. The menus are slower to use because they require more selections to get to a command, but they also contain more commands and options than the toolbars, as well as some commands not found on the Ribbon.

Remember that if you have just ended a command, you can restart that command by pressing ↵, by pressing the spacebar, or by right-clicking. When you right-click, a *context* menu appears near the cursor. The top item on this menu is Repeat *Command*, where *Command* is the last command used. For example, if you've just finished using the Erase command and you right-click, the top item of the context menu is Repeat Erase. If you've used a command recently, you can select that command by pausing the cursor over the Recent Input option and then selecting that command from the *cascading menu* that appears (see Figure 5.1).

FIGURE 5.1: The right-click context menu and Recent Input cascading menu

I'll introduce some of the other items on the context menu throughout the rest of the book. This menu is called a context menu because the items on it depend on the following:

▶ Whether a command is running

▶ Which command you're using

▶ Where you are in a command

In this chapter, I'll introduce you to several new commands and, through the step-by-step instructions, show some alternative methods for accomplishing tasks similar to those you have previously completed. You'll add front and back decks and steps, thresholds, and kitchen and bath fixtures to the cabin floor plan (see Figure 5.2). For each of these tasks, the focus will be on noticing which objects and geometry are already in the drawing that can make your job easier and on tools to help you accomplish the tasks more quickly and efficiently. As you work your way through the chapter, if you haven't already done so, activate the Dynamic Input button on the status bar and work with the dynamic display information shown in the drawing area.

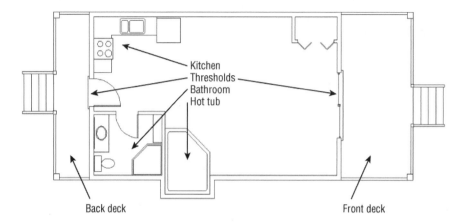

FIGURE 5.2: The cabin with front and back decks and steps, thresholds, kitchen, bathroom, and hot tub

Drawing the Thresholds

You draw the two thresholds, each with three simple lines. The trick is to see which part of the drawing you can effectively use to generate and position those lines. The thresholds extend 2″ (51 mm) beyond the outside wall line and run 3″ (76 mm) past either jamb line (see Figure 5.3). These are simple shapes to draw, but you'll learn a few new techniques as you create them.

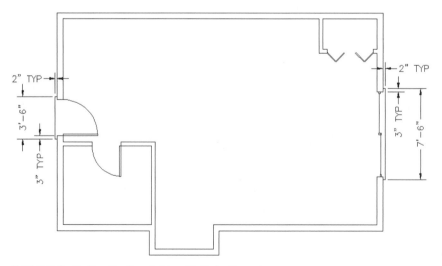

FIGURE 5.3: The thresholds with their dimensions

Drawing the Front Threshold

Thresholds generally are used on doorway openings when the level changes from one side of the opening to the other or to prevent rain and dust from entering the structure. This usually occurs at entrances that open from or to the outside. Although they are quite different in shape, each threshold for the cabin has the same geometry as the steps. The lip of each threshold is offset 2″ (51 mm) from the outside wall, and each edge runs 3″ (76 mm) past the doorjamb (see Figure 5.3). You'll use a temporary tracking point with polar tracking and direct entry to draw the three thresholds for the cabin.

As you can see in Figure 5.3, the front threshold is 7′-6″ (2286 mm) wide, extending 3″ (76 mm) past the doorway on each side. You can draw a line from the endpoint of one of the jamb lines down 3″ (76 mm) and then draw the perimeter of the threshold. Here's how you do it:

1. With AutoCAD running, open your cabin drawing (last saved as Cabin04c.dwg), and use the Zoom command options to achieve a view similar to Figure 5.4. The file is also available from this book's web page at www.sybex.com/go/autocad2010ner.

FIGURE 5.4: Zoomed in to the front opening

2. Check to be sure all buttons on the left side of the status bar, except Ortho Mode, Object Snap, and Dynamic Input, are still in their off positions. Start the Line command.

WAYS TO USE THE OBJECT SNAP TOOLS

You can access the Object Snap tools in several ways:

▶ The Object Snap context menu provides access to the object snaps. To open this menu, hold down the Shift key or Ctrl key and right-click.

▶ If you're using a mouse with a scroll wheel or a three-button mouse, you might be able to open the Object Snap menu by clicking on the wheel or the middle mouse button. If this doesn't work, set the mbuttonpan variable to zero. (Enter **mbuttonpan⏎ 0⏎.**) Be aware that you will no longer be able to pan by holding down the scroll wheel.

▶ When the menu bar is displayed, the Object Snap toolbar can be displayed by right-clicking on the Quick Access toolbar, then choosing Toolbars ➤ AutoCAD ➤ Object Snap.

▶ In most cases, you can enter the first three letters of any osnap to activate it, as in **end⏎** for Endpoint.

You need to start the threshold 3″ (76 mm) below the bottom jamb and inline with the outside wall line. Unfortunately, there is no feature to snap the cursor to at that point. The techniques that you've previously used would require offsetting the jamb line or starting the line at the jamb and drawing an overlapping line 3″ (76 mm) downward. Both of these methods would require you to erase the unnecessary line after the threshold is complete. Here, you will instead begin using the Object Snap Tracking tool to eliminate the need to create unnecessary geometry. With the Object Snap Tracking tool, you specify a location in the drawing area, called a *temporary tracking point*, relative to existing features or other locations.

3. Click the Object Snap Tracking button on the status bar.

In this case, because the threshold starts 3″ (76 mm) below the outside corner of the lower jamb, you'll use that corner as the temporary tracking point for the start point of the line.

4. Pause the cursor over the outside corner of the lower jamb until the endpoint osnap marker appears, followed by a small, gray cross inside that marker. Move the cursor directly downward, and you will see an "X" appear where the cursor appears directly below the reference point (see Figure 5.5). The gray cross indicates the temporary tracking point for the Object Snap Tracking tool, and the "X" indicates the point where the line will start.

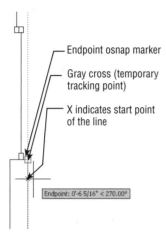

— Endpoint osnap marker

— Gray cross (temporary tracking point)

— X indicates start point of the line

Endpoint: 0'-6 5/16" < 270.00°

FIGURE 5.5: Pause the cursor over the endpoint to select the reference point.

5. Enter 3↵ (76↵) to use the direct entry method to start the first line 3″ (76 mm) below the temporary track point. With the Ortho mode turned on, the point selected is directly below the corner of the jamb.

6. Hold the crosshair cursor directly to the right of the last point; when you see the alignment path and tooltip, enter 2↵ (51↵) (see Figure 5.6). AutoCAD draws the bottom edge of the threshold. You've used direct entry with Ortho mode again, and you didn't have to enter either the relative polar or the Cartesian coordinates.

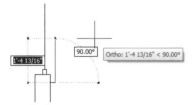

90.00°   Ortho: 1'-4 13/16" < 90.00°

1'-4 13/16"

FIGURE 5.6: Using direct input to draw the bottom edge of the threshold

7. Hold the crosshair cursor directly above the last point; when you see the alignment path and tooltip, enter 7'6″↵ (2286↵). AutoCAD draws the front edge of the threshold.

8. Select Perpendicular from the Object Snap context menu (Shift+right-click) and move the cursor to the outside wall line. When the Perpendicular icon appears on the wall line, as shown in Figure 5.7, click to draw the top edge of the threshold.

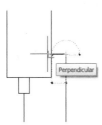

FIGURE 5.7: Use the Perpendicular osnap to draw the final line

9. Press ↵ to end the Line command. The completed front threshold looks like Figure 5.8.

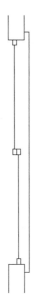

FIGURE 5.8: Completing the front threshold

10. Use the Zoom Previous command to view the completed front threshold with the whole floor plan.

Drawing the Back Threshold

The method of drawing the threshold for the back door is the same as the method used to draw the front threshold. You will use Ortho mode, direct input, and object snap tracking to draw the lines. Here is how it's done:

1. Zoom and pan until the back door fills the drawing area.

2. Start the Line command and place the cursor over the left corner of the lower jamb. Then, after the temporary tracking point cross appears inside the endpoint marker, move the cursor directly downward, as shown in Figure 5.9.

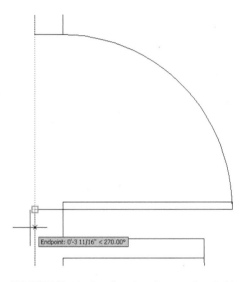

Endpoint: 0'-3 11/16" < 270.00°

FIGURE 5.9: Starting the rear threshold

3. Enter 3↵ (76↵) to set the start point of the line 3″ (76 mm) below the edge of the jamb.

4. Move the cursor directly to the left; then enter 2↵ (51↵) to draw the lower edge of the threshold.

5. Finish the threshold by moving the cursor directly upward and entering 3′6″↵ (1067↵); then use the Perpendicular object snap to draw to the edge of the threshold perpendicular to the outside wall. Press ↵ to end the Line command, and the back threshold should look like Figure 5.10.

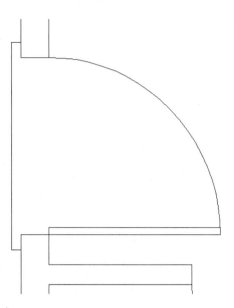

FIGURE 5.10: The completed back threshold

6. Use the Zoom Previous command to view the completed front and back thresholds with the whole floor plan.

This exercise may have seemed complicated when you drew the first threshold but was easier when you drew the second. Like many techniques available in AutoCAD, with a little practice, these methods can be used efficiently and become second nature. In the next exercise, you will draw the cabin's front deck and stairs; then you'll use the existing geometry to draw the back deck and stairs.

Drawing the Decks and Stairs

The decks consist of the platform, posts, railings, and a set of stairs. You'll begin by drawing polylines for the perimeter to facilitate the drawing of the railing lines using the Offset command; then you'll continue the construction using lines and the Offset and Trim commands. You will also begin using the Temporary Track Point osnap, an option with the Object Snap Tracking tool.

Drawing the Front Deck

Figure 5.11 shows the dimensions of the front deck you'll draw.

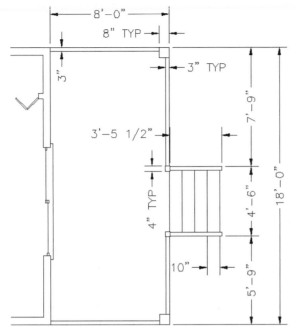

FIGURE 5.11: The dimensions of the front deck and stairs

 1. Right-click the Polar Tracking button on the status bar at the bottom of the screen, and then choose Settings from the context menu to open the Drafting Settings dialog box. By default, the Polar Tracking tab is active (see Figure 5.12).

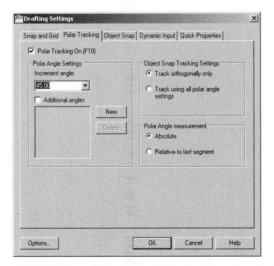

FIGURE 5.12: The Polar Tracking tab of the Drafting Settings dialog box

2. In the Polar Angle Settings area, change the Increment Angle to 45.00. On the right side, be sure that Absolute is selected in the Polar Angle Measurement area. Finally, in the upper-left corner, click the Polar Tracking On check box. This has the same effect as clicking the Polar Tracking button in the status bar. Click OK. The Polar Tracking button is turned on in the status bar and the Ortho mode is automatically turned off. Polar tracking is similar to Ortho mode but provides more angular increments to which you can snap the cursor.

3. Turn the Object Snap Tracking button off in the status bar.

The object snaps are also available from the Object Snap toolbar. One benefit of using the toolbar is that access to the non-running osnaps can remain visible on the screen without the need to open a menu and, if necessary, the toolbars can be docked to the perimeter of the drawing area or moved to a second monitor.

4. To open the Object Snap toolbar, you'll first need to display the menu bar. Click the down arrow in the Quick Access toolbar, then choose Show Menu Bar, as shown in Figure 5.13.

FIGURE 5.13: Displaying the menu bar

5. Expand the Tools menu, then click Toolbars ➢ AutoCAD ➢ Object Snap. You could also enter -toolbar↵ "object snap"↵ and choose

Show from the context menu, as shown in Figure 5.14. Be sure you enter the command exactly as shown, with the leading hyphen (-) before **toolbar** and the quotes surrounding **object snap**.

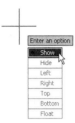

FIGURE 5.14: Exposing the Object Snap toolbar from the context menu

The Object Snap toolbar appears in the drawing area (see Figure 5.15).

FIGURE 5.15: The Object Snap toolbar

6. Start the Polyline command and draw a polyline from the lower-right corner of the cabin to a point 8′0″ (2438 mm) to the right.

7. Click the Snap To Perpendicular button in the Object Snap toolbar, place the cursor over the top outside horizontal line of the cabin, and when the Snap marker appears (see Figure 5.16), click to draw the vertical line of the deck's perimeter.

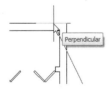

FIGURE 5.16: Drawing the vertical line perpendicular to the upper cabin wall

8. Click on the top-right corner of the cabin to complete the perimeter of the deck; then press ↵ to end the polyline command. Your drawing should look like Figure 5.17.

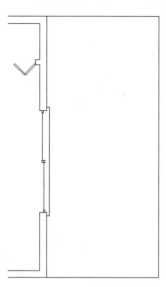

FIGURE 5.17: The perimeter of the front deck

9. Offset the perimeter 3″ (72 mm) to the inside to represent the inside and outside edges of the handrail, and then terminate the Offset command.

Drawing the Deck Posts

There are four posts on the deck: two 8″ (204 mm) posts at the corners that hold up the roof and two 4″ (102 mm) posts at the top of the stairs. You will use the Rectangle command to draw the posts and the Mirror command to copy them.

 1. Start the Rectangle command and, at the `Specify first corner point or:` prompt click on the endpoints where the lines form the lower-right corner of the deck. At the `Specify other corner point or:` prompt, enter -8,8↵ (-204,204) to draw the first 8″ (204 mm) post. The rectangle should be similar to Figure 5.18.

FIGURE 5.18: The first corner post

2. To create the opposite post, select the rectangle that you just drew and then start the Mirror command.

> **T I P** Notice how you can either start an AutoCAD command and then select objects, or select objects first and then start the command.

3. At the Specify first point of mirror line: prompt, click the Snap To Midpoint button on the Object Snap toolbar; then pause the cursor over either of the vertical handrail lines. When a feature is symmetrical like the deck, you can use the Midpoint snap to mirror objects about the center line.

4. Move the cursor directly to the left or right, as shown in Figure 5.19, to mirror the post; then click to execute the mirror; and then press ↵ to accept the No option for deleting the source object.

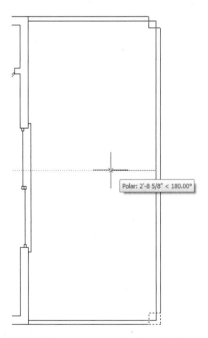

Polar: 2'-8 5/8" < 180.00°

FIGURE 5.19: The first deck posts are in place

5. Use the Trim command to trim the short polyline segments that fall within the posts. When you are finished, they should each look similar to Figure 5.20.

FIGURE 5.20: Trim the handrail lines to clean up the post.

The 4″ (102 mm) posts at the top of the stairs are centered on the 3″ (72 mm) handrails on the deck and on the stairs. To create the lower small post, you need to locate the bottom-right corner at a point ½″ (15 mm) to the right of the front handrail and 5′-8½″ (1740 mm) from the bottom-right corner of the deck.

1. Select the large lower post and start the Copy command.

2. Select the lower-right corner point as the base point and then, at the Specify second point or: prompt, enter .5,5′8.5″ (15,1740). Press ↵ to end the Copy command. The copied post will appear as shown in Figure 5.21.

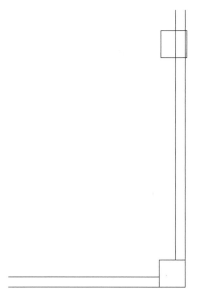

FIGURE 5.21: The copied deck post

3. Zoom in to the new post. The bottom-right corner of the post is located in the correct location, but the post is twice the size that it should be.

4. Start the Scale command by clicking the Scale button in the Modify panel; then select the new rectangle.

5. Set the lower-right corner as the base point; then move the cursor to see the effect when the scale is based from that corner. A copy of the selected object appears as shown in Figure 5.22.

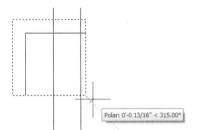

Polar: 0'-0 13/16" < 315.00°

FIGURE 5.22: A copy of the scaled object appears as you move the cursor

6. Enter 0.5↵ to scale the rectangle to 50 percent of its current size.

Drawing the Stairs

You could mirror the 4" (102 mm) rectangle now to create the reciprocal post, but we'll wait until the stair handrails are complete and then mirror both objects at once. The first stair handrail is 3" (76 mm) wide and centered on the 4" (102 mm) post, so you'll use a temporary tracking point to locate the first point of the line.

1. Start the Line command and click the Temporary Track Point button in the Object Snap toolbar, or enter tt↵.

2. Click on the lower-right corner of the small post to locate the temporary tracking point; then move the cursor directly upward and enter .5↵ (13↵) to place the start point ½" (13 mm) above the corner.

3. To complete the handrail, do the following:

a. Move the cursor directly to the right and enter 3'5.5↵ (1054↵).

b. Move the cursor directly upward and enter 3↵ (72↵).

c. Move the cursor directly to the left and enter 3'5.5↵ (1054↵). Your first handrail should look like Figure 5.23.

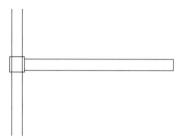

FIGURE 5.23: The first handrail

You can now mirror the post and railing to draw them on the oppo-site side of the stairway. You can't use the midpoint of the deck's perimeter line as one point of the mirror line, because the stair is centered on the front door and not on the deck. You can, however, use the midpoint of the front door's threshold.

1. Select the 4″ (102 mm) post and all three lines that make up the handrail. Try using a window selection (drag from left to right) to select the objects rather than picking them one at a time.

2. Start the Mirror command.

3. Use the Midpoint osnap, and then specify the midpoint of the vertical threshold line as the first point of the mirror line, as shown in Fig-ure 5.24.

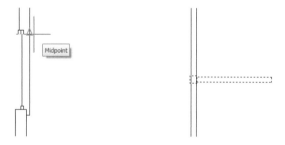

FIGURE 5.24: Using the midpoint of the threshold as the first mirror point

4. Move the cursor to the right; then click to specify the second point of the mirror line. Press ↵ to retain the source objects. Your deck should look like Figure 5.25.

5. Zoom in until you can see both stair handrails and posts.

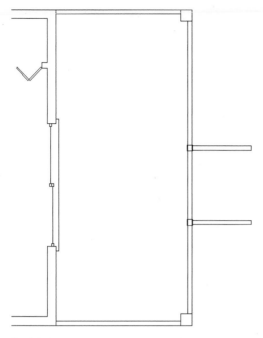

FIGURE 5.25: The deck with both handrails

6. Start the Offset command, and then set the offset distance to 10″ (254). This is the width of the step treads.

7. Offset the outside perimeter line and then the line you offset until you have a total of four offset lines, as shown in Figure 5.26. Press ↵ to end the Offset command.

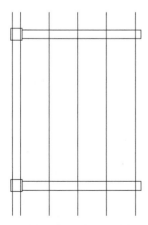

FIGURE 5.26: Offset the perimeter line to draw the stairs.

Now you will use the Trim command to trim away the stair lines that extend into and past the railings and the lines that pass through the 4″ (102 mm) posts.

8. Start the Trim command. Select both of the inside lines of the stairway handrails and the 4″(102 mm) post polylines as the cutting edge objects.

T I P   Make sure that you do not select the offset perimeter polylines as cutting edges. When polylines are selected as cutting edges and then as the trimmed objects as well, they are trimmed back to the endpoint nearest to the picked location.

9. Trim the four stair lines on both sides of the railing.

10. Of the two vertical lines that extend between the two posts, trim only the left vertical line.

11. Finally, trim away the four short lines that pass through the two 4″ (102 mm) posts. When the trimming is completed, your front stairway should look like Figure 5.27.

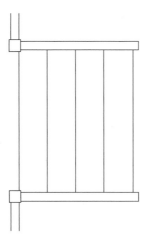

F I G U R E 5 . 2 7 : The completed front stairs

12. Zoom to the drawing's extents.

Drawing the Back Deck and Stairs

The deck, handrails, posts, and stairs at the rear portion of the cabin are similar to the same features at the front of the cabin. One of the most significant strengths of CAD software over traditional hand drafting is the ability to use existing geometry and linework in a drawing to create additional identical or similar objects. In this section, you will first mirror the front deck to the back of the cabin. I will then introduce you to the Stretch command to adjust the lines to match the cabin's structure. Figure 5.28 shows the dimensions of the rear deck that are different from those on the front deck.

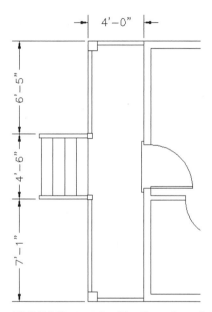

FIGURE 5.28: The dimensions of the rear deck and stairs

1. Start the Mirror command.

2. Use a crossing selection window to select all the components of the front deck, but do not select the cabin wall, front door, or threshold. If you inadvertently select an unwanted object, hold down the Shift key and pick the object again to deselect it. The dashed selected set should look like Figure 5.29.

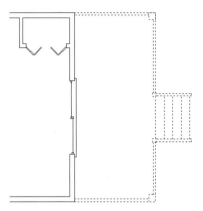

FIGURE 5.29: The Selected front deck and steps

3. At the Specify first point of mirror line: prompt, activate the Midpoint osnap and click near the midpoint of the top, outside wall line. Click when the Midpoint snap marker and tooltip appear.

4. Move the cursor downward. With Ortho mode active, the cursor is restricted to the 270° angle, causing the deck to be mirrored perfectly to the rear of the cabin, as shown in Figure 5.30.

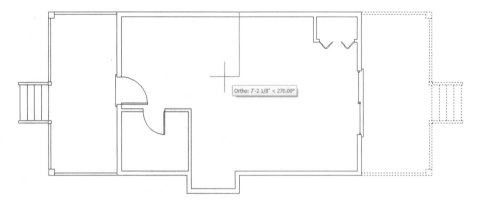

FIGURE 5.30: Mirroring the front deck to the rear of the cabin

5. Click to define the mirror line and press ↵ to retain the source objects. The front deck is mirrored to the back of the cabin.

The Stretch command is used to lengthen or shorten objects in the drawing area. The major restriction when using Stretch is that the objects must be selected with a crossing window or crossing polygon, so be sure to define your selection window from right to left or enter cr⏎ at the Select objects: prompt.

When part of an object resides inside the crossing window borders, the portion inside the window is moved, the portion crossing the border is stretched, and the portion outside the border is unaffected. When an object is completely inside the crossing window, it is affected as if the Move command is used. Figure 5.31 shows the result when the top portions of the objects in a drawing are selected and stretched. The far-left image shows a crossing selection window encompassing the entire top portion of the objects, and the middle-left image shows the result of stretching the object upward. The middle-right image shows a crossing selection window encompassing only the right half of the top portion of the objects, and the far-right image shows the result of stretching the object upward. Some objects, such as circles, ellipses, and blocks, cannot be stretched.

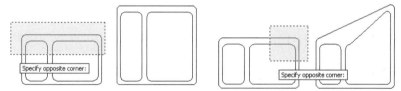

FIGURE 5.31: Selecting and stretching the entire top portion (left) and only the top-right portion (right)

Take the following steps to fix the rear deck and stairs using the Stretch command:

1. Zoom in to the rear deck and stairs.

2. Click the Stretch button in the Modify panel or enter stretch⏎ to start the Stretch command.

3. At the Select objects: prompt, place the cursor above the deck and to the right of the stairs, but be sure the point is to the left of the threshold.

4. At the Specify opposite corner: prompt, click a point outside and to the left of the deck, as shown in Figure 5.32. The deck objects ghost to indicate that they are selected. Press ⏎ to discontinue selecting objects.

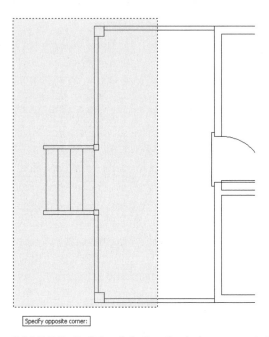

Specify opposite corner:

FIGURE 5.32: Selecting the deck components for the Stretch command

Like the Move command, Stretch requires you to specify a base point and a second point to define the result of the stretch. The selected objects are stretched to the same distance and angle as the relationship between those two points. For example, after selecting objects to stretch on the right side of the drawing area, you can select a base point on the left side of the drawing area and a second point two inches above the base point. The selected objects on the left are stretched upward two inches.

You can reference objects or features in the drawing area or select a random point for the base and specify the angle and distance for the second point.

> **5.** The open end of the deck needs to be stretched 4′-0″ (1220 mm) to the right. Pick a point anywhere in the drawing area, and then move the cursor to the right. You will see the deck stretching to the right while a ghosted version remains in place (see Figure.5.33).

> **6.** Enter 4′↵ (1220↵). The deck is stretched 4′-0″ (1220 mm) to the right.

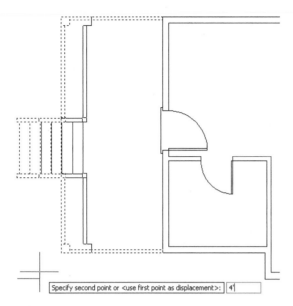

Specify second point or <use first point as displacement>: 4'|

FIGURE 5.33: The deck after specifying the base point for the Stretch command

Using Point Filters to Finish the Deck

To complete the back deck, you need to align the center of the stair with the center of the door. To do this, you will use the Stretch command along with the Midpoint object snap and the point filters. *Point filters*, also called *coordinate filters*, are a tool you can utilize to use only the X, Y, or Z value of a selected point in the drawing area. For example, suppose you want to stretch an object to the center of a rectangle but you don't know where that center location is located. To specify the correct location, you would use the X point filter and pick the midpoint of a horizontal line from the rectangle; then you'd use the Y point filter and pick the midpoint of a vertical line from the rectangle. The resulting location is at the intersection of the midpoint of the two sides of the rectangle at the center point. To finish the back deck, follow these steps:

1. Press ↵ or the spacebar to restart the Stretch command and drag a crossing selection window around the stairs, stair handrails, and stair posts, as shown in Figure 5.34.

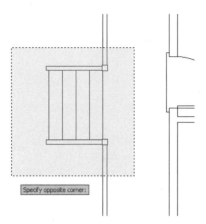

FIGURE 5.34: Select the stairs for the next Stretch command

---

2. At the `Specify base point or:` prompt, activate the Midpoint osnap and pick the midpoint of the top step.

3. At the `Specify second point or:` prompt, you need to pick a point that is horizontally (X) equal to the same location as the point you selected in step 2 and vertically (Y) equal to the midpoint of the threshold. Hold the Shift key down and right-click to open the Osnap context menu; then choose Point Filters ➤ .x, as shown in Figure 5.35.

FIGURE 5.35: Select the .x point filter from the Object Snap context menu.

The prompt in the Command window has .X of appended to indicate that AutoCAD will use only the X component of the next location picked.

4. Turn off Ortho mode, and click either endpoint of the top step. This point is in line with the midpoint you picked in step 2, so the stretch will not move the stairs horizontally.

Move the cursor around in the drawing area and you'll see that the movement of the stairs is now restricted to the y-axis. In the Command window, the notation (need YZ) is appended to the prompt, indicating that AutoCAD will use only the Y and Z components of the next location picked. Only the y-axis is referenced if you are using AutoCAD LT.

5. Click the Snap to Midpoint button in the Object Snap toolbar, and then click the midpoint of the threshold (see Figure 5.36).

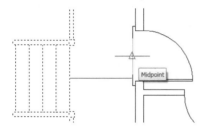

FIGURE 5.36: Select the midpoint of the threshold as the Y and Z components of the second point.

6. The stairs are moved vertically and centered on the back door. Zoom to the drawing's extents. Your drawing should look like Figure 5.37.

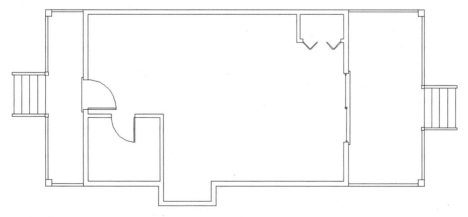

FIGURE 5.37: The cabin after completing the back deck

7. Save your file as Cabin05a.dwg.

Laying Out the Kitchen

The kitchen for the cabin will have a stove, a refrigerator, and a counter with a sink (see Figure 5.38). The refrigerator is set 2″ (51 mm) from the back wall. Approaching this drawing task, your goal is to think about the easiest and fastest way to complete it. The first step in deciding on an efficient approach is to ascertain what information you have about the various parts and what existing elements in the drawing will be available to assist you.

Figure 5.38 gives you the basic dimensions, and you'll get more detailed information about the sink and stove as you progress through the exercise.

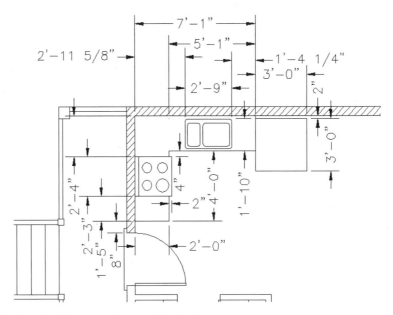

FIGURE 5.38: The general layout of the kitchen

Drawing the Counter

Although the counter is in two pieces, you'll draw it as one piece and then cut out a section for the stove. Try two ways to draw the counter to see which method is more efficient.

Object Snap Tracking and Direct Entry

The first drawing method uses object snap tracking and direct entry:

1. Continue with the drawing from the previous exercise or open Cabin05a.dwg from the book's web page.

2. Use a zoom window to zoom your view so that it is about the same magnification as Figure 5.39. On the status bar, click the Polar Tracking button to turn polar tracking back on if it isn't already on. The Object Snap, Object Snap Tracking, and Dynamic Input buttons should be in their on positions. The rest of the buttons should be off.

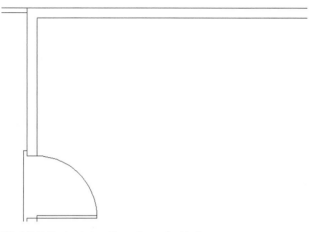

FIGURE 5.39: Zoom in to the kitchen area.

3. Start the Line command. Next, place the cursor near the lower end of the right-rear doorjamb line where the door swing meets the wall. A small cross appears on the point you choose, indicating the reference location for the object snap tracking.

4. Move the mouse upward; then enter 8↵ (204↵) to start the counter line 8″ (204 mm) from the corner of the jamb (see Figure 5.40).

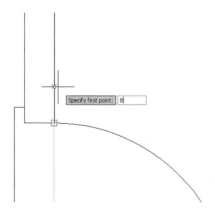

FIGURE 5.40: Setting the location for the first counter line

5. Hold the crosshair cursor directly to the right of the first point of the line, and enter **2'⏎** (**610⏎**) move the cursor straight up then enter **4'⏎** (**1220⏎**) (see Figure 5.38, shown earlier).

6. Hold the cursor to the right again, and enter **5'1"⏎** (**1550⏎**) to draw the long counter line that runs in front of the sink.

7. Select the Perpendicular osnap, and then pick the inside wall line, as shown in Figure 5.41, to complete the counter. Press ⏎ to end the Line command.

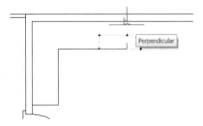

FIGURE 5.41: Completing the counter

Using Offset and Fillet

To do the same thing using the Offset command, you'll need to undo the effects of the preceding command. Because all lines were drawn in one cycle of the Line command, one use of the Undo command will undo the entire counter:

1. Click the Undo button on the Quick Access toolbar or enter **u⏎**. The counter you just drew should disappear. If you ended the Line command while drawing the counter and had to restart it before you finished, you might have to click the Undo button more than once. If you undo too much, click the Redo button, which is just to the right of the Undo button.

   Now draw the counter again, this time using the Offset and Fillet commands.

2. Offset both the left inside wall line and the top inside wall line 2' (610 mm) to the inside of the cabin.

3. Stop and then restart the Offset command, and offset the inside left wall line 7'-1" (2159 mm) to the right. Next, offset the inside top wall line 6'-0" (1829 mm) (the sum of the two counter dimensions and the stove dimension) downward (see Figure 5.42).

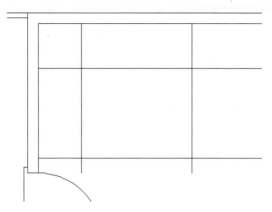

FIGURE 5.42: Offsetting wall lines to create the counter

T I P If the Fillet command has a nonzero radius setting that you want to keep, hold down the Shift key to set the radius to zero for one use of the command. After the command ends, the radius returns to its nonzero setting.

4. Use the Fillet command with a radius of zero to clean up the three corners. Be sure to click on the portions of the lines that you want to retain.

You can decide which of the two methods is more practical for you. Both are powerful techniques for laying out orthogonal patterns of lines for walls, counters, and other objects.

Undoing and Redoing in AutoCAD

AutoCAD has two Undo commands, and they operate quite differently:

▶ When you click the Undo button on the Quick Access toolbar, you're using the AutoCAD U command. You can also start it by entering **u**↵. The U command works like the Undo command for Windows-compliant applications by undoing the results of the previous commands one step at a time. Using the Ctrl+Z hotkey combination also executes the U command.

Continues

UNDOING AND REDOING IN AUTOCAD   *(Continued)*

▶ The Undo command in AutoCAD has many options, and you start it by entering **undo**↵. You use this approach when you want to undo everything you've done since you last saved your drawing or to undo back to a point in your drawing session that you specified earlier using the Mark option. Be careful when you use the Undo command; you can easily lose a lot of your work.

▶ The Oops command is a special undo tool that restores the last objects erased, even if the Erase command wasn't the last command executed.

▶ The Redo command will undo the effect of several undo's. So, if you undo a few steps too many, you can still get them back. The Redo tool must be used immediately after using the Undo tool.

▶ Both the Undo and Redo buttons in the Quick Access toolbar have small down arrows to their right. Clicking these arrows displays a drop-down menu showing a list of the recent commands used (Undo) or undone (Redo). When there are several commands to be undone or redone, selecting the command to be undone to may be faster than clicking the Undo or Redo button repeatedly.

Drawing the Stove and Refrigerator

The stove and refrigerator are simple rectangles. Here you will use the Temporary Tracking Point osnap to locate the first corner of each shape:

1. For the refrigerator, click the Rectangle button on the Draw panel, and then click the Temporary Track Point osnap button on the Object Snap toolbar. Use the Endpoint osnap to select a base point by placing the cursor near the upper end of the right side of the counter. Then hold the cursor directly below that point. When the dotted tracking path and the Track Point tooltip appear, enter 2↵ (51↵), as shown in Figure 5.43. This starts the rectangle 2″ (51 mm) from the back wall, along the side of the counter.

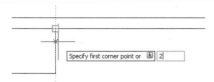

FIGURE 5.43: Locating the first corner of the rectangle

2. To specify the opposite corner of the rectangle, enter @36,-36↵ (@914,-914↵).

3. For the stove, right-click and choose Repeat RECTANG from the context menu that opens. Use the technique from step 1, but pick the lower end of the left side of the counter as the tracking point. Hold the cursor directly above that point, and enter 1′5″↵ or 17↵ (432↵). Then enter @26,27↵ (@660,686↵) to complete the rectangle.

4. Use the Trim command to trim away the front edge of the counter that passes through the stove. Your kitchen should look like Figure 5.44.

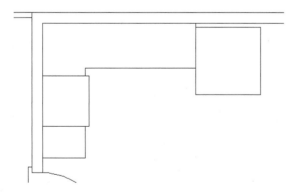

FIGURE 5.44: The stove and refrigerator made with rectangles

N O T E   Because the stove rectangle is drawn as a *polyline*, you need to select only one segment of it for all sides of the rectangle to be selected and, in this case, for them to become cutting edges.

Completing the Stove

The stove needs a little more detail. You need to add circles to represent the burners and a line off the back to indicate the control panel (see Figure 5.45). You locate the burners by their centers.

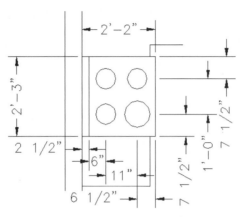

FIGURE 5.45: The details of the stove

1. Zoom in to a closer view of the stove. You need to draw a line along the back of the stove that is 2.5″ (64 mm) in from the wall line. Offset seems like the right command to use.

2. Offset the wall line to the right 2.5″ (64 mm). When you pick the line, pick it somewhere above or below the stove—otherwise, you might offset the stove rectangle. After it has been offset, trim it back to the sides of the stove (see Figure 5.46).

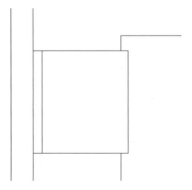

FIGURE 5.46: The stove with the control panel drawn

W A R N I N G   The back segment of the stove coincides with the wall. If you try to pick the wall line where the two lines coincide, you might pick the rectangle of the stove instead. You don't want to offset a line of the stove because it's a polyline. When you attempt to offset any segment of a polyline, all segments are offset and all corners are filleted automatically. This would be inconvenient in this situation because only one line segment needs to be offset. When you draw the sink, you'll learn a technique for selecting the line you want when two or more lines overlap or coincide.

The next step is to draw the circles that represent the burners. To do this, you will use one corner of the stove as the Object Snap Tracking reference point, using the Snap From osnap to locate the center of the first circle. Then you will copy and adjust the circles to create the remaining burners.

1. Make sure the Object Snap Tracking button is still turned on; then click the down arrow next to Circle in the Draw panel and look at the fly-out menu, shown in Figure 5.47, for a moment.

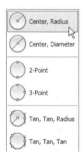

F I G U R E   5 . 4 7 : The Circle command's fly-out menu

You have six options for constructing a circle. The first two require you to specify a point as the center of the circle and to enter a radius or a diameter. You use the next two when you know two or three points that the circle must intersect. The last two options use tangents and a radius or just tangents to form a circle. Notice that each circle construction method has a unique icon on the left side of the fly-out menu. Whichever method was used last becomes the default method when you click the Circle button and its icon appears on the button.

2. Choose the Center, Radius option from the fly-out menu.

3. Click the Snap From osnap button from the Object Snap toolbar. Choose it from the Object Snap context menu or enter **from**↵. The command prompt changes from `Specify center point for circle or:` to `Base point:`.

4. Click on the bottom endpoint on the front of the control panel (see Figure 5.48) to set the reference point; then enter **@6,7.5**↵ (**@152,191**↵) to specify the center point of the first circle.

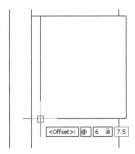

FIGURE 5.48: Setting the location for the first burner

Using Snap From

Unlike the Object Snap Tracking feature or the Temporary Track Point object snap, the Snap From osnap requires you to click in the drawing area to set the reference point. Another distinction between the tools is that the Snap From osnap does not restrict the cursor to orthogonal movements like the other two. Even if Dynamic Input is turned on, you still need to type the "@" symbol to enter relative coordinates.

5. At the `Specify radius of circle or:` prompt, enter **3.5**↵ (**89**↵) to draw a circle with its center 6″ (152 mm) from the back of the stove and 7½″ (191 mm) from the lower edge with a radius of 3.5″ (89 mm).

6. Start the Copy command. Select the circle, and then press ↵.

7. Click the Snap to Center osnap button or enter **cen**↵, and then click anywhere on the perimeter of, or inside, the circle.

8. Measured center-to-center, the back burners are 11″ (279 mm) apart from the front burners, and as seen from the front, the left burners are 12″ (305 mm) apart from the right burners. To draw the remaining burners using the center of the selected circle as the base point, enter **0,12**↵, **11,0**↵ (as shown in Figure 5.49), **11,12**↵↵ (**0,305**↵, **279,0**↵, **279,305**↵↵).

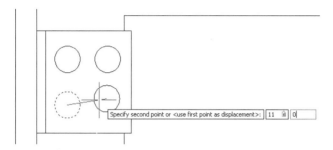

FIGURE 5.49: Copying the burners

Changing the Circle's Radius

The front-left burner is often larger than the other three; in this case, it has a radius of 4½″ (114 mm). Rather than draw the burner separate from the others, it will be easier to change the radius of the existing circle. In AutoCAD there are two ways to enter data to change an object's properties: the Properties palette and the Quick Properties dialog box.

The Properties palette, shown in Figure 5.50, is a comprehensive list of an object's properties, and any property values residing in a field with a white background can be changed from within the palette. Simply click in a field and enter in a new value, or in some cases such as the Color property, double-click the value to expand a list of choices. You can scroll through the palette to see categories and fields that extend beyond the visible limits of the palettes using the scroll bar on the left-hand side or using the scroll wheel on your mouse. The palette, and the categories within it, can be expanded or collapsed, and the palette itself can be set to Auto-Hide mode so that it disappears until the cursor pauses over it.

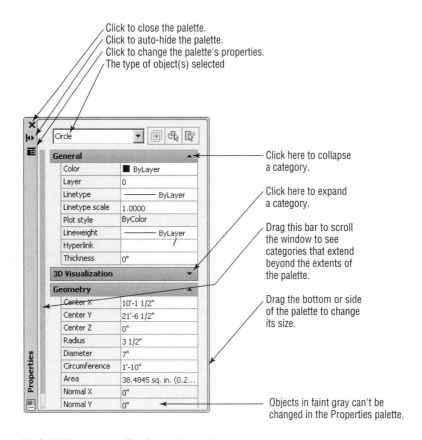

Click to close the palette.
Click to auto-hide the palette.
Click to change the palette's properties.
The type of object(s) selected

Click here to collapse
a category.

Click here to expand
a category.

Drag this bar to scroll
the window to see
categories that extend
beyond the extents of
the palette.

Drag the bottom or side
of the palette to change
its size.

Objects in faint gray can't be
changed in the Properties palette.

FIGURE 5.50: The Properties palette

The Quick Properties dialog box has a limited number of object properties listed; it shows the properties of the selected object that are most often adjusted by AutoCAD users. You can easily customize the Quick Properties dialog box to show the properties that you prefer for any specific type of object by selecting an object and then clicking the large button near the top-right corner (see Figure 5.51). While the Properties palette remains open whether an object is selected or not, turning on Quick Properties mode will cause the dialog box to appear when an object is selected and disappear when the selection set is empty. When you close the Quick Properties dialog box by clicking the X in the upper-right corner, another dialog box may appear asking your preferences for closing this particular dialog box. The Quick Properties feature is turned on by clicking the Quick Properties button at the bottom of the AutoCAD window.

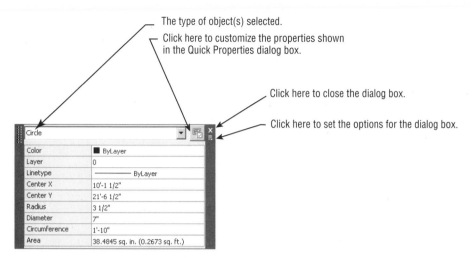

FIGURE 5.51: The expanded Quick Properties dialog box

1. Select the front-left burner. Five blue grips appear on the circle and at its center.

2. Right-click and choose Properties from the context menu, or click the View tab of the Ribbon and click the Properties button in the Palettes panel. Figure 5.52 shows the resulting Properties palette; you can readjust its size and position. Notice the drop-down list at the top of the Properties palette. This tells you that the currently selected object is a circle.

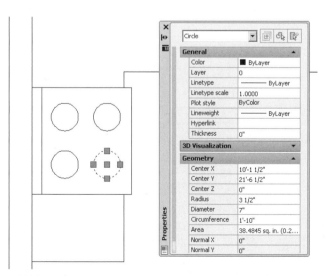

FIGURE 5.52: The Properties palette and the selected burner

3. Move down the categorized list of properties in the Geometry list and click Radius.

4. Highlight the 3 1/2″ (89) Radius setting. Change it to 4 1/2″ (114) and press ↵. The burner in the drawing is enlarged.

5. Click the X in the upper-left or upper-right corner of the Properties palette to close it. Then press the Esc key to deselect the circle.

6. Use Zoom Previous to see the whole kitchen with the completed stove (see Figure 5.53).

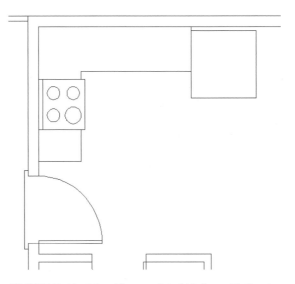

FIGURE 5.53: The completed kitchen with the stove

7. Save your file as Cabin05b.dwg.

With the stove finished, the final task in the kitchen is to draw the sink.

 N O T E   **The Properties palette and Quick Properties dialog box are important tools for working with objects in a drawing. You'll learn more about them in Chapter 6, "Using Layers to Organize Your Drawing," and you'll use them throughout the rest of this book.**

Drawing the Kitchen Sink

You'll draw a double sink with one basin larger than the other (see Figure 5.54). You'll use Offset, Fillet, and Trim to create the sink from the counter and wall lines.

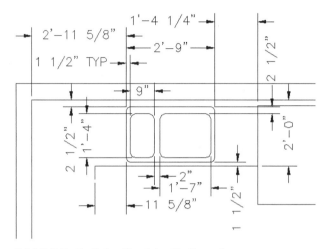

FIGURE 5.54: The sink with dimensions

1. Zoom in to the sink area, keeping the edges of the refrigerator and stove in view. Offset the inside wall line 2 ½" (64 mm) down and the front edge of the counter 1 ½" (38 mm) up.

2. Restart the Offset command, and set the offset distance to 16.25" (413). You're going to offset the right side of the counter 1'-4¼" (413 mm) to the left, but it coincides with the left side of the refrigerator. Hold down the Shift key and the spacebar as you pick that line. If the refrigerator becomes dashed (see Figure 5.55), pick the same line again. The selected line switches to the line representing the edge of the counter. When the counter edge is selected, release the Shift key and the spacebar. Press ↵ to complete the selection, and then finish the offset by picking a point to the left of the selected line. This selection technique is called *cycling*. It allows you to select one object that might coincide with another.

When you drew the detail onto the stove, you could have used selection cycling to select the wall line where it coincided with the stove outline. You didn't need to because you could easily select the wall line at a point where the stove outline wasn't interfering.

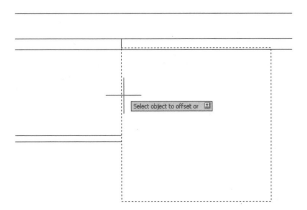

FIGURE 5.55: The refrigerator is selected while cycling through the selections.

3. Offset this new line 2'-9" (838 mm) to the left. This forms the outside edge of the sink (see the top of Figure 5.56).

4. Fillet the corners of this rectangle to clean them up, using a radius of zero.

5. Offset the left side, bottom, and right side of the sink 1.5" (38 mm) to the inside. Offset the top side 2.5" (64 mm) to the inside. Then, offset the new line on the left 9" (229) to the right and again 2" (51 mm) farther to the right. This forms the basis of the inside sink lines (see the middle of Figure 5.56).

6. Trim away the horizontal top and bottom inside sink lines between the two middle vertical sink lines. Then, fillet the four corners of each basin with a 2" (51 mm) radius to clean them up. Use the Multiple option of the Fillet command so that you won't need continually to restart the command.

7. Fillet all four outside sink corners with a 1.5" (38 mm) radius. This finishes the sink (see the bottom of Figure 5.56). Use Zoom Previous to view the whole kitchen with the completed sink.

This completes the kitchen area. You drew no new lines to complete this task because you created most of them by offsetting existing lines and then trimming or filleting them. Keep this in mind as you move on to the bathroom.

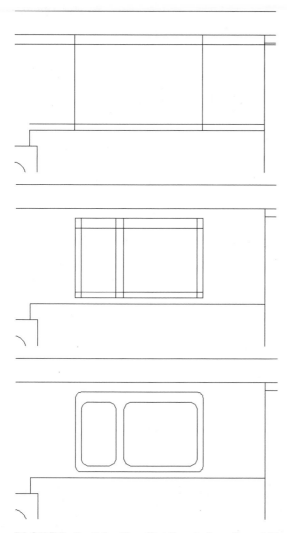

FIGURE 5.56: The offset lines to form the outside edge of the sink (top), the offset lines to form the inside edges of the sink (middle), and the finished sink (bottom)

Constructing the Bathroom

The bathroom has three fixtures: a sink, a shower, and a toilet as well as a mirror and a shelving unit. While you are drawing the bathroom, you'll draw the hot tub in the main room as well (see Figure 5.57). When drawing these fixtures, you'll use a few object snaps over and over again. You can set one or more of the osnap choices to be running continually until you turn them off. That way, you won't have to select them each time.

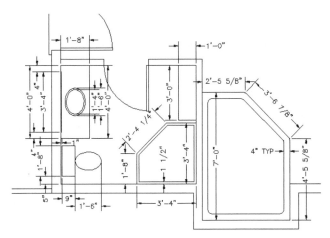

FIGURE 5.57: The bathroom fixtures and hot tub with dimensions

Setting Running Object Snaps

You'll set three osnaps to run continually for now, until you get used to how they work:

1. Right-click the Object Snap button on the status bar, and choose Settings from the context menu to open the Drafting Settings dialog box. By default, the Object Snap tab is current (see Figure 5.58).

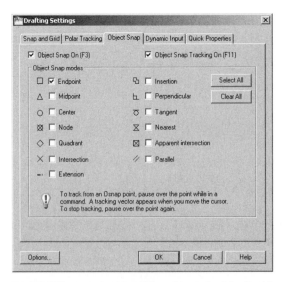

FIGURE 5.58: The Object Snap tab of the Drafting Settings dialog box

Each of the 13 osnap options has a check box and a symbol next to it. The symbol appears as a marker in the drawing when you select a particular osnap, and the cursor is near a point where you can use that osnap. You can select any number of osnaps to be running at a time.

N O T E   **You can choose a different color for the markers if you want. If you're using a dark background in the drawing area, use a bright color, such as yellow. For a white background, try blue.**

2. In the lower-left corner of the Drafting Settings dialog box, click Options to open the Options dialog box (see Figure 5.59); the Drafting tab should be on top. Then, at the bottom of the AutoSnap Settings area, click the Colors button to open the Drawing Window Colors dialog box. 2D Model Space and AutoSnap Marker will be selected. Open the Color drop-down list in the upper-right corner and select a color. Then click Apply & Close. While you're in the AutoSnap Settings area of the Drafting tab, make sure the Marker, Magnet, and Display AutoSnap Tooltip check boxes are selected. Also make sure that the Display AutoSnap Aperture Box is unchecked. You can change the size of the markers using the slider in the AutoSnap Marker Size area, but don't make them so large that working with them becomes cumbersome. Click OK.

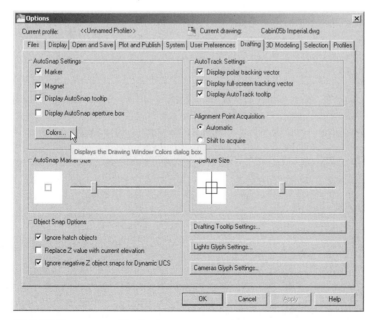

F I G U R E   5 . 5 9 : The Drafting tab of the Options dialog box

3. Back on the Object Snap tab of the Drafting Settings dialog box, click the check boxes next to Endpoint, Midpoint, and Intersection. Then, above the list and to the left, be sure the check box next to Object Snap On is selected.

4. Click OK to close the dialog box. These osnaps will now be active anytime you're prompted to select a point on the drawing. You can deactivate them by turning off the Object Snap button in the status bar.

Now you're ready to begin drawing the bathroom. The shower determines the placement of the other two items, so let's start there.

Drawing a Shower Unit

You'll start the shower unit with a rectangle and then trim away one corner. As you start this exercise, check the status bar. The Polar Tracking, Object Snap, Object Snap Tracking, and Dynamic Input buttons should be in their on positions. The rest of the buttons should be off. Follow these steps:

1. Enter z↵ e↵ or click the Zoom Extents button to zoom to the drawing's extents. Then use the Zoom Window or the scroll wheel to view the bathroom close-up.

2. Start the Rectangle command. For the first point, move the cursor to the lower-right inside corner of the room. As soon as Endpoint osnap marker appears on the endpoint you want to snap to, click. This places the first corner of the rectangle at the endpoint. For the second point, enter l -40,40↵ (-1016,1016↵).

 T I P   Remember, if you are not using Dynamic Input, you need to enter the @ symbol before entering relative coordinates. If you are not using Direct Input and don't get the rectangle you want after entering the relative coordinates for the second corner, click the Options button at the bottom of the Application menu to open the Options dialog box. Click the User Preferences tab. In the upper-right corner in the Priority For Coordinate Data Entry area, be sure that the button next to Keyboard Entry Except Scripts is active, and then click OK. Try the rectangle again.

3. Start the Line command, and move the cursor near the midpoint of the top line of the rectangle. Notice that a triangle, the Midpoint osnap marker, appears when you get near the midpoint of the line. When you see the triangle on the midpoint you want, click.

4. Move the cursor near the midpoint of the left side of the rectangle until you see the triangle appear at the midpoint location (see Figure 5.60). Click again. Press ⏎ to end the Line command.

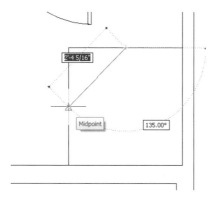

FIGURE 5.60: Using the Midpoint osnap to complete a line across the corner of the shower

5. Start the Trim command and, using the last line you created as a cutting edge, trim away the upper-left corner of the shower rectangle. The trimming requires only one pick because you're trimming a polyline. Press ⏎ to end the Trim command.

   You want to offset the shower inward evenly on all sides, but the perimeter now consists of an open polyline and a line. To close the polyline, you could use the Polyline command's Join option, as you did in an earlier exercise, or delete the line and direct the polyline to create a segment that closes its perimeter. For this exercise, you will do the latter.

6. Select and erase the diagonal line you used as a cutting edge to trim the shower.

7. Click the Edit Polyline button from the expanded Modify panel or enter pe⏎. At the Select polyline or [Multiple]: prompt, select any segment of the shower polyline. Enter c⏎ or choose the Close option and then press ⏎ to end the command. The Close option closes an open polyline by creating a straight segment between the open endpoints.

8. Offset the shower polyline inward 1 ½" (38 mm), as shown in Figure 5.61.

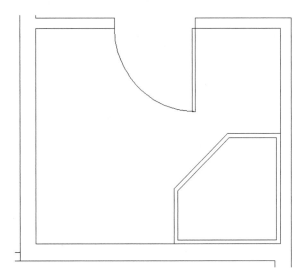

FIGURE 5.61: The offset shower polyline

Next you'll draw the sink to the right of the shower.

Drawing the Bathroom Sink and Mirror

You'll offset a line and draw an ellipse for this fixture while practicing using the Temporary Tracking Point osnap option in the process. The Endpoint and Midpoint osnaps are still running.

1. Zoom in to the sink area with a zoom window. Offset the top inside wall line down 4′ (1219 mm). Then offset the new line up 4″ (102 mm) and the top inside wall down 4″ (102 mm). These lines are the vertical limits of the sink counter and the mirror.

2. Offset the left inside wall 1′-8″ (508 mm) to the right, and then offset that same line ½″ (13 mm) to frame the counter and the mirror. Your sink area should look like Figure 5.62.

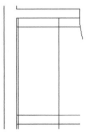

FIGURE 5.62: The offset shower polyline

3. Fillet the lines to form the sink counter and mirror. You will have to zoom into each end of the mirror to select the correct end of the mirror's sides to fillet the lines properly. Figure 5.63 shows the partially completed sink and mirror.

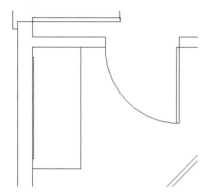

FIGURE 5.63: The sink and mirror

 4. Click the down arrow next to the Ellipse button on the Draw panel and choose the Center option, or enter el↵ c↵ to start the command from the command line.

5. Place the cursor near the midpoint of the bottom counter line. When the small cross appears in the osnap marker, the first tracking point is established.

6. Move the crosshair cursor to the midpoint of the vertical line that defines the front of the counter. When the cross appears in this osnap marker, move the cursor to the left to the point where the two dotted tracking point vectors intersect. A small, dark X appears at the intersection to indicate the point that AutoCAD will use for the center point of the ellipse (see Figure 5.64).

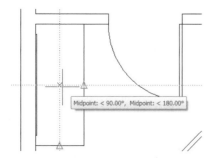

FIGURE 5.64: Defining the center point for the ellipse

7. Click to define the center point.

   Rather than using the direct entry method to define a point with the Object Snap Tracking tool, you've just used two different object snaps to define one point.

8. Hold the crosshair cursor directly to the right of the center point. Enter 5↵ (127↵). Hold the crosshair cursor directly above the center, and enter 7↵ (178↵). The ellipse is constructed, and the sink fixture is nearly complete.

9. Use the Offset tool to offset the ellipse 1″ (25 mm) to the outside (see Figure 5.65). Leave the view on your screen as it is for a moment.

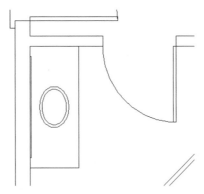

FIGURE 5.65: The completed sink fixture

 W A R N I N G Be aware that offsetting an ellipse does not create a new ellipse, but instead creates a polyline with several small segments.

The toilet and the shelves are the final fixtures necessary in the bathroom. You'll use the Ellipse command again, along with the Rectangle command, to draw them. You'll also learn about a couple of new display options.

Positioning the Toilet and Shelves

The shelves are a simple rectangle measuring 3′×1′ (914 mm×305 mm), and the toilet consists of a rectangle and an ellipse centered between the sink and the wall. The tank is offset 1″ (25 mm) from the back wall and is 9″×20″ (229 mm×508 mm). The ellipse representing the seat measures 18″ (457 mm) in one direction and 12″ (304 mm) in the other.

 1. On the Utilities panel, click the Pan button. The cursor changes to a small hand to indicate that you are in Pan Realtime mode. Position

the cursor in the lower part of the drawing area with the view still zoomed in on the sink.

2. Drag the cursor up and to the right. When the toilet area comes into view, release the mouse button. The drawing slides along with the movement of the cursor. If necessary, zoom in and then pan again until you have the toilet area centered in the drawing area.

T I P **You can also perform a** *pan*, **a lateral change in the viewing area with no change in zoom factor, by holding down the middle mouse button or scroll wheel. The** mbuttonpan **variable must be set to 1 (enter mbuttonpan⏎ 1⏎) for this functionality to be available. Now that most people use a wheel mouse, this manner of panning is becoming the preferred method. Rolling the wheel to zoom is also common.**

3. Right-click and choose Zoom from the context menu that opens. Back in the drawing, the cursor changes to a magnifying glass with plus and minus signs.

4. Position the Zoom Realtime cursor near the top of the drawing and hold down the left mouse button. Drag the cursor down, and watch the view being zoomed out in real time. Move the cursor up, still holding down the mouse button. Position the cursor in such a way that you have a good view of the toilet area and then release the mouse button. Right-click again, and choose Exit from the context menu to end the Zoom Realtime command.

With Zoom Realtime, moving the cursor to the left or right has no effect on the view. The magnification is controlled solely by the up-and-down motion.

These zooming options are convenient tools for adjusting the view of your drawing. Let's move on to the toilet first. You need to find a way to position the toilet accurately, centering it between the wall and shower. The midpoint of the left wall line isn't useful because the wall line runs behind the shower. You'll have to use a reference point to locate the starting point for the toilet tank. The lower-left corner of the tank is 5″ (127 mm) from the bottom wall and 1″ (25 mm) from the left wall. Because there is no osnap feature to define the location on the left wall, you will use the From osnap to locate the corner.

1. Start the Rectangle command and click the Snap From button in the Object Snap toolbar. Click on the lower-left inside corner of the bathroom to specify the reference point.

2. Enter **@1, 5⏎** (**@25,127⏎**) to place the first corner of the rectangle and then **9,20⏎** (**229,508⏎**) to draw the 9"×20" (229 mm×508 mm) toilet tank centered on the left wall (see the left of Figure 5.66).

3. Start the Ellipse command. The Command window displays a default prompt of Specify axis endpoint of ellipse or:. Using the Specify Axis Endpoint option and the running Midpoint osnap, you can easily define the ellipse's location and first axis from one end of the ellipse to the other.

4. Move the cursor near the midpoint of the right side of the tank, and when the triangle shows up there, click. This starts the ellipse.

5. Hold the crosshair cursor out to the right of the rectangle, and enter 1'6⏎ (457⏎). This sets the first axis. Now, as you move the crosshair cursor, you'll see that a line starts at the center of the ellipse, and the cursor's movement controls the size of the other axis. To designate the second axis, you need to enter the distance from the center of the axis to the end of it, or half the overall length of the axis.

6. Hold the crosshair cursor directly above or below the center point, and enter 6⏎ (152⏎). The ellipse is complete, so you've finished the toilet (see the right of Figure 5.66).

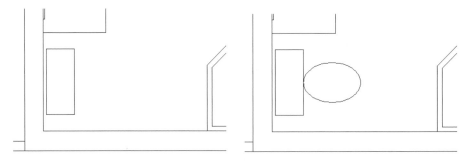

FIGURE 5.66: The toilet tank in place (left) and the completed toilet (right)

7. To complete the fixtures, construct the shelves by drawing a 3'-0"×1'-0" (914 mm×305 mm) rectangle from the upper-right corner of the bathroom. Figure 5.57 earlier in the chapter shows the proper orientation. Zoom out and your completed bathroom should look like Figure 5.67.

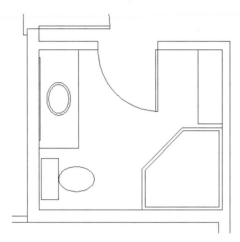

FIGURE 5.67: The completed bathroom fixtures

 T I P   You can snap the features of an ellipse or a circle using the Center or Quadrant object snaps. If an ellipse is rotated, the Quadrant points will be located at the two points where the curves are sharpest and the two points where the curves are flattest. The Quadrant snaps will always remain at the four points of a circle or arc that project vertically or horizontally from the center point regardless of the object's orientation.

Drawing the Hot Tub

What is a cabin without a hot tub to relax in? You'll complete the cabin fixtures by using a polyline to draw the outside perimeter of the hot tub, offsetting this polyline to the inside and then filleting the appropriate corners. Here's how it's done:

1. Make sure the Polar Tracking button is still turned on in the status bar; then start the Polyline command and click on the bottom-left inside corner of the pop-out to the right of the bathroom, as shown in Figure 5.68.

FIGURE 5.68: Starting the hot tub polyline

2. Click on the endpoint, to the right, on the opposite end of the pop-out.

3. Move the cursor directly above the last point and enter 4′5-5/8″↵ (1362↵) to draw the first vertical line. Refer to Figure 5.57 for the dimensions of the hot tub.

4. Earlier in this chapter, you set the polar tracking Increment Angle value to 45.00 in the Drafting Settings dialog box. This setting lets you easily place the cursor at 45° increments from a set point rather than at the 90° increments provided by using Ortho mode. Place the cursor above and to the left of the current last point, until the Polar Snap tooltip reads 135°; then enter 3′6-7/8″↵ (1089↵) to draw the diagonal line (see Figure 5.69).

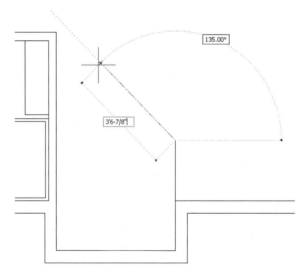

FIGURE 5.69: Use polar tracking and direct input to draw the diagonal line.

5. Use the Perpendicular osnap to draw the top horizontal line from the last point to the outside of the bathroom wall and enter c↵ to close the polyline.

6. Use the Offset command to offset the polyline 4″ (102 mm) to the inside.

7. Start the Fillet command and set the Radius value to 3″ (76); then fillet the two outside corners that project into the cabin (see Figure 5.70).

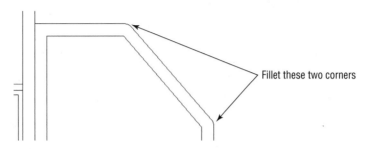

FIGURE 5.70: Fillet the two corners that extend into the cabin

8. Stop and then restart the Fillet command, but this time choose the Polyline option. Click the inside polyline to fillet all the corners at one time.

9. Zoom to the drawing's extents. Your cabin should look like Figure 5.71.

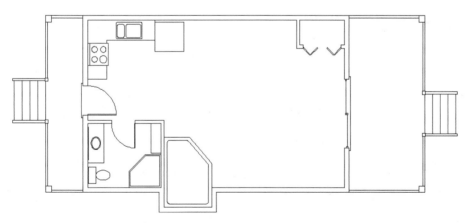

FIGURE 5.71: The completed floor plan zoomed to fill the screen

10. Save your drawing as Cabin05c.dwg.

USING PAN REALTIME AND ZOOM REALTIME

The Pan and Zoom buttons are next to each other on the Navigate panel. In addition to the panel buttons, you can start Pan by entering **p**↵ and Zoom Realtime by entering **z**↵↵. You can also start Pan or Zoom by right-clicking at the Command: prompt and then choosing Pan or Zoom from the context menu, or clicking the Pan or Zoom button in the middle of the status bar. If you try this, you'll find that it's easier than clicking the Pan or Zoom button.

Exit Ends the Zoom Realtime or Pan Realtime command.

Pan Switches to Pan Realtime from Zoom Realtime.

Zoom Switches to Zoom Realtime from Pan Realtime.

3D Orbit Is a special viewing tool for 3D that is covered in later chapters.

Zoom Window Allows you to make a zoom window without first ending Pan Realtime or Zoom Realtime. You pick a point, hold down the left mouse button, and then drag open a window in your drawing. When you release the button, you're zoomed into the window you made, and Pan Realtime or Zoom Realtime resumes.

Zoom Original Restores the view of your drawing that you had when you began Pan Realtime or Zoom Realtime.

Zoom Extents Zooms to the drawing extents.

To end Pan Realtime or Zoom Realtime, press the Esc key, press ↵, or right-click and choose Exit from the context menu.

When Pan Realtime or Zoom Realtime is running, AutoCAD is in a special mode that makes the status bar invisible and therefore unusable.

Using Parametric Constraints

ACAD ONLY Parametric constraints are a feature introduced in AutoCAD 2010 that allows you to constrain the features of one object to the features of another. This can eliminate the need to adjust several objects manually when their relationship to another object has changed. Although constraints can only be created in AutoCAD, the objects that are constrained are visible when the file is opened in AutoCAD LT.

Constraints are found in two different types: Geometric and Dimensional. Geometric constraints link the values or physical relationships, such as tangency or perpendicularity. For instance, you can use the Concentric constraint to link one circle to be centered around another. Once the constraint is set, moving one circle causes the other to be moved an equal distance and direction. There are 12 different geometric constraints, and any number can be used between different objects.

Dimensional constraints add a dimension between objects that specifies the distance, angle, radius, or diameter. Standard dimensions, which are covered in Chapter 12, "Dimensioning a Drawing," only reflect an object's parameters or its relationship to other objects. Dimensional constraints not only display the values, but changing the value changes the objects to match. In this exercise, you are going to add constraints to the stove to maintain the relationships between the burners.

1. Zoom in to the stove top.

2. Click the Parametric tab on the Ribbon; then click the Equal button in the Geometric panel.

3. At the `Select first object or [Multiple]:` prompt, enter **m⏎** to activate the Multiple option. All objects selected after the first one will be set equal to that first one.

4. Select one of the small circles, select the other two, and then press ⏎. A small equal (=) sign appears below each circle to identify it as an object using the Equal parametric constraint (see Figure 5.72).

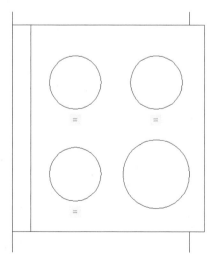

F I G U R E 5 . 7 2 : The stove with the Equal constraint added to the small burners

The constraints shown in the drawing area do not appear when the drawing is plotted. Plotting is covered in Chapter 15, "Printing an AutoCAD Drawing."

5. Select one of the small circles, right-click, and then choose Properties from the context menu to open the Properties panel.

6. Change the Radius, Diameter, or Circumference values and watch as all three circles change to match the new value.

7. Click the Undo button in the Quick Access toolbar to undo the modification, and then close the Properties panel.

8. Zoom to the drawing's extents.

N O T E   The parametric constraint markers are placed a set distance, in pixels, from the objects they influence. When you zoom out, the markers may appear disjointed from their objects, but the constraint is still functional.

9. Save your file as Cabin05d.dwg.

The bathroom and kitchen are complete, and you now have a fairly complete floor plan for the cabin. While completing the drawing tasks for this chapter, you were exposed to several new commands and techniques to add to those introduced in Chapter 4. You now have a set of tools that will take you a long way toward being able to lay out a drawing of any size.

Chapters 1 through 5 fill out the basic level of skills in AutoCAD that allow you to draw on the computer approximately as you would with pencil and vellum, although you might already see some of the advantages CAD offers over traditional board drafting. Beginning with the next chapter, I'll introduce you to concepts of AutoCAD that don't have a counterpart in board drafting. These features will take you to a new level of knowledge and skill, and you'll start to get an idea of what sets computer drafting apart.

If You Would Like More Practice...

The following are several additional exercises that will give you the opportunity to practice the skills and techniques you have learned.

Drawing the Cabin Again

As is true for almost any skill, the key to mastery is practice. Redrawing the entire cabin might seem daunting at this point when you think of how long it took you to get here. But if you try it all again, starting from Chapter 3, you'll find that it will take about half the time it did the first time. If you do it a third time, it'll take half that time. Once you understand the techniques and how the commands work, feel free to experiment with alternative techniques to accomplish tasks and with other options on the commands.

Drawing Something Else

If you have a specific project in mind that you would like to draw in AutoCAD, so much the better. Try drawing the floor plan of your home or a classroom.

Drawing Some Furniture for the Cabin

Once you put some furniture in the cabin, you'll quickly see how small it is! But it can still accept some basic furniture without seeming too cramped. You should be able to add the following:

▶ Kitchen—a table and chairs

▶ Living room—a short couch or love seat, coffee table, easy chair and a fireplace

▶ Bedroom—a double bed, chest, and nightstand

　Use a tape measure and go around your office or home to determine the approximate dimensions of each piece. The goal here is not so much to ensure accuracy of scale but to practice drawing in AutoCAD. Figure 5.73 shows the floor plan with these pieces of furniture. If you draw the bed shown here, try using the Spline tool for the curved, turned-down sheets. It's on the expanded Draw panel. You'll see how it works after a little experimentation.

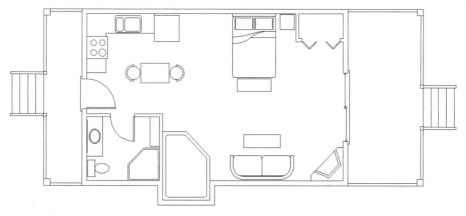

F I G U R E 5 . 7 3 : The floor plan with furniture

Drawing a Gasket

Figure 5.74 shows a gasket that is symmetrical around its vertical and horizontal axes. This symmetry will allow you to use the Mirror command to create much of the drawing.

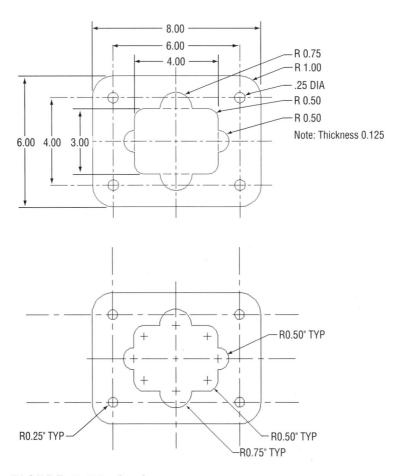

FIGURE 5.74: A gasket

The diagrams in Figure 5.75 summarize the steps.

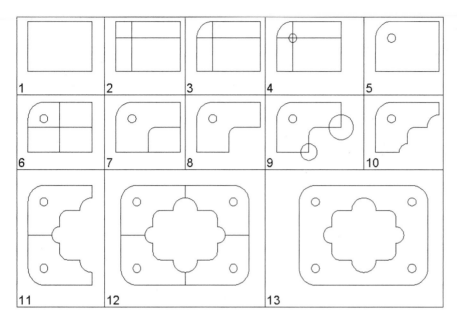

FIGURE 5.75: The 13 steps to creating the gasket

To draw the gasket, set Linear Units to Engineering with a precision of 0'-0.00". Set Angular Units to Decimal with a precision of 0.00. Now, follow these steps:

1. Use the Line command to draw a rectangle 4" wide and 3" high.

2. Offset the upper horizontal line and the left vertical line 1" to the inside of the rectangle.

3. Use Fillet with a radius set to 1" on the upper-left corner of the original rectangle.

4. Draw the circle with the 0.25" radius, using the intersection of the two offset lines as the center.

5. Erase the offset lines.

6. Offset the right vertical line 2" to the left and the bottom horizontal line 1.5" up.

7. Use Fillet with a radius of 0.50″ on the intersection of these two lines, retaining the right and lower segments.

8. Trim back the lower-right corner of the original rectangle.

9. Draw circles with 0.50″ and 0.75″ radii on the bottom and right sides of the shape.

10. Use Trim to remove unneeded lines.

11. Use Mirror to flip the shape down.

12. Use Mirror again to flip the shape to the right.

13. Erase unneeded lines. (Each line to be erased is really two lines.)

14. If you are using AutoCAD, and not LT, add the Equal constraint so that all four circles remain the same size.

If you choose to save this drawing, name it Gasket-05.dwg.

Drawing a Parking Lot

Figure 5.76 shows a parking lot partially bordered by sidewalks and streets.

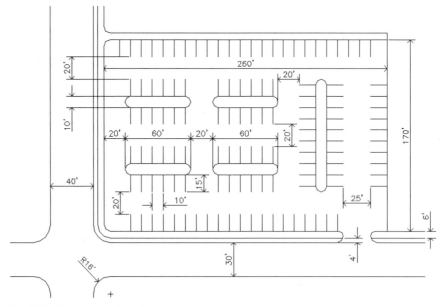

FIGURE 5.76: A parking lot

You'll get a lot of practice using the Offset and Fillet commands while completing this drawing. Guidelines will help you, so don't be afraid to use them. Note the tip at the end of this section. Here's a summary of the steps:

1. Set Linear and Angular units to Decimal, each with a precision of 0. Set the Linear units to Architectural. Assume that 1 linear decimal unit equals 1'. Set Polar Tracking to 90°, and turn it on. Set the Endpoint and Midpoint osnaps to be running. Set Snap to 10, Grid to 0, and Drawing Limits to 400, 250. Zoom All.

2. Use Grid and Snap to draw the large 260'×170' rectangle using the Line command and relative Cartesian coordinates as you did in Chapter 3. Turn off the Grid and Snap. Offset three of the lines 6' to the outside to make the sidewalk.

3. On two sides, offset the outer sidewalk line 4' to the outside to make the curb. Then, offset the curb lines 30' and 40' to make the street.

When using Decimal units as feet, you don't need to enter the foot sign (') when you enter distances.

4. Draw extra lines to make the street intersection.

5. Fillet and Trim lines to create the curved corners of the intersection and sidewalks.

6. Offset the lines of the inner rectangle to the inside to make guidelines for the parking strips and islands.

7. Use Fillet and Trim to finish the drawing.

8. If you choose to save this drawing, name it Parking Lot-05.dwg.

T I P   **Using Fillet on two parallel lines creates a semicircle to connect them. Try it on the islands in the parking area.**

Are You Experienced?

Now you can...

- ☑ use the Temporary Tracking Point and Snap From object snaps to create and use tracking points

- ☑ use the Perpendicular and Intersection osnaps

- ☑ set up and use running osnaps

- ☑ use the Stretch command

- ☑ use the Properties palette and the Quick Properties dialog box

- ☑ move around the drawing area with Zoom Realtime and Pan Realtime

- ☑ use point filters

- ☑ use the Circle and Ellipse commands

- ☑ move and duplicate objects with the Move and Copy commands.

- ☑ use geometric constraints

CHAPTER 6

Using Layers to Organize Your Drawing

▶ Creating new layers

▶ Assigning a color and a linetype to layers

▶ Moving existing objects onto a new layer

▶ Controlling the visibility of layers

▶ Working with linetypes

▶ Isolating objects by layer

▶ Using the Action Recorder

▶ Creating layer states

I n precomputer days, drafters used sets of transparent overlays on their drafting tables. They were sheets that stacked one on top of the other, and the drafters could see through several at a time. Specific kinds of information were drawn on each overlay. All of them related spatially so that several overlays might be drawn for the same floor plan. Drawings for each discipline, such as plumbing, electrical, or HVAC, as well as charts and tables, were drawn on separate overlays so that the floor plans did not have to be reproduced for every type of drawing produced. Each overlay had small holes punched near the corners so the drafter could position the overlay onto buttons, called *registration points*, that were taped to the drawing board. Because all overlays had holes punched at the same locations with respect to the drawing, information on the set of overlays was kept in alignment.

To help you organize your drawing, AutoCAD provides you with an amazing tool called *layers*, which is a computerized form of the transparent overlays, only much more powerful and flexible. In manual drafting, you could use only four or five overlays at a time before the information on the bottom overlay became unreadable. (Copying the drawing meant sending all the layers through the blueprint machine together.) In AutoCAD, you aren't limited in the number of layers you can use. You can have hundreds of layers, and complex CAD drawings often do.

Using Layers as an Organizing Tool

To understand what layers are and why they are so useful, think again about the transparent overlay sheets used in hand drafting. Each overlay is designed to be printed. The bottom sheet might be a basic floor plan. To create an overlay sheet for a structural drawing, the drafter traces over only the lines of the floor plan that the overlay needs and then adds new information pertinent to that sheet. For the next overlay, the drafter performs the same task again. Each sheet, then, contains some information in common as well as data unique to that sheet.

In AutoCAD, using layers allows you to generate all the sheets for a set of overlays from a single file (see Figure 6.1). Nothing needs to be drawn twice or traced. The wall layout is on one layer and the rooflines are on another. Doors are on a third. You can control the visibility of layers so that you can make all objects residing on a layer temporarily invisible. This feature lets you put all information keyed to a particular floor plan in one .dwg file. From that drawing, you can produce a series of derived drawings—such as the foundation plan, the second floor plan, the reflected ceiling plan, and the roof plan—by making different combinations of layers visible for each drawing or drawing layout (layouts are covered in Chapter 14, "Using Layouts to Set Up a Print"). When you make a print, you decide which layers will be visible. Consequently, in a set of drawings, each sheet based on the floor plan displays a unique combination of layers, all of which are in one file.

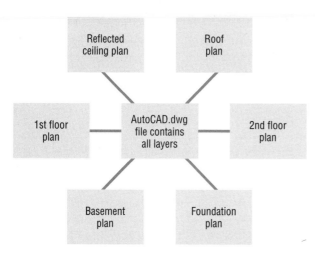

FIGURE 6.1: Several drawings can be created from one file.

As an organizing tool, layers allow you to classify the various objects in a computerized drawing—lines, arcs, circles, and so on—according to the component of the building they represent, such as doors, walls, windows, dimensions, and notes. Each layer is assigned a color, and all objects placed on the layer take on that assigned default color unless you specify a different color for the objects. This lets you easily distinguish between objects that represent separate components of the building (see Figure 6.2). You can quickly tell which layer a given object or group of objects is on.

FIGURE 6.2: Separate layers combined to make a drawing

First, you'll look at the procedure for achieving this level of organization, which is to set up the new layers and then move existing objects onto them. Following that, you'll learn how to create new objects on a specific layer and find out which objects reside on which layers.

Setting Up Layers

All AutoCAD drawings have one layer in common—layer 0. Layer 0 is the default layer in all new drawings. If you don't add any new layers to a drawing, everything you create in that drawing is on layer 0. In fact, everything so far in the cabin drawing has been drawn on layer 0.

 N O T E   Objects and layers are analogous to people and countries; just as all people must reside in some country, so too must all objects be on some layer.

All objects in AutoCAD are assigned a layer. In this book, I'll refer to objects assigned to a particular layer as *being on* that layer. You can place objects on a layer in two ways: you can move or copy them to the layer, or you can create them on the layer in the first place. You'll learn how to do both in this chapter. However, first you need to learn how to set up layers. To see how you do this, you'll create seven new layers for your cabin drawing—Walls, Doors, Steps, Deck, Fixtures, Headers, and Roof—and then move the existing objects in your drawing onto the first five of these layers. After that, you'll create new objects on the Headers and Roof layers. You'll begin by creating a few new layers:

1. Open AutoCAD and then open either Cabin05c.dwg or Cabin05d.dwg (depending on whether you completed the exercise explaining parametrics in the previous chapter). Make sure the Home tab is active and the Layers panel is in the Ribbon, centered just above the drawing area on your screen.

2. Expand the panel and you will see, as shown in Figure 6.3, that it contains several buttons, two drop-down lists, and a slider bar for controlling layers.

FIGURE 6.3: The expanded Layers panel

A *linetype* is the appearance style of a line, such as continuous, dashed, and dash-dot.

Several panels to the right is the Properties panel (see Figure 6.4), with four drop-down lists for controlling linetypes, colors, and other layer and object properties.

FIGURE 6.4: The expanded Properties panel

3. Click the Layer Properties button on the left end of the Layers panel to open the Layer Properties Manager dialog box (see Figure 6.5). Notice the large open area in the middle right of the dialog box with layer 0 listed at the top of the Name column. This is the Layer List box. All the layers in a drawing are listed here, along with their current states and properties. Cabin05d.dwg has only one layer so far.

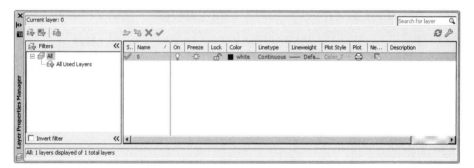

FIGURE 6.5: The Layer Properties Manager dialog box

To the left of the Layer List box is the Layer Filters tree view box, where you can define which layers to display in the Layer List box. The Layer Properties Manager dialog box has nine buttons along the top to perform layer and filter management tasks. You'll see an Invert Filter check box at the bottom of the dialog box.

Before setting up new layers, look for a moment at the Layer List box. The Layer Properties Manager dialog box is considered *modeless* because you can leave the dialog box open while you continue to work on your drawing. This means you can leave the dialog box open and move it away from your drawing area where it can remain constantly open, waiting for you to input changes without having to stop to open the dialog box each time. Being modeless also means that your changes are instantly reflected in the drawing area and you don't need to close the dialog box to see the effects of your actions.

Some dialog boxes, such as the Open and Options dialog boxes, are *modal* and must be closed prior to returning to your drawing.

Using the Layer List Box

Each layer has four properties—Color, Linetype, Lineweight, and Plot Style—that determine the appearance of the objects on that layer. You may need to resize the columns to see the complete column name. You do this by placing the cursor between the columns and dragging left or right. Look at the layer 0 row in the list and notice the square and the word *white* in the Color column. The square is black (or white if you have a black background for your drawing area), but the name of the color is white whether the square is black or white. Continuous is in the Linetype column. This tells you that layer 0 has been assigned the color White (meaning black or white) and the Continuous linetype by default.

N O T E   If you set up your drawing area so that the background is white, AutoCAD automatically changes the color assigned to white in the Layer List box to black, so lines that would ordinarily appear as white on a black background now appear as black on the white background. When you then switch to a black background, the black lines change to white lines. This allows the lines to be visible regardless of the background color, and AutoCAD doesn't have to assign a new color to a layer that has been assigned the White setting when you switch background colors.

The five columns to the left of the Color column are Status, Name, On, Freeze, and Lock. They each have icons or text in the layer 0 row. These columns represent some of the status modes—or *states*—of the layer, and they control whether objects on a layer are visible, whether they can be changed, or on which layer new objects are created. I'll discuss the visibility and status of layers later in this chapter, and I'll discuss the columns to the right of the Linetype column—Lineweight, Plot Style, Plot, and Description—in Chapter 15, "Printing an AutoCAD Drawing." Don't worry about them right now.

Creating New Layers and Assigning Colors

Let's create a few new layers, name them, and assign them colors:

1. In the toolbar at the top of the Layer Properties Manager, click the New Layer icon. A new layer named Layer1 appears in the list. The layer's name is highlighted, which means you can rename it by entering another name now.

2. Enter Walls↵. Layer1 changes to Walls. The row for the Walls layer should still be highlighted (see Figure 6.6).

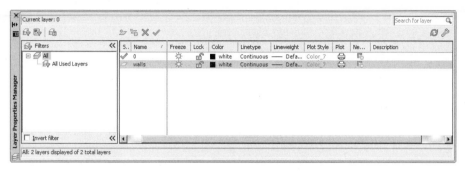

FIGURE 6.6: The Layer Properties Manager dialog box with a new layer named Walls

3. Click the word "white" in the Color column for the Walls row to open the Select Color dialog box (see Figure 6.7). Notice the three tabs at the top—Index Color, True Color, and Color Books. Each has a different selection of colors available to AutoCAD.

4. Be sure the Index Color tab is selected. You have three sets of color swatches and two buttons for making color choices. In the row of 9 color swatches, below the large group of 240 choices, click the cyan (turquoise) square. In the Color text box, "white" changes to "cyan," and the front rectangle in the lower-right corner takes on the color cyan.

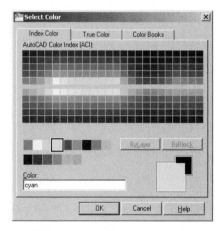

FIGURE 6.7: The Index Color tab in the Select Color dialog box

COLOR MODES

The Index Color tab provides the option to choose from the 256 distinct colors in the AutoCAD Color Index (ACI). Using the True Color tab, you can set each of the color parameters of the red, green, and blue (RGB) or Hue, Saturation, and Value (HSV) components of the final color to any value between 0 and of 255, resulting in over 16 million combinations. The Color Books tab lets you access thousands of color definitions that are provided by several color standards, such as Pantone and DIC. They are used to match the colors used on your system to physical swatches that are used by designers.

T I P   As you move the cursor over the available color swatches, the index color number, from 1 through 255, as well as the RGB values appear beneath the large field of 240 choices.

5. Click OK to close the Select Color dialog box. In the Layer List box of the Layer Properties Manager dialog box, you can see that the color square for the Walls layer has changed to cyan.

As you create your new list of layers and assign colors to them, notice how each color looks in your drawing. Some are easier to see on a screen with a light background, and others do better against a dark background. In this book, I'll assign colors that work well with a black background. If your system has a white background, you might want to use darker colors, which you can find in the array of 240 color swatches in the upper half of the Index Color tab.

You'll now continue creating new layers and assigning colors to them. You'll master this procedure as you add a new layer or two in each chapter throughout the rest of the book:

1. In the Layer Properties Manager dialog box, click the New Layer button, or right-click in the Layer List box and choose New Layer from the list of commands in the context menu.

2. Enter Doors↵ to change the name of the layer.

3. Pick the color square in the Doors row. When the Select Color dialog box opens, click the red square in the same row of color swatches where you previously found cyan. Click OK.

4. Repeat these steps, creating the following layers with their assigned colors. Pick the colors from the same row of color swatches that you have been using. Notice that when a new layer appears in the Layer List box, it initially takes on the properties of the layer that was previously selected.

 W A R N I N G   In the row of nine colors, the ninth swatch might not be clearly visible when it is close to the background color of the dialog box.

Layer Name	Color
Steps	8 (Gray)
Deck	Green
Fixtures	Magenta
Headers	Yellow
Roof	Blue

 T I P   Blue might or might not read well on a black background. If you don't like the way it looks, try picking a lighter shade of blue from the array of 240 colors on the Index Color tab.

When finished, the layer list should have eight layers with their assigned colors in the color squares of each row (see Figure 6.8). All layers are assigned the Continuous linetype by default. This is convenient because most building components are represented in the floor plan by continuous lines, but the roof—because of its position above the walls—needs to be represented by a dashed line. Later you'll assign the Dashed linetype to the Roof layer.

> With the cabin drawing, you'll start developing a basic set of layers. Once you learn how to manage the set you're using here, tackling more complex layering systems will come naturally. In more complex drawings, you might need several layers for variations of the same building component, landscape element, or machine part. You might replace the Walls layer, for example, with several layers, such as Existing Walls to Remain, Walls to Be Demolished, and New Walls.

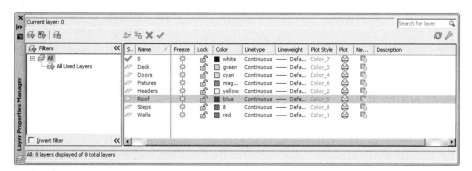

F I G U R E   6 . 8 : The Layer List box, in the Layer Properties Manager dialog box, with the seven new layers and layer 0

Naming Layers

You can name layers in a variety of ways. With their different color assignments, layers make it possible for you easily to distinguish which objects in your drawing represent walls or other parts of your building. Most offices follow a standard for organizing layers by name, color, and linetype. Both the International Organization for Standardization (ISO) and American Institute of Architects (AIA) publish layering standards, which are often adapted by architecture and mechanical firms and customized to fit their specific needs.

When you name layers, you can use uppercase and lowercase letters, and AutoCAD will preserve them. But AutoCAD doesn't distinguish between them and treats *Walls*, *WALLS*, and *walls* as the same layer.

Using AutoCAD's Traditional Colors

The traditional set of 255 colors for AutoCAD is set up in such a way that the first 7 colors are named (Red, Blue, and so on) and numbered (1 through 7), whereas the other 248 colors have only numbers.

As you saw on the Index Color tab of the Select Color dialog box, AutoCAD has three groupings of colors: a large array of swatches in the top half and two rows of swatches below. Moving the cursor over a swatch displays its AutoCAD number below the array as well as its red, green, blue (RGB) values. The RGB values are the amount of each color, a number from 0 (none) to 255 (all), that is mixed with the other two base colors to make the selected color. Click a swatch to assign it to the layer that has been selected in the Layer Properties Manager dialog box.

You should avoid using colors that resemble the background color, such as colors 250 or 18 with a black background. The objects with these colors could become visually lost in the drawing area. Be aware of this if your drawings might be sent to someone who doesn't use your color standards so that they can work efficiently with the drawings.

The Array of 240 Colors In the top half of the dialog box are colors numbered 10 through 249, arranged in 24 columns, each having 10 swatches.

The Row of 9 Standard Color Swatches This group includes colors 1 through 9. The first 7 colors in this group also have names: Red (1), Yellow (2), Green (3), Cyan (4), Blue (5), Magenta (6), and White/Black (7). Colors 8 and 9 have numbers only. Color 7 is named White, but it will be black if you're using a white background color.

Continues

USING AUTOCAD'S TRADITIONAL COLORS *(Continued)*

The Row of 6 Gray Shades These colors are often assigned screening values (such as 50 percent, 75 percent, and so on) numbering 250 through 255. As pure color assignments, they range from almost black to almost white.

These 255 colors, plus the background color, make up the traditional Auto-CAD 256-color palette. Two additional colors are in a group by themselves, Logical Colors, and are represented by buttons on the Index Color tab.

The two buttons in this grouping—ByLayer and ByBlock—represent two ways you can assign a color to objects—such as lines, circles, text, and so on—via the layer they are on or via the *block* they are part of, rather than to the objects themselves. (I'll cover blocks in the next chapter.) When you assign cyan to the Walls layer and place all objects representing walls on that layer, all wall objects are automatically assigned the color ByLayer and take on the color of their layer—in this case, cyan.

You can change the color of an object to one other than the assigned layer color by selecting the object and choosing a color from the Color Control drop-down list in the Properties panel. Setting an object's color directly is not always best practice, however, and you should try to maintain color assignments by layer whenever practical.

Looking at the Other Tabs in the Select Color Dialog Box

AutoCAD also supports a True Color palette and various Pantone, DIC, and RAL color groups. Although I won't cover these features in any depth in this book, let's take a quick look at them before moving on.

The True Color Tab With the Layer Properties Manager dialog box open, click one of the color swatches in the Layer List box to open the Select Color dialog box again. Then click the True Color tab. In the upper-right corner, the Color Model drop-down list displays either RGB or HSL. The red, green, blue (RGB) color model looks like the left side of Figure 6.9, and the hue, saturation, luminance (HSL) model looks like the right side of Figure 6.9.

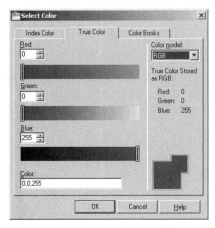 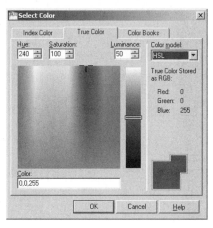

FIGURE 6.9: The True Color tab with the RGB color model (left) and the HSL color model (right)

The RGB option shows three horizontal color bands, one for each of the three primary colors. Move the sliders on each band to set a number from 0 to 255, or enter a number in the input box for each color. The three primary color values that combine to make up the final color appear at the bottom and on the right side, and the rectangles in the lower-right corner show the currently selected and previously selected color.

The HSL screen displays a rectangle of colors and a vertical band with a slider. Drag the crosshairs around on the rectangle. The color in the front rectangle in the lower-right corner changes as you move the crosshairs. Moving the crosshairs left or right takes the Hue value through a range of 361 values. Moving it up or down changes the percentage of saturation, or *intensity*, with the top of the rectangle representing 100 percent.

The slider to the right of the rectangle controls the luminance, which, like saturation, varies from 0 percent—representing black—to 100 percent, or white. A luminance of 100 percent maximizes a color's brightness but washes out all of the hue.

The Color text box displays the currently selected color's three RGB numbers. You can also specify a color by entering numbers in the individual input boxes for Hue, Saturation, and Luminance—or the boxes for Red, Green, and Blue in the RGB screen. You can use the up and down arrows in these boxes to scroll through the possible settings.

If you select a color using the RGB or HSL screen, that color appears in the Layer List box of the Layer Properties Manager dialog box by its three RGB numbers (see Figure 6.10).

The Color column might be compressed in such a way that the names of colors in the list are abbreviated. You can widen the column by dragging the divider at the right of the title farther to the right.

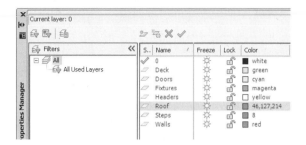

FIGURE 6.10: The Layer Properties Manager with the Roof layer assigned a color that is not part of the standard AutoCAD 255 color list

With the combination of 256 values for each of the three primary colors, you now have more than 16 million colors to choose from in AutoCAD.

The Color Books Tab The Color Books tab displays the colors of the selected color book (see the image on the left side of Figure 6.11). AutoCAD has 20 color books. Each book appears in the Color Book drop-down list at the top of the tab; the current book appears in the box. Below that, a set of colors that corresponds to the position of the slider is displayed in bars. Moving the slider to a new position displays another set of colors. Click a displayed color bar to select it, and then click OK. The color appears in the Layer Properties Manager Layer List box by its identifying name and number (see image on the right side of Figure 6.11).

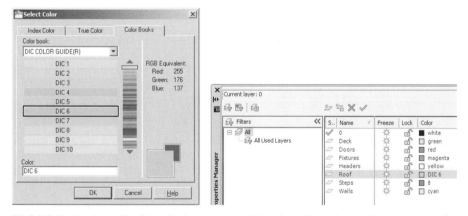

FIGURE 6.11: The Color Books tab in the Select Color dialog box (left) and the layer list with an assigned DIC number (right)

Later in the book, you'll be asked to create new layers and assign them colors of your choice. Use this opportunity to explore the True Color and Color Books tabs of the Select Color dialog box, and try using some of these colors in your drawing. Keep the Layer Properties Manager dialog box open. You'll use it to assign linetypes in the next section.

 You can delete selected layers using the Delete Layer button, shaped like a red X, in the Layer Properties Manager dialog box. You can delete only *empty* layers—those containing no objects. You can identify empty layers in the Layer Properties Manager by the grayed-out icon in the Status column.

Assigning Linetypes to Layers

When you assign a color to a layer, you can choose any color supported by your system. This is not so with linetypes. Each new drawing has only one linetype loaded into it by default (the Continuous linetype). You must load any other linetypes you need from an outside file:

1. In the Layer Properties Manager dialog box, click Continuous in the column for the Roof layer to open the Select Linetype dialog box (see Figure 6.12). In the Loaded Linetypes list, only Continuous appears. No other linetypes have been loaded into this drawing.

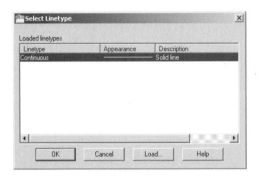

FIGURE 6.12: The Select Linetype dialog box

2. Click Load to open the Load Or Reload Linetypes dialog box. Scroll down the list to the Dashed, Dashed2, and DashedX2 linetypes (see Figure 6.13). Notice how, in this family, the dashed lines are different sizes.

T I P   You can select or deselect all the available linetypes in the Load Or Reload Linetypes dialog box by right-clicking and choosing Select All or Clear All from the context menu. You can also select multiple linetypes by holding down the Ctrl key and clicking.

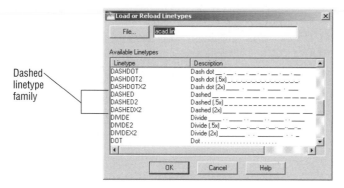

FIGURE 6.13: The list of available linetypes scrolled to the three Dashed linetypes

3. Click DASHED in the left column, and then click OK. You're returned to the Select Linetype dialog box. The Dashed linetype has been added to the Linetype list under Continuous (see Figure 6.14). Click Dashed to highlight it, and click OK. In the Layer Properties Manager dialog box, the Roof layer has been assigned the Dashed linetype (see Figure 6.15).

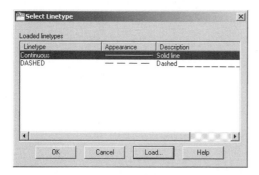

FIGURE 6.14: The Select Linetype dialog box with the Dashed linetype loaded

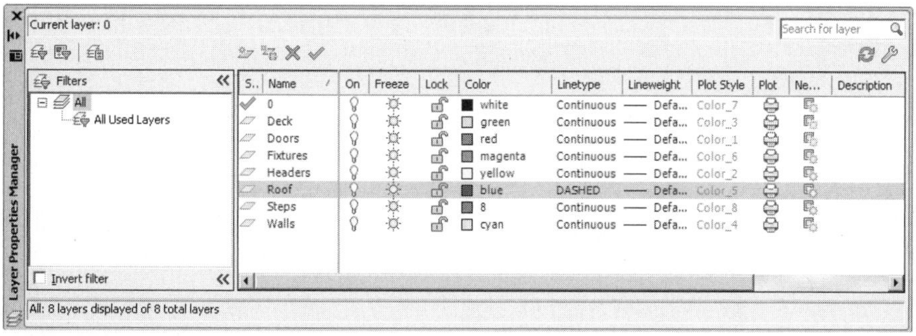

FIGURE 6.15: The Layer Properties Manager dialog box with the Roof layer assigned the Dashed linetype

AUTOCAD'S LINETYPES

The Available Linetypes list in the Load Or Reload Linetypes dialog box lists 45 linetypes. They fall into three groups:

Acad_ISO The first 14 linetypes are in the Acad_ISO family (ISO is the International Organization for Standardization). They are set up to be used in metric drawings and have *lineweight*, or pen-width, settings.

Standard Below the ISO linetypes are eight families of three linetypes each, mixed with seven special linetypes that contain graphic symbols. Each family has one basic linetype and two that are multiples of it: one has dashes twice the size (called, for example, Dashed × 2), and one has dashes half the size (called Dashed2). (See Figure 6.10, shown earlier.) Having an assortment of different sizes of one style of linetype is helpful for distinguishing between building components, such as foundation walls and beams, which, in addition to rooflines, might also need dashed lines.

Complex Mixed in with the Standard linetypes are seven linetypes that contain symbols, letters, or words. You can use these linetypes to indicate specific elements in the drawing, such as fences, hot-water lines, railroad tracks, and others.

It isn't difficult to create or acquire your own custom linetypes. You can do so in three ways:

Using Notepad Start the Windows Notepad program, and navigate to the Support folder for AutoCAD 2010. This is usually found at this location: `C:\Documents and Settings\`*your name*`\Application Data\ Autodesk\AutoCAD 2010\R18.0\enu\Support`. (LT users will see `AutoCAD LT` instead of AutoCAD 2010.)

Open the file named `acad.lin`, whose type is listed as AutoCAD Linetype Definition if you pause the cursor over the filename. It contains the definition codes for all the linetypes; they are easy to figure out. Copy an existing pattern and create your own. I recommend that you back up the `acad.lin` file before making any modifications to it.

Continues

AutoCAD's Linetypes *(Continued)*

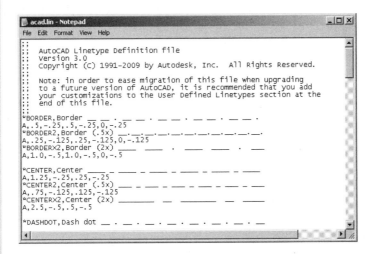

Using the Linetype Command Enter **-linetype**↵, (the "-" command prefix executes a command-line version of the command rather than a dialog-based version) and then enter **c**↵ for the Create option. You'll be guided through the steps to create your own .lin file or add to an existing file. To use the Linetype command, you need to know the definition codes. Use Notepad until you get a feel for the codes.

Use Existing Linetypes You can often find an acceptable linetype, created by other AutoCAD users, on the Internet or in various industry publications. Many are free and some are available at a reasonable cost. The line code is simply appended to the acad.lin file on your system.

Learning More About Lineweight

In the Layer Properties Manager dialog box is a column for the Lineweight property. When you first create a layer, it's assigned the default lineweight. Just as you assigned a color and a linetype for each new layer in the cabin drawing, you can also assign a lineweight. Once assigned, lineweights can be displayed so you can see how your drawing will look when printed.

Using the Current Layer as a Drawing Tool

Now is a good time to look at what it means for a layer to be *current*. Notice the green check mark above the Layer List box in the Layer Properties Manager dialog box. The same green check mark appears in the Status column in the layer 0 row. The name of the current layer, in this case, 0, appears in the upper-left corner of the dialog box.

At any time, one, and only one, layer is set as the current layer. When a layer is current, all objects you draw will be on the current layer and they will take on the properties assigned to that layer unless directed otherwise. Because Layer 0 is current—and has been current so far in this book—all objects that you have drawn so far are on layer 0 and have the linetype and color that are specified by default for layer 0: Continuous and White (or Black), respectively. If you make the Walls layer current, any new lines you draw will be Continuous and Cyan. If the Roof layer is current, any new lines will be Dashed and Blue. Here's how to make the Walls layer the current layer:

1. Click the Walls layer in the Layer List box to highlight it, and then click the Set Current green check mark above the Layer List box. Alternatively, you can double-click the Walls layer or highlight it and press Alt+C. The Walls layer replaces layer 0 as the current layer and the name appears in the text field at the top of the dialog box. The green check mark also appears next to the Walls layer in the Layer List box.

T I P   When the Status column is displayed, AutoCAD must evaluate the objects and layers at several times during the drawing process. This can cause a lag when the drawing is large and the list of layers is extensive. You can hide the Status, or any other column, by right-clicking the column name and then clicking any checked option in the context menu that appears.

2. Click the Auto-hide button near the top-left corner of the dialog box. Auto-hide causes the dialog box to collapse down to the title bar. To expand the dialog box temporarily, pause the cursor over the title bar; to permanently expand it, click Auto-hide again.

3. Look at the Layer drop-down list on the Ribbon's Layers panel. Most of the symbols you saw in the Layer List box, in the Layer Properties Manager dialog box, are on this drop-down list. The Walls layer is the visible entry on the list and has a cyan square (the color you assigned

to the Walls layer earlier). The layer is visible in this list when it's collapsed and no objects are selected in the current layer.

4. Now look at your drawing. Nothing has changed because the objects in the drawing are still on layer 0.

You need to move the objects in the drawing onto their proper layers. To do this, you'll use the Layer drop-down list on the Layers panel to assign each object to one of the new layers.

Assigning Objects to Layers

When assigning existing objects in the drawing to new layers, your strategy will be to begin by selecting several of the objects that belong on the same layer and that are easiest to select. You'll reassign them to their new layer using the Layer drop-down list. You'll then move to a set of objects that belong on a different layer or belong on the same layer as the previously selected object and are slightly more difficult to select, and so on.

1. In the drawing, click and drag a selection window down and to the left to use a crossing selection window to select the front deck, as shown in the top of Figure 6.16. See the next section, "Selecting Objects with Selection Windows," for a complete description of the window selection process.

2. Grips appear and the lines ghost, signaling that the objects have been selected. Hold the Shift key down and select the front stairs with a crossing selection, as shown in the middle image in Figure 6.16. Selecting objects with the Shift key pressed causes objects that are already selected to become unselected (removed from the selection set) while there is no effect on unselected objects.

3. The stair lines appear solid again. Repeat the process on the rear deck so that the deck is selected but the back stairs are not. The selected components should look like the bottom image in Figure 6.16.

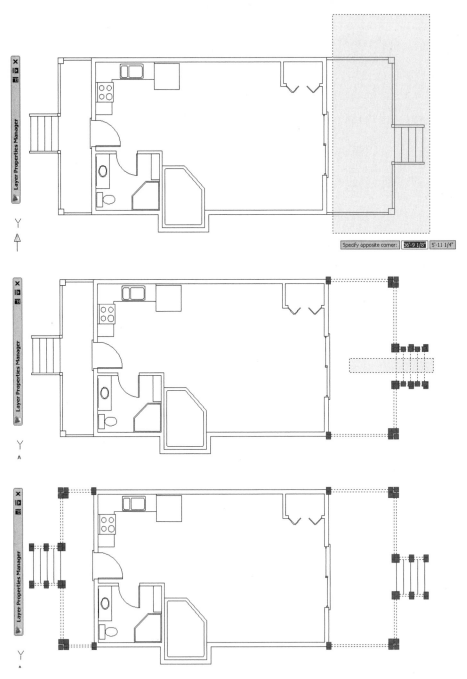

FIGURE 6.16: Selecting the front deck (top), deselecting the front stairs (middle), and the completed selection (bottom)

Notice also that in the Layer drop-down list, the layer being displayed now is layer 0 rather than Walls, the current layer. When objects are selected with no command running, the Layer drop-down list displays the layer to which the selected objects are currently assigned. If selected objects are on more than one layer, the Layer drop-down list is blank.

4. Click the Layer drop-down list to open it (see Figure 6.17).

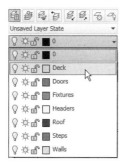

FIGURE 6.17: The expanded Layer drop-down list

5. Click the Deck layer. The list closes. The Deck layer appears in the Layer drop-down list. The deck lines have been moved to the Deck layer and are now green.

6. Press Esc to deselect the lines and remove the grips. The current layer, Walls, returns to the Layer drop-down list.

This is the process you need to go through for each object so it will be placed on the proper layer. In the next section, you'll move the thresholds and steps to the Steps layer. You'll select the threshold and steps by using a selection window.

Selecting Objects with Selection Windows

AutoCAD has two types of selection windows: the regular selection window and the crossing window. The crossing window is represented by dashed lines, and its interior is, by default, a semitransparent light green color. The regular window is represented by solid lines, and its interior is a semitransparent lavender color when using a white background and blue when using a black background.

By default, AutoCAD is set up so that whenever no command is running and the prompt in the Command window is Command:, you can pick objects one at a time or start a regular or crossing window. If you pick an object, it's selected and its grips appear. If you select a blank area of the drawing, this starts a selection window. If you then move the cursor to the right of the point just picked, you create a regular window. If you move the cursor to the left, you create a crossing window. You'll use both crossing and regular selection windows to select the thresholds and steps.

1. Zoom into the sliding-glass door area. Click the Object Snap button on the status bar to turn it off, if it isn't already off.

2. Hold the crosshair cursor above and to the right of the upper-right corner of the sliding-glass door threshold—still inside the perimeter of the deck—as shown on the left side of Figure 6.18. Click that point, and then move the cursor down and to the left until you have made a tall, thin crossing window that completely encloses the right edge of the threshold and is crossed on its left edge by the short horizontal connecting lines, as shown on the right side in Figure 6.18. Then click again. The three lines that make up the threshold are selected.

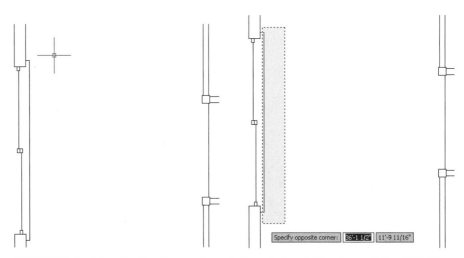

FIGURE 6.18: Starting the crossing selection window (left) and completing it (right)

3. Click the Layer drop-down list to open it, and then click the Steps layer. The front threshold is now on the Steps layer.

4. Using the Zoom Previous tool, from the Zoom fly-out menu in the Navigate panel (View tab), enter z↵ p↵ or simply use the scroll wheel to return to a view of the entire drawing. Zoom in to the threshold at the back door. You will use a regular selection window to select this threshold.

When you zoom or pan with the Zoom or Pan tool, the grips are deselected. When you zoom or pan using the scroll wheel, they are not.

5. Start a selection window slightly above and to the left of the threshold and drag down and to the right, as shown in Figure 6.19. Be sure to enclose the horizontal threshold lines completely.

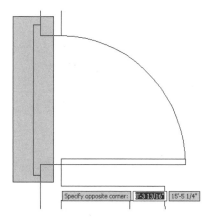

Specify opposite corner: | 3'-3 13/16" | 15'-5 1/4"

F I G U R E   6 . 1 9 : Selecting the threshold with a regular selection window

6. Move the selected lines to the Steps layer the same way you did in step number 3.

Using the Quick Properties Panel

The Quick Properties panel provides access to several of the most commonly changed parameters of the selected objects. You can quickly change the selected object's layer, color, and linetype as well as several parameters specific to the object selected. For example, the Radius parameter is available when a circle is selected and the Closed option is available when a polyline is selected. When multiple objects are selected, only the parameters common to all are displayed. You will use the Quick Properties panel to change the layer of the front and back stairs.

1. Use crossing selection windows to select all of the front and back stairs. The grips appear, indicating the objects are selected. For lines, grips appear at each endpoint and at the midpoint of each segment; for polylines, they appear at each endpoint. When endpoints of lines coincide, their grips overlap. When lines are very short, their grips might appear to overlap, but that is just the result of the zoom factor.

2. Click the Quick Properties button in the status bar. The Quick Properties panel opens in the drawing, as shown in Figure 6.20.

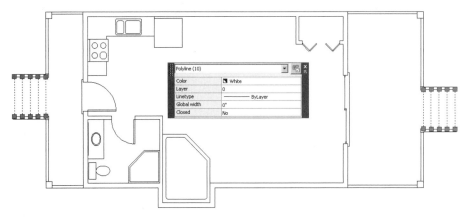

FIGURE 6.20: The Quick Properties panel

3. Click in the Layer field; then click to expand the Layer drop-down list and choose the Steps layer, as shown in Figure 6.21.

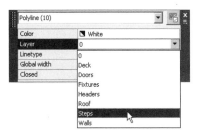

FIGURE 6.21: Assigning the objects to the Steps layer

All ten polylines representing the stairs are now on the Steps layer.

4. Press the Esc key to deselect the objects and remove the grips. Even when it is turned on, the Quick Properties panel disappears when no objects are selected.

Selecting the Doors and Swings

To select the doors and swings, you can use crossing windows. Let's examine this task closely to learn more valuable skills for selecting objects:

1. Place the crosshair cursor in a clear space below and to the right of the back door, and then pick that point to start the selection window. Move the cursor up and to the left until the crossing window crosses the back door and swing but doesn't cross the wall line, as shown in the top of Figure 6.22.

Grips have other uses besides signaling that an object has been selected. You'll learn about some of these as you progress through the chapters.

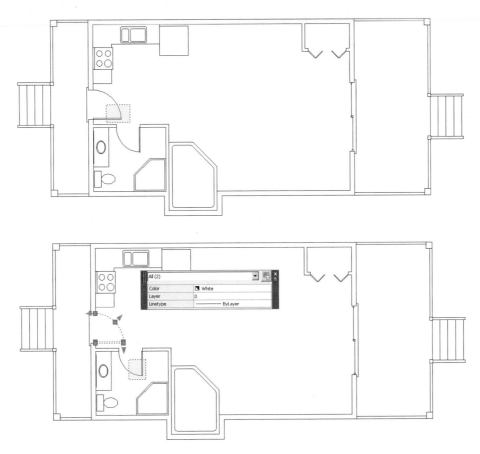

FIGURE 6.22: Using a crossing window to select the doors and swings: the back door (top), the bathroom door (bottom)

2. When you have the crossing window sized and positioned correctly, click again to select the back door and its swing. The Quick Properties panel reappears. Notice how the quantity of selected objects is shown in the top field but not the type of objects. This is because more than one type of object is currently selected.

3. Move to the bathroom, and position the crosshair cursor in the clear space below and to the right of the door. When the crosshair cursor is positioned, click. Then move the cursor up and to the left until the window you're creating crosses the bathroom door and swing without crossing any wall lines or any of the fixtures (see the bottom of Figure 6.22). Click in a clear space again. The bathroom door and swing are selected.

4. Select the four rectangles that make up the closet doors; then open the Layer drop-down list from either the Layers panel or the Quick Properties panel and select the Doors layer. Then press Esc to deselect the objects and remove the grips. The doors are now red and on the Doors layer (see Figure 6.23).

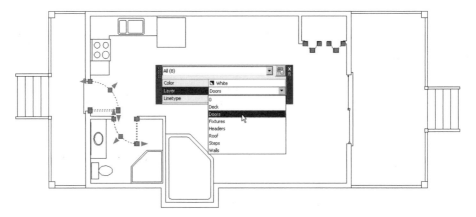

F I G U R E 6 . 2 3 : Using the Quick Properties panel's Layer drop-down list to change the layer of the door objects

For the sliding-glass door, it's awkward to create a crossing window from left to right because it might be difficult to position the pickbox between the threshold lines and the sliding door. In this situation, use a regular window to select the objects:

1. Zoom in to the sliding-glass door area.

2. Pick a point to the left of the balcony opening, just above the upper jamb line. Move the crosshairs down and to the right until the right edge of the window sits inside the wall but just to the right of the sliding-glass window frames, not encompassing the entire jamb. When your window is positioned as shown in Figure 6.24, click. The entire sliding-glass door assembly is selected but not the jambs, walls, threshold, or balcony. Many grips appear: 13 lines make up the sliding-glass door, and each has three grips; a grip at each endpoint and a grip at each midpoint. Many of the grips overlap.

3. Open the Layer drop-down list, and select the Doors layer.

4. Press Esc to deselect the objects and remove the grips, and then use Zoom Previous. You have a full view of the floor plan, and all doors are red and reside on the Doors layer.

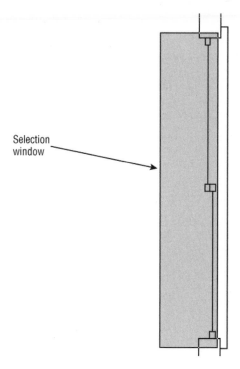

FIGURE 6.24: Using a regular selection window to select the sliding-glass door

The next task is to move the kitchen and bathroom counters and fixtures and the hot tub onto the Fixtures layer. In doing this, you'll learn how to deselect some objects from a group of selected objects.

Selecting the Kitchen and Bathroom Fixtures

Sometimes it's more efficient to select more objects than you want and then deselect those you don't want. You'll see how this is done when you select the kitchen and bathroom fixtures:

1. Pick a point in the kitchen area just below and to the right of the refrigerator but above the back door to start a crossing window.

2. Move the cursor to the top left and up until the upper-left corner of the crossing window is to the left of the left edge of the counter and inside the back wall, as shown in the top left of Figure 6.25. When you have it correct, click that point. The entire kitchen counter area and the inside wall lines are selected.

3. Move down to the bathroom, and pick a point inside the shower near the bottom-right corner, being careful not to touch any lines with the crosshair cursor.

4. Move the crosshair cursor up and to the left until the lower-left corner of the crossing window is in the middle of the sink (see the top right of Figure 6.25). When you have it positioned this way, click that point. All the bathroom fixtures, except the mirror, are selected.

5. From left to right, drag a regular window that encompasses the mirror, as shown in the bottom of Figure 6.25. It doesn't matter if the selection window surrounds objects that are already selected.

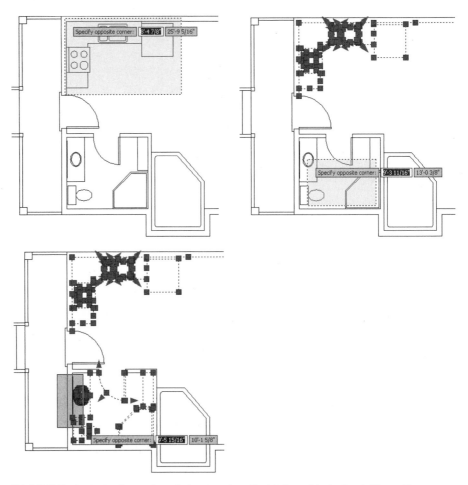

FIGURE 6.25: A crossing window to select the kitchen objects (top left), another crossing window to select the bathroom objects (top right), and a regular selection window selecting the mirror (bottom)

6. To complete the selection set, drag a crossing selection window that crosses both of the hot tub polylines that encroach into the living room.

7. Hold down the Shift key, and then pick the selected door and swing in the bathroom and the selected interior wall lines in the kitchen. Be careful to not pick a grip. As you pick the objects, their lines become solid again and their grips disappear, letting you know they have been deselected, or removed from the selection set (see Figure 6.26). Be sure to pick the inside wall lines in the kitchen where they don't coincide with the stove or counter.

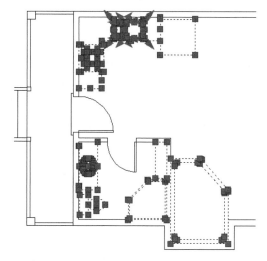

FIGURE 6.26: The completed selection set after removing the door swing and back wall line

8. Release the Shift key. Open the Layer drop-down list, and select the Fixtures layer. The fixtures are now on the Fixtures layer and are magenta.

9. Press the Esc key to deselect the objects.

The last objects to move onto a new layer are the wall lines. As the drawing is now, it won't be easy to select the wall lines because so many other objects in the drawing are in the way. However, these other objects are now on their own layers, whereas the wall lines are still on layer 0. If you make all your layers temporarily invisible except for the 0 and Walls layers, selecting the wall lines will be easy.

Before you do that, let's pause and look at the selection process. The sidebar "Selecting Objects in Your Drawing" summarizes the selection process and the tools I have covered so far.

SELECTING OBJECTS IN YOUR DRAWING

As you select objects in the cabin drawing to move them onto their pre-scribed layers, you use various selection tools. Mastering these important tools will greatly enhance your performance as an AutoCAD user. As you select objects by picking them and windowing them, you're building a *selection set*. You might want to remove objects from that selection set later. Here is a summary of the basic selection tools that you have used so far, with a couple of additions:

Picking This is the basic, bottom-line selection tool. Click the line, circle, or other object to select it. If no command is running, grips appear on the selected object and the object becomes dashed. If a command is running and you're being prompted with `Select objects:`, grips don't appear, but the object is selected and ghosts. In AutoCAD you can select objects and then issue a command, or you can issue the command first and then select the objects as directed.

Selecting a Window Automatically To start a window, click a location that is in an empty portion of the screen where there are no objects. To form a regular window, move your cursor to the right. To form a crossing window, move your cursor to the left. This feature is called *implied windowing*, and it works this way if no command is running or if one is running and the prompt says `Select objects:`.

If the geometry of your drawing makes forming a crossing or regular selection window difficult because of the need to move from right to left (crossing) or from left to right (regular), you can force one or the other by entering **c**↵ or **w**↵, respectively, but only if a command is running.

Removing Objects from a Selection Set At some point, you'll find it more efficient to select more objects than you want and then remove the unwanted ones. You can do this in three ways:

► To remove a couple of objects, hold down the Shift key and pick the objects.

► To remove objects from the selection set, hold down the Shift key and use one of the selection window types.

► If a command is running, enter **r**↵, and then use the selection tools (picking, windows, and so on) without the Shift key to remove objects from the selection set.

If you are in a command and need to add objects back to the selection set after removing some, enter **a**↵. This puts you back into selection mode, and you can continue adding objects to the set.

Turning Off and Freezing Layers

You can make layers invisible either by turning them off or by *freezing* them. When a layer is turned off or frozen, the objects on that layer are invisible. These two procedures operate in nearly the same way and perform about the same function, with one significant difference: objects on frozen layers cannot be selected with the All option, while objects on layers that are off can be selected. For example, if you enter e↵ a↵↵ to erase all objects, all the visible and invisible objects on the layers turned off are deleted, while the objects on frozen layers remain in the drawing but are still invisible. Here is a good rule to follow: If you want a layer to be invisible for only a short time, turn it off; if you prefer that it be invisible semi-permanently, freeze it.

For the task at hand, you'll turn off all the layers except layer 0 and the Walls layer. You'll then move the wall lines onto the Walls layer:

1. Click the Layer Properties button on the Layers panel to open the Layer Properties Manager dialog box, or expand the dialog box if it is still collapsed on your screen. Notice that layer 0 is still first in the list and that the other layers have been reorganized alphabetically (see the top of Figure 6.27). Also, notice the icons in the Status column: a green check mark signifies that the Walls layer is current; the light blue layer icons signify that those layers (0, Deck, Doors, Fixtures, and Steps) now have objects on them; and the light gray layer icons tell you that those layers (Headers and Roof) don't have any objects on them.

Layers beginning with numbers appear first, in numeric order. Following those are the rest of the layers, listed alphabetically.

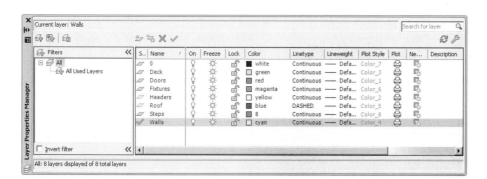

FIGURE 6.27: The layers, now listed alphabetically (top), and turning off the selected layers (next page)

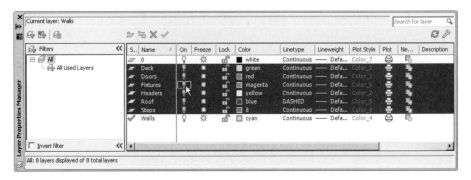

FIGURE 6.27 *(Continued)*

N O T E Because the Walls layer is current and has a green check mark in the Status column, you can't tell whether it has any objects on it. You have to make a different layer current and then check whether the Walls icon is blue or gray.

2. Click the Deck layer to highlight it. Then, hold down the Shift key and click the Steps layer. All layers are selected except Layer 0 and the Walls layer.

3. Move the arrow cursor over to the On column, which has a lit light bulb as a symbol for each layer row.

4. Click one of the light bulbs of the selected layers (see the bottom of Figure 6.27). The lit light bulb symbols all change to unlit bulbs except the ones for layer 0 and the Walls layer.

5. Collapse or close the Layer Properties Manager or simply move it out of the way. All objects in your drawing are invisible except the wall lines (see Figure 6.28). The wall lines are still on layer 0.

6. Start a regular selection window around the cabin by clicking the upper-left corner of the drawing area, above and to the left of any lines. Then click the lower-right corner in the same way. All the wall lines are selected and grips appear on all of them.

7. Open the Layer drop-down list, and then click the Walls layer. The walls move to the Walls layer and are now cyan. Press Esc to deselect the objects.

8. In the Layer Properties Manager dialog box, right-click any layer and choose Select All from the context menu. All layers are highlighted.

9. Click one of the unlit bulbs in the On column. All unlit bulbs become lit. Back in your drawing, all objects are now visible and on their correct layers (see Figure 6.29).

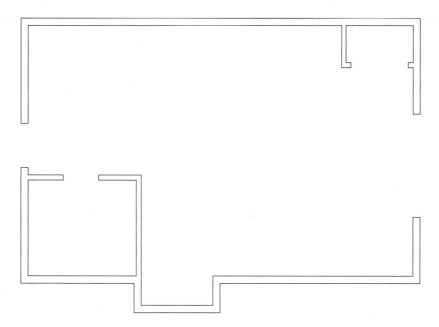

FIGURE 6.28: The floor plan with all layers turned off except the Walls layer and layer 0

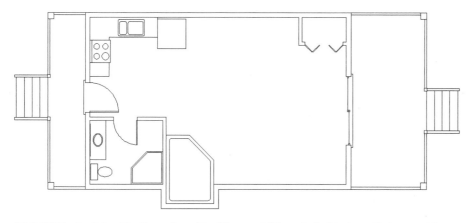

FIGURE 6.29: The floor plan with all layers visible and all objects on their correct layers

10. Save this drawing in your training folder as Cabin06a.dwg.

Two of your layers, Roof and Headers, still have no objects on them because these components haven't been drawn yet. You'll draw the headers now.

Drawing the Headers

Most door and window openings don't extend to the ceiling. The portion of the wall above the opening and below the ceiling is the *header*. The term comes from the name of the beam inside the wall that spans the opening. In a floor plan, wall lines usually stop at the door and window openings, but you need lines across the gap between jamb lines to show that an opening doesn't extend to the ceiling; hence, you'll create the header.

To draw headers directly onto the correct layer, you need to make the Headers layer current. As you've seen, you can use the Layer Properties Manager dialog box. But you can also use a shortcut, the Layer drop-down list in the Layers panel, which you have just been using to move objects from one layer to another:

1. Click anywhere on the Layer drop-down list, or click the down-arrow button on the right end. The drop-down list opens, displaying a list of the layers in your drawing. If you have more than 10 layers, a scroll bar becomes operational, giving you access to all the layers.

2. Click the Headers layer. The drop-down list closes. "Headers" now appears in the box (see Figure 6.30), telling you that the Headers layer has replaced Walls as the current layer.

FIGURE 6.30: The Headers layer is now shown as current in the Layers panel.

3. Turn on the Object Snap button on the status bar if necessary. The Endpoint, Midpoint, and Intersection osnaps are now active. If they aren't, right-click on the Object Snap button and, in the context menu, click on the osnaps that you want active.

 4. The doors and thresholds might be in your way, so you'll freeze those layers. You may not always know what layer a particular object resides on, so selecting with a pick rather than by layer name can be very useful. Click the Freeze button in the Layers panel.

5. At the `Select an object on the layer to be frozen or:` prompt, click one door or swing and one threshold. All the objects on the Doors and Steps layers temporarily disappear. Press Esc to end the Freeze command.

You need to draw two parallel lines across each of the three openings, from the endpoint of one jamb line to the corresponding endpoint of the jamb on the opposite side of the opening.

6. To start the Line command, enter l↵ or click the Line button in the Draw panel. Move the cursor near the upper end of the left jamb for the back door until the colored snap marker appears at the upper-left endpoint of the jamb line and then click.

7. Move the cursor to the left end of the lower jamb, and click to complete the line.

8. Right-click once to open a context menu near your cursor (see Figure 6.31).

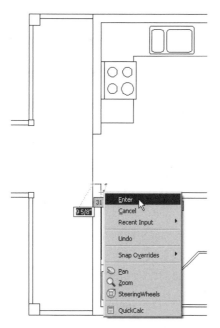

FIGURE 6.31: The right-click context menu for accessing recent and common commands

9. Choose Enter from the menu, and then right-click again to open another context menu at the cursor, as shown in Figure 6.32.

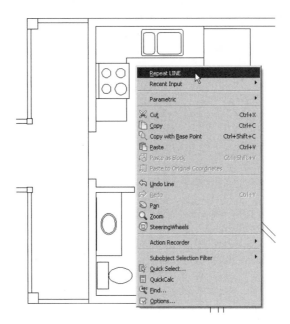

FIGURE 6.32: A second right-click context menu with additional commands available

10. Choose Repeat LINE.

11. Move to the right endpoint of the upper jamb line for the back door and, with the same technique used in steps 6 through 10, draw the lower header line across the opening. You can see the results in the left image of Figure 6.33.

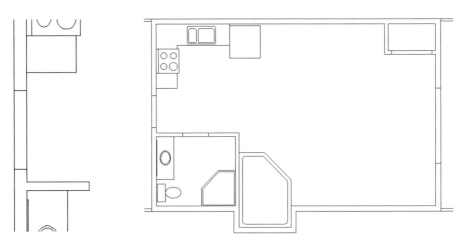

FIGURE 6.33: The header lines drawn for the back door opening (left) and for the rest of the doorway openings (right)

12. Keep using the same procedure to draw the rest of the header lines for the remaining three doorway openings.

The floor plan will look like the right image of Figure 6.33.

The Layer drop-down list box is a shortcut that allows you to pick a different layer quickly as the current layer and to turn off or turn on individual layers. To create new layers or to turn off many layers at a time, use the Layer Properties Manager dialog box. You'll learn about another tool for changing the current layer as you draw the rooflines.

Drawing the Roof

Before you start to draw the rooflines, refer to Figure 6.34 and note the lines representing different parts of the roof:

▶ Eight *eaves lines* around the perimeter of the building, representing the lowest edge of the roof

▶ One *ridgeline*, representing the peak of the roof

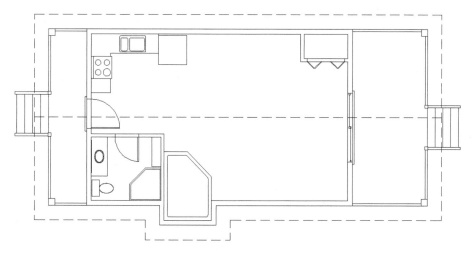

FIGURE 6.34: The floor plan with the rooflines

The roof for the cabin is called a *double-pitched roof* because the panels slope down to the eaves on only two sides. You'll start by drawing the eaves.

Creating the Eaves

Because the roof extends beyond the exterior walls the same distance on all sides of the building, you can generate the eaves lines by offsetting the outside wall lines:

1. Open the Layer drop-down list, and select Roof to make it current. Then start the Offset command. The second prompt line from the bottom of the command window says Layer=Source, meaning the objects created by the Offset command will be on the same layer as the object offset. Press the down arrow key, and choose the Layer option from the context menu (see the left image of Figure 6.35).

FIGURE 6.35: Choosing the Layer option (left) and the current option (right)

2. From the second context menu that appears, choose the Current option (see the right image of Figure 6.35). Offset lines will now be created on the current layer.

3. Enter 1"6↵ (457↵) to set the offset distance. Pick the upper-left, vertical, outside handrail polyline, and then pick a point to the left of that polyline to offset it to the outside. The L-shaped offset line is on the Roof layer.

4. Move to another side of the cabin, pick the lower-right outside handrail polyline, and offset it to the outside.

5. Repeat this process for the three outside wall lines that define the pop-out on the bottom of the cabin and the short horizontal outside wall line to the left of the pop-out. You have one offset element on each side of the cabin (see Figure 6.36). Press ↵ to end the Offset command.

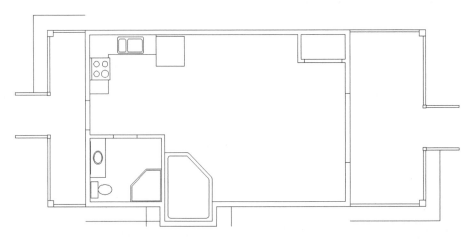

FIGURE 6.36: One outside wall line is offset to each side of the building.

6. Start the Fillet command. Make sure the radius is set to zero. If it is, go to step 7. If it isn't, enter **r**⏎, and then enter **0**⏎ to reset the radius (or use the Shift key to override the radius value).

7. Starting with the horizontal portion of the upper-left L-shaped polyline, click two of these newly offset lines that are on adjacent sides of the building. Work around the building in a clockwise manner, being sure to click the half of the line nearest the corner where the two selected lines will meet (see the top of Figure 6.37). The lines extend to meet each other and form a corner (see the bottom of Figure 6.37). The Fillet command ends.

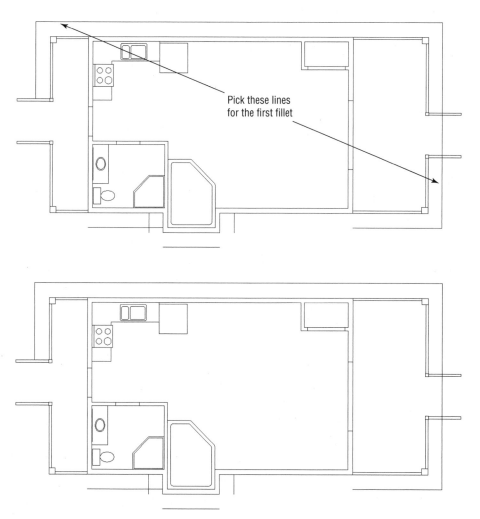

Pick these lines
for the first fillet

F I G U R E   6 . 3 7 : Picking lines to fillet one of the eaves' corners (top) and the result (bottom)

8. Press ↵ to restart the Fillet command, and then enter m↵ to select the Multiple option. Pick the remaining pairs of adjacent lines that will meet at the corners. When you try to fillet the final section, you'll get a warning at the command prompt that reads Lines belonging to polylines must be consecutive or separated by one segment and the command prompt returns to Select first object or:.

Although it looks as though the polyline has a single gap between two adjacent segments, in actuality the gap is between the first (vertical) segment and the eighth (horizontal) segment. You can't use the Pedit command's Close option yet because it would add an additional, diagonal segment from the polylines' existing endpoints. You could explode the pline into individual lines, execute the fillet and then use Pedit to join them, but in this case you'll use the polyline's grips to close the gap.

STARTING OBJECT SNAPS

By now, you know that you can activate a nonrunning osnap using the Shift+right-click menu or the Object Snap toolbar, or by typing the shortcut keys. From now on, I'll simply instruct you to activate a specific object snap and you can use the method that you prefer.

9. Press the Esc key to terminate the Fillet command. Click the polyline to select it and display its grips. You can temporarily turn off the Quick Properties panel by clicking the X in the upper-right corner, or turn it off completely by clicking the Object Properties button in the status bar.

10. Click the grip at the open left endpoint of the horizontal segment (see the top of Figure 6.38). The grip turns red to signify that it is *hot* and can be manipulated.

11. Start the Perpendicular osnap, place the cursor over the open, vertical segment; then, when the marker appears, click. The horizontal line is extended to the location perpendicular to the vertical line.

12. Select the grip at the open end of the vertical segment to make it hot; then click the open end of the horizontal line to move the first endpoint there (see the bottom of Figure 6.38).

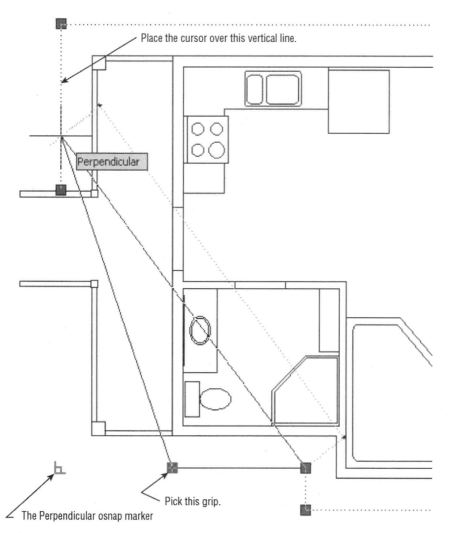

FIGURE 6.38: Using the grip to move the horizontal endpoint (top) and the vertical endpoint (next page)

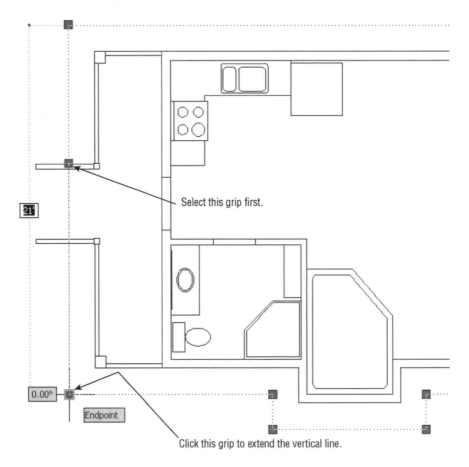

Select this grip first.

Click this grip to extend the vertical line.

FIGURE 6.38: *(Continued)*

13. Finally, with the polyline still selected, start the Pedit command, choose the Close option, and press ↵ to end the command. Visually, there is no difference in the perimeter of the roof, but AutoCAD no longer sees an open polyline. Closed polylines are almost always preferable in case you need to extrude a 2D object into a 3D object, and using closed polylines is generally a cleaner drafting practice. Your completed roof perimeter should look like Figure 6.39.

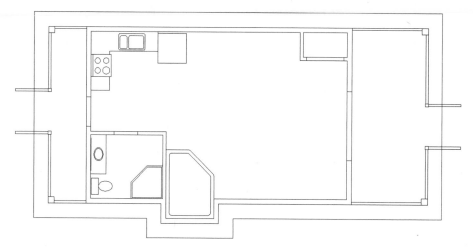

FIGURE 6.39: The completed eaves lines after filleting

Setting a Linetype Scale Factor

By default, the dashes in the Dashed linetype are set up to be ½″ (13 mm) long with ¼″ (6 mm) spaces. This is the correct size for a drawing that is close to actual size on your screen, such as the box you drew in Chapter 2. But for something that is the size of your cabin, you must increase the linetype scale to make the dashes large enough to see. If the dashes were 12″ (305 mm) long with 6″ (152 mm) spaces, they would at least be visible, although possibly not exactly the right size. To make such a change in the dash size, ask what you must multiply ½″ (13 mm) by to get 12″ (305 mm). The answer is 24, so that's your scale factor. AutoCAD stores a Linetype Scale Factor setting that controls the size of the dashes and spaces of noncontinuous linetypes. The default is 1.00, which gives you the ½″ (305 mm) dash, so you need to change the setting to 24:

N O T E The Imperial to Metric conversion is approximated.

1. Enter ltscale↵ or lts↵. The prompt in the Command window says
   `Enter new linetype scale factor <1.0000>:`.

2. Enter 24↵ to set the linetype scale factor to 24. Your drawing changes, and you can see the dashes (see Figure 6.40).

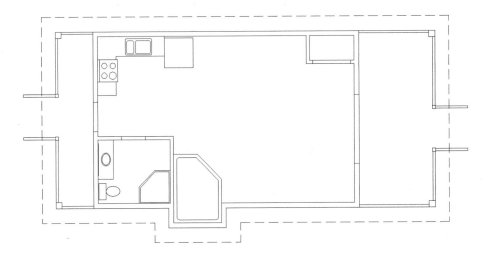

FIGURE 6.40: The eaves lines on the Roof layer with visible dashes

If you aren't satisfied with the dash size, restart the Ltscale command, and increase the scale factor for a longer dash or decrease it for a shorter one. This linetype scale factor is global, meaning that it affects every noncontinuous line in the drawing. There is also an individual scale factor for linetypes. You'll see that in the next section.

Assigning an Individual Linetype Scale Factor

Although the Ltscale command sets a linetype scale factor for all objects that do not use the Continuous linetype in the drawing, you can also adjust the dash and space sizes for individual objects. To change the dash and space size for the eaves lines of the roof to make them larger, follow these steps:

1. Start the Offset command and offset the eaves polyline to the outside of the cabin. This is only a temporary line for comparison.

2. End the Offset command and select the new polyline.

3. Right-click and choose Properties from the context menu, to open the Properties palette.

4. Click Linetype scale option to highlight the current scale of 1.0000, and enter 3↵. The selected polyline's linetype scale is increased, as shown in Figure 6.41.

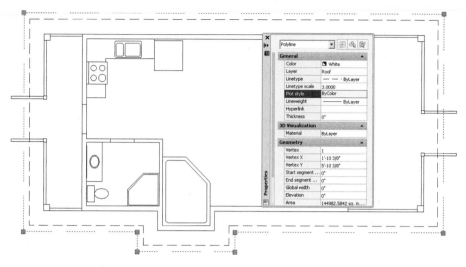

F I G U R E   6 . 4 1 : Changing the linetype scale for a single object

   5. Close the Properties palette, and delete the polyline with the larger
       dashes.

N O T E   **If no objects are selected and you set Linetype Scale in the Properties palette to a number other than 1.0000, any noncontinuous lines that
are subsequently drawn will be controlled by this new Linetype Scale setting.**

   This feature allows you to get subtle variations in the size of dashes and spaces
for individual noncontinuous lines. But remember that all lines are controlled
by an individual linetype scale factor and by the global linetype scale factor. The
actual size of the dashes and spaces for a particular line is a result of multiplying
the two linetype scale factors together. This additional flexibility requires you to
keep careful track of the variations you're making.

   To find out the current linetype scale value for new objects and the global linetype scale factor, follow these steps:

   1. Enter **ltype↵** to open the Linetype Manager dialog box.

   2. Make sure the Details area is visible at the bottom of the dialog box. If
       it isn't, click Show Details in the upper-right corner.

   3. Note the bottom-right corner. The current global and object line-
       type scales appear here (see Figure 6.42). You can also modify
       them here.

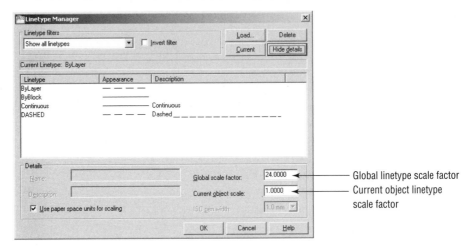

FIGURE 6.42: The Linetype Manager dialog box

    4. For now, click Cancel.

Drawing the Ridgeline

To finish the roof, you'll draw a single line to represent the peak of the roof that extends from the front of the cabin to the back. Because of the pop-out, the roof is not symmetrical, so the ridgeline will be centered on the two longest vertical sections. Look at the Linetype drop-down list on the Properties panel (see Figure 6.43). A dashed line with the name ByLayer appears there. ByLayer tells you that the current linetype will be whatever linetype has been assigned to the current layer. In the case of the Roof layer, the assigned linetype is Dashed. You'll read more about ByLayer later in this chapter.

FIGURE 6.43: The Linetype drop-down list

    1. Start the Line command and activate the Midpoint object snap.

    2. Start the line from the midpoint of the right vertical roofline. Start the Perpendicular osnap; then click on the vertical roofline on the opposite side of the cabin.

    3. Terminate the Line command. Your cabin should look like Figure 6.44.

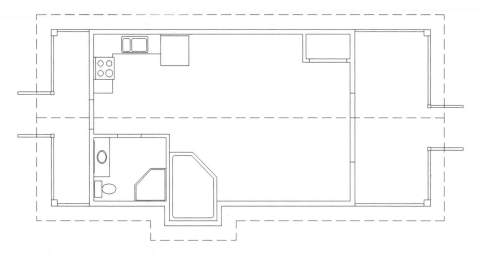

FIGURE 6.44: The completed roof

Using the Layer Walk Tool

Before saving this drawing, use the Make Object's Layer Current button to make the Doors layer current. You will use the Layer Walk tool to verify the contents of each layer by isolating them one at a time:

1. Expand the Layers panel, and click the Pin button in the lower-right corner. This causes the panel to stay open after the cursor moves off it, instead of auto-collapsing.

2. Expand the Layer drop-down list and click the Snowflake icon for the Doors and Steps layers to unfreeze those layers. Alternatively, when all layers must be thawed, you could click the Thaw All Layers button instead.

3. Click the Make Object's Layer Current button in the top row of buttons in the Layers pane. You'll get the Select object whose layer will become current: prompt.

4. Pick one of the door or swing lines. The Doors layer replaces Roof in the Layer drop-down list, telling you the Doors layer is now the current layer.

T I P The Make Object's Layer Current button works two ways. You can click the button and then select the object whose layer will become current, or you can select an object that's on the target layer and then click the button. If you select multiple objects using the latter method, they must all reside on the current layer or the tool will prompt you to select an object.

5. Click the Layer Walk button in the extended Layers panel to open the LayerWalk dialog box, shown in Figure 6.45.

FIGURE 6.45: The LayerWalk dialog box

6. Select a layer other than layer 0, and the drawing area shows only the objects on that layer. Use the up and down arrows to "walk" through the drawing's layers, verifying that the objects reside on the correct layers. Figure 6.46 shows the cabin drawing with the Fixtures layer selected (top).

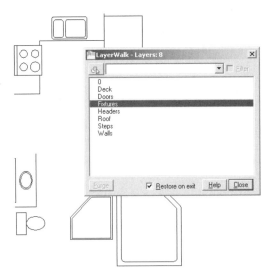

FIGURE 6.46: Displaying the contents of the Fixtures layer (top) and the Walls layer (next page)

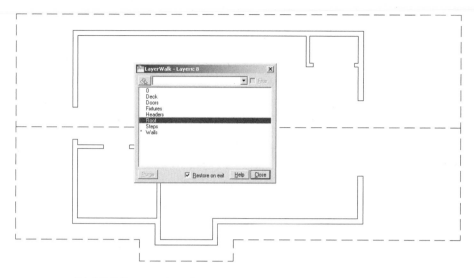

FIGURE 6.46: *(Continued)*

7. If you double-click a layer name, that layer stays displayed even when it isn't highlighted and an asterisk appears next to the layer name. Figure 6.46 (above) shows the cabin drawing with the Roof layer selected and the Walls layer locked on.

8. Close the LayerWalk dialog box.

9. Click the Unpin button to unpin the expanded Layers panel.

10. Save this drawing as Cabin06b.dwg.

By drawing the rooflines, you have completed most of the exercises for this chapter. The cabin floor plan is almost complete. In the next chapter, you'll complete the floor plan by placing windows in the external walls using a grouping tool called a *block*. The rest of this chapter contains a short discussion about color, linetypes, and lineweights and how they work with layers and objects. We'll also look at the Action Recorder feature to record and play back repetitive tasks.

Setting Properties of Layers and Objects

This section covers a few concepts you should consider when assigning properties to layers and objects.

Selecting Colors for Layers and Objects

First, you must decide whether you prefer a light or dark background color for the drawing area. This is generally a personal preference, but the lighting in your work area can be a contributing factor. Bright work areas usually make it difficult to read monitors easily, and with a dark background color on your screen in a brightly lit room, you'll often get distracting reflections on the screen. Eyestrain can result. Darkening your work area will usually minimize these effects. If that's not possible, you might have to live with a lighter background.

Next, look at the colors in your drawing. If the background of your drawing area is white, notice which colors are the easiest to read. For most monitors, yellow, light gray, and cyan are somewhat faded, while blue, green, red, and magenta are read easily. If your drawing area background is black, the blue is sometimes too dark to read easily, but the rest of the colors that you have used so far usually read well. This is one reason that most users prefer the black or at least a dark background color.

Assigning a Color or a Linetype to an Object Instead of a Layer

You can also assign properties of layers, such as color, linetype, and lineweights, to objects. For example, think about the Roof layer. It's assigned the Dashed linetype. A line on the Roof layer can be assigned the Continuous linetype, even though all other lines on the Roof layer are dashed. The same is true for color and lineweights. Occasionally, this makes sense, especially for linetypes, but that is the exception rather than the rule. To make such a change, select the line, open the Properties palette, and change the linetype from ByLayer to the linetype of your choice. You can also use the Properties toolbar to make quick changes to an object's appearance.

In this chapter, you have seen how to assign colors and linetypes to layers in order to control the way objects on those layers appear. That is the rule to follow. When objects are assigned properties that vary from those of their layer, the result can be confusing to someone working with your drawing file, because the objects don't appear to be on their assigned layer. If the object's properties match those of another layer, you can mistakenly think the object is on that layer.

Making a Color or a Linetype Current

If you look at the Properties panel for a moment, you'll see more such lists to the right of the Layer drop-down list. The first three are the Color, Linetype, and Lineweight controls. You use these tools to set a color, linetype, or lineweight to be current. When this is done, each object subsequently created will be assigned the current linetype, lineweight, and/or color, regardless of which linetype, lineweight, and color have been assigned to the current layer. If, for example, the Doors layer is set as the current layer and the Dashed linetype and green color are assigned as current, any lines drawn are dashed and green but still on the Doors layer. This isn't a good way to set up the system of layers, linetypes, and colors because of the obvious confusion it will create in your drawing, but beginners often accidentally do this.

The best way to maintain maximum control of your drawing is to keep the current linetype, lineweight, and color set to ByLayer, as they are by default. When you do this, colors and linetypes are controlled by the layers, and objects take on the color and linetype of the layers they are on. If this configuration is accidentally disturbed and objects are created with the wrong color or linetype, you can correct the situation without too much trouble. First, reset the current color, lineweight, and linetype to ByLayer by using the drop-down lists on the Properties panel. Next, select all problem objects; then use the Properties palette or Quick Properties panel to change the linetype, lineweight, or color to ByLayer. They will take on the color, lineweight, and linetype of the layer to which they have been assigned, and you can quickly tell whether they are on their proper layers.

Using the Action Recorder

One of the most useful tools in AutoCAD 2010 is the Action Recorder. With this feature, you can perform repetitive tasks and save the steps to a file, called a macro, which can be played back any time you need to repeat those steps in any drawing. For example, if you need to draw several countersunk holes in a plate at a specified distance, you can prompt the user for a start point, angle, diameter, and spacing, and then let AutoCAD do the work. The Action Recorder creates the macros for you without the need for you to learn macro programming. For this example, you will add two new layers to your drawing and then make one of them the current layer. The practice of adding your standards to somebody else's (a client, contractor, and so on) drawing is common. Follow these steps to create the action:

1. Click the Ribbon's Manage tab to display a series of panels that contain tools for managing a drawing's interface and standards.

2. Click the Record button in the Action Recorder panel. The Record button changes to a Stop button, and the panel pins itself open, as shown in Figure 6.47. A large red dot appears at the cursor to remind you that the actions are being recorded.

FIGURE 6.47: The Action Recorder panel as it appears when the actions are being recorded

3. You'll use the command line to start the layer command. The - prefix starts the command without opening the Layer Properties Manager dialog box. Enter -**layer**↵.

4. Enter **n**↵ or pick New from the list that appears at the cursor; then enter **Landscaping**↵ to name the new layer. Both methods for selecting an option work equally well.

5. Select the New option again and enter **Electrical**↵ to create and name the new layer.

6. Choose the Set option; then enter **Electrical**↵↵ to make the Electrical layer current and end the Layer command.

7. Click the Stop button to discontinue recording the actions. Your Action Recorder panel should look like Figure 6.48.

WARNING   Special characters, such as spaces or slashes, are not permitted in action filenames.

FIGURE 6.48: The Action Recorder after creating the new layers and setting the current layer

8. In the Action Macro dialog box that opens (see Figure 6.49), enter New_Layers↵ in the Action Macro Command Name field and add a description if you like.

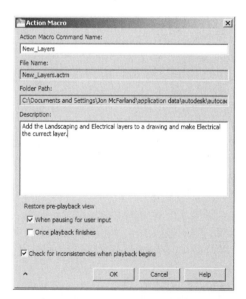

FIGURE 6.49: The Action Macro dialog box

9. Click OK and the macro is saved as New_Layers.actm in the C:\Documents and Settings*Your Name*\Application Data\ Autodesk\AutoCAD 2010\R18.0\enu\Support\Actions folder (a copy is also available on this book's web page).

10. Unpin the Action Recorder panel so that it can collapse.

11. Open a new drawing file, make sure the New_Layers macro name appears in the Available Action Macro field, and click the Play button, as shown in Figure 6.50.

FIGURE 6.50: Playing the New_Layers macro in the Action Recorder panel

12. Click Close when the Action Macro dialog box indicates the macro has run through completion (see Figure 6.51).

FIGURE 6.51: The Action Macro dialog box

13. Switch to the Home tab, and then open the Layer drop-down list in the Layers panel. You will see the new layers the macro created.

As you can see, action macros are easy to record and can save you time when repetitive tasks are required. You could have easily set the layers' colors and line-types, on/off statuses, or performed other layer-related tasks. The Action Recorder is quite powerful and can save a great amount of time when you use it to create macros specific to your needs. In the next section, you will look at a method of saving and recalling all the settings for the layers in your drawings. You can close the blank drawing without saving the changes.

Creating Layer States

Even a drawing that reads well when printed may get cluttered in the viewports, and it can become difficult to execute a command properly. This was evident ear-lier when the door swing made it harder than it should have been to create the headers. Often, you will find yourself freezing or turning off the same layers to execute a specific task and then making them visible again. In the course of your workday, you might issue the same sequence of layer commands dozens of times. To make this task more efficient, layer states are available. *Layer states* are named settings where you can save the conditions of the layers, such as On, Frozen, or Current, and restore them through the Layer States Manager dialog box. The following exercise demonstrates how to create a layer state that shows only the floor plan and not the roof or fixtures:

1. If you did not complete the previous Action Recorder exercise, create two layers in your drawing named Landscaping and Electrical.

2. In the Cabin drawing, make layer 0 the current layer.

3. From the Layer drop-down list or the Layer Properties Manager dialog box, freeze the Roof and Fixtures layers.

4. On the Layers panel, click the Layer States drop-down list, which currently shows Unsaved Layer State, and click on Manage Layer States, as shown in Figure 6.52.

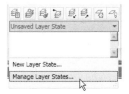

FIGURE 6.52: Accessing the Layer States Manager

The Layer States Manager dialog box opens (see Figure 6.53).

FIGURE 6.53: The Layer States Manager dialog box

5. Click the New button to create a new saved layer state. In the New Layer State to Save dialog box, enter **Floor Plan** in the New Layer State Name field. If you like, enter a description for the layer state as well (see Figure 6.54). Click the OK button when you are done.

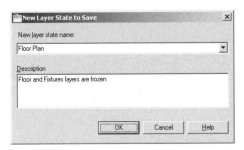

FIGURE 6.54: Saving a layer state in the New Layer State to Save dialog box

6. The new layer state appears in the Layer States Manager dialog box, as shown in Figure 6.55. Click the Close button to close the Layer States Manager dialog box.

FIGURE 6.55: The Layer States Manager dialog box showing the new layer state

7. Thaw the Roof and Fixtures layers. The objects on those layers become visible again.

8. Open the Layer States Manager dialog box again. Click the More Restore Options button, the right-facing arrow at the bottom-right corner, to display additional options. The items shown in the Layer Properties to Restore section are, when checked, the features of the layer state that are affected when it is restored. It is important to note that if you make changes to a layer's color or lineweight, those changes are lost when the layer state is restored if those features are checked here.

9. Uncheck the Color, Linetype, and Lineweight options (see Figure 6.56), and then click the Restore button.

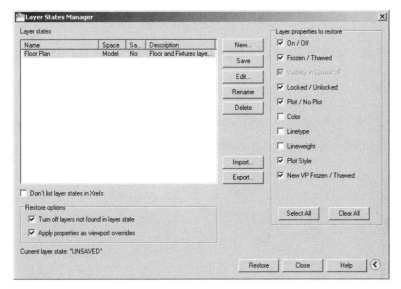

FIGURE 6.56: The Layer States Manager dialog box with the restore options selected

10. The Roof and Fixtures layers are frozen again (see Figure 6.57), and Floor Plan appears in the Layer State drop-down list.

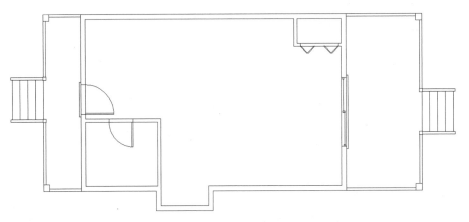

FIGURE 6.57: The cabin with the Roof and Fixtures layers frozen

11. Save this drawing as Cabin06c.dwg.

As you can see, saving layer states can reduce the number of steps it takes to restore a specific set of layer properties. In a complex drawing, it isn't uncommon to have a dozen or more saved layer states.

USING THE LAYER STATES MANAGER

You also use the Layer States Manager dialog box to manage existing layer states. Here are its features:

Layer States List Box Displays a list of previously saved layer states.

Restore Button Restores the layer state that is highlighted in the Layer States list box.

Edit Button Opens the Edit Layer State dialog box where the current layer state's properties are edited.

Delete Button Deletes a layer state. This doesn't affect the current layer setup.

Import Button Imports an .las file, from a .dwg, .dws, or .dwt file, as a new layer state in the current drawing.

Export Button Exports the chosen saved layer state to be saved as an .las file.

To modify a layer state, restore it to be the current layer state and then change it. To rename a layer state, highlight it, click its name, and enter the new name.

If You Would Like More Practice...

All trades and professions that use AutoCAD have their own standards for naming and organizing layers. The following suggestions urge you to apply this chapter's concepts to your individual use of the program.

Experimenting with Linetypes and Linetype Scales

Choose Save As to save Cabin06c.dwg to a new file called Cabin06c_Linetype.dwg. Then experiment with the linetypes and linetype scales (Global and Object) to get a feel for how the linetypes look and how the scales work. You won't be using this practice file again, so feel free to draw new objects that will make it convenient for you to work with linetypes. Here are some suggestions for linetypes to experiment with:

▶ Dashed2 or Dashed (0.5×)

▶ Dashed×2 or Dashed (2×)

▶ Hidden (as compared to Dashed)

▶ Phantom

▶ DashDot

▶ Fenceline2

▶ Hot_Water_Supply

Here is a summary of the steps to get a new linetype into your drawing:

1. Create a new layer or highlight an existing layer.

2. In the Layer Properties Manager, click the linetype name in the Linetype column for the chosen layer.

3. Click the Load button.

4. Highlight a linetype in the list and click OK.

5. Highlight the new linetype in the Linetype Manager dialog box and click OK.

6. Make the layer with the new linetype the current layer, and then click OK to close the Layer Properties Manager dialog box.

7. Draw objects.

Once you have a few linetypes represented in the drawing, open the Linetype Manager dialog box and experiment with the Global and Object linetype scale factors.

Setting Up Layers for Your Own Trade or Profession

Open a new drawing, and set up approximately 10 layers that you might use in your own profession. Assign colors and linetypes to them. Most activities that use CAD have some layers in common, such as Centerline, Border or Titleblock, Drawing Symbols, Dimensions, and Text or Lettering.

Are You Experienced?

Now you can...

☑ **create new layers and assign them a color and a linetype**

☑ **load a new linetype into your current drawing file**

☑ **move existing objects onto a new layer**

☑ **turn layers off and on**

☑ **freeze and thaw layers**

☑ **make a layer current and create objects on the current layer**

☑ **use the Walk tool to verify that objects are on the proper layers**

☑ **reset the linetype scale factor globally or for a selected object**

☑ **record action macros**

☑ **create layer states**

CHAPTER 7

Combining Objects into Blocks

- ▶ Creating and inserting blocks

- ▶ Using the Wblock command

- ▶ Detecting blocks in a drawing

- ▶ Working with AutoCAD's DesignCenter

- ▶ Controlling the appearance of palettes on your screen

C omputer drafting derives much of its efficiency from a feature that makes it possible to combine a collection of objects into an entity that behaves as a single object. AutoCAD calls these grouped objects a *block*. The AutoCAD tools that work specifically with blocks make it possible to do the following:

- ▶ Create a block in your current drawing
- ▶ Repeatedly place copies of a block in precise locations in your drawing
- ▶ Share blocks between drawings
- ▶ Create .dwg files either from blocks or from portions of your current drawing
- ▶ Store blocks on a palette for easy reuse in any drawing

In general, objects best suited to becoming part of a block are the components that are repeatedly used in your drawings. In architecture and construction, examples of these components are doors, windows, and fixtures; or drawing symbols, such as a North arrow; or labels for a section cut line (see Figure 7.1). In mechanical drawings, these can be countersunk and counterbored holes, screws, bolts, fasteners, switches, or any other objects that you find yourself repeatedly drawing. In your cabin drawing, you'll convert the doors with swings into blocks. You'll then create a new block that you'll use to place the windows in the cabin drawing. To accomplish these tasks, you need to learn two new commands: Block and Insert.

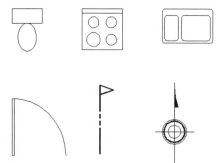

FIGURE 7.1: Examples of blocks often used in architectural drawings

Making a Block for a Door

When making a block, you create a *block definition*. This is an entity that is stored in the drawing file and consists of the following components:

- ▶ The block name
- ▶ An insertion point to help you place the block in the drawing
- ▶ The objects to be grouped into the block

You specify each of these in the course of using the Block command. When the command is completed, the objects are designated as a single block and the block definition is stored with the drawing file. You then insert additional copies of the block into the drawing using the Insert command.

N O T E In earlier chapters, I told you exactly what to click or enter to launch a command. Now that you're familiar with AutoCAD's interface, I'll simply instruct you to start a command or tool. In general, I'll refer to a command by the tooltip that appears when you place the cursor on the command's icon on the Ribbon or the command as it is entered at the Command: prompt. If the command doesn't have an icon on the Ribbon, I'll refer to its name on the associated menu or toolbar. In the rare case that the command doesn't appear in either place, I'll tell you what to enter in the Command window. Any command can be started by entering its name or an alias at the Command: **prompt.**

Before you create a block, you must consider the layers on which the objects to be blocked reside. When objects on Layer 0 are grouped into a block, they take on the color and linetype of the layer that is current when the block is inserted or the layer to which you move the block. Objects on other layers retain the properties of their original layers, regardless of which color or linetype has been assigned to the current layer. This is one characteristic that distinguishes Layer 0 from all other layers.

T I P The objects that compose blocks can reside on more than one layer.

As you define a block, you must decide which, if any, of the objects to be included in the block need to be on Layer 0 before they are blocked. If a block will always be on the same layer, the objects making up the block can remain on that layer. On the other hand, if a block may be inserted on several layers, the objects in the block need to be moved to Layer 0 before the block definition is created, to avoid confusion of colors and linetypes.

As you learn to make blocks for the doors, you'll also see how layers work in the process of creating block definitions. You'll create a block for the exterior swing door first, using the front door, and call it door3_0 to distinguish it from the smaller interior door. For the insertion point, you need to assign a point on or near the door that will facilitate its placement as a block in your drawing. The hinge point makes the best insertion point.

For this chapter, the Endpoint osnap should be running most of the time, and Polar Tracking should be off. Follow these steps to set up your drawing:

1. If you're continuing from the last chapter, skip to step 2. If you're starting a new session, once AutoCAD is running, click the Open button on

the Quick Access toolbar. In the Select File dialog box, highlight Cabin06c, and click Open. If this .dwg file isn't in the list, click the down arrow to the right of the Look In drop-down list at the top of the dialog box, navigate to your Training Data folder, and then select the file. This file is also available at www.sybex.com/go/autocad2010ner.

You're using the Freeze option for layers this time because you won't need to see the lines on the Roof, Fixtures, and Headers layers for a while. This might be a good time to consider creating another layer state.

2. Click the Layer drop-down list, and click the sun icon for the Headers layer to freeze it. The sun turns into a snowflake. Then click the Doors layer to close the list. The Doors layer is now current, and the headers, fixtures, and rooflines are no longer visible in the drawing (see Figure 7.2).

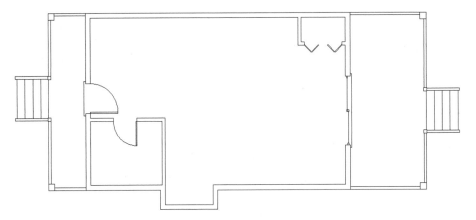

FIGURE 7.2: The floor plan with the Headers, Fixtures, and Roof layers frozen

3. Check the status bar, and make sure the Object Snap button is in the On position. Right-click the Object Snap button and make sure that, at a minimum, the Endpoint snap is running. If it isn't, click Endpoint on the context menu.

4. In the status bar, turn Polar Tracking off if it's on.

T I P   The features in the status bar and their particular options are AutoCAD settings and not saved as part of any particular drawing. Changes made on the status bar in one drawing are in effect when any subsequent drawings are opened or accessed.

5. You can also turn off Quick Properties to prevent the Quick Properties panel from opening whenever an object is selected.

Now you're ready to make blocks.

1. Click the Create button on the Ribbon's Block panel, located under the Insert tab, to open the Block Definition dialog box. Notice the flashing cursor in the Name text box. Type **door3_0**, but don't press ↵ (see Figure 7.3).

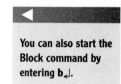

You can also start the Block command by entering **b**↵.

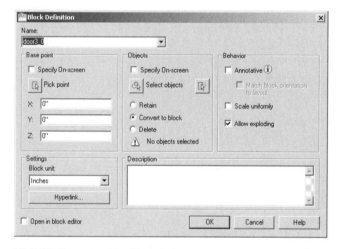

FIGURE 7.3: The Block Definition dialog box

2. Click the Pick Point button in the Base Point area. The dialog box temporarily closes, and you're returned to your drawing.

3. Use the scroll wheel on the mouse to zoom in to the back door area in your drawing.

4. Move the cursor to the back door area, and position it near the hinge point of the door. When the Endpoint marker appears on the hinge point (see Figure 7.4), click. This selects the insertion point for the door, and the Block Definition dialog box returns. The insertion point is the location, relative to the cursor, that the block references when it is inserted.

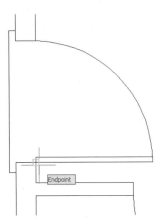

Endpoint

FIGURE 7.4: The back door opening when picking the hinge point as the insertion point

5. Click the Select Objects button in the Objects area. You're returned to the drawing again. The cursor changes to a pickbox, and the Command window displays the Select objects: prompt.

6. Select the door and swing, and then press ↵. You're returned to the Block Definition dialog box.

7. At the bottom of the Objects area, the count of selected objects appears. Just above that are three radio buttons. Click the Delete radio button if it's not already selected. The Delete option erases the selected objects after the block definition is created, requiring you to insert the block into the drawing. The Convert To Block option replaces objects with a block definition as soon as the block is created. In this situation, the Convert To Block option would be a better choice, but it's a good idea to get some practice using the Insert command, so click Delete.

8. Enter a description of the block in the Description field and make sure Inches or Millimeters is specified in the Block Unit drop-down list, depending on the units you are using. The Block Definition dialog box should look similar to Figure 7.5.

9. At the bottom of the dialog box, be sure the Open In Block Editor check box is not selected, and then click OK to close the dialog box. The door and swing disappear (see Figure 7.6).

You have now created a block definition, called door3_0. Block definitions are stored electronically with the drawing file. You need to insert the door3_0 block (known formally as a *block reference*) into the back door opening to replace the door and swing that were just deleted when the block was created.

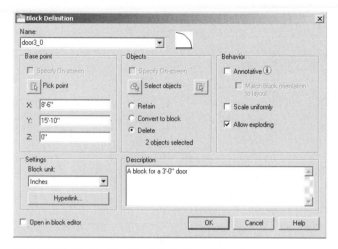

FIGURE 7.5: The Block Definition dialog box

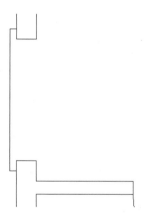

FIGURE 7.6: The back door area after creating the door3_0 block

Inserting the Door Block

You'll use the Insert command to place the door3_0 block back into the drawing.

1. On the Block panel, click the Insert button to open the Insert dialog box. At the top, the Name drop-down list contains the names of the blocks in the drawing. Open the list and select door3_0, which is the only block currently in the drawing. A preview of the block appears in the upper-right corner (see Figure 7.7). Below the Name list are three areas with the Specify On-Screen option. These are used for the insertion procedure.

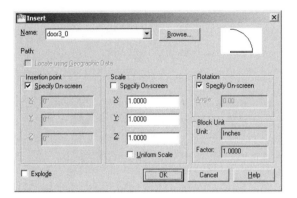

FIGURE 7.7: The Insert dialog box

2. Check the Specify On-screen options for the Insertion point and Rotation options, but leave Scale unchecked. (The scale of the door should not change unless it is used to flip the door, as shown in the next exercise.) Also, make sure the Explode check box in the lower-left corner is unchecked. Explode disassembles the block into its component parts upon insertion into the drawing.

3. Click OK. You're returned to your drawing, and the door3_0 block is now attached to the cursor, with the hinge point coinciding with the intersection of the crosshairs (see Figure 7.8). The Command window says Specify insertion point or [Basepoint/Scale/X/Y/Z/ Rotate]:.

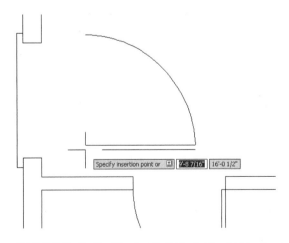

FIGURE 7.8: The door3_0 block attached to the cursor

4. With the Endpoint osnap running, move the cursor toward the right end of the lower jamb line in the back door opening. When the Endpoint marker appears at the jamb line's lower-right endpoint, click.

5. The door3_0 block is no longer attached to the cursor, and its insertion point has been placed at the right end of the lower jamb line. The block now rotates as you move the cursor (see the left of Figure 7.9). At the Specify rotation angle <0.00>: prompt, press ↵ again to accept the default angle of 0°. The door3_0 block properly appears in the drawing (see the right of Figure 7.9).

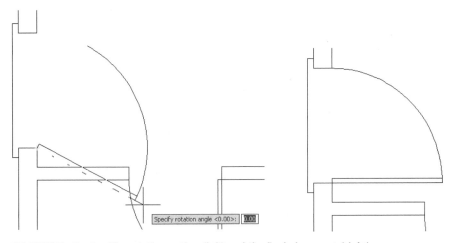

FIGURE 7.9: The rotation option (left) and the final placement (right)

Each time a block is inserted, you can specify the following on the screen or in the Insert dialog box:

- ► The location of the insertion point of the block

- ► The X and Y scale factors

- ► The Z scale factor in the dialog box (used for 3D drawings, in AutoCAD only)

- ► The rotation angle

As you insert blocks, you can stretch or flip them horizontally by specifying a negative X scale factor or vertically by specifying a negative Y scale factor, or you can rotate them from their original orientations. Because you created the door3_0 block from the door and swing that occupied the back door opening and the size was the same, inserting this block back into the back door opening

◄ Nothing has changed about the geometry of the door, but it's now a different kind of object. Before, it was a rectangle and an arc; now it's a block reference made up of a rectangle and an arc.

required no rotation, so you followed the defaults. You can insert the same block into the back door opening and flip the door horizontally by flipping the Y scale factor.

Flipping a Block While Inserting It

Flipping the block is only a temporary change, so you'll want to be able to get your drawing back to the state that it is in now quickly. To make that possible, you'll first use the Mark option of the Undo command. Mark sets a point in your drawing that you can return to, regardless of the number of subsequent steps that are taken, by using the Undo command's Back option. Follow these steps to set the Undo Mark:

1. Enter **undo**↵ at the Command: prompt. For this situation you cannot use the U command or press the Undo button on the Quick Access toolbar.

2. At the Enter the number of operations to undo or [Auto/Control/BEgin/End/Mark/Back] <1>: prompt, enter **m**↵ for the Mark option. The Undo command ends.

3. Use the Erase command to erase the door and swing, the door3_0 block, from the back door opening.

4. Click the Insert button in the Block panel or enter **i**↵. In the Insert dialog box, door3_0 should still be in the Name drop-down list. Check the Specify On-Screen option for the Scale option.

5. Click OK. You're returned to your drawing, and the door3_0 block is attached to the cursor.

6. Move the cursor to the right end of the upper jamb line. When the osnap marker appears at that endpoint (see the left of Figure 7.10), click. AutoCAD places the insertion point, and the prompt is now Enter X scale factor, specify opposite corner, or [Corner/XYZ]<1>:.

7. Press ↵ to accept the default X scale factor of 1. The prompt changes to Specify Y scale factor <use X scale factor:. To flip the door down so that it spans the door opening, you need to give the Y scale factor a value of −1.

8. Enter **-1**↵. Then press ↵ again to accept the default rotation angle of 0°. The Insert command ends, and the door3_0 block appears in the back door opening (see the right of Figure 7.10).

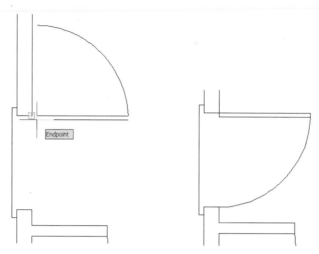

FIGURE 7.10: Placing the door3_0 insertion point (left) and the block after insertion (right)

9. You don't want the door hinged on the side where it is now, so you need to restore the block as it was inserted before you deleted it. Enter **undo↵** and then **b↵** to choose the Back option, which returns your drawing to the state it was in when you used the Mark option.

N O T E   When inserting a block, giving a value of –1 to the X or Y scale factor has the effect of flipping the block, much like the Mirror command did in Chapter 4, when you first drew the doors. Because you can flip or rotate the door3_0 block as it's inserted, you can use this block to place a door and swing in any 3'-0" opening, regardless of its orientation.

Doors are traditionally sorted into four categories, depending on which side the hinges and doorknob are on and which way the door swings open. To be able to use one door block for all openings of the same size, you need to know the following:

▶ How the door and swing in the block are oriented

▶ Where the hinge point is to be in the next opening

▶ How the block has to be flipped and/or rotated during the insertion process to fit properly in the next doorway opening

Blocking and Inserting the Interior Door

Because the interior door is smaller, you need to make a new block for it. You could insert the door3_0 block with a 5/6 scale factor, but this would also reduce the door thickness by the same factor, and you don't want that.

After you finish the swinging doors, I'll go into some detail about AutoCAD's *dynamic block*, which you can use for all swinging doors.

On the other hand, for consistency, it's a good idea to orient all door blocks the same way, and the bathroom door is turned relative to the door3_0 block. You'll move and rotate the bathroom door and its swing to orient it like the back door:

1. Use Zoom Window to define a window that encloses the bathroom door. The view changes to a close-up of the area enclosed in your window (see Figure 7.11).

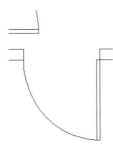

FIGURE 7.11: The result of a zoom window

2. Repeat a procedure similar to the one you used to make a block out of the back door and swing to make a block out of the bathroom door and swing. Here is a summary of the steps:

   a. Start the Block command. (Click the Create button on the Block panel.)

   b. In the dialog box, type **door2_6** to name the new block. Don't press ↵.

   c. Click the Pick Point button, and pick the hinge point of the bathroom door.

   d. Click the Select Objects button, and pick the door and swing. Then press ↵.

   e. In the Objects area, make sure the Delete radio button is selected.

   f. Make sure the Block Unit option is correct and add a description.

   g. Click OK. The door and swing disappear.

3. Insert the door2_6 block in the bathroom doorway opening. Follow the steps carefully. Here's a summary:

   a. Start the Insert command.

   b. Open the Name drop-down list, select door2_6, and then click OK.

   c. Pick the bottom end of the right jamb line.

   d. Accept the scale factors of 1 and the default 0 for the rotation.

 N O T E   If all your doors are at 90° angles, you can turn on Ortho mode to speed up the rotation process. With Ortho active, wherever you move the cursor at the `Specify rotation angle <0.00>:` prompt, the rotations are restricted to 90° increments.

4. Use the Zoom Extents tool to show all of the cabin in the drawing area (see Figure 7.12).

5. Save your drawing as Cabin07a.dwg.

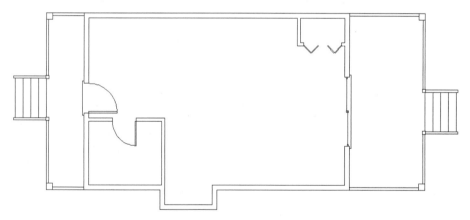

F I G U R E 7 . 1 2 : The floor plan with all swinging doors converted into blocks

 T I P   If you have trouble anticipating how a block such as the door block needs to be flipped or rotated during insertion, don't worry about it; just be sure to locate the insertion point accurately in the drawing. Then, after the block is inserted, you can flip or turn it by using the Mirror and Rotate commands.

THE FATE OF OBJECTS USED TO MAKE A BLOCK

The three radio buttons in the Objects area of the Block Definition dialog box represent the options you have for objects transformed into a block:

Retain The objects remain unblocked. Click this if you want to make several similar blocks from the same set of objects.

Convert To Block The objects become the block reference. Click this if the first use of the block has geometry identical to that of the set of objects it's replacing.

Delete The objects are automatically erased after the block has been defined. Click this if the first use of the block will be at a different scale, orientation, or location from the set of objects it's replacing.

This view looks the same as the view you started with at the beginning of this chapter (see Figure 7.2). Blocks look the same as other objects, and you can't detect them by sight. They're useful because you can use them over and over again in a drawing or in many drawings, and because the block is a combination of two or more (and sometimes many more) objects represented as a single object. Your next task is to learn how to detect a block, but first, I'll discuss AutoCAD's dynamic block feature.

Using Dynamic Blocks

Dynamic blocks are blocks whose appearance can be changed in a variety of ways, depending on how they are set up. Any block can be transformed into a dynamic block, and AutoCAD offers several sample dynamic blocks that have already been set up. Take a door block, for example. By adding extra parameters and controls to the block, you could use a single dynamic block for openings in a variety of preset sizes. The arc size would change but the thickness of the door would remain the same. After you insert a dynamic block, click it. In Figure 7.13, arrows appear at opposite sides of the opening to indicate that these are adjustable parameters. This is just an example and not steps for you to follow at this time.

When you click the arrow at the end of the door swing arc, the dynamics begin and markers appear below the opening (see Figure 7.14), indicating the preset sizes to which the door and swing can be changed. In this example, you can use the door for openings from 2'-0" to 3'-6", at 6" intervals. (The tooltip shows where the cursor is, not the door size.)

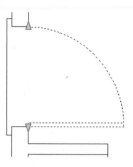

F I G U R E   7 . 1 3 : Arrows appear at the locations in a dynamic block where the parameters are adjustable.

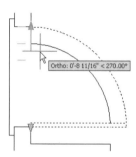

F I G U R E   7 . 1 4 : Markers appear at the increments where the door's swing can be adjusted.

Once you set a new size, the door and swing take on that size, as shown in Figure 7.15, whereas the door thickness remains the same. Now you can move this door to a smaller opening.

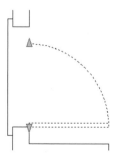

F I G U R E   7 . 1 5 : The dynamic door block with a smaller door and swing

Later in this chapter, when I introduce *palettes*, I'll show you where to find AutoCAD's sample dynamic blocks. For instructions on creating and using dynamic blocks, see Chapter 9, "Using Dynamic Blocks and Tables."

Finding Blocks in a Drawing

You can detect blocks in a drawing in at least three ways: by using grips, by using the List command, and by looking at the Properties palette.

Using Grips to Detect a Block

Grips appear on objects that are selected when no command is started. When an object that isn't a block is selected, grips appear at strategic places such as endpoints, midpoints, and center points. But if you select a block, by default only one grip appears, and it's always located at the block's insertion point. Because of this, clicking an object when no command is started is a quick way to see whether the object is a block:

1. At the Command: prompt, click one of the door swings. The door and swing turn into dashed lines, and a square blue grip appears at the hinge point, as shown in Figure 7.16.

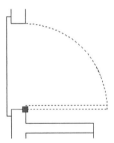

FIGURE 7.16: Blocks have only one grip, at the insertion point.

2. Press Esc to clear the grip.

3. Expand the Application menu, click the Options button at the bottom of the menu to open the Options dialog box, and then click the Selection tab. The Grips area is on the right side and Enable Grips Within Blocks is unchecked by default (see Figure 7.17). If this option is checked, grips appear on all objects in the block as if they weren't blocked when you click a block with no command running. Leave this setting unchecked.

   You can also change the size of the grip and any of the three color states. By default, unselected grips are blue, grips that you click to select are red, and grips over which you pause the cursor are green.

4. Click OK or Cancel to close the Options dialog box.

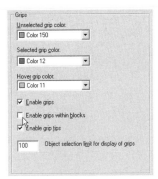

FIGURE 7.17: The Enable Grips Within Blocks option

We'll look at grips in more detail in Chapter 12, "Dimensioning a Drawing." You might need to know more about a block than just whether something is one. If that is the case, you'll need to use the List command.

Using the List Command to Detect a Block

You can use the List command to learn more about a block:

1. Click the List button in the expanded Properties panel, or enter li⏎ at the Command: prompt.

2. Click the back door block, and then press ⏎. The AutoCAD Text Window temporarily covers the drawing area (see Figure 7.18). In the Text Window, you can see the words BLOCK REFERENCE Layer: "DOORS", followed by 12 lines of text. These 13 lines describe the block you selected.

```
AutoCAD Text Window - Cabin07a Imperial.dwg                    _|□|X|
Edit

Command: _Options
Command:
Command:
Command: _list
Select objects: 1 found

Select objects:
                  BLOCK REFERENCE  Layer: "Doors"
                           Space: Model space
                  Color: 7 (white)    Linetype: "BYLAYER"
                  Handle = 232
      Block Name: "door3_0"
               at point, X=    8'-6"  Y=  15'-10"  Z=     0'-0"
  X scale factor:     1.0000
  Y scale factor:     1.0000
  rotation angle:     0.00
  Z scale factor:     1.0000
        InsUnits: Inches
  Unit conversion:    1.0000
  Scale uniformly: No
  Allow exploding: Yes

Command:                                             ◄| |   ►|
```

FIGURE 7.18: The AutoCAD Text Window

The information stored in the Text Window includes the following:

▶ What the object is (block reference)

▶ The layer the object is on (Doors layer)

▶ The name of the block (door3_0)

▶ The coordinates of the insertion point in the drawing

▶ The X, Y, and Z scale factors

▶ The rotation angle

3. Press F2. The AutoCAD Text Window closes.

T I P   The AutoCAD Text Window isn't exclusively for use with the List command. Instead, it is a constantly scrolling history of the command prompt. The F2 key acts as a toggle to turn the window on and off. You can even copy information from all but the bottom line for use inside or outside AutoCAD. The Text Window displays only one page of information at a time and then pauses while the Press ENTER to continue: prompt appears at the command line. Press ⏎ to continue. If you need to see information that has scrolled off the window, use the scroll bar on the right side or roll the mouse wheel to bring it back into view.

4. Right-click, and choose Repeat LIST from the context menu.

5. At the Select objects: prompt, click one of the steps that make up the back staircase, then click one of the wall lines, and finally press ⏎.

6. The Text Window appears again, and you can see information about the stair polyline that you selected.

7. If the last line reads Press ENTER to continue:, then the amount of information is too large for the Text Window. Press ⏎ to display the remaining information.

8. Press F2 several times to switch back and forth between the Text Window and the drawing or move the Text Window so that you can see the command line. Notice that the last two or three lines in the Text Window appear in the Command window at the bottom of the drawing (see Figure 7.19), depending on the size of your Command window.

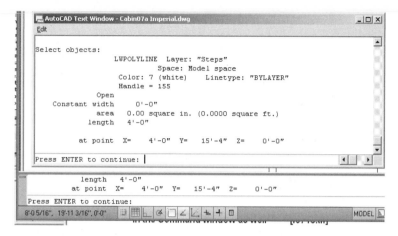

FIGURE 7.19: The bottom few lines of the Text Window appear in the Command window as well.

9. Press F2 to close the Text Window.

Using the Properties Palette to Examine a Block

In Chapter 6, you used the Properties palette to change the individual linetype scale for the roof objects. It can also be a tool for investigating objects in your drawing. When the Properties palette is open and only one object is selected, it displays data specific to the selected object. If multiple objects are selected, it shows only the data shared by those objects.

1. Select one of the door blocks.

2. Click the Properties button on the Palettes panel of the Ribbon's View tab, or right-click and choose Properties from the context menu. The Properties palette opens.

The data displayed on the palette is similar to that displayed when you used the List command, but it's in a slightly different form (see Figure 7.20). At the top of the dialog box, a drop-down list displays the type of object selected—in this case, a block reference. The fields that are white signify items that you can change directly in the palette, and items that are grayed out cannot be changed. You can't change any values in the AutoCAD Text Window.

Block insertion means the same thing as *block reference*, and both are casually called *blocks*.

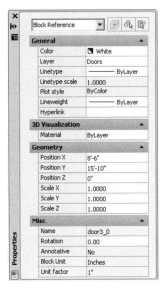

FIGURE 7.20: The Properties palette with a door block selected

3. Close the Properties palette by clicking the X in the upper-left or upper-right corner; then press Esc to deselect the door block.

T I P   The X you click to close the Properties palette is in the upper-left or upper-right corner of the palette if it's floating and in the upper-right corner if it's docked.

If you're ever working on a drawing that someone else created, these tools for finding out about objects will be invaluable. The next exercise on working with blocks involves placing windows in the walls of the cabin.

Creating a Window Block

You can create all the windows in the cabin floor plan from one block, even though the windows are four different sizes (see Figure 7.21). You'll create a window block and then go from room to room to insert the block into the walls:

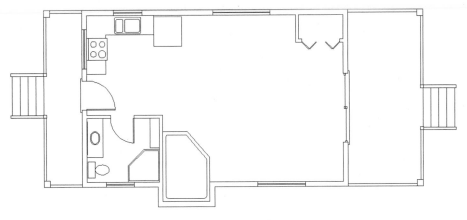

FIGURE 7.21: The cabin windows in the floor plan

1. Make Layer 0 the current layer.

2. Right-click the Object Snap button on the status bar and click the Midpoint and Perpendicular osnaps, if necessary, to set them as running osnaps, and then deselect Intersection. The osnap menu should look similar to Figure 7.22. Turn on the Object Snap option in the status bar.

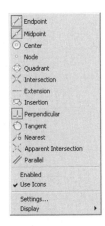

FIGURE 7.22: The osnap menu

3. Using a zoom window, zoom in to a horizontal section of wall where there are no jamb lines or intersections with other walls (see Figure 7.23). Because the widths of the windows in the cabin are multiples of 12″ (305 mm), you can insert a block made from a 12″

(305 mm)-wide window for each window, and you can apply an X scale factor to the block to make it the right width. The first step is to draw a 12″ (305 mm)-wide window inside the wall lines.

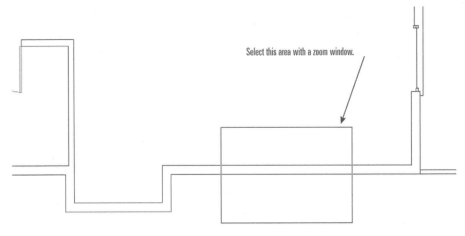

Select this area with a zoom window.

FIGURE 7.23: Making a zoom window

Use the Nearest osnap button when you want to locate a point somewhere on an object but aren't concerned exactly where on the object the point is located.

4. Start the Line command, and then click the Nearest osnap button on the Shift+right-click menu or enter **nea↵**. The Nearest osnap will allow you to start a line on one of the wall lines; it snaps the cursor to any part of any object under the cursor and guarantees that the objects form an intersection but do not cross.

5. Move the cursor to the upper wall line, a little to the left of the center of the screen and, with the hourglass-shaped marker displayed, as shown in Figure 7.24, click. A line begins on the upper wall line.

Nearest

FIGURE 7.24: Starting the line using the Nearest osnap

6. Move the cursor to the lower wall line. The Perpendicular marker appears directly below the point you previously picked. When it's displayed, click. The line is drawn between the wall lines, as shown in Figure 7.25. Press ↵ to end the Line command.

FIGURE 7.25: Drawing the first window line

7. Start the Offset command. Enter 12↵ (305) to set the offset distance to 12″ (305 mm). Pick the line you just drew, and then pick a point to the right of that line. The line is offset 12″ (305 mm) to the right. Press ↵ to end the Offset command.

8. Start the Line command again. Move the cursor near the midpoint of the line you first drew. When the Midpoint marker appears, click. Move the cursor near the midpoint of the line that was just offset. When the Perpendicular or Midpoint symbol appears, click. Press ↵ to end the Line command. Your drawing should look like Figure 7.26.

FIGURE 7.26: Completed lines for the window block

The three lines you've drawn will make up a window block. They represent the two jamb lines and the glass (usually called *glazing*). By varying the X scale factor from 2 to 6, you can create windows 2′ (610 mm), 3′ (915 mm), 4′ (1220 mm), 5′ (1525 mm), and 6′ (1830 mm) wide. This is a single-line representation, with no double lines to indicate the frames, so for scaling the blocks there is no thickness issue as there was with the doors.

Before you create the block, you need to decide the best place for the insertion point. For the doors, you chose the hinge point because you always know where it will be in the drawing. Locating a similar strategic point for the window is a little more difficult but certainly possible. You know the insertion point shouldn't be on the horizontal line representing the glazing, because it will always rest in the middle of the wall. There is no guideline in the drawing for the middle of the wall, and this would require a temporary tracking point every time a window is inserted. Windows are usually dimensioned to the midpoint of the glazing line rather than to either jamb line, so you don't want the insertion point to be at the endpoint of a jamb line. The insertion point needs to be positioned on a wall line but also lined up with the midpoint of the glazing line.

To locate this point, you'll use an object snap called Mid Between 2 Points. As the name suggests, the M2P osnap, as it's commonly called, snaps to a point midway between two other points you select. Follow these steps to set the base point for the window block along the outside wall line and midway between the window's edges:

1. Start the Block command by clicking the Create button in the Block panel.

2. In the Block Definition dialog box, enter **win-1** for the block name, and then click the Pick Point button.

3. Back in the drawing, Shift+right-click and then click the Mid Between 2 Points option in the context menu (this osnap is not available from the Object Snap toolbar), or enter **m2p↵**.

4. With the Endpoint osnap running, move the cursor to the lower end of the left window jamb (see Figure 7.27) and click when the Endpoint marker appears.

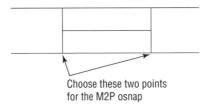

Choose these two points
for the M2P osnap

F I G U R E   7 . 2 7 : Select the two endpoints for the M2P osnap.

5. Click the lower end of the right jamb to define the insertion point midway between the two endpoints that you picked.

6. In the Block Definition dialog box, click the Select Objects button.

7. Back in the drawing, select the two jamb lines and the glazing line, then press ↵.

8. Back in the dialog box, be sure the Open In Block Editor check box at the bottom is unchecked, the Delete radio button is selected, and Units is set to Inches (Millimeters). Then click OK. The win-1 block has been defined, and the 12″ (305 mm) window has been erased.

9. Use Zoom Previous to zoom out to a view of the whole floor plan.

This completes the definition of the block that will represent the windows. The next task is to insert the win-1 block where the windows will be located and scale them properly.

UNDERSTANDING GROUPS

Another way you can make several objects act as one is to use the Group command. *Groups* differ from blocks in that they do not replace separate objects with a single definition but instead associate several objects by name so they react as if they are a single object. (Some similar programs use the term *named selection set* to represent what AutoCAD calls a group.) Selecting one member object from the group selects all the members. Unlike with objects in a block, you can add or remove members of a group and toggle the group to allow the individual members to be selected. Use groups when you know the association between the objects is not permanent, and use blocks when it might be. The procedure for creating a group is as follows:

1. Enter **group**⏎ at the command line to open the Object Grouping dialog box.

2. Enter a name for the group in the Group Name field.

3. Click the New< button in the Create Group area. The dialog box closes temporarily.

Continues

UNDERSTANDING GROUPS *(Continued)*

4. Select the objects to be added to the group, and then press ↵. The Object Grouping dialog box reopens, and the group name appears in the field at the top. Select the group name.

Clicking the Selectable button in the Change Group section (not the Selectable check box in the Create Group section) acts as a toggle that causes the group members to react to selection picks as if they are not members of a group. The Add< and Remove< buttons increase or decrease the membership of the group, and Explode destroys the group, leaving its member objects as individuals again.

Inserting the Window Block

Several factors come into play when deciding where to locate windows in a floor plan:

▶ The structure of the building

▶ The appearance of windows from outside the building

▶ The appearance of windows from inside a room

▶ The location of fixtures that might interfere with placement

▶ The sun angle and climate considerations

For this exercise, you'll work on the windows for each room, starting with the kitchen, and make a total of five windows at either 3'-0", 4'-0", 5'-0", or 6'-0" wide (see Figure 7.28).

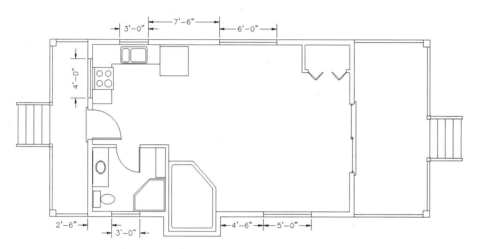

FIGURE 7.28: The cabin's window sizes and locations

Rotating a Block During Insertion

As you can see in Figure 7.28, the kitchen has windows on two walls: one 4'-0" (1220 mm) window centered over the stove in the back wall and one 3'-0" (915 mm) window centered over the sink in the top wall.

You'll make the 4" (1220 mm) window first:

1. Thaw the Fixtures layer; you'll need to see the sink and stove to place the windows properly.

2. Zoom in to a view of the kitchen so that you can see both walls, as shown in Figure 7.29.

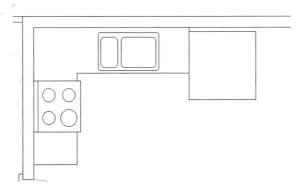

FIGURE 7.29: Zoom in to the kitchen.

3. Click the Polar Tracking button on the status bar to turn on polar tracking. Polar Tracking, Object Snap, Object Snap Tracking, and Dynamic Input should now be in their On positions.

4. Create a new layer by clicking the Layer Properties button and then clicking the New Layer button in the Layer Properties Manager dialog box. The new Layer1 layer appears and is highlighted. Enter **Windows↵** to rename the layer.

5. Click the Color swatch in the Windows row to open the Select Color dialog box, with the white swatch highlighted and *white* listed in the Color text box. Enter **30↵** to change the color to a bright orange. The Select Color dialog box closes.

6. With Windows still highlighted in the Layer Properties Manager dialog box, click the Set Current button, or double-click the name of the layer, to make the Windows layer current. Close or auto-hide the Layer Properties Manager.

7. Start the Insert command (click the Insert button in the Block panel). Open the Name drop-down list in the Insert dialog box. In the list of blocks, click win-1. Be sure all three Specify On-Screen check boxes are selected, and then click OK.

8. In your drawing, the 12″ (305 mm) window block is attached to the cursor at the insertion point (see Figure 7.30). Note that it's still in the same horizontal orientation that it was in when you defined the block. To fit it into the left wall, you'll need to rotate it as you insert it.

9. Move the cursor along the inside wall line near the midpoint of the stove. The stove line overlaps the wall line and the midpoints of each are close together. Make sure the cursor is over the stove's midpoint (the lower of the two, as shown at the left of Figure 7.31), and then click.

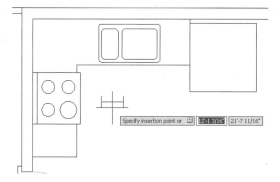

FIGURE 7.30: The win-1 block attached to the cursor

10. You're prompted for an X scale factor. This is a 4'-0" (1220 mm) window, so enter 4↵. For the Y scale factor, enter 1↵.

11. You're prompted for the rotation angle. The window block is now 4'-0" (1220 mm) wide and rotates with the movement of the cursor. Move the cursor so that it's directly above the insertion point. The polar tracking lines and tooltip appear (see the middle of Figure 7.31). They show you how the window will be positioned if the rotation stays at 90°. The window fits nicely into the wall here.

12. With the tracking line and tooltip visible, click. The win-1 block appears in the left wall. The Insert Block command ends (see the right of Figure 7.31).

The Y scale factor will be 1 for all the win-1 blocks because all walls that have windows are 6" wide—the same width as the win-1 block.

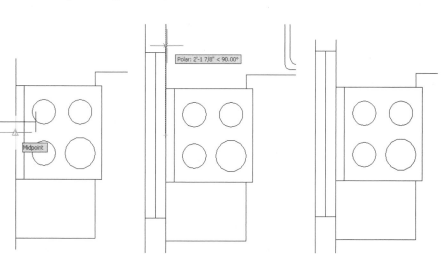

FIGURE 7.31: Selecting the stove's midpoint as the insertion point (left), rotating the win-1 block 90° (middle), and the final position (right)

Using Snap Tracking to Set the Insertion Point

The window over the sink is centered on the sink, but the sink line doesn't overlap the wall as did the stove line. You'll use the same snap tracking procedure that you used in Chapter 5 to set the window block's insertion point without the need to draw extraneous geometry. Refer to Figure 7.28, shown earlier, as a reference as you follow the procedure here:

1. Use the Pan and Zoom tools to get a better view of the top wall of the cabin.

   You want to create one 3'-0" (915 mm) window, centered over the sink. Be sure the Endpoint and Midpoint osnaps are running, and turn off the Perpendicular osnap.

2. Start the Insert command. Be sure win-1 is in the Name drop-down list, and check that all Specify On-Screen check boxes are marked. Click OK.

3. At the Specify insertion point: prompt, position the crosshair cursor over the intersection of the inside wall lines in the top-left corner of the cabin, as shown in Figure 7.32.

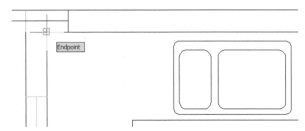

FIGURE 7.32: Setting the first tracking point to locate the window block

When Object Snap Tracking is turned on and the + appears at the object snap marker, a tracking point has been *acquired*. It remains acquired until you place the cursor directly on the object snap symbol a second time or until that part of the command is done.

4. When the temporary track point appears inside the Endpoint marker, move the cursor, without clicking, over the Midpoint marker for the topmost line of the sink.

5. When the temporary track point appears inside the Midpoint marker, move the cursor directly above that point to the intersection of the two track points. You have set, or *acquired,* two temporary tracking points without using the Temporary Tracking Point osnap.

6. When the crosshair reaches a point directly above the first tracking point, a vertical tracking line appears and the tooltip identifies the intersection of the two tracking lines as Endpoint: <0.00°, Midpoint: <90.00° (see Figure 7.33). When you see this tooltip, click. This places the insertion point on the inside wall line, centered over the sink.

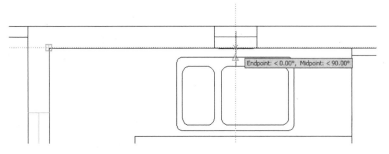

FIGURE 7.33: Setting the insertion point for the window block

7. At the X scale factor prompt, enter **3**↵. Then, at the Y scale factor prompt, enter **1**↵. Press ↵ again to accept the default rotation angle of 0°. The 3′-0″ (915 mm) window is inserted into the wall behind the sink. Your kitchen with the second window block inserted should look like Figure 7.34.

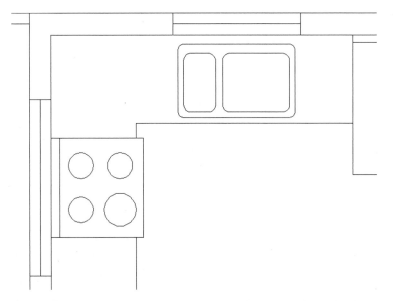

FIGURE 7.34: The kitchen after inserting the second window block

As you can see, using the Object Snap Tracking tool, you can quickly and precisely locate an insertion point even when a snappable feature doesn't exist.

T I P   When using object snap tracking, you'll inevitably acquire a tracking point that you don't need or want. To remove it, place the crosshair cursor on it momentarily. The tracking point will disappear.

Changing a Block's Scale Factor Using Object Properties

You've inserted two different-sized window blocks at two different rotations. Just three remain to be inserted: one in the bathroom and two in the living room. You'll copy the horizontal kitchen window into the living room and then use the Properties palette to change the block's scale, resulting in a 6'-0" (1830 mm) window.

1. Pan and zoom to get a good view of the kitchen and the top of the living room.

   Referring back to Figure 7.28, you see that the windows are 7'-6" (2286 mm) apart. Because the insertion points are centered horizontally in the blocks, the insertion points of the two windows are 12'-0" (3659 mm) apart. You need to copy the 3'-0" (915 mm) kitchen window 12'-0" (3659 mm) to the right.

2. Select the 3'-0" (915 mm) kitchen window and click the Copy tool in the Modify panel.

3. At the Specify base point: prompt, click anywhere in the drawing area. Clicking near the block that you are moving will keep everything visually compact.

4. Move the cursor directly to the right; then, at the Specify second point or <use first point as displacement>: prompt, enter 12'↵ (3659↵), as shown in Figure 7.35, and press ↵ again to terminate the Copy command.

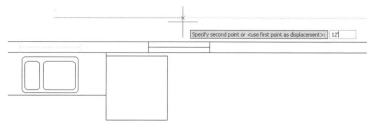

FIGURE 7.35: Copying the kitchen window 12' to the right

5. The window is copied 12'-0" (3659 mm) to the right. Select the new window block, right-click, and then choose Properties from the context menu to open the Properties palette.

6. In the Geometry rollout, locate the Scale X parameter and change its value to 6, as shown in Figure 7.36.

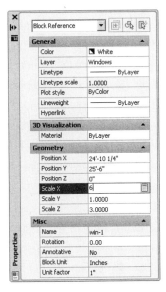

FIGURE 7.36: Change the block's X scale factor in the Properties palette.

7. The window in the living room is now 6'-0" (1830 mm) wide. Close the Properties palette, and press Esc to deselect the new window.

As you've seen, you can change many of an object's parameters, including the scale factors for a block definition, using the Properties palette.

Finishing the Windows

The last two windows to insert are both in the bottom wall, one in the living room and one in the bathroom. You'll use skills you've already developed to place them:

1. Use the Zoom and Pan tools to adjust your view of the drawing down to the bottom wall between the front wall and the hot tub. This window is 5'-0" (1525 mm) wide, and its insertion point is 7'-0" (2134 mm) (4'-6" + 2'-6") (1372 mm + 762 mm) from the pop-out for the hot tub.

2. Start the Insert command, verify that win-1 appears in the Name field, and click OK. Place the cursor over the intersection of the outside wall lines on the upper-right side of the pop-out, as shown in Figure 7.37.

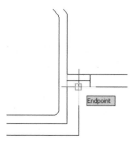

FIGURE 7.37: Selecting the first point to define the insertion point

3. Move the cursor directly to the right and enter 7'↵ (2134↵). The window is inserted 7'-0" (2134 mm) to the right of the corner. Give the new block an X scale factor of 5, a Y scale factor of 1, and a rotation of 0°. The new window appears as shown in Figure 7.38.

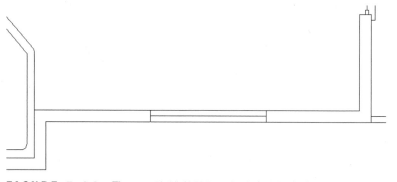

FIGURE 7.38: The new 5'-0" (1525 mm) window in the living room

T I P If you can't recall a typed-in command, you can enter the first letter or two of the command and then use the Tab key to cycle through all the Auto-CAD commands that begin with the letters you entered. When the correct command appears at the command prompt, press Enter to activate it.

The final window that you need to draw is the 3'-0" (915 mm) window in the bathroom. The insertion point is located 4'-0" (1220 mm)

from the bottom-left outside corner of the cabin. To create this window, you'll copy the living room window that you just drew and then change the X scale factor using the Properties palette.

4. Select the 5'-0" (1525 mm) window in the living room and start the Copy command.

5. At the Specify base point: prompt, hold down the Shift key and press the right mouse button to open the Object Snap context menu. Click the Insert icon to activate the Insertion Point object snap and temporarily disable the running osnaps.

6. Place the cursor over the window block until the Insert marker appears (see Figure 7.39); then click to define the base point for the Copy command as the insertion point of the block.

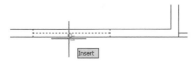

FIGURE 7.39: Snapping to the insertion point of the block

7. At the Specify second point or <use first point as displacement>: prompt, pause the cursor over the bottom-left outside corner of the cabin to acquire a temporary track point.

8. Move the cursor directly to the right, and enter 4'↵ (1220↵), as shown in Figure 7.40. The window is copied to its new location 4'-0" (1220 mm) from the corner. Press ↵ again to end the Copy command.

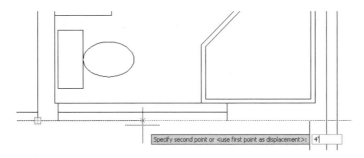

FIGURE 7.40: Setting the Copy command's second point 4' (1220 mm) from the corner

9. Select the new window and open the Properties palette; then change the Scale X parameter to 3.

10. The window resizes to 3′-0″ (915 mm) wide, as shown in Figure 7.41. Close the Properties palette and press Esc to end the Copy command.

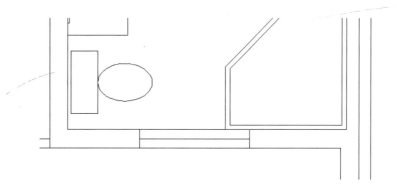

FIGURE 7.41: The new 3′-0″ (915 mm) window in the bathroom

 T I P   In a cluttered area, you can enter non↵ at any Select Point: or Select Objects: **prompt to disable all running osnaps for the duration of a single pick.**

---

 11. From the menu bar, choose View ➤ Zoom ➤ Extents to zoom out to the Extents of the drawing, displaying all the objects within the drawing area. This changes the view to include all the visible lines, and the view fills the drawing area.

12. Use the scroll wheel to zoom out a little from the Extents view so that all objects are set in slightly from the edge of the drawing area. Your drawing, with all the windows in place, should look like Figure 7.42.

13. Save this drawing as Cabin07b.dwg.

You have inserted five windows into the floor plan, each generated from the win-1 block. You created the win-1 block on Layer 0 and then made the Windows layer current, so each window block reference took on the characteristics of the Windows layer when it was inserted.

T I P All your windows are in 6″ (150 mm) thick walls, so they are all 6″ (150 mm) wide. But what if you want to put a window block in a 4″ (100 mm) wall between two interior rooms? You can still use the win-1 block. During insertion, you change the Y scale factor to 2/3 to reflect the change in thickness of the wall.

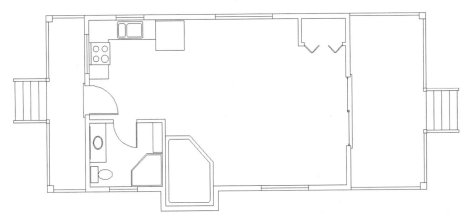

FIGURE 7.42: The cabin drawing after inserting the windows and adjusting the zoom factor

      You can disassociate the components of blocks by using the Explode command. The tool is found in the Modify panel or on the bottom item on the Modify menu. Exploding a block has the effect of reducing the block to the objects that make it up. Exploding the win-1 block reduces it to three lines, all on Layer 0. If you explode one of the door blocks, it's reduced to a rectangle and an arc, with both objects on the Doors layer because these components of the door block were on the Doors layer when you defined it.

> You can also start the Explode command by entering **explode**⏎.

Revising a Block

If you need to revise a block that has already been inserted in the drawing several times, choose a block whose X and Y scale factors are equal. You inserted all the windows using different X and Y scale factors, so to revise the win-1 block you'll need to insert that block one more time, this time using the same X and Y scale factors. You can then modify the objects that make up the win-1 block reference. When finished with the changes, you can save them to the block definition. This redefines the block and updates all associated block references.

Let's say that the client who's building the cabin finds out that double glazing is required in all windows. You'll want the windows to show two lines for the glass. If you revise the win-1 block definition, the changes you make in one block reference will be made in all six windows.

N O T E   Using standard commands, you can move, rotate, copy, erase, scale, and explode blocks. All objects in a block are associated and behave as if they were one object.

1. Click the Ribbon's Insert tab and then click the Block Editor button in the Block panel, or enter **bedit**↵ at the Command: prompt.

2. Select the win-1 block reference listed in the Edit Block Definition dialog box shown in Figure 7.43, and the block appears in the preview window.

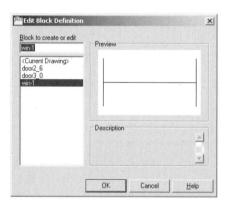

F I G U R E   7 . 4 3 : The Edit Block Definition dialog box

3. Click OK. In the drawing area, the rest of the drawing disappears, the background turns gray, and the Block Editor tab and panels appear in the Ribbon. Only the win-1 block and the Block Authoring Palettes remain (see Figure 7.44). You are now in the Block Editor mode.

4. Use the Offset command to offset the glazing line 0.5″ (13 mm) up and down. Then erase the original horizontal line (see Figure 7.45). This window block now has double glazing.

5. On the Open/Save panel, click the Save Block button.

6. In the Close panel, at the far right end of the Ribbon, click the Close button. The Block Editor closes and you are returned to the cabin drawing.

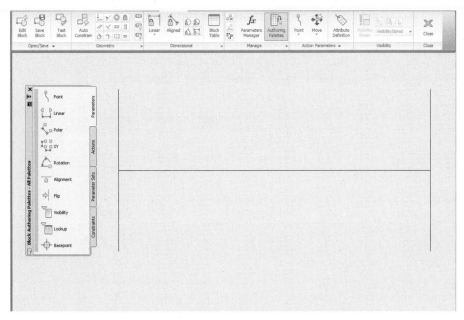

F I G U R E 7 . 4 4 : The drawing area and Ribbon in the Block Editor mode

F I G U R E 7 . 4 5 : The result of the modifications to the win-1 block

N O T E If you click the Close button without saving the changes to the block, an AutoCAD warning window appears providing you with the opportunity to save the changes or exit the Block Editor without saving the changes.

7. Use Zoom Previous tool to view the entire drawing. All windows in the cabin now have double glazing.

8. Zoom in to a closer look at the kitchen in order to view some of the modified window block references (see Figure 7.46).

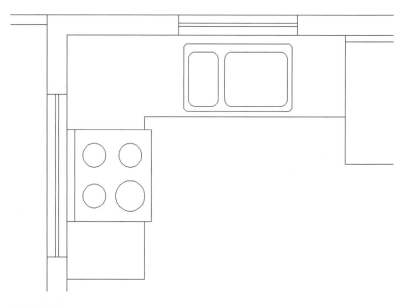

F I G U R E 7 . 4 6 : Zooming in to see the revised window blocks with double glazing

9. Use Zoom Previous to see a view of the entire floor plan. Save this drawing as Cabin07c.dwg.

Named objects are, quite simply, AutoCAD objects with names, such as blocks and layers. Lines, circles, and arcs don't have individual names, so they aren't named objects.

Sharing Information Between Drawings

You can transfer most of the information in a drawing to another drawing. You can do so in several ways, depending on the kind of information that you need to transfer. You can drag blocks and lines from one open drawing to another when both drawings are visible on the screen. You can copy layers, blocks, and other *named objects* from a closed drawing into an open one using the Design-Center. I'll demonstrate these two features—and touch on a few others—as I finish this chapter.

Dragging and Dropping Between Two Open Drawings

In AutoCAD, several drawings can be open at the same time, just like documents in a word processing program. You can control which one is visible, or you can tile two or more to be visible simultaneously. When more than one drawing is visible, you can drag objects from one drawing to another.

1. With Cabin07c.dwg as the current drawing, click the New button on the Quick Access toolbar. In the Select Template dialog box, click the arrow next to the Open button and then click the Open With No Template—Imperial (Metric) option. These actions open a blank drawing.

2. Click the View tab and then click the Tile Vertically button in the Windows panel. The new blank drawing (called Drawing*n*.dwg) appears alongside Cabin07c.dwg (see Figure 7.47).

Like most Windows-based programs, AutoCAD 2010 can have multiple files open in a session. When you open the Application menu and then click the Open Drawings button, a list of the open drawings is displayed. To bring the file you want in front of the others, click it.

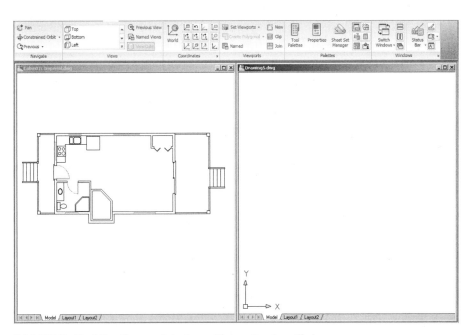

FIGURE 7.47: The user interface with two drawings tiled

Each drawing has a title bar, but only one drawing can be active at a time. At this time, the blank drawing (probably named Drawing1) should be active. If it is, its title bar is dark blue or some other color, and the Cabin07c.dwg title bar is grayed out. If your Cabin07c.dwg drawing is active instead, click once in the blank drawing.

The new drawing
might be called
Drawing2.dwg or
Drawing3.dwg. This
doesn't affect how the
exercise works.

3. Open the Application menu, and then click Drawing Utilities ➤ Units. In the Drawing Units dialog box, change the type of units in the Length area to Architectural (or Decimal if you are working in Metric), and then click OK.

4. Click the Cabin07c.dwg drawing to make it active.

5. Use Zoom Extents, and then use the scroll wheel to zoom out a little.

6. Use the Layer drop-down list to make the Walls layer current, and then turn off the Doors, Fixtures, Steps, and Windows layers. The walls and decks should be the only lines visible.

7. Use a selection window to select the cabin with its decks. Grips appear on all lines.

8. Place the cursor on one of the wall lines at a point where there are no grips, and then click and hold down the left mouse button and move the mouse. A copy of the selected cabin lines is attached to the mouse as if you had used the Move command (see Figure 7.48).

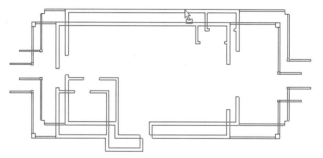

FIGURE 7.48: Dragging a selection of objects

9. Drag the cursor across the drawing to the center of the blank drawing, and then release the mouse button. The blank drawing is now active and contains the lines for the walls and decks (see Figure 7.49).

10. Zoom out so that you can see the entire drawing, and then enter ucsicon↵ off↵ to turn off the UCS icon.

11. Open the Layer drop-down list, and note that the new drawing (Drawing1.5dwg in the example) now has the Deck and Walls layers.

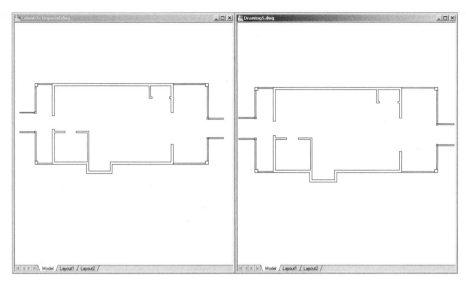

FIGURE 7.49: The result after dragging lines from one drawing to another

In this fashion, you can drag any visible objects from one drawing into another, including blocks. If you drag and drop a block, its definition is copied to the new drawing, along with all layers used by objects in the block. If you drag with the right mouse button, a context menu will appear, providing a few options for placing the objects in the receiving drawing.

Copying Objects Between Drawings

If you don't choose to have both open drawings visible at the same time, you can always use the Copy and Paste tools available in most Windows-based programs. Here's the general procedure:

1. Click the Maximize icon in the upper-right corner of the new drawing. The new drawing fills the screen.

2. Click the Switch Windows button in the Windows panel under the View tab. When the menu opens, notice at the bottom that the open drawings are displayed and the active one is checked (see Figure 7.50).

FIGURE 7.50: The Open Drawing menu with Drawing5.dwg active

3. Click the Cabin07c.dwg drawing. It replaces the new drawing as the active drawing and fills the screen. Turn on the layers you turned off previously. Leave the Headers and Roof layers frozen.

4. Select the fixtures in the kitchen and bath from this drawing using the selection tools you have learned, and then right-click and choose Copy With Base Point from the context menu. You're prompted to specify a base point in the Cabin07c.dwg drawing. Click the upper-left corner of the building using the Endpoint osnap. Press Esc to deselect the objects.

5. In the Window panel, click the Switch Windows button and then click Drawing*n*.dwg to make it active.

T I P   **You can also cycle through the open drawings by holding down the Ctrl key and then pressing the Tab key.**

---

6. Right-click and choose Paste from the context menu or press Ctrl+V. Pick the upper-left corner of the building using the Endpoint osnap. The fixtures are accurately positioned in the new drawing. If you check the layers, you'll see that the new drawing now has a Fixtures layer, in addition to the Walls and Deck layers.

Using AutoCAD's DesignCenter

The DesignCenter is a tool for copying named objects (blocks, layers, text styles, and so on) to an opened drawing from an unopened one. You can't copy lines, circles, and other unnamed objects unless they are part of a block. You'll see how this works by bringing some layers and a block into your new drawing from Cabin07c.dwg:

1. Make Cabin07c.dwg current, and then close it. Don't save changes. Maximize the window for your new drawing if it isn't already maximized.

 2. Click the Insert tab and click the DesignCenter button on the Content panel, or enter **dc**⏎ at the Command: prompt. The DesignCenter appears on the drawing area. It can be docked, floating, or if floating, hidden (see Figure 7.51). Your screen might not look exactly like the samples shown here. The tree diagram of file folders on the left might or might not be visible. Also, your DesignCenter might be wider or narrower.

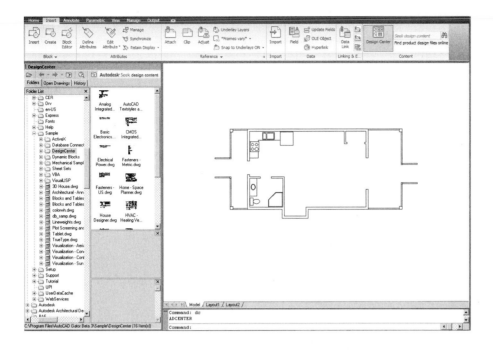

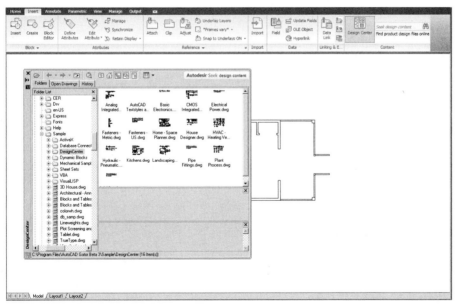

FIGURE 7.51: The DesignCenter docked (top), floating (bottom), and hidden (next page)

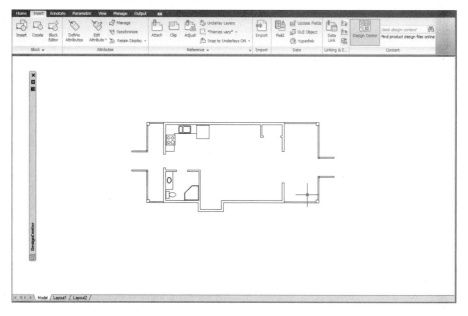

FIGURE 7.51 *(Continued)*

13. Click the Tree View Toggle button at the top of the DesignCenter (the fourth button from the right) a few times to close and open the file folder tree diagram. You can resize the DesignCenter horizontally (and vertically as well, if it's floating), and you can resize the subpanels inside. If Auto-Hide is on, the DesignCenter hides behind the title bar until you put your cursor on it. Leave the tree view open.

4. Click the Load button in the upper-left corner of the DesignCenter palette to open the Load dialog box. Navigate to your Training Data folder and open it.

5. Highlight Cabin07c.dwg, and click Open. The Load dialog box closes, and you are returned to your drawing. Now the left side of the DesignCenter lists your drawings in the Training Data folder and Cabin07c.dwg is highlighted; the right side of the DesignCenter shows the types of objects in Cabin07c.dwg that are available to be copied into the current drawing—in this case, Drawing4.dwg (see the top of Figure 7.52).

6. On the left side once again, click the + symbol to the left of Cabin07c.dwg. The list of named objects in the right panel now appears below Cabin07c.dwg in the tree view on the left. Click the

Layers icon on the left side. The list of layers in Cabin07c.dwg appears in the panel on the right (see the bottom of Figure 7.52).

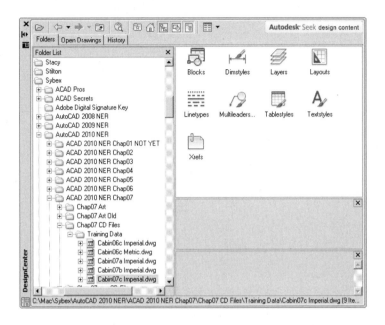

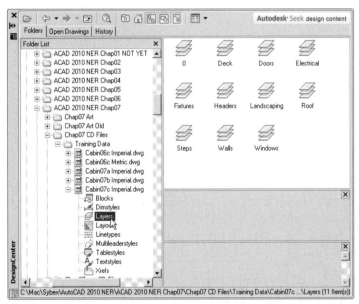

FIGURE 7.52: The DesignCenter displaying the files in the Training Data folder on the left and accessible objects on the right (top) and types of accessible objects on the left (bottom)

7. Click the Views button above the right window of the DesignCenter (the button on the far right). Choose List in the menu that opens. This changes the view of layers displayed from icons into a list.

8. Use the Shift and Ctrl keys to help you select all the layers except 0, Deck, Fixtures, and Walls (see Figure 7.53).

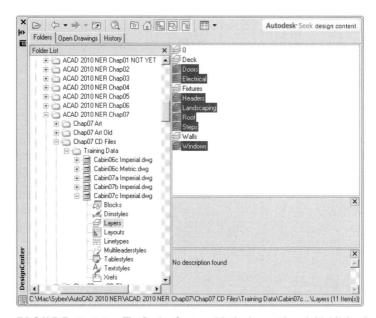

FIGURE 7.53: The DesignCenter with the layers to grab highlighted

9. Right-click on one of the highlighted layers in the right window, and choose Add Layer(s) from the context menu that opens.

10. Open the Layer drop-down list on the Layers panel. It now displays all the layers of the Cabin07c.dwg drawing, including those you just transferred to the Drawingn.dwg drawing.

Now let's see how this process works when you want to get a block from another drawing:

1. On the left side of the DesignCenter, click Blocks in the list under the Cabin07c.dwg drawing. On the right side, the list of blocks in that drawing appears (see the top of Figure 7.54).

> If you prefer dragging and dropping, click and hold the left mouse button, drag the cursor onto the drawing, and then release the mouse button.

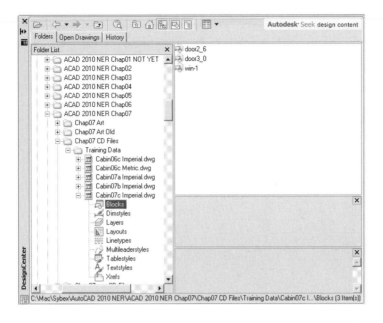

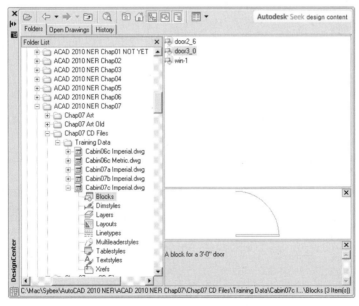

FIGURE 7.54: The DesignCenter with Blocks selected (top) and with the door3_0 block selected and Preview turned on (bottom)

2. Click door3_0 in the right panel, and then, if necessary, click the Preview button at the top of the DesignCenter. A picture of the block appears in the lower-right corner of the DesignCenter (see the bottom of Figure 7.54). You can resize the preview pane vertically.

3. Open the Layer list, and make Doors the current layer.

4. Dock the DesignCenter on the left side of the drawing area if it's not already there, and then zoom in to the back door area of the drawing (see Figure 7.55). The Endpoint osnap should be running.

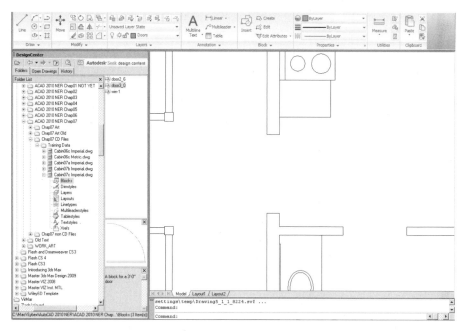

FIGURE 7.55: Zoomed in to the back door area with the DesignCenter docked

You can also right-click and drag a block from the DesignCenter into the current drawing. If you do this, a context menu appears. Click Insert Block. This opens the Insert dialog box, and you can complete the insertion procedure.

5. In the DesignCenter, click and drag door3_0 from the list to the drawing, and continue to hold the left mouse button down after the block appears at the cursor. As the cursor comes onto the drawing, the door3_0 block appears. Use the Endpoint osnap to locate the block at the opening, as you did earlier in this chapter (see Figure 7.56).

6. Click the Close icon in the upper-right corner of the DesignCenter to close it.

7. Keep your new drawing open in case you want to use it in the first few practice exercises at the end of this chapter. Otherwise, close it without saving it.

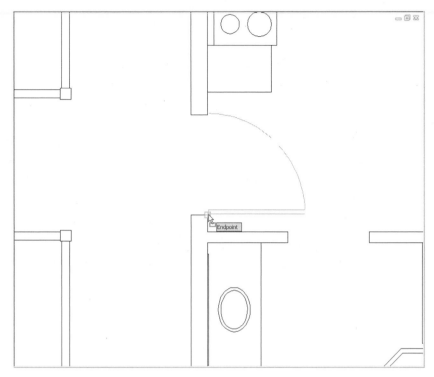

FIGURE 7.56: Dragging the door3_0 block into Drawing5 from the DesignCenter

By doing this insertion, you've now made the door3_0 block a part of your new drawing, and you can reinsert it in that drawing without the DesignCenter.

At the top of the DesignCenter window, the buttons on the left are tools for navigating through drives and folders to find the files you need to access; the buttons on the right give you options for viewing the named objects in the window.

DESIGNCENTER OPTIONS

Here's a brief description of the functions of the DesignCenter buttons, from left to right:

Load Opens the Load dialog box, which you use to navigate to the drive, folder, or file from which you want to borrow named AutoCAD objects.

Back Moves you one step back in your navigation procedure.

Forward Moves you one step forward in the navigation procedure that you have been using.

Continues

DesignCenter Options *(Continued)*

Up Moves up one level in the folder/file/named objects tree.

Search Opens a Search dialog box in which you can search for a file.

Favorites Displays a list of files and folders that you have previously set up.

Home Navigates to the DesignCenter folder in the AutoCAD program. This folder has subfolders of sample files that contain libraries of blocks and other named objects to import through the DesignCenter. You can designate a different Home folder by selecting the folder, right-clicking, and then choosing Set As Home from the context menu.

Tree View Toggle Opens or shuts the left panel that displays the logical tree of folders, files, and unnamed objects.

Preview Opens or shuts a preview window at the bottom of the right palette window. When you highlight a drawing or block in the palette window, a preview appears. You can resize the preview pane.

Description Displays or hides a previously written description of a block or drawing. You can resize the description pane.

Views Controls how the items in the palette window are displayed. There are four choices: Large Icons, Small Icons, List, and Details.

Other Ways to Share Information Between Drawings

You can transfer information between drawings in several other ways. This section looks at three of them. First, you can use the Wblock command to take a portion of a drawing and create a new drawing file from the selected objects. Second, you can insert any .dwg drawing file into any other drawing file. Finally, you can create *palettes* of blocks that can be accessed for any drawing.

Using the Wblock Command

To perform a Write Block, or Wblock, operation, you create a new file by telling AutoCAD which elements of the current drawing you want in the new file. Let's say you want to create a new .dwg file for the bathroom of the cabin. Here are the steps:

1. Open Cabin07c.dwg, and then pan and zoom to see the bathroom. Enter wblock↵ or w↵ to open the Write Block dialog box.

2. At the top, under Source, click the Objects radio button (see Figure 7.57).

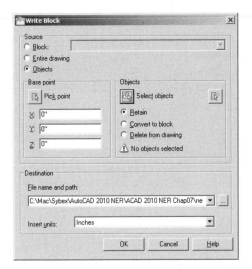

FIGURE 7.57: The Write Block dialog box

3. In the middle portion, the Base Point and Objects areas are similar to those for creating a block. For the Base Point, the default is 0,0,0. Click the Pick Point button, and in the drawing, pick the point at the inside, top-left corner of the bathroom.

4. In the Objects area, click the Select Objects button; then use a window as well as individual picks to select everything you want to include and press ↵. Click the Retain radio button in this area, if necessary, so that the selected objects aren't deleted from the current drawing.

If you select with a crossing window here, you'll get more than you need, but you can clean up the new drawing later.

5. In the Destination area, enter a filename—say, **bath**—for the new drawing, and choose a folder in which to save it.

6. In the Insert Units drop-down list, select Inches or Millimeters, in case the new drawing is used in a drawing that has units other than Architectural or Decimal.

7. Click OK. A preview window briefly appears, the command ends, and the selected material is now a new drawing file located in the folder that you specified.

8. Close the Cabin07c.dwg drawing without saving any changes.

You can use the Wblock command in three ways, which are available via radio buttons at the top of the Write Block dialog box. Here's a brief description of each:

Block To make a drawing file out of a block that's defined in the current drawing, select the name of the block from the drop-down list at the top and then follow the procedure in steps 4 through 6 in the preceding exercise. When you follow this procedure, the objects in the new drawing are no longer a block. Wblocking a block has the effect of exploding it.

Entire Drawing Click this button to *purge* a drawing of unwanted objects such as layers that have no objects on them and block definitions that have no references in the drawing. You aren't prompted to select anything except the information called for in the preceding steps 4 through 6. You can keep the same drawing name or enter a new one. A preferable way to accomplish the same task is to use the Purge command. Open the Application menu then click Drawing Utilities ➤ Purge or enter purge↵ to open the Purge dialog box, and select which features you wish to purge.

Objects You select which objects to use to create a new file, as in the preceding steps 1 through 6.

Inserting One Drawing into Another

When you insert a drawing into another drawing, it comes in as a block. You use the same Insert tool that you use to insert blocks, but in a slightly different way. For example, in the previous section you Wblocked a portion of Cabin07c.dwg and made a new file called bath.dwg. Now suppose you want to insert bath.dwg into a drawing that you'll call DrawingC.dwg. Once you've created DrawingC.dwg, use this procedure:

1. Make DrawingC.dwg current.

2. Start the Insert command.

3. In the Insert dialog box, click the Browse button, and then navigate to the folder containing bath.dwg.

4. Open that folder, highlight bath.dwg, and then click Open to return to the Insert dialog box. The drawing file that you selected is now displayed in the Name drop-down list. At this point, a copy of bath.dwg has been converted to a block definition in DrawingC.dwg.

5. Set the insertion parameters, and then click OK.

6. Finish the insertion procedure as if you were inserting a block.

You transfer blocks between drawings by dragging and dropping or by using the DesignCenter. You can also convert them into .dwg files by using the Wblock command, and you can insert them back into other .dwg files as blocks by using the Insert command. They become disassociated when they leave the drawing and can be inserted as a block when they enter another drawing.

Exploring AutoCAD's Palettes

AutoCAD provides a tool called *palettes* to make blocks and other features or tools easily accessible for any drawing. You'll now take a brief look at the sample palettes that come with AutoCAD and see how to manage them on the screen:

1. Open the Cabin07c.dwg drawing, and zoom to the drawing's extents. Then use the scroll wheel to zoom out a little.

2. If palettes aren't already visible in the drawing area, click the View tab and then click the Tool Palettes button in the Palettes panel to display the palettes (see Figure 7.58). You can also open the tool palettes from the menu bar by clicking Tools ➤ Palettes ➤ Tool Palettes, or by using the Ctrl+3 shortcut keys. They can be floating or docked on either side of the drawing area, and the navigation bar can be on the left or right side.

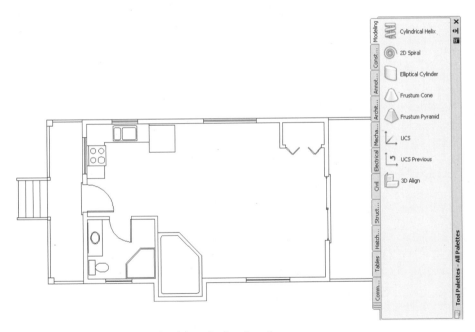

FIGURE 7.58: The tool palettes displayed on the screen

Your palettes might appear different from those shown in a couple of ways. The ones shown here are positioned on the right side but aren't docked there. Yours might be transparent, showing your drawing beneath them, or your palettes might be hidden and show only the title bar. In Figure 7.58, several tabs are on the left side, indicating the available palettes. On the right side is the palette title bar with control icons at the top and bottom.

On each palette is its content. The Hatches sample palette has hatch patterns and fills (discussed in Chapter 11, "Working with Hatches and Gradients"), and the Draw and Modify palettes contain commands from the Draw and Modify toolbars respectively.

3. Click the Architectural tab to display its content on the palette. Its tab might be abbreviated to read "Archit…," but pausing the cursor over the tab displays a tooltip showing the entire tab name.

Notice the scroll bar next to the title bar (see Figure 7.59). This appears when there is more content than the palette can show. Blocks that are shown with a lightning bolt symbol as part of the icon are dynamic blocks.

4. Move the cursor to the title bar. Right-click, and choose Transparency from the context menu to open the Transparency dialog box (see Figure 7.60). Here you can toggle transparency on and off and adjust the degree of transparency for the palettes.

FIGURE 7.59: The tool palettes with the Architectural tab active

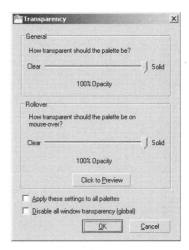

FIGURE 7.60: The Transparency dialog box

W A R N I N G AutoCAD might display a notification dialog box, rather than the Transparency dialog box, if your video driver and operating system combination is unable to display palette transparency.

5. Be sure the Disable All Window Transparency (Global) check box is not selected, and be sure the Opacity slider in the General section is at mid-position or a bit on the Solid side. Set the Rollover to 100% Opacity so the palette is solid whenever the cursor is over it. Click OK. Now the drawing is visible through the palettes (see Figure 7.61).

6. Right-click the palettes' title bar, and choose Auto-Hide from the context menu. When the menu closes, move the cursor off the palettes. The palettes disappear except for the title bar (see Figure 7.62). When you move the cursor back onto the title bar, the palettes reappear—a handy feature.

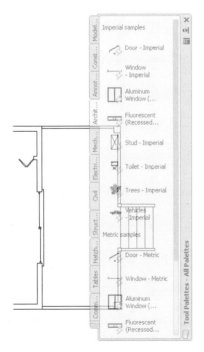

FIGURE 7.61: The palettes in Transparent mode

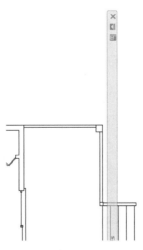

FIGURE 7.62: The palettes title bar with Auto-Hide on

7. Close the Cabin07c.dwg drawing without saving any changes.

With both Transparency and Auto-Hide active, the palettes are less intrusive and take up less screen area, but they remain easily accessible. In Chapter 11, you'll learn more about palettes and their properties and how to set up new palettes and change existing ones.

> **T I P**   When they are in floating mode, the Properties palette and Design-Center also have the Auto-Hide option.

This chapter has outlined the procedures for setting up and using blocks, the Wblock command, and AutoCAD's DesignCenter. Blocks follow a set of complex rules, some of which are beyond the scope of this book.

If You Would Like More Practice...

Here are some suggestions that will give you some practice in working with blocks, drag-and-drop procedures, and the DesignCenter:

- ▶ Make blocks out of any of the fixtures in the bathroom or kitchen. Try to decide on the best location to use for the insertion point of each fixture. Then insert them back into the Cabin07c.dwg drawing in their original locations. Create them on Layer 0, and then insert them on the Fixtures layer. Here's a list of the fixtures:

    - ▶ Shower

    - ▶ Bathroom sink and counter

    - ▶ Toilet

    - ▶ Stove

    - ▶ Kitchen sink

    - ▶ Refrigerator

    - ▶ Hot Tub

- ▶ At the end of Chapter 5, I suggested creating pieces of furniture for the kitchen, living room, and bedroom of the cabin. If you did that, it will be good practice to make blocks out of those pieces and insert them into the cabin floor plan. If you didn't do that exercise, you can do so now and then convert the pieces of furniture into blocks.

▶ Drag some of the dynamic blocks from the Civil, Structural, Electrical, Mechanical, Architectural, and Annotation sample palettes into the `Cabin07c.dwg` drawing, and experiment with them to see how they work. Figure 7.63 shows the cabin with a few trees and a car added from the Architectural palette.

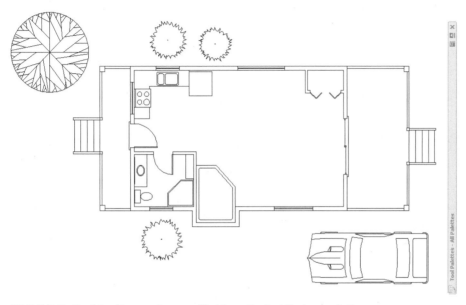

FIGURE 7.63: Trees and a car added from the Architectural palette

▶ If you work in a profession or trade not directly concerned with architecture or construction, develop a few blocks that you can use in your own work:

    ▶ Electrical diagrams consist of many simple symbols, each of which can be a block.

    ▶ Cams and gears—or gear teeth—and other engine parts that have been made into blocks can be assembled into a mechanical drawing.

    ▶ Plumbing diagrams, like electrical ones, use a variety of symbols repetitively—valves, meters, pumps, and joints. You can easily make them into blocks and then reassemble them into the diagram.

In each of these examples, choosing the most useful location for the insertion point will determine whether the block that you create will be a handy tool or a big frustration.

Are You Experienced?

Now you can...

☑ create blocks out of existing objects in your drawing

☑ insert blocks into your drawing

☑ vary the size and rotation of blocks as they are inserted

☑ detect blocks in a drawing

☑ use point filters to locate an insertion point

☑ revise a block

☑ drag and drop objects from one drawing to another

☑ use AutoCAD's DesignCenter

☑ use the Wblock command

☑ open palettes and control their appearance

CHAPTER 8

Controlling Text in a Drawing

- ▶ Setting up text styles

- ▶ Placing new text in the drawing

- ▶ Modifying text in a drawing

- ▶ Working with grid lines

- ▶ Managing single-line and multiline text

- ▶ Adding hyperlinks

- ▶ Using Spell Check

Y ou have many uses for text in your drawings, including titles of views, notes, and dimensions. It's not uncommon for the majority of a page to be covered with text outlining pertinent information, including legal and code requirements, construction or manufacturing information, and contact information for companies or individuals involved in the project. Each of these might require a different height, orientation, justification, and style of lettering. To control text, you'll need to learn how to do the following:

► Determine how the text will look by setting up text styles

► Specify where the text will be and enter it in the drawing

► Modify the text already in your drawing

AutoCAD offers two types of text objects: single-line and multiline. *Single-line text* makes a distinct object of each line of text, whether the line is one letter or many words. This type of text is useful for titles of drawings, titles of views within a drawing, room labels, and schedules. You use multiline text for dimensions, tables, and longer notes. With *multiline text*, AutoCAD treats a whole body of multiline text as one object, whether the text consists of one letter or many paragraphs.

The two types of text share the same text styles, but each has its own command for placing text in the drawing. When you modify text, you can use the same commands for either type of text, but the commands operate differently for multiline text than for single-line text. AutoCAD handles any text used in *dimensioning*—a process by which you indicate the sizes of various components in your drawing—differently from other text; I'll cover dimensioning in Chapter 12, "Dimensioning a Drawing."

You'll progress through this chapter by first looking at the process of setting up text styles. You'll then start placing and modifying single-line text in the cabin drawing. Finally, you'll look at the methods for creating and controlling multiline text as it's used for notes and tables. If you work in a non-AEC profession or trade, be assured that the features presented in this chapter will apply directly to your work. The basic principles of working with text in AutoCAD and LT "cross the curriculum" (an educational metaphor) and apply universally.

Setting Up Text Styles

In AutoCAD, a text style consists of a combination of a style name, a text font, a height, a width factor, an oblique angle, and a few other mostly static settings. You specify these text style properties with the help of a dialog box that opens when you start the Style command. You'll begin by setting up two text styles—one for labeling the rooms in the floor plan and the other for putting titles on the two views. You'll need a new layer for text:

1. Open the Cabin07c.dwg drawing.

2. Zoom out so that you can see the entire drawing.

3. Create a new layer named **Text1**. Assign it a color, and make it current.

4. Thaw all the other layers.

5. Click the Annotate tab to display the panels relevant to text and dimensioning and save the file as Cabin08a.dwg.

Your drawing should look like Figure 8.1.

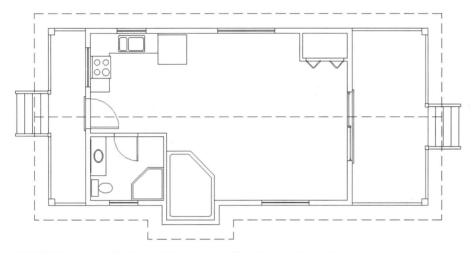

F I G U R E   8 . 1 : The Cabin08a drawing with all layers displayed

Determining Text and Drawing Scale

When you set up text styles for a drawing, you have to determine the height of the text letters. To make this determination, you first need to decide the scale at which the final drawing will be printed.

In traditional drafting, you can ignore the drawing scale and set the actual height of each kind of text. This is possible because, although the drawing is to a scale, the text doesn't have to conform to that scale and is drawn full size.

In AutoCAD, a feature called *layouts* makes it possible to set the height of text in the same way—that is, at the height at which it will be printed. You'll learn about using layouts in Chapter 14, "Using Layouts to Set Up a Print." In that chapter, you'll place text on layouts; in this chapter, I'll demonstrate how you use text without layouts. You'll place text in the cabin drawing. The drawing is actual size, but the text has to be much larger than actual size because both the drawing and its text will be scaled down by the same factor in the process of printing the drawing.

A layout is a drawing environment that has been overlaid on the drawing of your project. The layout and the drawing are part of the same file.

In this drawing, you'll use a final scale of 3/16″ = 1′-0″ (1 = 70). This scale has a true ratio of 1:64 (1:70) and a scale factor of 64 (see Table 8.1). If you want text to be 3/16″ (4.5 mm) high when you print the drawing at 3/16″ (1:70) scale, multiply 3/16″ (4.5 mm) by the scale factor of 64 (70) to get 12″ (310 mm) for the text height. You calculate the scale factor by inverting the scale fraction and multiplying it by 12 (310). You can check that calculated text height by studying the floor plan for a moment and noting the sizes of the building components represented in the drawing. The stair tread depth is 10″, and the text will be slightly larger.

TABLE 8.1: Standard Scales and Their Corresponding Ratios

Scale True	Scale Factor
1″ = 1′-0″	12
1/2″ = 1′-0″	24
1/4″ = 1′-0″	48
3/16″ = 1′-0″	64
1/8″ = 1′-0″	96
1/16″ = 1′-0″	192

Similarly, when using decimal units, the scale factor is derived by dividing the second number in the ratio by the first such as: 1:50 has a scale factor of 50 and 1:60 has a scale factor of 60.

Defining a Text Style for Room Labels

Now that you have a good idea of the required text height, it's time to define a new text style. Each new AutoCAD .dwg file comes with two predefined text styles: Standard and Annotative. You'll add two more. Follow these steps:

You can also start the Style command by opening the menu bar and choosing Format ➢ Text Style.

1. Expand the Text Style drop-down list in the Text panel, and choose Manage Text Style (see Figure 8.2) or enter st↵ to start the Style command.

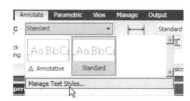

FIGURE 8.2: Starting the Style command

2. The Text Style dialog box opens (see Figure 8.3). In the Styles area, you'll see the default Standard text style as well as the Annotative text style.

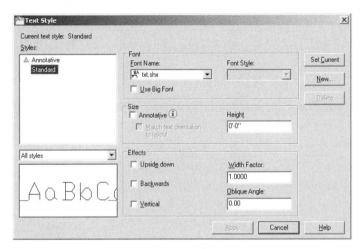

FIGURE 8.3: The Text Style dialog box in which text styles are set up

3. Click New to open the New Text Style dialog box. You'll see a highlighted Style Name text box set to *style1* in it. When you enter a new style name, it will replace style1.

4. Enter **Label↵** in the Style Name text box, as shown in Figure 8.4. The New Text Style dialog box closes, and in the Text Style dialog box, Label appears highlighted in the Styles list. You've created a new text style named Label. It has settings identical to those of the Standard text style, and it's now the current text style. Next you'll change some of the settings for this new style.

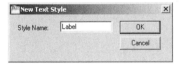

FIGURE 8.4: Setting the name for the new text style

5. Move down to the Font area, and click the Font Name drop-down list to open it. A list of fonts appears; the number of choices depends on

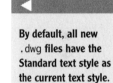

By default, all new .dwg files have the Standard text style as the current text style.

A font is a collection of text characters and symbols that all share a characteristic style of design and proportion.

what software is installed on your computer. AutoCAD can use both its native .shx (Compiled Shape) font files and Windows .ttf (True-Type font) files.

6. Scroll through the list until you find romans.shx, and then click it. The list closes, and in the Font Name text box the romans.shx font replaces the txt.shx font that was previously there. In the Preview area in the lower-left corner, a sample of the romans.shx font replaces that of the txt.shx font.

7. Press the Tab key a few times to move to the next text box. The Height setting is highlighted at the default of 0'-0" (0).

8. Enter 12 (305), and then press Tab again. A height of 1'-0" (305 mm) replaces the default height. Your Text Style dialog box should look like Figure 8.5.

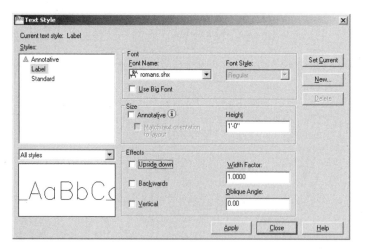

FIGURE 8.5: The Text Style dialog box after setting up the Label style

You won't need to change any of the other parameters that define the new text style. They can all stay at their default settings.

9. Click the Apply button at the bottom of the dialog box. The Label text style is saved with the current drawing and becomes the current text style. The current text style appears in the Text Style drop-down list in the Text panel, as shown in Figure 8.6.

FIGURE 8.6: The Text Style drop-down list after setting Label as the current style

N O T E The current text style is similar to the current layer. All text created while a text style is current will follow the parameters or settings of that text style.

When you define a new text style, you first name the new style. This has the effect of making a copy of the current text style settings, giving them the new name and making the new text style current. You then change the settings for this new style and save the changes by clicking Apply.

Defining a Second Text Style

Before you close the dialog box, define another text style:

1. Click the New button again.

2. In the New Text Style dialog box, enter **Title**, and click OK. A new text style called Title is created and is now the current text style. Its font, height, and other settings are a copy of the Label text style. Now you'll make changes to these settings to define the Title text style.

3. Click the current font, romans.shx. The drop-down list of fonts opens. Scroll up one font and click romand.shx. The list closes, and romand.shx appears as the chosen font.

4. Press Tab until the Height text box is highlighted, enter 18 (457), and then press Tab again. This changes the height parameter to 1'-6" (457 mm).

T I P If you press ↵ after entering the height, the new style is automatically applied, meaning it's saved and made the current text style. Don't do this if you need to change other settings for the style.

5. Click Apply, and then click Close.

Of the many fonts available in AutoCAD, you'll use only a few for your drawings. Some are set up for foreign languages or mapping symbols. Others would appear out of place on architectural or technical drawings but might be just right for an advertising brochure or a flier. Later in this chapter, you'll have a chance to experiment with the available fonts.

Refer to Figure 8.3 for a moment, and note that the Standard text style has a height of 0'-0" (0). When the current text style has a height set to 0, you're prompted to enter a height each time you begin to place single-line text in the drawing. The default height will be 3/16" (or 0.20 for decimal units and 2.5 for metric). Multiline text will use the default height of 3/16" unless you change it.

Now that you have two new text styles, you can start working with single-line text.

SHX and TTF Fonts

AutoCAD text styles can use either the AutoCAD .shx (Compiled Shape) font files or the Windows .ttf (TrueType font) files on your system. The .shx fonts are older files that were originally designed for use with pen plotters that required the pen tip to follow a precise vector. When you zoom into an AutoCAD font or print it large on a drawing, the straight line segments that comprise it become apparent. Two more fonts in the roman font family—romant (triplex) and romanc (complex)—have multiple, closely set lines and are used for larger text.

TrueType fonts are mathematical representations of vector formats and are common in most Windows applications. Many fonts are available, and you can use them with no loss of crispness regardless of the size of the font or the zoom factor in the drawing.

The .shx fonts are small files designed specifically to work with AutoCAD and do not significantly affect your system's performance. TrueType fonts usually look better but can affect workflow, especially when panning or zooming the view. If you must use .ttf fonts, such as in a large field of text where the serifs would make reading easier, turn off or freeze the text's layer when possible. In either case, anybody opening your drawing file must have all the included fonts on their system in order to see the drawing properly.

Using Single-Line Text

Your first task is to put titles in for the floor plan using the new Title text style.

Placing Titles of Views in the Drawing

The titles need to be centered approximately under each view. If you establish a vertical guideline through the middle of the drawing, you can use it to position the text. Guidelines aren't as elegant a solution as a temporary track point, but they are quick and don't require too much forethought. Here are the steps:

1. Pan the drawing up to create a little more room under the floor plan.

2. Set up your osnaps and status bar options so that Polar Tracking and Object Snap are on and the Endpoint and Midpoint osnaps are running. Drop a line from the midpoint of the ridgeline in the floor plan straight down to a point near the bottom of the screen.

3. Offset the horizontal, outside wall line, to the right of the pop-out in the floor plan down 6′ (1830 mm), as shown in Figure 8.7.

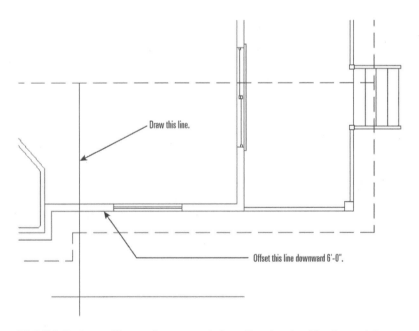

Draw this line.

Offset this line downward 6′-0″.

FIGURE 8.7: The new lines created after offsetting the ridge line and the pop-out

4. Click the down arrow below the Multiline text button in the Text panel and click the Single Line Text button in the fly-out menu, or enter **dt↵** to start the Dtext (Dynamic Text) command—the command used for single-line text.

5. The bottom line of text in the Command window says Specify start point of text or [Justify/Style]:. The line above it displays the name of the current text style and the style's height setting. The bottom line is the actual prompt, with three options. By default, the justification point is set to the lower-left corner of the text. You need to change it to the middle of the text to be able to center it on the guideline.

6. Enter **j↵** or press the down arrow on the keyboard until Justify is selected at the cursor prompt, and then press ↵. All the possible justification points appear in the prompt, as shown in Figure 8.8.

FIGURE 8.8: The single-line text justification options

7. Enter **c↵** to choose Center as the justification.

8. Use the Shift+right-click menu to choose the Intersection osnap, and pick the intersection of the guideline and the offset line.

9. For the rotation, press ↵ to accept the default angle of 0°, or enter **0↵** if 0° is not the default. A flashing I-shaped cursor superimposed over a narrow box appears at the intersection (see Figure 8.9).

10. With Caps Lock on, enter **FLOOR PLAN↵**. The text is centered at the intersection as you enter it, and the cursor moves down to allow you to enter another line (see the left image of Figure 8.10).

11. Press ↵ again to end the Dtext command. The text is centered relative to the vertical guideline and sits on the offset line (see the right image of Figure 8.10).

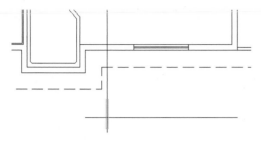

FIGURE 8.9: The text cursor sits on the guidelines.

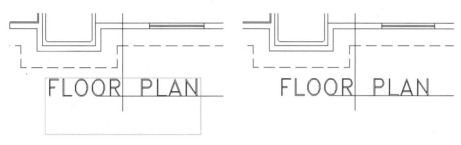

FIGURE 8.10: The first line of text is entered (left) and placed (right).

12. Erase the offset line and the vertical guideline. Your drawing will look like Figure 8.11.

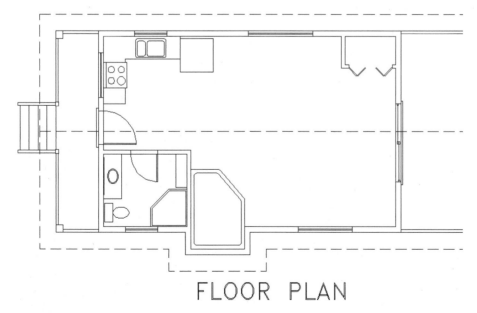

FIGURE 8.11: The drawing with the title complete

You specified a location for the text in two steps: first, you set the justification point of each line of text to be centered horizontally; second, you used the Intersection osnap to position the justification point at the intersection of the two guidelines. I'll discuss justification in more depth a little later in this chapter.

Next you'll move to the interior of the cabin floor plan and place the room labels in their respective rooms.

Placing Room Labels in the Floor Plan

Text for the room labels will use the Label text style, so you need to make that style current before you start placing text. You can accomplish this in the Text panel:

1. Click the Polar Tracking, Ortho Mode, and Object Snap buttons on the status bar to turn off these features.

2. Expand the Text Style drop-down list on the Text panel to display a list of all the text styles in the drawing. Click Label, as shown in Figure 8.12, to make Label the current style.

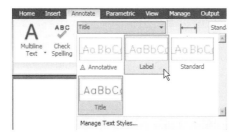

FIGURE 8.12: Selecting a new current text style in the Text panel

3. Start the Dtext command, and notice that the FLOOR PLAN text shows as dashed lines. If you press ↵ at the Specify start point of text or [Justify/Style]: prompt, the new text will be placed just below the last text line created.

4. Pick a point in the living room between the refrigerator and the closet.

5. Press ↵ at the rotation prompt. The text cursor appears at the point you picked.

6. With Caps Lock on, enter KITCHEN↵ LIVING ROOM↵ BATH↵↵. The Dtext command ends. You have three lines of text in the kitchen and living room area (see Figure 8.13).

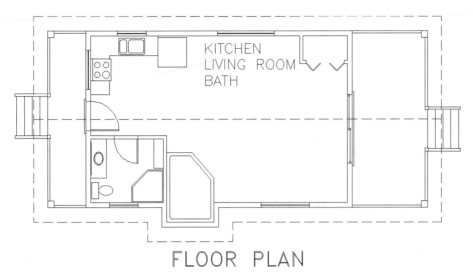

FLOOR PLAN

FIGURE 8.13: The three room labels placed in the cabin

For this text, you used the default Left justification and each line of text was positioned directly below the previous line at a spacing set by AutoCAD. In many cases, it's more efficient to enter a list of words or phrases first and then move the text to its appropriate location. That's what you're doing for this text. When you know the location of the insertion point for the next line, you can click that point, instead of pressing ↵ at the end of the current line. This starts the next line of text at the selected location.

Moving Text

You'll eyeball the final position of this text because it doesn't have to be exactly centered or lined up precisely with anything. It should just sit in the rooms in such a way that it's easily readable:

1. Click the BATH text. One grip appears at the justification point of the text.

2. Click the grip to activate it. The BATH text is attached to the cursor and moves with it (see the top of Figure 8.14). The Stretch command automatically starts. Because text can't be stretched, the Stretch command functions like the Move command.

3. Move the cursor below and outside the bathroom and just beyond the eave line, and then click to place text at its new location.

4. Press Esc to deselect the text and remove the grip (see the bottom of Figure 8.14). Then select the KITCHEN text.

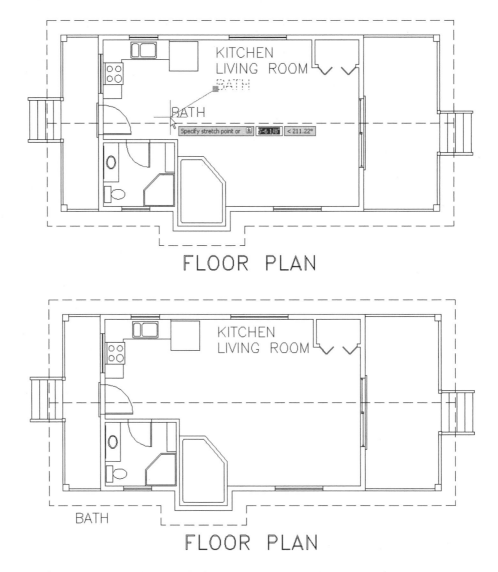

FIGURE 8.14: Moving the BATH text (top) and its new location (bottom)

> When you move text in this way, you're actually using the Stretch option of the grips feature. Because text can't be stretched, it just moves with the cursor.

5. Click the grip for the newly selected text.

6. Pick a point in the kitchen so that the KITCHEN text is positioned approximately at the center of the room. Press Esc to deselect the text.

7. Repeat this process to move the LIVING ROOM text to an appropriate location without crossing the roof line (see Figure 8.15).

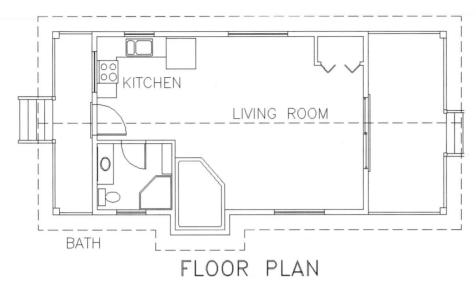

KITCHEN

LIVING ROOM

BATH

FLOOR PLAN

F I G U R E   8 . 1 5 : The LIVING ROOM and KITCHEN text moved to their proper positions

Adding a Leader to the Text

A *leader* is a short series of lines that run from a note or symbol to a corresponding feature in your drawing. Although leaders are normally associated with dimensions (covered in Chapter 12), you can also use them with plain text. The leaders that you draw manually will not, however, have the adaptability of actual dimension leaders, but are just simple geometry used to link two features in a drawing. In this situation, you want to associate the BATH text with the bathroom by drawing a polyline from the text to the room.

1. Press F8 to toggle Ortho Mode on.

2. Click the Home tab and then, in the Draw panel, click the Polyline button.

3. Draw a short horizontal segment from the right of the text approximately 8″ (200 mm) long, extending even further to the right.

4. Toggle Ortho Mode off again, click a second point inside the bathroom, and press ↵ to end the command. Your leader should look like the one shown in Figure 8.16.

   To terminate the polyline inside the bathroom, you'll place a donut at the endpoint. A *donut* is actually a closed, circular polyline with a width assigned to it. The width is determined by defining the outside diameter and inside diameter of the donut ring. When the inside diameter is set to zero, a closed, filled circle is created.

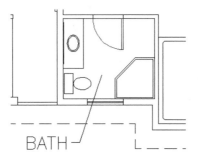

FIGURE 8.16: A leader extends from the text to the bathroom.

5. Expand the Draw panel and then click the Donut button.

6. At the Specify inside diameter of donut: prompt, enter 0↵.

7. At the Specify outside diameter of donut: prompt, enter 3↵ (75↵). A 3″ (75 mm) diameter, closed circle appears at the cursor.

8. Turn on the running osnaps and, at the Specify center of donut or: prompt, click the endpoint of the polyline inside the bathroom. Your bathroom, BATH text, and leader should look like Figure 8.17.

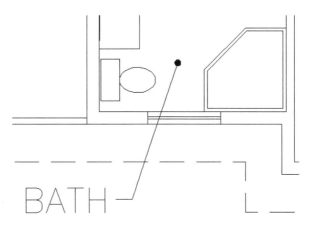

FIGURE 8.17: The bathroom, BATH text, and leader

9. Press ↵ to end the Donut command.

As you've seen, you can easily move text around the drawing using the grip at the insertion point. Often, however, you'll be unable to position it in the optimum location without the drawing looking crowded or sloppy. A leader can tie text to a specific feature adding readability to your drawing. Occasionally, the location of a line and text coincide and the conditions do not allow you to relocate the text. We are going to force a situation here where you'll need to erase parts of these lines around the text. To do this, you'll use the Break command and then, at the end of the exercise, revert the drawing back to its original configuration. If you do not want to complete the next section, save your drawing as Cabin08b.dwg and skip to the "Using Text in a Grid" section.

Breaking Lines

The Break command chops a line into two lines. When you're working with text that intersects a line, you'll usually want a gap between the lines after the break. The Break command provides this option as well as others. Follow these steps:

1. Enter **undo**↵ **m**↵ to set the undo mark so you can return your drawing to the state it is in now.

2. Select the LIVING ROOM text and move it so that it rests on the ridgeline, as shown in Figure 8.18.

FIGURE 8.18: The selected text overlapping the ridgeline

3. Turn off Object Snap, and click the Break button on the extended Modify panel.

4. Place the pickbox on the ridgeline just to the right of the text and click. The line ghosts, and the cursor changes to the crosshair cursor. You just selected the line to break and picked one of the break points.

5. Put the crosshair cursor on the roofline just to the left of the text, and pick that point. The line is broken around the text, and the Break command ends. As you can see in Figure 8.19, the text is easier to read now than it was when the line was running through it.

You can also start the Break command by entering br↵.

FIGURE 8.19: The ridgeline is broken on either side of the text.

6. You don't want to retain your drawing in its current state, so enter
   undo⏎ b⏎ to revert back to the undo point that you set with the Mark
   option.

7. Your drawing should look like Figure 8.20. Save your drawing as
   Cabin08b.dwg.

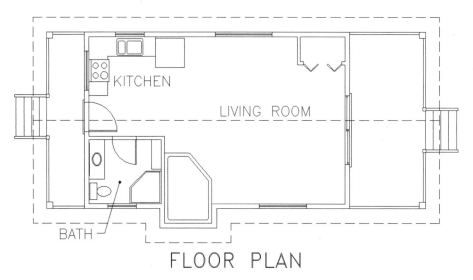

FIGURE 8.20: The cabin with the labels added

 T I P   The multiline text objects have a mask feature that creates an enve-
lope over and around the text, hiding the objects behind it. Unlike the break-
ing-lines approach, the masked objects reappear when you move the text.
Masking is not supported for single-line text, but the Text Mask utility is available in the Express Tools. Express Tools are not included with AutoCAD LT.

A CLOSER LOOK AT THE BREAK COMMAND

Use your own judgment to determine how far from the text a line must be broken back. You have to strike a balance between making the text easy to read and keeping what the broken line represents clear. For the bathroom, I directed you to keep the text completely out of the room because, if any lines of the fixtures had to be broken to accommodate the text, it might have made it difficult for a viewer to recognize that those lines represent a shower, sink, or a toilet.

Here are some other options for the Break command:

▶ Ordinarily, when you select a line to be broken, the point where you pick the line becomes the beginning of the break. If the point where the break needs to start is at the intersection of two lines, you must select the line to be broken somewhere other than at a break point. Otherwise, AutoCAD won't know which line you want to break. In that case, after selecting the line to break, enter **f**↵. You'll be prompted to pick the first point of the break, and the command continues. Now that AutoCAD knows which line you want to break, you can use the Intersection osnap to pick the intersection of two lines.

▶ To break a line into two segments without leaving a gap, click the Break At Point button, which is on the expanded Modify panel. You might want to do this to place one part of a line on a different layer from the rest of the line. To break the line this way, start the command, select the line to break, and then pick the point on the line where the break is to occur, using an osnap if necessary. AutoCAD makes the break and ends the command.

Using Text in a Grid

AutoCAD provides a grid of dots or lines, which you worked with in Chapter 3. The grid is a tool for visualizing the size of the drawing area and for drawing lines whose geometry conforms to the spacing of the dots or lines. Many floor plans have a separate *structural* grid, created specifically for the project and made up of lines running vertically and horizontally through key structural components of the building. At one end of each grid line, a circle or a hexagon is placed and a letter or number is centered in the shape to identify it. This kind of grid is usually reserved for large, complex drawings, but you'll put a small grid on the cabin floor plan to learn the basic method for laying one out:

1. Create a new layer called **Grid**. Assign it a unique color, and make it current.

2. Offset the roofline polyline 10′ (3050 mm); then pan and zoom as necessary so that the cabin is centered on screen and takes up only about 75 percent of the drawing area.

3. Turn Object Snap on if it's off; set the Endpoint, Midpoint, and Perpendicular osnaps to be running; and then start the Line command.

4. Draw lines from the upper-left and upper-right inside corners of the walls up to the offset roof line. Then draw lines from the left upper and lower inside corners of the exterior walls to the vertical offset line on the left (see Figure 8.21).

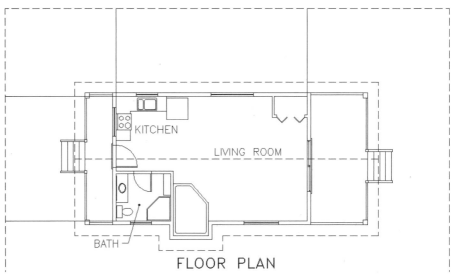

FIGURE 8.21: The first grid lines

5. The grid lines need to be centered on the structural member they are identifying, in this case an 8×8 (204×204) column. Start the offset command, enter e↵ y↵ to set the Erase parameter, and then set the offset distance to 4″ (102 mm). Now, when an object is offset, the original is erased.

6. Offset each of the grid lines 4″ (102 mm) toward the inside of the cabin. You may notice that the toilet will interfere with the new column in the lower-left corner of the cabin. Move the toilet up 4″ (102 mm) to add clearance and then adjust the size of the sink counter and mirror as well.

7. Now you need to draw grid lines for the posts at the corners of the decks. Draw lines from the horizontal midpoint of the top-right and top-left deck posts vertically to the offset roofline.

8. Next, draw lines from the upper-left and lower-left deck posts horizontally to the offset roof line. This time add a jog to each column line so that their endpoints are not too close to the endpoints of the existing horizontal column lines (see Figure 8.22). You need to leave space for the column tag and don't want them to overlap.

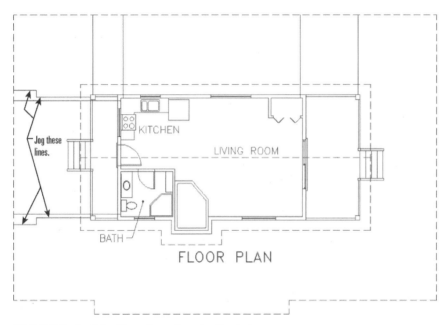

FIGURE 8.22: The column lines for the deck posts

 T I P Use the F8 key to toggle Ortho mode on and off to keep the jogged lines straight.

9. The column lines should not extend all the way to the cabin; there should be a gap to keep the drawing from getting congested and confusing. Offset the original roofline, without erasing the original, 6″ (150 mm) to the outside and then trim all eight column lines back to this new Polyline, as shown in Figure 8.23. You may need to zoom in to the end of each line being trimmed to ensure that the correct object is selected for trimming.

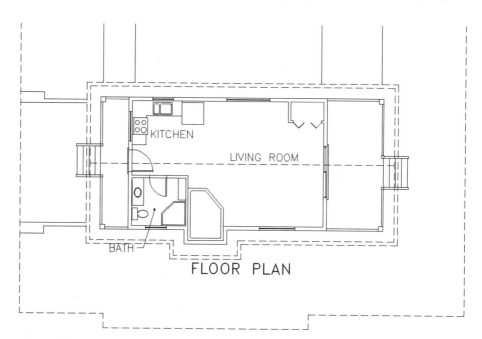

FIGURE 8.23: The column lines are trimmed back to the newly offset rooflines.

10. Erase the offset rooflines you created in steps 4 and 9, and then zoom out to a view that includes the floor plan and the grid lines (see Figure 8.24).

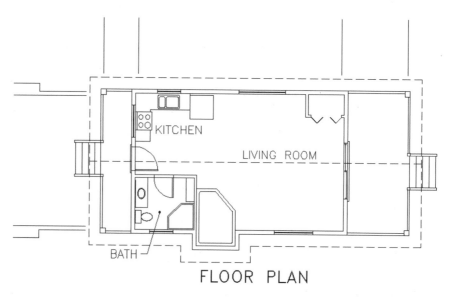

FIGURE 8.24: The cabin with the completed grid lines drawn and the offset roof lines deleted

This completes the grid lines. To finish the grid, you need to add a circle with a letter or a number in it to the left or upper end of the lines. You'll use letters across the top and numbers running down the side:

1. In the Draw panel, expand the Circle fly-out menu and click 2-Point. The 2-Point option draws a circle defined by selecting two opposite points of the circle's diameter.

2. At the `Specify first end point of circle's diameter:` prompt, pick the upper end of the leftmost vertical grid line.

3. Make sure Dynamic Input is on. Then move the cursor directly above the last point and enter **2' (610)** or enter **2'<90↵ (610<90)** at the `Specify second end point of circle's diameter:` prompt. This places a circle 2' (610 mm) in diameter at the top of the grid line (see the left image of Figure 8.25).

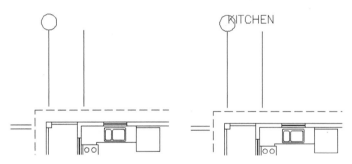

FIGURE 8.25: The circle on the grid line (left) and the KITCHEN text copied to the circle (right)

4. Click the KITCHEN text. A grip appears.

5. Click the grip; type c, for *copy*; and press ↵.

6. Activate the Center osnap, and click the circle on the grid. The KITCHEN text appears on the circle, with the lower-left corner of the text at the center of the circle (see the right image of Figure 8.25). Press Esc twice, once to end the Stretch function and again to clear the grip.

7. Click the copy of the KITCHEN text that is now on the grid, right-click to bring up the context menu, and then click Properties to open the Properties palette. Text appears on the drop-down list at the top, telling you that you've selected a text object.

This might seem like a roundabout way to generate letters for the grid symbols, but this exercise is meant to show you how easy it is to use text from one part of the drawing for a completely different text purpose. It's a handy technique, as long as you want to use a font that has been chosen for a previously defined text style. A faster way to do this is to use the Single Line Text command with the Justify setting set to Middle, use the Center osnap to place the text cursor at the center of the circle, and then enter A↵↵.

8. Use the Properties palette to make the following changes to the KITCHEN text:

   a. Change Layer, in the General rollout, from Text1 to Grid.

   b. Change Contents, in the Text rollout, from KITCHEN to A.

   c. Change the Justify setting from Left to Middle.

For each change, follow these steps in the Properties palette:

1. Click the category in the left column that needs to change. If the setting is on a drop-down list, an arrow appears in the right column.

2. Click the down arrow to open the list. In the case of the KITCHEN text, just highlight it because there is no drop-down list.

3. Click the new setting or enter it.

4. When you've finished, close the Properties palette and press Esc to deselect the text.

The KITCHEN text changes to the letter *A*, is centered in the grid circle, and moves to the Grid layer (see Figure 8.26).

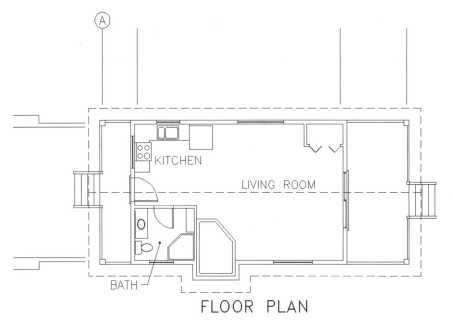

F I G U R E   8 . 2 6 : The grid circle with the letter A

You used the Center osnap on the KITCHEN text to position its justification point at the center of the circle. You then modified the justification point from the Left position (which is short for Base Left) to the Middle position (short for Middle Center). The Middle position is the middle of the line of text, horizontally and vertically. So what you did had the effect of centering the text in the circle. You'll now look at text justification briefly.

Justifying Text

Each line of single-line text is an object. It has a justification point, which is similar to the insertion points on blocks. When drawing, you can use the Insert osnap to locate the justification point of text precisely (or the insertion point of blocks) and thereby control the text's position on the drawing. When you use the Single Line Text or Dtext command, the default justification point is the lower-left corner of the line of text. At the Dtext prompt (`Specify start point of text or [Justify/Style]:`), if you enter j↵, you get the prompt `Enter an option [Align/Fit/Center/Middle/Right/TL/TC/TR/ML/MC/MR/BL/BC/BR]:`. These are your justification options.

Figure 8.27 shows most of these options. The dots are in three columns—left, center, and right—and in four rows—top, middle, lower, and base. The names of the justification locations are based on these columns and rows. For example, you have TL for Top Left, MR for Middle Right, and so on. The third row down doesn't use the name Lower; it simply goes by Left, Center, and Right. Left is the default justification position, so it's not in the list of options. The Middle position sometimes coincides with the Middle Center position, but not always. For example, if a line of text has *descenders*—portions of lowercase letters that drop below the baseline, such as *j* and *p*—the Middle position drops below the Middle Center position. Finally, the lowest row, the *Base row*, sits just below the letters at the lowest point of any descenders.

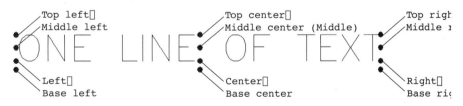

F I G U R E 8 . 2 7 : The justification points on a line of text

Finishing the Grid

To finish the grid, you need to copy the grid circle with its text to each grid line and then change the text:

1. Be sure the Endpoint osnap is still running. Then, at the command prompt, select the letter *A* and the circle. Grips appear: two for the text, one at the original justification point and one at the new justification point; one at the center of the circle; and one at each of the circle's quadrant points.

2. Click the grip at the bottom of the circle to activate it.

3. Right-click, and choose Move from the context menu; right-click again, and choose Copy to activate the copy option.

4. Pick the top end of each vertical grid line; then right-click and choose Enter to terminate the command (see Figure 8.28).

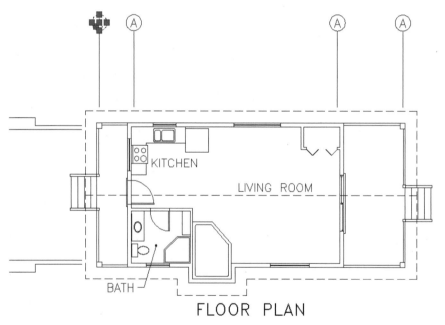

FIGURE 8.28: The grid circle and letter are copied to the top of all three vertical lines.

5. Move back to the original grid circle and select the grip on the right side of the circle to activate it.

6. Repeat steps 3 and 4 to copy the original grid circle and letter to the left end of each horizontal grid line.

7. Press Esc to deselect the objects and remove the grips. Then, if necessary, use the Stretch command to adjust the jogged lines and eliminate any overlap.

Now you'll use the Ddedit command to change the text in each circle.

You can also start the Ddedit command by opening the menu bar and choosing Modify ➢ Object ➢ Text ➢ Edit, or by entering **ddedit**↵ or the alias **ed**↵. These methods display additional command-line options.

8. Be sure Caps Lock is on, and then double-click the letter *A* in the second grid circle from the left on the top row. The text now has a blue background to indicate that it is being edited.

9. Enter B↵. The *A* changes to *B*.

T I P Editing text is one of the situations where pressing the spacebar does not have the same effect as pressing ↵.

10. Click the *A* in the next circle to the right, and then enter C↵. The *A* changes to a *C*.

11. Repeat this process for the remaining five grid circle letters, changing them to *D*, *1*, *2*, *3*, and *4*. Press ↵ to end the Edit Text command. The letters and numbers are all in place, and the grid is complete (see Figure 8.29).

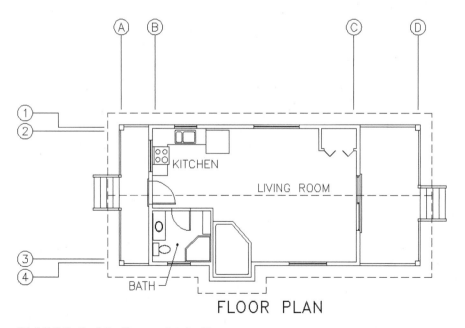

F I G U R E 8 . 2 9 : The completed grid

12. Save this drawing as Cabin08c.dwg.

Often, it's easier to copy existing text and modify it than to create new text, and grips are a handy way to copy text. Using the Edit Text command (technically called Ddedit) is a quick way to modify the wording of short lines of text, meaning those that consist of a word or a few letters. The Properties palette is useful for changing all aspects of a line of text.

For the next exercise with text, you'll get a chance to set up some more new text styles, place text precisely, and use the Ddedit command again to modify text content. You'll do all this while you develop a title block for your drawing.

Creating a Title Block and Border

The first step in creating a title block and border for the cabin drawing is deciding on a sheet size for printing the final drawing. Because many people have access to 8.5″×11″ (210×297) format printers, you'll use that sheet size. So if you print the drawing at a scale of 3/16″ = 1′-0″ (1 = 60), will it fit on the sheet?

To answer that question, you have to ask how big an area will fit on an 8.5″×11″ (210 mm×297 mm) sheet at 3/16″ = 1′-0″ (1:60) scale? The answer is quite simple: if every inch (millimeter) on the sheet represents 64″ (60 mm) in the drawing (12″ / (3/16″)) (60/1), you multiply each dimension of the sheet in inches (millimeters) by 64″ (60) per inch. For this sheet, you multiply 8.5″×64″ (210 mm×60) per inch to get 544″ (12,600 mm) or 45′-4″. You multiply 11″×64″ (297 mm×60) per inch to get 704″ (17,820 mm) or 58′-8″. So, the 8.5″×11″ (210 mm×297 mm) sheet represents a rectangle with dimensions of approximately 45′×58′ (12,600 mm×17,820 mm) at a scale of 3/16″ = 1′-0″ (1:60) (usually called *three-sixteenths inch scale*). You won't be able to show the entire column lines at this scale but, when I discuss layouts in Chapter 14, you will learn how to display the content of a single drawing at different scales. Even when you account for the unprintable area around the perimeter of the sheet, there should be plenty of room for your cabin drawing. This is the information you need to start creating the title block.

Drawing the Border

The border of the drawing will be set in from the edge of the sheet. Here are the steps:

1. Create a new layer called **Tblk1**. Leave the default color assigned, and make this layer current.

2. Start the Rectangle command (used in Chapter 4 to make the doors).

3. At the prompt, enter 0,0↵. Then enter 58′,45′ ↵ (17820,12600↵).

   This draws a rectangle that may extend off the top of the screen.

4. Use Zoom Extents to zoom out until the entire rectangle is visible in the drawing area (see Figure 8.30).

You need to fit the drawing into the rectangle as if you were fitting it on a sheet of paper. The easiest and safest way to do this is to move the rectangle over to enclose the drawing. You'll leave plenty of room for the elevations that you will draw in a later chapter.

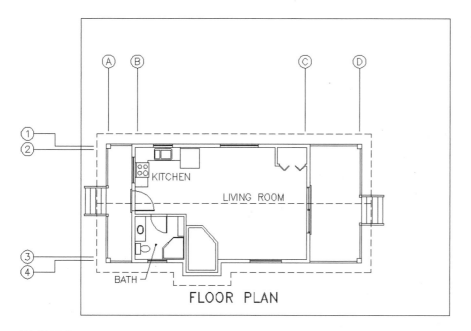

FIGURE 8.30: Zooming out to include the entire rectangle

5. At the command prompt, click the rectangle to select it. Grips appear at the corners of the rectangle.

6. Click the lower-left grip. Press the spacebar once to switch from Stretch mode to Move mode. Then move the rectangle over the drawing (see the top of Figure 8.31).

7. When the rectangle is approximately in the position shown in the bottom of Figure 8.31, click. Press Esc to deselect the rectangle. The rectangle is positioned around the drawing and represents the edge of the sheet.

Once you activate a grip and the Stretch function begins, pressing the space-bar toggles through the other four commands in this order: Move, Rotate, Scale, Mirror.

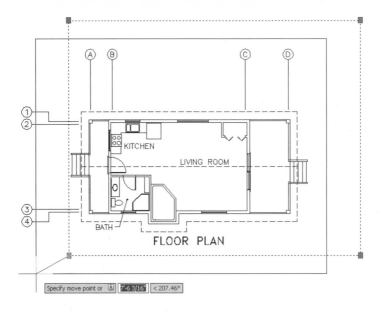

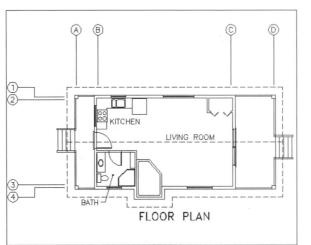

FIGURE 8.31: Moving the rectangle with grips (top) and the results (bottom)

8. You need a border set in from the edge. Offset the rectangle 2′ (600 mm) to the inside. With a scale of 3/16″ = 1′-0″ (1 = 60), each 1′-0″ (60 mm) on the drawing will be represented by 3/16″ (1 mm) on the sheet. So a 2′ (600 mm) offset distance will create an offset of 3/8″ (10 mm) on the printed sheet.

9. Double-click the inside rectangle to start the Pedit command.

10. Enter w↵2↵↵ (50↵↵). This command sets the width of the inside rectangle's segments to 2″ (50 mm).

11. Move both rectangles to center the cabin. Use Zoom Extents, and then zoom out a little to create a view in which the drawing with its border nearly fills the screen (see Figure 8.32). The outer rectangle represents the edge of the sheet of paper, and the thicker, inner rectangle is the drawing's border.

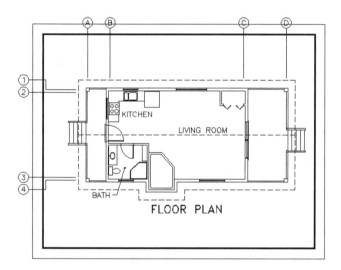

FIGURE 8.32: The drawing with its border

Constructing a Title Block

The *title block* is a box that contains general information about a drawing, such as the name of the project, the design company, and the date of the drawing. It will be set up in the lower-right corner of the border and will use the same special line, the *polyline*, which is created when the Rectangle command is executed.

You first used the Rectangle command in Chapter 4 for drawing the doors. At that time, I mentioned that rectangles created with the Rectangle command consist of a polyline whose four segments are grouped as one object. In step 10 of the previous section, you saw that these segments could have varying widths.

▶

You can also start the Polyline command by entering pl↵ or by choosing Draw ➢ Polyline from the menu bar.

The *Polyline command*, nicknamed the Pline command, allows you to draw continuous straight and curved line segments of varying widths, with all segments behaving as if they were one object.

When you explode a polyline using the Explode command, the segments lose any width they have and become independent lines. The ability of a polyline to have a width makes it useful in constructing title blocks. You'll use the Pline command to draw the various lines that make up the title block, and then you'll fill in the text:

1. Zoom in to a view of the lower third of your drawing, including the bottom of the border. Be sure the Endpoint and Perpendicular osnaps are running.

2. Click the Polyline icon on the Draw panel. The Specify start point: prompt appears in the Command window.

3. Click the Polar Tracking button on the status bar to turn on polar tracking. Hold the cursor over the lower-left corner of the inner border, and when the vertical tracking point appears, move the cursor directly above that point and enter 10'↵ (3050↵). This starts a polyline on the left side of the border 10' (3050 mm) above the lower-left corner.

4. Notice the bottom two lines of text in the Command window. The upper one tells you the width set for the polyline, currently 0'-0" (0). The lower one says Specify next point or [Arc/Halfwidth/Length/Undo/Width]:, listing the options for the Polyline command with the default option being to pick a second point. This is the time to set the line width.

5. Enter w↵, and then enter 2↵↵ (50↵↵). This sets the starting and ending widths of polyline segments to 2" (50 mm). The original polyline command prompt returns.

6. Hold the crosshair cursor on the right side of the border. When the Perpendicular osnap marker appears on the border line, click. Then press ↵ to terminate the command. The first polyline segment is drawn (see Figure 8.33). The 2" (50 mm) width setting will stay until you change it and will be saved with the drawing file.

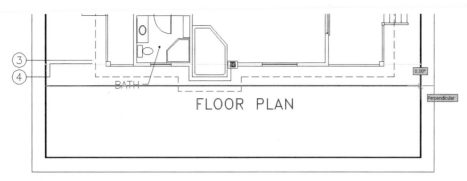

FIGURE 8.33: Drawing the first polyline for the title bar

7. Restart the Polyline command. Pause the cursor over the bottom-right corner of the border to set the temporary track point, move it directly to the left, and enter **16′⏎** (**4875⏎**) to start the polyline 16′ (4875 mm) from the corner.

8. Move the cursor to the last polyline that you drew and, when the Perpendicular osnap marker appears, click. The left edge of the title block is drawn (see the top of Figure 8.34). Press ⏎ to end the Polyline, or Pline, command.

9. Trim the left half of the upper horizontal pline drawn back to the pline just drawn.

10. Offset the horizontal pline down 3′-6″ (1065 mm), offset this new line down 2′-6″ (762 mm), and then offset this new line down 2′ (610 mm). (See the middle of Figure 8.34.)

11. Start the Pline command. Using Midpoint osnap, start a pline at the midpoint of the third horizontal line down. Then end the segment at the bottom of the border, taking advantage of the running Perpendicular osnap. Press ⏎ to end the Pline command.

12. Trim the right side of the line just above the bottom of the border, back to the line you just drew (see the bottom of Figure 8.34).

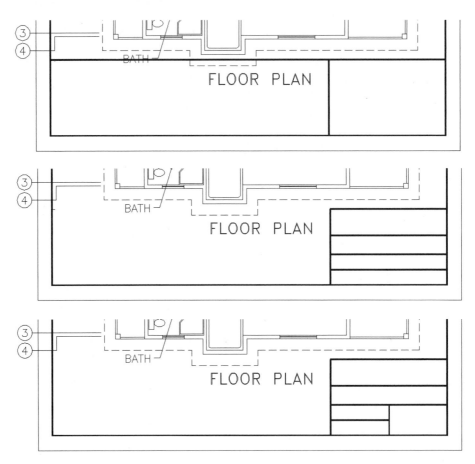

FIGURE 8.34: Building the title block: the left edge (top), the horizontal lines (middle), and the last line trimmed (bottom)

The lines for the title block are almost done. Some of the plines might look wider than others. The monitor distorting the picture at the current view almost certainly causes this. By zooming in, you can assure yourself that everything is correct.

1. Zoom in to a close view of the title block. Notice that the intersection of the outer lines in the upper-left corner doesn't seem clean.

2. Zoom in to that corner using a zoom window (see the left of Figure 8.35). The lines don't intersect in a clean corner because they are two separate polylines. You need to join them as one.

 3. Click the Edit Polyline button on the expanded Modify panel or enter pe↵ to start the Polyline Edit (Pedit) command, and select one of the two lines. When a pline is thicker than the pickbox, you must place

the pickbox on the edge of the polyline to select it, not over the middle of it.

4. Click Join or enter j↵ to activate the Join option, and then select the other pline and press ↵. This corrects the corner (see the right of Figure 8.35). Enter x↵ or just press ↵ to end the Pedit command.

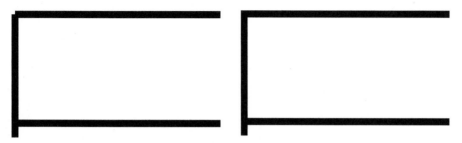

FIGURE 8.35: Zoomed into the upper-left corner (left) and the corner corrected (right)

5. Use Zoom Previous and then use Zoom with the scroll wheel to zoom out enough to see the entire title block (see Figure 8.36).

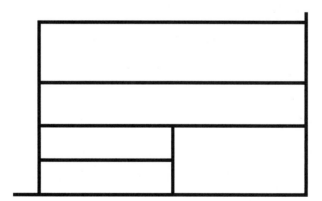

FIGURE 8.36: The completed lines of the title block after zooming out

Putting Text in the Title Block

The title block has five boxes that will each contain distinct pieces of information. The large one at the top will contain the name of the project. Below that will be the name of the company producing the drawing—your company. (If you don't have a company name, make one up.) Below that on the left will be the initials of the person (you) who drew this drawing, and below that will be the date.

In the lower-right corner will be the sheet number, in case more than one sheet is required for this project. This follows a standard format. Most title block layouts contain this information and more, depending on the complexity of the job.

You need to put labels in some of the boxes to identify what information will appear there. For this, you need to set up a new text style.

1. Expand the Text Style drop-down list, on the Text panel under the Ribbon's Annotate tab, and click Manage Text Styles.

2. The Label text style should still be current. If not, then select it. Click New, enter **Tblk-label**, and then click OK. Leave the font set to romans.shx, but change the height to 8″ (204). Click Apply and then Close. Tblk-label is the current text style.

3. Be sure Caps Lock is on, and start the Single Line Text or Dtext command. Click the None osnap button in the Shift+right-click menu, or enter **non**↵. Then pick a point in the upper-left corner of the upper box of the title block. It doesn't have to be the perfect location now; you can fix it after you see the text. The None osnap prevents you from picking a feature that exists in your drawing.

4. Press ↵ at the rotation prompt. Enter **PROJECT:**↵↵. PROJECT: appears in the upper box (see the left of Figure 8.37).

5. If necessary, move this text to the upper-left corner, as far as possible, while still allowing it to be readable. It will help if Polar Tracking and Object Snap are temporarily turned off.

T I P   If you have running osnaps and need to have them off for one pick, you can click the Snap to None osnap button. Doing so cancels all running osnaps for the next pick. If you need running osnaps turned off for several picks, click the Object Snap button on the status bar. Click it again when you want the running osnaps to become active.

6. Use the Copy command to copy this text to the bottom two boxes on the left, using the endpoint of the horizontal lines above each of the boxes as the base and displacement points. This keeps each piece of text in the same position relative to the upper-left corner of each box.

7. Double-click the upper of the two copies of text to start the Ddedit command.

8. Enter **DRAWN BY:** and press ↵. Pick the lower copy of text. The Edit Text dialog box returns.

9. Enter **DATE:** and press ↵. Press ↵ to end the Ddedit command. Doing this changes the text, so three of the boxes have their proper labels (see the right of Figure 8.37).

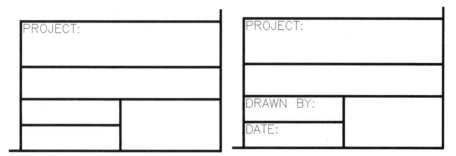

FIGURE 8.37: One line of text placed (left) and the text changed to the correct wording (right)

Using the Ddedit command is a quick way to change the wording of text and to correct spelling. You have to change one line at a time, but the command keeps running until you stop it. You can also change the Contents text box in the Properties palette.

The next area to work on is the lower-right box. This is where the sheet number appears, and it's usually displayed in such a way that the person reading the drawing can tell not only the page number of the current sheet but also the number of sheets being used for the project. You'll create a new text style for this box:

1. Open the Text Style dialog box and click New.

2. Turn off Caps Lock, then enter **Sheet_No** and click OK. For the font, select romand.shx. Change the height to 1′-1″ (330). Click Apply, and then click Close. Sheet_No is now the current text style.

3. Start the Dtext command, and enter **j**↵. Then enter **tc**↵ to set the justification to the top center of the text. Pick a point near the top-center of the large box in the bottom-right corner of the title box (see Figure 8.38). Use the None osnap if necessary.

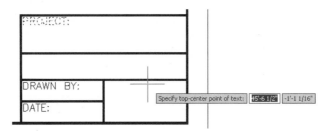

F I G U R E 8 . 3 8 : Positioning the text insertion point for the large box in the title block

4. Press ↵ at the rotation prompt. Turn Caps Lock back on, and then enter **SHEET:**↵ **1 of 1**↵↵. (When you get to the *of*, turn off Caps Lock or hold down the Shift key while typing.) This inserts the text into the box and centers it horizontally.

5. With polar tracking on, use the Move command to move the text down and center it vertically in the box (see Figure 8.39). Remember, when you select the text to move it, you have to pick each line because they are two separate objects.

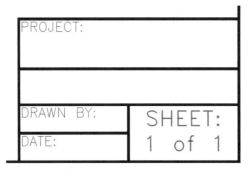

F I G U R E 8 . 3 9 : The text after being inserted and centered vertically

Now it's time for you to experiment. Use the techniques you just learned to fill in the text for the other four boxes. Feel free to try other fonts, but you'll have to adjust the height for each text style so that the text fits in its box. Some guidelines for height follow:

 T I P When the Font Name input box is highlighted, use the up and down arrows on the keyboard to scroll through the fonts and watch the preview window to see what the font looks like.

Box	Recommended Height of Text
Project	1'-8" (510 mm)
Company	1'-0" (305 mm)
Drawn By	0'-10" (254 mm)
Date	0'-10" (254 mm)

You can use the same style for all text with the same properties, but you'll have to set up a new style for each new font or height you choose unless you set up a style with a height of 0'-0" (0). In that case, you'll be prompted for the height each time you start to place text in the drawing. This is the recommended way to operate for the top two boxes because it will give consistency to the text even when heights vary. You might try several fonts and then come back to this technique at the end. I also recommend you use a relatively simple font for the text in the Drawn By and Date boxes.

Try these fonts:

▶ romant.shx or romanc.shx

▶ Any of the swis721 series

▶ Times New Roman

▶ Technic

▶ SansSerif

▶ CityBlueprint or CountryBlueprint

▶ Arial

In the top two boxes, you can center the text vertically and horizontally if you draw a line diagonally across the box, choose Middle Center as a justification for the text, and use the Midpoint osnap to snap to the diagonal line when you start the text. For the Drawn By and Date boxes, centering the text horizontally isn't advisable because the label text already in the boxes takes up too much space. However, you can use the diagonal line to center it and then move the text to the right until it makes a good fit. Using polar tracking will keep the new text vertically centered.

Be careful in your use of running osnaps as you position text. If you're eyeballing the final location, it's best to have no running osnaps. On the other hand, if you're precisely locating justification points by snapping to lines and other objects, you might try having the following osnaps running: Endpoint,

Intersection, Perpendicular, and Insertion, with Midpoint optional. When you finish, your title block should look something like Figure 8.40.

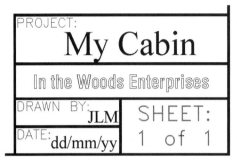

FIGURE 8.40: The completed title block

If you're going to design your own company title block, be ready to spend a little time setting it up and deciding which fonts will give the look that best reflects the image you want to project. You can then use this title block on all your subsequent projects.

Use Zoom to Extents, and then zoom out a little to view the entire drawing. Save this drawing (see Figure 8.41) as Cabin80d.dwg.

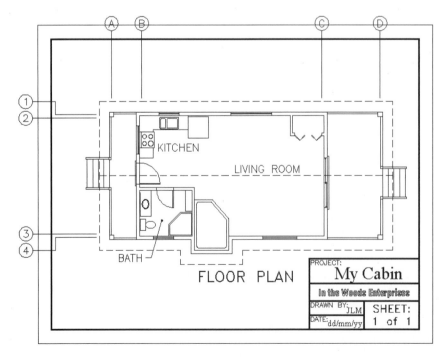

FIGURE 8.41: The latest version of the cabin drawing

Looking at AutoCAD's Title Blocks

Now that you've created a title block and a border, you'll briefly look at the title blocks and borders that AutoCAD provides in its template files and see how you can use these files to set up a new drawing. Follow these steps:

1. Click the New icon on the Quick Access toolbar to open the Select Template dialog box.

2. Double-click `Tutorial-iArch.dwt` or `Tutorial-mArch.dwt` for an imperial or metric template. The new drawing appears with a title block and border (see Figure 8.42). In addition, this sheet has extra lines and area along the right edge for listing revisions to the drawing and company information.

FIGURE 8.42: A new drawing made from the Tutorial-iArch template

3. Zoom in to the title block on the lower part of the drawing, as shown in Figure 8.43. Notice that it has spaces for the scale and sheet number, among other information, and that some areas are left blank.

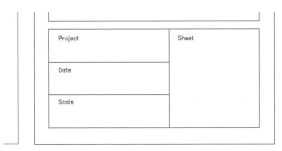

FIGURE 8.43: A close-up of the architectural drawing template

4. Close this drawing, and click the New button again to look at some of the other template files on the list. Don't worry about the part of the template name that identifies plot style types. I'll cover this in Chapter 15, "Printing an AutoCAD Drawing." The background for the template files is gray because they use *layouts*, which I'll introduce in Chapter 14, "Using Layouts to Set Up a Print."

When you open a new drawing by selecting a template file, AutoCAD uses the template file as the basis of your new drawing. It copies the information in the template file onto the new drawing file and names the new drawing Drawing1, Drawing2, and so on. You can convert any drawing into a template file. Simply choose Save As ➤ AutoCAD Drawing Template from the Application menu. The new file will have the .dwt extension. You can store it in AutoCAD's Template folder or any folder you choose. When you click Save, the Template Options dialog box opens, giving you the options of writing a description of the new template file and choosing whether the template will use metric or English units (see Figure 8.44).

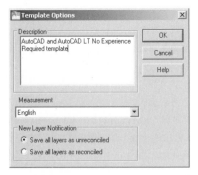

FIGURE 8.44: The Template Options dialog box

The final section of this chapter introduces you to multiline text, which you'll also work with as you learn about dimensions in the next chapter, and it introduces you to AutoCAD's spelling checker.

Using Multiline Text

Multiline text (often referred to as *Mtext*) is more complex than single-line text. You can use it in the same way you used single-line text in this chapter, but it can do more. When you have several lines of text or when you need certain words within a line of text to appear differently than the adjacent words, multi-line text is the best feature to use.

A paragraph of multiline text is a single entity. The text wraps around, and you can easily modify the length of a line after you place the text in the drawing. Within the multiline text entity, all text can be edited and behaves as if it were in a word processor. You can give a special word or letter of the text its own text style or color. Everything you learned about defining a new text style applies to multiline text, because both kinds of text use the same text styles. Just as polylines become lines when exploded, multiline text is reduced to single-line text when exploded.

Dimensions use multiline text, and any text that is imported into an AutoCAD drawing from a word processing document or text editor becomes multiline text in the drawing. In this section, you'll learn how to place a paragraph of multiline text in the cabin drawing and then modify it. In Chapter 12, you'll work with dimension text and text with leader lines, both of which use multiline text.

Use the Explode command to turn multiline text into single-line text, to unblock objects in a block reference, and to convert a polyline into regular lines. Click the Explode button on the Modify panel to start the command.

T I P   If you are using AutoCAD and have the Express Tools installed, the Txt2mtxt command (on the menu bar, click Express ➤ Text ➤ Convert Text to Mtext) changes the selected Dtext objects into Mtext objects. When multiples lines of Dtext are selected, they are converted into a single Mtext object. LT does not have the Express Tools available.

You'll start by adding a note in the lower-left corner of the Cabin08d drawing, using the Multiline Text command:

1. Click the Make Object's Layer Current button on the Layers panel. Then click the FLOOR PLAN text to make the Text1 layer current. Zoom in to the blank area to the left of the title block in the lower-left corner of the cabin drawing.

2. Click the Object Snap button on the status bar to disable any running osnaps temporarily. Then, under the Annotate tab, click the Multiline Text button on the Text panel. The Command window displays the

name of the current text style and height and prompts you to specify a first corner.

3. Select a point near the left border line in line with the top of the title block. The prompt now says `Specify opposite corner or [Height/Justify/Line spacing/Rotation/Style/Width/Columns]:`. These are all the options for the Multiline Text command.

4. If the current style is Label, go on to step 5. Otherwise, expand the Text Style drop-down list and choose Label.

5. Unlike single-line text, Mtext uses a window to define the width of the text, rather than a point for the justification point. Drag open a window that fills the space between the left border and the left side of the pop-out. This defines the line width for the multiline text (see Figure 8.45). Click to finish the window.

FIGURE 8.45: Making a multiline text window

6. The Text Editor tab and its associated panels appear in the ribbon. In the Style and Formatting panels, you can see the current text style and its font and height, as shown in Figure 8.46. Just above the rectangle you defined, the Multiline Text Editor opens. This is where you'll enter the text.

FIGURE 8.46: The Style and Formatting panels on the Text Editor tab

7. Enter the following text, using single spacing and pressing ⏎ only at the end of the first line and at the end of each note. Lines that are longer than the window that you dragged out will wrap automatically:

GENERAL NOTES:

All work shall be in accordance with the 2000 Ed. Uniform Building Code and all local ordinances.

Roof can be built steeper for climates with heavy snowfall.

All windows to be double-paned.

8. When you've finished, click a blank spot in the drawing area. The text appears in the drawing (see the top left of Figure 8.47). The window you specified was used only to define the line length. Its height doesn't control how far down the text comes; that is determined by how much text you enter. Before you adjust the text to fit the area, you will have AutoCAD add numbering to the notes.

9. Double-click anywhere on the new text to display the Multiline Text Editor and the MText panels.

10. Move the cursor to the upper-left corner of the window containing the text and in front of the *A* in the first word (*All*) of the first note. Hold down the left mouse button, and drag to the right and down until all the remaining text is highlighted. Release the mouse button.

11. Expand the Bullets and Numbering drop-down list in the Paragraph panel and then choose Numbered from the cascading menu that pops up (see the top right of Figure 8.47).

12. The note numbers appear. Click the Close Text Editor button on the Close panel; then select the text object and open the Properties palette.

13. In the Text rollout, highlight the Text Height input field and change the value from 1' (305) to 9" (230), and press ⏎. AutoCAD redraws the text smaller.

14. Use the grip at the upper-right corner of the text to stretch the text box further to the right. The text reconfigures to fit the new constraints (see the bottom of Figure 8.47).

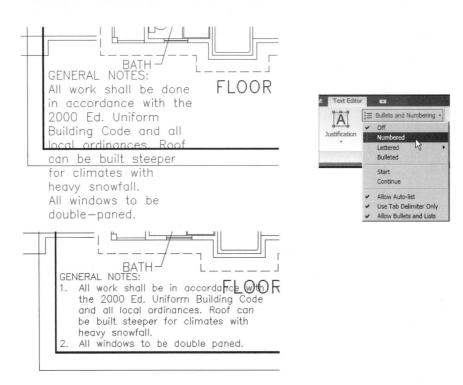

F I G U R E 8 . 4 7 : Mtext in the drawing (top left), adding the note numbers (top right), and the modified text (bottom)

15. Double-click the Mtext again. The Text Editor tab opens.

16. Highlight all the text again. In the Font drop-down list on the For-matting panel, select SansSerif as the current font. The selected text changes to the new font.

17. Click a point in the drawing area. The Mtext in the drawing becomes more compact, and there is room for more notes.

18. Move the text and title block down and to the left until the cabin fits neatly within the upper-border area and the notes are unobstructed (see Figure 8.48).

A
B
C
D
1
2
3
4
KITCHEN
LIVING ROOM
BATH
FLOOR PLAN
GENERAL NOTES:
1. All work shall be done in accordance with the 2000 Ed. Uniform Building Code and all local ordinances. Roof can be built steeper for climates with heavy snowfall.
2. All windows to be double-paned.
PROJECT:
My Cabin
In the Woods Enterprises
DRAWN BY: JLM
SHEET:
DATE: dd/mm/yy
1 of 1

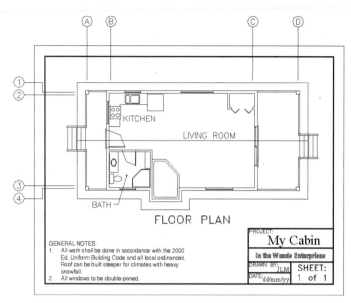

FIGURE 8.48: The results of a font modification

SansSerif is a TrueType font supported by Windows. When used in AutoCAD drawings, it can be italic or bold. To see how to change individual words within the text, you'll underline and bold the "Uniform Building Code" text:

1. Zoom in to and double-click the Mtext again.

B

U

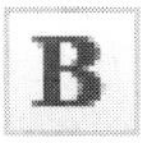

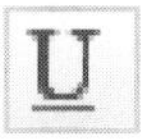

2. Use the same technique as you did earlier to highlight only the "Uniform Building Code" text. Then click the Bold and Underline buttons on the Formatting panel. This underlines the selected text and displays the bold feature.

3. Click in the drawing area. AutoCAD redraws the text with the changes (see Figure 8.49).

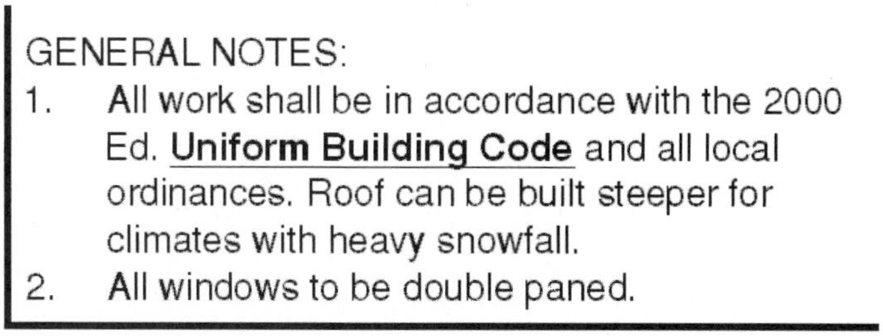

GENERAL NOTES:
1. All work shall be in accordance with the 2000 Ed. **Uniform Building Code** and all local ordinances. Roof can be built steeper for climates with heavy snowfall.
2. All windows to be double paned.

FIGURE 8.49: The Mtext with individual words modified

You can also italicize individual words and give them a different color or height from the rest of the Mtext by using the other tools on the Multiline Text panel. I encourage you to experiment with all these tools to become familiar with them.

You can easily alter the length of a line to make the Mtext fit more conveniently on the drawing. Let's say you've decided to put your company logo to the left of the title block. You need to squeeze the text into a narrower space. You have some extra room at the bottom, so you should be able to do it:

1. Move the Mtext up slightly, and then click the Mtext to select it. Two square grips appear at the upper corners of the body of Mtext and one arrow-shaped grip appears centered at the bottom.

2. On the status bar, be sure Polar Tracking and Object Snap are off. Then click the bottom-center grip to activate it.

3. Slowly move the cursor down as far as you can without causing the text box to dip below the border (see the top of Figure 8.50) and then click.

4. Select the upper-right grip, move it as far as you can to the left without causing the Mtext to form another column to the right of the existing column, and then click (see the bottom of Figure 8.50).

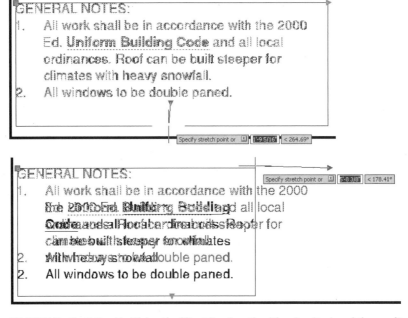

FIGURE 8.50: Modifying the Mtext line length with grips (top) and the results (bottom)

5. Reposition the text as necessary.

The ruler at the top of the Mtext Editor window has two sliding indicators for setting indentions. The top indicator is for the first line in the Mtext object and the first line after each ⏎. The bottom indicator is for the rest of the text. You set that one in a little to the left to make the note numbers stand out. Follow these steps:

1. Double-click the text again.

2. In the Mtext Editor window, highlight the two notes.

3. Use the mouse to slide the bottom indicator on the ruler one notch to the left (see Figure 8.51). Click outside the text to save the changes. The notes are now a bit closer to the numbers.

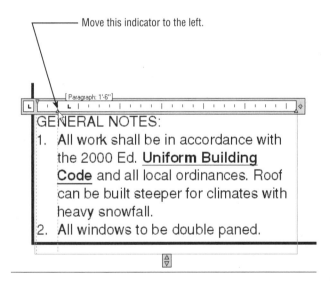

FIGURE 8.51: Adjusting the paragraph slider on the ruler and the result

Adding a Hyperlink

You have the ability to add *hyperlinks*, links to web pages or files, to the body of an Mtext object. When a hyperlink to a URL exists, anyone with the drawing open can hold down the Ctrl button and click the link to open the associated page in their web browser. Hyperlinks can also point to local or network files, causing the file's associated application to open when they are clicked. Here is the procedure for adding a hyperlink:

1. Double-click the Mtext object.

2. Highlight the text where you want the hyperlink to appear.

3. Right-click and choose Insert Field from the context menu (see Figure 8.52), or click the Field button in the Insert panel.

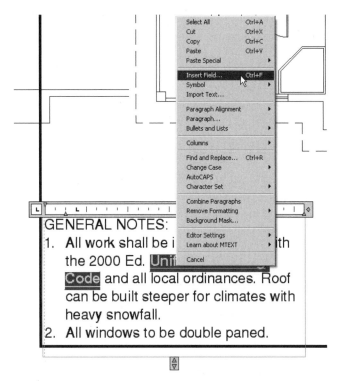

FIGURE 8.52: Inserting a field into an Mtext object

4. In the Field Names section of the Field dialog box that opens, select Hyperlink. In the Text to Display field, enter the text that you want to appear in the tooltip when the cursor hovers over the hyperlink (see Figure 8.53). In this case, it will be the same.

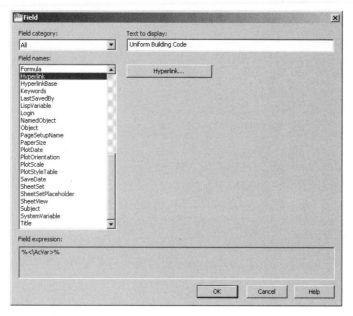

FIGURE 8.53: The Field dialog box

5. Click the Hyperlink button; then, in the Edit Hyperlink dialog box (see Figure 8.54), you can do any of the following:

▶ Enter the web page or filename and path in the Type The File Or Web Page Name box.

▶ Click the File button under Browse For to select a file to which to link the text.

▶ Click the Web Page button under Browse For to navigate to the web page to which you want to link the text.

Perform one of these options, click the OK button to close this dialog box, and then click OK to close the Field dialog box.

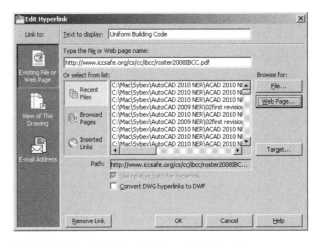

FIGURE 8.54: The Edit Hyperlink dialog box

6. Click a blank area to deselect the Mtext. The link appears as text with a gray background; the background doesn't appear in a printed drawing.

7. Hold the Ctrl key down, and hover the cursor over the gray background (see Figure 8.55). The cursor changes to the hyperlink cursor, and instructions to follow the link appear on a tooltip. With Ctrl still pressed, click the background. This minimizes AutoCAD, opens your browser, and navigates to the selected web page.

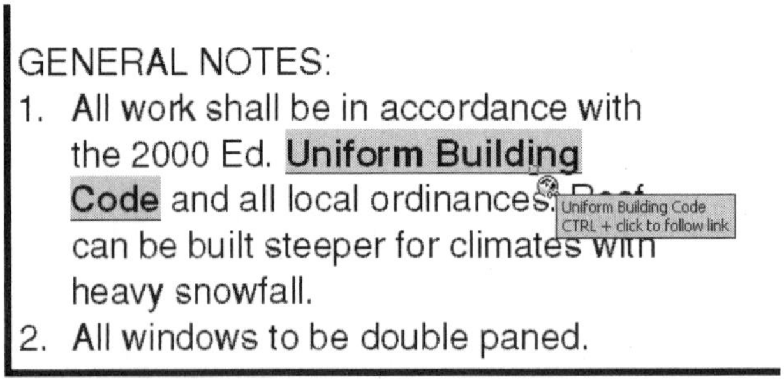

GENERAL NOTES:
1. All work shall be in accordance with the 2000 Ed. **Uniform Building Code** and all local ordinances. Roof can be built steeper for climates with heavy snowfall.
2. All windows to be double paned.

Uniform Building Code
CTRL + click to follow link

FIGURE 8.55: Selecting a hyperlink embedded in Mtext

8. Perform a Zoom Extents, and then save this drawing as Cabin08e.dwg. Your drawing should look like Figure 8.56.

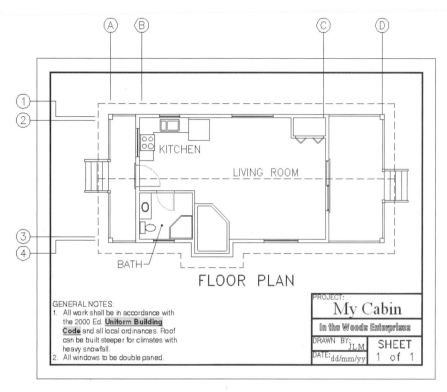

FIGURE 8.56: The cabin with the text added

Using the Spell-Check Feature

Like most programs with word processing capability, AutoCAD includes a spell-check feature to identify potential spelling errors. The spell check can be run to look for errors in a selected single-line or multiline text object. There is also a real-time spell-check feature to spot misspellings as you type and to suggest alternative words. Follow these steps to see the spell-check feature in action:

1. Zoom into the notes at the bottom of the drawing area and move them up enough to allow space for one more line of text. Expand the Mtext window down to accommodate the next line of text.

2. Double-click the notes, place the cursor just past the period at the end of the second note, and enter ↵**Soler panels, by SolCorp, are available.**↵ ↵. The third numbered note is appended to the others.

3. Notice how the words *Soler* and *SolCorp* are underlined with a dashed line (see Figure 8.57). This is how the real-time spell-check tool identifies the words the AutoCAD dictionary doesn't recognize.

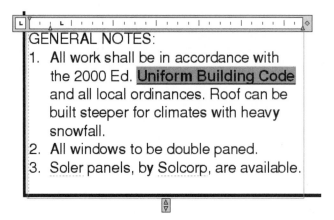

FIGURE 8.57: The new line of text with the misspelled words

4. Position the cursor in the word *Soler*, and right-click to open a context menu. At the top of the menu are spelling suggestions. Click or pause the cursor over the More Suggestions options; then click Solar, as shown in Figure 8.58. *Soler* is replaced with *Solar* in the selected Mtext.

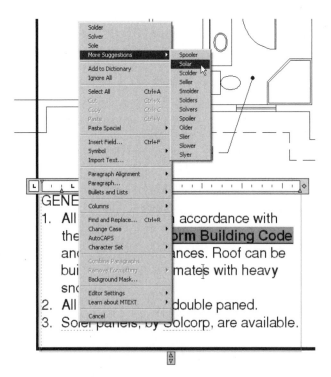

FIGURE 8.58: Using the context menu to replace a misspelled word

Many words that you frequently use, such as company, city, or individual names, may not exist in the AutoCAD dictionary and will be flagged as misspelled words. You can easily add words to the dictionary to eliminate these words from being flagged repeatedly.

5. Put the cursor in the word SolCorp, and right-click to open the context menu. Near the top of the menu, click Add To Dictionary (see Figure 8.59). SolCorp is added to the AutoCAD dictionary and is no longer underlined.

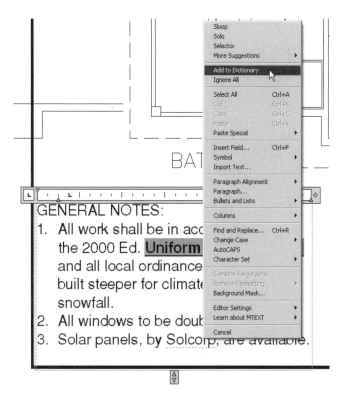

FIGURE 8.59: Adding a word to the AutoCAD dictionary

Spell-Checking an Entire Drawing

Often, drawings can have many separate text elements in the form of single-line text, multiline text, and dimensions. Although you can select each object individually, you can also run the Spell Check tool on the entire drawing. Here's how:

1. Make sure nothing is selected in the drawing. Then, under the Annotate tab, click the Check Spelling button in the Text panel.

2. In the Check Spelling dialog box that opens, choose Entire Drawing in the Where To Check drop-down list and then click Start. AutoCAD checks the entire drawing for words that do not exist in the dictionary, highlights them, and offers suggestions for misspelled words, as shown in Figure 8.60.

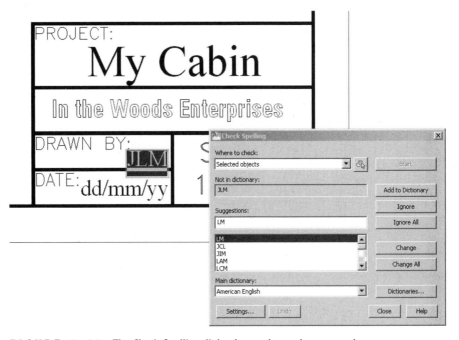

FIGURE 8.60: The Check Spelling dialog box and an unknown word

3. When an unknown word is identified, you can:

   ▶ Click Add To Dictionary to add the word to the AutoCAD dictionary.

   ▶ Click Ignore to take no action and continue searching the drawing for misspelled words.

   ▶ Click Ignore All to take no action and continue searching the drawing for misspelled words, ignoring all occurrences of the same word.

► Select a word in the Suggestions list and then click Change to replace the flagged word with the suggested word.

► Select a word in the Suggestions list and then click Change All to replace the flagged word with the suggested word and automatically substitute all occurrences of the flagged word for the suggested word.

4. When the spell-checking task is finished, click OK in the Spell Check Complete dialog box and click Close in the Check Spelling dialog box.

5. Perform a Zoom Extents, and then save this drawing as Cabin08f.dwg.

Exploring Other Aspects of Multiline Text

Multiline text has several other features that I can only touch on in this book. I encourage you to experiment with any features that you might find useful to your work.

Using Justification Points

Mtext has justification points similar to those of single-line text, and they behave the same way. The default justification point for Mtext, however, is the upper-left corner of the body of text, and the available options are for nine points distributed around the perimeter of the body of text and at the center (see Figure 8.61).

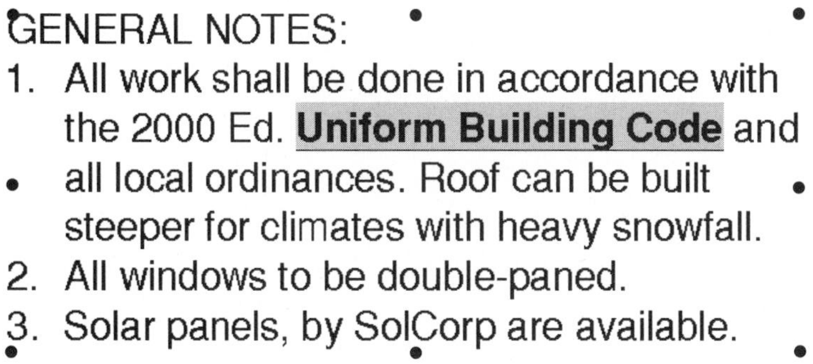

GENERAL NOTES: •   •
1. All work shall be done in accordance with
    the 2000 Ed. **Uniform Building Code** and
•   all local ordinances. Roof can be built   •
    steeper for climates with heavy snowfall.
2. All windows to be double-paned.
3. Solar panels, by SolCorp are available.
•   •   •

FIGURE 8.61: Justification points for Mtext

When you need to modify the justification of Mtext, double-click the text to open the Mtext Editor and display the Text Editor tab and panels. In the Paragraph panel, click the Justification button and then click the justification preference from the fly-out menu, as shown in Figure 8.62. I'll describe the other items on this menu in the upcoming "Tools for Modifying Multiline Text" sidebar.

FIGURE 8.62: Justification points for Mtext

Adding Special Characters

With Mtext, you can add special characters—the degree symbol, the diameter symbol, and so on—that aren't included in most font character packages. You'll have a chance to do this in Chapter 12, "Dimensioning a Drawing."

If you want to experiment with the Mtext in the cabin drawing, make a copy of it, and place it outside of the title block. Double-click it and see what you can learn about the Multiline Text Editor, the tools found in the panels located under the Multiline Text tab, and the Mtext shortcut menu. The "Tools for Modifying Multiline Text" sidebar summarizes the features of the latter two.

TOOLS FOR MODIFYING MULTILINE TEXT

Here's a brief summary of the various features of the Multiline Text tab's panels that are available whenever Mtext is selected with a double-click:

The Style Panel

Style List Lists all existing text styles in the drawing file.

Continues

TOOLS FOR MODIFYING MULTILINE TEXT *(Continued)*

Annotative Button Toggles the Annotative property for text and dimensions. This property can cause the text to scale automatically as necessary. Chapter 12 covers annotation.

Text Height Drop-down Text Box Sets the height for selected text or sets the height for subsequently entered text.

The Formatting Panel

Bold, Italic, Underline, and Overline Buttons Changes selected text or sets up for subsequently entered text.

Make Uppercase and Make Lowercase Buttons Changes the case of the selected text to all upper- or all lowercase.

Font Drop-down List Sets the font for the selected text or sets the font for subsequently entered text.

Color Drop-down List Changes the color of a selected portion of text or sets a color for subsequently entered text.

Background Mask Button Sets the parameters for using a background mask to hide objects behind the text.

Oblique Angle Spinner Buttons Sets the selected text to an oblique angle off the vertical, from −85° to the left to 85° to the right.

Tracking Spinner Buttons Adjusts the spacing between selected letters from a minimum of 75 percent of the default spacing to a maximum of four times the default spacing.

Width Factor Spinner Buttons Adjusts the width of selected letters and the spacing between them from a minimum of 10 percent of the default width and spacing to a maximum of 10 times the default.

The Paragraph Panel

Justification Button Displays a menu with the nine Mtext justification choices.

Bullets and Numbering Button Opens a fly-out menu for controlling numbering and bullets.

Line Spacing Button Opens a fly-out menu for controlling spacing between lines of text.

Continues

TOOLS FOR MODIFYING MULTILINE TEXT *(Continued)*

Paragraph Button Opens up by clicking on the arrow on the right. Opens the Paragraph dialog box where you can set tab and paragraph spacing, indents, and other paragraph-related parameters.

Left, Center, Right, Justify, and Distribute Buttons Justifies the selected text accordingly.

The Insert Panel

Columns Button Opens a menu for controlling the column options.

Symbol Button Opens a menu of symbols to insert into the Mtext where the cursor rests.

Field Button Begins the process of inserting a field in the Mtext in place of selected text or where the cursor rests in the text.

The Spell Check Panel

Spell Check Button Runs the Spell Check utility.

Edit Dictionaries Opens the Dictionaries dialog box where custom dictionaries can be selected and edited.

The Tools Panel

Find & Replace Button Opens the Find and Replace dialog box where you can specify a text string to search for and the text string that will replace it.

Import Text Imports a word processing or text file into an AutoCAD drawing. The maximum size allowed is 32KB, so the smallest document possible in some versions of Microsoft Word is too large. You can, however, use files in text-only or RTF formats. Clicking the Import Text button opens the Select File dialog box that displays only files with the .txt and .rtf extensions. You can bring in text files with other extensions if you enter the full filename with its extension and if they aren't larger than 32KB. Text comes in as Mtext and uses the current text style, height setting, and layer. The imported file might not retain complex code fields for such elements as tabs, multiple margin indents, and so on.

AutoCAPS When checked, capitalizes all text.

The Options Panel

More Displays a menu with several options for adjusting the parameters for text, Mtext, and the Mtext editor.

Continues

TOOLS FOR MODIFYING MULTILINE TEXT *(Continued)*

Ruler Button Toggles the ruler above the Mtext to be visible or invisible.

Undo Button Undoes the last editing action.

Redo Button Redoes the last undo.

The Close Panel

Close Button Deselects the Mtext and closes the Multiline Text tab.

The Mtext Context Menu

The features of the Mtext context menu, the menu that appears when you place your cursor in the text or highlight text and right-click, are as follows:

Spelling Suggestions If the highlighted text is not in the dictionary, then a set of suggested words is displayed along with a cascading menu with additional word options.

Add To Dictionary and Ignore All Two more actions available when misspelled words are highlighted.

Select All Selects and highlights all the text in the selected Mtext object.

Cut Copies the selected text to the Windows Clipboard and deletes it from the Mtext object.

Copy Copies the selected text to the Windows Clipboard.

Paste Pastes text from the Windows Clipboard to the cursor location in the Mtext objects.

Paste Special Displays a submenu containing additional methods for pasting content into an Mtext object.

Insert Field Opens the Field dialog box, which you use to insert a field into the selected text. If you select text containing a field, this menu item changes to three menu items: Edit Field, Update Field, and Convert Field To Text.

Symbol Imports symbols (such as diameter, degree, and so on) that aren't available in the font you're using.

Import Text Imports a word processing or text file into an AutoCAD drawing. The maximum size allowed is 32KB, so the smallest document possible in some versions of Microsoft Word is too large. You can, however, use files in text-only or RTF formats. Clicking the Import Text button opens the

Continues

TOOLS FOR MODIFYING MULTILINE TEXT *(Continued)*

Select File dialog box that displays only files with the `.txt` and `.rtf` extensions. You can bring in text files with other extensions if you enter the full filename with its extension and if they aren't larger than 32KB. Text comes in as Mtext and uses the current text style, height setting, and layer. The imported file might not retain complex code fields for such elements as tabs, multiple margin indents, and so on.

Paragraph Alignment Sets the justification for the selected Mtext.

Paragraph Opens the Paragraph dialog box. It has settings for indenting the first line and subsequent paragraphs of Mtext (similar to what the sliders do on the ruler above the Mtext Editor window) and tab stop positions.

Bullets and Lists Opens a fly-out menu that offers various options for using the listing features.

Columns Provides access to the column parameters.

Find and Replace Opens the Replace dialog box, in which you search for a word or a series of words (text string) and replace them with text that you specify.

Change Case Changes the case of all highlighted text to uppercase or lowercase.

AutoCAPS When checked, capitalizes all text.

Character Set Opens a menu of several languages. When applicable, the codes of the selected language are applied to selected text.

Combine Paragraphs Joins highlighted individual paragraphs into one paragraph.

Remove Formatting Removes formatting, such as bold, underline, and so on, from highlighted text.

Background Mask Opens the Background Mask dialog box in which you specify color for and activate a background mask to go behind the selected Mtext object.

Editor Settings Opens a menu where you can select whether certain features appear, such as the ruler or toolbar.

Learn About MTEXT Opens the New Features Workshop at the lesson regarding Mtext.

Cancel Closes the menu.

If You Would Like More Practice...

Trades and professions other than architecture and construction use text with AutoCAD and LT in the same way as demonstrated in this chapter.

For more practice using single-line text, follow these steps:

1. Close all drawings, and then open Cabin04c-addon.dwg.

2. Using the DesignCenter, bring in the Title and Label text styles from the Cabin08e drawing while it's closed.

3. Place labels on the features that were added:

   ▶ Use the Title text style to identify the addition as GARAGE.

   ▶ Use the Label text style to give the features the following names: WALKWAY, STORAGE, OFFICE, and CAR.

For more practice using Mtext, follow these steps:

1. Open Cabin08f.dwg, and zoom in to the blank space between the notes and the title block.

2. Create a new text style called Description that uses the Times New Roman font and a height of 8″ (204 mm).

3. Start Mtext, and specify a rectangle for the text that covers the area between the notes and the title bar.

4. Enter the following text exactly as shown here, spelling errors and all:

   This is a design for a small vaction cabin. It contains approximately 380 square feet of living space and includes one bedroom and one bath. It can be adopted to provide shelter in all climates and can be modified to allow constuction that uses local building materials. Please sund all inquiries to the manufacturer.

5. Double-click the new text, and make these changes:

   a. Correct all spelling errors using the Spell Check tool or real-time spell checking.

   b. Change *square feet* to sq. ft.

   c. Bold the following: *one bedroom, one bath, all climates,* and *local building materials.*

   d. Italicize the last sentence.

Are You Experienced?

Now you can...

- ☑ set up text styles
- ☑ place single-line text in a drawing for titles and room labels
- ☑ create a structural grid for a drawing
- ☑ modify single-line text
- ☑ construct a title block and place text in it
- ☑ open AutoCAD template files
- ☑ place Mtext in a drawing
- ☑ modify Mtext in several ways
- ☑ add a hyperlink to an Mtext object
- ☑ check the spelling in a drawing

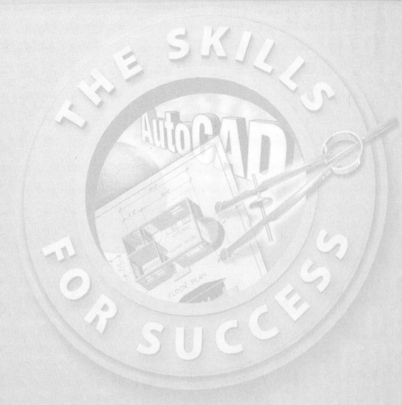

CHAPTER 9

Using Dynamic Blocks and Tables

- ▶ Adding block attributes
- ▶ Calculating area
- ▶ Adding fields as attributes
- ▶ Creating dynamic blocks
- ▶ Creating tables

I n Chapter 7, you explored creating and using blocks to combine separate objects into a single, complex object to aid in selecting objects and editing properties. Chapter 8 covered the addition of text into drawings. In this chapter, you will expand your knowledge of blocks and use text inside blocks and tables to display information about specific features of the drawing.

The blocks you've worked with have been static collections of objects that you have inserted throughout your drawing as doors or windows. Each instance of the same block was visually identical to the others, and you were able to scale the window blocks along one axis and without distortion to fit the walls. Blocks can also contain textual information, called *attributes*, specific to an individual block instance. Blocks do not have to remain static and unchanging. In this chapter, you will learn how to define your blocks so that they can change as required, without needing to explode the blocks and modify the component objects.

After exploring blocks further, you'll learn how to create a table to act as a door schedule, displaying the door type, unit price, and total cost. A *schedule* is a chart in a drawing that contains logically organized information about a particular component of a project, such as a steel base plate, valve, bolt or screw, door, window, or room finish. Each of these has its own schedule. Information in a door schedule, for example, might include size, material, finish, location, and type of jamb.

Using Attributes for a Grid

The grid lines for a building are usually located at the center lines of structural components, such as walls or columns. You can identify columns in buildings by letter and number, specifying the intersection of the two grid lines. In the cabin drawing, you used grid lines to indicate the outside edges of exterior walls and the center lines of interior walls. Grids generally have a circle or a hexagon with a number or letter in it at the end of each grid line, with the numbers running in one direction (horizontally or vertically) and letters in the other.

A simple but handy use of attributes is to make the letter or number in the circle an attribute and then make a block out of the attribute and circle. By redoing the grid symbols in the cabin drawing, you'll learn how to set up attributes and create a new block that can be used in any other drawing:

1. Open Cabin8f.dwg. The drawing consists of the floor plan with a structural grid, notes, and a title block. Make sure the Grid layer is current, and then freeze the Tblk1 and Text1 layers.

2. Zoom in to the floor plan, keeping the grid visible. In this case, the letters run horizontally across the top and the numbers run vertically along the side.

3. Erase all the circles, letters, and numbers in the grid except those for *A* and *1*. Leave the grid lines intact (see Figure 9.1).

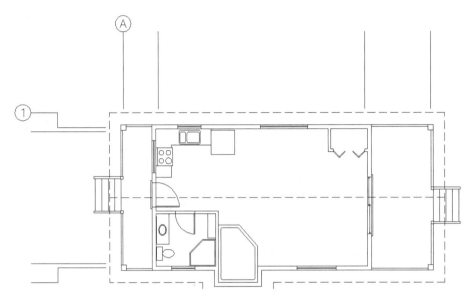

FIGURE 9.1: The floor plan of `Cabin8f` with all but two grid symbols erased

4. Select the letter *A*, right-click, and choose Properties. The Properties palette displays information about the text (see Figure 9.2). You need to know the text style and the height: Label and 1′ (305).

FIGURE 9.2: The Properties palette for the text

5. Close or minimize the Properties palette, and then erase *A* and *1*, but not the circles.

6. Start the Scale command. Select the top, left circle and press ↵.

7. At the Specify base point: prompt, use the Endpoint osnap, and pick the endpoint of the grid line where it meets the circle. Enter **1.25**↵. This enlarges the circle by 25 percent.

8. Repeat steps 6 and 7 for the circle on the left side.

9. Expand the Block panel; then click the Define Attributes button to start the Attdef command and open the Attribute Definition dialog box (see Figure 9.3). In the Attribute area are three text boxes: Tag, Prompt, and Default. The cursor is flashing in the Tag text box. Think of the letter in the grid circle. It's a grid letter, which is a tag that provides the visual textual information.

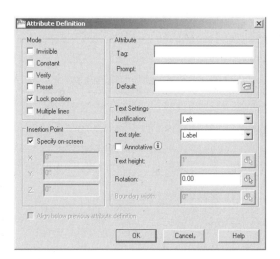

FIGURE 9.3: The Attribute Definition dialog box

10. Enter **grid_letter**. Don't press ↵.

11. Press the Tab key to move to the Prompt text box. Here you enter a prompt that will ask the future user who will be setting up a grid for the text to input for the tag.

12. Enter **Enter grid letter**, again without pressing ↵. Press Tab to move to the Default text box. Here you enter a default or sample value that

will be used if the future user presses ⏎ instead of entering a new value. You want it capitalized in this case, so enter **A**. This sets up the attribute so that the user setting up the grid will be prompted to enter the grid letter and will be given a default of *A*. The capital *A* lets the user know that the letter should be uppercase.

13. The lower portion of the dialog box is where you set up parameters for the attribute text: location in the drawing, justification, text style, height, and rotation. Click the Justification drop-down list, and select Middle Center.

14. Choose Label in the Text Style list box. Because the Label text style's height is set to a value other than 0′0″ (0), the Text Height text box in the Attribute Definition dialog box is grayed out. Make sure Invisible is not checked in the Mode area. Figure 9.4 shows what you should see.

F I G U R E 9 . 4 : The Attribute Definition dialog box showing the appropriate values

15. Click OK. Doing so returns you to the drawing to pick an insertion point. Back in the drawing, use the Center osnap, and click the circle at the top of the grid. GRID_LETTER is centered over the circle (see Figure 9.5), and the Attdef command ends.

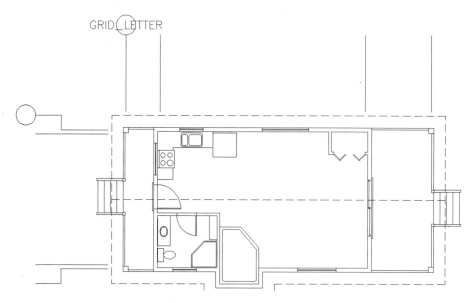

FIGURE 9.5: The first attribute definition placed in the grid circle

The text over the circle is called the *attribute definition*. Its function in Auto-CAD is similar to that of a block definition. When you made the win-1 block for the windows, the definition was a 12″ (305 mm)-long window with an insertion point. When the win-1 block is inserted, you can use the original block definition to make windows of various sizes. The same is true for the attribute definition. When it becomes part of a block that's inserted, the attribute can be any letter you want. You'll see that happen in a minute.

First make a similar attribute definition for the numbered grid symbol:

1. Click the Define Attributes button again or enter **att↵** to start the Attribute Definition command. The Attribute Definition dialog box opens again.

2. Repeat steps 10 to 15 from the preceding exercise, using the following guidelines:

    a. Enter **grid_number** in the Tag text box.

    b. Enter **Enter grid number** in the Prompt text box.

    c. Enter **1** in the Default text box.

    d. Select Middle Center from the Justification drop-down list.

    e. Click OK, use the Center osnap, and click the grid circle on the left.

The second attribute definition is centered over the circle on the left side (see Figure 9.6).

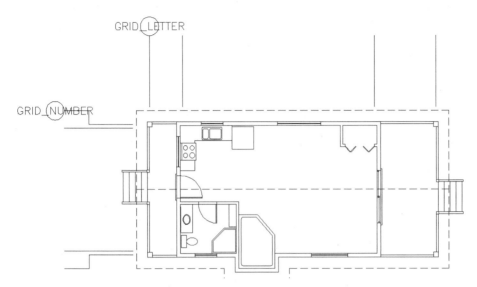

FIGURE 9.6: The second attribute definition is placed.

You now have two attribute definitions and are ready to make each of them part of a block that includes the circle over which they're currently centered.

Defining Blocks with Attributes

You have to define two blocks for the grid symbols and their attributes. The insertion point for the block used for the top of the grid should be at the lowest point of the circle. The insertion point for the block used for the left side should be at the point on the circle farthest to the right. Follow these steps:

1. Click the Create button on the Block panel to start the Block command, and open the Block Definition dialog box.

2. In the Name drop-down list, enter **grid-v** (for vertical) and then click the Pick Point button in the Base Point area.

3. In the drawing, use the Endpoint osnap and select the grid line that ends at the circle on top.

4. In the Block Definition dialog box that reopens, click the Select Objects button in the Objects area.

5. In the drawing, select the circle and attribute definition on the top. Press ↵.

6. In the Block Definition dialog box, be sure the Delete button is selected in the Objects area and click OK. The block is defined and includes the attribute definition. In the drawing, the top circle and attribute definition have been deleted.

7. Click the Create button again. Repeat steps 2–6 to define a second block for the circle and attribute definition on the left side. Use the following guidelines:

   a. Enter **grid-h** in the Name drop-down list.

   b. Click Pick Point. Use the Endpoint osnap, and pick the horizontal grid line that ends at the rightmost point of the grid circle on the left of the floor plan.

   c. When selecting objects, select the circle on the left and its attribute definition.

When you complete the command, you have a second block definition that includes an attribute definition and no grid circles in the drawing.

Inserting Blocks with Attributes

Let's insert these blocks (which are now grid symbols) at the endpoints of the grid lines. As you insert them, you'll assign them the appropriate letter or number, but first you'll make sure that AutoCAD uses a dialog box to prompt for the user input:

1. Be sure the Endpoint osnap is running, and then enter **attdia**↵.

2. If the value in the angle brackets is set to 0, press ↵. Otherwise, enter 0↵.

3. Click the Insert button in the Block panel or enter i↵. In the Insert dialog box, open the Name drop-down list, and select grid-v.

4. Be sure the Specify On-Screen box is checked for Insertion Point but not for Scale and Rotation, so that those values remain constant among the blocks and you're not prompted to change them. Click OK.

5. Click the leftmost vertical grid line in the drawing. Now look at the bottom line in the Command window or the command prompt at the cursor, as shown in Figure 9.7.

The `attdia` variable defines whether the Insert command opens a dialog box or prompts the user, at the Command prompt, for attribute information. When it is set to 0, no dialog box is used.

This is the text you entered in the Attribute Definition dialog box for the prompt. *A* is the text you entered as the default value. The last line also appears at the command prompt attached to the cursor. To accept the default value for this grid line, press ↵.

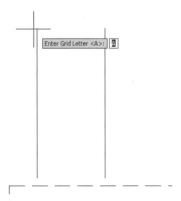

FIGURE 9.7: The command prompt shows the values for the Prompt and Default options specified.

6. Pressing ↵ inserts the grid symbol at the endpoint of the leftmost vertical grid line (see Figure 9.8).

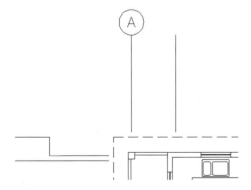

FIGURE 9.8: The first grid symbol block is inserted.

7. Press ↵ to restart the Insert command. Click OK to accept grid-v as the current block to be inserted.

8. Click the grid line to the right of the one you just selected.

9. At the `Enter grid letter <A>:` prompt, enter B↵. The second grid symbol is inserted on a grid line, and the letter *B* is located in the circle. Be sure to use a capital *B* here; the tag will not prevent you from using a lowercase letter, but drawing standards require consistency.

10. Repeat steps 7–9 to insert the other two grid symbols across the top of the floor plan, incrementing the values for each.

11. Continue repeating steps 7–9, but select the grid-h block for the four grid symbols that run down the left side of the floor plan. The results should look like Figure 9.9.

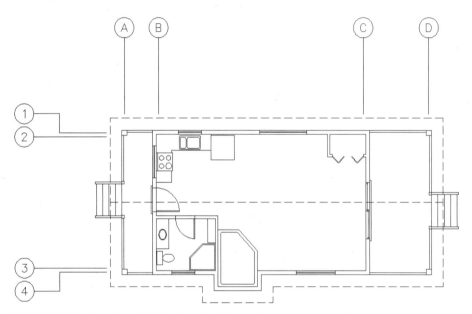

FIGURE 9.9: The grid with all symbols inserted

 12. If the circles overlap, use the Stretch command (see Figure 9.10) to stretch the short horizontal and vertical lines and the circle away from the long, straight grid lines.

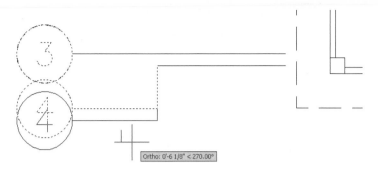

FIGURE 9.10: Use the Stretch command to relocate the grid symbol.

Editing Attribute Text

To illustrate how you can edit attribute text, let's assume you decide to change the C grid symbol to B1. You must then change the D symbol to C. Here are the steps:

1. Double-click the C grid symbol. Doing so opens the Enhanced Attribute Editor dialog box shown in Figure 9.11. You can change several items here, but you want to change only the Value parameter.

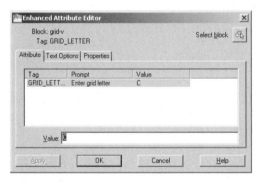

FIGURE 9.11: The Enhanced Attribute Editor dialog box

2. Be sure the Attribute tab is selected. Highlight C in the Value text box, enter **B1**, and then click the Apply button. B1 replaces C in the larger window where the tag, prompt, and value appear together. Click OK to close the dialog box.

N O T E   Because you set the justification point for the attribute text to Middle Center and located the text at the center of the grid circle, the B1 text is centered in the circle just like the single letters.

3. Double-click the D grid symbol.

4. In the Enhanced Attribute Editor dialog box, repeat step 2 to change D to C. The attributes are updated (see Figure 9.12).

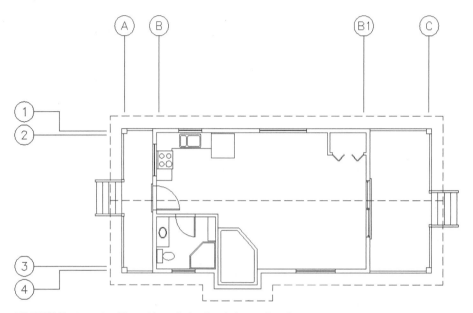

FIGURE 9.12: The grid symbols after being updated

The exercises in this chapter so far have illustrated the basic procedures for defining, inserting, and changing attributes. You can apply these same procedures to the process of setting up a title block in which attributes are used for text that changes from one sheet to the next. You can now move to a more complex application of the attribute feature to see its full power.

Setting Up Multiple Attributes in a Block

The cabin has three rooms and two decks, with the kitchen and living room sharing the same space. Each room has a different area and floor covering. You can store this information, along with the room name, in the drawing as attributes. You'll set up a block that consists of three attributes (name, area, and covering). You'll then insert the block back into the floor plan. As you may remember, the text style for the room labels is LABEL. You'll use that for the attributes.

You have to erase the room labels for now, but it will be handy to mark their justification points. That way, you can insert the attribute exactly where the label text is now. Follow these steps:

1. Thaw the Text1 layer. With the Grid layer current, from the menu bar, choose Format ➤ Point Style or enter **ddptype**↵ to open the Point Style dialog box (see Figure 9.13).

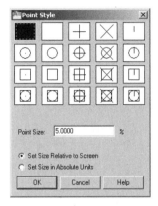

> A point is a single location in space, defined by an X, Y, and Z position, with no area or volume. The Point Style dialog box determines how the marker at the point location appears. By default, the point appears as a single pixel, which can be visually lost in the drawing.

FIGURE 9.13: The Point Style dialog box

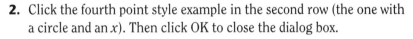

2. Click the fourth point style example in the second row (the one with a circle and an *x*). Then click OK to close the dialog box.

3. Set the Insertion osnap to be running, and then click the Multiple Points button on the expanded Draw panel to start the Point command. Place the cursor on the LIVING ROOM text. When the Insertion symbol appears at the lower-left corner, click to place the point object. Don't end the command yet.

4. Repeat step 3 for the KITCHEN and BATH labels. The decks don't have any associated text in this drawing, so you can place the attribute anywhere you want. Press Esc to end the Point command.

5. Erase the LIVING ROOM, KITCHEN, and BATH labels. The drawing should look like Figure 9.14.

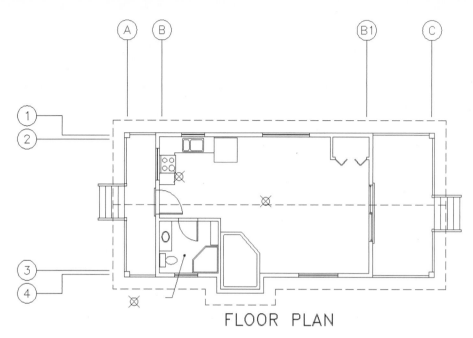

FLOOR PLAN

FIGURE 9.14: The floor plan with markers for insertion points and three room labels erased

6. Make Layer 0 current. Click the Define Attributes button to open the Attribute Definition dialog box.

7. For Tag, enter **rm_name**. For Prompt, enter **Room name**. For Default, enter **LIVING ROOM**. (This default value will remind the user to use all uppercase letters.)

8. In the bottom half of the dialog box, the settings for the text stay the same. Click OK.

9. In the drawing, click above the cabin and between the B and B1 grid lines. This places the first attribute definition in the drawing (see Figure 9.15). Because you're going to make a block out of it and reinsert it into the rooms, you don't have to place the attribute definition where the room labels are; any open area in the drawing is fine.

10. Press ⏎ to restart the Attdef command. For this attribute, enter **rm_area** for Tag. For Prompt, enter **Area of room**, and for Default, enter **10.00 Sq. Ft. (10.00 M2)**. This will show the user the proper format for the area.

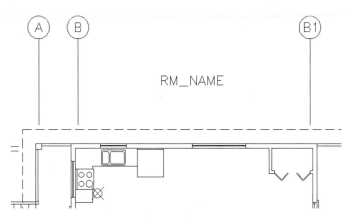

FIGURE 9.15: The room name attribute definition placed in the drawing

11. In the Mode area, click to activate Invisible. The Invisible mode makes the attribute values invisible in the drawing, but they're still stored there and can be accessed when required.

12. In the lower-left corner of the dialog box, click the Align Below Previous Attribute Definition check box. All the text options fade out (see Figure 9.16). The style is the same as that of the first attribute, and this attribute definition will appear right below the first one.

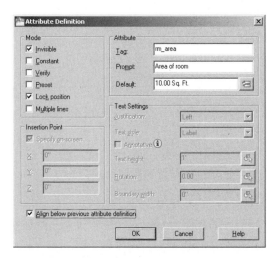

FIGURE 9.16: Setting the proper values in the Attribute Definition dialog box

13. Click OK. The second attribute definition appears in the drawing below the first one.

14. Repeat steps 10–13 to define the third attribute. For Tag, enter **rm_floor**. For Prompt, enter **Floor Material**. For Default, enter **Wood Parquet**. Be sure the Invisible mode is still checked, and select the Align Below Previous Attribute Definition check box. Click OK. All three attribute definitions are now in the drawing (see Figure 9.17).

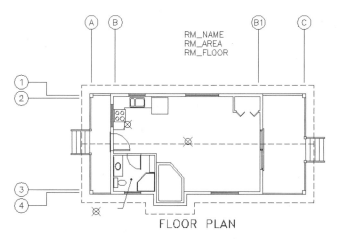

F I G U R E   9 . 1 7 : The floor plan with all three attribute definitions

Now you'll make a block out of the three attributes.

Defining a Block with Multiple Attributes

A block with attributes usually includes lines or other geometrical objects along with the attribute definitions, but it doesn't have to do so. In this case, the three attribute definitions are the sole content of the block, and the block's insertion point is the justification point for the first attribute: the room label text. Follow these steps to define the block:

1. Click the Create button to start the Block command.

2. In the Block Definition dialog box, enter **room_info** for the name.

3. Click the Pick Point button. In the drawing, use the Insert osnap and choose the top attribute definition. Doing so aligns the justification point of this attribute with the insertion point of the block.

4. Back in the Block Definition dialog box, click the Select Objects button. In the drawing, pick each attribute definition individually in the order you created them. Selecting them in this order causes them to be listed in the Enter Attributes dialog box in the same order.

5. Press ↵ after selecting the last attribute definition. Then, after being sure Delete is still selected, click OK in the dialog box. The room_info block is defined, and the attribute definitions are deleted from the drawing.

6. Save your drawing as Cabin09a.dwg.

You're almost ready to insert the room_info block in each of the three rooms and near the balcony. But first you need to calculate the area of each room.

Calculating Areas

You can calculate areas in a drawing by using the Hatch command in conjunction with the Properties palette or by using the Area command. Because area calculations are made over and over again in design, construction, and manufacturing, the Area command is an important tool. You can calculate an overall area and then subtract subareas from it, or you can add subareas together to make a total. Chapter 11 covers hatches.

For this exercise, you'll use the Area command to calculate the areas of the five floor spaces in the floor plan. You need to write down the areas after you make the calculations. Follow these steps:

1. Make a new layer named **Area**, and make it the current layer.

2. Freeze all the other layers except Deck, Windows, and Walls. Your drawing should look like Figure 9.18.

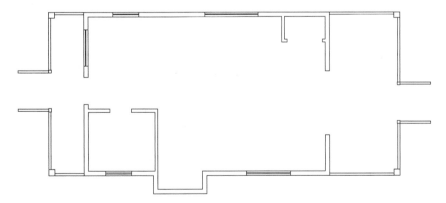

FIGURE 9.18: The floor plan with all layers turned off except Area, Deck, Walls, and Windows

   T I P   When you want to select all the layers in a drawing except a few, select those few layers in the Layer Properties Manager, right-click, and choose Invert Selection from the context menu. The unselected layers become selected and the selected layers are deselected.

3. Make sure that the Endpoint osnap is running.

4. Draw a closed polyline around the inside of each room. To delineate the kitchen from the living room, use the left edge of the large window near the closet as the right edge of the kitchen and use the bathroom wall as the lower limit.

5. Draw a polyline around each of the decks using the Perpendicular object snap to draw the segments through the posts on the decks' outside corners. Your cabin should be divided as shown in Figure 9.19.

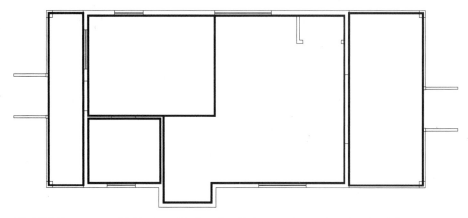

FIGURE 9.19: Divide the cabin into five distinct sections using closed polylines.

Now that the perimeter lines are drawn, you need to calculate the area bound by them:

1. In the Utilities panel, click the Area button or, if it isn't visible, click the down arrow under the large button on the left side of the panel and choose Area from the fly-out menu, as shown in Figure 9.20.

FIGURE 9.20: Starting the Area command

2. At the `Specify first corner point or [Object/Add area/Sub-tract area/eXit]:` prompt, enter o↵ to switch to Object mode and then select the bathroom polyline.

3. The area of the polyline turns green in the drawing area. Press the F2 key to open the AutoCAD Text Window, which displays the results of your calculation: `Area = 7176.00 square in. (49.8333 square ft.)`, `Perimeter = 28'-4'. (Area = 4455000, Perimeter = 8460)`. You'll also notice that you're not actually in the Area command; you're in the Area option of the Measuregeom (Measure Geometry) command. This command has replaced several of the measurement tools in AutoCAD 2010.

4. Write down the area in square feet to check against the number calculated in the next section. Press ↵ to restart the Area option, enter o↵, and then click the kitchen polyline. The area should be 135.7674 square feet (12660810). Write down this number. (You can round it to two decimal places; you just want them to verify the numbers that AutoCAD will calculate.)

5. Repeat this process for the living room where the area should be 278.5660 square feet (26201990). Write down 278.57 (26201990).

6. Repeat this process one last time for the front and back decks. The areas should be 135.63 square feet (12648636) and 65.63 square feet (6126516), respectively.

7. Thaw all the layers except Tblk1 and make the Text1 layer current.

 N O T E   The Add and Subtract options in the Area prompt allow you to add together areas you have calculated and to subtract areas from each other. If you're going to add or subtract areas, enter a↵ after you start the Area command. Then, after each calculation, you'll be given the Add and Subtract options. If you don't enter a at the beginning, you can make only one calculation at a time.

To use the Properties palette to calculate an area, select the polyline to be measured, open the Properties palette, and then scroll down to the Area readout in the Geometry rollout. The area appears in square inches and square feet. This also works for hatch patterns, which I'll cover in Chapter 11.

Inserting the Room_Info Block

You have five areas calculated and recorded, and you are ready to insert the room_info block. When you inserted the grid symbols as blocks with attributes earlier in this chapter, the prompts for the attribute text appeared in the Command window. With multiple attributes in a block, it's more convenient to display all the prompts in a dialog box. Let's change the setting that makes the dialog box replace the command prompts:

1. Enter **attdia**↵. At the prompt, enter **1**↵. This allows the dialog box containing the prompts to open during the insertion process.

2. Set the Node osnap to be the only one running, and make sure the Object Snap button is turned on. The Node osnap snaps the cursor to a point object.

3. Click the Insert button in the Block panel. In the Insert dialog box, select room_info from the Name drop-down list and then click OK. Select the point object that marks the justification point for the LIVING ROOM label text to open the Edit Attributes dialog box (see Figure 9.21).

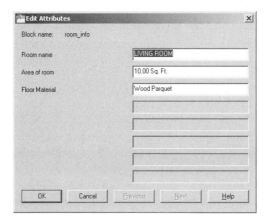

FIGURE 9.21: The Edit Attributes dialog box

4. The only change you need to make is the value for Area Of Room. The defaults are correct for the other two items.

5. Rather than inputting text, you'll instruct the attribute to read the Area parameter from the polyline. Press the Tab key to highlight the Area Of Room box, right-click, and choose Insert Field from the context menu, as shown in Figure 9.22.

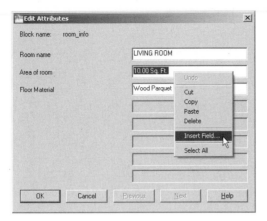

FIGURE 9.22: Inserting a field as an attribute

6. The Field dialog box opens. Select Object in the Field names column, and click the Select object button (see Figure 9.23). The dialog box closes so that you can pick the object that the field will reference.

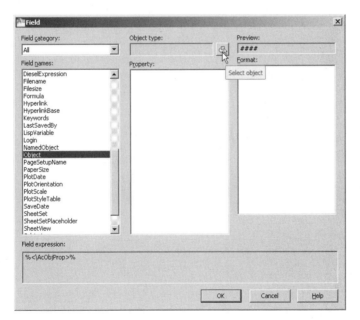

FIGURE 9.23: Click Select Object in the Field dialog box.

7. Select the polyline that follows the perimeter of the living room. The Field dialog box reopens with additional content in its list boxes.

8. Select Area in the Property column, Architectural (Decimal) in the Format column, and 0.00 in the Precision drop-down list. The correct area measurement appears in the top-right corner of the dialog box (see Figure 9.24).

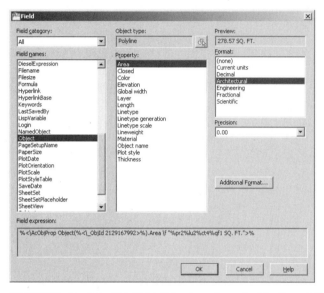

FIGURE 9.24: The Field dialog box after selecting the polyline and choosing the property and format

If you're working in Architectural units, you can skip to step 13, but if you're working in metric units, continue with the next step.

9. Notice the value in the Preview window in the top-right corner of the dialog box. The number is much too large to be defining the area of the living room in square meters; instead, it's showing the area in square millimeters. So you need to multiply the value calculated by a conversion factor to display the correct value.

10. Click the Additional Format button to open the Additional Format dialog box. One square meter equals 1,000,000 square millimeters (1000× 1000), so each square millimeter is 1/1,000,000 of a square meter. To figure out the conversion factor needed to convert square inches into square feet, divide 1 by 1,000,000 and you'll come up with 0.000001.

11. Enter **0.000001** in the Conversion Factor field. To identify the units, enter **M2** in the Suffix field. Be sure to place a space prior to the "M" to ensure a gap between the suffix and the calculated area. Your Additional Format dialog box should look like Figure 9.25.

FIGURE 9.25: The Additional Format dialog box

12. Click OK to close the Additional Format dialog box and note that the Preview section in the Field dialog box now shows the correct value of 26.20 M2, as you can see in Figure 9.26.

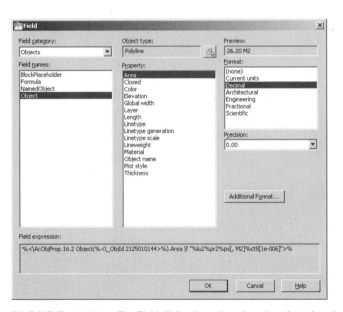

FIGURE 9.26: The Field dialog box after changing the values in the Additional Format dialog box

13. Click OK to close the Field dialog box and return to the Edit Attributes dialog box. The Area Of Room value is now shown with a gray background, as you can see in Figure 9.27, to identify it as a field rather than a text element.

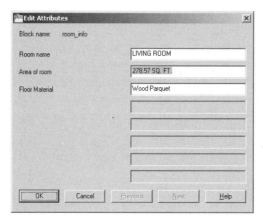

FIGURE 9.27: The Edit Attributes dialog box with a field for the Area Of Room value

14. Click OK to insert the room_info block into the drawing in the living room. The room label is the only visible attribute (see Figure 9.28). You set the other two attributes to be invisible.

FIGURE 9.28: The first room_info block is inserted.

Editing Attributes

The remaining four block insertions are identical to the first one, with just a few specific changes: changing the room name and referencing a different polyline. Follow these steps to copy and modify the block and attributes that you've created:

1. Select the LIVING ROOM attribute and, using the Node osnap, copy it to the node at the insertion point for the BATH text.

2. Double-click the new attribute to open the Enhanced Attribute Editor dialog box and select the RM_AREA row, as shown in Figure 9.29.

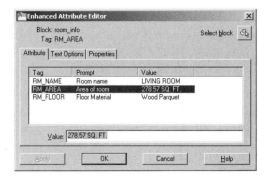

FIGURE 9.29: Select the RM_AREA row in the Enhanced Attribute Editor.

3. Double-click the 278.57 SF (26.20 M2) value with the gray background at the bottom of the dialog box to open the Field dialog box, where you can edit the preferences and references.

4. Click the Select Object button near the Object Type field. Both dialog boxes disappear and the cursor turns into a pickbox. Select the polyline that follows the perimeter of the bathroom.

5. When the Field dialog box reappears, only if you're using metric units, click the Additional Format button; then repeat steps 10 and 11 from the previous exercise.

6. Click OK to close the Field dialog box and return to the Enhanced Attribute Editor dialog box. Select the RM_NAME row and then, at the bottom of the dialog box, highlight LIVING ROOM and enter BATH to replace the text. Change the floor material to Tile.

7. Click OK to close the dialog box. The revised BATH attribute is now properly placed in the drawing.

8. Repeat steps 1 through 7, substituting **KITCHEN**, **FRONT DECK**, and **BACK DECK** for the room name attribute and selecting the appropriate polyline as a reference for each block. There are no node point objects for the deck text, so you can just rotate and place the attribute a little left of center on the appropriate deck. For the decks, change the floor material to Cedar Planks. Metric users will need to open the Additional Format dialog box for each block and add the conversion factor and suffix for each block. When you are done, your cabin should look like Figure 9.30.

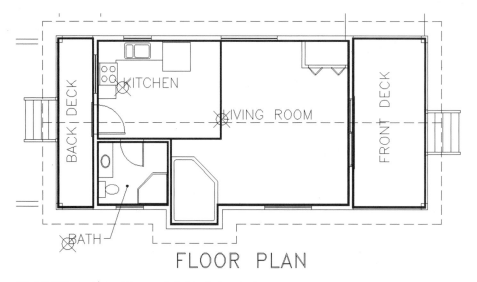

FIGURE 9.30: All room_info blocks inserted

EDITING TOOLS FOR ATTRIBUTES

The attribute-editing tools seem complicated at first because their names are similar, but they are easily distinguishable once you get used to them and know how to use them. Here are descriptions of five attribute-editing tools:

The Edit Attributes Dialog Box

This is the same dialog box displayed in the process of inserting a block that has attributes, if the attdia setting is set to 1. It is used to change attribute values only. Enter **attedit**⏎ to use it to edit values of attributes already in your drawing. You will be prompted to select a block reference in your drawing. When you do that, the Edit Attributes dialog box appears.

Continues

Editing Tools for Attributes *(Continued)*

The Enhanced Attribute Editor Dialog Box

With this dialog box, you can edit values and the properties of the attribute text—such as color, layer, text style, and so on. When you enter **eattedit**↵, click Modify ➣ Objects ➣ Attribute ➣ Single or click the Edit Attributes (Single) button in the Block panel and then pick a block that has attributes, the dialog box opens. Double-clicking the block has the same effect.

The Properties Palette

Use the Properties palette to edit most properties of attribute definitions. Select the attribute definition, and then right-click and choose Properties to open the Properties palette. Then scroll down to the Attributes rollout.

The Block Attribute Manager

Click the Manage Attributes button in the expanded Block panel to open the Block Attribute Manager dialog box. There you can select a block and edit the various parts of each attribute definition that the block contains, such as the tag, prompt, and value.

The −attedit Command

You can also edit more than one attribute at a time by clicking the Edit Attributes (Multiple) from the Block panel, or by choosing Modify ➣ Object ➣ Attribute ➣ Global, or by entering -attedit↵. The prompt reads Edit attributes one at a time? [Yes/No] <Y>. If you accept the default of Yes, you're taken through a series of options for selecting attributes to edit. Select the attributes to edit, and then press ↵ to end the selection process. A large *x* appears at the insertion point of one of the selected attributes. At this point, you get the following prompt: Enter an option [Value/Position/Height/Angle/Style/Layer/Color/Next] <N>:, allowing you to modify any of the characteristics listed in the prompt for the attribute with the *x*. Press ↵ to move to the next selected attribute.

If you respond to the first prompt with No, you're taken through a similar set of selection options. You're then asked to enter a current value to be changed and to enter the new value after the change. You can change the values of attributes globally by using the −attedit command this way.

Controlling the Visibility of Attributes

The floor plan looks the same as it did at the beginning of this exercise, except for the addition of the deck labels. But it includes more than meets the eye. What was regular text is now an attribute, and your drawing is "smarter" than it was before. The next few steps illustrate the display controls for the visible and invisible attributes:

1. Expand the Block panel, click the down arrow next to the Retain Attribute display button, and click Display All, as shown in Figure 9.31.

FIGURE 9.31: Selecting the Display All option

All the attributes, including those designated as invisible, appear with the room labels (see Figure 9.32).

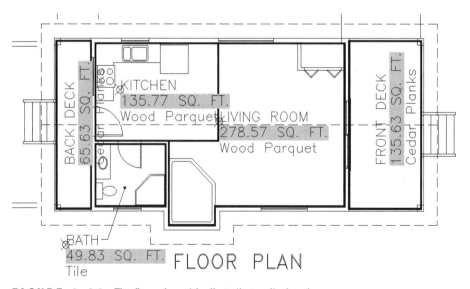

FIGURE 9.32: The floor plan with all attributes displayed

Like the hyperlink you added to the notes in Chapter 8, the fields are shown with a gray background, but this background does not appear in the printed drawings. As you can see, one of the benefits of using attributes over simple text is the ability to control their visibility, but their true strength is the ability to output attribute values to spreadsheets or databases. When you use fields and formulas (covered in the "Creating a Table" section later in this chapter), the attribute can adjust its values as the circumstances change.

2. Start the Stretch command and drag a crossing window enclosing part of the front deck, as shown in Figure 9.33.

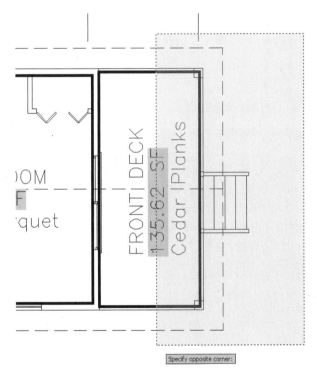

FIGURE 9.33: Select part of the front deck with the Stretch command.

3. Pick any location in the drawing area as the base point, move the cursor to the right, and then click to stretch the deck, as shown in Figure 9.34. Use Ortho mode or polar tracking to stretch the objects directly to the right.

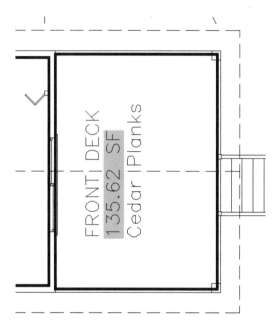

FIGURE 9.34: The front deck after stretching it to the right

4. The deck is now larger, but the attribute showing the area remains at its previous value. Attributes need to be instructed to reevaluate or regenerate themselves. This can happen whenever a drawing is opened or when the Regen or Regenall commands are issued. From the menu bar, choose View ➤ Regen All or enter **regenall**⏎. The area updates to show the true value for the associated polyline (see Figure 9.35).

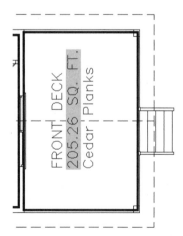

FIGURE 9.35: The front deck after issuing the Regenall command

5. You don't want the deck at this larger size, so click the Undo button in the Quick Access toolbar or press **u**↵ until your drawing is in the state it was just before the Stretch command was executed.

6. The visibility of the attributes, as you defined them in the Attribute Definition dialog box, is called their *normal* state. To return them to this state, click the down arrow next to the Display All Attributes in the expanded Block panel and then click Retain Display (see Figure 9.36) or choose View ➤ Display ➤ Attribute Display ➤ Normal from the menu bar.

FIGURE 9.36: Returning the attribute display to normal

7. All the attributes return to their normal state (see Figure 9.37). Save this drawing as Cabin09b.dwg.

FLOOR PLAN

FIGURE 9.37: All the attributes in their normal state

The Display All Attributes and Hide All Attributes options make all attributes in a drawing visible or invisible, regardless of how you set the Visible/Invisible mode in the attribute definition. The Normal setting allows an attribute to be displayed only if the Visible/Invisible mode was set to Visible in the definition.

Exploring Other Uses for Attributes

Along with grid symbols and room, window, and door schedules, another common use for attributes is in standardized title blocks, particularly in facilities management and interior design. You can specify every piece of office furniture in a building with attributes. You can then extract the data and send it to a furniture specifier that inputs the data into its databases and completes the order. The big office furniture manufacturers sell their own proprietary software that works with AutoCAD and automatically sets up attributes when you insert their blocks of the furniture, which they have predrawn and included in the software package.

Attributes are also being used more and more in maps drawn in AutoCAD, which are then imported into geographical information system (GIS) software (a powerful analysis and presentation tool). When map symbols, such as building numbers, are blocks containing an attribute, they're transformed in the GIS program in such a way that you can set up links between the map features (buildings) and database tables that contain information about the map features. In this way, you can perform analyses on the database tables, and the results automatically appear graphically on the map. (For example, you could quickly locate all buildings that have a total usable area greater than a specified square footage.)

In the next section, you'll go through an exercise that demonstrates how you can create dynamic blocks that vary their appearance based on user input.

Creating a Dynamic Block

In Chapter 7, you created blocks for the windows and doors. However, because of its schematic appearance, you were not able to scale the door block as you did with the window block. Scaling the door and swing would have allowed one door block to fit into any size opening, but it would have also scaled the thickness of the door differently for each door width. Dynamic blocks are standard blocks with additional functionality to allow certain features to change without affecting all objects in the block. The door blocks are an excellent opportunity to explore the abilities of AutoCAD's dynamic blocks.

The basic procedure for setting up a dynamic block has the following stages:

1. Create the block using the Block command.

2. Right-click the block, and choose Block Editor.

3. Click a parameter, and follow the Command window prompts to create the parameter.

4. Click the Actions tab, and click an action to associate with the parameter; then, follow the Command window prompts to set up the action.

5. Use the Properties palette to rename and specify settings for the parameter and any actions associated with it.

6. Save your work back to the block definition, and close the Block Editor.

You'll work through this process by converting the door3_0 block from Cabin09B into a dynamic block in a new drawing:

1. With Cabin09B as the current drawing, zoom in to the floor plan at the back of the cabin. From the menu bar choose Edit ➤ Copy With Base Point; then use the Insert osnap to select the insertion point of the back door block as the base point. Select the back door block, and press ↵. This copies the door block to the Windows Clipboard.

2. Start a new drawing, and change the Length units to Architectural (Decimal). Then, from the menu bar choose Edit ➤ Paste, and when prompted to specify the base point, enter 0,0↵.

3. Zoom to extents, and then zoom out a bit to give yourself some room to work around the objects. Turn off the UCS icon (**uscicon**↵ **off**↵).

4. Select the door block, right-click, and choose Block Editor from the context menu. The drawing area turns gray, and the Block Authoring palettes open to indicate that you are in the Block Editor.

5. Pan the view, and adjust the Block Authoring palettes so that your screen looks similar to Figure 9.38.

You want to be able to use this door block for openings of the following widths: 2'-0", 2'-6", 3'-0", and 3'-6"(609 mm, 762 mm, 915 mm, and 1068 mm).

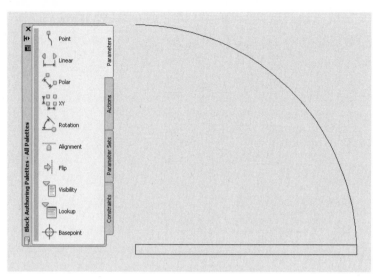

FIGURE 9.38: The door block in the Block Editor

Setting Up Parameters and Actions

You'll use the Linear parameter to set up the 6″ (153 mm) increments for the door width. Then you'll associate a Stretch action with that parameter to allow the door width to change, and you'll associate a Scale action to allow the door swing to change. Follow these steps:

1. Be sure Parameters is the active palette in the Block Authoring Palettes, and then click the Linear Parameter icon (see Figure 9.39).

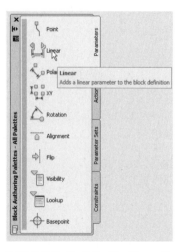

FIGURE 9.39: The Linear Parameter in the Block Authoring palettes

2. Make sure the Endpoint osnap is running, click the lower-left corner of the door, and then click the open endpoint of the door swing.

3. Move the cursor to position the dimension symbol a little to the left of the door block, and then click to place it (see Figure 9.40).

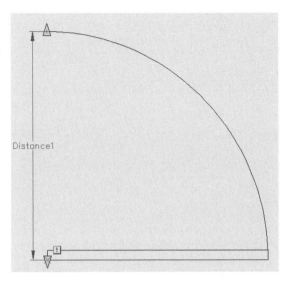

Distance1

FIGURE 9.40: The Linear parameter is placed.

Note the small exclamation symbol on a square yellow background. This reminds you that no action has been associated with this parameter. You'll set up the Stretch action first:

1. Click the Actions tab on the Block Authoring palettes, and then click the Stretch icon.

2. Click the Distance parameter to the left of the door, and then click the up-pointing arrow at the end of the door swing.

3. At the `Specify first corner of stretch frame or [CPolygon]:` prompt, form a crossing polygon around the right half of the door, clicking each of the opposing corners rather than clicking and dragging, as shown in Figure 9.41.

4. At the `Select objects:` prompt, select the door and press ↵. The Stretch action icon appears near the end of the door swing.

5. Click the Scale Action icon on the Actions palette, select the Distance parameter again, select the arc, and then press ↵. The Scale action icon appears next to the Stretch action icon.

6. Minimize the Block Authoring palettes.

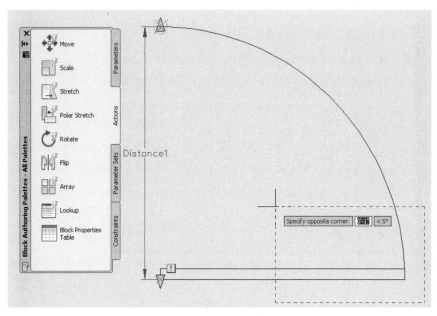

FIGURE 9.41: The crossing polygon for the Stretch action

This completes your work with the Block Authoring palettes. You'll accomplish the rest of the tasks with the Properties palette.

Fine-Tuning the Dynamic Block with the Properties Palette

The Distance linear parameter shows the width of the opening and is perpendicular to the door's width. You need to set up an offset angle so the door width changes as the opening width changes. Then you need to set up the incremental widths and rename the parameter and actions. You'll set up the increments first:

1. Select the Distance parameter and then open the Properties palette.

2. In the Property Labels section on the palette, change Distance Name from Distance1 to **Door Opening**.

3. Scroll down to the Value Set section, and click the text box for Dist Type where it says None. Then open the drop-down list and select Increment.

4. Moving down, line by line, set Dist Increment to **6″ (153)**, Dist Minimum to **2′ (609)**, and Dist Maximum to **3′6″ (1068)**, as shown in Figure 9.42.

FIGURE 9.42: Change the parameters in the Properties dialog box

5. Deselect the Distance parameter. It now has the increment markers for the door opening widths (see Figure 9.43).

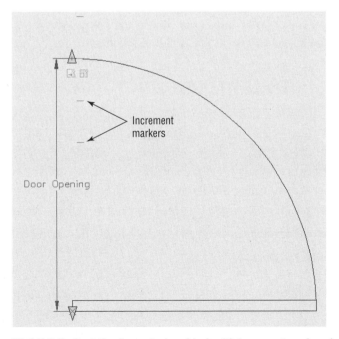

FIGURE 9.43: Dynamic door block with increment markers for the opening widths

Now, the final task is to fine-tune the Stretch and Scale actions that control the door size and swing:

1. Click the Stretch action symbol near the end of the door swing. The symbol, the Distance parameter, and the window you drew earlier ghost.

2. In the Properties palette, scroll down to the Overrides section; for Angle Offset, enter 270↵. This is the direction the door will stretch relative to movement of the open end of the door swing arc. The Distance multiplier stays at 1.0000 because you don't want the width of the door to change in the same proportion as the width of the opening.

3. In the Misc section, change Action Name from Stretch to **Door Size**.

4. Deselect this action, and select the Scale action.

5. In the Misc section of the Properties palette, change Action Name from Scale to **Door Swing Size**.

6. Close the Properties palette, and click the Save Block button in the Open/Save panel under the Block Editor tab.

7. Click the Close button at the right end of the Ribbon to return to the drawing.

8. Save the drawing as DynDoor.dwg in the same folder as your other Chapter 9 drawings, and then close the drawing.

Inserting a Dynamic Block

When you use this block in your floor plans, insert it just as you would a regular door block. Then copy it to the various doorway openings in the plan, orient it, and adjust its size to fit the openings. You can easily edit dynamic blocks, which are a versatile feature to have at your disposal.

You'll use the dynamic door block that you just created to replace the doors in your cabin:

1. In the Cabin09b drawing, delete the two existing swing doors, make the Doors layer current, and then and then freeze the Area, Roof, Headers, Grid, Fixtures, and Text1 layers. Your drawing should look like Figure 9.44.

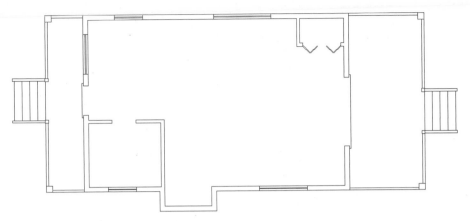

FIGURE 9.44: The cabin drawing with most of the layers frozen and the doors deleted

The door block that you created in the DynDoor drawing is based on the door3_0 block that already exists in the current drawing. Even if there is no such block inserted in the drawing, the block definition remains part of the drawing file. You will delete the block definition using the Purge dialog box.

2. On the Application menu click Drawing Utilities ➤ Purge or enter purge↵ to open the Purge dialog box.

3. Click the plus sign to expand the Blocks entry to see the two door blocks (see Figure 9.45). Select the Blocks entry, check the Purge Nested Items option, and make sure Confirm Each Object To Be Purged is unchecked. Click the Purge button, and then close the dialog box.

T I P   You can purge only those objects and features that do not exist in the drawing, such as deleted blocks, empty layers, or linetypes that are not used. Some items, including Layer 0 and the Standard text style, can't be purged. AutoCAD can also accumulate registered applications (regapps), usually from third-party applications or features no longer used in the current drawing, and geometry lines with a length of 0. To eliminate these, you must enter -purge↵ to start Purge without the dialog box and then enter r↵ or z↵. The All option (a↵) will not purge these types of objects. Run Purge often to eliminate accumulated junk in your drawing that contributes to larger file sizes and slower performance.

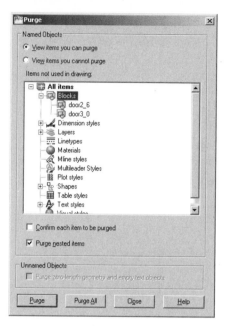

FIGURE 9.45: Deleting the block references with the Purge dialog box

4. With the Endpoint osnap running, click the Insert button in the Block panel.

5. Click the Browse button in the Insert dialog box that opens. Using Browse, you can insert any AutoCAD drawing into another as a block.

6. In the Select Drawing File dialog box, navigate to the folder where you placed the DynDoor drawing (see Figure 9.46). Select it, and then click the Open button.

7. Click OK in the Insert dialog box. The dynamic door block appears attached to the cursor. Click the lower-right corner of the back door opening to insert the block. This is a 3'-0" (915 mm) door opening, so you don't need to modify the block.

8. Press ⏎ to restart the Insert command. In the Insert dialog box, check the Specify On-Screen options under Rotation and Scale and make sure Uniform Scale is unchecked.

9. Click the lower-right corner of the bathroom opening to place the door and enter 1 for the X scale, -1 for the Y scale, and 270⏎ at the rotation prompt. The door is placed properly, but as shown in Figure 9.47, the default size is too large for the opening.

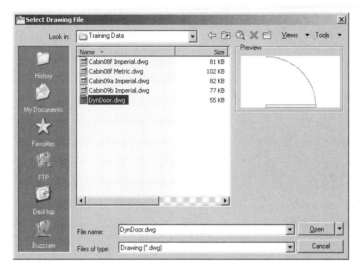

FIGURE 9.46: Selecting the DynDoor block for insertion

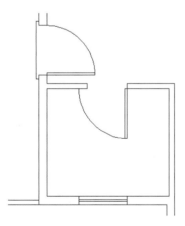

FIGURE 9.47: The door must be resized to fit.

10. Explode the two door blocks that you just inserted. In this case, you're not exploding the dynamic door block itself; you're exploding the drawing file that it is nested in so that you can access the block's dynamic properties.

T I P   The Explode option is at the lower-left corner of the Insert dialog box. Checking it prior to inserting the block eliminates the need to explode it after the block is inserted. If this option is selected when inserting a nondynamic block, that block is broken up into its component objects. Checking the Explode option also prevents the block from being inserted with the axes scaled unevenly.

11. Select the bathroom door block, and the blue dynamic arrows appear (see Figure 9.48).

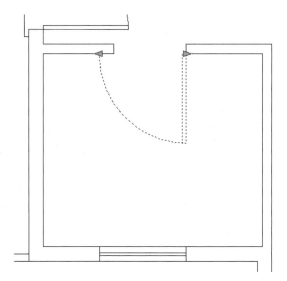

FIGURE 9.48: The dynamic block's resizing arrows

12. Select the left arrow, and drag it up to the corner of the opening. Notice how the length of the door changes as well (see Figure 9.49).

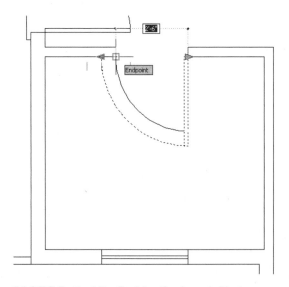

FIGURE 9.49: Resizing the dynamic block

13. Click to set the door size, and then press Esc to deselect the door. The door block is scaled properly with no distortion to the width of the door itself (see Figure 9.50).

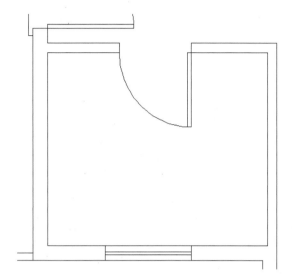

FIGURE 9.50: The dynamic door block scaled to fit the 2′6″ door opening

14. Save your drawing as Cabin09C.dwg.

This completes the section on dynamic blocks. If you want to experiment with the dynamic block feature, examine the sample dynamic blocks to see how they work and are set up, and try to create one of your own. In the next section, I'll cover the methods for creating a table.

Creating a Table

Most professions that use AutoCAD use tables to consolidate and display data in organized formats. Architectural construction documents usually include at least three basic tables: door, window, and room finish schedules. These are usually drawn in table form, and they display the various construction and material specifications for each door or window type or for each room. In mechanical drawings the bill of materials and other specifications can be found in tables. To illustrate the AutoCAD tools for creating tables, you'll construct a simple door schedule for the cabin.

You create tables in AutoCAD by first creating a table style and then creating a table using that style. It's a process similar to that of defining a text style and then inserting text in a drawing using that style.

Defining a Table Style

Table styles are more complex than text styles. They include parameters for width and height of rows and columns and, among other elements, at least one text style.

1. Make Cabin9c the current drawing if it isn't already.

2. Create a new layer called Tables, assign it color number 7, and make it the current layer.

3. Click the Annotate tab; then click the small arrow in the Tables panel's title bar to open the Table Style dialog box (see Figure 9.51).

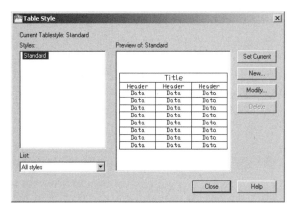

FIGURE 9.51: The Table Style dialog box

On the left is the Styles list box. It displays all the defined table styles. To the right of that is a Preview Of: window that displays the current table style—in this case, the Standard style because it's the only one defined so far. Below the Styles list box is a drop-down list called List that gives you options for which table styles to display. To the right of the preview window are four buttons.

4. Click the New button to open the Create New Table Style dialog box. In the New Style Name text box, enter **Door Schedule**, as shown in Figure 9.52, to create a new table style name, and click Continue.

FIGURE 9.52: Naming the new table style

5. The New Table Style dialog box opens with Door Schedule in the title bar (see Figure 9.53). The new style you're defining will be like the Standard style with the changes you make here. The drop-down list in the Cell styles section contains the three parts of the sample table at the bottom-right corner of the dialog box: Data, Header, and Title.

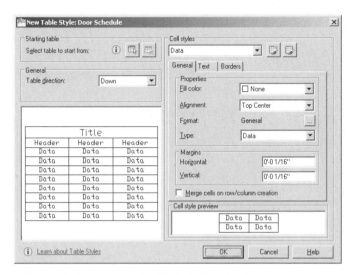

FIGURE 9.53: The New Table Style dialog box

You can specify text and line characteristics for each of the three parts. Be sure the Data option is active in the Cell Style area.

T I P Not only can each table have its own style, but each cell can have a distinct style as well. Using the Launches The Create A New Cell Style Dialog Box and Launches The Manage Cell Styles Dialog Box buttons in the top-right corner of the New Table Style dialog box, you can design and apply any number of cell styles within a table.

6. Click the Text tab, and then click the Text Style button to the right of the Text Style drop-down list to open the Text Style dialog box. You want a new text style for the door schedule.

7. Define a new style called Table, and use the Arial font and a 0'-0" (0) height. A Height value here allows you to control the height in the New Table Style dialog box. Click Apply, and then click Close. The table style now appears in the Text Style drop-down list, and the data cells in the two preview windows now show the Arial font.

8. Set Text Height to 6″ (152). Leave Text Color and Text Angle at their default settings.

9. Switch to the General tab, click the button in the Format row and, in the Table Cell Format dialog box, change Data Type to Text and Format to (None), as shown in Figure 9.54; then click OK. The selected data type prevents numeric data from justifying to the right, rather than following the specified Middle Center option.

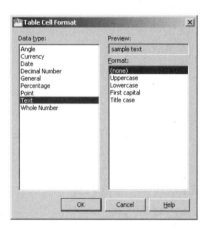

F I G U R E   9 . 5 4 : Changing the data format in the Table Cell Format dialog box

10. Change Alignment to Middle Center. The General tab should look like Figure 9.55.

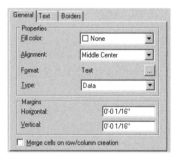

F I G U R E   9 . 5 5 : The General tab of the New Table Style dialog box

11. In the Cell Styles drop-down list at the top of the dialog box, choose Header to expose its parameters. In the Text tab, choose the same text style (Table), and set the height to 9″ (229).

12. Choose Title from the Cell Styles drop-down list, select the Table text style again, and set the height to 12″ (305). In the General tab, set the Horizontal and Vertical Margins to 4″ (102).

    You'll leave the Border properties at their default settings. These control the visibility of the horizontal and vertical lines of the table, their lineweights, and their colors. Your profession or discipline might have its own standard for these parameters.

13. In the General section, on the left side of the dialog box, make sure Table Direction is set to Down. Click OK to save the new table style.

14. Back in the Table Style dialog box, in the Styles list, click Door Schedule to highlight it, and then click the Set Current button to make it the current table style (see Figure 9.56). Click Close.

Now, let's look at the geometry of the new table.

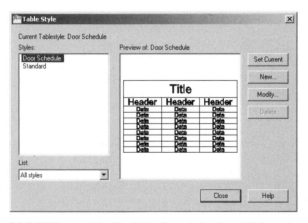

FIGURE 9.56: The Table Style dialog box with Door Schedule as the current table style

Designing a Table

The parameters in the Door Schedule table style have set the height of the rows. You now need to determine the width of the columns and figure out how many columns and rows you need for the door schedule. You do this as you insert a new table. Remember that Door Schedule is the current table style. Follow these steps:

1. Zoom and pan so that you can see the area below the cabin. The table won't fit inside the title block perimeter, but I'll show you how to give it its own title block in Chapter 14.

2. In the Annotate tab's Tables panel, click the Table button to open the Insert Table dialog box (see Figure 9.57). In the Table Style area, Door Schedule appears in the Table Style drop-down list because it's now the current table style. An abstract version of the table appears below in the preview area.

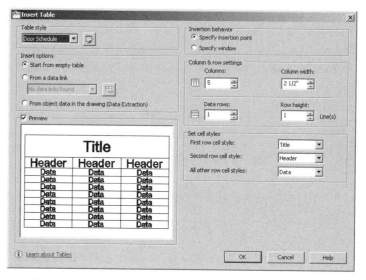

FIGURE 9.57: The Insert Table dialog box

3. On the right side, click the Specify Window radio button if necessary. You'll make a window to define the extents of the table. Below, in the Column & Row Settings area, click the Columns and Row Height radio buttons. You need to define only the number of columns in the table. You won't worry about the row height for now; it's determined by the number of lines of text, and you're using only one line of text.

4. You'll have six categories to describe the doors, so set the Columns box to 6. Each column is initially set to the same width. You can adjust it later. Click OK.

5. Back in the drawing, turn off Object Snap and Polar Tracking on the status bar. Then click a point left-of-center and below the cabin. This establishes the upper-left corner of the new table, so make sure it's below the extents of the title block border.

6. Drag the cursor across the drawing and down until the screen displays a table that has eight rows (six data rows, a header row and title row) and then release the mouse button (see Figure 9.58). The new table appears; its title bar has a flashing cursor and a light gray background.

It has a dark gray background above and to the left of the table; the columns are lettered and the rows are numbered. The Text Editor tab and panels appear in the Ribbon.

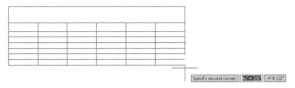

Specify second corner:

FIGURE 9.58: The new table inserted in the drawing

7. With Caps Lock on, enter **DOOR SCHEDULE**↵. The cursor moves to the upper-left cell on the table. This is the row for the column headers.

8. With Caps Lock on, enter **SYM**, and press the Tab key to highlight the next column header to the right. Moving across the header row, enter (in caps) **NAME** and press the Tab key; enter **H&W** and press the Tab key; enter **TYPE** and press the Tab key; enter **MAT'L** and press the Tab key; and then enter **COST**↵. This completes the row of column heads (see the top of Figure 9.59).

9. Partially fill in the data for the door schedule that's shown at the bottom of Figure 9.59 in the same manner. Pressing the Tab key instead of ↵ moves the activated cell left to right across each row and then down to the next row. Pressing ↵ moves the activated cell down each column and then ends the command. For the Glass and Aluminum material, don't press ↵ to move to the next line, simply keep typing and the text is wrapped automatically and the cell height is changed to accommodate the additional lines of text.

DOOR SCHEDULE					
SYM	NAME	H&W	TYPE	MAT'L	COST

DOOR SCHEDULE					
SYM	NAME	H&W	TYPE	MAT'L	COST
1	Front	7' x 7'	Sliding	Glass and Aluminum	
2	Back	3' x 7'			
3	Bath	2'6 x 7'			
4	Closet	4' x 7'			

FIGURE 9.59: The table with its title and column heads (top) and the table partially filled in (bottom)

SETTING THE CELL STYLE

If a cell justification doesn't appear correctly, or you want to change the style of a cell or range of cells, select the cells you want to change. In the Cell Styles panel under the Table Cell tab, expand the Cell Justification fly-out button and choose the appropriate style.

10. You don't have to enter everything from scratch; it's easy to copy the contents of one cell into other cells. Enter **Swinging** in cell D4 and then highlight the text. Press Ctrl+C to copy the highlighted text to the Windows Clipboard. Deselect the current cell, and then select the cell below it by clicking in cell D5. Press Ctrl+V to paste the word Swinging into the selected cell.

11. Complete the Type and Material columns, as shown in Figure 9.60.

DOOR SCHEDULE					
SYM	NAME	H&W	TYPE	MAT'L	COST
1	Front	7' x 7'	Sliding	Glass and Aluminum	
2	Back	3' x 7'	Swinging	Wood SC	
3	Bath	2'6 x 7'	Swinging	Wood HC	
4	Closet	4' x 7'	Bi-Fold	Wood HC	

FIGURE 9.60: The table with its text-based cells filled in

Adding a Formula

Currently, all the data cells are configured to hold text information and not numbers. You will now change the Cost column to read the information as numbers and then sum the values in the bottom cell with a formula:

1. Select all the cells below the Cost header in column F by clicking in cell F3, holding down the Shift key, and then clicking in cell F8.

2. Right-click, and choose Data Format from the context menu.

3. In the Table Cell Format dialog box that opens, choose Currency for Data Type; then choose 0.00 from the Precision drop-down list (see Figure 9.61). If necessary, change the Symbol value to the symbol of your local currency. Click OK to close the dialog box.

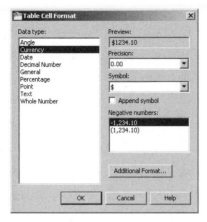

FIGURE 9.61: Formatting the table cells

4. In the Cost column, enter **350** for the front door, **105** for the back door, **85** for the bathroom door, and **65** for the closet door. AutoCAD automatically formats the numbers to two decimal places and adds a dollar sign to each, as shown in Figure 9.62.

DOOR SCHEDULE					
SYM	NAME	H&W	TYPE	MAT'L	COST
1	Front	7' x 7'	Sliding	Glass and Aluminum	$350.00
2	Back	3' x 7'	Swinging	Wood SC	$105.00
3	Bath	2'6 x 7'	Swinging	Wood HC	$85.00
4	Closet	4' x 7'	Bi-Fold	Wood HC	$65.00

FIGURE 9.62: The Cost column filled in

5. Click in the empty cell at the bottom of the Cost column to select it. In the Insert panel, click the Formula button and then choose Sum, as shown in Figure 9.63.

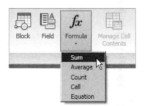

FIGURE 9.63: Adding a formula to the cell

As in a spreadsheet, a Sum formula adds the values of all the cells in a selected region.

6. At the Select first corner of table cell range: prompt, click in cell F3, the first door cost cell. At the Select second corner of table cell range: prompt, click in cell F6, the bottom door cost cell.

7. The formula "=SUM(F3:F6)" appears in cell F8. Click anywhere outside the table to deselect the cell and display its calculated value of $605.00, as shown in Figure 9.64.

SYM	NAME	H&W	TYPE	MAT'L	COST
	DOOR SCHEDULE				
1	Front	7' x 7'	Sliding	Glass and Aluminum	$350.00
2	Back	3' x 7'	Swinging	Wood SC	$105.00
3	Bath	2'6 x 7'	Swinging	Wood HC	$85.00
4	Closet	4' x 7'	Bi-Fold	Wood HC	$65.00
					$605.00

F I G U R E   9 . 6 4 : The completed table

 W A R N I N G   You would expect that the formatting assigned to the cell previously would carry through to the formula, but it doesn't always. You might need to reformat individual cells as required.

The table is finished and now you just need to do a little cleanup in your drawing to avoid any problems in the future and to tie elements in the drawing back to the table.

1. Thaw the Text1 and Tblk1 layers; then move your table, as required, so that it doesn't overlap the notes or title block.

2. You need a symbol for each door that corresponds with each number in the SYM column. With the Tables layer current, draw a circle with a radius of 8″ (204).

3. Press the Single Line Text button in the Annotation panel under the Home tab. Right-click and choose the Justify option from the context menu, and then choose the Middle option so the text will be centered around the insertion point.

4. Activate the Center osnap and then click the circle. Set the height to 10″ (254) and the rotation angle to 0. When the blinking cursor appears at the center of the circle, enter 1↵↵. The number 1 is centered in the circle.

5. Move the symbol near the front door, as shown in Figure 9.65, and then copy it to locations near the other three doors.

FIGURE 9.65: The first door symbol placed by the front door

6. Edit each of the symbol's numbers so they correspond with their entry in the SYM column. Your drawing should look like Figure 9.66.

FLOOR PLAN

FIGURE 9.66: The cabin with the door symbols added

7. Thaw the Grid layer; then select and delete the point objects you used to place your room name blocks.

8. Save this drawing as Cabin09d.dwg.

This concludes the chapter on dynamic blocks and tables. In the next chapter, you'll look at adding the elevations to the drawings.

This has been a quick tour of the features of attributes and the commands used to set them up and modify the data they contain. In the process, you saw several ways you can use them in an AutoCAD drawing. If you continue to work with attributes, you'll find them to be a powerful tool and a way to link information in your AutoCAD drawing to other applications. You also explored the methods for creating dynamic blocks that change as required to match your drawing's needs. Finally, you created a table to display the door schedule information and added a formula to calculate the total cost.

If You Would Like More Practice...

Blocks and attributes are commonly used in title blocks. For more practice using attributes, you can try the following:

- ▶ Replace the title block text with attributes.
- ▶ Add attributes to the window blocks.
- ▶ Experiment with the dynamic block functionality by creating window blocks that can be dragged to the appropriate width without resorting to scaling the blocks.
- ▶ Add a window schedule to calculate the cost of the cabin's windows.

Are You Experienced?

Now you can...

- ☑ **set up blocks with attributes**
- ☑ **control the visibility of the attributes**
- ☑ **calculate the area of an enclosed space**
- ☑ **create dynamic blocks**
- ☑ **define a table style**
- ☑ **create a table complete with formulas**

CHAPTER 10

Generating Elevations

▶ Drawing an exterior elevation from a floor plan

▶ Using grips to copy objects

▶ Setting up, naming, and saving user coordinate systems and views

▶ Transferring lines from one elevation to another

▶ Moving and rotating elevations

N ow that you have created all the building components that will be in the floor plan, it's a good time to draw the exterior elevations. *Elevations* are horizontal views of the building, seen as if you were standing facing the building instead of looking down at it, as you do with a floor plan. An elevation view shows you how windows and doors fit into the walls and gives you an idea of how the building will look from the outside. In most architectural design projects, the drawings include at least four exterior elevations: front, back, and one for each side.

I'll go over how to create the South elevation first. Then I'll discuss some of the considerations necessary to complete the other elevations, and you'll have an opportunity to draw them on your own.

In mechanical drawing, the item being drawn is often a machine part or a fixture. The drafter uses orthographic projection to illustrate various views of the object and calls them *front view, top view, side view*, and so on, instead of elevations and plans. An exercise later in this chapter will give you practice with orthographic projection, but the procedure will be the same, whether you're drawing buildings or mechanical objects.

> Orthographic projection is a method for illustrating an object in views set at right angles to each other—front, top, side, back, and so on.

Drawing the South Elevation

You draw the elevation using techniques similar to those used on a traditional drafting board. You'll draw the south elevation view of the cabin directly below the floor plan by dropping lines down from key points on the floor plan and intersecting them with horizontal lines representing the heights of the corresponding components in the elevation. Figure 10.1 shows those heights. For this project, we'll consider the top of the screen to be north.

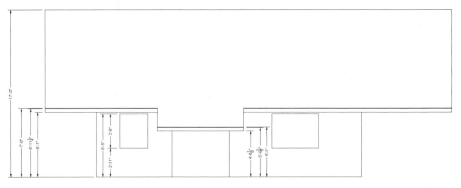

FIGURE 10.1: The south elevation with heights of components

Follow these steps:

1. Open Cabin09D.dwg.

2. Create a new layer called S-elev. Assign it color 42, and make it current.

3. Freeze the Grid, Tables, Tblk1, and Text1 layers. The Area layer should already be frozen, but check it and freeze it too if it is still thawed. Thaw the Roof layer.

4. Offset the bottom horizontal wall line to the right of the pop-out 30′ (9144 mm) down. The offset line may be off the screen.

5. Perform a Zoom Extents; then zoom out just enough to bring the offset wall line up off the bottom edge of the drawing area.

6. Select the object and, when the grips are visible, click the left grip. Use the Perpendicular osnap to stretch the line to the left extent of the building, as shown in Figure 10.2.

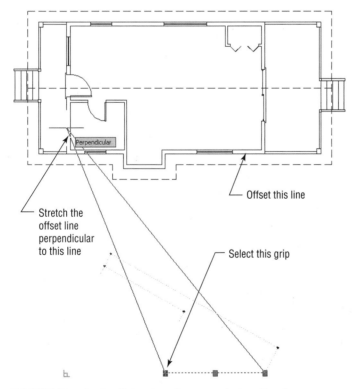

FIGURE 10.2: Using the grip to stretch the offset line

7. Deselect the offset line. When done, your drawing should look like Figure 10.3.

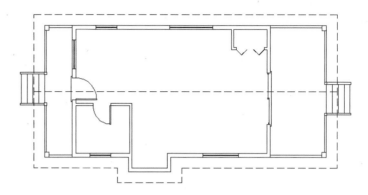

FIGURE 10.3: The floor plan with space below it for the south elevation

Setting Up Lines for the Heights

The line you offset establishes a baseline to represent the ground or the bottom of the cabin. You can now offset the other height lines from the baseline or from other height lines:

A soffit is the underside of the roof overhang that extends from the outside edge of the roof back to the wall.

1. Check the status bar to make sure that Polar Tracking, Object Snap, and Dynamic Input are in their on positions while the other buttons are off. The Endpoint osnap should be running.

2. Change the layer of the offset line from Walls to S-elev. Offset the base line 6'-7" (2007 mm) up to mark the lowest edge of the roof supports and the bottom edge of the soffit. Then offset the same line 6'-11 ¼" (2115 mm) and again 7'-0"(2134 mm) to establish the lower and upper heights of the roof covering respectively. Finally, offset the base line up 17'-0" (5182 mm) to mark the ridgeline of the roof. The lines should look like those shown in Figure 10.4.

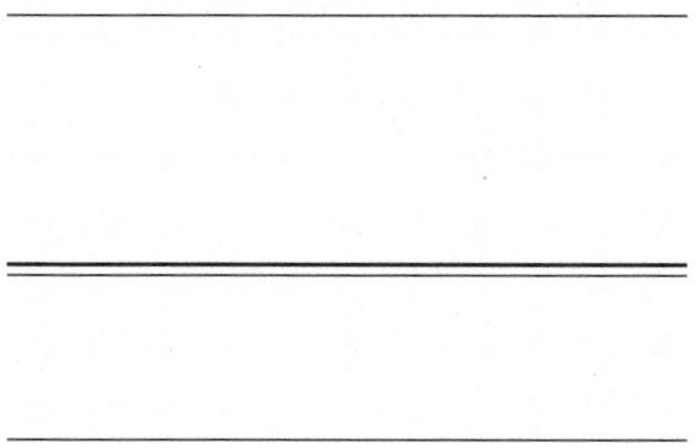

FIGURE 10.4: Lines representing different heights in the elevation

3. Offset the base line 2'-11" (889 mm) to represent the bottom of the windows, and then offset the offset line 3'-6" (1069 mm) to mark the top.

4. To complete the lines representing different heights in the elevation, copy the three horizontal roof lines down 1'-11" (584 mm). These will be the lines at the edge of the roof where it covers the pop-out (see Figure 10.5; note that two of the lines appear to be at the same height). Use a crossing selection window to select the lines; be sure not to select the line representing the tops of the windows.

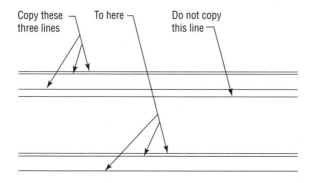

FIGURE 10.5: The horizontal height lines for the elevation in place

Each of these lines represents the height of one or more components of the cabin. Now you'll drop lines down from the points in the floor plan that coincide with components that will be visible in the elevation. The south elevation will consist of the exterior walls, two windows, the pop-out, and the roof.

Using Grips to Copy Lines

In the following steps, you'll use grips to copy the dropped lines:

1. Start a line from the lower-left corner of the exterior walls in the floor plan. Select the Perpendicular osnap, and click the ground line. Press ↲ to end the Line command.

2. Select the line you just drew. The grips appear on the line's midpoint and endpoints (see Figure 10.6).

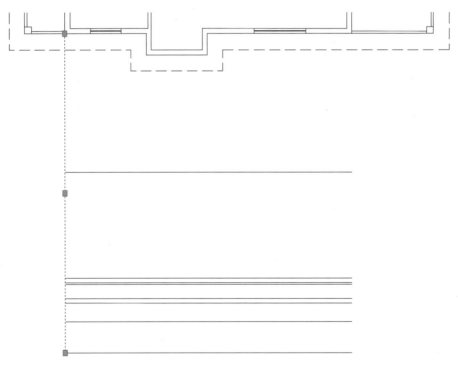

FIGURE 10.6: Select the line dropped from the floor plan.

The Stretch command is a modifying tool that you use to lengthen or shorten lines and other objects. You'll have another chance to use it in Chapter 11, "Working with Hatches and Gradients."

3. Click the grip on the upper endpoint. The grip changes color from blue to red, and the prompt changes to Specify stretch point or [Base point/Copy/Undo/eXit]:. This is the Stretch command,

which is activated by grips. Any time you activate a grip, the Stretch command automatically starts.

4. Right-click and choose Move from the context menu. Right-click again, and choose Copy from the context menu. This selects the Copy option. You'll use the Move command with its Copy option to copy the line you just selected.

5. With the Endpoint osnap running, select the three corners of the building (the far end and the two corners at the pop-out) and the four corners of the roof on the south side of the building. The line is copied to each of these corners.

6. Pick the four endpoints of the window openings in the floor plan to copy the line there as well.

7. Press Esc twice to end the command and deselect the line. Your drawing resembles Figure 10.7.

In the next section, you'll trim and extend the lines as necessary to continue the elevation drawing.

Each of the commands that work with grips has a Copy option, which keeps the original object as is while you modify the copy. You can copy with grips in several ways that aren't possible with the regular Copy command.

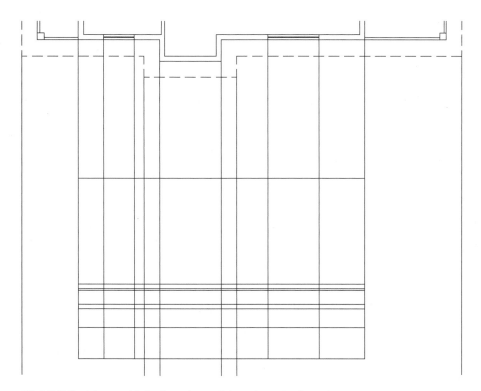

FIGURE 10.7: All the lines dropped down from the floor plan

GETTING A GRIP ON GRIPS

In Chapter 7, you saw how to use grips to detect whether an object is a block. Grips actually serve a larger function. The grips feature is a tool for editing objects quickly, using one or more of the following five commands: Stretch, Move, Rotate, Scale, and Mirror. These commands operate a little differently when using grips than when using them otherwise.

The commands can also perform a few more tasks with the help of grips. Each command has a Copy option. So, for example, if you rotate an object with grips, you can keep the original object unchanged while you make multiple copies of the object in various angles of rotation. You can't do this by using the Rotate command in the regular way or by using the regular Copy command.

To use grips, follow these steps:

1. When no commands have been started, click an object that you want to modify.

2. Click the grip that will be the base point for the command's execution.

3. Right-click at this point, and choose any of the five commands from the context menu that opens on the drawing area. (You can also cycle through the five commands by pressing the spacebar and watching the Command prompt.)

4. When you see the command you need, execute the necessary option.

5. Enter x↵ when you're finished.

6. Press Esc to deselect the object.

The key to being able to use grips efficiently is knowing which grip to select to start the process. This requires a good understanding of the five commands that work with grips.

This book doesn't cover grips in depth, but it introduces you to the basics. You'll get a chance to use the Move command with grips in this chapter, and you'll use grips again when we get to Chapter 12, "Dimensioning a Drawing."

Keep the following in mind when working with grips:

▶ Each of the five commands available for use with grips requires a base point. For Mirror, the base point is the first point of the mirror line. By default, the base point is the grip that you select to activate the process, but you can change base points. After selecting a grip, enter **b**↵ and pick a different point to serve as a base point, then continue the command.

▶ When you use the Copy option with the Move command, you're essentially using the regular Copy command.

Trimming Lines in the Elevation

The next task is to extend and trim the appropriate lines in the elevation. You'll start by extending the roof lines:

1. Click the Extend button in the Modify panel, and then click both of the lines dropped from the left and right extents of the roof and press ↵. These are the boundary edges.

2. Click once on each end of the top four horizontal lines—the ridge-line, the top and bottom of the roof covering, and the bottom of the soffit (see Figure 10.8).

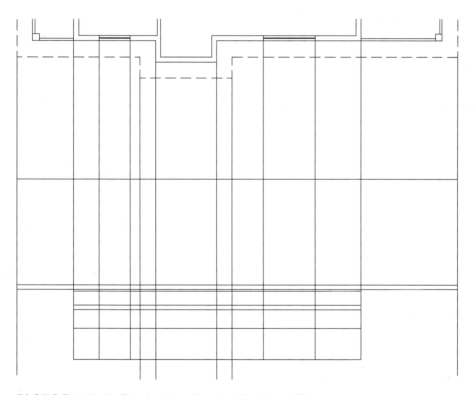

FIGURE 10.8: The elevation after extending the roof lines

3. Start the Trim command; then select as the cutting edges the four vertical lines that were dropped from the roof corners and the seven horizontal lines that represent the roof, as shown in the top of Figure 10.9.

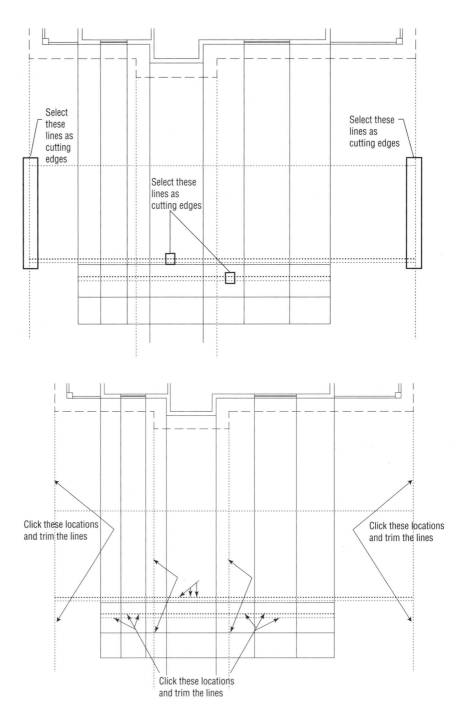

FIGURE 10.9: The cutting edges for trimming the roof lines (top) and selecting the trim points (bottom)

4. Press ↵ and click the lines at the locations shown in the bottom of Figure 10.9 to trim the line and complete the roof. Be sure not to trim the horizontal line that represents the top of the window. When completed, your elevation should look like Figure 10.10.

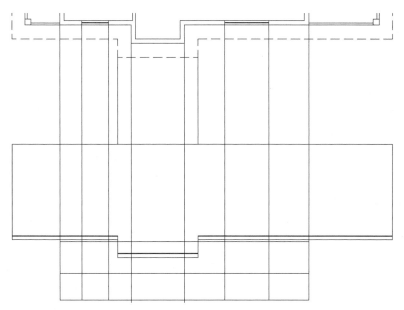

FIGURE 10.10: The elevation after trimming the roof lines

5. Start the Trim command again, and select the six lines that represent the boundaries of the windows (see Figure 10.11).

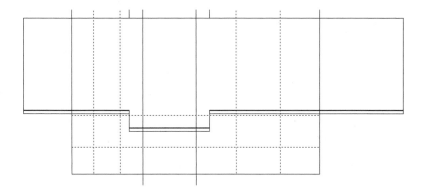

FIGURE 10.11: Selecting the window lines with the Trim command

6. Trim all the line segments that extend beyond the limits of the windows. When you are done, the south elevation should look like Figure 10.12.

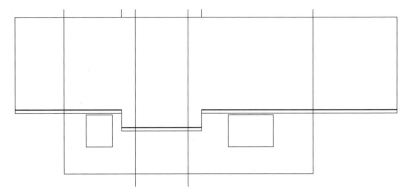

FIGURE 10.12: The elevation after trimming the roof lines

7. The final steps for this section are to trim away the vertical lines that were dropped from the corners of the elevation. Trim these to the soffit lines. Also trim the base line and erase any remaining lines between the floor plan and the elevation. When you're done, your drawing should look like Figure 10.13.

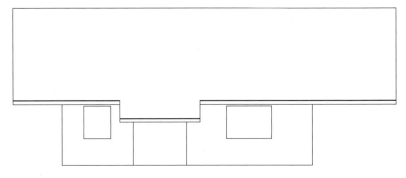

FIGURE 10.13: The cabin after trimming the window lines and erasing any unnecessary lines

Save this drawing as Cabin10a.dwg.

This is the basic process for generating an elevation: drop lines down from the floor plan, and trim the lines that need to be trimmed. The trick is to learn to see the picture you want somewhere among all the crossed lines and then to be able to use the Trim command accurately to cut away the appropriate lines.

Tips for Using the Trim and Extend Commands

Trim and Extend are sister commands. Here are a few tips on how they work:

Basic Operation Both commands involve two steps: selecting cutting edges (Trim) or boundary edges (Extend) and then selecting the lines to be trimmed or extended. Select the cutting or boundary edges first, and then press ↵. Next, pick lines to trim or extend. Press ↵ to end the commands. You can use the Fence option or a selection window to select several lines to trim or extend at one time.

Trimming and Extending in the Same Command If you find that a cutting edge for trimming can also serve as a boundary edge for extending, hold down the Shift key and click a line to extend it to the cutting edge. The opposite is true for the Extend command.

Correcting Errors It's easy to make a mistake in selecting cutting or boundary edges or in trimming and extending. You can correct a mistake in two ways:

▶ If you select the wrong cutting or boundary edge, enter r↵ and then choose the lines again that were picked in error. They will lose their highlighting. If you need to keep selecting cutting or boundary edges, enter a↵ and select new lines. When finished, press ↵ to move to the second part of the command.

▶ If you trim or extend a line incorrectly, enter u↵ or right-click and choose Undo from the context menu. This undoes the last trim. Click Undo again if you need to untrim or unextend more lines. When you have made all the corrections, continue trimming or extending. Press ↵ to end the command.

If the command ended and you click the Undo button, you will undo all trimming or extending that was done in the preceding command.

Drawing the Decks in Elevation

The cabin sits on an 18″ (457 mm) foundation (which you'll add in the "Drawing the Supports and Foundation" section later in the chapter), with the surrounding land falling away from it at a slight angle. On the front and back sides are decks with stairways to step up to the door levels. In this section, you'll draw the front deck first, mirror it to the other end, and then adjust the second deck to match the conditions at the back of the cabin.

Drawing the Front Deck

Figure 10.14 shows the dimensions required to draw the horizontal elements of the stairway while most vertical lines are dropped from the floor plan.

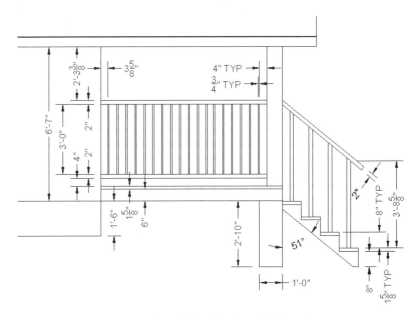

FIGURE 10.14: The front deck and stairs with dimensions

Follow these steps to draw the front deck:

1. Make the Deck layer current.

2. Draw a horizontal line from the elevation's bottom-right corner of the wall directly to the right. Make sure the line extends beyond the limits of the stairway in the floor plan.

3. Draw lines from the corner post, the stairs, and the end of the railing in the floor plan downward, well past the base line, as shown in Figure 10.15.

4. Zoom in to the right end of the cabin elevation. Here you're going to first offset the horizontal line several times and then trim the resulting lines back to the lines that represent the post. Start the Offset command, offset the horizontal line upward 6″ (152 mm), and press e to exit the command.

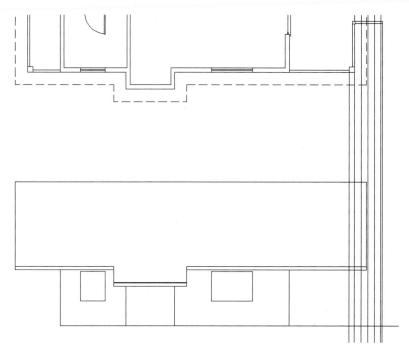

FIGURE 10.15: The lines drawn from the edge of the wall and down from the floor plan

5. Repeat step 5 five times, offsetting the original line 7 5/8″ (194 mm), 11 5/8″ (295 mm), 1′-1 5/8″ (346 mm), 4′-1 5/8″ (1260 mm), and 4′-3 5/8″ (1312 mm), respectively. The right end of your elevation should look like Figure 10.16.

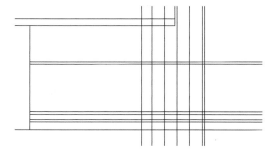

FIGURE 10.16: The offset lines for the stairs

6. Start the Trim command and select the two post lines, the soffit line, and the third horizontal deck line from the bottom as the cutting edges (see Figure 10.17).

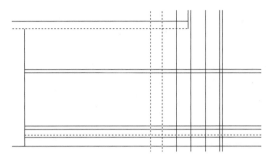

FIGURE   10.17: Select the cutting edges for the Trim command

7. Trim all the deck horizontal lines to the right post line, and then trim the top four deck lines again, this time to the left post line. Trim the vertical post lines back to the soffit line on top and the third horizontal deck line below. Next, draw a short vertical line from the bottom of the right post line to the lowest horizontal line, as shown in Figure 10.18.

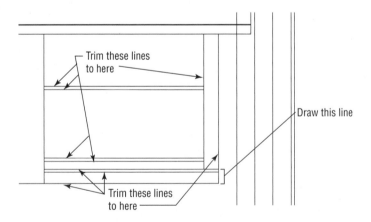

FIGURE   10.18: The deck and post lines after trimming them back to their proper lengths

Drawing the Railing Posts

The railing posts are ¾″ (20 mm) square components that are 3′-0″ (915 mm) long and spaced with a 4″ (102 mm) gap between each one. Once the first object is drawn, it's simple to use the Endpoint osnap to copy the remaining posts. Here's how:

1. Offset the left post line 4″ (102 mm) to the left, and then offset this line another ¾″ (20 mm).

2. Trim these two lines back to the lower edge of the upper rail and to the upper edge of the lower rail (see Figure 10.19).

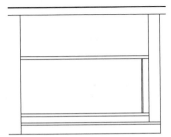

FIGURE 10.19: Draw the first railing post

3. Start the Copy command, and select the two railing post lines. Using the Endpoint osnap, select the right endpoint of the lower railing as the base point and the lower endpoint of the left railing post line where it meets the railing as the second point, as shown in Figure 10.20.

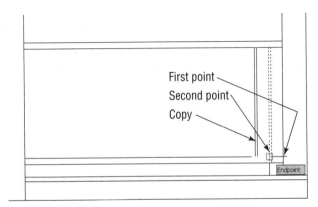

FIGURE 10.20: Copy the railing post to the left using the Endpoint osnaps

4. With the Copy command still running, repeatedly select the bottom endpoint of the previous, left railing post until there is no longer room for another post between the railings; then terminate the command. Your completed railings should look like those shown in Figure 10.21.

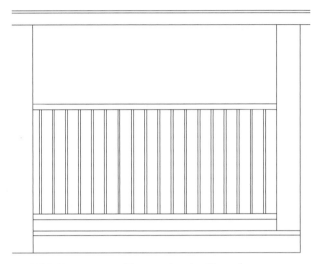

FIGURE 10.21: The completed railings

Drawing the Stairs

There are four steps leading up to the cabin, each with an 8″ (204 mm) rise and a 1 5/8″ (41 mm) thick tread. The 10″ (254 mm) length of the steps, also called the run, is based on the lines dropped from the steps in the floor plan.

1. Using Object Snap Tracking and direct input, draw a line from a point 8″ below the top of the deck directly to the right, well beyond the last vertical step line, as shown in Figure 10.22.

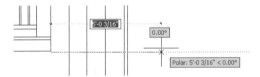

FIGURE 10.22: Drawing the first step tread

2. Using the Offset command, make three copies of this line, each one 8″ (204 mm) below the previous. These lines are the tops of the stair treads.

3. Offset each of the stair tread lines downward 1 5/8″ (41 mm) (see Figure 10.23).

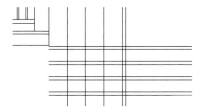

FIGURE 10.23: Offset the lines downward

4. Using the vertical step lines as cutting edges, trim each of the steps to its proper 10″ (254 mm) length. Try using a crossing window to select multiple lines to trim at one time.

5. Next, use the horizontal step lines as cutting edges to trim back the vertical lines, leaving the short, vertical line between each step intact. Your stairway should look like Figure 10.24.

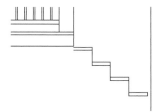

FIGURE 10.24: The steps after trimming away the extraneous lines

6. For the stringer, the support for the steps, you need a line that matches the angle between each step. Draw a line from the top-right corner of the first step to the top-right corner of the last step, and then offset this line 10″ (254 mm) so the copy appears below the stairs, as shown in Figure 10.25.

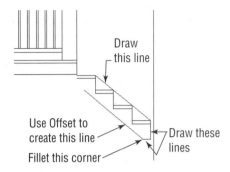

FIGURE 10.25: Drawing the stringer

7. Draw a line from the bottom of the lowest step tread 8″ (204 mm) downward and then a few feet directly to the left. Fillet the bottom-left corner of the stringer with a radius of 0, as shown in Figure 10.25.

8. The last parts of the stairway to draw are the 2″ (51 mm) railing posts and the handrail. Move the angled line at the top of the stairs up 3′-6″ (1067 mm) and then offset it upward 2″ (51 mm).

9. Extend the upper line until it intersects the post on the left and the last remaining vertical line dropped from the floor plan. Extend the lower line only to the post on the left, as shown in Figure 10.26.

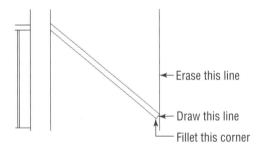

FIGURE 10.26: Finishing the stair rail

10. Draw a line from the right endpoint of the upper railing line perpendicular to the lower line, then fillet the corner. Erase the vertical line that extends from the floor plan.

11. To create the posts, draw a line from the midpoint of a stair tread upward and then offset it 1″ (25.5 mm) to the left and right. Erase the original line and then trim or extend the other two lines until they intersect with the lower railing line.

12. Using the top-right corner of each step as a reference point, copy the post to the other three steps. When you're done, your deck should look like Figure 10.27.

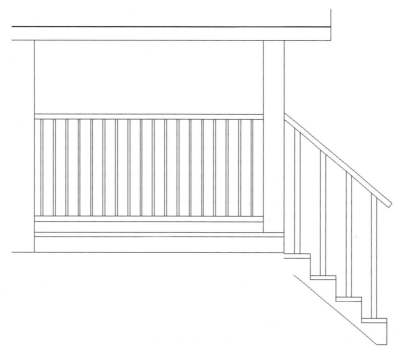

FIGURE 10.27: The stairway, deck, posts, and railings

Drawing the Supports and Foundation

The cabin rests on a foundation and the decks are supported by concrete posts. You can quickly draw these with the Rectangle command using object snaps and the Object Snap Tracking tool.

1. Make a new layer named **Foundation**, assign it a color, and make it current.

2. Start the Rectangle command, and draw a rectangle with the first point at the right end of the lowest horizontal deck line and the second point 1′ (305 mm) to the left and 2′-10″ (864 mm) below (-1′,-2′-10″) or (-305,-864) that point.

3. Extend the lower stringer line until it intersects the support post, as shown in Figure 10.28.

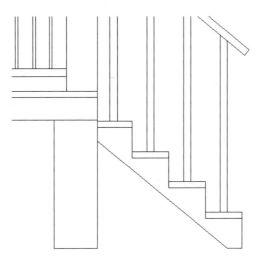

FIGURE 10.28: The extended stringer and the first deck support post

4. Zoom out so that you can see the entire cabin, and start the Rectangle command again.

5. At the Specify first corner point or: prompt, click the lower-right corner of the cabin's exterior wall.

6. At the Specify other corner point or: prompt, pause the cursor over the lower-left corner of the cabin's exterior wall until the temporary track point appears. Then move the cursor directly downward and enter 18↵ (457↵). The foundation rectangle is shown in Figure 10.29.

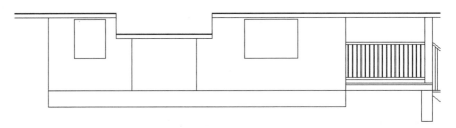

FIGURE 10.29: The completed foundation rectangle

Mirroring the Deck

From this view, the decks, stairways, post, and supports are nearly symmetrical, making the Mirror tool an excellent choice for creating most of the objects on the back deck. The front deck is wider than the back deck, but an efficient use of the Erase and Trim commands can quickly fix that.

1. Start the Mirror command, and then select all the components of the deck, stairs, railings, posts, and the concrete support.

2. At the Specify first point of mirror line: prompt, use the Midpoint osnap to select the midpoint of the roof.

3. At the Specify second point of mirror line: prompt, pick a point directly below the first point.

   The components on the right remain ghosted, while the new components on the left appear solid, as shown in Figure 10.30.

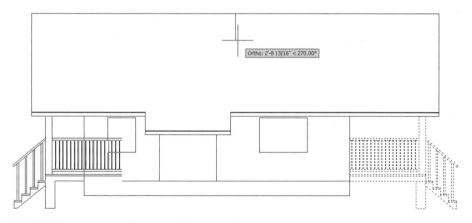

FIGURE 10.30: The front deck mirrored to the back of the cabin

4. When prompted whether to erase source objects, press ↵ to accept the default No option to retain the selected objects on the right.

5. Zoom in to the back deck. Erase any posts that exist past the leftmost exterior wall, and trim the horizontal deck lines back to that wall line, including the line that overlaps the top of the foundation. Your back deck should look like Figure 10.31.

FIGURE 10.31: The back deck after trimming and erasing unneeded lines

Cleaning Up the Drawing

The south elevation is essentially finished. All that remains is to make sure the objects reside on the proper layers. Many of the lines were drawn on the S-elev layer, and they need to be moved to their proper layers.

1. Select all the roof and soffit lines, and move them to the Roof layer. While they are still selected, select Continuous as the linetype in the Properties panel.

2. Select the steps, stringers, stair handrails, and stair handrail posts and move them to the Steps layer. The top of Figure 10.32 shows the objects on the Roof, Steps, and Foundation layers. The bottom of Figure 10.32 shows the objects on the S-elev and Deck layers.

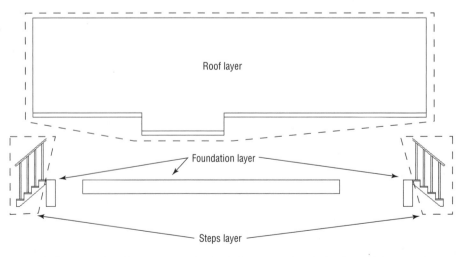

FIGURE 10.32: The objects on the Roof, Steps, and Foundation layers (above) and on the S-elev and Deck layers (next page)

FIGURE 10.32 *(Continued)*

3. Save this drawing as Cabin10b.dwg.

Generating the Other Elevations

The full set of drawings that contractors use to construct a building includes an elevation for each side of the building. In traditional drafting, the elevations are usually drawn on separate sheets. This requires transferring measurements from one drawing to another by taping drawings next to each other, turning the floor plan around to orient it to each elevation, and using several other cumbersome techniques. You do it about the same way on the computer, but it's much easier to move the drawing around. You'll be more accurate, and you can quickly borrow parts from one elevation to use in another.

Making the Opposite Elevation

Because the north elevation shares components and sizes with the south elevation, you can mirror the front elevation to the rear of the building and then make the necessary changes:

1. Open Cabin10b.dwg if it's not already open. You need to change the view to include space above the floor plan for the elevation on the opposite side of the building.

2. Use the Pan tool, or hold down the scroll wheel to move the view of the floor plan to the middle of the screen. Then zoom out the view enough to include the front elevation.

3. Start the Mirror command. Use a window to select the south elevation and press ↵.

4. For the mirror line, select the Midpoint osnap and pick the left edge line of the ridge line in the floor plan.

5. With polar tracking on, hold the crosshair cursor directly to the right of the point you just picked (see the top of Figure 10.33), and pick another point. At the Erase source objects?[Yes/No]<N>: prompt, press ↵ to accept the default of No. The first side elevation is mirrored to the opposite side of the cabin (see the bottom of Figure 10.33).

The user coordinate system (UCS) defines the positive X and Y directions relative to your drawing. A drawing can have several UCSs but can use only one at a time. The world coordinate system (WCS) is the default UCS for all new drawings and remains available in all drawings.

You can now make the necessary changes to the new elevation so that it correctly describes the south elevation of the cabin. However, you might find it easier to work if the view is right side up.

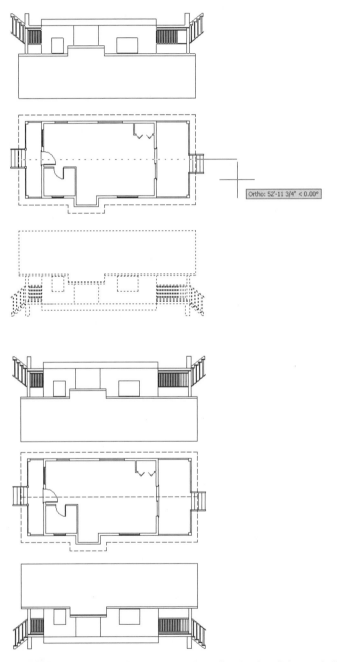

FIGURE 10.33: Specifying a mirror line (top) and the result (bottom)

6. Click the View tab then, in the Coordinates panel, click the Show UCS button. Then choose the Show UCS Icon option from the fly-out menu to execute the UCSICON command and turn on the UCS icon that you turned off earlier. This button may be located under the fly-out menu exposed by clicking the down arrow next to a similar-looking button (see Figure 10.34).

FIGURE 10.34: Showing the UCS icon

Take a look at the icon, currently located at the origin, for a moment. The two arrows in the icon show the positive X and Y directions of the current UCS. That is the WCS, which is the default system for all Auto-CAD drawings. You'll change the orientation of the icon to the drawing and then change the orientation of the drawing to the screen.

7. Click the Z button in the Coordinates panel and enter 180↙. This rotates the icon 180° around the z-axis to an upside-down position. The square box at the intersection of the x- and y-axes disappears, meaning that you're no longer using the default WCS. (See Figure 10.35.)

FIGURE 10.35: The UCS icon showing the UCS rotated 180°

8. From the Menu bar, choose View ➤ 3D Views ➤ Plan View ➤ Current UCS or enter plan↙ c↙. The entire drawing is rotated 180°, and the mirrored elevation is now right side up. Note that the UCS icon is now oriented the way it used to be, but the square in the icon is still missing. This signals that the current UCS is not the WCS.

You used the UCS command to reorient the UCS icon relative to the drawing. You then used the Current option of the Plan command to reorient the drawing on the screen so that the positive X and Y directions of the current UCS are directed to the right and upward, respectively. This process is a little bit like turning your monitor upside down to get the correct orientation, but it's easier.

9. Zoom in to display the lower edge of the floor plan and the mirrored elevation (see Figure 10.36). Now you can work on the rear elevation.

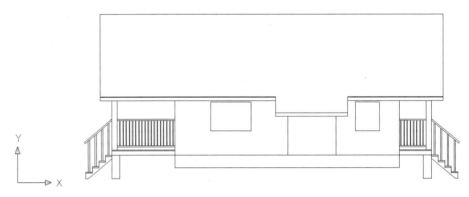

FIGURE 10.36: The cabin drawing rotated 180° and zoomed in

Revising the New South Elevation

A brief inspection will tell you that the decks and stairs don't need any changes. The windows and roof need revisions and the pop-out doesn't exist on this side of the cabin:

▶ The two remaining windows need resizing and repositioning.

▶ The roof needs to be a series of straight, unbroken lines.

▶ The vertical pop-out lines and the pop-out roof extension need to be deleted.

You can accomplish these tasks quickly by using commands with which you're now familiar:

1. Make a new layer named **N-elev**, assign it the same color as S-elev, and make it current.

2. Change all lines on the S-elev layer that exist on this elevation to the N-elev layer. (Try using the Isolate and Unisolate commands from the Layers panel.)

3. Erase the vertical lines from the remaining windows, and then drop lines down from the jambs of the two windows in the floor plan, past the bottoms of the windows in elevation (see the top of Figure 10.37).

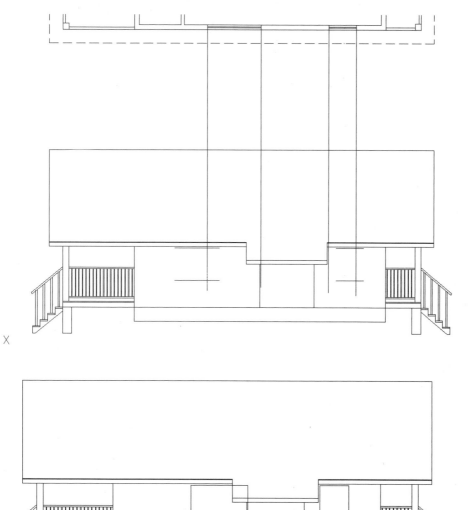

FIGURE 10.37: Erase the vertical window lines and drop new lines (top), and the revised windows after filleting the corners (bottom)

4. Use the Fillet command to construct the new windows. Pick the lines carefully, especially around the pop-out area. Your south elevations should look like the bottom of Figure 10.37.

5. Delete the vertical pop-out lines, the three short roof lines over the pop-out, the three roof lines to the right of the pop-out, and the two short vertical lines that connect the main roof with the pop-out roof (see the top of Figure 10.38).

6. Use the Extend command to extend the three remaining roof lines to the left, vertical roofline, as shown in the bottom of Figure 10.38.

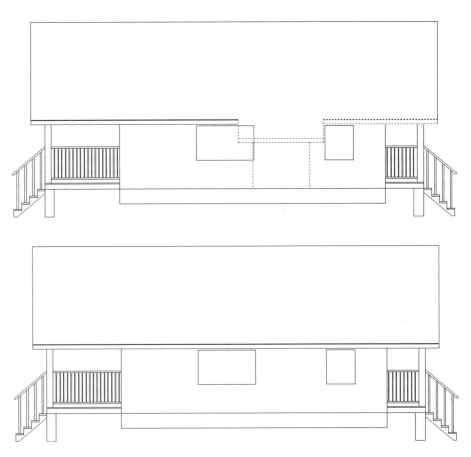

FIGURE 10.38: Erase the unwanted pop-out and roof lines (top), and extend the remaining roofline (bottom).

You need to save the UCS you used to work on this elevation so that you can quickly return to it in the future, from the WCS or from any other UCS you might be in.

7. Click the UCS Settings button in the lower-right corner of the Coordinates panel to open the UCS dialog box. Click the Named UCSs tab, then click the current UCS name (currently named *Unnamed*) once to enter the highlight the text. Then enter **North_elev↵** (see Figure 10.39). This will allow you to recall it if you need to work on this elevation again. Click OK to exit the dialog box.

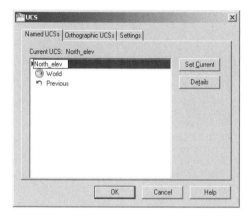

FIGURE 10.39: The UCS dialog box

T I P You can save any UCS in this way. The WCS is a permanent part of all drawings, so you never need to save it.

8. You can also save the view to be able to recall it quickly. Click the Named Views button in the Views panel, or open the View Manager dialog box. You can also start the View command by entering v↵.

9. Click New to open the New View / Shot Properties dialog box.

10. In the View name text box, enter **North_elev** (see Figure 10.40). Click the Current display radio button and click OK. Back in the View Manager dialog box, North_elev appears in the list of views. Click OK again. Now you can restore the drawing to its original orientation, with the side elevation below the floor plan and right side up. You do this by opening the View Manager, selecting North_elev, and clicking Set Current.

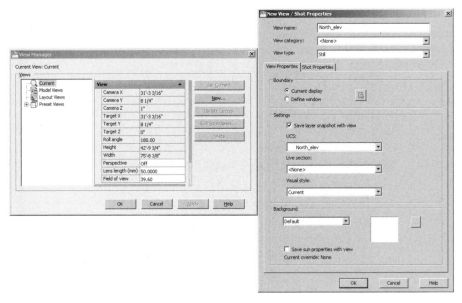

FIGURE 10.40: Saving a view in the View Manager and New View / Shot Properties dialog boxes

T I P   You can name and save any view of your drawing and then restore it later.

11. Click the World button in the Coordinates panel, or enter **ucs↵↵** to restore the WCS as the current coordinate system.

12. Choose View ➤ 3D Views ➤ Plan View ➤ Current UCS from the Menu bar. This zooms to Extents view and displays a plan view of the drawing with the X and Y positive directions in their default orientation. You can also enter **plan↵↵** to restore the plan view of the WCS.

You created a new UCS as a tool to flip the drawing upside down without changing its orientation with respect to the WCS. Now you'll use it again to create the front and back elevations.

Making the Front and Back Elevations

You can generate the front and back elevations using techniques similar to those you have been using for two side elevations. You need to be able to transfer the heights of building components from one of the side elevations to either of the remaining elevations. To do this, you'll make a copy of the first elevation you drew, rotate it 90°, and then line it up so you can transfer the heights to the front elevation. It's quite easy:

1. Zoom out slightly, and then zoom in to a view of the floor plan and the first elevation. Pan the drawing so that the floor plan and elevation are on the left part of the drawing area. You need to transfer the height data from the side elevation to the front elevation. To ensure that the front elevation is the same distance from the floor plan as the side elevation, you'll use a 45° line that extends down and to the right from the rightmost and lowermost lines in the floor plan.

2. Turn on polar tracking and be sure Increment Angle is set to 45°. Also make sure that the Object Snap Tracking button on the status bar is toggled on. Then set the Endpoint osnap to running and be sure the Midpoint osnap isn't running.

3. Start the Line command. Move the crosshair cursor to the bottom-right corner of the front stairway handrail in the floor plan. Hold it there for a moment. A cross appears at the intersection point. Don't click yet.

4. Move the crosshair cursor to the lower-right corner of the roof pop-out in the floor plan, and hold it there until a cross appears at that point. Don't click yet.

5. Move the crosshair cursor to a point directly to the right of the corner of the roof pop-out and directly under the intersection point of the handrail (see the top of Figure 10.41). Vertical and horizontal tracking lines appear and intersect where the crosshair cursor is positioned, and a small *x* appears at the intersection. A tracking tooltip also appears.

6. Click to start a line at this point.

7. Move the crosshair cursor down, away from this point and to the right at a negative 45° angle (or a positive 315° angle). When the 45° polar tracking path appears, enter 40'⏎ (**12200**). Press ⏎ again. This completes the diagonal reference line (see the bottom of Figure 10.41).

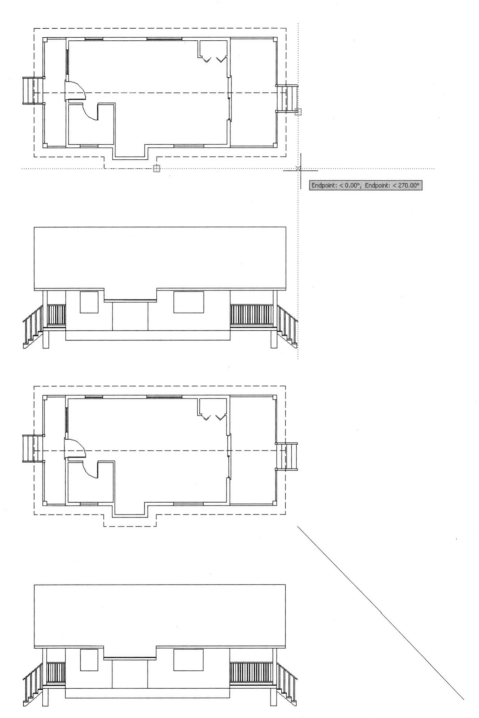

Endpoint: < 0.00°, Endpoint: < 270.00°

F I G U R E   1 0 . 4 1 : Starting a diagonal reference line with tracking points (top) and the completed diagonal line (bottom)

8. Start the Copy command, and select the entire south elevation and nothing else. Then press ↲.

9. For the base point, select the left endpoint of the base line of the cabin.

10. For the second point, pick the Intersection osnap, and place the cursor on the diagonal line. When the *x* symbol with three dots appears at the cursor, click. Then move the cursor to any point on the base line of the south elevation. An *x* appears on the diagonal line where the ground line would intersect it if it were longer (see the top of Figure 10.42). This is called the *implied intersection*. The implied intersection is a distinct object snap in itself, and it is also the osnap that is used when the Intersection osnap is specified but an intersection is not clicked. This is why the three dots appeared after the x symbols.

11. When the *x* appears, click to locate the copy. Press Esc to end the Copy command. Zoom out to include the copy, and then use Zoom Window to include the floor plan and south elevations (see the bottom of Figure 10.42). Press Esc to terminate the Copy command.

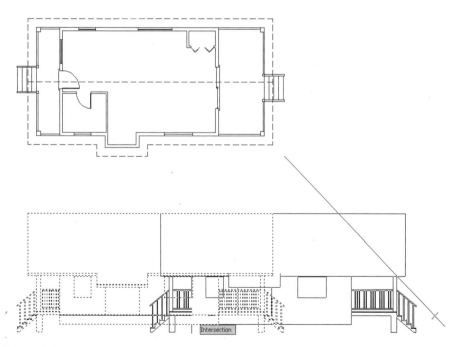

F I G U R E   1 0 . 4 2 : Making a copy of the side elevation (above) and adjusting the view (next page)

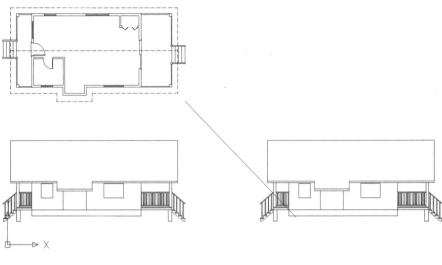

FIGURE 10.42 *(Continued)*

12. Start the Rotate command, and select the copy of the south elevation; then press ↵. Activate the Intersection osnap, and click the intersection of the diagonal line with the base line as you did in steps 9 and 10. For the angle of rotation, enter **90**↵ (see the top of Figure 10.43).

13. Start the Move command and, when prompted to select objects, enter **p**↵↵ to select the most recently selected objects. The rotated elevation is selected. For the base point, click a point in a blank space to the right of the rotated elevation and on the upper part of the drawing area. For the second point, move the cursor down using polar tracking until the last step on the elevation is lower than the roof pop-out in the plan view and then click.

14. Zoom out and use Zoom Window to adjust the view (see the bottom of Figure 10.43).

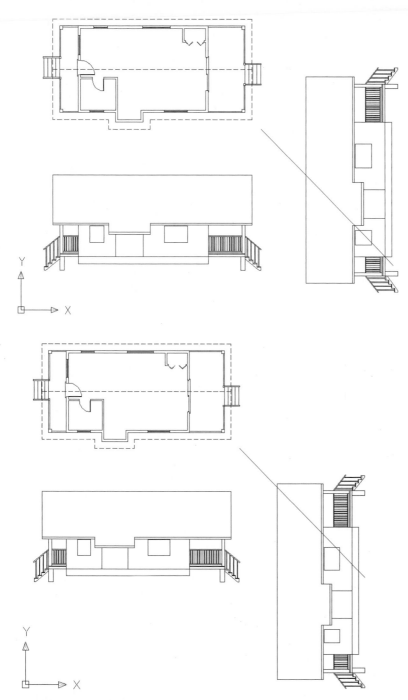

FIGURE 10.43: Rotating the copy (top) and the moving the copy with the view adjusted (bottom)

The rest of the process for creating the front elevation is straightforward and uses routines you have just learned. Here's a summary of the steps:

1. Set up a new UCS for the front elevation showing the East side of the cabin. (Click the Z button in the Coordinates panel, and then enter 90↵.) Use the Plan command to rotate the drawing to the current UCS.

2. Make a new layer named E_elev, make it current, and place the elevation walls on this layer.

3. Drop lines from the floor plan across the drawing area and height lines, which you'll draw from the copied elevation.

4. Trim or fillet these lines as required, and add any necessary lines.

   ▶ Draw the roof first and remember that there is a thin layer of roof covering (see the top of Figure 10.44).

   ▶ Draw the wall, door, and foundation next. You won't be able to get the height line for the sliding-glass door from the side elevation. It's 7'-3" (2210 mm) from the top of the deck (see the middle of Figure 10.44).

   ▶ Finally, draw the pop-out, deck, railings and support posts. The railing posts have the same size and spacing on the front of the deck as they do on the sides, and the support post measures 1'-0" (305 mm) across. This can create a congested drawing, and you may want to draw the guide lines only as necessary to draw each component and then erase them. (See the bottom of Figure 10.44.)

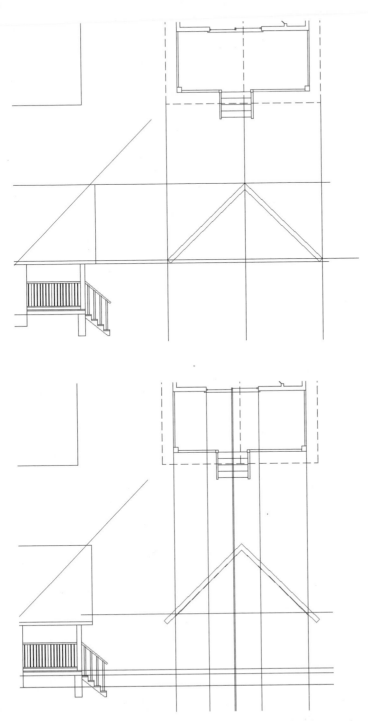

FIGURE 10.44: Incrementally drawing the front elevation starting with the roof (top); the wall, door, and foundation (bottom); and finally the deck (next page)

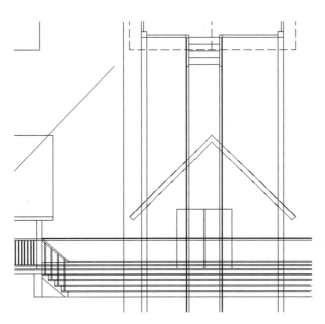

FIGURE 10.44 *(Continued)*

5. Erase or trim away any lines that represent objects that are visually behind any objects in the foreground. For instance, the portions of the foundation that are behind the steps or support posts or the vertical door lines that are behind the railings.

6. Make sure all the objects reside on the proper layers, and change the roof objects' linetype to Continuous.

7. When you're done, the east elevation should look like Figure 10.45.

8. Erase the copy of the south elevation and the diagonal transfer line.

9. Name and save the UCS and view (call them both East_elev).

T I P   When creating elevations, you might accidentally draw a line over an existing line. To catch this error, start the Erase command and use a crossing window to select the suspect line. In the Command window, the number of objects selected appears. If more than one line has been selected, cancel, restart the Erase command, and pick the line again. This time, only the extra line is selected and you can erase it. If more than two lines are on top of each other, repeat the process.

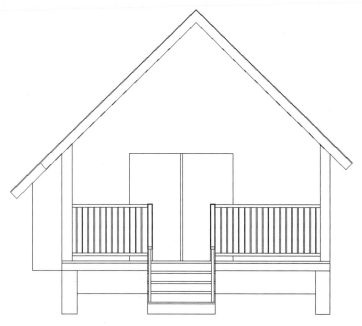

FIGURE 10.45: The completed east elevation

You can create the rear elevation from a mirrored image of the front elevation. Here are the steps:

1. Mirror the front elevation to the opposite side.

2. Set up a UCS for the left elevation. (Click the Z button in the UCS panel, and then enter 180↵.) Use the Plan command to rotate the drawing to the current UCS.

3. Revise the elevation to match the left side of the cabin.

   ▶ Temporarily move the railing posts a known distance and angle away from their current locations.

   ▶ Use the Stretch command and Perpendicular osnap to stretch the stairway and railings to match the stairway location on the back of the cabin as shown on the floor plan.

   ▶ Move the railing posts back to their original locations.

   ▶ Add or delete posts as required.

   ▶ Delete the sliding door frame that divides the left and right panels, and then adjust the door to match the extents shown on the plan view.

▶ Move the wall lines to a new layer named **W_elev**.

▶ Add the window with the lower edge at 2'-11" (889 mm) above the base line and the top edge at 7'-11" (2413 mm) above the base line. When you're done, the elevation should look like Figure 10.46.

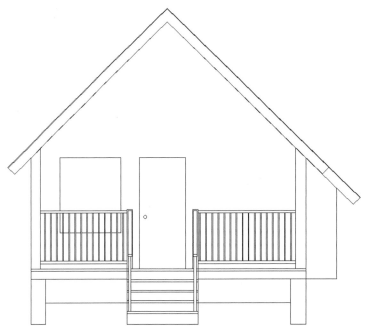

FIGURE 10.46: The completed rear elevation

4. Name and save the UCS and view (call them both **West_elev**).

When you have completed all the elevations, follow these steps to clean up and save the drawing:

1. Return to the WCS.

2. Display the Plan view.

3. Erase any remaining construction lines.

4. Thaw the Text1 layer, and then move the notes down and to the left so they no longer overlap any elevation.

5. Copy and rotate the FLOOR PLAN label under each of the plans, and edit the content appropriately.

6. Zoom out slightly for a full view of all elevations. The drawing looks like Figure 10.47.

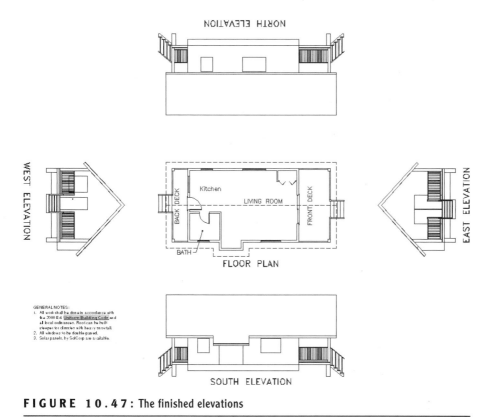

FIGURE 10.47: The finished elevations

7. Save the drawing as Cabin10c.dwg.

Considering Drawing Scale Issues

This last view raises several questions: How will these drawings best fit on a page? How many pages will it take to illustrate these drawings? What size sheet should you use? At what scale will the drawing be printed? In traditional hand drafting, you wouldn't be able to draw the first line without answers to some of these questions. You have completed a great deal of the drawing on the computer without having to make decisions about scale and sheet size because, in AutoCAD, you draw in real-world scale or full-scale. This means that when you tell AutoCAD to draw a 10′ (3048 mm) line, it draws the line 10′ (3048 mm) long. If you inquire how long the line is, AutoCAD will tell you that it's 10′ (3048 mm) long. Your current view of the line might be to a certain scale, but that changes every time you zoom in or out. The line is stored in the computer as 10′ (3048 mm) long.

You need to make decisions about scale when you're choosing the sheet size, putting text and dimensions on the drawing, or using hatch patterns and noncontinuous linetypes. (Chapter 11 covers hatch patterns, and Chapter 12 covers dimensioning.) Because you have a dashed linetype in the drawing, you had to make a choice about scale in Chapter 6, when you assigned a linetype scale factor of 24 to the drawing. You chose that number because when the drawing consisted of only the floor plan and the view was zoomed as large as possible while still having all objects visible, the scale of the drawing was about ½″ = 1′-0″. That scale has a true ratio of 1:24, or a scale factor of 24. You'll get further into scale factors and true ratios of scales in the next chapter.

If you look at your Cabin10c drawing with all elevations visible on the screen, the dashes in the dashed lines look like they might be too small, so you might need to increase the linetype scale factor. If you were to thaw the title block's layer now, you would see that your drawings won't all fit. Don't worry about that yet. Beginning with the next chapter, and right on through the end of this book, you'll need to make decisions about scale each step of the way.

Drawing Interior Elevations

You construct interior elevations using the same techniques you learned for constructing exterior elevations. You drop lines from a floor plan through offset height lines and then trim them away. Interior elevations usually include fixtures, built-in cabinets, and built-in shelves, and they show finishes. Each elevation consists of one wall and can include a side view of items on an adjacent wall if the item extends into the corner. Not all walls appear in an elevation—usually only those that require special treatment or illustrate special building components. You might use one elevation to show a wall that has a window and to describe how the window is treated or finished, and then assume that all other windows in the building will be treated in the same way unless noted otherwise.

In the next chapter, you'll learn how to use hatch patterns and fills to enhance floor plans and elevations.

If You Would Like More Practice...

Here are three exercises for practicing the techniques you learned in this chapter. The last one will give you practice in basic orthogonal projection.

Exterior elevations Open Cabin10c.dwg and revise each elevation adding 1 1/2≤ frames around the windows and doors. Add mullions, the dividers between window panes, to separate each window into four equal panes and add a rectangular window to the back door. Figure 10.48 shows the revised south elevation with the features added to the windows.

SOUTH ELEVATION

FIGURE 10.48: The revised south elevation

Interior elevations For some practice with interior elevations, try drawing one or two elevations. You can measure the heights and sizes of various fixtures in your own home or office as a guide.

Orthogonal projection Draw the three views of the block shown in Figure 10.49 following the procedures you used for the cabin elevations, except that in this case, you'll use the procedure that mechanical drafters employ—that is, draw the front view first, and then develop the top and right side views from the front view. The completed drawing, named Chap10 Block.dwg, can be found on the book's website, www.sybex.com/go/autocad2010ner.

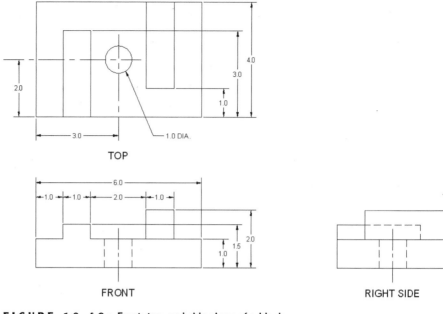

FIGURE 10.49: Front, top, and side views of a block

Are You Experienced?

Now you can...

- ☑ **draw exterior elevations from a floor plan**

- ☑ **use grips to copy objects**

- ☑ **add detail to an elevation**

- ☑ **set up, name, and save a UCS and a view**

- ☑ **transfer height lines from one elevation to another**

- ☑ **copy, move, rotate, and mirror elevations**

CHAPTER 11

Working with Hatches, Gradients, and Tool Palettes

- ▶ Selecting a predefined hatch pattern and applying it to a drawing
- ▶ Setting up and applying user-defined hatch patterns
- ▶ Modifying the scale and shape of a hatch pattern
- ▶ Specifying the origin of a hatch pattern
- ▶ Filling an enclosed area with a solid color
- ▶ Filling an enclosed area with a gradient
- ▶ Setting up and using palettes and palette tools

Hatches can be abstract patterns of lines, they can be solid *fills*, or they can resemble the surfaces of various building materials. Gradients are visual features that shift from one solid color to another over a specified distance. To give the appearance of texture to a drawing, an AutoCAD user can hatch in areas or fill them in with a solid color or gradient. Solid fills in a drawing can provide a shaded effect when printed using *screening*, printing an object using less than 100 percent ink density that results in a look quite different from the solid appearance of the AutoCAD drawing on the screen. Chapter 15, "Printing an AutoCAD Drawing," covers screening and other printing issues.

In an architectural floor plan, the inner sides of full-height walls are often hatched or filled to distinguish them from low walls in the foreground. Wood or tile floors can be hatched to a parquet or tile pattern. In a site plan, hatches distinguish between areas with different ground covers, such as grass, gravel, or concrete. When you're working with elevations, you can hatch almost any surface to show shading and shadows. Realistic hatch patterns can illustrate the surfaces of concrete, stucco, or shingles. Hatches and fills are widely used in mechanical, landscaping, civil, structural, and architectural details as a tool to aid in clear communication. Be sure that your hatch patterns add to the readability of your drawings and do not hinder it by making the drawings appear cluttered.

To learn how to hatch and fill areas, you'll start with some of the visible surfaces in the south elevation of the cabin. You'll then move to the floor plan, hatch the floors, and put hatch patterns and fills in the walls and a gradient on the balcony. You'll use the Hatch And Gradient dialog box for all hatches and gradients. It's a tool with many options that you can use to create a sense of depth or texture in your drawings.

A key part of a hatch pattern is the boundary of the pattern. You define the area being hatched through a procedure called *ray casting* in which AutoCAD searches the drawing for lines or objects to serve as the hatch boundary.

Hatching the South Elevation

Hatches and fills should be on their own layers so they can be turned off or frozen without also making other objects invisible. You'll begin the exercise by creating new layers for the hatches and assigning colors to them:

1. Open the Cabin10c.dwg drawing or, if you completed the "If You Want More Practice" section in the previous chapter, open your drawing with the additional window and door features. Cabin10d.dwg, from this chapter's website files, has this additional content. It should contain the floor plan, elevations, and the general notes.

T I P   To see the visual effect of putting hatch patterns on the south elevation well, change the background color for the drawing area to white. Click
the Options button at the bottom of the Application menu to open the Options
dialog box, and then click the Display tab. Click the Colors button and choose
2D Model Space in the Context list, Uniform Background in the Interface Element list, and White in the Color list to make the change.

2. Set up four new layers as follows:

Layer Name	Color
Hatch-elev-brown	42
Hatch-elev-gray	Gray (8)
Hatch-elev-black	Black (White) (7)
Hatch-noplot	60

3. For the Hatch-noplot layer only, click the printer icon in the Plot column of the Layer Properties Manager.

The icon changes to a printer with a red circle with a line through it.
The objects on that layer will not appear in print regardless of
whether they are visible in the drawing area.

4. Make the Hatch-elev-gray layer current. Now any new objects you
   create will be assigned to this layer.

5. Click the Hatch button on the Draw panel to open the Hatch and
   Gradient dialog box (see Figure 11.1). Be sure the expansion arrow in
   the lower-right corner is pointing to the left. If it isn't, click it to
   expand the dialog box to its full size. You'll use this dialog box to
   choose a pattern, set up the pattern's properties, and determine the
   method for specifying the boundary of the area to be hatched. The
   Hatch tab should be active. If it's not, click the tab. Predefined and
   ANSI31 should appear in the Type and Pattern drop-down lists,
   respectively. If not, open the lists and select those options.

You can also start the
Hatch command by
entering h↵.

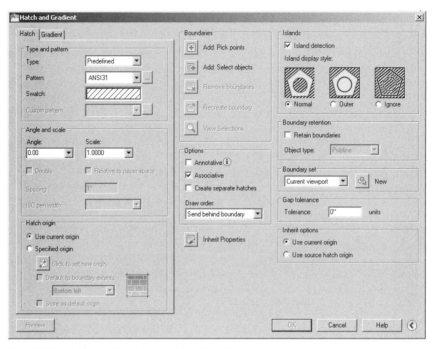

FIGURE 11.1: The Hatch and Gradient dialog box

6. Move to the right of the Pattern drop-down list, and click the Browse button to open the Hatch Pattern Palette dialog box (see Figure 11.2). This palette is where you select the specific hatch pattern that you'll use. Of the four tabs, ANSI is active and the ANSI31 pattern is highlighted.

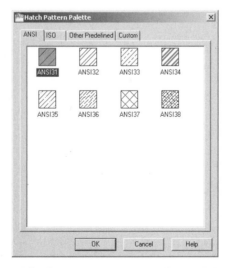

FIGURE 11.2: The Hatch Pattern Palette dialog box

7. Click the Other Predefined tab. Find the AR-RROOF pattern, click it, and then click OK. Back in the Hatch and Gradient dialog box, note that AR-RROOF has replaced ANSI31 in the Pattern drop-down list. A new pattern appears in the Swatch preview box, which is below the Pattern list (see Figure 11.3).

   You can change the Scale and Angle settings in their drop-down lists, which are below the Swatch preview box. In the Angle drop-down list, the preset angle of 0.00 is fine, but you need to adjust the Scale setting.

8. The Scale drop-down list contains preset scale factors that range from 0.2500 to 2.0000 (0.25 to 2). To set the scale to 6, you have to enter it manually. In the Scale drop-down list, select 1.0000 (1) and enter **6**, but do not press ↲; just proceed to step 9 and continue the procedure. (That is, create the hatch and then press ↲. The next time you open the dialog box in the current drawing, you'll see that 6 has been added to the drop-down list and is displayed as 6.0000 (6).)

9. In the Options section in the middle of the dialog box, check the Associative option. Associative hatches automatically update the areas they cover whenever their boundaries change. If you delete any component of the boundary, however, the hatch becomes nonassociative.

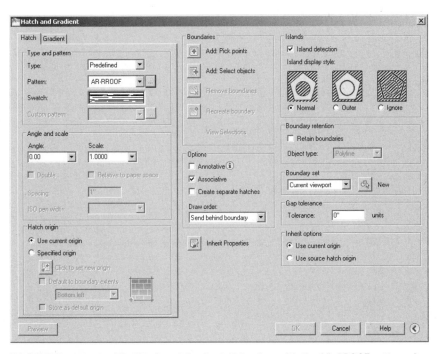

FIGURE 11.3: The Hatch and Gradient dialog box with the AR-RROOF pattern chosen

10. Move to the upper middle of the dialog box, and click the Add: Pick Points button. This returns you to the drawing.

11. In the south elevation view, click the middle of the roof area. The lines that form the boundary of the roof area become dashed, displaying an outline of the area to be hatched (see Figure 11.4).

SOUTH ELEVATION

FIGURE 11.4: The roof's boundary is selected.

12. Right-click and choose Preview from the context menu. In the preview drawing, look at how the hatch will appear. This hatch looks fine for now (see Figure 11.5).

SOUTH ELEVATION

FIGURE 11.5: The finished hatch pattern in the roof area

13. Press ↵ or right-click to accept this hatch. The hatch is now placed in the roof area.

14. Zoom in to a view of just the south elevation. Notice how the appearance of the hatch pattern gets more detailed as the roof gets larger on the screen.

Looking at Hatch Patterns

Let's take a short tour through the available patterns:

1. Start the Hatch command.

2. In the Hatch and Gradient dialog box, be sure that the Hatch tab is active. Then click the Browse button next to the Pattern drop-down list to open the Hatch Pattern Palette dialog box.

3. Make the Other Predefined tab active if it isn't already. Look at the display of hatch patterns. Eleven pattern names begin with *AR-*, including the one just used. These patterns have been designed to look like architectural and building materials, which is why you see the AR prefix. In addition to the roof pattern you just used, you'll see several masonry wall patterns, a couple of floor patterns, and one pattern each for concrete, wood shakes, and sand.

4. Scroll down the display and observe the other non-AR patterns. They're geometrical patterns, some of which use common conventions to represent various materials.

5. Click the ANSI tab and look at a few of the ANSI patterns. These are abstract line patterns developed by the American National Standards Institute, and they are widely used by public and private design offices in the United States.

6. Click the ISO tab. These are also abstract line patterns developed by another organization: the International Organization for Standardization. The Custom tab is empty unless custom hatch patterns have been loaded into your copy of AutoCAD.

7. Click Cancel in the Hatch Pattern Palette dialog box. Click Cancel again to close the Hatch and Gradient dialog box.

As you work with hatch patterns, you'll need to adjust the scale factor for each pattern so the patterns will look right when the drawing is printed. The AR patterns are drawn to be used with the scale factor set approximately to the default of one to one (displayed as 1.0000 (1)) and should need only minor adjustment. However, even though the treatment you just chose for the roof is an AR pattern, it is something of an anomaly. Instead of using it as is, you had to change its scale factor to 6.0000 (6) to make it look right in the drawing.

T I P   When you're using one of the AR patterns, leave the scale factor at 1.0000 until you preview the hatch; then you can make changes. This rule also applies to the 14 ISO patterns displayed on the ISO tab of the Hatch Pattern Palette dialog box.

For the rest of the non-AR patterns, you'll need to assign a scale factor that imitates the true ratio of the scale at which you expect to print the drawing. Table 11.1 gives the true ratios of some of the standard scales used in architecture and construction. When using metric units, the scales are simple ratios (1:50, 1:100, and so on.)

T A B L E   1 1 . 1 : Standard Scales and Their Corresponding Ratios

Scale	True Scale Factor
1" = 1'-0"	12
1/2" = 1'-0"	24
1/4" = 1'-0"	48
1/8" = 1'-0"	96
1/16" = 1'-0"	192

The scale is traditionally written by mixing inches with feet in the expression, which causes some confusion. For example, the third scale in the table, commonly called quarter-inch scale, shows that a quarter inch equals one foot. A true ratio of this scale must express the relationship using the same units, as in $\frac{1}{4}'' = 1'\text{-}0''$ Simplifying this expression to have no fractions, you can translate it to, say, $1'' = 48''$. This is how you arrive at the true scale factor of 48, or the true ratio of 1:48.

As you continue through this chapter, take special note of the various scale factors used for different hatch patterns.

Hatching the Rest of the South Elevation

You'll apply hatches to the foundation, support posts, wall, and ground. You'll then work with some special effects.

Using a Concrete Hatch on the Foundation

For the foundation hatch, keep the Hatch-elev-gray layer current. Follow these steps:

1. Start the Hatch command. Then click the preview swatch below the Pattern drop-down list in the Hatch and Gradient dialog box. This has the same effect as clicking the Browse button next to the Pattern drop-down list.

2. Activate the Other Predefined tab. Find and select the AR-CONC pattern and click OK.

3. Open the Scale drop-down list, and select 1.0000 (1).

4. In the Options section, check the Create Separate Hatches option. When multiple areas are selected for hatching, this option creates a distinct hatch in each area rather than a single hatch consisting of multiple, noncontiguous hatched areas.

5. Click Add: Pick Points. Then, in the drawing, click once in each rectangle representing the foundation and the support posts. The borders of these areas change to dashes.

6. Press ↵ and click the Preview button in the bottom-left corner of the dialog box. After reviewing the patterns, right-click again to accept the hatches. The concrete hatch pattern is applied to the foundation and support areas (see Figure 11.6).

SOUTH ELEVATION

FIGURE 11.6: The south elevation with a concrete hatch pattern added to the foundation and support posts

Hatching the Wall

For the walls, you'll use the AR-RSHKE pattern, which looks like wood shingles (often called *shakes*). You'll need to account for the openings in the wall for the windows and the pattern change at the pop-out. Here are the steps:

1. Change the current layer to Hatch-elev-brown.

2. Start the Hatch command, and go through the same process to apply a hatch to the wall. Here is a summary of the steps:

   a. Click the Browse button.

   b. Activate the Other Predefined tab, and select the AR-RSHKE pattern.

   c. Set Scale to 1, and click Add: Pick Points.

   d. Pick once any place on the pop-out wall and once on the wall on each side, anywhere that's not inside a window or a window frame.

   e. Right-click and choose Preview.

3. The wall is hatched (see the top of Figure 11.7), but it is not done very well. There is no visual evidence that the pop-out is on a different plane than the two other walls. Zoom in to one of the windows and you'll see that, after skipping the frame, the hatch spans the window pane areas, as shown in the bottom of Figure 11.7).

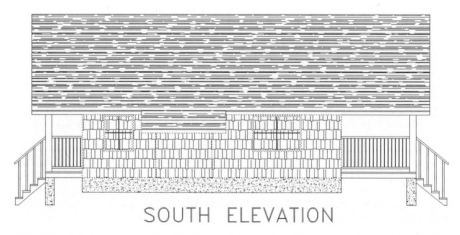

SOUTH ELEVATION

FIGURE 11.7: The completed hatching of the south wall (above) and the hatch spanning the window panes

Continues

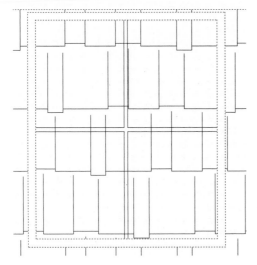

FIGURE 11.7 *(Continued)*

4. Press Esc to return to the Hatch and Gradient dialog box.

   Refer to the bottom of Figure 11.7 and notice how, like the boundary of the wall and the window frame, the inner, closed areas are also dashed. AutoCAD refers to these nested, closed areas as *islands*, and you must instruct the program how to hatch them. For example, should the hatch pattern stop at the first island it encounters and discontinue filling in the areas altogether? Should it ignore any islands and fill the boundary completely? Should it stop at the perimeter of the first island, skip the area between that island and the perimeter of the next, and then restart the hatch pattern inside the next nested boundary? The third option is the default solution; unless you direct otherwise, AutoCAD will alternate hatching in every other closed island area.

5. In the Islands area, click the Outer radio button or graphic, as shown in Figure 11.8. This instructs AutoCAD to stop the hatch at the first island and disregard any nested islands.

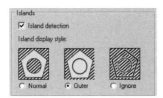

FIGURE 11.8: Choosing the Outer island detection option

6. You want to hatch the pop-out area separately to distinguish it from the others, so you need to remove its boundary from the currently hatched areas. In the Boundaries area, click the Remove Boundaries button.

7. The dialog box disappears. Pick one of the horizontal boundary lines of the pop-out (see Figure 11.9), one of the lines that isn't shared with the two other walls, and then press ↵ to return to the Hatch and Gradient dialog box.

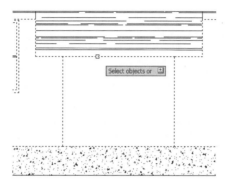

FIGURE 11.9: Removing one of the hatch boundaries

8. Click the Preview button at the lower-left corner of the dialog box, and then right-click to accept the hatch. The hatch stops at the first island, as shown in Figure 11.10, and is omitted in the pop-out.

SOUTH ELEVATION

FIGURE 11.10: The hatching of the south wall minus the pop-out and the islands

T I P Using the Preview option is not required each time you create a hatch, but it's a useful tool. It can prevent you from having to erase or undo and then re-create a hatch.

Hatching the Pop-out

Hatch patterns, or simply *hatches,* are a constantly repeating series of lines with a constantly repeating pattern that fill a designated area. The hatch has a base point, or origin (usually at the drawing's origin of 0,0), that is the starting point for the pattern that is emitted equally in all directions. If you hatch two overlapping areas with separate hatches, the hatches in the overlapping areas will be identical. This is the problem with the pop-out: even though the pop-out wall was a different hatched area than the areas on either side, the pattern appeared continuous because all three hatches share the same origin. In this section, you'll apply the hatch pattern to the pop-out and then edit the origin.

1. Start the Hatch command and apply the hatch to the pop-out area.

2. Zoom in to the pop-out and double-click the hatch pattern. Instead of opening the Properties palette, double-clicking a hatch pattern opens the Hatch Edit dialog box, which is identical to the Hatch and Gradient dialog box.

 3. In the Hatch Origin area, click the Click To Set New Origin button. The dialog box disappears. Enter **6,1↵** (**152,25**) to move the origin 6″ (152 mm) to the right and 1″ (25 mm) up, and reopen the Hatch Edit dialog box.

4. Click Preview. The hatch pattern is revised to reflect the new origin point and the pop-out no longer meshes seamlessly with the hatches on either side, as shown in Figure 11.11.

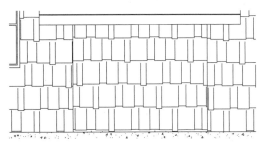

FIGURE 11.11: The pop-out with the revised hatch pattern

5. Right-click or press ↵ to accept the hatch.

Using a Solid Fill Hatch

The windows will be hatched with a solid fill. You apply this hatch in the same way as the other hatches you've been using, except that you don't have a choice of scale or angle:

1. Make Hatch-elev-black the current layer.

2. Start the Hatch command, and then click the Swatch sample box. Make sure the Other Predefined tab is active, and select the first pattern, SOLID. Click OK. Back in the Hatch and Gradient dialog box, note that the text boxes for Angle and Scale aren't available. These don't apply to solid fills.

3. Click Add: Pick Points. In the drawing, select a point in the middle of each of the glass panes or the middle of the window if you didn't draw the mullions.

4. Right-click, choose Preview to inspect the hatch, and then right-click again. The windows have a solid black (or white) fill (see Figure 11.12).

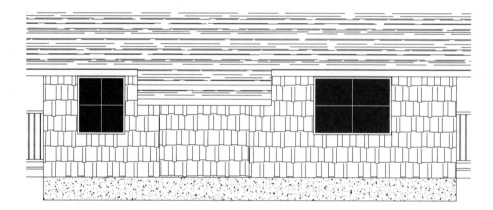

SOUTH ELEVATION

FIGURE 11.12: The windows with a solid fill hatch

 TIP Depending on the quality and resolution of your monitor, solid fills can appear to flow over thin, nonhatched areas. This is only an illusion; the hatch actually stops at the border, as you can see if you zoom into an area in question.

Adding Special Effects

To finish this elevation, you need to show shading to give the impression that the roof overhangs the wall.

Implying Shading with a Gradient

When shaded surfaces are illustrated on an exterior elevation, they give a three-dimensional quality to the surface. You'll put some additional hatching at the top portion of the wall to illustrate the shading caused by the roof overhang.

You need to hatch the top 2′-0″ (610 mm) of the wall with a gradient. To determine the boundary line of the hatch, you'll turn off the layer that has the shake pattern. You'll then create a guideline to serve as the lower boundary of the hatch:

1. Make the Hatch-noplot layer current, and then turn off the Hatch-elev-brown layer.

2. Use the Rectangle command to draw rectangles that extend from the corners, where the roof and vertical lines meet, to 2′-0″ (610 mm) below the lowest three roof lines. Figure 11.13 shows the rectangles to draw in bold and the windows hidden for clarity.

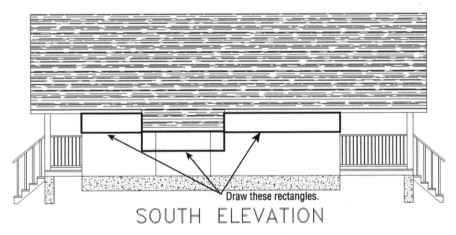

Draw these rectangles.

SOUTH ELEVATION

FIGURE 11.13: Creating the boundaries for the forthcoming gradient

3. Make the Hatch-elev-black layer current, and then start the Hatch command. In the Hatch and Gradient dialog box, click the Gradient tab. This is similar in layout to the Hatch tab (see Figure 11.14).

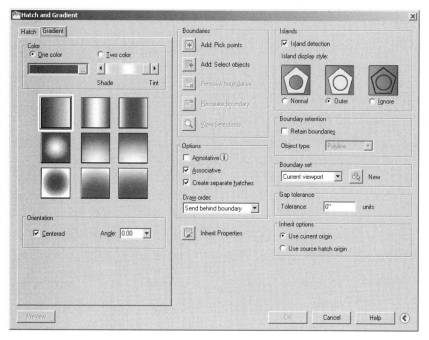

FIGURE 11.14: The Gradient tab of the Hatch and Gradient dialog box

4. In the Color area, make sure One Color is selected and then click the Browse button next to the color swatch to open the Select Color dialog box. Unlike hatches, gradients do not get their color from the layer they are on; you must explicitly select the color. Click the Index Color tab, select color 250 in the bottom row of swatches (see Figure 11.15), and then click OK. The gradient samples turn shades of gray.

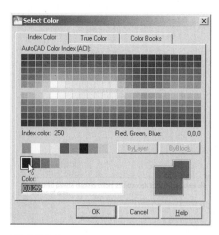

FIGURE 11.15: Selecting the gradient color

5. Click the middle sample pattern in the column on the right (see Figure 11.16). This causes the gradient to shift from opaque to clear, in a linear fashion, from top to bottom.

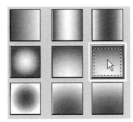

FIGURE 11.16: Selecting the gradient color

6. Click the Add: Select Objects button, and then click the two rectangles that you drew on either side of the pop-out. Using the Select Objects option, you can select closed polylines, circles, or ellipses as the boundary objects. Preview the hatch, and then accept it.

7. Repeat step 6, making sure the Gradient tab is active, but this time selecting the rectangle under the pop-out.

8. When creating hatches, AutoCAD may not always initially display the result properly. Enter **regen**↵ to force AutoCAD to reevaluate the drawing and refresh the drawing area. Your gradients should look like Figure 11.17. The gradient obscures the windows, but you'll fix that in the next couple of steps.

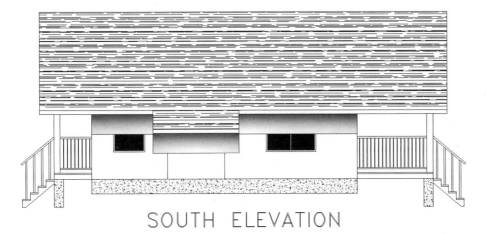

SOUTH ELEVATION

FIGURE 11.17: The gradient shaded effect

9. Turn on the Hatch-elev-brown layer. The shakes return, but the gradient hides a portion of them.

Although all objects in your drawing so far reside on the same plane, like lines on a piece of paper, visually one object may appear to be on top of another. You can rearrange the order of the objects by selecting them and then changing their location in the stacking order. You need to move the shading behind the hatch pattern.

10. Select all the gradients. In the Modify panel, click the down arrow next to the far right icon in the top row and then choose Send To Back, as shown in Figure 11.18, or enter **draworder↵ b↵** at the command prompt.

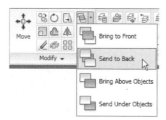

FIGURE 11.18: Sending the gradient objects behind the others in the drawing

The gradient moves behind the shakes (see Figure 11.19). Don't worry about the gradient boundaries; they won't appear when the drawing is plotted.

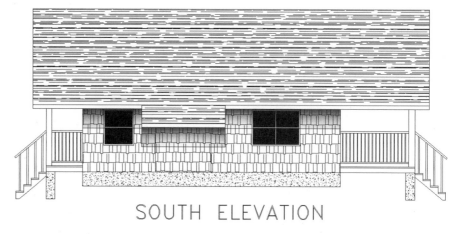

SOUTH ELEVATION

FIGURE 11.19: The gradient shaded effect after moving the gradients to the back

11. Save this drawing as Cabin11a.dwg.

Using Hatches in the Floor Plan

In the floor plan, you can use hatches to fill in the walls or to indicate various kinds of floor surfaces. You'll start with the floors.

Hatching the Floors

So far, you've used only predefined hatch patterns—the 69 patterns that come with AutoCAD. You can also use a *user-defined pattern*, which is a series of parallel lines that you can set at any spacing and angle. If you want to illustrate square floor tile, select the Double option of the user-defined pattern, which uses two sets of parallel lines—one perpendicular to the other, resulting in a tiled effect.

Creating the User-Defined Hatch Pattern

You'll use the user-defined pattern for a couple of rooms and then return to the predefined patterns. Follow these steps:

1. With Cabin11a open, zoom in to the floor plan and thaw the Headers and Fixtures layers. You can use the header lines to help form a boundary line across an entryway to a room and to keep the hatch pattern from extending to another room.

2. With the floor plan in full view, freeze the Roof layer and then zoom in to the bathroom. Even if the rooflines are dashed, they will still form a boundary to a hatch.

3. Create a new layer called **Hatch-plan-floor**. Assign it color 142, and make it current.

4. Start the Hatch command. Be sure the Hatch tab is active.

5. Open the Type drop-down list, and select User Defined. The list closes, and User Defined replaces Predefined as the current pattern type. The Pattern and Scale drop-down lists aren't available, but the Spacing text box is.

6. In the Spacing text box, change 1″ (1) to 9″ (229). Slightly above and to the left of that, click the Double check box to activate it (see Figure 11.20).

FIGURE 11.20: Defining the hatch pattern

7. Click Add: Pick Points. Back in the drawing, be sure no osnaps are running, then click a point in the bathroom floor, not touching the fixture lines or the door. Click the floor between the door swing and the door, being careful to not touch the door.

8. Right-click, and choose Preview from the shortcut menu. The tiled hatch pattern should fill the bathroom floor and stop at the header while not encroaching into the door or fixtures (see Figure 11.21). If the tile pattern looks OK, right-click again to accept it.

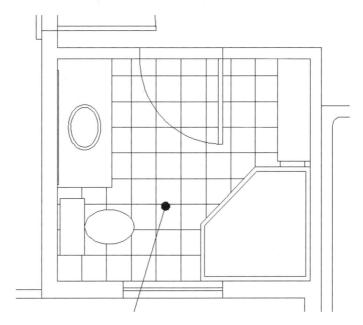

FIGURE 11.21: The tiled hatch pattern in place

Note that the user-defined pattern has no scale factor to worry about. You simply set the distance between lines in the Spacing text box.

 WARNING   If you can't get the Hatch command to hatch the desired area, you might have left a gap between some of the lines serving as the hatch boundary. This can prevent AutoCAD from being able to find the boundary you intend to use. Zoom in to the areas where objects meet, and check to see that there are no gaps or increase the Gap Tolerance value on the right side of the dialog box.

Controlling the Origin of the Hatch Pattern

Often, a designer wants to lay out the tile pattern such that the pattern is centered in the room or starts along one particular edge. For this project, the tiles are set to start in the center of the room and move out to the edges, where they're cut to fit. You'll change the hatch pattern's origin to set this up in the kitchen:

1. Use the Pan and Zoom tools to slide the drawing up until the kitchen occupies the screen. Thaw the Area layer.

2. Turn Object Snap Tracking on (on the status bar), and set the Midpoint osnap to be running.

 3. Start the Hatch command. In the Hatch Origin area in the lower-left corner, select the Specified Origin radio button, and then click the Click To Set New Origin button.

4. Back in the drawing, place the cursor at the midpoint of the right side of the area polyline. The tracking point appears inside the triangular Midpoint osnap symbol. Don't click.

5. Move the cursor to the upper, horizontal polyline segment and do the same thing. Then move the cursor straight down until it's positioned directly to the left of the first acquired tracking point and below the second. When the cursor is positioned properly, two tracking lines and a tooltip appear (see the top of Figure 11.22). Click. This sets the origin of any subsequently created hatch patterns at the center of this room and reopens the Hatch and Gradient dialog box.

6. The User Defined pattern type is still current, and the spacing is set to 9″ (229). Change the spacing to 12″ (305). Be sure Double is still checked.

7. In the Islands area, choose Ignore so the hatch will span across the room name block and then click Add: Pick Points.

8. In the drawing, pick a point anywhere in the middle of the kitchen and also between the door swing and the door, similar to what you did in the bathroom. Right-click and choose Preview.

9. Inspect the drawing to see whether the hatch looks right, and then right-click again. This places the hatch of 12″ (305 mm) tiles in the kitchen (see the bottom of Figure 11.22). Notice how the pattern is centered left to right and top to bottom.

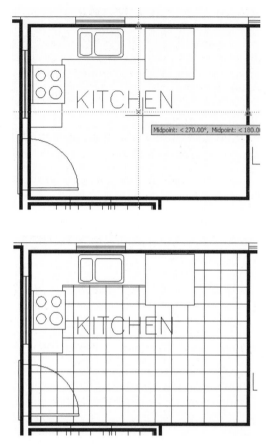

FIGURE 11.22: Hatching the kitchen: the two tracking lines (top) and the finished, centered hatch (bottom)

Each time you change the origin in the Hatch and Gradient dialog box, all subsequent hatch patterns will use the new setting as their origin. For most hatches, the origin isn't important, but if you need to control the location of tiles or specific points of other hatch patterns, you can reset the hatch origin before you create the hatch by clicking Click To Set New Origin and then entering 0,0↵.

Finishing the Hatches for the Floors

To finish hatching the floors, you'll use a parquet pattern from the set of predefined patterns in the living room and another user-defined pattern on the two decks:

1. Use Pan and Zoom to adjust the view so it includes the living room.

2. Start the Hatch command, and set the current pattern type to Predefined.

3. Click the Browse button, and activate the Other Predefined tab. Select the AR-PARQ1 pattern. Set the scale to 1, and be sure the angle is set to 0 and Island is set to Ignore.

4. Click Add: Pick Points, and then click anywhere in the living room, inside the closet, and inside the triangles formed by the bi-fold doors.

5. Right-click and choose Preview from the menu. The squares look a little small.

6. Press Esc to return to the Hatch and Gradient dialog box. Reset the scale to 1.33.

7. Click the Preview button. This looks better. Right-click to accept the hatch. The parquet pattern is placed in the living room (see Figure 11.23).

FLOOR PLAN

FIGURE 11.23: The parquet hatch in the living room

T I P   If you find the text difficult to read with the dense hatch pattern, you have a few options. You can place a rectangle on the Hatch-noplot layer around the text and then instruct AutoCAD to respect the islands they create; you can change the text to a filled-in, TrueType font that stands out better; or you can instruct AutoCAD to plot the text denser than the hatches.

8. Freeze the Area layer.

9. Start the Hatch command. In the Hatch Origin area, be sure Specified Origin is selected, and then click the Click To Set New Origin button. Use the Endpoint osnap and pick the lower-left inside corner of the front deck.

10. Back in the Hatch and Gradient dialog box, set User Defined to be the pattern type.

11. Clear the Double check box. Set Angle to 90° and the spacing to 6″ (152). Click Add: Pick Points.

12. Click anywhere on the front deck.

13. Right-click and then choose Preview. Right-click again. The front deck is hatched with parallel lines that are 6″ apart (see Figure 11.24).

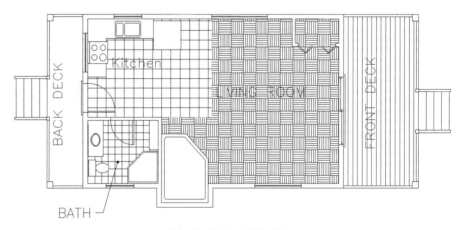

FIGURE 11.24: The user-defined hatch pattern on the front deck

14. Repeat steps 9 through 13 on the back deck using the lower-right corner of the deck as the hatch origin.

15. The transition between the kitchen and the living room floor coverings isn't as clean and evident as it could be. Draw a polyline with a width of 0 from the corner of the bathroom, perpendicular to the living room window opening and then directly to that window, as shown in bold in Figure 11.25.

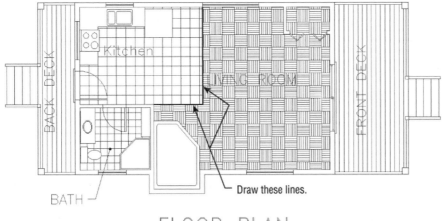

FIGURE 11.25: The hatch pattern on the rear deck and the line between the living room and kitchen

16. Save the drawing as `Cabin11b`.

Modifying the Shape of Hatch Patterns

The next exercise will demonstrate how hatches are associative. An *associative* hatch pattern automatically updates when you modify the part of a drawing that is serving as the boundary for the pattern. You'll be changing the current drawing, so before you begin making those changes, save the drawing as it is. Follow these steps:

1. Zoom out and pan to get the floor plan and the north and south elevations in the view.

2. Thaw the Roof and Area layers. You'll use the Stretch command to modify the plan and two side elevations.

3. Turn on polar tracking.

 4. Click the Stretch button on the Modify panel.

5. Pick a point above and to the right of the stairway in the north elevation. Drag a window down and to the left until a crossing selection window lands between the two closet doors in the floor plan and ends below the cabin in the south elevation (see the left image of Figure 11.26). Click to complete the window. Then press ↵ to finish the selection process.

6. For the base point, choose a point in the blank area to the right of the selection and click.

7. Move the cursor directly to the right of the point you picked; then enter 5'↵ (1524↵).

8. The living room and roof are now longer, and the hatch patterns have expanded to fill the new areas (see the right image of Figure 11.26).

9. Save this drawing as Cabin11b Stretched.dwg.

Hatches are a necessary part of many drawings. You've seen a few of the possibilities AutoCAD offers for using them in plans and elevations.

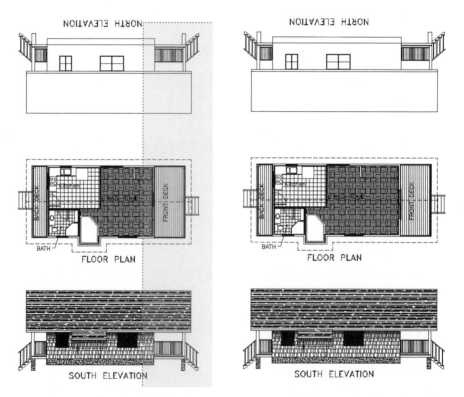

F I G U R E 1 1 . 2 6 : The crossing selection window (left) and the modified cabin with the adjusted hatch patterns (right)

Creating and Managing Tool Palettes

If you find yourself using particular hatch patterns over and over in various drawings, wouldn't it be advantageous to have them available at a moment's notice instead of setting them up each time? AutoCAD's tool palettes let you do just that. Now you'll go through the process of setting up a couple of palettes and customizing them to contain specific hatch patterns, blocks, and commands that are used with the cabin drawings. From these exercises, you'll get the information you need to set up your own custom palettes.

Creating a New Tool Palette

You'll create a new tool palette and then populate it with the blocks you've used so far in the cabin drawing:

1. Open the Cabin11b.dwg file, and thaw the Roof layer.

2. Click the View ribbon tab, and then click the Tool Palettes icon on the Palettes panel to display the palettes on the screen. Then place the cursor on a blank space on the palettes, right-click, and choose New Palette, as shown in Figure 11.27. A new blank palette displays with a small text box on it.

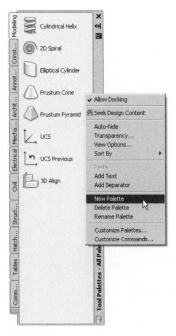

FIGURE 11.27: Creating a new tool palette

3. Enter **Cabin Blocks**↵ to name the new palette.

4. Open the DesignCenter by clicking its button on the Palettes panel or by entering **adc**↵.

5. On the left side of the DesignCenter, navigate to the Cabin11b drawing under the Folders tab or the Open Drawings tab. When you find it, click the + sign to its left. The list of drawing content types in it opens below the drawing.

6. Select Blocks from this list. Now the right side of the DesignCenter displays the six blocks in Cabin11b, either as small images or by name only.

7. Click the arrow on the Views button in the DesignCenter toolbar, and choose Large Icons as the view option to see a display like Figure 11.28.

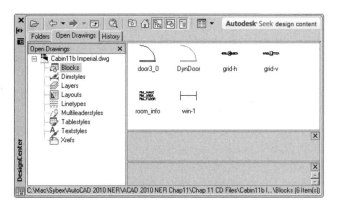

FIGURE 11.28: The DesignCenter with the Large Icons view enabled

8. Select door3_0, and then hold down the Shift key and click win-1 to select all six blocks. Click and drag the six blocks over to the Cabin Blocks palette. Small images of the blocks appear on the new palette (see Figure 11.29), and they're now available for any drawing. Simply drag a block off the palette onto the drawing. You can then fine-tune its location, rotate it, and so forth. Any layers used by the block are also brought into the drawing.

N O T E Small blocks, such as the grid circles, may not display properly in the tool palettes.

9. Place the cursor on door3_0 on the new palette, right-click, and then select Properties to open the Tool Properties dialog box. It displays information about door3_0 and provides a means to change many parameters (see Figure 11.30).

FIGURE 11.29:
The Cabin Blocks tool palette you've just created

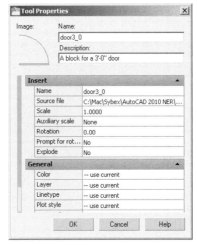

FIGURE 11.30:
The Tool Properties dialog box

10. Close the Tool Properties dialog box.

Setting Up a Palette for Hatches

To create a palette for hatches, you'll create and name a new palette using the same procedure as in the preceding section, but the hatches get onto the palette in a different way:

1. Right-click a blank space on the Cabin Blocks palette, choose New Palette, and then enter **Cabin Hatches**⏎ in the text box.

2. Zoom in on the south elevation of the cabin, and click the roof hatch to display a grip.

3. Move the cursor to a portion of the roof hatch that isn't close to the grip, and then click and drag the hatch pattern over to the new palette (see Figure 11.31).

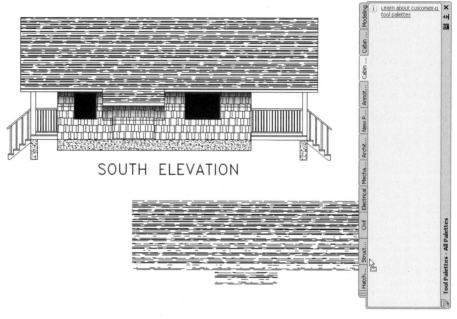

SOUTH ELEVATION

FIGURE 11.31: Copying the roof hatch to the new palette

4. When the cursor is over the palette and a horizontal line appears there, release the mouse button. The roof hatch is now positioned on the palette and available for use in any drawing. Simply drag it off the palette and into the enclosed area in the drawing that you want to hatch with the pattern.

5. Place the cursor on the new swatch of AR-RROOF, right-click, and choose Properties. The Tool Properties dialog box opens (see Figure 11.32).

6. Change the name from AR-RROOF to **Cabin Roof**. Enter a description of what the hatch represents, such as **Cabin roof, south elevation,** or **shakes.** Notice that the hatch has the angle and scale used on the roof and that it's also on the Hatch-elev-gray layer. Use the slider at the left to view all the properties. Click OK to close the dialog box and update the palette (see Figure 11.33).

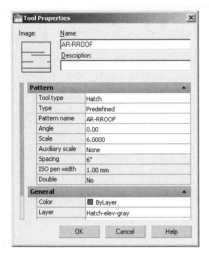

FIGURE 11.32:
The Tool Properties dialog box for the hatch pattern

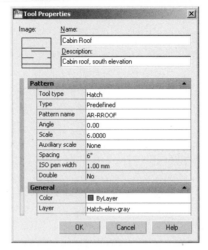

FIGURE 11.33:
The Cabin Hatches palette after the first hatch is renamed

By using the Tool Properties dialog box, you can also give hatches color. You can place all the hatches that you've used for the cabin so far on the palette in the same manner. They retain the properties they had in the original drawing, but by using the Tool Properties dialog box, you can change those properties.

Creating a Palette for Commands

Take a moment to look at a few of the sample palettes that come with AutoCAD, and check the properties of some of the items that you see. In addition to blocks and hatches, there are also command icons. These are placed on the palette in a slightly different way from blocks and hatches:

1. Right-click the Cabin Hatches palette in a blank area, and choose New Palette from the context menu.

2. Name the new palette **Commands.**

3. Be sure that any objects created by the commands you want to place on the Commands palette are visible on your screen. If they aren't in the drawing area, pan or zoom to display them or create new ones.

4. Click an object, such as a line that you want to be able to reproduce with a single command, and then drag it to the palette just as you

dragged the hatches in the previous section. This adds the object's creation command to the palette.

5. Drag several additional objects of various kinds onto the Commands palette (see Figure 11.34).

FIGURE 11.34: The Commands palette with four command icons

When you need to use one of these commands, click the icon on the palette.

If you set the palettes to Auto-hide, they fold under the palette title bar. When you put your cursor on the bar, the palettes display and then hide a moment after your cursor moves off the palettes. To activate Auto-hide, right-click the palette title bar and choose Auto-hide from the context menu, or click the Auto-hide button under the X at the top of the palette's title bar.

This has been a brief introduction to the palette feature. I encourage you to experiment with the various options to become familiar with them so that you can use them as you find the need. Try right-clicking a blank portion of a palette and investigating the commands available on the resulting context menu. From this menu, you can delete any palette and you can copy and paste tools from one palette to another.

If You Would Like More Practice...

If you would like to practice what you've learned in this chapter, here are a couple of extra exercises.

Creating the Hatch Patterns for the Other Elevations

To create your hatch pattern for the roof, make these changes and additions to Cabin11b.dwg:

1. Make the Hatch-elev-brown layer current, and thaw the roof layer.

2. Start the Hatch command.

3. Click the Inherit Properties button, and then click the hatch pattern on either side of the pop-out in the south elevation. At the Pick internal point: prompt, press ↵. This copies that hatch's properties to the Hatch and Gradient dialog box.

4. Make sure Outer is selected in the Islands area, and change the Angle to 180.

5. Click Add: Pick Points and pick a point inside the wall in the north elevation. The hatch appears rotated 180° to match the rotation of the view.

6. Repeat the previous process, changing the rotation, pattern, and layer until all the hatches and gradients in the south elevation appear in the other three elevations except the roof pattern, which only appears in the north and south.

   ▶ Make sure you're on the correct layer when creating the new hatches.

   ▶ You'll need to draw additional rectangles on the Hatch-noplot layer to constrain the new gradients. Use polylines to draw the boundaries in the east and west elevations.

   ▶ Make sure Create Separate Hatches is selected when you create the hatch patterns for the windows.

WARNING   When layers are added to a drawing after a named view is saved, you must select that named view in the View Manager dialog box and then click the Update Layers button to display the layers correctly when you set the view to current.

When you are done, the remaining elevations should look similar to those in Figure 11.35.

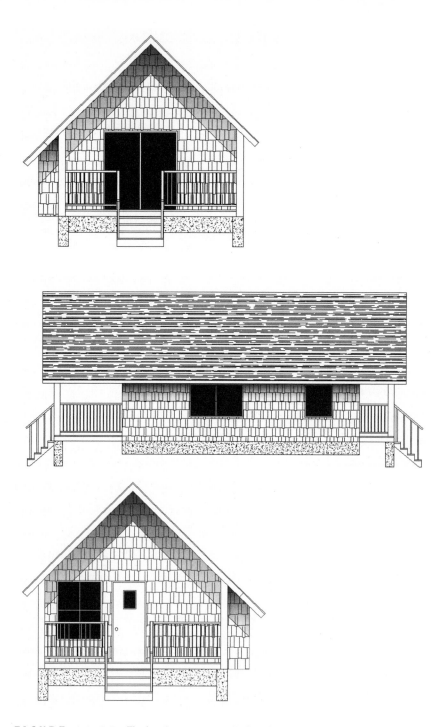

FIGURE 11.35: The hatch patterns applied to the east elevation (top), the north elevation (middle), and the west elevation (bottom)

7. Set the UCS back to World, and use the Plan command to reorient the drawing area.

8. Save this drawing as Cabin11c.dwg.

Creating Your Hatch Palette

It's true that you can use any hatch pattern to represent anything you want, but most professions follow some sort of standard, even if loosely. The ANSI31 pattern of parallel lines is probably the most widely used pattern. Although according to the ANSI standard, it "officially" represents Iron, Brick, and Stone Masonry, and it's universally accepted as any cross-section view of any material—that is, the part of the object that was sliced through to make the view.

In this exercise, you'll create a new palette of hatches that you might use in your work. Use the same method demonstrated in the previous section of this chapter:

1. Open the DesignCenter and, under the Folders tab, find and select acad.pat. If you performed a typical installation of AutoCAD, the file should be in the C:\Program Files\AutoCAD 2010\UserData-Cache\Support folder. LT users should substitute AutoCAD LT 2010 for AutoCAD 2010 in the path. Open that file.

2. Use the Large Icons view to view the patterns on the right side of the DesignCenter.

3. On the right side of your screen, create a new tool palette and name it Hatches.

4. Back in the DesignCenter, scroll through and drag any patterns you might use over to the new Hatches palette.

5. Close the DesignCenter.

6. Hold the cursor briefly over the name of each hatch to display a tooltip that describes the name and purpose of the hatch.

7. If you've brought any patterns to the palette that you don't want there after all, right-click each of them and choose Delete from the context menu. Don't worry about changing any of the properties, such as Scale or Rotation. That will come later, as you begin to use these hatches in your own work.

8. Check out the tools on the Hatches And Fills sample palette that comes with AutoCAD. To access a list of all the available sample palettes, move the cursor over to the tabs that identify each palette.

Then move it down just below the lowest tab where you see the edges of the tabs that are hidden. Click the edges of the hidden tabs, and choose a palette from the list to be brought forward and displayed as the top tab.

9. Right-click some of the hatches or fills, and note how the rotation and scale vary for hatches that look the same on the palette. One hatch, such as ANSI31, might be repeated several times on the same palette, with each occurrence having a different scale or rotation. Notice that the names of the hatches and fills have been removed from the sample hatch palette. Can you figure out how to do this in your own palette or how to store the names?

Are You Experienced?

Now you can...

☑ **create a predefined hatch pattern and apply it to a drawing**

☑ **set up and apply user-defined hatch patterns**

☑ **modify the scale of a hatch pattern**

☑ **modify the shape of a hatch pattern**

☑ **adjust the orientation of a hatch pattern**

☑ **control the origin of a hatch pattern**

☑ **apply solid fills and gradients**

☑ **create and populate a tool palette with blocks, hatches, or commands**

CHAPTER 12

Dimensioning a Drawing

▶ Setting up a dimension style

▶ Dimensioning the floor plan of the cabin

▶ Modifying existing dimensions

▶ Setting up a multileader style

▶ Modifying existing dimension styles

D
imensions are the final ingredient to include with your cabin drawing. To introduce you to dimensioning, I'll follow a pattern similar to the one I used in Chapter 8, "Controlling Text in a Drawing." You will first create a dimension style that contains the properties for the dimensions, and then you will add the dimensions themselves.

Introducing Dimension Styles

Dimension styles are similar to text styles but give you more options to control. You set them up in the same way, but many parameters control the various parts of dimensions, including the dimension text.

Before you start setting up a dimension style, you need to make a few changes to your drawing to prepare it for dimensioning:

1. Open Cabin11c.dwg, the cabin with the hatch patterns added to all the views, and zoom in to the upper half of the drawing. If you didn't complete the "If You Would Like More Practice" section in the previous chapter, you can download the file from the book's website or continue with the Cabin11b.dwg file you created.

2. Create a new layer called **Dim1**. Assign white as its color, and make it current.

3. Freeze all the remaining layers except 0, Deck, Doors, Roof, Steps, Text1, Walls, Windows, Foundation, and all the elevations.

4. Set the Endpoint and Midpoint object snaps to be running.

5. Set the status bar so that only the Object Snap and Dynamic Input buttons are in their on positions.

6. Click the Annotate tab. Your drawing will look like Figure 12.1.

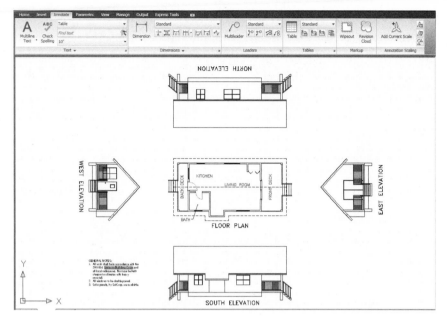

FIGURE 12.1: The cabin floor plan and elevations with the Annotate panels at the top of the drawing area

Making a New Dimension Style

Each dimension has several components: the dimension line, arrows or tick marks, extension lines, and the dimension text (see Figure 12.2). An extensive set of variables stored with each drawing file control the appearance and location of these components. You work with these variables through a series of dialog boxes designed to make setting up a dimension style as easy and trouble free as possible. Remember that AutoCAD is designed to be used by drafters from many trades and professions, each of which has its own standards for drafting. To satisfy these users' widely varied needs, AutoCAD dimensioning features have many options and settings for controlling the appearance and placement of dimensions in drawings.

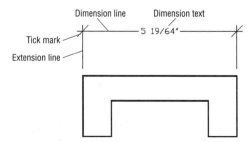

FIGURE 12.2: The parts of a dimension

Naming a Dimension Style

Every dimension variable has a default setting, and these variables as a group constitute the default Standard dimension style. As in defining text styles, the procedure is to copy the Standard dimension style and rename the copy—in effect making a new style that is a copy of the default style. You then make changes to this new style so it has the settings you need to dimension your drawing and save it. Follow these steps:

1. Click the Dimension Style button, the arrow at right end of the Dimensions panel's title bar, to open the Dimension Style Manager dialog box (see Figure 12.3). On the top left in the Styles list box, you'll see Standard highlighted, or ISO-25 if your drawing is in metric.

2. With Standard (ISO-25) highlighted in the Styles window, click the New button on the right side of the Dimension Style Manager dialog box to open the Create New Dimension Style dialog box shown in Figure 12.4.

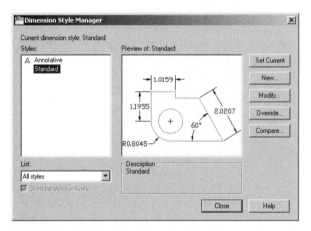

FIGURE 12.3: The Dimension Style Manager dialog box

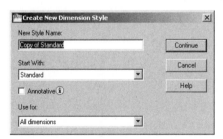

FIGURE 12.4: The Create New Dimension Style dialog box

3. In the New Style Name field, Copy of Standard (ISO-25) is highlighted. Enter **DimPlan**, but don't press ⏎ yet.

Notice that Standard (ISO-25) is in the Start With drop-down list just below. Because it's the current dimension style in this drawing, the new dimension style you're about to define will begin as a copy of the Standard style. This is similar to the way in which new text styles are defined (as you saw in Chapter 8). The Use For drop-down list allows you to choose the kinds of dimensions to which the new style will be applied. In this case, it's all dimensions, so you don't need to change this setting.

4. Click the Continue button. The Create New Dimension Style dialog box is replaced by the New Dimension Style: DimPlan dialog box (see Figure 12.5). It has seven tabs containing parameters that define the dimension style. You have created a new dimension style that is a copy of the Standard style, and now you'll make the changes necessary to set up DimPlan to work as the main dimension style for the floor plan of the cabin.

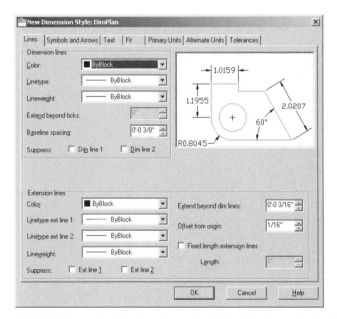

FIGURE 12.5: The New Dimension Style dialog box with DimPlan as the current style and Lines as the active tab

5. Be sure the Lines tab is active (on top). If it's not, click it.

Using the Lines Tab

You'll use the Lines tab to control the appearance of the dimension and extension lines. In most cases, the color, linetype, and lineweight should stay at their default ByBlock value, indicating that an object inherits its color from the block containing it.

1. In the Extension lines area, change the Offset from origin setting from 1/16″(0.63) to 1/8″ (1.25) to increase the gap between the beginning of the extension line and the object being dimensioned.

Setting Up the Symbols and Arrows Tab

The Symbols and Arrows tab has settings that control the appearance of arrowheads and other symbols related to dimensioning:

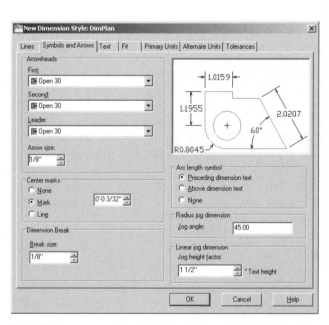

1. Click the Symbols and Arrows tab and then, in the Arrowheads area, click the down arrow in the First drop-down list to open the list of arrowheads.

2. Click the Open 30 option. The drop-down list closes with Open 30 displayed in the First and Second drop-down lists. In the preview window to the right, a graphic displays samples using the new arrowhead type.

3. Select Open 30 from the Leader drop-down list as well.

4. Set the Arrow Size parameter to 1/8″ (3.5). After the changes, the tab should look like Figure 12.6.

> **Tick marks are often used in the architecture profession. This list contains options for several kinds of arrowheads, dots, and so on.**

FIGURE 12.6: The Symbols and Arrows tab with the settings for the DimPlan style

Making Changes in the Text Tab

The settings in the Text tab control the appearance of dimension text and how it's located relative to the dimension and extension lines:

1. Click the Text tab in the New Dimension Style dialog box. Settings in three areas affect the appearance and location of dimension text. Look ahead to Figure 12.7 to see the Text tab. The preview window appears in all tabs and is updated automatically as you modify settings. Move to the Text Appearance area in the upper-left corner of the dialog box, where six settings control how the text looks. You're concerned with only two of them.

2. Click the Browse button that sits at the right end of the Text Style drop-down list to open the Text Style dialog box. Set up a new text style called **Dim** that has the following parameters:

   ▶ Arial font

   ▶ 0'-0" (0) height

   ▶ 0.8000 width factor

   ▶ All other settings at their default

   If you need a reminder about creating text styles, refer to Chapter 8. Apply this text style, click the Set Current button, and then close the Text Style dialog box.

3. Back in the Text tab, open the Text Style drop-down list and select the new Dim style from the list.

T I P   Setting the text height to 0'0" (0) in the Text Style dialog box allows the Text Height parameter of the dimension style to dictate the actual height of the text in the drawing. This allows many different dimension styles to use the same text style, each producing text with different heights. If you give the text a non-zero height in the Text Style dialog box, then that height is always used and the Text Height parameter of the dimension style is disregarded.

Some trades and professions use the Centered option for vertical text placement and the Horizontal option for text alignment.

4. Set the Text Height value to 1/8" (3.5).

5. Move down to the Text Placement area. These settings determine where the text is located, vertically and horizontally, relative to the dimension line. You need to change two settings here; make sure both the Horizontal and Vertical options are set to Centered.

6. Move to the Text Alignment area. The radio buttons control whether dimension text is aligned horizontally or with the direction of the dimension line. The ISO Standard option aligns text depending on whether the text can fit between the extension lines. Only one of the buttons can be active at a time. Horizontal should already be active. Click the Aligned With Dimension Line button. Notice how the appearance and location of the text changes in the preview window. This finishes your work in this tab; the settings should look like those in Figure 12.7.

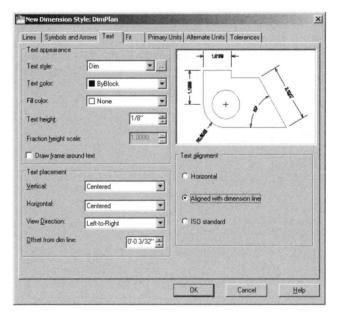

FIGURE 12.7: The Text tab with settings for the DimPlan style

This dialog box has four more tabs with settings, but you'll be making changes in only two of them: Fit and Primary Units.

Working with Settings on the Fit Tab

The settings on the Fit tab control the overall scale factor of the dimension style and how the text and arrowheads are placed when the extension lines are too close together for both text and arrows to fit:

1. Click the Fit tab in the New Dimension Style dialog box. Figure 12.8 shows the Fit tab as you'll set it.

> For your own work, you might have to experiment with the settings on this tab.

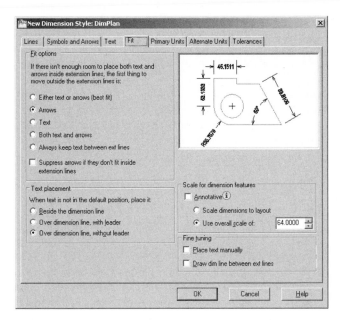

FIGURE 12.8: The new settings in the Fit tab

2. In the upper-left corner, in the Fit Options area, click the Arrows radio button. This causes the arrows to be moved from between the extension lines to outside the dimension lines when they won't fit properly.

3. In the Text Placement area, click the Over Dimension Line, Without Leader radio button.

4. Move to the Scale For Dimension Features area. Be sure the Use Overall Scale Of radio button is active. Set the scale to 64 (70). In the Fine Tuning area, uncheck Draw Dim Line Between the Ext Lines. The settings on the Fit tab should look like those in Figure 12.8.

Setting Up the Primary Units Tab (Architectural)

If your drawing is set up to use Architectural units, continue with this section. If you are using decimal units, skip this section and continue with the next section, "Setting Up the Primary Units Tab (Metric)." In the preview window, you might have noticed that the numbers in the dimension text maintain a decimal format with four decimal places, rather than the feet and inches format of the current architectural units. Dimensions have their own units setting, independent of the basic units for the drawing as a whole. On the Primary Units tab, you'll set the dimension units:

1. Click the Primary Units tab, and take a peek ahead at Figure 12.9 to see how it's organized. It has two areas: Linear Dimensions and Angular Dimensions, each of which has several types of settings.

2. In the Linear Dimensions area, starting at the top, make the following changes:

   a. Change the Unit Format setting from Decimal to Architectural.

   b. Change the Precision setting to 0'-0 1/8".

   c. Change the Fraction Format setting to Diagonal.

3. In the Zero Suppression area, uncheck 0 inches.

N O T E Zero Suppression controls whether the zero is shown for feet when the dimensioned distance is less than one foot and also whether the zero is shown for inches when the distance is a whole number of feet. For the cabin drawing, you'll suppress the zero for feet, but you'll show the zero for inches. As a result, 9" will appear as 9", and 3' will appear as 3"-0'.

4. In the Angular Dimensions area, leave Decimal Degrees as the Units Format setting and change Precision to two decimal places, as you did for the basic drawing units in Chapter 3, "Setting Up a Drawing." For now, leave the Zero Suppression area as it is. After these changes, the Primary Units tab looks like Figure 12.9.

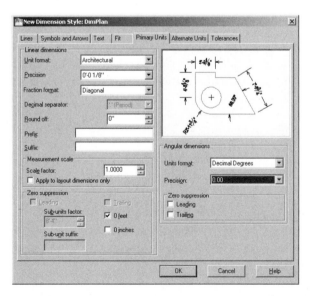

FIGURE 12.9: The Primary Units tab after changes have been made

Setting Up the Primary Units Tab (Metric)

If your drawing is set up to use Architectural units, and you've completed the previous section, then skip this section and continue with the next section, "Completing the Dimension Style Setup." In the preview window, you might have noticed that the numbers in the dimension text maintain a decimal format with four decimal places rather than the feet and inches format of the current architectural units. Dimensions have their own units setting, independent of the basic units for the drawing as a whole. On the Primary Units tab, you'll set the dimension units:

1. Click the Primary Units tab, and take a peek ahead at Figure 12.10 to see how it's organized. It has two areas: Linear Dimensions and Angular Dimensions, each of which has several types of settings.

2. In the Linear Dimensions area, starting at the top, make the following changes:

   a. Make sure Unit Format is set to Decimal.

   b. Change the Precision setting to 0.

   c. In the Suffix box, enter **mm⏎**, making sure you add a space before the first m.

3. In the Zero Suppression area, make sure Leading is checked and Trailing is not.

> **N O T E** Zero Suppression controls whether the zero is shown for measurements when the dimensioned distance is less than one millimeter and whether the zero is shown when the final digits, to the right of the decimal point in the dimension, are zeros. For the cabin drawing, you'll suppress the trailing zeros but not the leading zeros. As a result, .9500 will appear as 0.95 with Precision set to 0. This won't be a factor during these exercises.

4. In the Angular Dimensions area, leave Decimal Degrees as the Units Format setting and change Precision to two decimal places, as you did for the basic drawing units in Chapter 3. For now, leave the Zero Suppression area as it is. After these changes, the Primary Units tab looks like Figure 12.10.

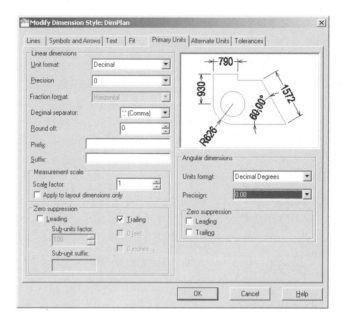

FIGURE 12.10: The Primary Units tab after changes have been made

Completing the Dimension Style Setup

Of the last two tabs, any industry involved in global projects may use the Alternate Units tab, and the mechanical engineering trades and professions use the Tolerances tab. You won't need to make any changes to these tabs for this tutorial, but you'll take a brief look at them in the following sections.

It's time to save these setting changes to the new DimPlan dimension style and begin dimensioning the cabin:

1. Click the OK button at the bottom of the New Dimension Style dialog box. You're returned to the Dimension Style Manager dialog box (see Figure 12.11).

   DimPlan appears with a gray background in the Styles list box, along with Standard and Annotative. In the lower-right corner of the dialog box, in the Description area, you'll see the name of the new style. See Table 12.1, later in this section, as a reference for the differences between the Standard style that you started with and the DimPlan style.

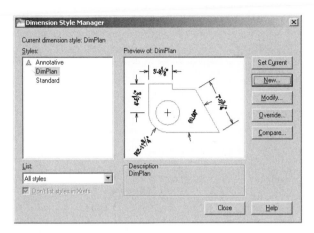

FIGURE 12.11: The Dimension Style Manager dialog box with
DimPlan listed

2. Click DimPlan to highlight it in a dark blue; then click the Set Current button. Finally, click the Close button. You're returned to your drawing, and the Dimensions panel displays DimPlan in the Dimension Style drop-down list, as shown in Figure 12.12. This indicates that DimPlan is now the current dimension style.

FIGURE 12.12: The Dimensions panel showing DimPlan as the current
dimension style

3. Save your drawing as `cabin12a.dwg`.

You have made changes to 16 settings that control dimensions. This isn't too many, considering that there are more than 50 dimension settings. Table 12.1 summarizes the changes you've made so that the dimensions will work with the cabin drawing.

T A B L E 1 2 . 1 Changes Made So Far

Tab	Option	Default Setting	DimPlan Setting
Lines	Offset From Origin	0'-0 1/16" (0.63)	0'-0 1/8" (1.25)
Symbols and Arrows	First	Closed Filled	Open 30
	Second	Closed Filled	Open 30
	Leader	Closed Filled	Open 30
	Ext. Line – Extend Beyond Ticks	3/16" (2.5)	1/8" (3.5)
	Arrow Size	3/16" (2.5)	1/8" (3.5)
Text	Text Style	Standard	Dim
	Text Alignment	Horizontal	Aligned With Dimension Line
	Text Height	3/16" (2.5)	1/8" (3.5)
Fit	Fit Options	Either Text or Arrow (Best Fit)	Arrows
	Text Placement	Beside The Dimension Line	Over Dimension Line, Without Leader
	Overall Scale	1.0000 (1)	64.0000 (70)
Primary Units	Unit Format	Decimal	Architectural (Decimal)
	Fraction Format	Horizontal	Diagonal
	Zero Suppression	Feet, Inches (Trailing Only)	Feet only
	Angular Precision	Zero decimal places	Two decimal places

You'll change a few more settings throughout the rest of this chapter as you begin to dimension the cabin in the next set of exercises. We'll now look briefly at the Alternate Units and Tolerances tabs.

N O T E The next two sections describe dimensioning features that you won't use in the cabin project. If you would rather begin dimensioning the cabin and look at this material later, skip to the "Placing Dimensions on the Drawing" section.

Exploring the Alternate Units Tab

If your work requires your dimensions to display both metric and architectural units, use the Alternate Units tab in the New Dimension Style dialog box or the Modify Dimension Style dialog box when you are changing an existing style. In the example shown in Figure 12.13, the primary units setting is Architectural (Decimal). Now you'll set up the alternate units:

1. Click the Dimension Style button on the Dimensions panel.

2. Highlight DimPlan in the Dimension Style Manager, if it's not already highlighted.

3. Click the Modify button to open the Modify Dimension Style dialog box. This is identical to the New Dimension Style dialog box that you used in the previous sections.

4. Click the Alternate Units tab. (Look ahead to Figure 12.13 to see what the style will look like when you're finished here.) You'll make only three or four changes on this tab.

5. In the upper-left corner of the tab, select the Display Alternate Units check box. This makes the rest of the settings on the tab available to you for making changes.

6. If Decimal (Architectural) isn't displayed in the Unit Format drop-down list, select it.

7. If Precision isn't set to 0 (0'-0 1/8″), open that drop-down list and select that level of precision.

8. If the alternate units is Decimal, then set Multiplier For Alt Units to 25.4. This makes millimeters the alternate units. If the alternate units is Architectural, then set Multiplier For Alt Units to 0.039370. This makes inches the alternate units.

9. In the lower-right quarter of the tab, in the Placement area, select Below Primary Value. This has the effect of placing the alternate units below the primary units and on the opposite side of the dimension line. The tab should look like Figure 12.13.

If you want centi-meters to be the alternate units, change the Multiplier For Alt Units setting to 2.54 and set Precision to 0.00.

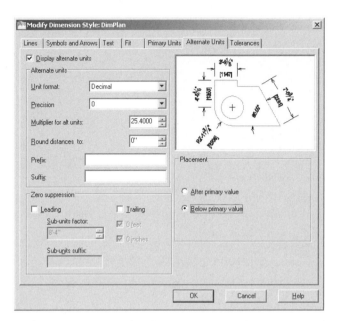

FIGURE 12.13: The Alternate Units tab after being set up for millimeters

10. Uncheck the Display Alternate Units check box; you don't need use these settings. You won't be using alternate units when you dimension the cabin.

Exploring the Tolerances Tab

AutoCAD offers features whose options help you create several kinds of *tolerances* (allowable variances from the stated dimension). These are very common in the machining and manufacturing industries where it's understood that the dimensions given are only approximations of the part fabricated. Tolerances are usually measured in thousandths of an inch or hundredths of a millimeter. The Tolerances tab provides four methods for creating what are called *lateral tolerances*, the traditional kind of tolerance that most drafts people use. This is the *plus or minus* kind of tolerance. Open the Modify Dimension Style dialog box, click the Tolerances tab, and look at the choices in the Method drop-down list, shown in Figure 12.14.

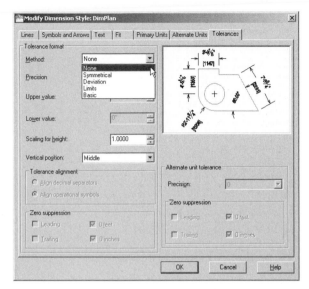

FIGURE 12.14: The Tolerances tab, showing the Method drop-down list options

Each of these is a method for displaying a plus or minus type of tolerance:

None No tolerances are displayed.

Symmetrical This method is for a single plus or minus expression after the base dimension. It's used when the upper allowable limit of deviation is identical to that for the lower limit, as in 1.0625 ± 0.0025.

Deviation This method is for the instance in which the upper allowable deviation is different from that of the lower deviation. For example, the upper limit of the deviation can be +0.0025, and the lower limit can be –0.0005. The two deviation limits are stacked and follow the base dimension.

Limits In this method, the tolerances are added to or subtracted from the base dimension, resulting in maximum and minimum total values. The maximum is placed over the minimum. In the example for the Symmetrical method, 1.0650 is the maximum and on top of 1.0600, the minimum.

Basic The base dimension is left by itself, and a box is drawn around it indicating that the tolerances are general, apply to several or all dimensions in boxes, and are noted somewhere else in the drawing. Often, basic dimensions appear when a dimension is theoretical or not exact.

When you select one of these options, one or more of the settings below become available. If you select Deviation or Limits, all settings become available:

Precision Controls the overall precision of the tolerances.

Upper Value and Lower Value The actual values of the tolerances.

Scaling For Height The height of the tolerance text. A value of 1 here sets the tolerance text to match that of the base dimension. A value greater than 1 makes the tolerance text greater than the base dimension text, and a value less than 1 makes it smaller than the base dimension text.

Vertical Position Where the base dimension is placed vertically relative to the tolerances. It can be in line with the upper or lower tolerance or in the middle.

At the bottom, when checked the Zero Suppression options (which are not available when Basic is the tolerance format) suppress extra zeros that occur before or after the decimal point. If you set up the Tolerances tab as shown in the top of Figure 12.15, a dimension looks like the one shown in the bottom of Figure 12.15.

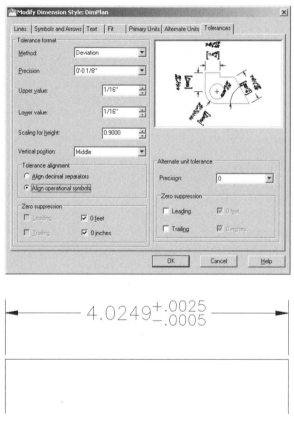

FIGURE 12.15: The Tolerances tab with some settings changed (top) and a dimension with deviation tolerances (bottom)

A more complex family of tolerances is available through the Dimensions panel. It's called *geometric tolerancing* and involves setting up a series of boxes that contain symbols and numbers that describe tolerance parameters for form, position, and other geometric features. Usually two to six boxes appear in a row, with the possibility of multiple rows. These all constitute the *feature control frame*, which eventually is inserted in the drawing and attached in some way to the relevant dimension. Follow these steps:

1. Click the Tolerance button on the expanded Dimensions panel to open the Geometric Tolerance dialog box (see Figure 12.16), in which you set up the feature control frame. The black squares will contain symbols, and the white rectangles are for tolerance or datum values or for reference numbers.

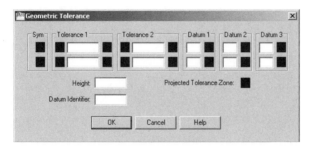

FIGURE 12.16: The Geometric Tolerance dialog box

2. Click in the top Sym box on the left to open the Symbol dialog box, which contains 14 standard symbols that describe the characteristic form or position for which the tolerance is being used. When you select one of the symbols, the window closes, and the symbol is inserted into the SYM box. Click the icon in the top row that consists of two concentric circles, as shown in Figure 12.17.

FIGURE 12.17: The Symbol dialog box

3. Click the top-left black square in the Tolerance 1 area. This inserts a diameter symbol.

4. Click the top-right black square of Tolerance 1. The Material Condition dialog box (see Figure 12.18) opens and displays the three material condition options. When you click one, it's inserted in the top-right square of Tolerance 1.

FIGURE 12.18: The Material Condition dialog box

If you need them, you can insert any of these three symbols in Tolerance 2 and Datum 1, 2, or 3.

5. Fill in the actual tolerance value(s) and datum references in the text boxes. (See Figure 12.19.)

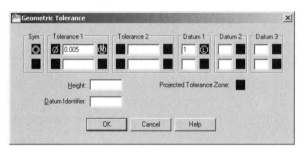

FIGURE 12.19: The Geometric Tolerance dialog box with a few values provided

6. When you're finished, click OK. You can insert the feature control frame into your drawing like a block and reference it to a part or a dimension, as shown in Figure 12.20.

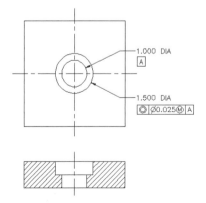

FIGURE 12.20: Geometric dimensioning on a machined part

This exercise was intended to show you the tools that AutoCAD provides for setting up the most commonly used lateral and geometric tolerances when you use the Tolerances tab in the Modify Dimension Style dialog box and the Tolerance button on the Dimensions panel. My intention here isn't to explain the methodology of geometric tolerances or the meanings of the various symbols, numbers, and letters used in them. That is a subject beyond the scope of this book.

Placing Dimensions on the Drawing

Upon returning to your drawing, it should still look almost exactly like Figure 12.1 (shown earlier), and it should have the following:

- ▶ A new layer called Dim1, which is current

- ▶ A new dimension style called DimPlan, which is current and is now displayed in the drop-down list on the Dimensions panel

- ▶ Most of the layers frozen

- ▶ The Endpoint osnap running (other osnaps may be running, but only Endpoint is important to this exercise)

- ▶ On the status bar: Ortho Mode, Polar Tracking, and Object Snap Tracking off

- ▶ A new text style called Dim, which is current

Placing Horizontal Dimensions

First, you'll dimension across the top of the plan, from the corner of the building to the closet wall, and then to the other features on that wall. Then you'll dimension the decks and roof.

1. Click the Linear button at the left side of the Dimensions panel to activate the Dimlinear command. If the Linear button isn't visible, click the down arrow below the current dimension command and then choose Linear from the drop-down list. The prompt says Specify first extension line origin or <select object>:.

2. Pick the upper-right corner of the cabin walls. The prompt changes to Specify second extension line origin:. At this point, zoom in to the closet area.

3. Activate the Perpendicular osnap, place the cursor over the outside of the closet wall as shown in Figure 12.21, and then click.

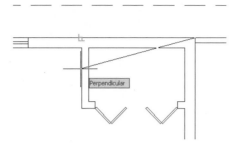

FIGURE 12.21: Selecting the wall with the Perpendicular osnap

4. At the Specify dimension line location or: prompt, click a point above the roof line to place the dimension in the drawing (see the top of Figure 12.22). Also notice that the left extension line starts perpendicular to the wall you picked.

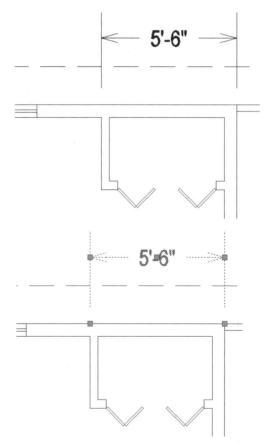

FIGURE 12.22: The dimension attached to the cursor (top) and the grips associated with a dimension (bottom)

5. Click anywhere on the new dimension. The dimension becomes dashed and five grips appear (see the bottom of Figure 12.22). When you need to adjust a dimension, click and drag the necessary grip. You'll learn more about using grips to modify dimensions in the "Modifying Dimensions" section later in this chapter.

6. Press Esc to deselect the dimension.

Your first dimension is completed.

When dimensioning a drawing, you usually dimension to the outside or center line of the objects and to each significant feature. The next dimension will run from the left side of the first dimension to the right side of the window.

N O T E Studs are the vertical 2″×4″ (51 mm×102 mm) or 2″×6″ (51 mm× 152 mm) members in the framing of a wall. When dimensioning buildings that have stud walls, architects usually dimension to the face of the stud rather than the outside surface of the wall material, but I won't go into that level of detail in this book.

Using the Continue Command

AutoCAD has an automatic way of placing adjacent dimensions in line with one another—the Continue command. You use it as follows:

1. Zoom out, and pan until you have a view of the upper wall and roofline, with space above them for dimensions (see Figure 12.23).

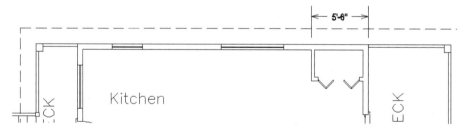

F I G U R E   1 2 . 2 3 : The result of zooming and panning for a view of the top of the floor plan

2. Click the Continue button on the Dimensions panel. If it's not visible, then click the down arrow next to the Baseline button and choose Continue from the fly-out menu. The prompt says Specify a second extension line origin or [Undo/Select] <Select>:. All you need to do here is pick a point for the right end of the dimension—in this case, the right corner of the nearest window.

3. Click the right corner of the living room window. This draws the second dimension in line with the first (see Figure 12.24). Note that the same prompt has returned to the Command window. You can keep picking points to place the next adjacent dimension in line.

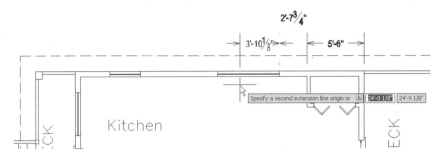

FIGURE 12.24: Using the Continue command

4. Continue adding dimensions with the Continue command by clicking, moving right to left, the endpoints of the window openings, the endpoint of the wall, and the end of the deck.

5. Use the Linear tool to add a dimension for the width of the front deck and the Perpendicular osnap to align the dimension lines. When you're done, your dimensions should look like the top of Figure 12.25.

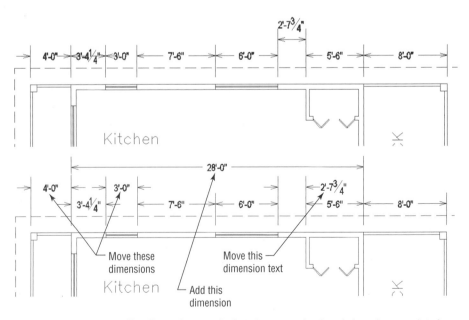

FIGURE 12.25: The dimension attached to the cursor (top) and the grips associated with a dimension (bottom)

6. Some of the dimensions, particularly on the left end of the cabin, appear cluttered with some of the arrowheads and text overlapping. Select the dimensions that need adjustment and use the grips near the arrows or at the text to adjust the dimension line or text location (see the bottom of Figure 12.25).

7. Finally, add a linear dimension from the end of the front deck to the beginning of the cabin and another overall dimension from one end of the cabin to another (see the bottom of Figure 12.25).

With the Continue command, you can dimension along a wall of a building quickly just by picking points. AutoCAD assumes that the last extension line specified for the previous dimension will coincide with the first extension line of the next dimension. If the extension line from which you need to continue isn't the last one specified, press ↵ at the prompt, pick the extension line from which you want to continue, and resume the command.

Another automation strategy that you can use with linear dimensions is the Baseline command.

Using the Baseline Command

The Baseline command gets its name from a style of dimensioning called *baseline*, in which all dimensions begin at the same point (see Figure 12.26). Each dimension is stacked above the previous one. Because of the automatic stacking, you can use the Baseline command for overall dimensions. AutoCAD will stack the overall dimension a set height above the incremental dimensions.

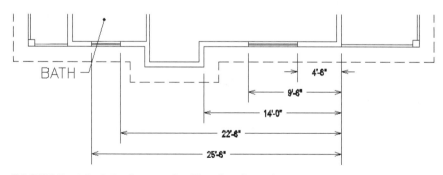

FIGURE 12.26: An example of baseline dimensions

The steps for creating baseline dimensions are listed here:

1. Create a linear dimension.

2. Click the down arrow next to the Continue button in the Dimensions panel, and then click the Baseline option. The prompt says Specify a

second extension line origin or [Undo/Select] <Select>:,
just like the first prompt for the Continue command.

3. Pick the next feature to be dimensioned.

4. Repeat step 3 as necessary to add the required dimensions.

5. Press Esc to end the Baseline command.

Setting Up Vertical Dimensions

Because you can use the Linear command for vertical and horizontal dimensions, you can follow the steps in the previous exercise to do the vertical dimensions on the right side of the floor plan. The only difference from the horizontal dimensioning is that you need two sets of dimensions: one for the wall and another for the deck. The following steps will take you through the process of placing the first vertical dimension. You'll then be able to finish the rest of them by yourself.

1. Pan and zoom to get a good view of the right side of the floor plan, including the front deck (see Figure 12.27).

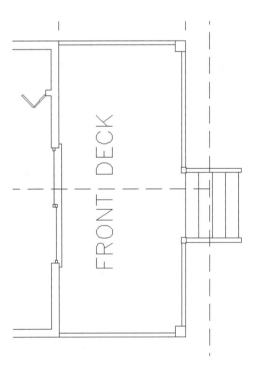

FIGURE 12.27: The result of zooming and panning for a view of the right side of the floor plan

2. Click the Linear button, and then start a vertical dimension from the top of the right exterior wall.

3. Place the second point at the endpoint on the opening of the sliding door. Click to place the dimension between the wall and the FRONT DECK text. Adjust the location of the text if needed (see the left image of Figure 12.28).

T I P   AutoCAD can sometimes be conservative when deciding whether both text and arrows can fit between the extension lines. Try moving the text a bit toward one of the extension lines in one of the 4'-6" dimensions and notice how the arrows move from outside the extension lines to inside.

4. Use the Continue command and grips to draw and edit the remaining two dimensions for the front of the cabin (see the right image of Figure 12.28).

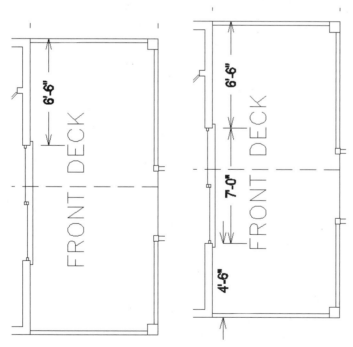

FIGURE   12.28: The dimension drawn to the start of the sliding door opening (left) and the completed first set of vertical dimensions (right)

5. Using a similar procedure, draw the vertical dimensions for the front deck, placing the dimensions to the right of the deck. Add a horizontal dimension showing the length of the stairway. When you're done, your dimensions should look like those in Figure 12.29.

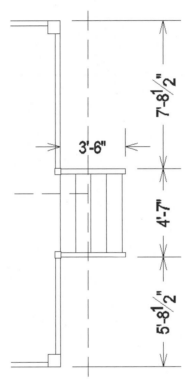

FIGURE 12.29: The dimensions for the front deck

Finishing the Dimensions

You place the rest of the horizontal and vertical dimensions using procedures similar to the one you used to complete the horizontal dimensions. Here is a summary of the steps:

1. Use the Linear and Continue commands to add horizontal dimensions to the bottom side of the building. Move the title and label text as required to display the dimensions clearly.

2. Add dimensions to the rear of the cabin and for the rear deck.

3. Dimension the roof.

4. Dimension the inside of the bathroom. After starting the Linear command, press ⏎ to allow the selection of an object, rather than a starting point for a dimension. Click one of the vertical walls, and then click to place the dimension.

The completed dimensions will be similar to Figure 12.30.

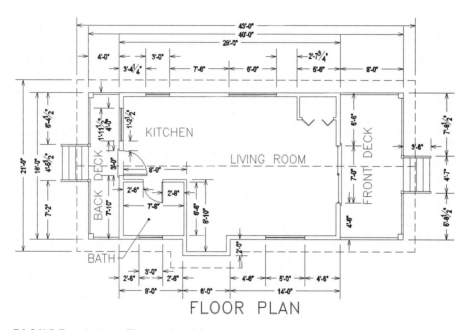

FIGURE 12.30: The completed dimensions

5. Save your drawing as cabin12b.dwg.

Using Other Types of Dimensions

AutoCAD provides tools for placing radial and angular dimensions on the drawing and for placing linear dimensions that are neither vertical nor horizontal. You'll make some temporary changes to the cabin file that you just saved, so that you can explore these tools and then close the drawing without saving it:

1. Make Layer 0 current.

2. Freeze the Dim1, Deck, Steps, and Text1 layers.

3. Use the Fillet command to fillet the top-right corner of the roof with a radius of 5'-0" (1525 mm).

4. Start the Line command, and then pick the lower-right corner of the roof as the start point.

5. Activate the Nearest osnap, and pick a point on the roof's ridgeline. The right end of the cabin should look like Figure 12.31.

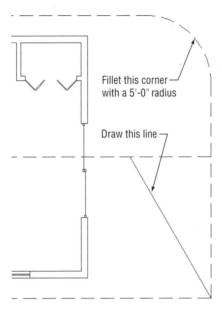

FIGURE 12.31: The right end of the cabin after implementing some temporary changes

Using Radial Dimensions

On the drop-down menu on the left side of the Dimensions panel are icons for Radius, Diameter, and Arc Length dimensions. They all operate the same way and are controlled by the same settings.

Adding a Radius Dimension

Follow these steps to place a radius dimension at the filleted corner, measuring the distance from the curve to the center point:

1. Click the Osnap button on the status bar to disable any running osnaps temporarily.

 2. Click the arrow below the Linear button, and then click the Radius button to start the Dimradius command.

N O T E   Most of the commands used for dimensioning are prefaced with a *dim* when you enter them at the command line; that is, dim is part of the command name. For example, when you click the Radius button on the Dimension toolbar or choose Dimension ➤ Radius from the menu bar, you see _dimradius in the Command window to let you know that you have started the Dimradius command. You can also start this command by entering **dimradius**↵ or **dra**↵ (the command alias).

3. Click the inside filleted corner well above the midpoint. The radius dimension appears, and the text is attached to the cursor. Where you pick on the curve determines the angle of the radius dimension (see Figure 12.32).

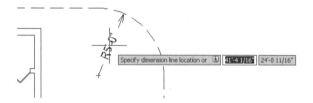

F I G U R E   1 2 . 3 2 : The radius dimension initially positioned on the curve

4. Click to place the radius text in the dimension. The "R" prefix indicates that this is a radius dimension.

Adding a Diameter Dimension

Similar to the radius dimension, a diameter dimension measures the distance from one side of a circle or arc, through the center point, to the other end. Follow these steps to place a diameter at the filleted corner:

1. Erase the radius dimension.

2. Click the arrow below the Radius button, and then click the Diameter button to start the Dimdiameter command.

3. Click the inside filleted corner near the location where it meets the vertical wall. The diameter dimension appears and the text is attached to the cursor.

4. Click to place the radius text in the dimension. The Ø prefix indicates that this is a diameter dimension. Where you pick on the curve determines the angle of the radius dimension (see Figure 12.33).

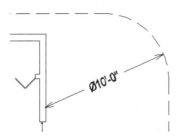

FIGURE 12.33: The diameter dimension positioned on the curve

Add an Arc Length

An arc length dimension measures the length of an arc or polyline arc segment. As shown in Figure 12.34, an arc symbol, or *cap*, precedes the text to identify it as an arc length dimension. Follow these steps to place an arc length dimension at the filleted corner:

TIP   You can change the location of the arc length symbol, from in front of the text to over it, or eliminate it altogether in the Symbols and Arrows tab of the Modify Dimension style dialog box.

1. Erase the radius dimension.

2. Click the arrow below the Diameter button, and then click the Arc Length button to start the Dimarc command.

3. Click anywhere on the arc at the filleted corner and the arc length dimension appears attached to the cursor.

4. Click to locate the dimension (see Figure 12.34).

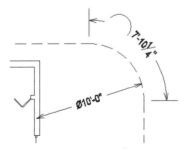

FIGURE 12.34: The arc length dimension positioned on the curve

SETTING UP PARENT AND CHILD DIMENSIONING STYLES

The DimPlan dimension style that you set up at the beginning of this chapter applies to all dimensions and is called the parent dimension style. You can change settings in this dimension style for particular types of dimensions, such as the radial type. This makes a child dimension style. The child version is based on the parent version, but it has a few settings that are different. In this way, all your dimensions will be made using the DimPlan dimension style, but radial dimensions will use a child version of the style. Once you create a child dimension style from the parent style, you refer to both styles by the same name and you call them a dimension style *family*. Follow these steps to set up a child dimension style for radial dimensions:

1. Click the Dimension Style button at the right end of the Dimensions panel to open the Dimension Style Manager dialog box.

2. With the parent style highlighted in the Styles list, click the New button to open the Create New Dimension Style dialog box.

3. Open the Use For drop-down list, select the type of dimensions for which you want to set up a child style, and then click the Continue button. The New Dimension Style dialog box opens and has the seven tabs you worked with earlier. Its title bar now includes the type of dimension you just identified, and the preview window shows a preview of that dimension type only.

4. Click the tabs and make the desired parameter changes.

5. Click OK to close the New Dimension Style dialog box.

6. In the Dimension Style Manager dialog box, notice the Styles list; the current dimension style now has a child style indented below it:

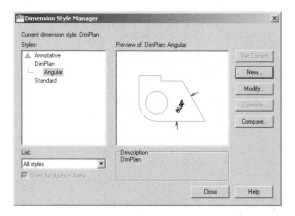

7. Click Close to close the Dimension Style Manager dialog box.

Using Aligned and Angular Dimensions

To become familiar with the aligned and angular dimension types, you'll experiment with the line you drew from the opposite corner of the roof in the previous exercise.

Using Aligned Dimensions

Aligned dimensions are linear dimensions that aren't horizontal or vertical. You place them in the same way that you place horizontal or vertical dimensions with the Linear command. You can also use the Baseline and Continue commands with aligned dimensions.

Use the Aligned command, which works just like the Linear dimension command, to dimension the line you drew at the beginning of this exercise. Follow these steps to add an aligned dimension:

1. Zoom in to the lower-right corner of the cabin roof.

2. Click the down arrow on the right side of the Dimensions panel, and then click the Aligned button.

3. Press ↵ to switch to Pick mode. The cursor changes to a pickbox.

4. Pick the diagonal line. The dimension appears attached to the cursor.

5. Click to place the dimension. Your drawing should look similar to Figure 12.35.

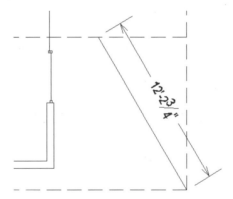

FIGURE 12.35: An aligned dimension added to the cabin drawing

Using Angular Dimensions

The angular dimension is the only basic dimension type that uses angles in the dimension text instead of linear measurements. Try making an angular dimension on your own. First turn off running osnaps.

You can start the Angular command by clicking the Angular button from the drop-down menu on the Dimensions panel. Follow the prompts, and pick the angle line you drew and the lower, horizontal roofline to dimension the angle between them.

Figure 12.36 show the angular dimension on the roof.

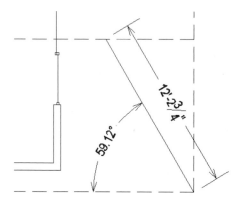

FIGURE 12.36: The roof with the angular dimension added

Using Ordinate Dimensions

Ordinate dimensions are widely used by the mechanical and civil engineering professions and related trades. They differ from the kind of dimensioning you have been doing so far in this chapter in that ordinate dimensioning specifies x- and y-coordinate values for specific points in a drawing based on an absolute or relative Cartesian coordinate system, rather than on a distance between two points. This method is used to dimension centers of holes in sheet metal or machine parts and to locate surveying points on an area map.

You don't need ordinate dimensions in the cabin project, so you'll now go through a quick exercise in setting them up to dimension the holes in a steel plate. Doing so will give you a glimpse of the tools that AutoCAD provides for this type of work. (If you aren't interested in ordinate dimensioning, move on to the next section, "Using Leader Lines," to modify the dimensions you've already created for the cabin.)

1. Open a new drawing, and leave the units at the default of Decimal with a precision of four decimal places. Turn polar tracking on.

2. Set up a new text style, and set 0.125 as the height. Click Apply and then Close to make it the current text style.

3. Draw a rectangle using 0,0 as the first point and 6,–4 as the second.

4. Use Zoom To Extents, and then zoom out to see the area around the object. Turn off the UCS icon.

5. Somewhere in the upper-left quadrant of the rectangle, draw a circle with a radius of 0.35 units. Then, using Polar Tracking or Ortho mode, copy that circle once directly to the right, once directly below the original, and to two other locations that are not aligned with any other circle, so the configuration looks something like the top of Figure 12.37.

6. Set the Endpoint and Center osnaps to be running, and turn on Ortho mode.

   What you are concerned with in ordinate dimensioning isn't how far the holes are from each other but how far the x- and y-coordinates of the centers of the holes are from a reference point on the plate. You'll use the upper-left corner of the plate as a reference point, or *datum point*, because it's positioned at the origin of the drawing, or at the 0,0 point.

 7. Click the Ordinate button on the drop-down menu on the Dimensions panel.

8. Click the upper-left corner of the rectangular plate, and then move the cursor straight up above the point you picked. When you're about an inch above the plate, click again. This sets the first ordinate dimension (see the top left of Figure 12.37).

9. Press the spacebar to repeat the Dimordinate command, and then repeat step 8 for the four circles near the middle or upper portions of the plate, using their centers as points to snap to and aligning the ordinate dimensions by eye. The lower circle is in vertical alignment with the one above it, so it needs no horizontal dimension. Place an ordinate dimension on the upper-right corner of the plate to finish. Press the F8 key to toggle Ortho mode off if you need to jog an extension line. The result should look like the top right of Figure 12.37.

10. Repeat this procedure for the y-ordinate dimensions. Once again, ignore any circles that are in vertical alignment, but include the upper-left and lower-left corners of the plate (see the bottom of Figure 12.37).

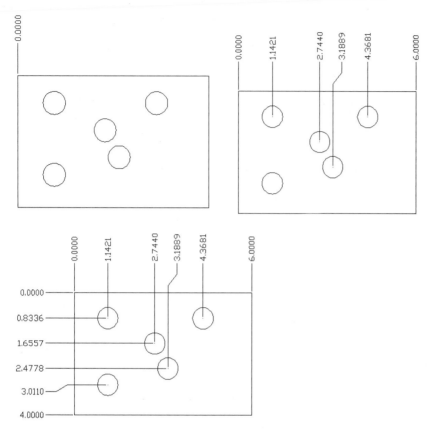

FIGURE 12.37: Placing the first ordinate dimension (top left), finishing up the x-coordinate dimensions (top right), and placing the y-coordinate dimensions (bottom)

In civil engineering, ordinate dimensions are used almost the same way but displayed differently. A datum reference point is used, but the dimensions are displayed at each point. This is because the points are a set of surveying points spread randomly over a large area, and the datum or reference point might be miles away (see Figure 12.38).

When you change settings for a dimension style, dimensions created when that style was current automatically update to reflect the changes. You'll modify more dimensions in the next section.

You have been introduced to the basic types of dimensions—linear, radial, leader, and angular—and some auxiliary dimensions—baseline, continue, and aligned—that are special cases of the linear type. You can also use the baseline and continuous dimensions with angular dimensions.

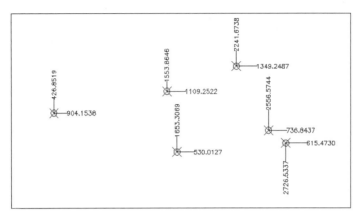

FIGURE 12.38: A sample surveyor's datum points with ordinate dimensions

Using Leader Lines

You will use the Multileader command to draw an arrow to features in the drawing to add descriptive information. Multileaders are not part of the dimension family, and you can find them on the Multileaders panel. Before you create a leader, you need to create a multileader style:

1. You don't need to save the changes from the previous exercise so, if it's still open, close the Cabin12b.dwg without saving it and then reopen the file.

2. Click the Multileader Style Manager button at the right end of the Leaders panel's title bar.

3. Click the New button in the Multileader Style Manager. In the Create New Multileader Style dialog box that opens, enter **DimPlan Leader** in the New Style Name text box and then click Continue (see Figure 12.39).

4. The Modify Multileader Style dialog opens (see Figure 12.40). This is where you define the leader properties. In the Leader Format tab, expand the Symbol drop-down list in the Arrowhead section, and choose Open 30. Set Size to 1/8″ (3.5).

5. Click the Leader Structure tab. The landing is the horizontal line at the end of the leader, just before the text. Make sure the Set Landing Distance option is checked, and then enter **3/16″ (0.36)** in the text box.

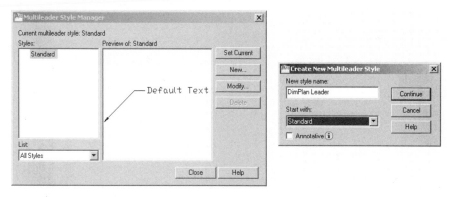

FIGURE 12.39: Creating a new multileader style

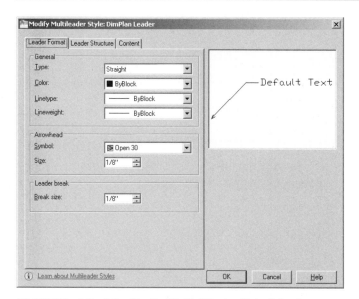

FIGURE 12.40: The Modify Multileader Style dialog box

6. In the Scale area, make sure the Specify Scale radio button is selected and then click in the text box and enter 64↵ (70↵).

7. Switch to the Content tab. Expand the Text Style drop-down list, choose Dim, and set the text height to 1/8″ (3.5).

8. In the Leader Connection area, set both the Left Attachment and Right Attachment options to Middle of Top Line. This places the middle of the top line of the leader text even with the landing.

9. Set the Landing Gap value to 1/8″ (3.5).

10. Click the OK button.

11. In the Multileader Style Manager, the DimPlan Leader style appears in the Styles list box (see Figure 12.41). Select it, click Set Current, and then click the Close button.

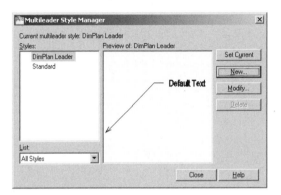

FIGURE 12.41: The DimPlan Leader multileader style shown in the Multi-leader Style Manager

Adding the Leaders

To add the leaders to the drawing, follow these steps:

1. Zoom in to the front deck.

2. Click the Multileader button on the Multileaders panel.

3. Activate the Endpoint osnap, if necessary, and then click the top-right corner of the top-right deck post.

4. At the Specify leader landing location: prompt, click a point above and to the right of the deck. The Text Editor tab and panels replace the Annotate tab and panels in the Ribbon, and a flashing vertical cursor appears to the right of the landing, as shown in Figure 12.42.

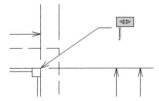

FIGURE 12.42: The flashing vertical cursor indicates that AutoCAD is waiting for text input

5. Enter Use only pressure treated lumber for deck and supports, and then drag the right arrow near the text to adjust the width of the multiline text object, as shown in Figure 12.43. Click a blank spot in the drawing area to complete the text and return to the Annotate tab.

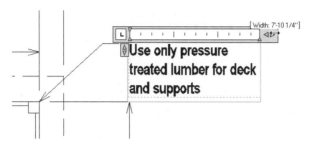

FIGURE 12.43: Adjust the width of the multiline text object.

T I P   To reposition a leader without moving the arrow, click it and then click the grip at the middle of the landing. Then move the cursor. When you do, the text, landing, and one end of the leader line will all move with it.

6. Pan to the right so that you can see the two windows on the north side of the cabin.

7. Add a leader that starts at the right edge of the 3′ (915 mm) window and then extends below and to the right. Enter All windows to be double paned at the text prompt, adjust the width of the text, and then click a blank spot in the drawing area (see Figure 12.44).

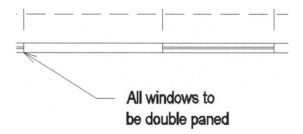

FIGURE 12.44: The multileader pointing to the first window

8. Several leader lines can extend from a single landing. Click the Add Leader button on the Leaders panel, and then at the Select a multileader: prompt, click the last leader you made. An arrowhead with a leader appears attached to the cursor and anchored to the

landing. Click the left corner of the window to the right and then press ↵.

N O T E   AutoCAD may place the second leader on the right side of the text if it determines that the leader fits better there. If this happens, click the multileader to select it and then move the text to the right. The second leader will reposition itself to the left side of the text.

9. Reposition the text as necessary. Your drawing should look similar to Figure 12.45.

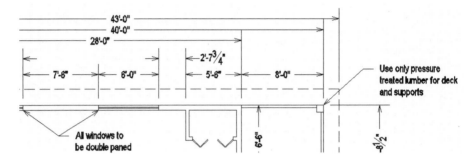

F I G U R E   1 2 . 4 5 : The cabin drawing with leaders

10. Save this drawing as `Cabin12c.dwg`.

The final part of this chapter will be devoted to teaching you a few techniques for modifying dimensions.

Modifying Dimensions

You can use several commands and grips to modify dimensions, depending on the desired change. Specifically, you can do the following:

▶ You can change the dimension text content.

▶ You can move the dimension text relative to the dimension line.

▶ You can move the dimension or extension lines.

▶ You can change the dimension style settings for a dimension or a group of dimensions.

▶ You can revise a dimension style.

The best way to understand how to modify dimensions is to try a few.

Modifying Dimension Text

You can modify any aspect of the dimension text. You'll look at how to change the content first.

Editing Dimension Text Content

To change the content of text for one dimension, or to add text before or after the dimension, you can use the Properties or Quick Properties palette. You'll change the text in the horizontal dimensions for the cabin and walls using Quick Properties:

1. Zoom and pan until your view of the floor plan is similar to Figure 12.46.

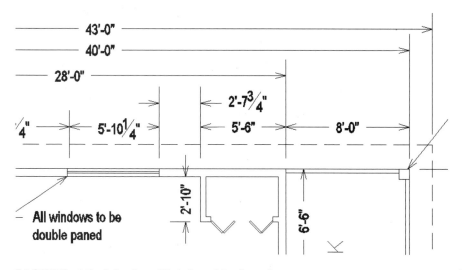

FIGURE 12.46: A modified view of the floor plan

 2. Select the horizontal 40'-0" (8550 mm) cabin dimension near the top of the drawing, then click the Quick Properties button in the Status Bar.

 TIP The procedure shown here can also be done in the Text rollout of the Properties palette.

3. Highlight the Text Override field, and enter **<> verify in field**↵. The phrase is appended to the dimension (see the top of Figure 12.47). The <> instructs AutoCAD to add the phrase to the dimension text; if

you had not prefixed the override with <>, then the phrase would have replaced the dimension text entirely.

4. Press the Esc key, and then click the 5'-6" (1670 mm) dimension, measuring the distance from the end of the cabin to the closet wall.

5. In the Text Override box, enter <> %%P↵. The ± symbol is now appended to the text (see the bottom of Figure 12.47).

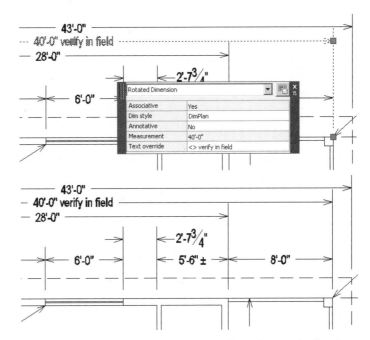

FIGURE 12.47: Adding a phrase to dimension text (top) and a special character (bottom)

Unless you have memorized all the ASCII symbol codes, it might be easier to insert symbols into dimension text using the text editing tools command. To do this, choose Modify ➤ Object ➤ Text ➤ Edit from the menu bar, or enter **ddedit**↵ and then select the dimension text. The text is highlighted and the Text Editor tab is activated. Place the cursor where you want the symbol to appear, and then click the Symbol button in the Insert panel to see a list of available symbols to choose from and their related ASCII codes. Click the symbol name to be added (see Figure 12.48).

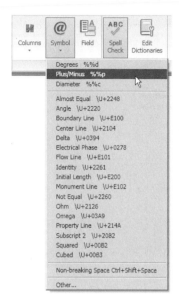

FIGURE 12.48: Inserting symbols from the Text Editor tab

Next you'll learn about moving a dimension.

Moving Dimensions

You can use grips to move dimensions. You used grips to move the dimension lines when you were putting in the vertical and horizontal dimensions. This time, you'll move the dimension line and the text:

1. Zoom in to a view of the upper-left side of the floor plan until you have a view that includes the left window and the top of the rear deck and their dimensions.

2. Select the 3'-0" (915 mm) window dimension. Its grips appear.

3. Click the grip on the right arrowhead to activate it.

4. Move the cursor down until the dimension text is just below the roofline. Click again to fix it there.

5. Click the grip that's on the text and, with polar tracking on, move the text to the right, outside of the extension line; then click to place it. Press Esc to deselect the dimension (see the top of Figure 12.49).

6. Select either of the leader lines pointing to the two windows. The leaders, landing, and leader text ghost and the grips appear.

7. Click the grip at the tip of the left leader, then move the grip to the end of the inner pane of the left window (see the bottom of Figure 12.49).

8. Click the grip at the tip of the right leader, and move the grip to the left end of the inner pane of the right window (also shown at the bottom of Figure 12.49).

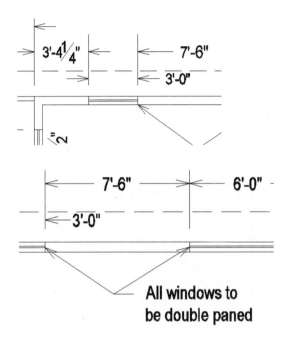

FIGURE 12.49: Moving the window dimensions with grips: the linear dimension (top) and the leaders (bottom)

Using Dimension Overrides

You can suppress the left extension line with the Properties palette, which allows you to change a setting in the dimension style for one dimension without altering the style settings. Follow these steps:

1. Thaw the Headers layer.

   Notice how the white (or black), left extension line for the 8′-0″ (2350 mm) dimension, measuring the width of the bath room, coincides with the header line. You could use the Draw Order tools to move the dimension behind the header, but that may still result in a visibly overlapping condition when the drawing is printed. In this case, you'll suppress the extension line, rendering it invisible.

2. Double-click the 8'-0" (2350 mm) dimension to open the Properties palette.

3. Scroll down to the Lines & Arrows rollout. If this section isn't open, click the arrow to the right.

4. Scroll down the list of settings in this section, and click Ext Line 1. Then click the down arrow to the right to open the drop-down list. Click Off. This suppresses the left extension line of the dimension (see Figure 12.50).

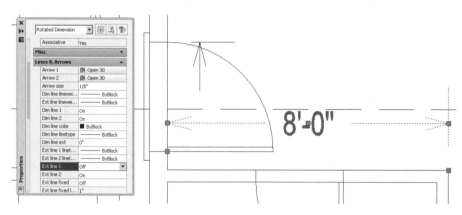

FIGURE 12.50: The 8'-0" (2350 mm) dimension with the left extension line suppressed

5. Close the Properties palette. Press Esc to deselect the dimension.

To illustrate how dimension overrides work, you suppressed an extension line without having to alter the dimension style. Extension lines are usually the thinnest lines in a drawing. It's usually not critical that they be suppressed if they coincide with other lines, because the other lines will overwrite them in a print.

However, in this example, the left extension line of the 8'-0" (2350 mm) dimension for the bathroom dimension coincides with the line representing the header of the back door. If the Headers layer is turned off or frozen, you will have to unsuppress the extension line of this dimension so that it will be visible spanning the door opening. Also, if you dimension to a noncontinuous line, such as a hidden line, use the dimension style override features to assign special linetypes to extension lines. In the practice exercises at the end of this chapter, you'll get a chance to learn how to incorporate center lines into your dimensions.

Dimensioning Short Distances

When you have to dimension distances so short that both the text and the arrows can't fit between the extension lines, a dimension style setting determines where they are placed. To see how this works, you'll add dimensions to the deck dimensioning the widths of the handrails and posts as well as the thickness of an interior wall. Then make a change in the Fit tab to alter the DimPlan dimension style to change where it places text that doesn't fit between the extension lines:

1. Zoom and pan to a view of the upper portion of the front deck so that the horizontal dimensions above the floor plan are visible (see Figure 12.51).

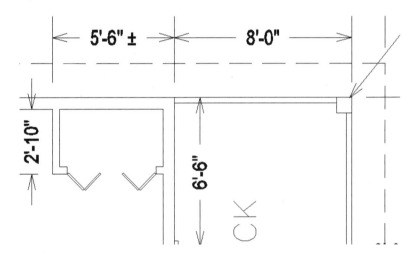

FIGURE 12.51: The new view of the upper-right floor plan and its dimensions

2. Activate the running osnaps if necessary, click the Linear button, and pick the upper-left corner of the deck post. Then pick the lower-left corner of the same deck post. Place the dimension line about 2′ (610 mm) to the left of the deck post. The 8″ (204 mm) dimension is placed even farther to the left of the point you selected (see Figure 12.52).

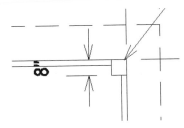

FIGURE 12.52: The text for the short dimension is not placed near the dimension lines.

 TIP Several of the dimensioning commands are also available on the Annotation panel under the Home tab.

3. Open the Dimension Style Manager dialog box, click the Modify button, and then, in the Modify Dimension Style dialog box, click the Fit tab.

4. In the Text Placement area, select the Beside The Dimension Line radio button (see Figure 12.53); click OK and then Close to shut both dialog boxes.

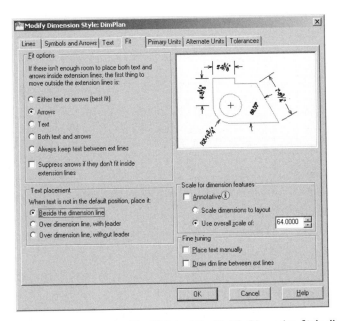

FIGURE 12.53: The Fit tab of the Modify Dimension Style dialog box after making the change

The dimension changes to reflect the modification to the style (see Figure 12.54). This is a global change that will affect all future dimensions.

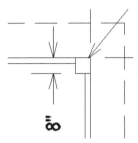

FIGURE 12.54: The short dimension after changing the style

5. Add another dimension measuring the width of the horizontal handrail, and add the text **TYP** after the dimension text, as shown in Figure 12.55. Refer to the "Modifying Dimension Text" section if you need a refresher.

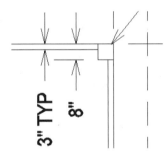

FIGURE 12.55: The handrail dimension after adding the "TYP" text

6. Make any adjustments necessary to make the drawing readable, and then save the drawing as Cabin12d.dwg.

This concludes the exercises for dimensions in this chapter. Working successfully with dimensions in your drawing requires an investment of time to become familiar with the commands and settings that control how dimensions appear, how they are placed in the drawing, and how they are modified. The exercises in this chapter have led you through the basics of the dimensioning process. For a more in-depth discussion of dimensions, you can refer to *Mastering AutoCAD 2010 and AutoCAD LT 2010* by George Omura (Wiley, 2009).

The next chapter will introduce you to external references, a tool for viewing a drawing from within another drawing.

If You Would Like More Practice...

In the first practice exercise, you'll get a chance to use the dimensioning tools that you just learned. After that is a short exercise that shows a technique for incorporating center lines into dimensions.

Dimensioning the Garage Addition

Try dimensioning the garage addition to the cabin that was shown at the end of Chapter 4 (Cabin04c-addon). Use the same techniques and standards of dimensioning that you used in this chapter to dimension the cabin; use the DimPlan dimension style you set up and used in this chapter.

1. Open Cabin04c-addon.dwg. Then use the DesignCenter to bring over the DimPlan dimension style, the Dim text style, the DimPlan Leader multileader style, and the Dim1 layer.

2. Dimension to the outside edges of exterior walls, the edges of the openings, and the center lines of interior walls.

3. Drag a Room_Info block and a room label from the cabin drawing into the garage drawing, and then copy and modify them as required.

4. If the leader does not display properly, check the Overall Scale value in the Properties panel and make sure it is set to 64 (70). When you're done, the drawing should look similar to Figure 12.56.

5. When you're finished, save this drawing as Cabin12d-addon.dwg.

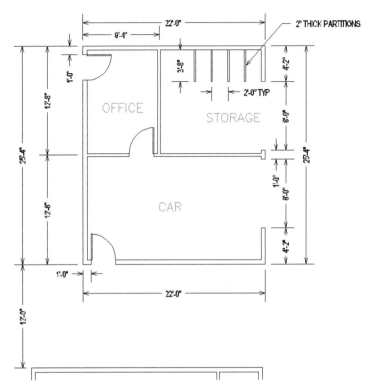

F I G U R E   1 2 . 5 6 : The walkway and garage dimensioned

Dimensioning to a Centerline

This exercise will show you how to use center lines as replacements for extension lines in dimensions. I'll use as many of the default settings for AutoCAD as I can to give you a look at what *out-of-the-box*, or *vanilla*, AutoCAD looks like; that is, how drawings look if you use the default settings for text styles, dimension styles, units, and so forth. The drawing you'll make is similar to the one you made in Chapter 2, but you know so much more now:

1. Choose File ➤ New from the Application menu; then, in the Create New Drawing dialog box, select the acad.dwt template.

2. Start the Rectangle command, and click a point in the lower-left quadrant of the drawing area. For the second point, enter @6,2↵.

3. Turn off the UCS icon, use Zoom To Extents, and then zoom out a bit. Pan to move the new rectangle down a little (see Figure 12.57).

FIGURE 12.57: The rectangle after panning down

You want to dimension from the upper-left corner of the rectangle to the center of the upper horizontal line and then to the upper-right corner. You'll select the Dimension command from the menu bar and use the default dimension settings:

1. Create a new layer called **Dim**, accept the White color, and make Dim current. Set the Endpoint and Midpoint osnaps to be running, and then click the Linear button in the Dimensions panel or in the Annotation panel under the Home tab. Click the upper-left corner of the rectangle, and then click the midpoint of the upper horizontal line of the rectangle. Drag the dimension line up to a point about one unit above the upper line of the rectangle, and click. This places the first dimension.

2. Click the dimension to make grips appear. Click the grip that is at the midpoint of the upper horizontal line of the rectangle, and with polar tracking on, drag it down to a point below the rectangle. Press Esc to deselect the dimension.

3. Click the Continue button, and select the upper-right corner of the rectangle. Doing so places the second dimension. Press Esc to end the command.

4. On the Properties panel, open the Linetype drop-down list and select Other. In the Linetype Manager dialog box, click the Load button.

5. In the Load Or Reload Linetypes dialog box, scroll down, find and click Center2, and then click OK. The Center2 linetype now appears in the Linetype Manager dialog box. Click OK.

6. Double-click the left dimension to open the Properties palette. In the Lines & Arrows rollout, click Ext Line 2 Linetype. Open the drop-down list, and select Center2. Press Esc to deselect the dimension.

7. Select the right dimension. On the Properties palette, return to the Lines & Arrows rollout, and click Ext Line 1 Linetype. Open the drop-down list, and select Center2. Press Esc to close the Properties palette.

Now there is a center line through the rectangle that's part of the dimensions. As a final touch, you'll put a center line symbol at the top of the center line by using the MText command:

1. Start the Multiline Text command, and make a small defining window somewhere in a blank portion of the drawing area.

2. Right-click the drawing area and select Symbol in the context menu that appears, then select Center Line. A center line symbol now appears in the Multiline Text editor. Highlight it, and change its height from 0.2000 to 0.4000 in the Text Height text box in the Text Style panel, as shown in Figure 12.58.

FIGURE 12.58: Changing the height of the center line symbol

 3. With the text still highlighted, click the Justification button in the Paragraph panel. From the fly-out menu that appears, click Bottom Center (see Figure 12.59).

FIGURE 12.59: Setting the Justification for the center line symbol

4. Click the Close Text Editor button in the Close panel to execute the changes and close the Multiline Text tab.

5. Click the center line symbol to activate the grips. Click the lower-middle grip, and then click the upper end of the center line. This locates the symbol properly.

6. Turn off running osnaps, be sure polar tracking is on, and click the same grip you did in the previous step. Move the symbol up slightly to create a space between it and the center line (see Figure 12.60).

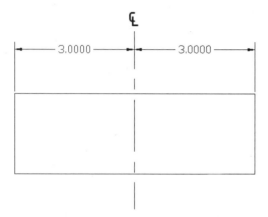

FIGURE 12.60: The center line symbol and a center line used as part of two dimensions

This completes the exercise. You can save the drawing if you wish.

Doing Other Exercises

Use the skills you've learned in this chapter to do the following:

► Set up a dimension style for your own use.

► Dimension a drawing as you would in your own profession or trade.

► Dimension any of the other drawings offered in previous chapters, such as the block, the gasket, or the parking lot.

► Add dimensions to the cabin elevations.

Are You Experienced?

Now you can...

- ☑ create a new dimension style
- ☑ place vertical and horizontal dimensions in a drawing
- ☑ use radial, aligned, and angular dimensions
- ☑ create a multileader style
- ☑ create multileader lines for notes
- ☑ modify dimension text
- ☑ override a dimension style
- ☑ modify a dimension style

CHAPTER 13

Managing External References

- ▶ Understanding external references

- ▶ Creating external references

- ▶ Editing external references

- ▶ Converting external references into blocks

T he floor plan of a complex building project might actually be a composite of several AutoCAD files that are linked together as external references to the current drawing. This enables parts of a drawing to be worked on at different workstations (or in different offices) while remaining linked to a central host file. In mechanical engineering, a drawing might similarly be a composite of the various subparts that make up an assembly.

External references, or *xrefs*, are .dwg files that have been temporarily connected to the current drawing and are used as reference information. The externally referenced drawing is visible in the current drawing. You can manipulate its layers, colors, linetypes, and visibility, and you can modify its objects, but it isn't a permanent part of the current drawing. Changes made to the xref's appearance, such as color or linetype, in the current drawing are not reflected in the xref source drawing.

External references are similar to blocks in that they behave as single objects and are inserted into a drawing in the same way. But blocks are part of the current drawing file, and external references aren't.

Blocks can be exploded back to their component parts, but external references can't; however, external references can be converted into blocks and become permanent parts of the current drawing. In Chapter 7, you were able to modify the window block and, in so doing, update all instances of the window block in the drawing without having to explode the block. With an external reference, you can apply the same updating mechanism. You can also edit an externally referenced drawing while in the drawing that references it. To manage external references, you need to learn how to set up an xref, manipulate its appearance in the host drawing, and update it.

Before you set up the xref, you'll create a site plan for the cabin. You'll then externally reference the site plan drawing into the cabin drawing. In Figure 13.1, the lines of the site plan constitute the xref, and the rest of the objects are part of the host drawing. After these exercises, you'll look at a few ways that design offices use external references.

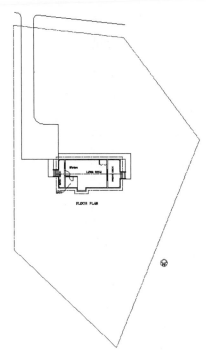

FIGURE 13.1: The cabin with the site plan as an external reference

Drawing a Site Plan

The site plan you'll use has been simplified so that you can draw it with a minimum of steps and get on with the external referencing. The following are the essential elements:

▶ Property lines

▶ Access road to the site

▶ North arrow

▶ Indication of where the building is located on the site

The first step is to draw the property lines.

Using Surveyor's Units

You draw property lines using surveyor's units for angles and decimal feet for linear units. In laying out the property lines, you'll use relative polar coordinates: you'll enter coordinates in the format @*distance*<*angle*, in which the distance is in feet and hundredths of a foot and the angle is in surveyor's units to the nearest minute.

Introducing Surveyor's Units

Surveyor's units, called *bearings* in civil engineering, describe the direction of a line from its beginning point. The direction (bearing), described as a deviation from the north or south toward the east or west, is given as an angular measurement in degrees, minutes, and seconds. The angles used in a bearing can never be greater than 90°, so bearing lines must be headed in one of the four directional quadrants: northeasterly, northwesterly, southeasterly, or southwesterly. If north is set to be at the top of a plot plan, then south is down, east is to the right, and west is to the left. Therefore, when a line from its beginning goes up and to the right, it's headed in a northeasterly direction; when a line from its beginning goes down and to the left, it's headed in a southwesterly direction; and so on. A line that is headed in a northeasterly direction with a deviation from true north of 30° and 30 minutes is shown as N30d30′E in AutoCAD notation. Figure 13.2 shown examples of a line drawn using surveyor's units.

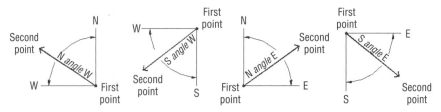

FIGURE 13.2: Drawing a line using surveyor's units

With the surveyor's unit system, a sloping line that has an up-and-to-the-left direction has a down-and-to-the-right direction if you start from the opposite end. So, in laying out property lines, it's important to move in the same direction (clockwise or counterclockwise) as you progress from one segment to the next.

Laying Out the Property Lines

You'll set up a new drawing and then start at the upper-right corner of the property lines, working your way around counterclockwise:

1. Open Cabin12d.dwg from your Training Data folder (or the folder in which your training files are stored). From the Application menu, choose Save As ➢ AutoCAD file, and save the drawing as Cabin13a.dwg.

2. Click the New button on the Quick Access toolbar, and open a new file using the acad.dwt template using the Open With No Template— Imperial option even if your cabin drawing is using decimal units.

   All the units in these first few sections are noted as architectural and, in a later section, I'll show you how to bring in a drawing using a different scale.

3. From the Application menu click Drawing Units ➢ Units to open the Drawing Units dialog box. Change the Precision value in the Length area to two decimal places (0.00).

4. In the Angle area, open the Type drop-down list and select Surveyor's Units. Then change the Precision value to the nearest minute (N 0d00′ E). Your Drawing Units dialog box should look like Figure 13.3. Click OK.

You're using decimal linear units in such a way that 1 decimal unit represents 1 foot. In AutoCAD and LT, the foot symbol (′) is used only with architectural and engineering units.

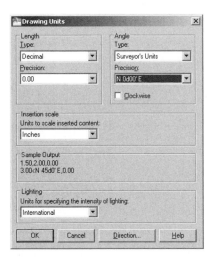

FIGURE 13.3: The Drawing Units dialog box set up to use surveyor's units

You'll need an area of about 250′×150′ for the site plan.

5. From the menu bar, choose Format ➤ Drawing Limits. Press ⏎ to accept the default of 0.00,0.00 for the lower-left corner. Enter **250,150**⏎. Don't use the foot sign.

6. Right-click the Snap Mode button on the status bar and choose Settings. Change Snap Spacing to 10.00, and change Grid Spacing to 0.00. Then select the Grid On check box to turn on the grid, but leave Snap off. Click OK.

7. Enter **z**⏎ **e**⏎ to zoom to the drawing's extents (see Figure 13.4). Your drawing may show a different drawing name in the title bar.

FIGURE 13.4: The site drawing with the grid on

8. Create a new layer called **Prop_Line**. Assign it the color number 172 and make it current.

9. Turn on Dynamic Input in the status bar.

10. Start the Line command. For the first point, enter **220,130**⏎. This starts a line near the upper-right corner of the grid.

11. Be sure Snap is turned off. Then enter the following:

@140<n90dw↵

@90<s42d30′w↵

@140<s67d30′e↵

@80<n52d49′e↵

c↵

The property lines are completed (see Figure 13.5).

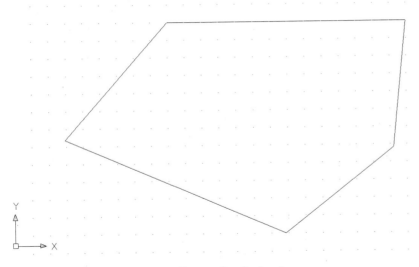

FIGURE 13.5: The property lines on the site drawing

Drawing the Driveway

The driveway is 8′ wide and set in 5′ from the horizontal property line. The access road is 8′ from the parallel property line. The intersection of the access road line and the driveway lines forms corners, each with a 3′ radius. The driveway extends 70′ in from the upper-right corner of the property.

Let's lay this out now:

1. Open the Drawing Units dialog box again. Change the Length units to Architectural and the Angle units to Decimal Degrees. Then set the Length Precision to 0′-0 1/16″ and the angular precision to 0.00. Click OK.

2. Because of the way AutoCAD translates decimal units to inches, your drawing is now only 1/12th the size it needs to be. Use the Distance command, under the Measure drop-down menu on the Utilities panel, and follow the prompts to check it. You'll have to scale it up.

3. Click the Scale button on the Modify panel.

N O T E   You can also start the Scale command by entering sc↵.

4. Enter all↵↵ to select all the objects in the scene. For the base point, enter 0,0↵.

5. At the Specify scale factor or [Copy/Reference]: prompt, enter 12↵. Then click Grid Display on the status bar to turn off the grid.

6. Zoom to the drawing's extents, and then zoom out a little more. The drawing looks the same, but now it's the correct size. Check it with the Distance command, or dimension some of the lines. Delete any dimensions that you make (the value will appear in the Command window).

7. Offset the upper-horizontal property line 5′ down. Offset this new line 8′ down.

8. Offset the rightmost property line 8′ to the right (see the top of Figure 13.6) to show the limits of the access road.

9. Create a new layer called **Road**. Assign it the color White, and make the Road layer current.

10. Select the three new lines, open the Layer drop-down list in the Layers panel, and click the Road layer to move the selected lines to the Road layer. Press Esc to deselect the lines.

11. Extend the driveway lines to the access road line. Trim the access road line between the driveway lines.

12. Fillet the two corners where the driveway meets the road using a 3′ radius (see the bottom of Figure 13.6).

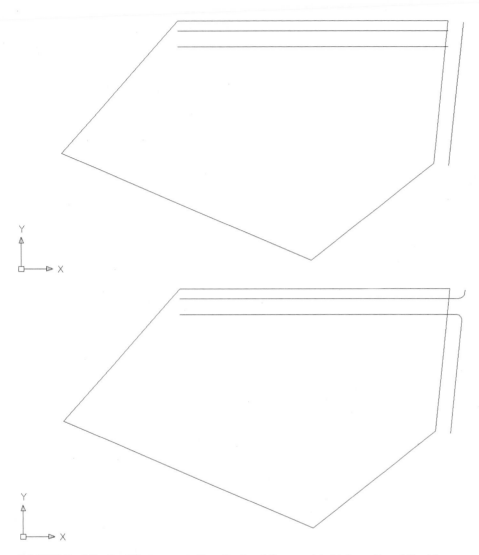

FIGURE 13.6: Offset property lines (top) and the completed intersection of the driveway and access road (bottom)

Finishing the Driveway

A key element of any site plan is information that shows how the building is positioned on the site relative to the property lines. Surveyors stake out property lines. The building contractor then takes measurements off the stakes to locate one or two corners of the building. In this site, you need only one corner because you're assuming the front door of the cabin is facing due east. A close look at Figure 13.1, shown earlier in this chapter, shows that the end of the driveway lines up with the top-rear corner of the cabin. Extending from the driveway are sidewalks that run to the front and rear steps. This locates the cabin on the site (see Figure 13.7).

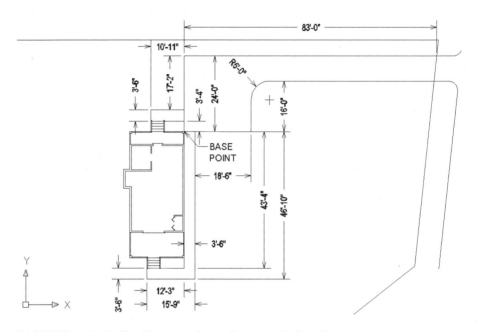

F I G U R E   1 3 . 7 : The driveway and patio lined up with the cabin

Imagine the site being on the bluff of a hill overlooking land that falls away to the south and west, providing a spectacular view in that direction. To accommodate this view, you'll want to change the orientation of the site drawing when you externally reference it into the cabin drawing:

1. On the status bar, turn on Object Snap Tracking and make sure the Endpoint osnap is running. Then start a line with the first point 83′-0″ to the left of the intersection of the upper driveway line and the property line.

2. Draw the line straight down 24′-0″. Draw another line 22′-0″ to the right; then end the Line command.

3. Offset the vertical line 22′-0″ to the right. This will mark the end of the driveway.

4. Fillet the intersection of the upper driveway line and the left vertical line with a radius of 0 and the intersection of the lower driveway line and the right vertical line with a radius of 6'-0" (see Figure 13.8).

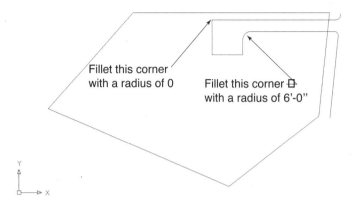

FIGURE 13.8: The completed driveway

5. To draw the rear sidewalk, use object snap tracking to draw a line that starts 3'-4" up from the lower-left corner of the driveway to a point 10'-11" to the left. Continue by drawing a line straight up 3'-6" and then 10'-11" back to the right before you terminate the Line command. See the top of Figure 13.9. You can refer back to Figure 13.7 to see the dimensions if necessary.

6. To draw the side and front sidewalk, start the Line command again. Then pick the lower-left corner of the driveway as the first point.

7. Either use the direct-entry method using the distances below to draw the remaining sidewalk lines, or enter the distances and angles as shown:

43'-4" <270↵

12'-3"<180↵

3'-6"<270↵

15'-9"<0↵

46'-10"<90↵

8. The bottom of Figure 13.9 shows the completed side and front sidewalk. Press ↵ to end the command.

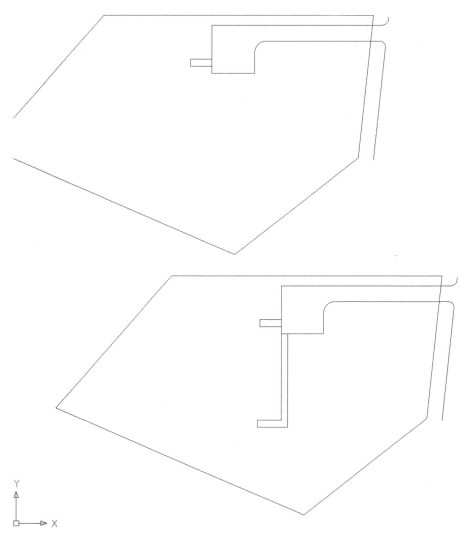

FIGURE 13.9: The first sidewalk (top) and the second sidewalk (bottom)

Adding a North Arrow

We've been identifying east to the right of the cabin and north to the top. Now you'll add a north arrow to identify the directions to anybody looking at your drawing. Here's how:

1. Make Layer 0 current and then open the DesignCenter.

2. Click the Folders tab and then navigate to the Program Files/AutoCAD 2010/Sample/DesignCenter/Landscaping.dwg file. Expand the

drawing contents in the left pane of the DesignCenter. Then click Blocks to display the list of blocks in the right pane.

3. Select the North Arrow block in the right pane, as shown in Figure 13.10.

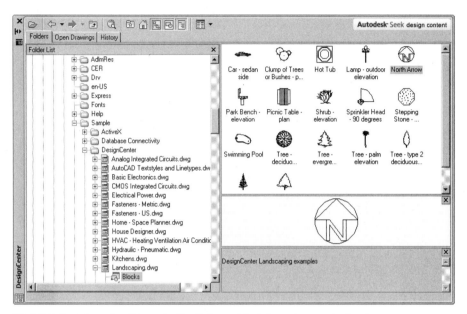

FIGURE 13.10: Select the North Arrow block from the sample drawing.

4. Drag the block into the left side of your drawing, and then close the DesignCenter.

5. The north arrow is a little small, so scale it up to twice its current size and rotate it so that it points to the right.

6. Open the Layer Properties Manager dialog box and change the linetype for the Prop_Line layer to PHANTOM. (You'll have to load this linetype; review Chapter 6 if necessary.)

7. Enter **ltscale⏎**, and then enter **100⏎**. You'll see the PHANTOM linetype for the property lines.

8. Finally, you need to set the base point; that is, the location that will be attached to the cursor when this drawing is inserted as a block or external reference. Type **base⏎**, and click the lower-left corner of the driveway. Refer to Figure 13.7, if necessary. Your drawing should look like Figure 13.11.

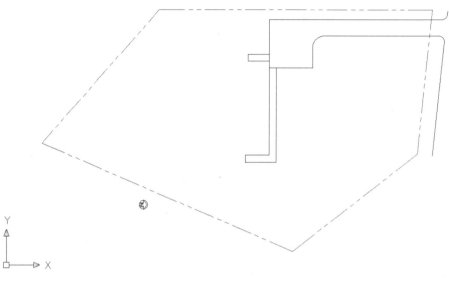

FIGURE 13.11: The completed site plan

9. Save this drawing in your Training Data folder as Site13a.dwg.

This completes the site plan. The next step is to attach the site plan as an external reference into the cabin drawing.

Setting Up an External Reference

When you set up an external reference, you go through a process similar to that of inserting a block into a drawing, as you did in Chapter 7. You select the drawing to be referenced and specify the location of its insertion point. There are options for the X scale factor, Y scale factor, and rotation angle, as there are for inserting blocks. Here, as with blocks, you can set up the command so that it uses the defaults for these options without prompting you for your approval.

Using the External References Palette

You can run all external reference operations through the External References palette, which you can open by clicking the Insert tab and then clicking the External References button on the Reference panel, or by entering xr↵. The External References palette also references image files and DWF or DGN underlay files as well as other AutoCAD drawings. DWF files are image files produced by several Autodesk products and are similar to Adobe PDF files. Files that have the .dgn extension are drawings created with the MicroStation CAD software.

The following two series of steps will guide you through the process of attaching Site13a.dwg to Cabin13a.dwg as an xref:

1. With Cabin13a as the current drawing, zoom to the drawing's extents and then create a new layer called Site. Assign color 162 as the layer color, and make the Site layer current.

2. Click the Insert tab, and then click the External References button at the end of the title bar of the Reference panel to open the External References palette.

3. Click the Attach DWG button in the palette toolbar, as shown in Figure 13.12.

FIGURE 13.12: The Attach DWG button on the External References palette

4. In the Select Reference File dialog box that opens, locate the Training Data folder (or the folder in which your training files are stored), and select Site13a.dwg. A thumbnail image of the drawing appears in the Preview window, as shown in Figure 13.13.

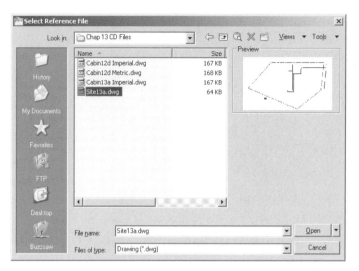

FIGURE 13.13: Select the xref in the Select Reference File dialog box.

5. Click Open to open the External Reference dialog box, and then click the Show Details button in the bottom-left corner to display the reference paths (see Figure 13.14).

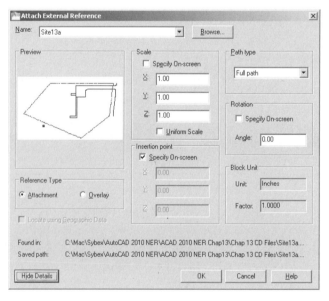

FIGURE 13.14: The External Reference dialog box with Site13a as the named reference

The file being referenced, Site13a, appears in the Name drop-down list at the top of the dialog box, with the full path of the file's location at the bottom. The right side of the dialog box contains three options for the insertion process, which are like those in the Insert dialog box that you used for inserting blocks in Chapter 7. Note that only the insertion point is set to be specified on the screen. The Scale and Rotation options should be set to use their default settings. If they aren't, click the appropriate check boxes so that this dialog box matches that in the previous graphic. Continue as follows:

1. Make sure Attachment is selected in the Reference Type area, and set the path type to Relative Path.

   With the Full Path option selected, the referenced file is located at the absolute path specified and other users of the drawing must have the same file structure. The Relative Path option selects the file from a folder location, relative to the path used by the current file, with the current drawing location at the top of the path structure.

2. Click OK. You return to your drawing, and the site plan drawing appears and moves with the base point attached to the crosshair cursor.

3. Click at the top-left corner of the rear deck post to be the insertion point, and then zoom to the drawing's extents. The xref drawing is attached and appears in the site plan (see Figure 13.15).

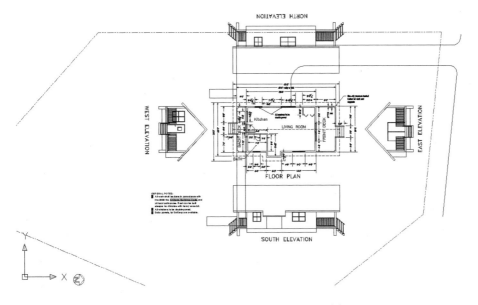

FIGURE 13.15: The Site13a drawing attached to the Cabin13a drawing

Organizing the Drawing Objects

The attached xref appears exactly as it did when it was the current drawing. The drawing is cluttered now, and when you use this file as part of a site plan, or part of the cabin drawing, you don't want all the information to be visible. In fact, you want most of the information to be invisible. You'll accomplish this by freezing many of the layers in the drawing viewports, as explained in the next chapter. For now, you'll just move the elevations and notes out of the site area using a layer state to return to the current layer configuration. Here's how:

1. In the Layers Properties Manager, click the Layer States Manager button, or expand the Layer State drop-down list in the Layers panel and choose Manage Layer States.

2. In the Layer States Manager dialog box, click New and then name this new state: **Plan and Elev No Hatch**.

3. Click OK to close the New Layer State to Save dialog box, and then Close to save the layer state and return to the drawing.

4. Turn on and thaw all the layers.

5. Carefully move the elevations and notes outside of the property line. Figure 13.16 shows the elevations stacked on the right side of the drawing area.

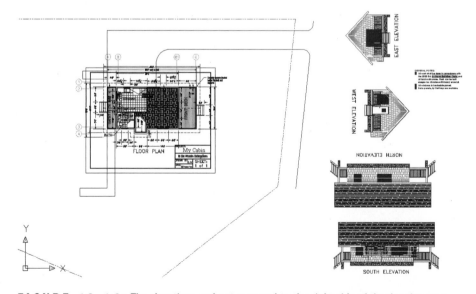

FIGURE 13.16: The elevations and notes moved to the right side of the drawing area

6. Open the Layer States Manager again, select the Plan and Elev No Hatch state, and click the Restore button. The layers return to their conditions when the layer state was saved.

Moving and Rotating an Xref

Now you need to rotate the site plan to match the orientation of the cabin:

1. Freeze the Dim1 layer.

2. Start the Rotate command, click the site plan, and then press ⏎.

3. To specify the insertion point of the xref as the rotation point, activate the Insert object snap, and then click any object from the site plan.

4. At the Specify rotation angle or: prompt, enter 90⏎. The site plan is rotated 90° counterclockwise, matching the orientation of the cabin (see Figure 13.17).

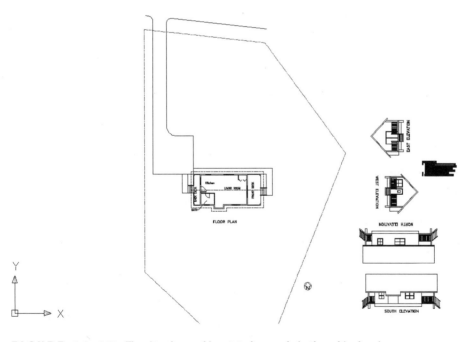

FIGURE 13.17: The site plan xref is rotated properly in the cabin drawing.

You have established Site13a as an external reference in this drawing. The next step is to make revisions to Site13a and see how they are reflected in the host drawing.

Modifying an Xref Drawing

You can modify an xref drawing by making it the current drawing, making the modification, saving the changes, making the host drawing current, and reloading the xref. AutoCAD users can also modify an xref by using a special modification command while the host drawing is current. This section demonstrates both methods. You'll start by opening Site13a.dwg and adjusting the width of the road. Then you'll make Cabin13a current again and use AutoCAD to modify the site plan as an xref, changing the property line and moving the North arrow.

Modifying an Xref by Making It the Current Drawing

The longest part of the driveway is 8'-0" wide, and we want to increase that to 10'-0". You'll make the change in the site plan drawing and then reload it into the cabin drawing:

1. With Site13a as the current drawing, zoom in to the area that includes the road and the driveway.

2. Offset the lower road line 2' downward, as shown in the top of Figure 13.18.

3. Fillet the right side with a radius of 3' and the left at 6'.

4. Delete the original line and radii. Your driveway is now 10' wide, as shown in the bottom of Figure 13.18.

FIGURE 13.18: Offset the lower driveway line (above), fillet the new lines, and delete the existing radii (next page).

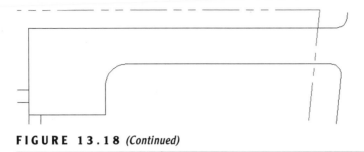

FIGURE 13.18 *(Continued)*

5. Save the Site13a drawing.

Although you'll make more later, this concludes the modifications you'll make to the site plan in this exercise. Now you can return to the cabin drawing.

6. Switch to the Cabin13a file. A balloon message appears at the bottom of the AutoCAD window (see Figure 13.19), pointing to the Manage Xrefs icon in the tool tray. This indicates that an externally referenced drawing has been saved after it was attached to the current drawing. You could click the blue link text to reload the file, but for this exercise, you will look at the External References palette and reload it from there.

FIGURE 13.19: The balloon message indicating the xref has changed

7. Open the External References palette, as shown in Figure 13.20, and stretch it to make it wider. The palette shows most of the pertinent information regarding the externally referenced files in the scene, including the status. When you pause the cursor over a reference, a cue card appears displaying a thumbnail image and additional information about that file. In this case, the palette indicates that Site13a needs reloading.

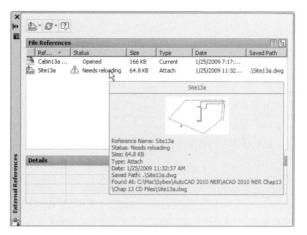

FIGURE 13.20: The External References palette showing the status of the xrefs

8. Select the Site13a xref in the palette, right-click, and choose Reload from the context menu. This causes AutoCAD to reevaluate the external reference and update the current drawing. The cabin drawing now shows the 10′-wide access road from the site plan drawing (see Figure 13.21).

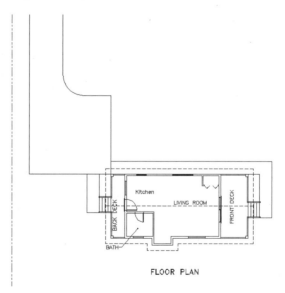

FIGURE 13.21: The cabin drawing with the updated site plan xref

9. Close the Site13a file, but leave the Cabin13a file open.

10. Save the cabin drawing as Cabin13b.dwg.

In this exercise, you saw how a host drawing is updated when the drawing that is externally referenced is made current, modified, saved, and then reloaded as an xref. Layers become an even more important tool when using external references. You can set them up one way in the actual drawing and another way in the xref of that drawing in a host file. In fact, you can externally reference the same drawing into any number of host files; have the layer characteristics of visibility, color, and linetype be different in each host file; and save them as such with each host file. External referencing is a powerful feature of AutoCAD, and you'll learn more about the possible applications of this tool toward the end of this chapter.

Modifying an Xref from Within the Host Drawing

In Chapter 7, you used the Xref And Block In-Place Editing tool to update the window block. You can use the same tool here for editing an xref while the host drawing is the current drawing. You can't create a new layer with this tool, but many of the regular editing commands are available when you use it. You'll make a few modifications to the site plan xref to illustrate this feature.

1. In the Cabin13b file, make Layer 0 current.

2. Zoom in to see the cabin and the lower portion of the property line (see Figure 13.22).

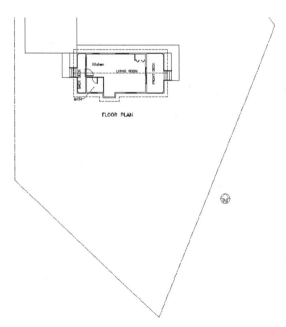

FIGURE 13.22: The cabin and the lower portion of the property line

N O T E   The Edit In-Place command edits both blocks and xrefs. So, in Auto-CAD's technical vocabulary for this command and its prompts, both blocks and xrefs are referred to as *references*.

3. Click the Insert tab and click the Edit Reference button in the expanded Reference panel. You're prompted to select the reference to edit. Click any object from the site plan xref. Alternatively, you can double-click the xref directly instead of accessing the tool from the Ribbon.

4. The Reference Edit dialog box opens (see Figure 13.23). On the Identify Reference tab, Site13a is listed as the selected xref with the North Arrow blocks shown as a nested reference. A preview window illustrates the xref drawing.

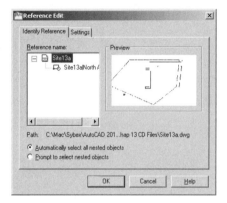

FIGURE 13.23: The Reference Edit dialog box

5. Click OK. The Edit Reference panel appears at the right end of the Ribbon.

W A R N I N G   If you have the AutoSave tool set to save your drawing automatically periodically (Application menu ➢ Options ➢ Open and Save ➢ File Safety Precautions ➢ Automatic Save or savetime↵), this feature is disabled during reference editing.

You're now free to use many of the Draw and Modify commands on the site plan drawing that you just selected.

6. Open the Layer Properties Manager, and notice that several new layers now appear.

At the top are 0Prop_Line and 0Road, and lower in the list are Site-RefEdit0, Site13a|Prop_Line and Site13a|Road. The layer names separated by the pipe (|) symbol indicate that these are layers from the externally referenced Site13 drawing and are referred to as *xref-dependent*. Site13|Prop_Line and Site13a|Road appear in the Layer Properties Manager even when you are not editing an xref in-place. One restriction in the layer tools is that you can't make an xref-dependent layer current in the host drawing. The layers at the top of dialog box, the ones with the $ symbols, are temporary and will hold any objects created on them in the editing session and then shift those objects to the proper xref layer at the conclusion of the editing session.

7. Make the 0Prop_Line layer current, and then offset the lower-right diagonal property line 10'-0" (3048 mm) to the right (see Figure 13.24).

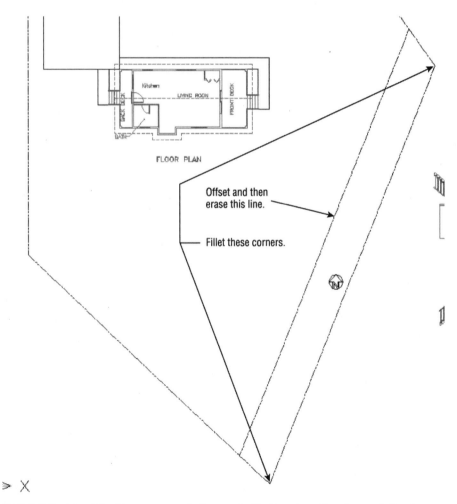

FIGURE 13.24: The new property line created in the externally referenced site plan

8. Fillet the two lines that intersected with the line you just offset to the newly created line using a radius of 0. Erase the original line (see Figure 13.24).

9. Select the North arrow and move it closer to the floor plan, just to the right of the label.

10. Expand the Edit Reference panel, and click the Save Changes button.

   When the warning dialog box opens, click OK. Your changes to the site plan are now saved back to the Site13a file and the Edit In-Place tool is terminated.

11. Use Zoom To Extents, and then zoom out a little to a view of the whole site (see Figure 13.25). Save this drawing. It's still named Cabin13b.dwg.

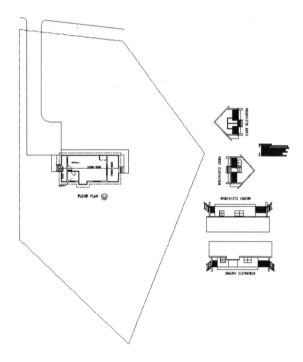

FIGURE 13.25: The Site13b drawing with the revised xref of the site plan

In this exercise, you saw how a host drawing is updated when its external reference is changed and how you can control the appearance of objects in the xref drawing from the host drawing by working with the xref-dependent layers. You also saw how you can modify objects in the xref from the host drawing by using the in-place xref editing tool. A drawing can serve as an external reference in several host drawings at the same time and have a different appearance in each one, including location, rotation, and scale. The results of in-place xref editing, however, must be saved back to the original drawing in order to be viewed in the xref. In-place xref editing is usually done only when the results are meant to be permanent changes in the original source drawing.

Adding an Image to a Drawing

Not only can you externally reference other drawing files into the current drawing, but you can also reference image files. Using this feature, you can add digital photographs or scanned images, such as artist renderings and construction forms, to a drawing. The procedure is similar to adding an externally referenced drawing; just follow these steps:

1. Create a new layer named **Image**, make it current, and then open the External References palette.

2. Right-click a blank area in the File References area below the existing filenames, and choose Attach Image from the context menu to open the Select Image File dialog box. You can also click the down arrow next to the Attach DWG button and choose Attach Image from the context menu.

3. Most of the common image file formats are compatible with AutoCAD 2010. Navigate to the file that you want to attach, and then click the Open button (see Figure 13.26). A .jpg file is included with the files on this book's web page, www.sybex.com/go/autocad2010ner.

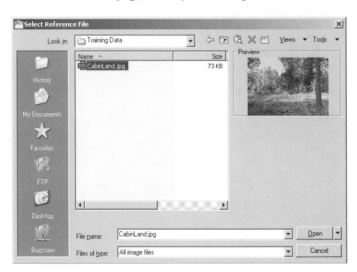

FIGURE 13.26: Selecting the image to be referenced in the Select Reference File dialog box

T I P   When you select an image file, a preview appears in the Select Reference File dialog box. You can use the arrow buttons on the keyboard to change the selection and associated preview image quickly.

4. In the Attach Image dialog box that opens, similar to the External Reference dialog box that you saw earlier in this chapter, select Relative Path and the path type. Check the Specify On-Screen options for both Scale and Insertion point (see Figure 13.27), and then click OK.

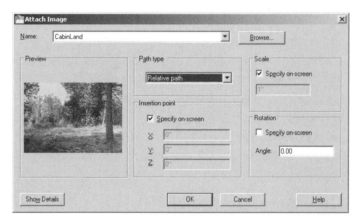

FIGURE 13.27: Select Relative Path and the path type in the Attach Image dialog box.

5. In the drawing area, click once to designate the lower-left corner of the image, move the cursor, and then click again to create the rectangular frame for the image. The image appears inside the frame (see Figure 13.28). The exact size and location of the frame are unimportant for this exercise, so ignore them for now. In the next chapter, you will decide how to view the image in the context of the rest of the drawing.

FIGURE 13.28: Placing the referenced image in the drawing

The imageframe variable determines the visibility of the image frame and how it reacts when clicked. Setting the variable to 0 (zero) causes the frame to be invisible and also prevents the image from being selected or edited. Setting the variable to 1 displays the frame, allows it to be selected, and also shows the frame when the drawing is plotted (plotting is covered in Chapter 15). Setting imageframe to 2 displays the frame in the viewport and allows it to be selected, but does not show the frame when the drawing is plotted. This variable affects all the images in the drawing.

6. Enter imageframe↵2↵ to set the variable to 2.

7. Save the cabin drawing as Cabin13c.dwg, and then close the file.

That's all there is to adding images to AutoCAD drawings. You can move and rotate the image using the same tools as with any other object. You can resize the image by selecting the frame and adjusting the grips. You get access to some rudimentary image-editing tools when you double-click the image frame. Feel free to experiment with them, but do not be concerned about altering the image file; these adjustments affect only the image's display inside AutoCAD.

Putting Xrefs to Use

External references have many different uses. I'll describe two common applications to illustrate their range.

Suppose you're working on a project as an interior designer and a subcontractor to the lead architect. The architect gives you a drawing of a floor plan that is still undergoing changes. You load this file onto your hard drive in a specially designated folder, and then you externally reference it into your drawing as a background—a drawing to be used as a reference to draw over. You can now proceed to lay out furniture, partitions, and so on while the architect is still refining the floor plan.

At an agreed-on time, the architect gives you a revised version of the floor plan. You overwrite the one that you have on your computer with the latest version. You can then reload the xref into your furniture layout drawing, and the newer version of the floor plan will be the background. In this example, the lead architect might also send the same versions of the floor plan to the structural and mechanical engineers and the landscape architect, all of whom are working on the project and using the architect's floor plan as an xref in their respective host drawings (see Figure 13.29).

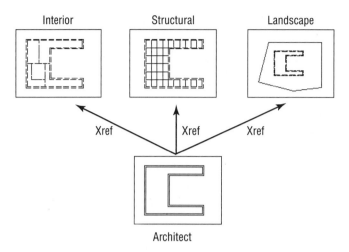

FIGURE 13.29: A single floor plan as an xref to three subcontractors

Xrefs are often used when parts of a job are being done in an office where a network is in place. Suppose a project involves work on several buildings that are all on the same site. If the project uses xrefs, each building can be externally referenced to the site plan. This keeps the site plan drawing file from getting too large and allows the project work to be divided among different workstations; in addition, the project manager can open the host site plan and keep track of progress on the whole project (see Figure 13.30).

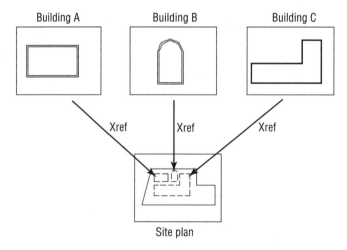

FIGURE 13.30: Three buildings as xrefs to a single site plan

These two applications for setting up xrefs in relation to a host file are applicable to almost any profession or trade using AutoCAD.

Exploring Additional Xref Features

You have seen how you can modify an xref in the host or the original drawing and how to bring in images. A few other features of external references deserve mention.

Setting the Xref Path

When you attach an xref to the host drawing, AutoCAD stores the name of the xref and its path.

N O T E   The path of a drawing file is the name of the drive, folder, and subfolder where a file is stored, followed by the name of the drawing.

Each time you open the host drawing, AutoCAD searches for any xrefs saved with the host file and displays them in the host drawing. If the xref drawing is moved to a new folder after the xref has been attached to a host, AutoCAD won't be able to find the xref and can't display it. To avoid that situation, you must update the host drawing with the new path to the xref file. Let's go through a quick exercise to illustrate how this works:

1. Use Windows Explorer to create a new subfolder called Xref within the Training Data folder you previously set up. Move Site13a.dwg to this folder.

2. Return to AutoCAD, and open Cabin13c.dwg again. The xref doesn't show up, and the References—Unresolved Reference Files dialog box opens (see Figure 13.31).

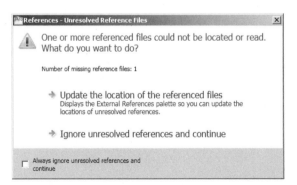

FIGURE 13.31: References—Unresolved Reference Files dialog box

AutoCAD is unable to find the xref because the path has changed.

3. Click the Update the Location Of The Referenced Files option to open the External References palette.

4. In the File References area where xrefs are listed, the path appears for each xref under the heading Saved Path (see Figure 13.32). The ".\" preceding the filename indicates that the current file path is relative and in the same folder as the current drawing. You can slide the scroll bar to the right—or widen the palette—to see the full path. Notice also that the Status column for this xref reads "Not Found."

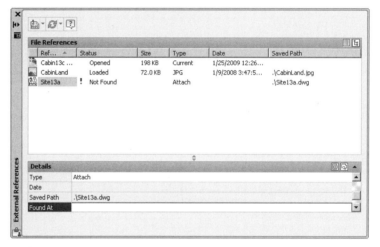

FIGURE 13.32: The missing xref is identified in the External References palette.

5. Click the Site13a xref to highlight it. Move down to the Details area, and click the blank space to the right of Found At. A button with three dots appears at the right end of the blank space.

6. Click the button. This opens the Select New Path dialog box. Find the Site13a drawing in the new Xref folder. Highlight it and click Open.

7. Back in the External References palette, the path has been updated to reflect the current location for Site13a. Move or minimize the palette and then perform a Zoom Extents. You can see that the xref is restored in your drawing.

W A R N I N G   When you're working with xrefs, be careful where you store files that are acting as xrefs to other files. All the files' paths must remain valid for the xrefs to be located.

Binding Xrefs

On occasion, you'll want to attach an xref to the host drawing permanently. If you send your drawing files to a printing service to be plotted, including a set of xref files can complicate things. Also, for archiving finished work, it might be better to reduce the number of files. There might also be occasions when the xref has been revised for the last time and no longer needs to be a separate file. In all these situations, you'll use the Bind command to convert an external reference into a block that is stored permanently in the host drawing:

1. In the External References palette, right-click Site13a in the File References list.

2. Choose Bind from the context menu to open the Bind Xrefs dialog box (see Figure 13.33).

FIGURE 13.33: The Bind Xrefs dialog box

The two options in the Bind Type area have to do with how layers are treated when an xref is bound to the host drawing. The default is Bind. It sets the xref layers to be maintained as unique layers in the host drawing. With the Insert option, layers that have the same name in the two drawings are combined into one layer. None of the layers in Site13a has the same name as any layers in Cabin13c. Let's use the Insert option.

3. Change the Bind Type to Insert and click OK. The xref disappears from the File References list.

4. Close the External References palette. Your drawing looks unchanged.

5. Click the site plan, and then open the Properties palette. The field at the top of the palette identifies the site plan as a block reference, as shown in Figure 13.34.

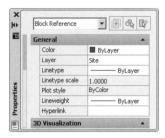

FIGURE 13.34: The top of the Properties palette with the former xref selected

6. Open the Layer Properties Manager. Figure 13.35 shows that the site plan's layers have all become layers in the Cabin13c drawing and no longer have the Site13a| prefix.

FIGURE 13.35: The Layer Properties manager showing the new layers

7. Click the Insert button in the Block panel. In the Insert dialog box, open the Name drop-down list. Site13a is listed here as a block, along with the window and door blocks that you created in Chapter 7 and the grid and north arrow blocks. A few additional blocks might be on the list. These blocks are used by the dimensions in the drawing.

8. Close the drop-down list by clicking a blank portion of the dialog box. Then click Cancel to return to your drawing. The site plan is now a permanent part of the Cabin13c drawing. If you need to make changes to the site plan part of the drawing, you can explode it and use the Modify commands. Or, you can use the In-Place Xref and Block Edit tool that you used previously in Chapter 7 to modify the window block.

9. You do not want to save the changes in this drawing. Click the Close button in the top-right corner of the drawing area, and then click No in the dialog box that opens.

10. Move the Site13a file back into the Training Data folder where it was prior to starting the exercises in the "Exploring Additional Xref Features" section.

This has been a quick tour of the basic operations used to set up and control external references. There are more features and commands for working with xrefs than I've covered here, but you now know enough to start working with them.

Exploring Other Xref Features

What follows are a few additional operations and features that you might find useful when you delve more deeply into external references. Play around a little, and see what you can do:

▶ Externally referenced drawings can also be hosts and have drawings externally referenced to them. These are called *nested* xrefs. There is no practical limit to the number of levels of nested xrefs that a drawing can have.

▶ You can't explode an xref, but you can detach it from the host. The Detach command is on the context menu that appears when you right-click an xref in the External References palette.

▶ Large, complex drawings that are externally referenced often have their insertion points coordinated in such a way that all xrefs are attached at the 0,0 point of the host drawing. This helps keep drawings aligned properly. By default, any drawing that is externally referenced into a host drawing uses 0,0 as its insertion point. However, you can change the coordinates of the insertion point with the Base command. With the drawing you want to change current, enter base↵ and enter the coordinates for the new insertion point.

▶ You can limit which layers, and to some degree, which objects in a drawing are externally referenced in the host drawing by using indexing and demand loading.

▶ A host drawing can be externally referenced into the drawing that has been externally referenced into the host, causing a circular reference. This is called an *overlay* and is an option in the Attach Xref dialog box. Overlays ignore circular xrefs.

▶ If you freeze the layer that was current when an xref was attached, the entire xref is frozen. Turning off this same layer has no effect on the visibility of the xref.

▶ The Unload option, available when you right-click a reference in the External References palette, lets you deactivate xrefs without detaching them from the host file. They stay on the list of xrefs and can be reloaded at any time with the Reload option. This option can be useful when you're working with complex drawings that have many xrefs.

If You Would Like More Practice...

In this chapter, you externally referenced the site plan drawing into the cabin drawing as an architect who was designing the project might have done. If you were the architect, you might want to have several additional drawings. Try doing this:

1. Create several new drawings of furniture and a shed. Each object is to have its own layer. Make more than one drawing for some of the objects, such as two beds or tables.

2. Add digital images on their own layers that show real-world examples of the furniture.

3. Externally reference all the furniture and shed drawings into the cabin drawing.

4. Use the Layer States Manager, as covered in Chapter 6, to create layer states for each combination of furniture.

Are You Experienced?

Now you can...

☑ **draw a basic site plan**

☑ **use surveyor's units to lay out a property line**

☑ **attach an external reference**

☑ **revise a drawing that is externally referenced**

☑ **modify an xref from the host drawing**

☑ **insert image files into an AutoCAD drawing**

☑ **update an xref path**

☑ **bind an xref to a host file**

CHAPTER 14

Using Layouts to Set Up a Print

- ▶ Putting a title block in a layout
- ▶ Setting up viewports in a layout
- ▶ Locking the display of viewports
- ▶ Controlling visibility in viewports
- ▶ Adding text in a layout

Chapter 13 introduced external references, which are useful and powerful tools for viewing a second drawing from within the current drawing. In this chapter, you'll learn to use external references in Layout display mode, which will allow you to get even more mileage out of them. External references help you combine several drawings into a composite; layouts allow you to set up and print several views of the same file. The layout is a view of your drawing as it will sit on a sheet of paper when printed.

Each layout has a designated printer and paper size for the print. You adjust the positioning of the drawing and the scale of the print. The part that is difficult to understand is the way two scales are juxtaposed in the same file: the scale of the drawing on the printed paper (usually a standard scale used by architects, such as 3/16″ or ¼″ = 1′-0″ (or 1 = 60), and the scale of the layout, which is almost always 1:1, or the actual size of the paper. Other professionals, such as mechanical or civil engineers, set up their drawings the same way. They may use a different set of standard scales for the drawing on the printed paper, but the layout almost always remains 1:1.

One way to visualize how a layout works is to think of it as a second drawing, or a specialized layer, that has been laid over the top of your current drawing. Each layout that you create will have one or more viewports—special windows through which you will view your project at a scale to be printed. The layouts are usually at a scale of 1:1 (actual size) and contain some of the information that you originally included with the building lines, such as the border and title block, notes, the scale, North arrow, and so on.

Think for a moment about drawing the floor plan of a building on a traditional drafting table. You draw the building to a scale such as 3/16″ = 1′-0″ (1 = 60). Then, on the same sheet of paper, you print a note using letters that are, say, 3/16″ (5 mm) high. If you looked at those letters as being on the same scale as the building, they would measure 1′ (300 mm) high, and that's what we've been doing on the cabin drawing so far. But in traditional drafting, you don't think that way; instead, you work with two scales in the drawing without thinking about it. So a letter is 3/16″ (5 mm) high (actual size), and a part of the building that measures 3/16″ (5 mm) on the paper is thought of as being 1′ (300 mm) long, at a scale of 3/16″ = 1′-0″ (1 = 60). Layouts are designed to let you juggle two or more scales in a drawing in the same way in order to set up the drawing to be printed.

Setting Up Layouts

You will begin working with Cabin13c.dwg, the complete cabin drawing so far. All the layers will be turned on and thawed, and you will use layouts to control the layer visibility (see Figure 14.1). This drawing is essentially complete and ready to print. For now, you will modify this drawing and create layouts for it to get a basic understanding of what layouts are and how they are activated and set up. Then, in the next chapter, you'll print this drawing both with and without a layout.

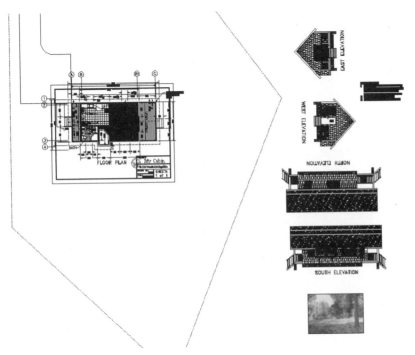

FIGURE 14.1: Cabin13c.dwg **with all layers visible**

In setting up a new layout, you will use an 8.5″×11″ (210 mm×297 mm) sheet:

1. Open Cabin13c.dwg, and thaw the Tblk1 layer. Notice the border of the drawing and the rectangle just outside the border that represents the edge of the sheet of paper on which the print will be made. You will recall from Chapter 8 that when you constructed the border and title block for this drawing, you had to calculate the size of the border for a scale of 3/16″ = 1′-0″ (1 = 70). This was based on a rectangle 58′ (17,700 mm) wide by 45′ (13,700) high, which you then offset 2′ (610 mm) to make the border. With layouts, you don't have to make this kind of calculation; you draw the border actual size.

2. To ensure that your system looks like the one described here, you'll turn off the layout tabs if they're turned on. From the Application menu, click Options and then click the Display tab of the Options dialog box. Make sure the Display Layout and Model Tabs option in the Layout Elements area is unchecked.

3. Before creating a new layout, you should set the AutoCAD interface to display the layouts easily. Right-click an empty area on the status bar and click Paper/Model to turn on this option, if necessary, as shown in Figure 14.2.

F I G U R E 1 4 . 2 : Turn on the Paper/Model option in the context menu.

The Model and Layout buttons appear in the middle of the status bar. Clicking these buttons is how you quickly switch between displaying a layout and looking at model space, which is the way you have been using AutoCAD up to this point.

Each layout has settings that spell out which plotting device is to be used to print the layout and how the print will appear. You specify these settings through a page setup that becomes associated with the layout. See the sidebar "Understanding Model Space and Paper Space" later in this chapter for a more in-depth understanding of the concepts.

N O T E   I use the terms *print* and *plot* interchangeably in this book, as I do *printer* and *plotter*. In the past, *plot* and *plotter* referred to large-format devices and media, but that's not necessarily true today. Print and printing are more widely used now because of changes in the technology of the large-format devices.

4. Click the Layout button in the status bar (the tooltip reads "Layout1") to switch from model space to view the drawing through the layout. The appearance of the drawing area changes to show your cabin inside a white rectangle, sitting in front of a gray background.

Your drawing has two borders along the perimeter of the white rectangle (one dashed and one solid). If the UCS icon consists of two arrows inside the solid border (see the top of Figure 14.3), then you are currently working in model space. If the UCS icon is shaped like a triangle and located in the portion of the drawing area (see the bottom of Figure 14.3), then you are currently working in paper space. The solid line is the boundary to the viewport, and the dashed line is the limit of the printable area.

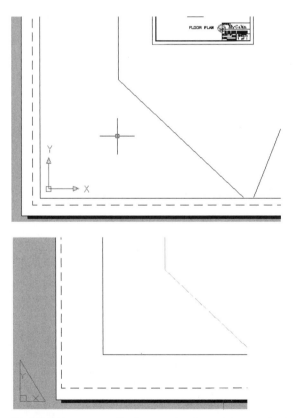

FIGURE 14.3: The layout when in model space (top) and when in paper space (bottom)

5. If you are in model space, move your cursor outside of the inner, solid rectangle and double-click, or enter **ps↵** to switch to paper space.

Setting the Layout Parameters

The paper shown—that is, the white rectangle—is the default size and orientation for the ACAD.dwt template. You'll need to set the parameters to match your printer.

1. Click the Quick View Layouts button next to the Layout button in the status bar to turn on the option. Small thumbnail representations of the existing layouts appear at the bottom of the drawing area, as shown in Figure 14.4.

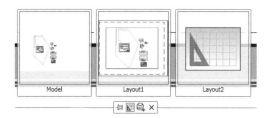

FIGURE 14.4: The drawing's layouts shown using the Quick View Layouts tool

This chapter is designed so that you can follow along even if you don't have a printer hooked up to your computer or if your printer isn't the one referred to in the text. Substitute the parameters specific to your printer where appropriate.

2. Place the cursor over the Layout1 thumbnail. It turns blue and two icons appear within its frame to indicate that any changes will affect that layout only.

3. Right-click, and then click the Page Setup Manager option in the context menu. After a moment, the Page Setup Manager dialog box opens (see the top of Figure 14.5). This is where you create a new page setup, or assign an existing one, to be associated with a new or selected layout.

4. Click New to open the New Page Setup dialog box. In the New Page Setup Name text box, enter **Cabin Floor Plan** and click OK.

5. This opens the Page Setup dialog box, which has Layout1 added to the title bar (see the bottom of Figure 14.5). The dialog box has 10 areas containing settings that control how the drawing will fit on the printed page and what part of the drawing is printed.

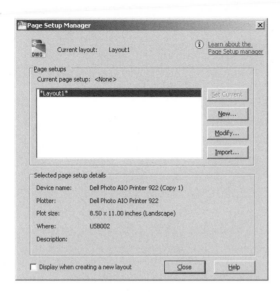

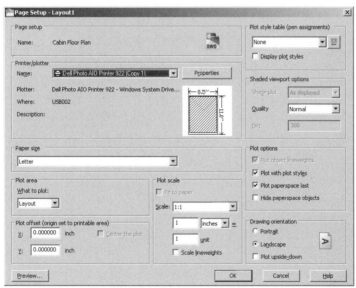

FIGURE 14.5: The Page Setup Manager dialog box (top) and the Page Setup dialog box (bottom)

6. In the Paper Size area, be sure the drop-down list is set to Letter (A4). In the Printer/Plotter area, Dell Photo AIO Printer 922 (Copy 1) is the selected printer here, but yours will likely be different. (If you have not created a page setup previously, None will be selected.) If your computer is linked to more than one printer, make sure you choose a printer that takes 8.5″×11″ (210 mm×297 mm) paper.

To open the Plotter Configuration Editor dialog box (see Figure 14.6), click the Properties button next to the Name drop-down list. Click the Device And Document Settings tab. In the upper area, highlight Modify Standard Paper Sizes (Printable Area). In the Modify Standard Paper Sizes area below, scroll down to Letter (A4) size and highlight it. At the bottom of this area are displays of data about the Letter sheet size including, in the example, Printable Area: 7.94″×10.34″ (201.6 mm×280.3 mm) in this case. This shows the maximum area that your printer can print on an 8.5″×11″ (210 mm×297 mm) sheet of paper and thus gives you an idea of how close to the edge of the paper the printer will print. Jot down the printable area. Yours may be different.

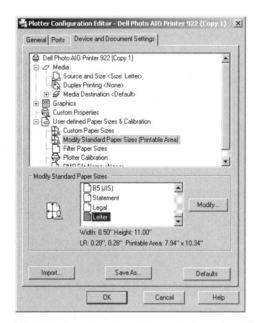

F I G U R E   1 4 . 6 : The Plotter Configuration Editor dialog box

Click Cancel to close this dialog box.

UNDERSTANDING MODEL SPACE AND PAPER SPACE

So far in this book, you have been drawing in model space. You have created all the drawing's information—lines, dimensions, text, the title block, and so on—in model space. In most production environments, everything that must be drawn to scale is placed in model space and other items, such as the title block, are placed in paper space, or the space that resides in the layout tabs. Think of *model space* as the real world where everything is drawn at full scale.

Paper space is located outside of the model space world and is the size of the paper on which you intend to plot the drawing. While in paper space, you can look into model space through a window called a *viewport*. The appearance of the objects seen through the viewport is determined by the viewport scale. At a 3/16″ = 1′(1 = 70) viewport scale, all model space objects seen through the view appear at 1/64th (1/70th) their drawn size. Each viewport can be set to its own scale.

While you are in a paper space layout, you can draw and edit objects in either paper space or in model space through the viewport. While you are in model space, you can only draw and edit in model space.

---

7. Back in the Page Setup dialog box, move to the Drawing Orientation area (lower-right corner) and select Landscape.

8. Under Plot Area, you'll see a drop-down list with four options for selecting which portion of the drawing area is to be plotted. Be sure that Layout is selected.

9. In the Plot Scale area, the scale to be used is 1:1. If it's not already selected, open the Scale drop-down list and select 1:1 from the list of preset scale choices.

10. In the Page Setup area (upper-left corner), Cabin Floor Plan appears as the current page setup. You'll ignore the other areas of this dialog box for now.

11. Click OK. You are returned to the Page Setup Manager dialog box. Cabin Floor Plan is now on the Page Setups list.

The Scale drop-down list contains several preset scales and a Custom option. To delete unnecessary scales, add new ones, edit existing ones, or rearrange the order of the listing, choose Format ➣ Scale List from the Menu bar or enter scalelistedit↵ to open the Edit Scale List dialog box.

12. Highlight Cabin Floor plan, and click Set Current. The layout area behind the dialog box changes to match the parameters you set in the Page Setup dialog box. Click Close to close the Page Setup Manager dialog box. You are returned to your drawing, and Layout1 appears (see Figure 14.7).

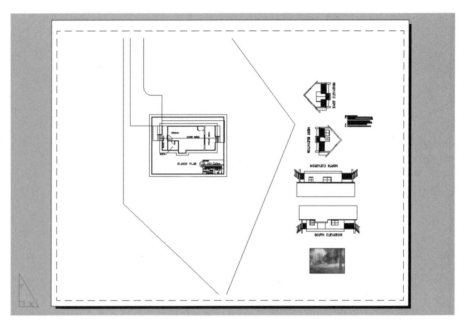

FIGURE 14.7: Layout1 for the cabin

13. You don't want the current viewport, the window that lets you see your drawing from the layout. You will make your own shortly. Make sure that you're in paper space, then enter e↵ all↵ to select all the objects in the layout. In the Command window, you can see that the only the viewport is selected. Press ↵ to erase the viewport. Everything disappears, but don't worry—your cabin drawing is intact.

14. Save your drawing as Cabin14a.dwg.

With the way I have set up AutoCAD for this book, the drawing area now displays a white sheet of paper resting on a gray background. You'll be changing two elements in the layout: you'll cut a new viewport and move the title block into the layout. The viewport creates a hole, or a window, in the layout so that you can see through the layout to the drawing of the building. You can think of the building as residing "underneath" the layout. Near the outer edge of the white rectangle is a rectangle of dashed lines. This represents the 7.94″×10.34″ (201.6 mm×280.3 mm) printable area of your printer. Everything within the dashed border will be printed.

 To work on the cabin itself, you need to move the cursor into model space. You can do this in two ways. One way is to click the Model button. This temporarily removes the layout and leaves you with just the drawing, or model. The other way is to switch to model space while a layout is active. You'll try that method now.

Creating the Paper Space Viewport

Now that the original viewport has been deleted, you need to be able to view the model hidden behind it. You will do this by creating a new viewport that won't show up when you plot the drawing. Here's how:

1. Open the Layer Properties Manager, create a new layer named **VP**, assign it the color red, and make VP the current layer.

 2. Click the printer icon in the Plot column to set this as a nonplotting layer. You want to be able to see the viewport objects on the screen, but you don't want to see them in prints of the drawings.

 A red circle with a line through it appears near the icon to indicate that objects on the layer will not plot.

> **T I P**   It's useful to assign the layer on which you place your viewport a color that will stand out in your drawing, so you are reminded that the viewports, while essential parts of the drawing, are usually designed to be invisible.

---

 3. Click the View tab and then, in the Viewports panel, click the New button.

4. In the Viewports dialog box that opens, click the New Viewports tab and then, in the Standard Viewports window, select Single (see Figure 14.8) and click OK.

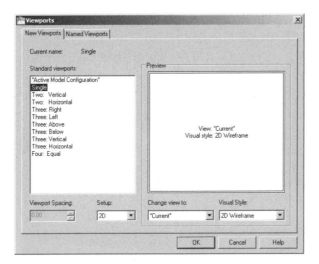

FIGURE 14.8: The Viewports dialog box

5. At the Specify First Corner: prompt, click a point near the upper-left corner of the layout, just inside the dashed rectangle.

6. At the Specify Opposite Corner: prompt, click a point near the lower-right corner of the layout. Your cabin drawing appears in the new viewport (see Figure 14.9).

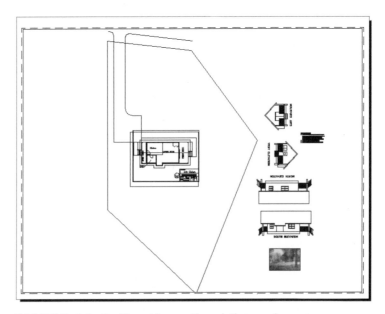

FIGURE 14.9: The cabin seen through the new viewport

7. Place your cursor over an object inside the cabin, click just once, and then move the cursor. Rather than selecting the object, you began a selection window. Drag the window around some of the objects near the cabin, and then click again. Nothing is selected.

8. Move the cursor over both the white and gray areas of the drawing window and notice how the crosshairs appear over both.

This informs you that you are currently working in paper space and can select only paper space objects such as the viewport (once you move them into paper space in the next section), the title block, and border. To work on the cabin itself, you need to change to model space. You can do this in two ways. One is to click the Model button. This temporarily removes the layout and leaves you with just the drawing, or model. The other way is to switch to model space while a layout is active.

When you activate model space while a layout is active, it is like opening a window and reaching through the opening to touch the drawing of the building behind the window.

9. Place your cursor within the viewport area and this time double-click. The viewport border becomes bolder and, when you move the cursor beyond the viewport, the cursor changes from a crosshair to an arrow. You are now in model space and are able to select the model space objects, but not any objects that reside in paper space.

N O T E   You can control the visibility of the UCS icon in each viewport and in paper space by clicking the View tab and then clicking the arrow at the right end of the Coordinates pane's title bar to open the UCS dialog box. In the dialog box, click the On option in the Settings tab.

10. Double-click the cursor outside of the viewport. The crosshair cursor returns, and you are back in paper space.

T I P   You can also click the MODEL button in the middle of the status bar to move from model space to paper space. When you are in paper space, this button changes to PAPER, and it will toggle you back to the current model space viewport.

Moving the Border to the Layout

You have already created the title block in model space, so you just need to move it to the layout. As in any other Windows program, you can use the cut, copy, and paste tools to move objects between model and paper space.

There is also the Change Space tool for the specific purpose of moving objects from within a viewport to the current paper space layout, or vice versa. When the Change Space tool is used, the objects that are moved are scaled appropriately so that they appear just as they did in the previous space. For example, a 4' (1200 mm)-diameter circle in a model space viewport that is scaled to ¼" = 1'-0" (1 = 60) appears to be 1" (20 mm) in diameter when the drawing is plotted at a scale of 1:1. When you use the Change Space tool and transfer the circle to paper space, it actually becomes a 1" (20 mm)-diameter circle in the layout. Here is the procedure for transferring the title block from model space to paper space:

1. Open the Layer Properties Manager and thaw and turn on all layers.

2. Switch to model space to zoom in to the floor plan area until the title block and border fits just within the viewport boundary, as shown in Figure 14.10.

3. Select all the title block objects, including the border and text. You can accomplish most of this quickly using a window selection window around the lower-right corner of the title block, as shown in Figure 14.11, and then clicking the border. Try not to select any of the other objects in the drawing, but if you do, deselect them using the Shift key.

 4. In the Home tab, expand the Modify panel and click the Change Space button.

5. It doesn't appear as if anything happened, but the title block has been moved to paper space and paper space is now active. Verify that you are in paper space by noticing that the UCS icon is now triangular, and then select some of the title block objects. The title block is selectable in paper space.

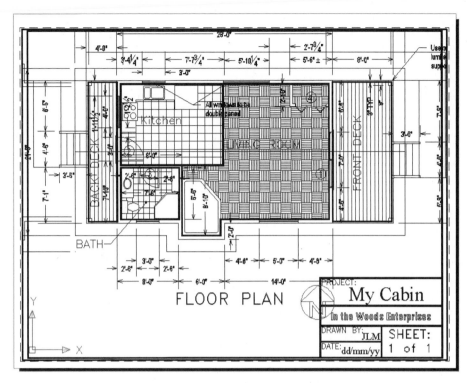

FIGURE 14.10: The cabin zoomed to show the title block and floor plan

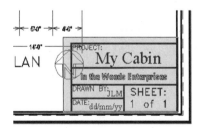

FIGURE 14.11: Selecting the title block with a selection window

6. Using the Endpoint object snap, adjust the title block and border so that the corners of the title block coincide with the corners of the viewport. Your drawing should look like Figure 14.12.

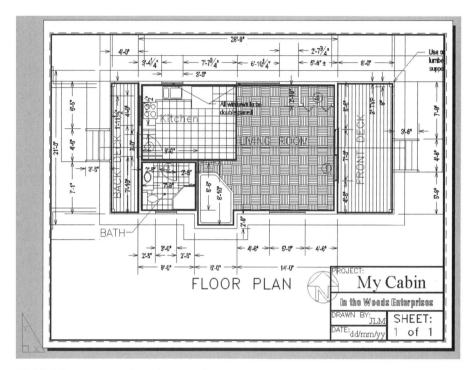

FIGURE 14.12: The cabin seen through the new viewport

Setting the Viewport Scale

The layout is set to print to an 8.5″×11″ (210 mm×297 mm) paper, and you want the contents of the viewport to plot to a specific scale. In this section, you will adjust the viewport scale to display the model space objects at 3/16″ = 1′ (1 = 70) by assigning a viewport scale.

1. Select the viewport. You know that the viewport is selected, and not the border polyline, when the Viewport Scale button appears in the status bar.

2. If you are using metric units, skip this step and go on to step 3. If you are using architectural units, then click the Viewport Scale button and, from the drop-down list, choose 3/16″ = 1′-0″ (see Figure 14.13). The viewport scales to 3/16″ = 1′-0″, and the scale is reflected on the status bar.

T I P   You can also change the viewport scale by selecting the viewport and changing the Standard Scale value in the Properties palette or Quick Properties panel.

FIGURE 14.13: Selecting the viewport scale

3. If you are using metric units, then double-click in the viewport and enter z↵ **1/70xp**↵. This instructs AutoCAD to scale the viewport to display objects at 1/70th the scale relative to the paper space layout. This was necessary because there is no 1/70 scale in the Scale drop-down list.

4. Double-click in the viewport, if necessary, to switch to model space and then use the Pan tool inside the viewport to adjust the position of the cabin so that the floor plan is centered (see Figure 14.14).

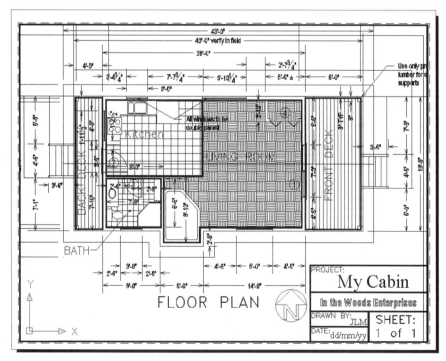

FIGURE 14.14: The cabin drawing zoomed into the floor plan

5. The scene is a bit cluttered, but that will be rectified in a later section. Double-click the gray area outside the title block to switch back to paper space.

T I P Items such as tables and notes can go either in model space, as shown in this exercise, or in paper space. When they are in paper space, it's easy to develop and maintain a consistent text or table style that appears the same in all drawings. When notes and tables are in model space, you have the flexibility to change their sizes simply by zooming in or out in the viewport. Model space objects can also be shown in any number of layouts in the same drawing. You'll develop your own standard, or adhere to your company's standard, for note and table placement.

Copying the Layouts

The layout that you made is an excellent starting point. You will add a few items from the DesignCenter, adjust the title block information, and then duplicate the layouts several times to accommodate the different views of your cabin. Each time a layout is copied, all of its contents, including the viewports and their settings, are copied with it. These copies are not interdependent, and any changes made to one are not reflected in the others.

N O T E You can delete all the paper space layouts, but you can't delete model space.

Adding Content from the DesignCenter

Before you copy the layouts, you'll add a block from the DesignCenter and edit its attributes.

1. Make Layer 0 current.

2. Open the DesignCenter, click the Folders tab, and navigate to Program Files ➤ AutoCAD 2010 ➤ Sample ➤ Dynamic Blocks ➤ Annotation – Imperial.dwg ➤ Blocks. If your drawing is in metric, navigate to Annotation – Metric.dwg.

3. Click and drag the Drawing Title block (see Figure 14.15) into your layout, and close the DesignCenter.

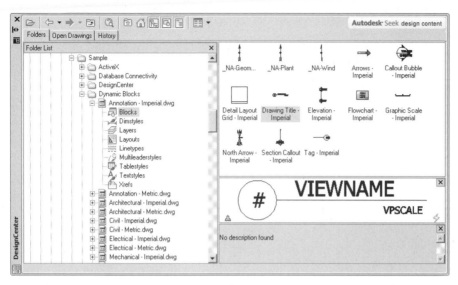

FIGURE 14.15: Selecting the Drawing Title block from the DesignCenter

4. Double-click the block, and in the Enhanced Attribute Editor dialog box, change the Viewport Scale, Drawing Name, and View Number values to 3/16″ = 1′-0″ (1:70), Floor Plan, and 1, respectively (see Figure 14.16); then click OK.

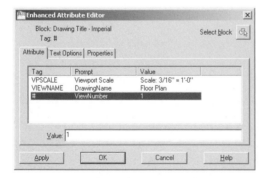

FIGURE 14.16: Changing the Drawing Title block's attributes

5. The new block adds a scale to the view title, something that should always be included in a drawing. Enter model space, erase the existing FLOOR PLAN text, and switch back to paper space.

Renaming, Deleting, and Adding Viewports

You have one layout that you don't need (Layout2) and one layout that you need to rename and make several copies of (Layout1). Here's how:

1. Click the Quick View Layouts button to display the layout thumbnails; then right-click the Layout2 tab. The drawing area changes to show the contents of that layout and the context menu opens.

2. Click Delete on the context menu, and then click OK in the warning dialog box that opens. The layout is removed from the drawing.

3. Click the Quick View Layouts button again, right-click Layout1, and then click Rename to highlight the name of the layout. Enter **Cabin Floor Plan**↵, as shown in Figure 14.17, to rename the layout. You can also double-click the viewport name to rename it. Always give your layouts descriptive names to help identify them when you are searching for particular content.

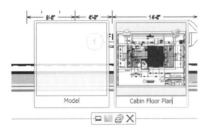

FIGURE 14.17: Renaming the layout

4. Right-click the layout thumbnail again; then choose Move or Copy from the context menu.

5. In the Move Or Copy dialog box that opens, select the (Move To End) item in the Before Layout list box. You can use this dialog box to copy a layout or to rearrange the order of the existing layouts. Click the Create A Copy option in the lower-left corner. Your dialog box should look like the one shown in Figure 14.18. Click OK.

6. Use the Quick View Layouts tool again, and you'll see a copy of the layout appears to the right of the original with "(2)" appended to its title.

7. Copy the layout six more times for a total of eight paper space layouts and one model space option. All the layouts are identical at this point.

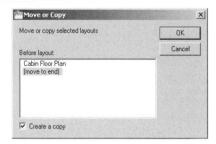

FIGURE 14.18: The Move Or Copy dialog box

8. Rename the seven layout copies to: **Plan Mat, Plan Notes, South Elev, East Elev, North Elev, West Elev,** and **Site Plan** (see Figure 14.19).

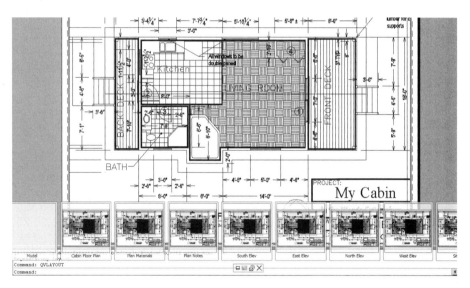

FIGURE 14.19: There are now eight layout tabs for the cabin drawing.

9. Click the Cabin Floor Plan layout to make it current and save your drawing as Cabin14b.dwg.

Adjusting a Viewport's Contents

The model space for the drawing is too cluttered to be useful. A drawing that looks like this would not be acceptable in most production environments, and one of the strengths of AutoCAD is its ability to adjust existing objects in the drawing easily. In this section, you will spread out the objects in model space and then specify which viewports display which layers.

1. Use the Quick View Layouts tool, and then click the Model layout on the far left to view the drawing in model space.

2. Make sure there isn't any obviously conflicting content and make any necessary adjustments, such as fixing overlapping views. For example, in the files from the book's web page, the image overlaps the table. Your drawing should look similar to Figure 14.20.

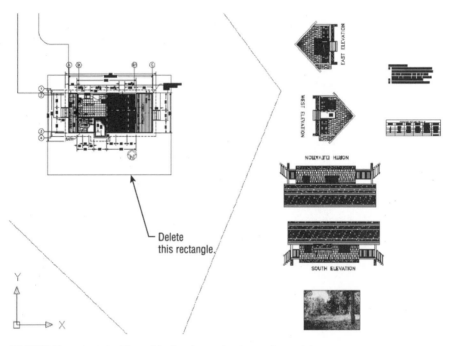

— Delete
this rectangle.

FIGURE 14.20: The cabin drawing as it appears in model space

N O T E   The viewports in layouts are described as *floating* because they can be moved around. They always reside in the layout portion of the drawing. There is another kind of viewport in AutoCAD called a model space or *tiled* viewport, which is fixed and exists only in model space. If you want more information on this subject, search for the phrase "set model space viewports" in the AutoCAD help system. For brevity, in this chapter I refer to floating viewports simply as viewports.

3. Delete the rectangle that is left over from the original, model-space title block (see Figure 14.20). Click Quick View Layouts, and then click the Cabin Floor Plan layout to make it current. Double-click the 1 of 1 text in the Sheet section of the title block, and edit it to read 1 of 8.

4. Double-click inside the viewport area. The goal here is to not display any objects that do not pertain to the current layout. This is where a well-thought-out and carefully followed layering scheme really pays some dividends.

5. In the Layers panel, click the Freeze button and then place your cursor back into the viewport area. The cursor is now a pickbox.

6. Click a hatch pattern for one of the floor materials; all the hatch patterns disappear. You did not freeze the Hatch-plan-floor layer in the drawing by picking the hatch; you froze the Hatch-plan-floor layer only in this particular viewport.

7. Open the Layer Properties Manager, and locate the Hatch-plan-floor layer. As you can see in Figure 14.21, the Freeze column shows the layer as thawed, but the VP Freeze column on the right shows the Hatch-plan-floor as frozen. All columns that start with VP relate only to the active viewport. When the Model tab is selected, these columns do not appear in the Layer Properties Manager. If you switched to the Model tab, you would see the Hatch-plan-floor layer is still visible.

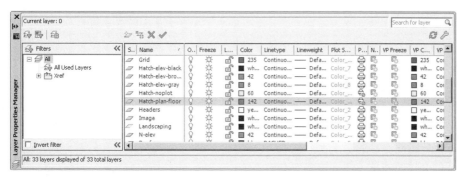

FIGURE 14.21: The Layer Properties Manager showing the status of the Hatch-plan-floor layer

8. Click the Freeze button again, and then click a door number symbol and a visible grid line to freeze these features in the viewport as well.

9. In the Layer Properties Manager, click the icon in the VP Freeze column for the Area layer to freeze the polylines used to calculate the floor plan areas. Freeze all three layers with names that start with "Site."

Setting the Linetype Scale

You may have noticed that the rooflines appear continuous rather than dashed. This is because the two variables that control linetype appearance, ltscale (line-type scale) and psltscale (paper space linetype scale), are both set to 1. With this configuration, the noncontinuous linetypes will appear the same in both model space and paper space.

1. To change the scale of the dashed rooflines, enter **ltscale**↵ 0.4↵. The roofline appears dashed again.

2. Adjust the dimensions so they fit within the viewport. You can pan without changing the viewport scale factor, but zooming will change it. You can reset the scale factor using the Viewport Scale drop-down list in the status bar.

3. Click the Esc key to terminate any active command, and then double-click outside the title block to enter paper space. Your drawing should look similar to Figure 14.22.

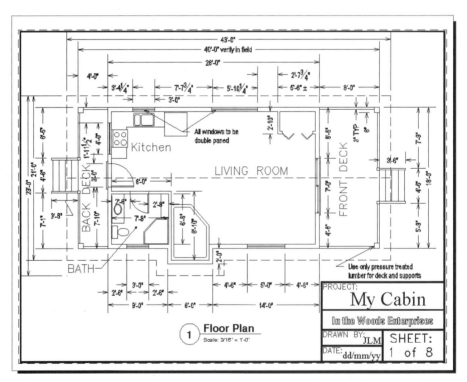

FIGURE 14.22: The Cabin Floor Plan layout after selectively freezing layers in the viewport

Adjusting the Other Viewports

Each of the remaining layouts has a specific purpose, and each requires a different set of layer conditions. You will use the same tools in the other viewports as you did for the viewport in the Cabin Floor Plan layout:

1. Make the Plan Mat layout active. This looks like the preceding tab before you made adjustments to the content that it displayed.

2. Double-click in the viewport and then, using the Freeze button and the Layer Properties Manager, freeze the following layers: Area, Dim1, Grid, Site, Site13a|Prop_Line, Site13a|Road, and Tables in the viewport only. Notice how you must use the Layer Properties Manager to freeze the Site layer when clicking the North arrow doesn't work. This is because the objects in the block are on the Site layer, but the block itself is on layer 0.

3. Switch to paper space and change the SHEET number to 2 of 8.

4. Double-click the Drawing Title block, and change the View Number to 2 and the Drawing Name to **Floor Plan Materials**.

5. The Drawing Title block is a dynamic block. Click it and then drag the right end of the horizontal line to the right until it extends underneath the entire title. (See Figure 14.23.)

FIGURE 14.23: Adjusting the Drawing Title dynamic block

Your drawing should look similar to Figure 14.24.

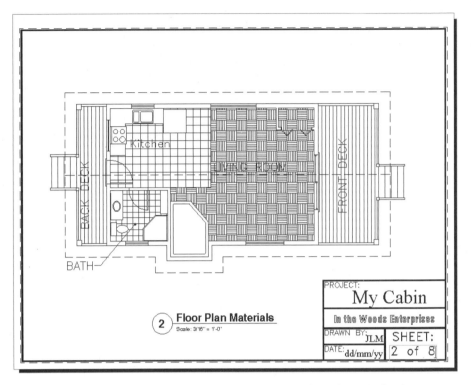

FIGURE 14.24: The Plan Mat layout after selectively freezing layers in the viewport

Adjusting the Plan Notes Layout

The Plan Notes layout is the first layout that requires more than one viewport. Here is a summary of the steps to clean up the drawing:

1. Make the Plan Notes layout active.

2. Inside the viewport, freeze the following layers: Area, Dim1, Hatch-plan-floor, Site, Site13a|Prop_Line, and Site13a|Road.

3. In the status bar, click the Viewport Scale button and choose 1/8″ = 1′-0″ (1:100). The viewport zooms out to reflect the smaller scale.

4. Switch to paper space and change the SHEET number to 3 of 8.

5. Double-click the Drawing Title block and change the View Number to 3, the Drawing Name to **Floor Plan Doors**, and the scale to 1/8″ = 1′-0″ (1:100). Then adjust the length of the horizontal line in the block until it extends underneath the entire title.

6. Select the viewport and, using the grips, adjust it so that it fits more closely to the floor plan. Your drawing should look similar to Figure 14.25.

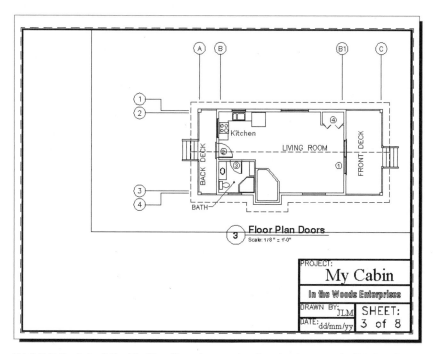

FIGURE 14.25: The Plan Notes layout after freezing layers and adjusting the viewport

7. Make the VP layer current, then create a new viewport (refer to the "Creating the Paper Space Viewport" section if you need a refresher) in the lower-left corner of the layout. The viewport should measure about 2″×4½″ (50 mm×115 mm) (look ahead to Figure 14.26).

8. The viewport displays all the model space contents. Zoom in to display only the table.

9. Copy this viewport, double-click inside the new viewport, and then pan and zoom until the General Notes fill the viewport.

10. Copy the Drawing Title block under the new viewports, and edit the attributes as shown in Figure 14.26.

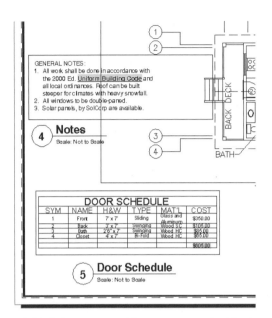

F I G U R E   1 4 . 2 6 : The new notes and table viewports

Adjusting the South Elev Layout

The south elevation is the only one drawn without rotating the UCS, so it will be the quickest to isolate in a layout. Here's how:

1. Make the South Elev layout active.

2. Pan in the viewport so that the south elevation is centered in the viewport.

3. You shouldn't need to freeze any layers for the elevations unless the tables, notes, or image encroaches in the viewport. If so, freeze the layers as appropriate.

4. Delete the SOUTH ELEVATION text.

5. Switch to paper space, and change the SHEET number to 4 of 8.

6. Double-click the Drawing Title block and change the View Number to 6 and the Drawing Name to **South Elevation**. Then adjust the length of the horizontal line in the block until it extends underneath the entire title. Move the Drawing Title block closer to the elevation. Your layout should look like Figure 14.27.

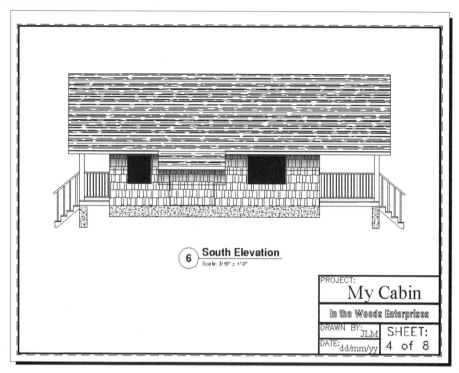

F I G U R E   1 4 . 2 7 : The South Elev layout after freezing layers and adjusting the viewport

Adjusting the Other Elevation Layouts

The remaining elevations were each drawn with a rotated User Coordinate System (UCS) so that they appeared in the correct orientation while you were drawing them; however, they are rotated when looking at the drawing in the World Coordinate System (WCS). In a similar fashion, you'll rotate the UCS in the viewports to view:

1. Make the East Elev layout active, and double-click inside the viewport.

2. To rotate the UCS, click the View tab and then click the Z button in the Coordinates panel. Enter 90↵ at the Specify Rotation Angle About Z Axis: prompt.

3. To use the Plan command to rotate the view to match the UCS, enter plan↵↵.

4. Click the Viewport Scale button, and choose 3/16″ = 1′-0″ if your units are architectural or double-click in the viewport and enter **z**↵ **1/70xp**↵; then exit model space. Pan in the viewport so that the east elevation is centered.

5. You shouldn't need to freeze any layers for the elevations unless the tables, notes, or image encroach in the viewport. If so, freeze the layers as appropriate. Move the objects that make up the east elevation, if necessary, so that nothing else is visible in the viewport, or adjust the viewport so that its boundary is closer to the objects.

6. Delete the EAST ELEVATION text.

7. Switch to paper space, and change the SHEET number to 5 of 8.

8. Double-click the Drawing Title block and change the View Number to 7 and the Drawing Name to **East Elevation**. Adjust the length of the horizontal line in the block until it extends underneath the entire title, and move the block closer to the elevation. Your layout should look like Figure 14.28.

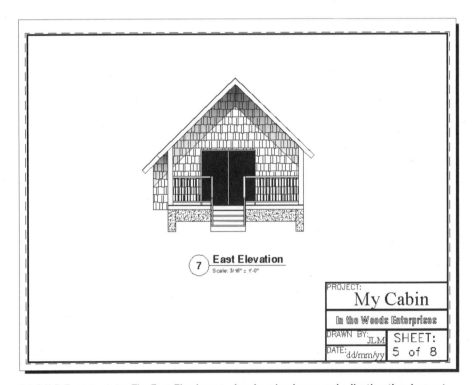

FIGURE 14.28: The East Elev layout after freezing layers and adjusting the viewport

9. Repeat steps 1 through 8 for the two remaining elevation layouts, substituting the appropriate text and values as required. For example, the viewport in the North Elev layout must be rotated 180° and the West Elev layout 270° or –90°.

When the elevations are completed, the North Elev layout should look like the top of Figure 14.29 and the West Elev layout should look like the bottom of Figure 14.29.

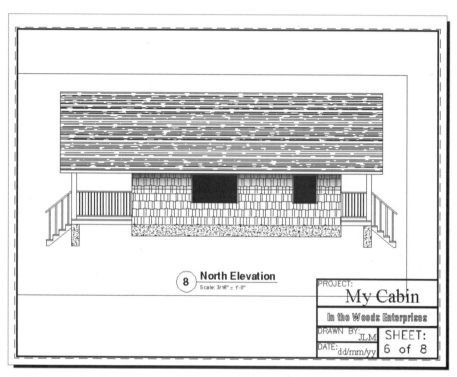

FIGURE 14.29: The North Elev layout (above) and the West Elev layout (next page)

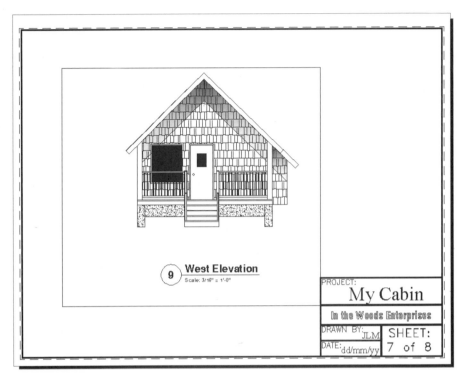

FIGURE 14.29 *(Continued)*

Setting Up the Site Plan Viewport

The site plan should show the cabin plan, the driveway, the access road, and the image but not the elevations or much of the information shown on the previous layouts. Because of the odd shape of the property line, you'll delete the current viewport, draw a polyline, and turn that polyline into a viewport. Here's how:

1. Make the Site Plan layout active.

2. Double-click inside the viewport, zoom to the drawing's extents, and then double-click outside of the viewport to switch back to paper space.

3. Make the VP layer current; then start the Polyline command and draw a closed polyline that roughly follows the shape of the property as shown in Figure 14.30. The exact shape isn't important because the viewport scale isn't properly set yet.

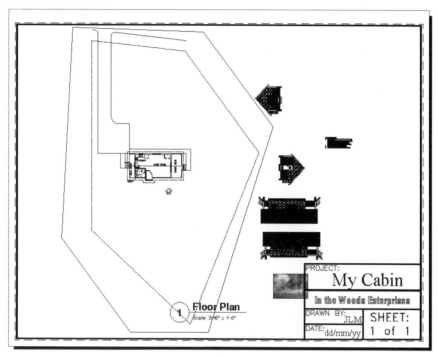

PROJECT:
My Cabin
In the Woods Enterprises
DRAWN BY: JLM   SHEET:
DATE: dd/mm/yy   1 of 1

1 Floor Plan
Scale: 3/16" = 1'-0"

F I G U R E   1 4 . 3 0 : Draw a polyline around the property.

4. To turn the polyline into a viewport, first click the View tab. Next click the Create From Object button in the Viewports panel and then click the polyline. You may need to click the down arrow next to the Create Polygonal button to select the Create From Object button from the fly-out menu.

The new viewport displays the model space contents as well as the original viewport.

T I P The Create Polygonal button can also be used to draw the viewport directly, but the Polyline tool provides greater control in the shape of the viewport, by allowing arc segments, and it allows the viewports to have a width in situations where they are visible when plotted.

5. Delete the rectangular viewport.

Defining a New Viewport Scale

Scales that use the convention *fraction"* = 1'-0" are said to be using an architectural scale. Site plans generally use an engineering scale, which use the convention 1" = *number* ', where *number* is a multiple of 10. For this site plan, you'll define a new viewport scale and add it to the Viewport Scale drop-down list.

1. Select the viewport, click the Viewport Scale button, and choose Custom to open the Edit Scale List dialog box, as shown in Figure 14.31.

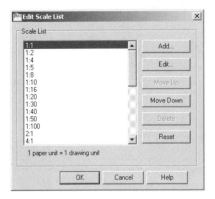

FIGURE 14.31: The Edit Scale List dialog box

2. Click the Add button to open the Add Scale dialog box.

3. The best engineering scale for the site plan, found through experimentation, is 1" = 30'-0" (1 = 400). This calculates to a ratio of 1" = 360" (1 = 400). In the Name Appearing In The Scale List box, enter 1" = 30" (1:400) but don't press ↵ yet.

4. In the lower part of the dialog box, set the Paper Units to 1 (1) and the Drawing Units to 360 (400), as shown in Figure 14.32.

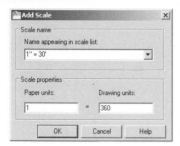

FIGURE 14.32: The Add Scale dialog box

5. Click OK in each of the dialog boxes to accept the changes and close them.

6. Select the viewport again, click the Viewport Scale button, and then choose 1" = 30' (1:400). The viewport scale changes to match the scale selected.

7. Pan in the viewport or select the viewport in paper space and adjust its endpoints so that only the site information is displayed.

8. Using the Freeze button or the Layer Properties Manager, freeze the following layers in the viewport only: Area, Dim1, Doors, Fixtures, Grid, Hatch-plan-floor, Roof, Tables, Text1, and Windows.

9. Switch to paper space, and change the SHEET number to 8 of 8.

10. Double-click the Drawing Title block and change the View Number to 10, the Drawing Name to **Site Plan**, and the Viewport Scale to 1" = 30' (1:400).

11. Create a new viewport and zoom in to see the referenced image file; then copy and edit the Drawing Title block. Your layout should look similar to Figure 14.33.

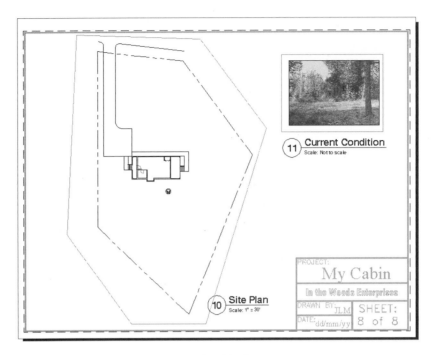

FIGURE 14.33: The completed Site Plan layout

12. Save your drawing as Cabin14c.dwg.

You've made a set of eight drawings, complete with scaled viewports and designated content. In the next section, you will look at a couple of ways to protect the drawing from accidental errors.

Locking and Turning Viewports Off

One of the common errors that you will make when working with viewports is zooming or panning while in a viewport and then failing to return the viewport to its proper appearance. You can prevent yourself, or anyone else, from editing the viewport view by *locking* the viewport. This feature doesn't prevent you from editing the content of the viewport—just how you access and view it. When you execute a pan or zoom while inside a locked viewport, AutoCAD temporarily exits the viewport, pans or zooms the equivalent amount in paper space, and then returns to model space. There is a slight lag in time when panning or zooming with this feature on, but it is much less than the time you may spend correcting, replotting, or reissuing a set of drawings that have viewports at the wrong scale factor. Follow this procedure to lock a viewport:

1. Use the Quick View Layouts tool to make the Cabin Floor Plan layout active.

2. Select the viewport, and then click the Lock/Unlock Viewport button next to the Viewport Scale button on the status bar.

The open lock icon changes to a closed lock. The viewport is now locked.

3. Repeat step 2 for all the viewports that show the cabin in the remaining layouts.

WHAT YOU DO IN MODEL SPACE AND PAPER SPACE (LAYOUTS)

Here's a partial list of some of the tasks you do in the two environments.

Model Space

You can do the following tasks in model space:

- Zoom to a scale in a viewport.
- Work on the building (or the project you are drawing).
- Make a viewport current.
- Control layer visibility globally for the drawing.

Paper Space (Layouts)

You can do the following tasks in paper space:

- Create viewports.
- Modify the size and location of viewports.
- Use the Viewports toolbar to set a viewport's scale.
- Lock/unlock the scale of the display in a viewport.
- Turn viewports on or off.

Turning Off Viewports

Beyond controlling the visibility of layers in each viewport, you can also turn off a viewport so that all model space objects within it are invisible:

1. Make the Plan Notes layout current, and then select the viewport that shows the table.

2. Right-click and choose Display Viewport Objects; then click No. The contents of the viewport disappear. You can accomplish the same result in the Properties palette by opening the drop-down list next to the On option in the Misc rollout and clicking No (see Figure 14.34).

3. Turn the viewport back on.

4. Save this drawing as Cabin14d.dwg.

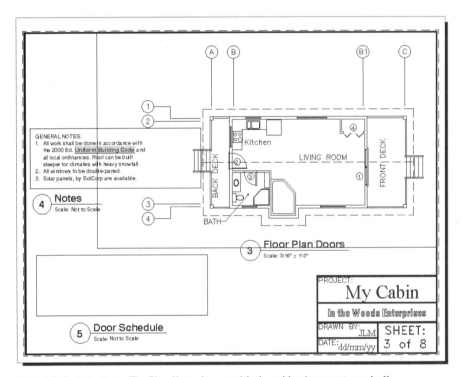

FIGURE 14.34: The Plan Notes layout with the table viewport turned off

Being able to turn off viewports can be an advantage for a complex drawing with many viewports or for one with a lot of information in each viewport. Remember that, even though all the layouts in this drawing are based on one drawing, AutoCAD is drawing at least part of that drawing in each viewport. In a complex drawing this can slow down the computer, so it's handy to be able to temporarily turn off any viewports on which you aren't working. It's also an easy way to check which objects are in model space and which are on the layout (or in paper space).

You will work with the viewports and layouts again in the next chapter, where you will round out your knowledge of 2D AutoCAD by learning the principles of plotting and printing AutoCAD drawings.

If You Would Like More Practice...

Create another layout for the cabin drawing that has a landscape orientation and is sized to fit a 30″×42″ paper. Create four or more viewports: one for the site plan and the others for various views of the drawing. Your new layout may look something like Figure 14.35.

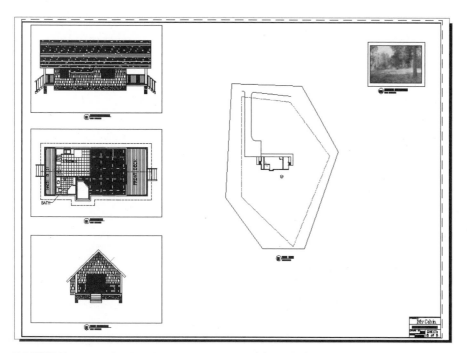

F I G U R E 1 4 . 3 5 : An additional layout for Cabin14d.dwg

Save this drawing as Cabin14-extra.dwg.

Are You Experienced?

Now you can...

☑ create a layout and associate it with a page setup

☑ move objects between paper space and model space

☑ set up viewports on layouts

☑ control layer visibility in individual viewports

☑ zoom to a scale in a viewport

☑ lock the display of a viewport

☑ turn viewports off and on

CHAPTER 15

Printing an AutoCAD Drawing

▶ Setting up a drawing to be printed

▶ Using the Plot dialog box

▶ Assigning lineweights to layers in your drawing

▶ Selecting the part of your drawing to print

▶ Previewing a print

▶ Printing a layout

▶ Publishing multiple layouts

▶ Looking at plot styles

W ith today's equipment, there is no difference between printing and plotting. *Printing* used to refer to smaller-format printers and *plotting* referred to pen plotters, most of which were for plotting large sheets. But the terms are now used interchangeably. Pen plotters have universally been virtually replaced by large-format inkjet or laser plotters with a few additional settings not commonly found on other printing devices. Otherwise, as far as AutoCAD is concerned, the differences between plotters and laser, inkjet, and electrostatic printers are minimal. In this book, printing and plotting have the same meaning.

Getting your drawing onto paper can be easy, if your computer is connected to a printer that has been set up to print AutoCAD drawings and AutoCAD has been configured to work with your printer. If these conditions have been met, you can easily manage printing with the tools you'll learn about in this chapter. If you don't have the initial setup in place, you'll need to set up your system to make AutoCAD work properly with your printer or find out how your system is set up to print.

You'll be using a couple of standard setup configurations between AutoCAD and printers to move through the exercises. You might or might not be able to follow each step to completion, depending on whether you have access to an 8.5"×11" (210 mm×297 mm) laser or inkjet printer, a larger-format plotter, or both.

You will print the Cabin14d.dwg drawing from a layout at its default 8 ½"×11" (210 mm×297 mm) sheet and at 30"×42" (762 mm× 1067 mm) sheet size.

Even if your printer won't let you print in these formats, I suggest you follow along with the text. You'll at least be able to preview how your drawing would look if printed in these formats, and you'll be taking large strides toward learning how to set up and make prints of your drawings. The purpose of this chapter is to give you the basic principles for printing, regardless of whether you have access to a printer.

Using the Plot Dialog Box

The job of getting your AutoCAD file onto hard copy can be broken down into five tasks. You'll need to tell AutoCAD the following:

▶ The printing device you'll use

▶ The lineweight assigned to each object in your drawing

▶ The portion of your drawing you're printing

▶ The sheet size to which you're printing

▶ The scale, orientation, and placement of the print on the sheet

You handle most of these tasks in the Plot dialog box:

1. Open Cabin14d.dwg (see Figure 15.1). Click the Cabin Floor Plan layout to make it active. Ensure that you are in paper space.

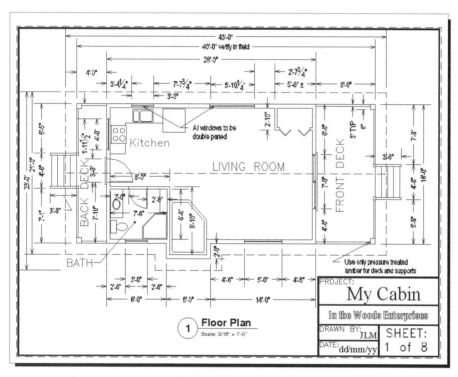

FIGURE 15.1: The Cabin14d.dwg drawing showing the floor plan

2. Click the Output tab, and then click the Plot button on the Plot panel to open the Plot dialog box. The title bar includes the name of the layout because, in this case, you're printing a drawing from paper space. If you print from model space, the title bar displays the word "Model." This dialog box is similar to the Page Setup dialog box that you worked with in Chapter 14, "Using Layouts to Set Up a Print," when you were setting up layouts (see Figure 15.2).

You can also open the Plot dialog box by pressing Ctrl+P, or by entering **plot**↵ or **print**↵.

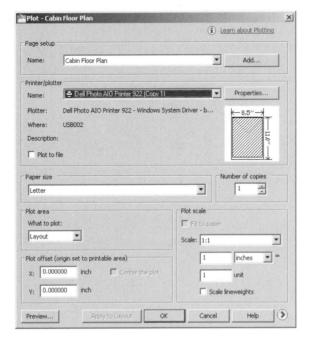

FIGURE 15.2: The Plot dialog box

This dialog box has some differences, however:

▶ The dialog box is smaller, but you can expand it to include four more areas of information and settings on the right side. (Yours might open in this expanded form.)

▶ It has an additional area called Number Of Copies.

UNRECONCILED LAYERS

If you receive a Layer Notification Warning dialog box or a notification bubble stating that you have unreconciled layers, you should address the situation before plotting the drawing. Unreconciled layers are new layers that have been added since the last time the drawing was saved, the Plot command was used, or a layer state was saved. The purpose of the warning or notification is to cause you to look at these new layers and determine whether any action is required. Open the Layer Properties Manager, and click Unreconciled New Layers in the left pane to display the list in the right pane. Select all the layers shown, right-click, choose Reconcile Layer from the context menu, and then close the Layer Properties Manager. All layers are now reconciled, and the warnings should discontinue until you add any new layers.

First you'll take a quick tour of this dialog box. Then you'll start setting up to print.

You'll see seven areas of settings on this unexpanded version of the dialog box. Some of the buttons and boxes won't be activated. I'll mention others only in passing, because their functions are for more advanced techniques than those covered in this book. These functions are available when in model space as well.

Printer/Plotter

In this area, the Name drop-down list contains the various printing devices to which AutoCAD has been configured, with the current one, the Dell Photo AIO Printer 922 (Copy 1), displayed in Figure 15.2. (Yours might say None or display a different printer.) Just below the list, the name of the driver and the assigned port or network path and asset name are displayed for the selected printer. Clicking the Properties button to the right opens the Plotter Configuration Editor dialog box, which has three tabs of data specific to the current printer. You must have a default printer assigned for the Properties button to be available. Most of this will already be set up by your Windows operating system. Back in the Plot dialog box, when selected, the Plot To File check box directs AutoCAD to make and save the print as a .plt file, rather than sending it to a printer. Many reproduction service bureaus prefer to receive .plt files to print, rather than Auto-CAD .dwg files with all their required support and externally referenced files (fonts, images, external references, and so on).

Paper Size and Number of Copies

In the Paper Size area, the drop-down list contains paper sizes that the current plot device can recognize. To the right is the Number Of Copies area, which is self-explanatory. When you have a large run of pages to print, it's prudent to print a single copy of each, check for errors or omissions, and then print multiple copies of each page.

Plot Area

In the Plot Area section, a drop-down list contains the options for specifying which portions of your drawing to print. You have already decided which layers will be visible when the print is made by freezing the layers in each viewport whose objects you don't want to print. Now you must decide how to designate the area of the drawing to be printed. As you go through the options, it's useful to think about the choices with regard to two printing possibilities: printing the whole drawing and printing just the floor plan. Using layouts removes much of the guesswork from the plotting process.

To illustrate how these options work, we'll make a couple of assumptions. First, the 1:1 Scale option is selected in the Plot Scale area, so AutoCAD will try to print the drawing at full scale. Second, the drawing will be in landscape orientation.

1. In the Plot Scale area, expand the Scale drop-down list and select 1:1.

 2. Click the right-pointing arrow in the lower-right corner to expand the dialog box.

 Make sure Landscape is selected in the Drawing Orientation section, and then click the left-pointing arrow to collapse the expansion.

The Display Option

The Display option on the What To Plot drop-down list prints what's currently on the screen, including the blank area around the drawing. With the sheet in landscape orientation and with the origin in the lower-left corner of the paper space area, choose this option. Click the Preview button in the lower-left corner of the Plot dialog box. The plot preview will look like Figure 15.3. The drawing doesn't fit well on the sheet with this option. It's oriented and sized correctly, but with the beginning of the plot area in the lower-right corner of the paper space area, it's printed above and to the right of where it should be. A considerable amount of clipping has also occurred, and much of the drawing is not displayed. Printing to Display is a quick method of plotting everything that is shown in the layout but is rarely the best solution when plotting in model space. Right-click and choose Exit, or press the Esc key, to exit the preview mode.

The Extents Option

When you select the Extents option, AutoCAD tries to fill the sheet with all visible objects in the drawing. Choose the Extents option, and then click the Preview button; the results will look similar to Figure 15.4.

This is closer to acceptable than the Display option, but it's not quite right. The border is off center because the extents of the drawing begin at the lower-left corner white area in paper space that represents the actual paper. This is a good method to use if the border is not plotted or if there is no border at all. Be aware that if any objects exist in paper space to the left or below the drawing area, these will shift the beginning of the extents and reduce the amount of the actual drawing area that is visible. Click Esc to return to the Plot dialog box.

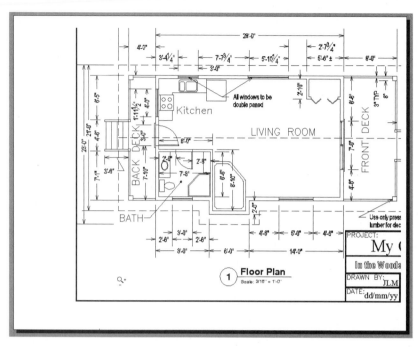

FIGURE 15.3: The cabin drawing printed to Display

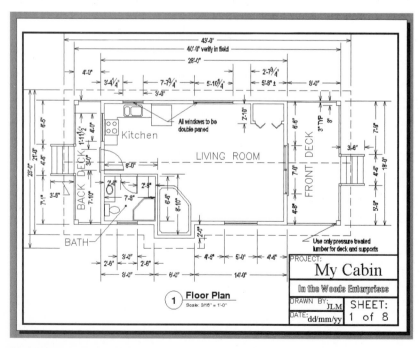

FIGURE 15.4: The drawing printed to Extents

The Limits Option

Do you remember the drawing limits for the cabin drawing that you set in Chapter 3, "Setting Up a Drawing"? As a refresher, perform the following steps:

1. Click Cancel to cancel the plot and close the Plot dialog box, and then click the Model button in the status bar. Plotting to Limits is not available in a layout.

2. Zoom in to the floor plan and start the Plot command again. If necessary, assign the same plotter and then choose Limits from the What To Plot drop-down list. In the Plot Scale section, click the Fit To Paper option—plotting at 1:1 in model space would result in only a miniscule portion of the vast drawing area actually getting plotted. When you print to Limits, AutoCAD prints only what lies within the limits, and it pushes what's within the limits to the corner that is the origin of the print.

3. Click the right-facing arrow in the lower-right corner, and make sure Landscape is selected in the Drawing Orientation area. Then click the Preview button in the lower-left corner (see Figure 15.5). This print won't work here because the limits don't cover the entire drawing, and the title block has already been moved into paper space. Printing to Limits can be a good tool for setting up a print, but you'll usually reset the limits from their original defining coordinates to new ones for the actual print.

4. Right-click, and choose Exit from the context menu to exit the preview.

If you are in a layout of a .dwg file, the Limits option is replaced by Layout in the What To Plot drop-down list under the Plot Area.

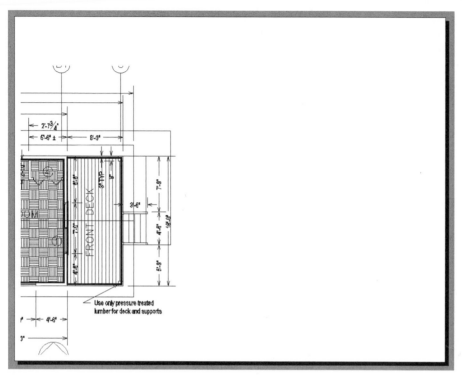

FIGURE 15.5: A preview of the drawing printed to Limits

The View Option

When printing to View, you tell AutoCAD to print a previously defined view that was saved with the drawing. When plotting from model space, the View option isn't displayed in the What To Plot drop-down list if you haven't defined and saved any views yet. The View option is never available when plotting from paper space.

1. Expand the What To Plot drop-down list, and click View. A new drop-down list appears to the right.

2. Expand the new drop-down list, and choose East_elev.

3. Click the Preview button, and the preview should look similar to Figure 15.6. A view is always taken from the same fixed location. In the preceding chapter, you moved several components of the cabin drawing and might need to update the named views to reflect this. The View option for What To Plot is a valuable tool for setting up partial prints of a drawing.

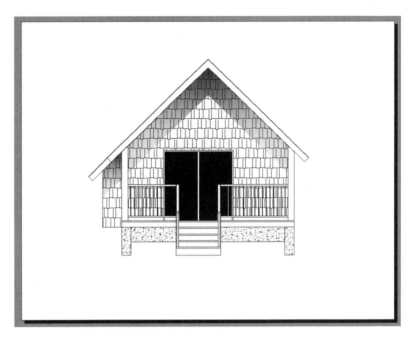

FIGURE 15.6: Plotting model space to a named view (East_elev)

4. Press Esc to exit the preview, and then click Cancel to close the Plot dialog box.

The Window Option

Using a window to define the area of a plot is the most flexible of the five methods described so far. It's like using a zoom window in the drawing. When you select this option, you're returned to your drawing where you'll make a window around the area you want to print. When you return to the Plot dialog box, a Window button appears in the right side of the Plot Area section (see Figure 15.7), in case you need to redefine the window.

FIGURE 15.7: The Plot Area section in the Plot dialog box with its drop-down list open and the Window button displayed next to it

AutoCAD will print only what is in the window you made, regardless of how it fits on the sheet. This method is similar to the View method just discussed. The difference is that the View method prints a previously defined view (one that was possibly defined by a window, but could also be defined in other ways), and the Window method prints what is included in a window that you define as you're setting up the plot. The window used by the Window method can't be saved and recalled at a later time.

These are the five ways to specify what to print in paper or model space. You'll use the Window option in the exercise to print a portion of the drawing from model space. Later in this chapter, you will revisit and plot from the layouts.

The Layout Option

One of the greatest benefits of layouts is the ability to see on the screen exactly what will be printed. This is the purpose of the Layout option in the Plot dialog box. When printed at a scale of 1:1, and on the paper size designated in the Page Setup dialog box, the printed drawing will look as it does in the layout. The layout option is discussed further in the "Printing a Drawing Using Layouts" section later in this chapter.

Plot Scale

On the right side of the Plot dialog box is the Plot Scale area, where you control the scale of the plot. When the Fit To Paper check box is selected, AutoCAD takes whatever area you have chosen to print and automatically scales it so that it will fit on the selected page size. When this option is unchecked, the Scale drop-down list becomes available. This list contains several preset scales to choose from plus a Custom option and any scales that you've added. Some of the scales in the list are displayed as pure ratios, such as 1:50. Others are shown in their standard format, such as ¼″ = 1′-0″. Below the drop-down list is a pair of text boxes for setting up a custom scale. When you choose a preset scale, these text boxes display the true ratio of that scale.

To set up a custom scale, you choose the units you're using in your drawing (inches or millimeters), and enter a plotted distance in the text box, just below the Scale drop-down list. Then, in the Units text box below that, enter the number of units in your drawing that will be represented by the distance you entered in the text box above. The inches (or millimeters) distance is an actual distance on the plotted drawing, and the units distance is the distance the plotted units represent. For 1/4″ scale (¼″ = 1′-0″), you can enter several combinations:

= Text Box	Units Text Box
1/4 inches	1′
1 inches	4′
1 inches	48 inches

Plot Offset and Plot Options

Below Plot Area is the Plot Offset (Origin Set to Printable Area) area, which contains two text boxes and a check box. Select the Center The Plot check box to center the plot on the printed sheet. If this check box isn't selected, by default AutoCAD places the lower-left corner (or the origin) of the area you have specified to plot at the lower-left corner (or origin) of the printable area of the current paper size. By changing the settings in the X and Y text boxes, you can move the drawing horizontally or vertically to fit on the page as you want. When the Center The Plot check box is selected, the X and Y text boxes are disabled for input but display the offset distance from the lower-left corner of the sheet that was necessary to center the drawing.

Just as each drawing has an origin (0,0), each plotter creates an origin for the plot. Usually it's in the lower-left or upper-left corner, but not always. When the plot is being made, the printer first locates the origin and starts the print there, moving laterally from the origin in the opposite direction of the paper feed. If the origin is in the lower-left corner, the print might come out looking like the top of Figure 15.8. If the origin is the upper-left corner, the print will look like the middle of Figure 15.8. The origin point has less of an impact as plotter technology develops. Many machines already have a self-centering capability.

By using the X and Y settings in the Plot Offset area, you can make one margin wider for a binding. To center your drawing on the page, select the Center The Plot check box (see the bottom of Figure 15.8). If layouts are set up and being used for printing, they determine this setting and the Center The Plot check box is unavailable.

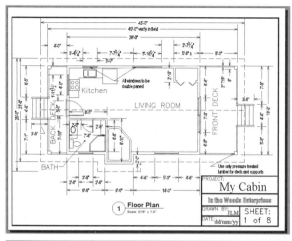

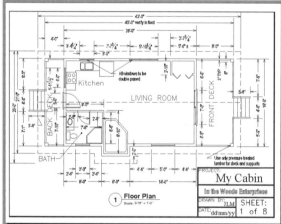

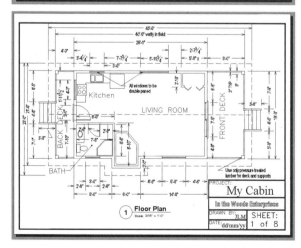

FIGURE 15.8: A print with its origin in the lower-left corner (top), in the upper-left corner (middle), and with the drawing centered (bottom)

T I P   Usually, 8.5″×11″ (210 mm×297 mm) format printers are configured for portrait orientation. If your drawing is also set to that orientation,
the origin of the plot will be in the lower-left corner. If your drawing is in the
landscape orientation, as in the example, the plot origin will move to the
upper-left corner of the page because the plot is rotated to fit on the page.

Setting the material to be printed accurately on the page will be a result of
trial and error and getting to know your printer. We'll return to this topic
shortly when we show how to get ready to print.

The Expanded Plot Dialog Box

If the Plot dialog box hasn't already been expanded, click the right-facing
arrow in the lower-right corner to expand it to include four additional
areas in a stack on the right. For now, we're primarily interested in the area on
the bottom, Drawing Orientation (see Figure 15.9).

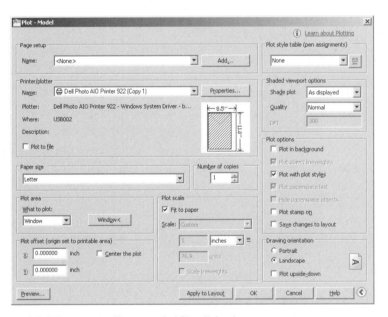

F I G U R E   1 5 . 9 : The expanded Plot dialog box

Drawing Orientation   The settings in this area are self-explanatory. The radio
buttons serve as a toggle between the portrait and landscape orientation, and the
Plot Upside-Down check box is an on/off toggle.

Plot Options   This area has seven check boxes that define how the plot is executed. These options shouldn't concern you now.

Shaded Viewport Options This area has settings to control the plot for renderings and shaded views (not available in AutoCAD LT), and will be covered in later chapters.

Plot Style Table (Pen Assignments) This is where the color and weight of linetypes are defined. We'll discuss plot styles and pen assignments later in this chapter.

You have taken a quick tour of the Plot dialog box, and you still have a drawing, Cabin14d.dwg, to print. Let's print it. As you set up the print, refer to this section for an explanation of the steps, if necessary.

Printing a Drawing

Your first task is to print Cabin14d.dwg from model space at a scale of 3/16″ = 1′-0″ (1 = 70) on an 8.5″×11″ (210 mm×297 mm) format printer. In this exercise, you'll use the default system printer, which is set up for an 8.5″×11″ (210 mm×297 mm) format printer. If you have an 8.5″×11″ (210 mm×297 mm) format printer, you should be able to follow the steps. If you don't have a printer, you can still get familiar with printing by following along with the steps.

The first step is to freeze some layers and assign lineweights to the remaining visible layers.

Determining Lineweights for a Drawing

Click Cancel to close the Plot dialog box, and look at the Cabin14d drawing as a whole. You need to decide on weights for the various lines. The floor plan is drawn as if a cut were made horizontally through the building just below the tops of the window and door openings. Everything that was cut will be given a heavy line. Objects above and below the cut will be given progressively lighter lines, depending on how far above or below the cut the objects are located.

In this system, the walls, windows, and doors will be heaviest. The roof, headers, fixtures, deck, and steps will be lighter. For emphasis, you'll make the walls a little heavier than the windows and doors. The hatch pattern will be very light, and the outline of the various components will be heavier for emphasis. Text and the title block information will use a medium lineweight. These are general guidelines; weights will vary with each drawing.

 N O T E Lineweight standards vary for each trade and profession that uses AutoCAD. Details usually follow a system that is independent from the one used by other drawings in the same set. Section lines, hidden lines, center lines, cutting plane lines, break lines, and so on will all be assigned specific lineweights.

You'll use four lineweights for this drawing, as shown in Table 15.1.

TABLE 15.1: The Four Lineweights Used in the Cabin Drawing

Weight	Thickness in Inches
Very light	0.005 (0.13 mm)
Light	0.008 (0.20 mm)
Medium	0.010 (0.25 mm)
Heavy	0.014 (0.35 mm)

In Cabin14d, 26 layers are visible in the floor plan, site plan, and the elevation layouts as they currently set up. Their lineweights will be assigned as shown in Table 15.2.

TABLE 15.2: Lineweights Associated with the Layers in the Current Cabin Drawing

Layer	Lineweight	Layer	Lineweight
0	Light	N-elev	Medium
Deck	Medium	Roof	Very light
Dim1	Very light	S-elev	Medium
Doors	Medium	Site	Medium
E-elev	Medium	Site13a|Prop_line	Medium
Fixtures	Light	Site13a|Road	Medium
Foundation	Light	Steps	Light
Grid	Medium	Tables	Medium
Hatch-elev-black	Very light	Tblk1	Medium
Hatch-elev-brown	Very light	Text1	Medium
Hatch-elev-gray	Very light	W-elev	Medium
Hatch-plan-floor	Very light	Walls	Heavy
Headers	Light	Windows	Medium

When you look at the lineweights currently assigned to these layers and at the thickness you need for these lineweights, you can generate a third chart that shows what lineweight needs to be assigned to each group of layers, as shown in Table 15.3.

T A B L E   1 5 . 3 : The Thickness of Each Lineweight and the Assigned Layers

Thickness	Layers
0.005 (0.13)	Dim1, plotting Hatch layers, Roof
0.008 (0.20)	0, Fixtures, Foundation, Headers, Steps
0.010 (0.25)	Deck, Doors, E-elev, Grid, N-elev, S-elev, Tables, Tblk1, Text1, W-elev, Windows and all three Site layers
0.014 (0.35)	Walls

Now it's time to freeze the unwanted layers and assign the lineweights to the remaining layers in the drawing:

1. Open the Layer Properties Manager, and make the VP layer current.

2. The VP, Area, Defpoints, and Hatch-noplot layers do not plot, so you don't need to be concerned with them at this time, but verify that they are set to not plot. The Electrical and Landscaping layers are empty.

3. Click the Dim1 layer to highlight it. Hold down the Ctrl key, and click the three Hatch-elev layers and the Roof layer to select them. Then release the Ctrl key.

4. In the Lineweight column of the Layer Properties Manager dialog box, click one of the highlighted Default words in the lineweight column to open the Lineweight dialog box (see Figure 15.10).

F I G U R E   1 5 . 1 0 : Assigning a lineweight in the Lineweight dialog box

N O T E   **If your lineweight units are shown in millimeters instead of inches, click Cancel, enter lwunits↵ 0↵, and then reopen the Lineweight dialog box.**

5. Click 0.005″ (0.13 mm). Then click OK. The Lineweight dialog box closes. In the Layer Properties Manager dialog box, the five highlighted layers now have a lineweight of 0.005″ (0.13 mm) assigned to them (see Figure 15.11).

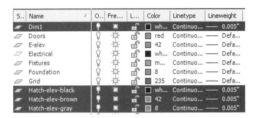

F I G U R E   1 5 . 1 1 : The new lineweight is shown in the Layer Properties Manager.

6. Click the Fixtures layer near the layer's name.

7. Hold down the Ctrl key; click Foundation, Headers, and Steps.

8. Click one of the highlighted Default words. The Lineweight dialog box opens.

9. Click 0.008″ (0.20 mm), and click OK. The newly highlighted layers now have a lineweight of 0.008″ (0.20 mm) assigned to them.

10. Select the Deck, Doors, Tblk1, Text1, Windows, and all four elevation layers, and set their thicknesses to 0.010″ (0.25 mm).

11. Click the Walls layer, and use the same procedure to assign it the thickness of 0.014″ (0.35 mm).

12. Set the linetype scale to 24 (ltscale↵ 24↵). The rooflines become dashed in model space.

You have assigned the lineweights. When the print is complete, you can judge whether these lineweight assignments are acceptable or need to be adjusted. In an office, a lot of time is invested in developing a lineweight standard that can be used in most drawings.

Setting Other Properties of Layers

Two other properties of layers deserve to be mentioned: Plot and Description. Both columns appear at the far-right end of the Layer Properties Manager dialog box.

The Plot feature is a toggle that controls whether the objects on a layer are printed. By default, the control is on. When this feature is turned off for a particular layer, objects on that layer aren't printed but remain visible on the screen. You used this feature to make the VP and Hatch-noplot layers unplottable and, in the future, you might designate a layer set not to print for in-house notes and data that you don't intend to be seen by those who will eventually view your printed drawings.

A Description column appears at the far right of the Layer List window. Clicking in this column on the blue bar of a highlighted layer opens a text box in which you can enter a description of the layer. Layer names are often in code or use abbreviations that don't fully describe what objects are on that layer. Here's a place to remedy that.

Setting Up the Other Parameters for the Print

Now that you have set the lineweights, it's time to move to the Plot dialog box and complete the setting changes you need to make in order to print this drawing. You'll use the Window option to select what you'll print.

1. In the Layer Properties Manager, select the Grid, Hatch-plan-floor, Tables, and all three Site layers. Then click the printer icon, under the Plot column, in the row of one of the selected layers. Those layers will no longer print.

2. Start the Plot command.

3. In the Plot dialog box, check the Printer/Plotter area to be sure you have the correct printer displayed in the drop-down list. Also check the Paper Size area to be sure you have Letter (A4) as the selected paper size. Then move down to the Plot Area section, open the What To Plot drop-down list, and select Window.

4. In the drawing, turn off Object Snap. To start the window, pick a point just above and to the right of the topmost and rightmost dimensions.

5. To complete the window, click a point below and to the left of the bottommost and leftmost dimensions. Back in the Plot dialog box,

Window is displayed in the What To Plot drop-down list, and a new Window button appears on the right side of the Plot Area section. Click this button if you need to redo the window after viewing a preview of the plot.

6. If you have not already done so, click the right-pointing arrow in the lower-right corner of the Plot dialog box to display another column of plotting options. In the Drawing Orientation area in the lower-right corner, be sure Landscape is selected.

7. In the Plot Scale area, uncheck Fit To Paper and, if you're using Architectural units, open the Scale drop-down list, and select 3/16″ = 1′-0″. Notice that the text boxes below now read 0.1875 and 12, a form of the true ratio for 3/16″ scale. If you're using decimal units, choose Custom from the Scale drop-down list and enter 1 in the upper text field and 70 in the lower.

8. In the Plot Offset area, click the Center The Plot check box. Your dialog box should look like Figure 15.12.

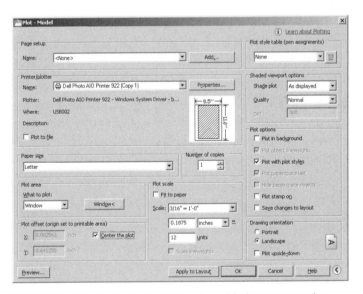

FIGURE 15.12: The Plot dialog box with the current settings

This completes the setup for your first plot. Before you waste paper, it's a good idea to preview how it will look as a result of the setup changes.

Previewing a Print

The Preview feature gives you the opportunity to view your drawing exactly as it will print.

1. Click the Preview button in the lower-left corner of the Plot dialog box. The computer takes a moment to calculate the plot and then displays a full view of your drawing as it will fit on the page (see Figure 15.13). If a Plot Scale Confirm dialog box opens, click Continue.

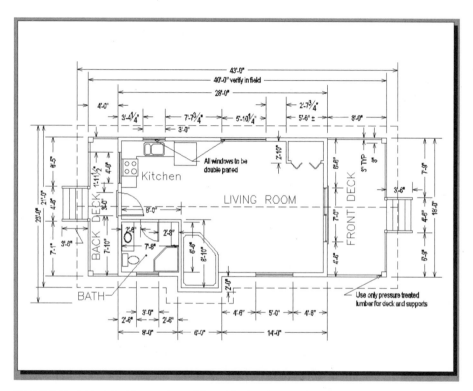

FIGURE 15.13: The preview of the cabin drawing, ready to print

2. Right-click and choose Zoom Window from the context menu.

3. Make a window that encloses the bathroom, hot tub, and a couple of the dimensions. You have to click and hold down the mouse button, drag open the window, and then release the button. The new view displays the lineweights you have set up (see Figure 15.14).

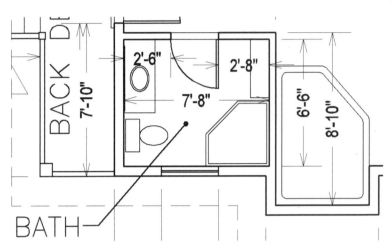

FIGURE 15.14: The zoomed-in view of the cabin showing the lineweights

4. Right-click and choose Zoom Original from the context menu to return to the first preview view.

5. Right-click again, and choose Exit to return to the Plot dialog box. If your print was oriented correctly on the sheet, you're ready to print. If not, recheck the setup steps for errors.

6. At the bottom of the Plot dialog box, click the Apply To Layout button and then click OK. The computer begins calculating the print and eventually sends it to the printer.

 7. After the print is done, a notification balloon appears at the lower-right corner of the AutoCAD window (see Figure 15.15). You can turn notifications on and off by right-clicking the Plot/Publish Detail icon in the AutoCAD tray and choosing the appropriate option.

FIGURE 15.15: The notification balloon indicating that the plot is complete

8. Save this drawing as Cabin15a.dwg.

When your print comes out, it should look like Figure 15.13 (shown earlier). Check the lineweights of the various components on the print. You might have to make adjustments for your particular printer.

Next you'll plot the drawing using the layouts you created in Chapter 14.

On the right side of the Printer/Plotter area of the Plot dialog box, AutoCAD displays a partial preview of the plot in diagram form, as you set it up. If there is problem with the setup, it displays red lines to warn you, but sometimes it isn't accurate. It's better to use the Preview feature, which provides you with a WYSIWYG view of the plot.

N O T E   You can change a setting in the Lineweight Settings dialog box to be able to see lineweights in your drawing before you preview a plot, but they aren't very accurate unless you're using layouts. When you print from model space, you have to preview the drawing from the Plot dialog box to see how the lineweights look.

Printing a Drawing Using Layouts

As a comparison to the preceding exercise, you'll print the drawing from the layouts. When a layout has been set up properly and is active, you print at a scale of 1:1. The elements of the drawing on the layout are then printed at actual size, and the model space portion of the drawing is printed at the scale to which the viewport has been set. Follow these steps:

1. Click the Cabin Floor Plan layout using the Quick View Layouts tool. For a review of layouts and viewports, see Chapter 14. Your layout should look like Figure 15.16.

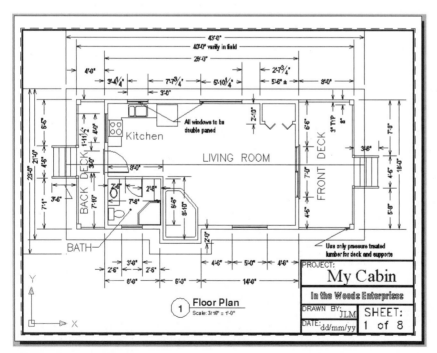

F I G U R E   1 5 . 1 6 : The cabin drawing ready for printing from a layout

2. Open the Layer Properties Manager dialog box, and make all layers plottable except VP, Hatch-noplot, and Area; the Defpoints layer is inherently non-plotting.

3. Make sure you are in paper space to start the Plot command.

4. You're using the same printer, paper size, and orientation as before, so make sure those parameters are the same.

5. Make sure that in the Plot Area section, the current choice displayed in the What To Plot drop-down list is Layout instead of Limits.

6. In the Plot Scale area, the scale has been set to 1:1. This is what you want.

7. In the Plot Offset area, the Center The Plot check box is grayed out; it isn't needed when using a layout to plot.

   There are no changes to make. Because this layout was set up for printing when it was created, all the settings in the Plot dialog box are automatically set correctly.

8. In the lower-left corner, select Preview. Your preview should look like Figure 15.17. Notice how the preview looks exactly like the layout, but without the dashed frame.

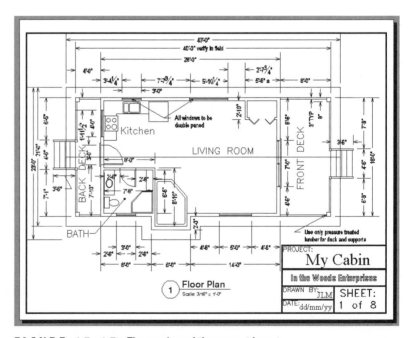

FIGURE 15.17: The preview of the current layout

9. Right-click and choose Exit to close the preview window. Click OK to start the print. If you don't have a printer, or if you're just following along, click Cancel to cancel the print at this point.

This exercise shows that once a layout has been created, most of the setup work for printing is already done for you. This greatly simplifies the printing process because the parameters of the print are determined before the Plot command begins.

Printing a Drawing with Multiple Viewports

Multiple viewports in a layout don't require special handling. The print is made with the layout active at a scale of 1:1. For the next print, you'll use a different printer—one that can handle larger sheet sizes. If you don't have access to a large-format printer, you can still configure AutoCAD for one and preview how the print would look.

Printing with a Large-Format Printer

The procedure here varies little from the one you just followed to print the layout at a 1:1 scale. Here you will scale the viewport up to fit on a larger sheet for presentation purposes:

1. Change the linetype scale back to 0.4, and then save the current drawing to your Training Data folder as Cabin15b.dwg.

2. This drawing has several layouts. In this exercise, you'll print the site plan, so be sure the Site Plan layout is active (see Figure 15.18).

N O T E   In a true production environment, it might be a better choice to create a large-format layout to accommodate large-format plots.

3. Switch to paper space if necessary, and then start the Plot command.

4. In the Plot dialog box, expand the Plotter Name drop-down list and, if you have one, select a large-format plotter. In the Paper Size area, choose any large-size paper that is recognized by the plotter. In this example, I'm using a 30″×42″ (762 mm×1067 mm) sheet size.

5. In the Plot Area section, choose Extents and then click the Center the Plot option.

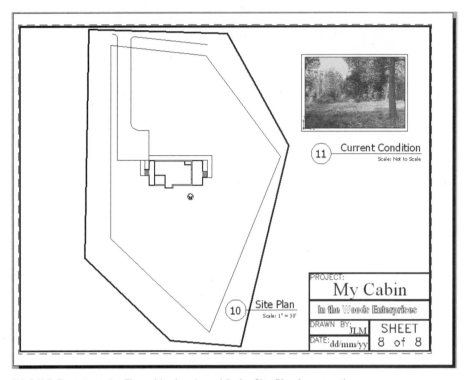

FIGURE 15.18: The cabin drawing with the Site Plan layout active

6. In the Plot Scale area, check the Fit To Paper option and then check Scale Lineweights. This option causes AutoCAD to scale the lineweights relative to the amount the layout is scaled to fit to the paper.

7. Click the Preview button. The white area around the border isn't even (see Figure 15.19). This is because the aspect ratio of the layout is different from that of the 30″×42″ (762 mm×1067 mm) paper.

8. Right-click and choose Exit from the context menu to cancel the preview. If you have a large-format printer configured and can plot this drawing at full size, click OK to start the print. Otherwise, click Cancel.

9. Save this drawing as `Cabin15b.dwg`. For the last exercise in this chapter, you'll set up AutoCAD to print all the paper space layouts at one time.

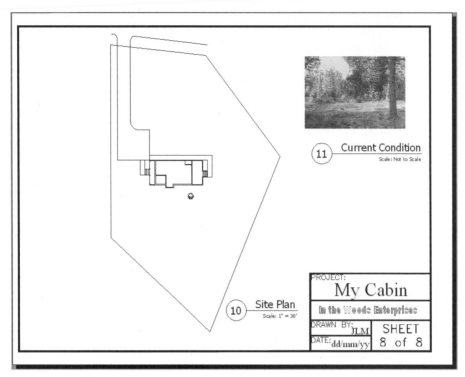

FIGURE 15.19: Preview of the Cabin Site layout

Publishing Multiple Layouts

In AutoCAD terminology, you *plot* a single layout or view one or more times. The terms *publishing* and *batch plotting* are interchangeable and refer to assigning several layouts or views to plot in sequence one or more times. In this exercise, you will publish all your layouts at one time.

 1. Click the Output tab and then click the Batch Plot button in the Plot panel. Choose the Publish option from the Application menu, or enter **publish↵**, to open the Publish dialog box (see Figure 15.20). This shows all the layouts, including model space for all open drawings.

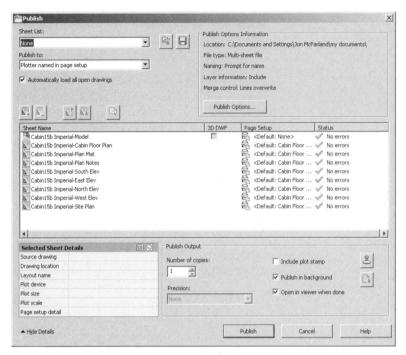

FIGURE 15.20: The Publish dialog box

2. You don't want to plot the objects from model space, so select the Model layout in the Sheet Name list and then click the Remove Sheet button.

3. To prevent the Model sheet from automatically being added in the future, right-click, and then uncheck the Include Model When Adding Sheets option in the context menu.

   In the Page Setup column, you can see that all the layouts are set to <Default:Cabin Floor Plan>. This indicates that all the layouts will use the original page setup designated when the first layout, Cabin Floor Plan, was created. Remember, the other layouts were copied from this original layout.

4. Click the Publish button at the bottom of the dialog box. In the Save Sheet List dialog box, click Yes. This provides you with the opportunity to save this publishing job as a Drawing Set Description (.dsd) file so that it can be reloaded with the Load Sheet List button. It's not always necessary to plot all the layouts in a drawing every time you use the Publish tool. By creating .dsd files for frequently published

layout combinations, you can reduce the amount of time required to produce hard-copy prints.

5. In the Save List As dialog box that opens, name the .dsd file and navigate to your current working directory to place it and then click Save.

6. The Publish dialog box closes and the plots begin. If a Processing Background Job dialog box appears, click OK. An extensive number of plots can take a while to finish, depending on the size and complexity of the drawings and speed of the printer. The publish operation takes place in the background so you can continue to work on your drawings as the publishing occurs.

7. You can click the Plot and Publish Details button in the bottom-right corner of the AutoCAD window to see information regarding the current and previous plots.

Only one publish operation can occur at one time. If you start one operation before the previous one is completed, you will see the Job Already In Progress dialog box, shown in Figure 15.21, indicating that you must wait before starting the next one.

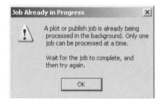

FIGURE 15.21: The Job Already In Progress dialog box

A Few Words about Plot Styles

So far in this chapter, you have assigned lineweights to layers. We have assumed that any printer is monochromatic and converts all colors in an AutoCAD drawing to black. Laser printers usually are monochromatic, but they might print the lighter colors in your drawing as screened. If you have access to a large-format inkjet plotter, you might have the option to print in monochrome or color. In that case, you might have objects in your drawing that are one color, but you want them printed in another color. Plot styles offer a means to handle these kinds of situations. You don't have to use plot styles in AutoCAD, but you might need to work on a drawing that uses them. We'll finish this chapter with a tour of the various dialog boxes and procedures for setting up and assigning plot styles.

Introducing Plot-Style Table Files

For LT, the path is similar but uses an `AutoCAD LT 2010` folder and one called `R15` instead of `R18.0`.

A plot style is a group of settings that is assigned to a layer, a color, or an object. It determines how that layer, color, or object is printed. Plot styles are grouped into plot-style tables that are saved as files on your hard drive. Two kinds of plot styles exist:

- Color-dependent, which are assigned to colors in your drawing
- Named, which are assigned to layers or objects

Leave AutoCAD for a moment, and use Windows Explorer to navigate to the following folder: `C:\Documents and Settings\`*`your name`*`\Application Data\Autodesk\AutoCAD 2010\R18.0\enu\Plotters`. Open the subfolder called `Plot Styles`; Figure 15.22 shows its contents. Thirteen plot-style table files are already set up. Nine of them are color-dependent plot-style table files, with the extension `.ctb`; and four are named plot-style table files, with the extension `.stb`. (If you can't see the `.ctb` and `.stb` extensions, choose Tools ➢ Folder Options ➢ View, and uncheck Hide Extensions For Known File Types.) Finally, you'll see a shortcut to the Add-A-Plot Style Table Wizard, which you use to set up custom plot-style tables. Close Windows Explorer, and return to AutoCAD.

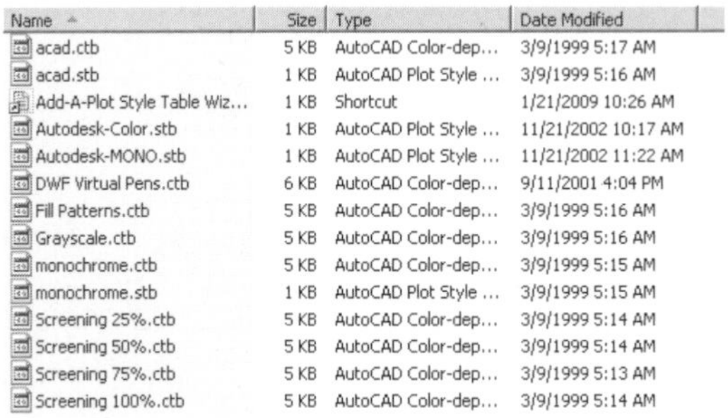

Name	Size	Type	Date Modified
acad.ctb	5 KB	AutoCAD Color-dep...	3/9/1999 5:17 AM
acad.stb	1 KB	AutoCAD Plot Style ...	3/9/1999 5:16 AM
Add-A-Plot Style Table Wiz...	1 KB	Shortcut	1/21/2009 10:26 AM
Autodesk-Color.stb	1 KB	AutoCAD Plot Style ...	11/21/2002 10:17 AM
Autodesk-MONO.stb	1 KB	AutoCAD Plot Style ...	11/21/2002 11:22 AM
DWF Virtual Pens.ctb	6 KB	AutoCAD Color-dep...	9/11/2001 4:04 PM
Fill Patterns.ctb	5 KB	AutoCAD Color-dep...	3/9/1999 5:16 AM
Grayscale.ctb	5 KB	AutoCAD Color-dep...	3/9/1999 5:16 AM
monochrome.ctb	5 KB	AutoCAD Color-dep...	3/9/1999 5:15 AM
monochrome.stb	1 KB	AutoCAD Plot Style ...	3/9/1999 5:15 AM
Screening 25%.ctb	5 KB	AutoCAD Color-dep...	3/9/1999 5:14 AM
Screening 50%.ctb	5 KB	AutoCAD Color-dep...	3/9/1999 5:14 AM
Screening 75%.ctb	5 KB	AutoCAD Color-dep...	3/9/1999 5:13 AM
Screening 100%.ctb	5 KB	AutoCAD Color-dep...	3/9/1999 5:14 AM

FIGURE 15.22: The contents of the `Plot Styles` folder

Understanding How Plot-Style Table Files Are Organized

Plot-style table files are assigned to a drawing and contain all the plot styles needed to control how that drawing is printed. Color-dependent plot styles control printing parameters through color. There are 255 of them in each color-dependent plot-style table, one for each color. Named plot-style tables, on the other hand, have only as many plot styles as are necessary, possibly only two or three. You'll now look at a plot-style table and see how it's organized:

1. Open the Plot dialog box.

2. Expand the dialog box if necessary, and choose acad.ctb from the Plot Style Table drop-down list in the top-right corner (see Figure 15.23).

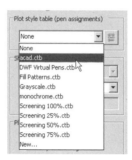

FIGURE 15.23: Assigning a color-dependent plot style to the drawing

 3. Click the Edit Plot Style button next to the drop-down list to open the Plot Style Table Editor dialog box with acad.ctb in its title bar (see Figure 15.24). This dialog box has three tabs. The General tab displays information and a Description text box for input.

FIGURE 15.24: The General tab of the Plot Style Table Editor dialog box for the acad.ctb file

4. Click the Table View tab (see Figure 15.25). Now you see the plot styles across the top and the plot style properties listed down the left side. This tab organizes the information like a spreadsheet. Use the scroll bar to assure yourself that there are 255 plot styles. Notice that each plot style has 12 properties plus a text box for a description. This tab displays the plot-style information in a way that gives you an overview of the table as a whole.

FIGURE 15.25: The Table View tab of the Plot Style Table Editor dialog box for the `acad.ctb` file

5. Click the Form View tab (see Figure 15.26). The same information is organized in a slightly different way. Here the plot styles are listed in the box on the left. You can highlight one or more plot styles at a time. The properties of the highlighted styles appear on the right. This view is set up to modify the properties of chosen plot styles. Notice that the first property, Color, has Use Object Color assigned for all plot styles. This means that red objects are plotted in red, blue in blue, and so on. You can override this by expanding the drop-down list and selecting another color.

6. Close the Plot Style Table Editor, assign the color-dependent mono-chrome.ctb to the drawing, then open the file for editing. Click the Table View tab. Now look at the Color property. All plot styles have the color Black assigned (see Figure 15.27).

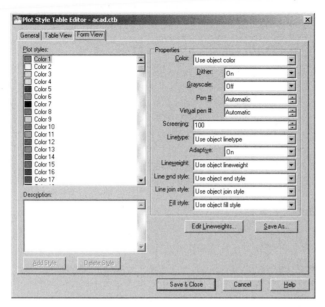

FIGURE 15.26: The Form View tab of the Plot Style Table Editor dialog box for the `acad.ctb` file

FIGURE 15.27: The Table View tab of the Plot Style Table Editor dialog box for the `monochrome.ctb` file

7. Click Cancel to close the Plot Style Table Editor dialog box, and close the Plot Styles dialog box.

7 1 0   Chapter 15 • Printing an AutoCAD Drawing

The monochrome.ctb file will print all colors in your drawing as black, but they won't change the colors in the AutoCAD file.

Assigning Plot-Style Tables to Drawings

Each drawing can be assigned only one kind of plot-style table file: color-dependent or named. This is determined when the drawing is first created.

N O T E   Even though the type of plot style for a new drawing is fixed in the Plot Style Table Settings dialog box, two utility commands let you switch the type of plot style that a drawing can have and assign a different one. They are the Convertpstyles and Convertctb commands.

Follow these steps:

1. Open the Application menu, and click the Options button in the lower-right corner.

2. This opens the Options dialog box; click the Plot And Publish tab. Then click the Plot Style Table Settings button near the lower-right corner of the dialog box. Doing so opens the Plot Style Table Settings dialog box.

    In the uppermost area are the two radio buttons that control which type of plot style a drawing will accept, color-dependent or named (see Figure 15.28). New drawings will accept only the type of plot style that is selected here.

FIGURE 15.28: The Plot Style Table Settings dialog box

3. Below the radio buttons is the Default Plot Style Table drop-down list. Here you can select a plot-style table file (of the type selected by the radio buttons) to be assigned automatically to new drawings. One of the options is None.

4. Close the Plot Style Table Settings dialog box. Then close the Options dialog box.

Throughout this book, all the drawings that you created (or downloaded) were set up to use color-dependent plot styles, so you can assign this type of plot style to the drawing. Usually you do this by assigning a particular plot-style table file to a layout or to model space. To finish our tour, and this chapter, you'll assign one of the available plot-style table files to the Cabin15b.dwg drawing and use the Preview option to see the results:

1. Make Cabin15b.dwg the current drawing if it isn't already.

2. Click the Cabin Floor Plan layout to make it current.

3. Start the Plot command, and make sure the extension of the dialog box at the right is open. If it's not, click the right-pointing arrow in the lower-right corner to open it. In the upper-right corner, make sure None is displayed in the Plot Style Table drop-down list and then click the Preview button. AutoCAD displays the preview in the same colors used in the drawing (see Figure 15.29).

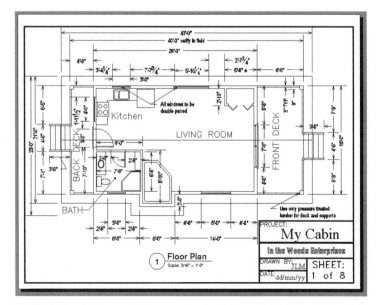

FIGURE 15.29: Preview of the Cabin Floor Plan layout without a plot-style table assigned to it

4. Exit the Preview display, and then click the Cancel button to cancel the plot.

5. With the Output tab active, click the Page Setup Manager button in the Plot panel. In the Page Setup Manager dialog box, highlight Cabin Floor Plan in the Page Setups list, and click Modify. Doing so opens the Page Setup dialog box.

6. Notice that in the Plot Style Table (Pen Assignments) area, None is selected. No plot-style table file has been assigned to this layout.

7. Open the drop-down list.

All the available .ctb (color-dependent plot-style table) files are listed. You can choose one or click New at the bottom of the list and create your own. Once one is chosen, you can click the Edit button to modify it and make a new plot style out of it.

8. Select monochrome.ctb, as shown in Figure 15.30.

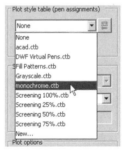

FIGURE 15.30: Assigning the monochrome.ctb file to the layout

9. Click Preview in the lower-left corner. All lines and filled areas in the drawing are solid black (see Figure 15.31).

10. Exit the Preview window.

11. Repeat steps 5–10, and select a different .ctb file from the Plot Style Table drop-down list. (I recommend trying Screening 50%.ctb and Grayscale.ctb.) When you get back to the preview, you'll see the difference.

12. Exit the Plot dialog box, and save the drawing as Cabin15c.dwg.

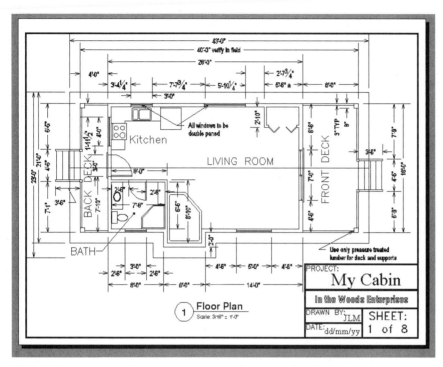

FIGURE 15.31: Preview with the `monochrome.ctb` plot-style table assigned to Layout1

Summing Up

This chapter has been a quick tour and introduction to the plot-style feature, which helps control how your drawing will plot. Getting consistently good output from your AutoCAD drawings involves an investment of time by you, or the office CAD manager/information technologist, to set up the best configuration of your printers and AutoCAD. As you have seen, layouts provide a good tool for setting up plots, once the configuration is right.

The next two chapters cover drawing in 3D (for AutoCAD users only). You'll also find a glossary of terms related to AutoCAD, AutoCAD LT, building construction, and design that have been discussed in the book. This book's web page (www.sybex.com/go/autocad2010ner) offers a collection of all AutoCAD drawing and adjunct files that you'll use or generate throughout the course of this book.

For readers who do not wish to continue learning the 3D aspects of AutoCAD, I hope you have found the book useful in helping you learn AutoCAD 2010 and AutoCAD LT 2010. Good luck using AutoCAD in your future. Please contact Sybex with any questions that arise while you work your way through the book (www.sybex.com/go/autocad2010ner).

Are You Experienced?

Now you can...

☑ set up a drawing to be printed

☑ assign lineweights to layers in your drawing

☑ select the area of your drawing to print

☑ choose a sheet size to print your drawing on

☑ control the orientation and origin of the print

☑ set the scale of the print

☑ preview a print

☑ print a layout

☑ publish multiple layouts

☑ navigate through the plot-style features

CHAPTER 16

Creating 3D Geometry

▷ **Setting up a 3D workspace**

▷ **Using the Polysolid tool**

▷ **Using the Boolean functions**

▷ **Extruding 2D objects**

▷ **Creating 3D surfaces**

▷ **Navigating in a 3D environment**

LT has a few 3D viewing tools but none of the 3D solid modeling tools that AutoCAD supports. Therefore, this chapter doesn't apply to LT.

Nothing in AutoCAD is quite as fascinating as drawing in 3D. Compared with a traditional 3D rendering of a building on a drafting board that uses vanishing points and projection planes, a true 3D computerized model of a building that can be rotated and viewed from any angle, inside and out, offers a world of difference. Nevertheless, many architectural firms still use the drafting board to create 3D illustrations for presentation drawings, even though they use AutoCAD for their construction drawings.

That being said, architectural firms are increasingly using AutoCAD's 3D features to create complex 3D models that are rendered, calculating the effects of light and materials and outputting the result as an image file. Acquiring some skills in working in 3D is becoming an employment requirement, and it's also a lot of fun. This chapter covers 3D modeling, and Chapter 17 introduces materials and rendering.

Constructing a 3D model of a building requires many of the tools that you've been using throughout this book and some new ones that you'll be introduced to in this chapter. Your competence in using the basic drawing, editing, and display commands is critical to your successful study of 3D for two reasons. At first, drawing in 3D can seem more complex and difficult than drawing in 2D, and it can be frustrating until you get used to it. If you aren't familiar with the basic commands, you'll become that much more frustrated. Second, accuracy is critical in 3D drawing. The effect of errors is compounded, so you must be in the habit of using tools, such as the osnap modes, to maximize your precision.

Don't be discouraged; just be warned. Drawing in 3D is a fascinating and enjoyable process, and the results you get can be astounding. I sincerely encourage you to make the effort to learn some of the basic 3D skills presented here.

Many 3D software packages are on the market today, and some are better for drawing buildings than others. Often, because of the precision that AutoCAD provides, a 3D `.dwg` file is exported to one of these specialized 3D packages for further work, after being laid out in AutoCAD. Two other Autodesk products, 3ds Max and 3ds Max Design, are designed to work with AutoCAD `.dwg` files and maintain a constant link with AutoCAD-produced files. Sometimes drawings are created in 2D, converted to 3D, and then refined into a shaded, colored, and textured renderings with specific lights and shadows. In this chapter, you'll look at the basic techniques of *solid modeling* and we'll touch on a couple of tools used in *surface modeling*. In the process, you'll learn some techniques for viewing a 3D model.

Modeling in 3D

You'll begin by building a 3D model of the cabin, using several techniques for creating 3D *solids* and *surfaces*. When you use solid modeling tools, the objects you create are solid, like lumps of clay. They can be added together or subtracted from one another to form more complex shapes. By contrast, 3D surfaces are composites of two-dimensional planes that stretch over a frame of lines the way a tent surface stretches over the frame inside.

As you construct these 3D objects, you'll become more familiar with the user coordinate system (UCS), learn how it's used with 3D, and begin using the basic methods of viewing a 3D model.

Setting Up a 3D Workspace

So far, you've been using the 2D Drafting & Annotation workspace to create your drawings. Your first task in transitioning into 3D begins by switching to a new work-space for working in 3D and changing how AutoCAD displays the available tools.

Let's start with Cabin15c.dwg. This is the version of the cabin that you saved at the end of the last chapter. If you haven't been following through the whole book and saving your work progressively, you can download this file from this book's page on the Sybex website, www.sybex.com/go/autocad2010ner. Follow these steps to switch the workspace:

1. If AutoCAD displays the Initial Setup dialog box when you start the program, choose Architecture from the list of industries in the first window and then click the Next button (see Figure 16.1).

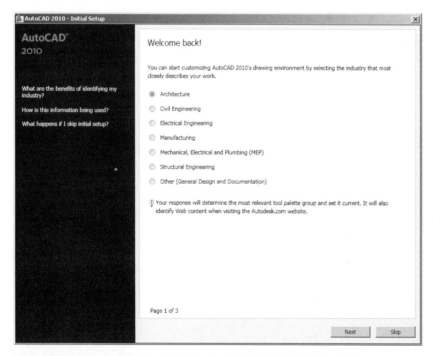

FIGURE 16.1: Choosing the industry in the first Initial Setup window

2. The second Initial Setup window contains a list of tool categories that can be displayed in the workspace. Check the 3D Modeling and Photorealistic Rendering options, as shown in Figure 16.2, and then click Next.

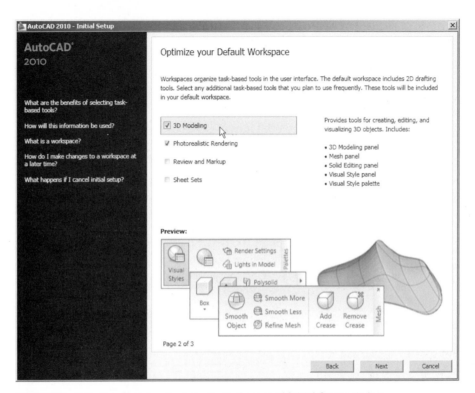

FIGURE 16.2: Choosing the industry in the second Initial Setup window

3. In the third window, make sure the Use AutoCAD 2010's Default Drawing Template File is selected and then click Start AutoCAD 2010 (see Figure 16.3).

4. If the Initial Setup dialog box is not shown, open the Options dialog box from the Application menu and then click the Initial Setup button at the bottom of the User Preferences tab (see Figure 16.4). If you set up the drawing here, rather than when you start up AutoCAD, you will see a Finish button on the third screen, rather than the Start AutoCAD 2010 button.

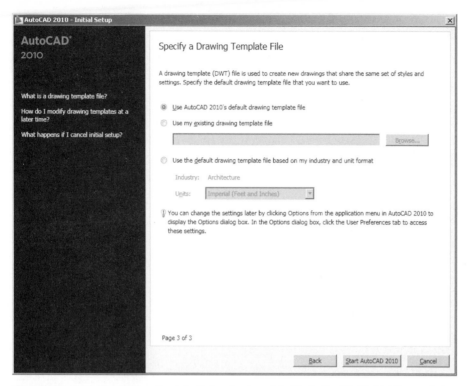

FIGURE 16.3: Setting the default drawing template file in the third Initial Setup window

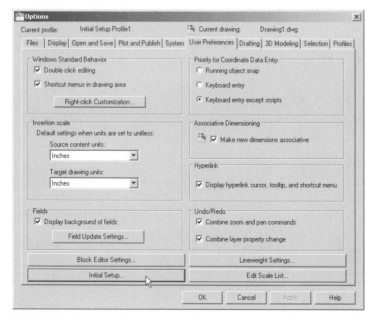

FIGURE 16.4: The User Preferences tab of the Options dialog box

5. Open Cabin15c.dwg; then click the Model button in the status bar to switch to model space. If you don't see the Model button, open the Options dialog box and uncheck the Display Layout and Model Tabs option on the Display tab.

6. Zoom in to the floor plan, make the Walls layer current, and freeze all other layers. Your drawing and AutoCAD setup will look like Figure 16.5.

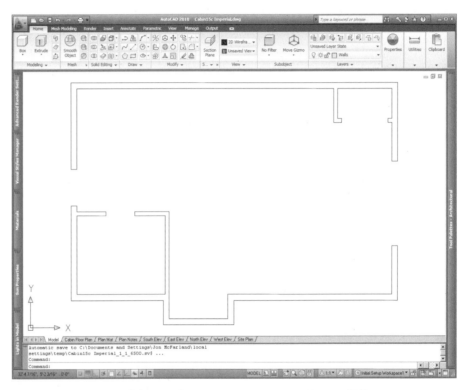

FIGURE 16.5: Cabin15c.dwg with all layers turned off except Walls

Try to start thinking of it in three dimensions. The entire drawing is on a flat plane parallel to the monitor screen. When you add elements in the third dimension, they project straight out of the screen toward you if they have a positive dimension and straight through the screen if they have a negative dimension. The line of direction is perpendicular to the plane of the screen and is called the z-axis. You're familiar with the x- and y-axes, which run left and right and up and down, respectively; think of the z-axis as running into and out of the screen.

7. If the UCS icon isn't visible on your screen, click the View tab and then click the Show UCS Icon button on the Coordinates panel. The UCS icon appears again. You turned it off in Chapter 5 and then used it in Chapter 10 to help construct some of the elevations. You'll use it again in a moment, but for now, keep an eye on it as the drawing changes. Remember that the icon's arrows indicate the positive direction for the x-, y-, and (in 3D) z-axes.

8. Click the Workspace Switching button on the right side of the status bar, select Save Current As, and enter a name in the Save Workspace dialog box that opens. If the workspace changes, you can return to the current setup by clicking the Workspace Switching button and choosing the saved workspace from the menu.

Now you'll change the view from a plan view of the drawing—looking straight down at it—to one in which you're looking down at it from an angle. There are several preselected viewpoints, and here you'll switch to one of them.

9. In the View panel under the Home tab, expand the 3D Navigation drop-down list and choose Southwest Isometric, as shown in Figure 16.6. The name of the view may be clipped by the border of the drop-down list.

FIGURE 16.6: Select the Southwest Isometric view from the 3D Navigation drop-down list.

The view changes to look like Figure 16.7. Notice how the UCS icon has altered with the change of view. The X and Y arrows still run parallel to the side and front of the cabin, but the icon and the floor plan are now at an angle to the screen, and the z-axis is visible. The crosshair cursor is now colored and also displays the z-axis.

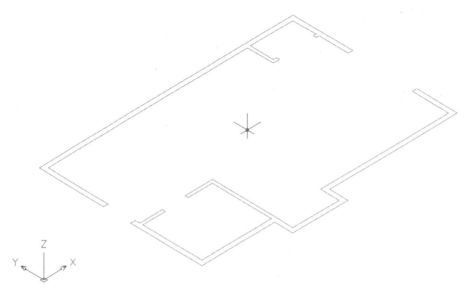

FIGURE 16.7: The walls as seen from the Southwest Isometric view

Setting the Visual Style

Just as you were able to fine-tune and customize your 2D workspace as you worked your way through the earlier chapters, you can do the same with the 3D workspace. Make a few changes now by changing the Visual Style, which defines the way the objects are displayed in the drawing area:

1. Expand the Tool palettes, and then click the X in the upper-right corner to turn them off for now. You won't use the palettes much in the next few pages, and when you need them, you can easily open them again.

2. In the drawing area, zoom to extents, zoom out a little, and pan down to create some space above the floor plan for the 3D walls.

N O T E   A common convention in 3D graphics is to color vectors or other axes to indicate elements, so that red indicates the x-axis, green indicates the y-axis, and blue indicates the z-axis. The phrase used to remember this is "RGB = XYZ." You'll see this convention used several times in this and the next chapter.

3. Open the Visual Styles drop-down list on the View panel, and select 3D Wireframe, as shown in Figure 16.8.

FIGURE 16.8: Selecting the 3D Wireframe visual style

The drawing area takes on a gray background and the UCS icon changes to have a chunkier, three-color appearance. A navigation tool called the ViewCube appears in the top-right corner (see Figure 16.9). I'll cover navigating in a 3D scene later in this chapter.

When you assign colors for 3D layers in the following pages, avoid using grays or other colors that are similar to the gray 3D background color.

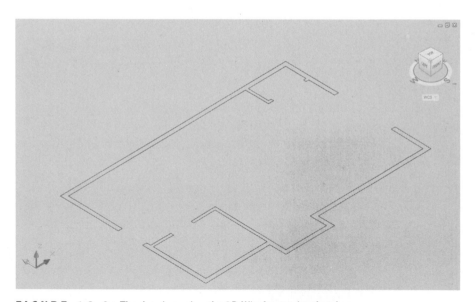

FIGURE 16.9: The drawing using the 3D Wireframe visual style

Making the Walls

The main task ahead is to create a 3D model of the cabin. You'll use solid elements for the cabin's walls, doors, windows, floor, decks, and steps. You'll learn several ways of viewing your work as you progress. To make the walls, you'll start with the polysolid object and then, like a sculptor, remove from the polysolid everything that isn't an interior or exterior wall. The elements to be removed are the void spaces for the doors and windows. Follow these steps:

1. Set the Endpoint osnap to be running. Create a new layer called 3D-Walls-Ext, assign it color 22, and make it current.

T I P   The Layers button isn't available in the 3D Modeling workspace. To open the Layer Properties Manager, you can click Layer on the Format menu or enter la↵.

2. Click the Polysolid tool on the Modeling panel on the far left side of the Home tab. AutoCAD may pause briefly as it loads the 3D specific applications.

3. At the Command: _Polysolid 0'-4", Width = 0'-0 1/4", Justifi-cation = Center Specify start point or [Object/Height/Width/Justify] <Object>: prompt, enter h↵ 7"7-1/4"↵ (2318↵) to set the object height to 7'-7¼" (2318 mm). This is the height where the inside faces of the exterior walls meet the roof.

4. The exterior walls are 6" (150 mm) thick, so the polysolid object should be 6" (150 mm) thick as well. Enter w↵ and then 6↵ (150↵) at the Specify width < 0'-0 1/4">: prompt.

5. The Justification option determines the side of the polysolid for which you will pick the endpoints. You will be picking the outside lines of the cabin in a counterclockwise order, so the justification must be set to Right. Enter j↵ r↵.

6. You're now ready to begin creating the walls. Click the corner of the cabin nearest to the bottom of the screen, and then move the cursor. The first wall appears and it is tied to the cursor, as shown in Figure 16.10.

7. Moving in the counterclockwise direction, click each of the endpoints along the outside perimeter of the cabin until only one segment sepa-rates the last segment from the first. Your drawing should look like Figure 16.11.

8. Right-click and choose Close from the context menu to close the polysolid.

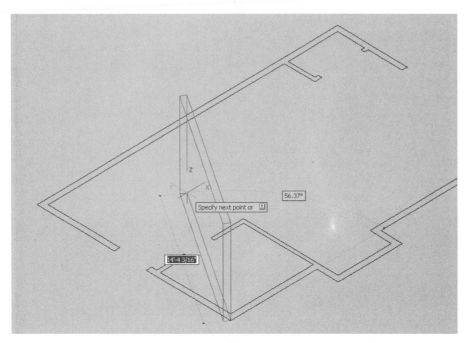

FIGURE 16.10: Starting the first polysolid wall

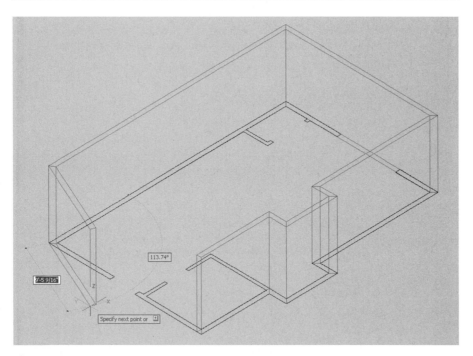

FIGURE 16.11: The exterior walls drawn with polysolids

Adding the Interior Walls

The interior cabin walls are thinner than the exterior walls and will probably have a different material assigned to them. You will make a new layer for these walls and change the polysolid parameters.

1. Create a new layer called **3D-Walls-Int**, assign it color 44, and make it the current layer.

2. Zoom into the lower-left corner of the cabin so that you can see the bathroom walls.

3. Start the Polysolid command again.

4. Press the down arrow on the keyboard to expose the context menu at the cursor, and then click the Width option, as shown in Figure 16.12.

You can also start the
Polysolid command
by entering **psolid↵**.

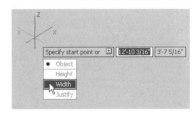

FIGURE 16.12: Choosing the Width option from the context menu

Enter 4↵ (100↵) to change the width to 4″ (100 mm).

5. Starting with the endpoint of the interior wall nearest to the back door, draw the two walls that enclose the bathroom. Right-click and choose Enter to terminate the command. If you have trouble clicking to the correct endpoints, temporarily freeze the 3D-Walls-Ext layer, create the new wall, and then thaw the layer.

6. Press the spacebar to restart the command, and then draw the two walls that surround the closet, starting at the endpoint that is farthest from the sliding glass door. Make sure that it is justified properly, and then zoom to the drawing's extents. Your drawing should look similar to Figure 16.13.

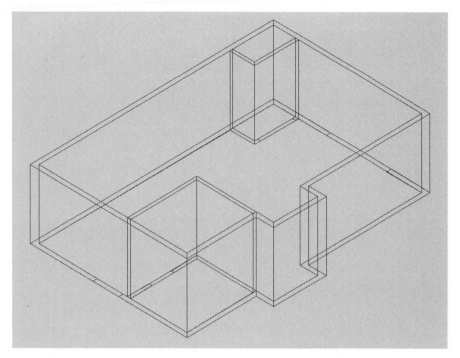

FIGURE 16.13: The cabin with all the walls drawn as polysolids

Creating the Door and Window Block-Outs

Before you add the geometry for the doors and windows, you must make the openings in the walls. You accomplish this using the Boolean tools; the features used to create a single object from the volumes of two overlapping objects, called *operands*. There are three Boolean functions: union, subtraction, and intersection. Union combines the two volumes, subtraction deletes one object and the overlapping volume shared with the other, and intersection deletes both objects, leaving only the shared volume behind. For the doors and windows, you will make block-outs; that is, you'll make solid boxes the size of the openings and then use the Subtract command to create the voids by removing the boxes as well as the volume they share with the walls. The boxes act as block-outs—volumes that are to be deleted—and their only function is to help delete part of the polysolid wall.

N O T E   See Figure 10.1 in Chapter 10 for the window elevations above the floor.

   1. Make a new layer named **Door_Win_Bool**, and set it as the current layer. Freeze the two 3D-Wall layers, and thaw the Windows layer.

2. Use the Visual Styles drop-down list to set the style to Conceptual, as shown in Figure 16.14. This is a flat-shaded style with bold lines.

FIGURE 16.14: Selecting the Conceptual visual style

3. Zoom in to the cabin so that you can see the back door and the kitchen window.

 4. Click the Box button in the Modeling panel of the Ribbon, or enter **box**⏎ at the command prompt. If Box is not shown, click the down arrow below the tool on the far left side of the panel and choose it from the fly-out menu. You will be making a block-out that will act as the operand that is removed from the polysolid.

 N O T E   Boxes, as well as cylinders, cones, and the other 3D objects on the fly-out are known as "primitives," and they are often used as the building blocks of more complex objects.

5. The box object requires three items of information to be constructed: two points that define the opposing corners of the object's footprint and a height value. At the prompts, click two opposite corners of the back door opening, as shown in Figure 16.15.

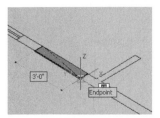

FIGURE 16.15: Defining the footprint of the back door

6. At the Specify height or [2Point]: prompt, enter 7′6↵ (2286↵). The box appears in place (see Figure 16.16).

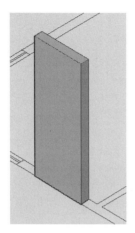

FIGURE 16.16: The first door operand created in place

When I instruct you to *pick* an object when working in 3D, you need to click an edge of the object or a line that helps define the object. If you try to select a surface, the selection may not be recognized.

7. Repeat steps 4 through 6 to create the block-outs for two internal doors and the sliding-glass door.

8. When using the Boolean functions, it's best not to have a situation where the two operands have coplanar faces. Select the box at the back door. The box's grips appear all around the base and a single grip at the top.

Dragging the triangular grips changes the lengths of the sides of the box but doesn't change the angles between the sides. The square grips move the corners of the box or the box itself, and the single top grip changes the box's height.

9. Click the triangular grip on the front of the box, and drag it forward to pull the front of the box out from the front of the cabin. It doesn't have to be a great distance, just enough so that the box and the frozen polysolid don't share the same plane.

10. Drag the rear triangular grip backward, and position it off the inside of the exterior wall. The base of the door should look similar to Figure 16.17.

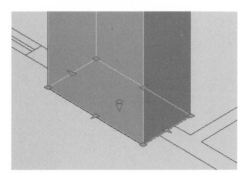

FIGURE 16.17: The base of the door after dragging the grips

11. Repeat the process for the other three door block-outs so that each is thicker than their associated opening. Your screen should look similar to Figure 16.18.

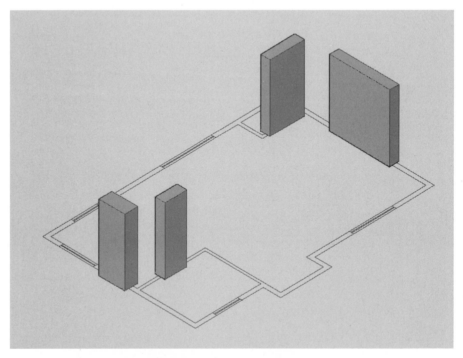

FIGURE 16.18: All the thick door block-outs in place

Creating the Window Block-Outs

As you might expect, making the window block-outs will be just like making the doorway openings. The only difference is that the bottoms of the window openings sit at a different height above the 2D floor plan. Here are the steps:

1. Using the same procedure as in the previous section, create the boxes for all the window block-outs, with each box set to 3'-6" (1067 mm) tall.

T I P   After you make the first window box, the default height for the Box command is the correct height for the remaining windows. When prompted for the height, just press the spacebar or ⏎.

2. Change the thicknesses of the boxes so they overlap the thickness of the outside walls. Your drawing should look like Figure 16.19.

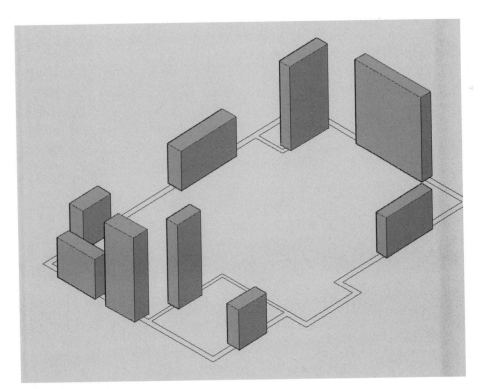

F I G U R E   1 6 . 1 9 : The drawing with all the block-outs in place

3. Save your drawing as Cabin16a.dwg.

Moving and Rotating in 3D

When you moved objects in the 2D portion of this book, terms like "left" and "right" or "up" and "down" were acceptable to use because all movements were associated with the sides of the drawing area. Even when you rotated the views in Chapter 10 it was so you could relate movements to the screen more easily. When working in 3D, however, these terms are no longer easily translated from your intent to proper movement on the screen. Let's take the back door block-out for example. If I told you to move it "forward," would that mean into the cabin, away from the cabin, or toward the bottom of the screen? You see what the problem is. When the viewpoint is significantly different than what you may expect, say, from the bottom or the back, then *front* or *back* may be even more confusing.

The First Right-Hand Rule

To help you stay oriented in 3D space, the UCS becomes more important. Each colored axis of the UCS icon points in the positive direction for that particular axis. To understand whether a movement, particularly in the z-axis, is in the positive direction, you should be familiar with the first of two "right-hand rules." This rule relates your hand to the UCS and helps clarify the axis directions. Start by extending the thumb and index finger on your right hand to form an "L" shape; then project your middle finger perpendicular to your palm as shown in Figure 16.20. The rule states: When your thumb is pointing in the positive X direction and your index finger is pointing in the positive Y direction, your middle finger must be pointing in the positive Z direction.

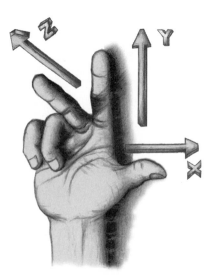

FIGURE 16.20: Use the first right-hand rule to identify x-, y-, and z-axes.

To apply this to the window block-outs in our cabin example, compare your right hand to the UCS icon in the drawing area. With your thumb pointing toward the cabin, and your index finger pointing away from the cabin and to the left, your middle finger then points toward the top of the screen. This indicates that the window block-outs, which are currently resting on the ground plane with the door block-out, need to be moved in the positive Z direction.

1. Click the 3D Move tool in the Modify panel. With the 3D Move tool you move objects using the Move grip tool, which looks similar to the UCS icon.

2. At the Select objects: prompt, select the bathroom window block-out and then press ↵ to end the selection process. The Move grip tool appears at the center of the box, as shown in Figure 16.21.

3. Move the cursor over each of the colored axes of the Move grip tool and notice that the axis turns yellow to indicate that it is current and a vector appears in line with the axis, as shown in Figure 16.22. When a vector is visible, all movements, either indicated with the cursor and a mouse click or input from the keyboard, are constrained to the axis indicated.

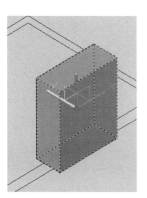

FIGURE 16.21: The Move grip tool at the center of the box

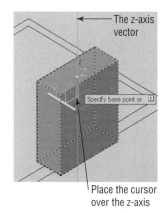

FIGURE 16.22: The z-axis vector indicating that moves are restricted to the z-axis

4. Move the cursor over the blue z-axis. Then, when the axis vector appears, click and move the box in the positive Z direction, and enter 2'11↵ (889↵). The box moves 2'-11″(889 mm) above the wall lines.

T I P **You can also use the standard Move tool and enter @0,0,2'11** (@0,0,889) to move the box 2'-11″ (889 mm) along the z-axis.

5. Start the 3D Move tool again, and this time pick the four remaining window block-outs.

6. Move the cursor directly above the Move grip tool and then click and drag the z-axis. Notice that all four boxes are moving and each leaves a ghosted version of itself at its original location (see Figure 16.23). Enter 2'11↵ (889↵) to move the selected block-outs.

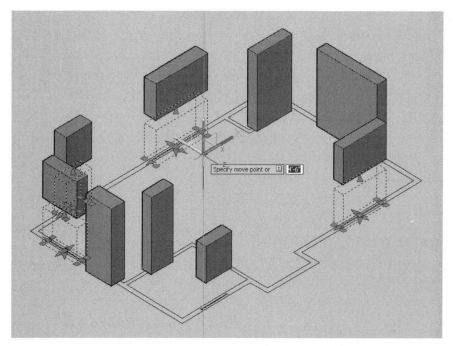

F I G U R E   1 6 . 2 3 : Move the remaining block-outs 2'-11" (889 mm) in the positive Z direction.

7. A move operation in a 3D view can sometimes be deceiving. Use the 3D Navigation drop-down list in the View panel to switch to the Top view, and make sure the block-outs are all located properly. If they are, then switch back to the southwest view. If they're not, undo to the point before the move and try it again.

Cutting the Openings

You are ready to start the Boolean processes and cut the openings in the walls. When prompted to select an object, be sure to click on the edge of the 3D objects and not a face, or the selection may not be successful.

1. Thaw the two 3D-Wall layers, and freeze the Windows layer.

2. Click the Subtract button on the Solid Editing panel, or enter subtract↵.

3. At the Select solids and regions to subtract from.. Select objects: prompt, select the exterior wall and then press ↵ to end the selection process. You can perform the Boolean functions on several objects at one time, but first you will do it to only one.

4. At the Select solids, surfaces and regions to subtract.. Select objects: prompt, select the back door and then press ↵. The door block-out, and the volume that it shared with the wall, are subtracted from the exterior wall (see Figure 16.24).

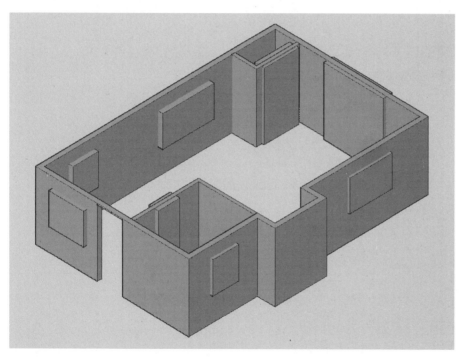

FIGURE 16.24: The back door subtracted from the exterior wall of the cabin

5. Start the Subtract command again, and select the exterior wall again.

TIP   If you have trouble seeing the window block-outs, temporarily switch to the 3D Wireframe visual style, execute the Boolean operation, and then switch back to the Conceptual style.

6. When prompted for the objects to subtract, select all the remaining exterior door and window block-outs and then press ↵. All the openings appear on the cabin's exterior walls, as shown in Figure 16.25.

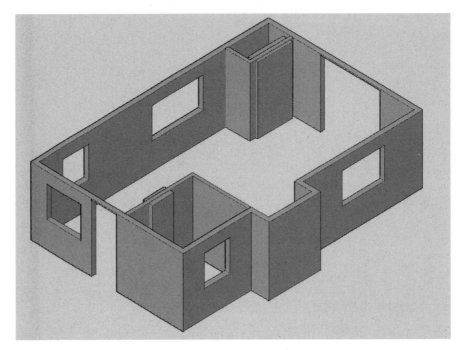

FIGURE 16.25: All the exterior openings created for the cabin

7. Repeat the subtraction process on the two interior walls to remove the bathroom and closet door volumes.

Creating the Floor, Foundation, and Thresholds

In designing the cabin, you didn't draw a floor but one was implied. The three exterior doorway openings have thresholds that indicate a small change in level from the cabin floor down to the decks. You'll now create additional objects to make the floor, foundation and supports, and the thresholds. Follow these steps:

1. Continuing from the previous set of steps, open the Layer Properties Manager and do the following:

a. Create new layers called 3D-Floor, 3D-Foundation, and 3D-Thresh; make 3D-Thresh current; and give each layer a unique color.

b. Freeze the two 3D-Walls layers.

c. Thaw the Steps layer.

To see where you're going, look ahead to Figure 16.28. You'll use the Extrude command to create a series of solids that represent the thresholds and boxes for the steps and the floor.

2. Zoom in the back door opening and its threshold.

3. Draw a polyline around the perimeter of the threshold using the Close option to make the last segment. The polyline is shown wider than necessary in Figure 16.26 for clarity only.

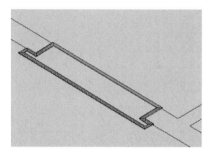

FIGURE 16.26: A polyline drawn around the perimeter of the threshold

4. The Extrude tool extends a 2D object in the Z direction, creating surfaces on the newly formed sides and end caps. Click the Extrude tool in the Modeling panel, select the threshold polyline, and then press ↵. At the Specify height of extrusion or [Direction/Path/Taper angle] <-1'-0">: prompt, enter **1.05**↵ (**27**↵). The first threshold is completed, as shown in Figure 16.27.

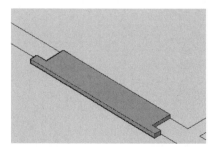

FIGURE 16.27: The extruded polyline

5. Make a similar extruded threshold for the sliding-glass door.

6. Make the 3D-Floor layer current. To make the floor, first draw a polyline around the inside perimeter of the cabin, ignoring the interior walls and thresholds.

7. Start the Extrude command, select the floor polyline, and then extrude it 1″ (25 mm) (see Figure 16.28).

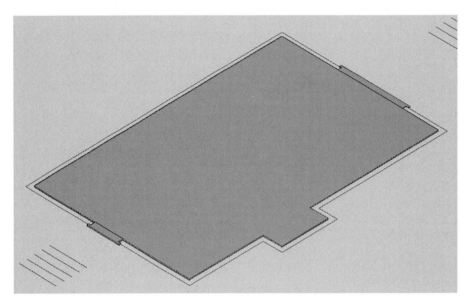

FIGURE 16.28: The 3D floor with the thresholds

Creating the Foundation and Supports

The cabin's foundation is an 18″ (457 mm)-thick concrete slab that sits directly on the ground. The foundation supports the structure except where the pop-out projects out from the side wall. At the outside corners of each deck are concrete support posts. All the objects are placed on the 3D-Foundation layer.

1. Make the 3D-Foundation layer current, and thaw the Deck layer.

2. Freeze the 3D-Floor and 3D-Thresh layers.

3. Draw a closed polyline around the outside perimeter of the cabin, making sure you span the pop-out area as if it didn't exist. Alternatively, you could use the Rectangle command.

4. Extrude the polyline 18″ (457 mm) in the negative Z direction. You can do this with Dynamic Input active by dragging the extrusion in the

negative direction and entering 18↵ (457↵) or by dragging it in the positive direction and entering -18↵ (-457↵).

5. Using the Rectangle command, draw a 12"×12" (305 mm×305 mm) rectangle at each of the four outside corners of the decks. The outside corner of each rectangle should match the outside corner of each deck post corner.

6. Start the Extrude command, select all four rectangles, and then extrude them 2'-10" (864 mm) in the negative Z direction. When you're done, the foundation and supports should look like Figure 16.29.

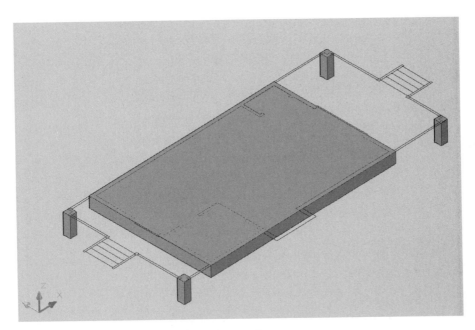

FIGURE 16.29: The foundation and supports

7. Save your drawing as cabin16b.dwg.

Building the Windows

Now that the openings are in place and the foundation is complete, you just need to build the geometry for the doors and windows. These can be as complete as you like them with sills, drip grooves, tapered panels, kick plates, and so on. For the exercise in this book, however, you'll create fairly simple frames, door panels, and glazing.

1. Make a new layer named **3D-Win-Frame**, and set it as the current layer. Freeze the 3D-Foundation layer, thaw the 3D-Wall-Ext layer, and then zoom into the kitchen window near the back door.

2. Click the Allow/Disallow Dynamic UCS button in the status bar to turn on Dynamic UCS mode. When you are in a command, Dynamic UCS causes the current UCS to adapt to the orientation of whichever face the cursor is over. This is important because, when using creation tools like the Box command, the footprint is made in the X and Y plane and the height is projected along the z-axis. When Dynamic UCS is active, the UCS shown at the cursor overrides the UCS shown by the UCS icon.

3. Start the Box command, and then move your cursor near the UCS icon. Notice that the color-coded axes of the crosshairs match the orientation and colors (RGB=XYZ) of the UCS icon axes. Next, move the cursor over the faces on the back wall of the cabin and see that the blue z-axis now points in the same direction as the UCS icon's y-axis. This identifies the orientation of that particular wall's face.

4. With the Endpoint osnap active, click the lower-left outside corner of the kitchen window, and then move the cursor away from that corner. The box starts to form with its orientation parallel to the outside wall, and the UCS icon temporarily changes its orientation (see the top of Figure 16.30). Click the opposite outside corner of the window for the base of the new box (see the bottom of Figure 16.30).

5. At the Specify height or [2Point]>: prompt, move the cursor until you can see the box projecting out from the wall and then enter -4↵ (-100). The box's Height parameter projects it 4" (100 mm) into the window opening. You can switch to a Wireframe visual style to see this more clearly.

6. Turn off Dynamic UCS, select the box, and move it 1" (25 mm) in the positive X direction to center it in the wall.

7. The box you just made will be the frame for the kitchen window. Now you need to make a block-out to subtract from the box to create the opening for the glazing. Copy the box you just made and move it in front of the back wall, and then select the copy to expose its grips. Use ortho mode, keyboard input, or the Move grip tool to ensure that the box is moved along the x-axis only.

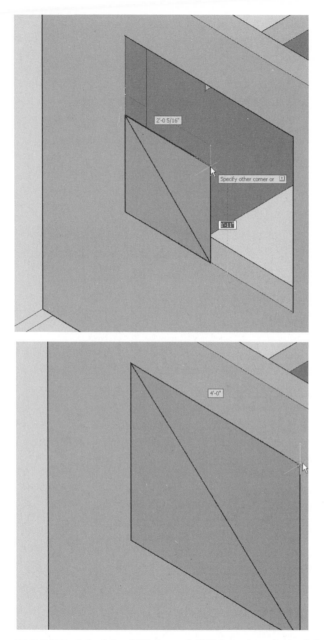

FIGURE 16.30: With Dynamic UCS turned on, the box's base is oriented parallel to the wall (top); the box's base is completed (bottom).

8. Turn on Polar Tracking, and then select each of the four outward-pointing triangular grips along the perimeter and move them 1″ (25 mm) toward the inside of the box (see the top image of Figure 16.31).

Click the triangular grip on the back of the box, and drag it until the box extends all the way through the back wall (see the bottom image of Figure 16.31).

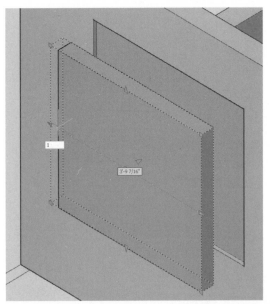

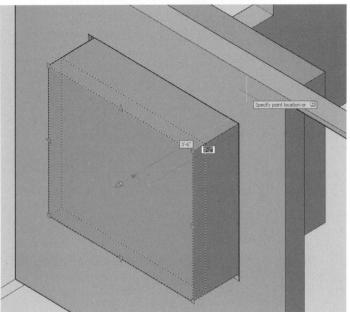

FIGURE 16.31: Moving the block-out's perimeter grips to shrink it slightly (top); the box's increased depth (bottom)

Switch to the 3D Wireframe visual style and then, using the Subtract Boolean function, subtract the block-out from the frame. Switch back to the Conceptual visual style, and your window should look similar to Figure 16.32.

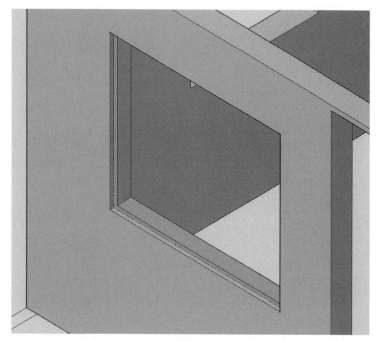

FIGURE 16.32: The completed kitchen window frame

10. Create a new layer named 3D-Glazing, give it a light blue color, and make it current.

11. A polyline can be drawn only in the XY plane, but a 3D polyline can be drawn along any axis. Click the 3D Polyline button in the Draw panel, enter **3dpoly↵** at the command line, or choose Draw ➤ 3D Polyline from the menu bar.

12. Turn on the Midpoint running osnap, and then draw the 3D polyline using the midpoints of the frame's four, 4″ (100 mm)-wide inner corners. Switch to the 3D Wireframe visual style and freeze the 3D-Wall-Ext layer if you have trouble locating the midpoints. Be sure to switch back to the Conceptual visual style and thaw the layer when you are done.

13. Use the Extrude tool to extrude the glazing 0.25″ (6 mm). If you have trouble selecting the 3D Polyline, use the Last option at the Select Objects: prompt. Your kitchen window should look like Figure 16.33.

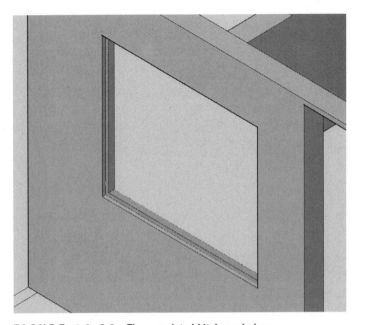

FIGURE 16.33: The completed kitchen window

Rotating in 3D (the Second Right-Hand Rule)

When you rotated objects in a 2D environment, all the rotations were perpendicular to the screen and you never had to consider the axis around which the object was rotating. Because all 2D rotations happened in the XY plane, the objects were rotated around the z-axis. Positive rotations were in the counterclockwise direction, and negative rotations were clockwise. In 3D, however, rotation can occur around any axis and you need to understand whether a rotation should be in the positive or negative direction. Use the second right-hand rule to understand how the rotation direction is identified in a 3D environment. It states that if you grasp an axis with your right hand with your thumb pointing in the positive direction, then your fingers will be curled in the positive rotation direction. Figure 16.34 illustrates this concept.

FIGURE 16.34: The right-hand rule as it applies to rotations

To rotate an object in 3D, you use the 3D Rotate tool, called a gripper, shown in Figure 16.35. It consists of three intersecting circular bands, the center of which is the pivot point of the rotation. Each band is color coded (RGB=XYZ) to identify the axis around which the objects are rotated. When you're prompted for a rotation axis, clicking the green band, for example, restricts the rotation to the y-axis.

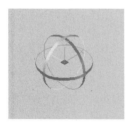

FIGURE 16.35: The 3D Rotate gripper

Completing the Windows

When Boolean operations are used, the component objects, called operands, are not replaced with the resulting object; they just become subobjects of it. You always have the ability to edit the operands and alter the object itself. Here's how:

1. Copy the existing window frame and glazing, and move the copy in front of the 5′-0″ (1525 mm) window on the south side of the cabin; then zoom into that window.

2. With the two objects selected, click the 3D Rotate tool in the Modify panel.

3. At the Specify base point: prompt, click the endpoint of the lower corner of the frame nearest to the cabin. The 3D Rotate gripper relocates to the specified corner.

4. At the Pick a rotation axis: prompt, click the blue z-axis ring. It turns yellow to indicate that it is the currently selected axis, and a blue line is emitted from the 3D Rotate grip tool to identify the pivot axis.

5. Imagine your right hand gripping the blue axis line with your thumb pointing upward, as in the hand shown in Figure 16.34. This shows you that a positive rotation, the direction your fingers are pointing in, is required to rotate the window counterclockwise. Enter **90↵** at the Specify angle start point or type an angle: prompt (see Figure 16.36). The window rotates 90°.

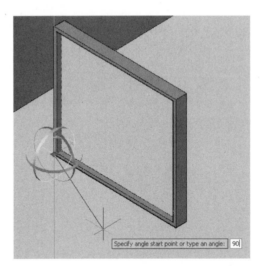

Specify angle start point or type an angle: 90

FIGURE 16.36: Rotating the window 90° counterclockwise

This window is currently 4'-0" (1220 mm) wide, while the opening is 5'-0" (1525 mm) wide. You can correct the discrepancy by editing the subobjects of the window frame. Subobjects are selected by holding the Ctrl key down while selecting an object. Follow these steps:

1. Turn running object snaps off and turn Polar Tracking on.

2. Select the window frame, right-click and choose Properties, then, in the Solid History rollout, choose Yes for the Show History option. See Figure 16.37.

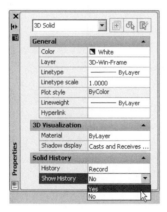

FIGURE 16.37: In the Properties palette, set the Show History property to Yes.

An outline of the box, used to subtract the volume for the opening, appears as shown in Figure 16.38.

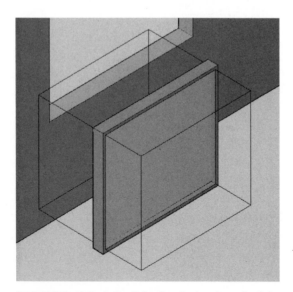

FIGURE 16.38: Selecting the box from the Subtract Boolean operation

N O T E   The object that you are editing is the window frame and the operand is the subobject. You must hold down the Ctrl key when selecting a subobject to expose its grips.

3. Hold the Ctrl key down, and then click to select the box operand and expose its grips. Click one of the triangular grips that control the width of the box, drag it to make the box wider, and then enter **12↵** (**305↵**) to stretch the box 12″ (305 mm) in the X direction, as shown in Figure 16.39.

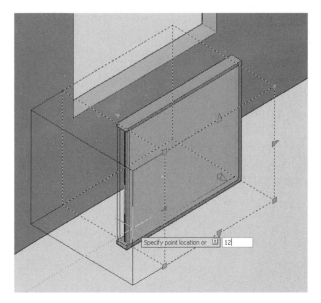

FIGURE 16.39: Adjusting the size of the box from the Subtract Boolean operation

The side of the window frame disappeared because the box operand that subtracted part of the frame operand now completely envelops the left side of the frame. You can fix this by adjusting the size of the frame operand.

4. Hold the Ctrl key down, and click the window frame to select it and expose the grips.

5. Click the triangular grip on the same side that you selected for the box operand, drag the grip to make the frame larger, and enter **12↵** (**305↵**), as shown in Figure 16.40. The frame is extended 12″ (305 mm).

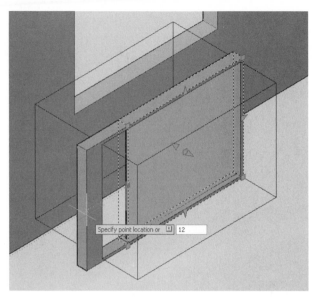

FIGURE 16.40: Adjusting the size of the window frame

6. Select the glazing, and then select each of the two exposed endpoints and move them 12″ (305 mm) to extend them to the new frame size (see Figure 16.41).

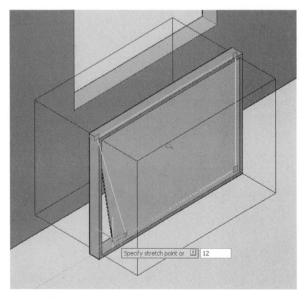

FIGURE 16.41: Adjusting the size of the window glazing

7. Finally, you need to move the new window into the opening. Turn on the running object snaps; select the frame and glazing. Pick the lower-left front corner of the frame as the first move point and the lower-left front corner of the opening as the second point. The window is moved into place, as shown in Figure 16.42.

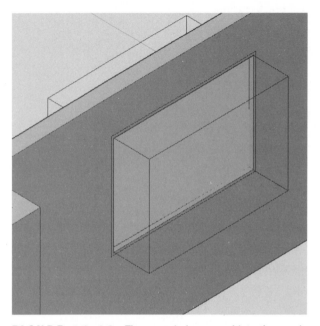

FIGURE 16.42: The new window moved into the opening

8. The frame is flush with the outside wall. Use the 3D Move tool to move it 1" (25 mm) in the positive Y direction.

9. Turn off Show History in the Properties palette.

Repeat the process in this section to make two of the other three rectangular windows in the cabin. Two of the windows are 3'-0" (915 mm) wide, and you can simply copy one into the opening of the other. When you're done, your drawing should look similar to Figure 16.43.

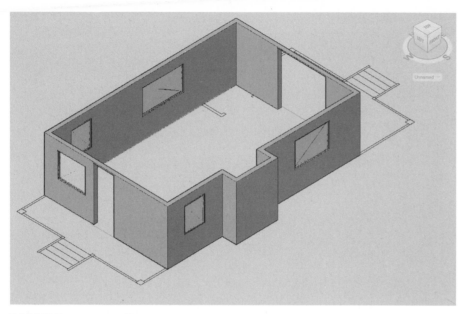

FIGURE 16.43: The cabin after all the rectangular windows and frames are finished

Adding the Pivot and Bi-Fold Doors

For this exercise, you will represent the two pivot doors with simple boxes and the two bi-fold doors with extruded polylines. Later, if you choose, you can add knobs and glass panes.

1. Add a new layer named 3D-Pivot-Doors, and make it current. Thaw the 3D-Thresh layer.

2. Zoom into the back door. Rather than moving the primitives as you have been doing, here you'll use object tracking to place the start point.

3. Switch to the 3D Wireframe visual style, turn on Object Snap Tracking mode in the status bar, and make sure the Polar Tracking and Intersection running object snaps are on as well.

4. Start the Box command, and then, at the Specify first corner or [Center]: prompt, place your cursor near the bottom-left outside corner of the front door where it meets the top of the threshold, until the small cross in the intersection marker appears. Move the cursor in the X direction until the tracking vector appears, and then enter 2↵ (51↵) to set the first corner of the door 2″ (51 mm) from the corner of the opening (see Figure 16.44).

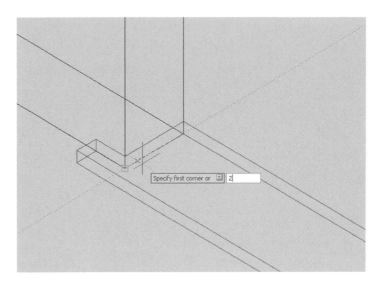

FIGURE 16.44: Locating the first corner of the door box

5. Enter @2,-36↵ (@51,-915) to place the second point of the 3'-0" (915 mm) door. Give the door a height of 7'-6" (2286), the distance from the top of the threshold to the bottom of the door opening.

6. Thaw the 3D-Walls-Int layer; then use a similar process to add the bathroom door, with these differences:

▶ The door is only 2'-6" (762 mm) wide.

▶ The door is only 1½" (38 mm) thick.

▶ The door is 7'-5" (2261 mm) tall.

▶ Offset the door 1¼" (32 mm).

▶ Start or move the door 1" (25 mm) above the bottom corner to accommodate the 1" (25 mm)-thick floor.

7. Zoom in to the bi-fold closet doors.

8. Freeze the 3D-Wall-Int layer and thaw the Doors layer. Start the Boundary command from the expanded Draw panel. Like the Hatch command, Boundary locates the perimeter of a closed area, but draws a polyline around it rather than drawing a pattern within it.

9. In the Boundary Creation dialog box that opens (see Figure 16.45), make sure that Polyline is selected in the Object Type drop-down list, then click the Pick Points button.

FIGURE 16.45: The Boundary Creation dialog box

10. Click inside each of the rectangles that represent the doors to create a new polyline. Thaw the 3D-Wall-Int layer and freeze the Doors layer.

N O T E   In step 8, you were required to freeze the 3D-Wall-Int layer before using the Boundary command and then thaw it afterward. This is because if you look at the closet area from the top, the upper edge of the header crosses the corners of each rectangle. When AutoCAD processes the boundary perimeter, it does so as if viewing the XY plane of the drawing and doesn't account for differences in the Z elevation of the objects. From the top, it looks as if the closet header would form one edge of the closed boundary. Try step 8 without freezing the 3D-Wall-Int layer and see the difference.

11. Move the four polylines 1″ in the Z direction so they rest at the same level as the top of the floor.

12. Start the Extrude tool, and extrude each polyline 7′-5″ (2260 mm).

13. Zoom out and switch to the Conceptual visual style. Your cabin should look like Figure 16.46.

14. Save your drawing as cabin16c.dwg.

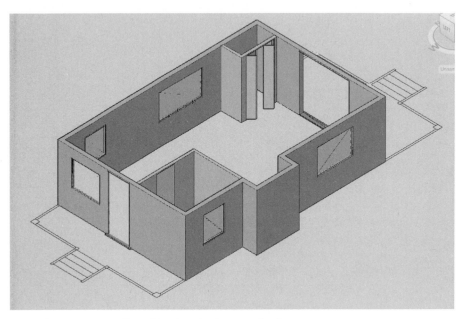

FIGURE 16.46: The cabin after the doors are in place

Navigating with the ViewCube

Changing the viewpoint used to view your drawings is especially important in a 3D environment because you are more likely to encounter a situation where foreground objects obscure background objects. The ViewCube, the tool in the upper-right corner of the drawing area, is used to access common views quickly, return to a saved view, or navigate freely in the drawing area.

The ViewCube (see Figure 16.47) consists of a center cube with each face labeled to identify the orthographic view that it represents. Clicking any of these labeled faces changes the viewpoint in the drawing area to display the objects from that point of view, based on the World Coordinate System (WCS). For example, clicking the ViewCube face labeled TOP changes the drawing area to display the cabin from the top, with the x-axis pointing to the right and the y-axis pointing to the top of your screen.

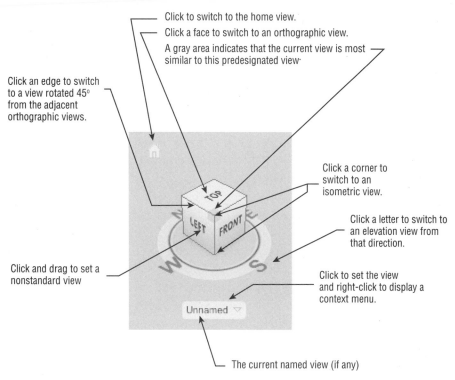

Click to switch to the home view.

Click a face to switch to an orthographic view.

A gray area indicates that the current view is most similar to this predesignated view·

Click an edge to switch to a view rotated 45° from the adjacent orthographic views.

Click a corner to switch to an isometric view.

Click a letter to switch to an elevation view from that direction.

Click and drag to set a nonstandard view

Click to set the view and right-click to display a context menu.

The current named view (if any)

FIGURE 16.47: The functions of the ViewCube

Clicking the face labeled FRONT changes the drawing area to display the cabin from the front, the view you designated as the south elevation, with the x-axis pointing to the right and the z-axis pointing to the top. The orthographic views are not the only viewpoints that you can access from the ViewCube. Clicking on any corner (see the left image in Figure 16.48) changes the drawing area to display the objects from an isometric vantage point that is a combination of the three labeled faces. Clicking on the corner at the intersection of the TOP, FRONT, and LEFT faces produces a view identical to the Southwest Isometric view you selected from the Viewpoint drop-down list. That corner is currently gray, indicating that it is the viewpoint most similar to the current view.

FIGURE 16.48: Clicking a ViewCube corner (left); clicking a ViewCube Edge (right)

Clicking any of the edges (see the right image in Figure 16.48) changes the drawing area to display the objects rotated 45 degrees from one of the adjacent orthographic views. Clicking on any of the ViewCube features not only changes the view but also executes a Zoom Extents command, displaying all of the visible objects in the drawing area. You'll usually perform a Zoom after using the View-Cube. Clicking and dragging the ViewCube changes the viewpoint freely without any constraints.

Surrounding the cube is a ring with the compass directions indicated. Clicking on any of the letters switches the view in the drawing area to a view from that direction. For example, clicking the letter E on the ring displays the east elevation of the cabin. This is a view showing the 3D cabin from the east and not the 2D east elevation that you drew. You can click and drag the ring to rotate the view in a freeform manner.

The ViewCube also provides access to the named UCSs that you created in Chapter 10 and, when a named UCS or the WCS is current, displays the name below the compass ring. Clicking on the rectangle shape below the ViewCube opens a context menu (see the left image in Figure 16.49) where you can select the current view. Right-clicking on the rectangle shape opens a context menu where you can, among other things, set the ViewCube settings and designate the current view as the home view (see the right image in Figure 16.49).

FIGURE 16.49: Selecting the current view from the ViewCube (left); accessing the right-click context menu (right)

You can quickly switch to the home view by clicking the house icon, which is visible when the cursor is over the ViewCube.

Switching to a predesignated view is quick and can often provide the vantage point that you need, but you may need to view your objects from a specific, non-standard location.

 T I P   Holding down the Ctrl key while holding down and dragging with the scroll wheel has a similar function as dragging the ViewCube.

Adding the Sliding Door

The remaining door to add is the sliding door on the front of the cabin. Although this is a door, the procedure for creating it will be more like that for the windows you've already made. Here are the steps:

1. Click and drag the ViewCube to the left and slightly upward to display the front of the cabin; then zoom in to the front door. Your view should look similar to Figure 16.50.

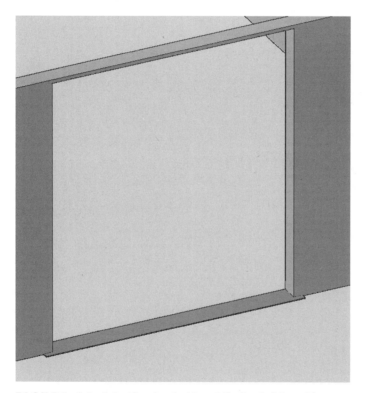

FIGURE 16.50: The view looking at the front of the cabin

2. Make the 3D-Win-Frame layer current.

3. Create a box that is 3'-7" (1092 mm) wide, 2" (51 mm) thick, and 7'-5.95" (2259 mm) tall, and place it 1" (25 mm) in on the right edge of the patio opening on top of the threshold.

4. Create a block-out that is 4″ (102 mm) smaller than the width and height of the frame you just drew, but significantly deeper. Then center it on the window frame, as shown in Figure 16.51. Some display roughness may occur where the block-out and frame meet, but this is just a function of the Conceptual visual style and the thin faces shown.

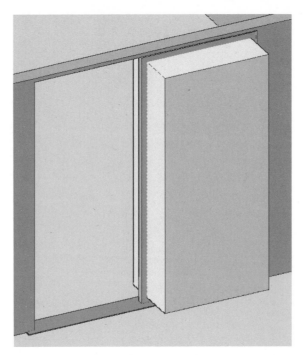

F I G U R E   1 6 . 5 1 : The first sliding-door frame and block-out

5. Subtract the block-out from the window frame.

6. Set the 3D-Glazing layer as current. Use a 3D polyline tool to create the boundary to the glazing, extrude it, and then center it in the frame.

7. Copy the frame until it butts the opening on the left and then move it 2″ (51 mm) toward the inside of the cabin so that the two door frames are offset (see Figure 16.52).

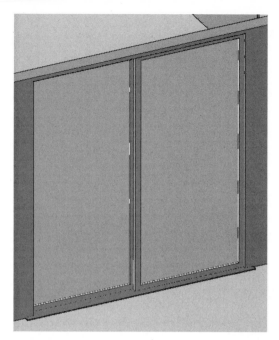

FIGURE 16.52: The completed sliding door with two offset panels

Building the Decks

You're nearly done modeling the cabin. The next step is to make the two decks using basic shapes and copying redundant objects. Follow these steps to create the front deck:

1. Make a new layer called **3D-Deck**, assign it color 240, make it current, and then thaw the 3D Foundation layer and freeze the other 3D layers except 3D-Walls-Ext and 3D-Thresh.

2. Click the Box tool and create a box to represent floor of the deck. Use the Endpoint osnap to locate the two opposite corners of the deck, and then give the box a height of -1 5/8″ (-41 mm). Your model should look like Figure 16.53.

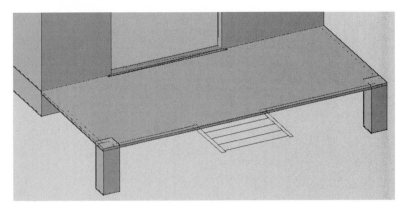

FIGURE 16.53: The beginning of the deck

3. Draw a box that follows the perimeter of the railing on the left side of the deck, and make this box 2″ (51 mm) tall. Move the box 4″ (102 mm) in the Z direction to represent the lower railing; then copy it and move the copy 3′-2″ (965 mm) higher to represent the upper railing. Your railings should look like those in Figure 16.54.

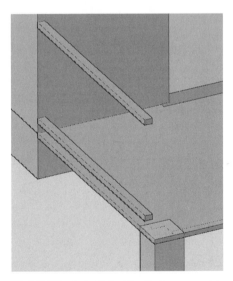

FIGURE 16.54: The first upper and lower railings

4. Repeat the process to create the two sets of railings at the front of the deck, on the left side of the stairs; then copy both sets to the opposite side of the deck. Switch to the right and top views with the ViewCube to check your work, adjust the size of the railings on the right side of

the steps, and then use the Zoom Previous command (z↵ p↵) to return to the current view (see Figure 16.55).

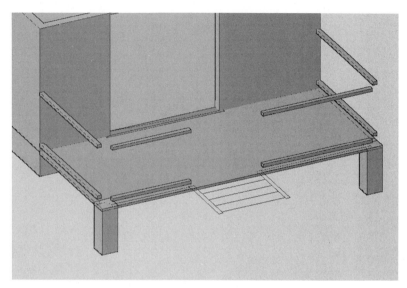

FIGURE 16.55: The railings in place and adjusted for size

5. To draw the first railing post, click the down arrow below the Box button in the Modeling panel and choose Cylinder from the fly-out menu. At the Specify center point of base or: prompt, click the midpoint of the first lower railing that you drew where it meets the exterior wall, and enter 3/8↵ (9.5↵) for the radius (see Figure 16.56).

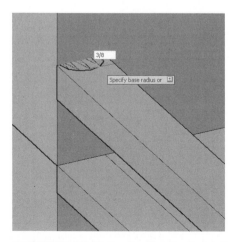

FIGURE 16.56: Creating the first railing post cylinder

6. At the Specify height or: prompt, make sure the cursor is above the cylinder's base, and then enter 3' ↵ (914↵).

7. To fill in the row of posts, move the first post 3 5/8" (92 mm) in the X direction and then copy it 20 times, at 4" (102 mm) increments in the X direction. The first set of railing posts should look like those shown in Figure 16.57.

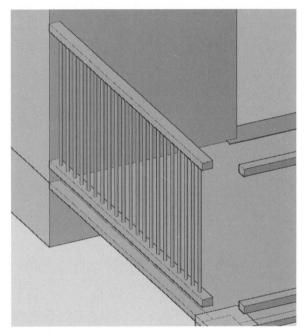

FIGURE 16.57: The first set of railing posts

8. Repeat steps 5 through 7 to draw the posts along the front of the deck, adjusting the count and the direction appropriately; then copy the posts from the left side of the deck to the right. Add any new post as required. The completed railing posts should look like those shown in Figure 16.58.

9. Zoom in to the front-left corner of the deck, where the support post sits. Use the Box tool to draw the 8"×8" (204 mm×204 mm) post and give it a height of 7'-8" (2337). You may need to adjust the height later when the roof is applied.

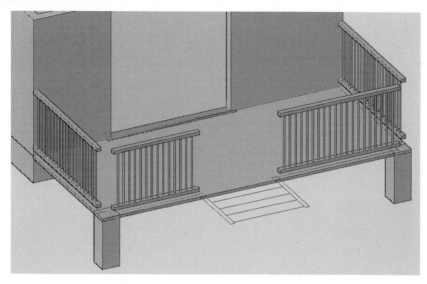

FIGURE 16.58: The completed railing posts

10. Copy the post to the opposite side of the deck and adjust the placement as necessary. Figure 16.59 shows the two support posts in place.

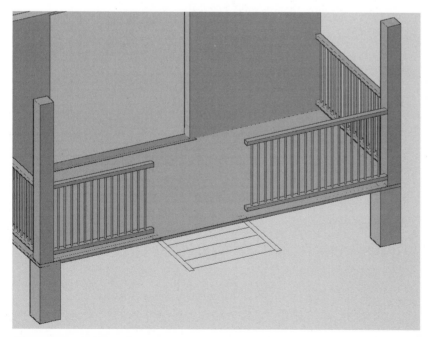

FIGURE 16.59: The support posts in place

Building the Steps

The steps and the step railings and posts transition from the ground level to the top of the deck. In this section, you'll build and move the stairs and create and then rotate the handrail.

1. Make a new layer named 3D-**Steps** and make it current.

2. Zoom in to see the steps clearly; then switch to the 3D Wireframe visual style. When you drew the steps in the plan view, the lines defining their width were trimmed back to the edge of the handrail. In reality, the steps extend all the way to the outside edges of the handrails.

3. Use the Box tool and Object Snap Tracking or the Apparent Intersection osnap to draw the four steps. Give each box a height of -1 5/8″ (-41 mm). Switch back to the Conceptual visual style. Your steps should look like those in Figure 16.60.

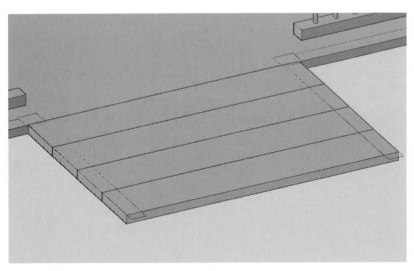

FIGURE 16.60: The front deck steps before setting their elevations

4. Move the step furthest from the deck 24″ (609 mm) in the negative Z direction, the second 16″ (406 mm), and the third one 8″ (203 mm). The top step remains flush with the top of the deck.

5. To draw a polyline that you'll extrude to become the stringer (the support for the steps), you'll use a 3D Polyline (see Figure 16.61). Follow these steps:

   a. Click the 3D Polyline button in the Draw panel.

b. Using the Object Snap Tracking tool, start the polyline 8″ (203 mm) below the back of the top step.

c. Use the Endpoint object snap to snap to the corner of the top step.

d. Follow the bottom and back edges of the steps until you reach the front of the bottom step.

e. Continue the polyline in the negative Z direction 8″ (203 mm) and then in the negative X direction 8″ (203 mm).

f. Enter c↵ to close the polyline.

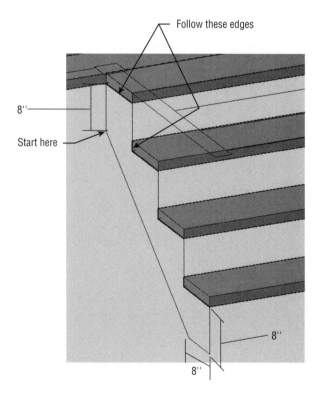

FIGURE 16.61: Drawing the stringer

6. Extrude the stringer 2″ (51 mm), and move it 2″ (51 mm) in the positive Y direction so that it's tucked under the steps a bit.

7. Copy or mirror the stringer to the opposite side of the steps. The completed steps should look like those shown in Figure 16.62.

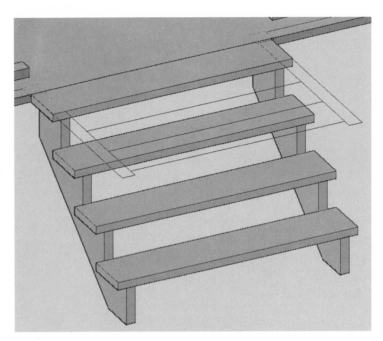

FIGURE 16.62: The completed steps

Creating the Stair Handrails

To create the handrails for the stairs, you'll first draw the vertical posts, create a box at the end of one of one of them, and then rotate it into place. Using the Dynamic UCS tool will ensure that the box is created in the correct orientation.

1. Zoom into the top of the stairs and draw a 3'-9" (1143 mm)-tall box, using the rectangle at the end of the railing to define the footprint.

2. Click the Allow/Disallow Dynamic UCS button in the status bar to turn it on.

3. Start the Box command, pick a point on the front surface of the post, and then specify a 2"×2" (51 mm×51 mm) base and a 4'-6" (1372 mm) height for the box. The box is created perpendicular to the front surface of the post.

4. Move the handrail so that it is centered on the post and 1" (25 mm) from the top, as shown in Figure 16.63.

5. Start the 3D Rotate tool, and select the handrail.

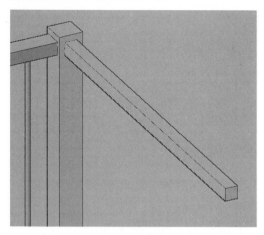

FIGURE 16.63: The box drawn perpendicular to the post

6. At the Specify base point: prompt, pick the midpoint of the handrail where it meets the post. At the Pick rotation axis: prompt, click the green y-axis ring; then, at the Specify angle start point or type an angle: prompt, enter -39↵. The handrail rotates into place.

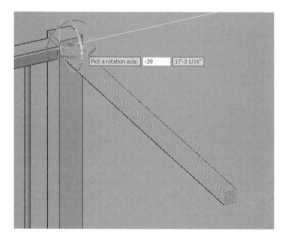

FIGURE 16.64: Rotating the handrail into place

7. The last items to build for this handrail are the 1″ (25 mm) posts that support it. Draw two cylinders with a ½″ (12.5 mm) radius and a height of about 2′ (610 mm) and space them evenly on the top step, centered under the handrail. Using the grips, adjust the height of each post so that they end inside the handrail.

8. Using the endpoints of the steps as a reference, copy the posts to the other steps and then copy the handrail and posts to the opposite side of the steps. When you are done, the completed steps should look like Figure 16.65.

FIGURE 16.65: The completed steps

Adding the Skirt

The final piece to add to the deck is a skirt, a linear member that acts as a connection surface for the structure and a visual shield so the residents can't see under the deck. With the modeling skills and experience that you picked up in the previous chapter, this should be a quick fix by building a skirt around the three open sides of the decks to obscure the underside. Here's how:

1. Switch to the 3D Wireframe visual style, and make sure that the Endpoint running osnap is active.

2. Make the 3D-Deck layer current.

3. Draw a 2″×6″ (51 mm×153 mm) box on the side and front of the deck just below the surface, as shown in Figure 16.66. The figure is shown in the Conceptual visual style for clarity. The boxes should span the distance from the foundation to the support post and between the support posts, respectively.

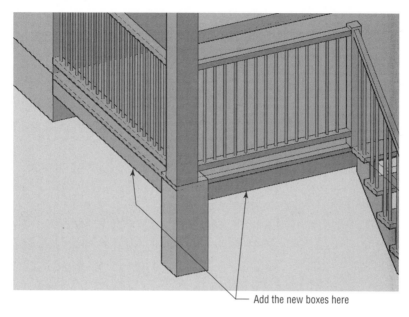

Add the new boxes here

FIGURE 16.66: The 2″×6″ skirt added below the deck

4. Copy the shorter box to the opposite side of the deck.

5. Change the visual style back to Conceptual, and your completed deck should look like Figure 16.67.

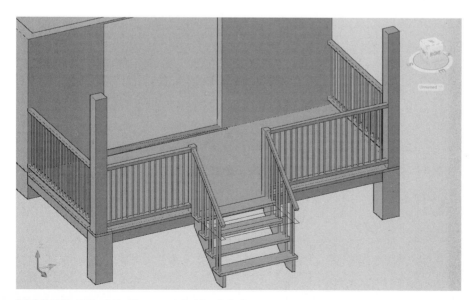

FIGURE 16.67: The completed front deck

Mirroring the Front Deck

Because the front deck is similar to the back deck, you can mirror all the objects that you've already worked hard to create to the back of the cabin, similar to the way you did in the 2D section of the book. Once the objects are in place, you can edit them to meet the design criteria. Follow these steps to mirror the deck:

1. Freeze all the layers except 3D-Deck and 3D-Steps; then thaw the Walls layer.

 2. Click the face labeled TOP in the ViewCube to switch to a plan view of the cabin. In the Layer Properties Manager, click the open lock icon in the Lock column next to Walls so that objects on the Walls layer can't be selected or modified.

 3. Select all the deck and step objects; then click the Mirror tool in the expanded Modify panel.

4. For the first point of the mirror line, select the midpoint of the long outside wall on the north side of the cabin, the wall that has the closet attached to the inside of it. For the second point, pick a point directly to the right. Press ⏎ to accept the default option not to delete the original objects. (See Figure 16.68.)

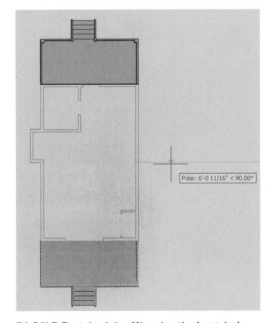

FIGURE 16.68: Mirroring the front deck

5. Move the cursor over the ViewCube, then click the counterclockwise-facing arrow in the top-right corner of the ViewCube to rotate the view 90° around the z-axis to give the cabin plan a more familiar orientation.

6. Thaw and lock the Deck layer; then zoom in to the back deck.

7. Change to the 3D Wireframe visual style.

8. Delete any of the handrail posts that exist between the 8″ (204 mm) 3D support posts and the 8″ (204 mm) 2D support posts (see Figure 16.69) on both sides of the deck.

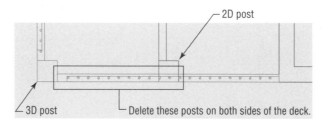

FIGURE 16.69: Delete the posts shown

9. Click the Move tool from the Modify panel, and drag a crossing window, dragging from right to left around the front of the deck and the stairs, as shown in Figure 16.70.

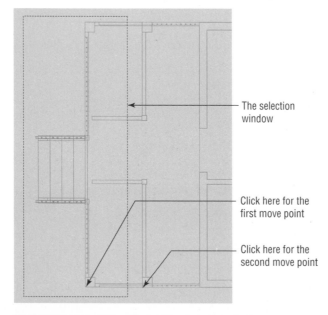

FIGURE 16.70: Moving the deck to make it narrower

10. Move the deck 4'-0" (1220 mm) in the X direction to fit the narrower rear deck's size. The floor, railings, and skirt project into the cabin.

11. Select the deck floor, horizontal railing, and horizontal skirts; then, using the triangular grips, move their right ends 4' (1220 mm) to the left, so they extend only to the back wall of the cabin. Figure 16.71 shows the back of the cabin after adjusting the features.

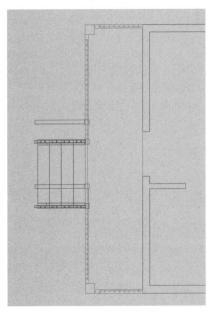

FIGURE 16.71: The rear deck after adjusting the handrails, skirts and deck floor

12. Delete the 3/4" (20 mm) handrail posts in the vertical row on the north side of the 3D steps between the 4" (102 mm) 3D vertical post and the 4" (102 mm) 2D vertical post (see Figure 16.72).

13. Using the Move command, move the steps into place, as shown in Figure 16.72. Add any new posts that are required on the south side of the steps. Use the triangular grips to adjust the lengths of the railings as required.

14. Change to the Conceptual visual style, and drag the ViewCube to get a good look at the new deck; it should look like Figure 16.73.

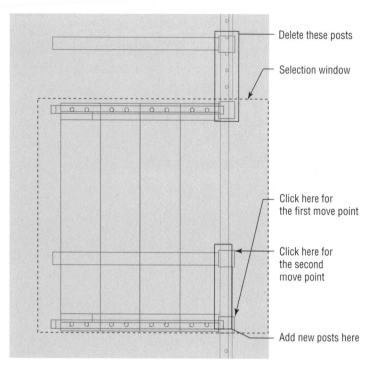

Delete these posts

Selection window

Click here for
the first move point

Click here for
the second
move point

Add new posts here

FIGURE 16.72: Moving the deck to make it narrower

FIGURE 16.73: The completed back deck

15. Save your drawing as cabin16d.dwg.

Putting a Roof on the Cabin

You'll finish the 3D model of the cabin by constructing a roof. The surface of the roof will be a different color from the roof structure, so you'll make them as two separate objects, each on its own layer. Both objects will be extruded from the east elevation, and you'll use the Boolean Subtract function to cut the roof in the areas where it doesn't project as far as it does over the pop-out. Follow these steps:

1. Create two new layers: **3D-Roof-Surface** with color 32 and **3D-Roof-Deck** with color 114. Make 3D-Roof-Surface current.

2. Thaw the 3D-Walls-Ext and Roof layers.

3. Click the rectangle below the ViewCube, and click East-elev from the context menu. The UCS changes and East-elev is shown in the View-Cube rectangle. Enter **plan↵ c↵** to orient the drawing area to the UCS; then zoom in to the east elevation (see Figure 16.74).

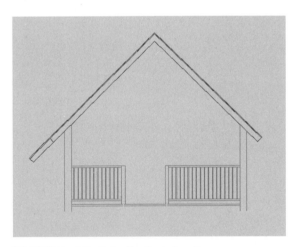

FIGURE 16.74: The East elevation

4. Use the Endpoint osnap and carefully draw a closed polyline around the thin roof surface. Make sure that the pline follows both the inner and outer surfaces of the roof covering and extends to the limits of the pop-out. There should be a total of six picks and then the Close option.

5. Make the 3D-Roof-Deck layer current, and then draw a closed polyline around the perimeter of the roof deck in the east elevation.

6. Drag the ViewCube and then click the corner that is shared by the TOP, FRONT, and RIGHT faces to change the view; then zoom in to the east elevation.

7. Use the Extrude tool to extrude the two polylines that you just drew 43′ (13110 mm), as shown in Figure 16.75.

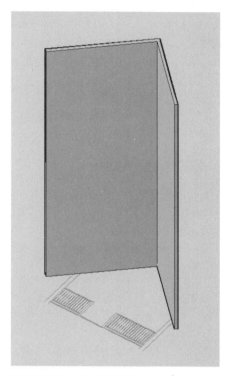

FIGURE 16.75: The extruded roof polylines

8. The Extrude tool creates the extrusion in the current layer, so select the thinner of the two extrusions and move it to the 3D-Roof-Surface layer using the Properties palette.

9. Use the 3D Rotate tool to rotate both objects 90° around the y-axis so that they match the orientation of the cabin.

Adjusting the Cabin Walls

The cabin walls were drawn with a constant height. In this section, you'll create the peaks at the front and back of the cabin to accommodate the roof. To accomplish this, you will add segmentation to the top of the walls using the Slice tool and then move the new edges in the z-axis. Here's how:

1. Freeze the 3D-Deck and 3D-Steps layers.

 2. Click the Slice button on the Solid Editing panel.

3. At the Select objects to slice: prompt, pick the exterior walls.

4. The Slice tool uses a plane with an infinite depth to cut the selected objects, so you need two points to define the plane. At the Specify start point of slicing plane or: prompt, use the Midpoint osnap to pick the midpoint of the top of the front wall, as shown in the top image of Figure 16.76.

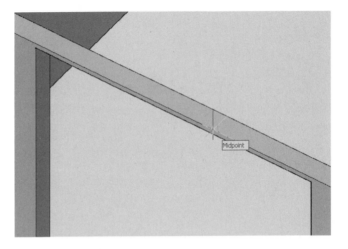

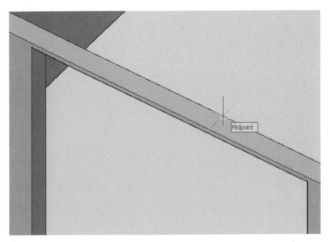

FIGURE 16.76: Selecting the first Slice point (top); selecting the second Slice point (bottom)

5. At the Specify second point on plane: prompt, pick the midpoint of the top of the back wall, as shown in the bottom image of Figure 16.76.

6. The Slice tool can display both sides of the sliced object or it can delete one of the sides. In this case, you want to keep both sides. At the Specify a point on desired side or [keep Both sides]: prompt, press ↵ or enter b↵ to retain both sides. The new edges appear on the walls (see Figure 16.77) and there are now two sets of exterior walls; one on the south side of the cabin and one on the north. Notice that the slice is centered on the wall, but not centered over the doorway.

FIGURE 16.77: The new edges created with the Slice tool

Just as you were able to edit the size of a box object by dragging its grips, you can do the same with nonprimitive objects. The grips are available at the edges, faces, and vertices; the points where two or more edges end. You access the subobjects by holding down the Ctrl key and clicking on the grip location. The grips won't appear until you click.

7. Zoom in to the newly sliced area on the front wall. Hold the Ctrl key down and click the middle of the top edge. The small rectangular, red edge grip appears as shown in Figure 16.78.

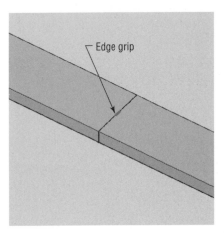

FIGURE 16.78: Exposing the edge grip

8. Click the grip, and enter @0,0,8′2-1/4↵ (@0,0,2496) to move the edge 8′-2¼″ (2496 mm) along the z-axis. The faces bound by the edge are adjusted accordingly and form one half of the peak, as shown in Figure 16.79.

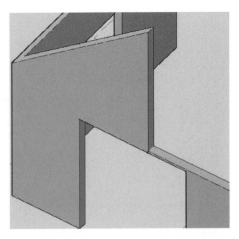

FIGURE 16.79: Creating half the peak

9. Adjust the edge on the other side of the front wall in the same manner. Zoom out and you'll see that adjusting one end of the sliced object adjusted the other, and the peak is already constructed at the back of the cabin (see Figure 16.80).

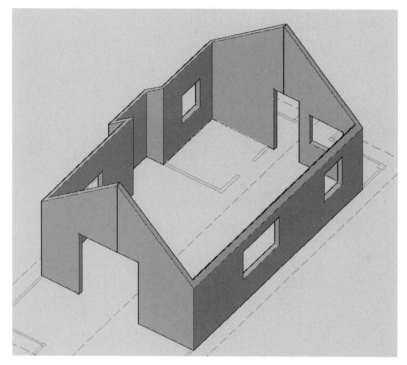

FIGURE 16.80: Both peaks are completed.

10. Use the Endpoint osnap to move the two roof objects so that the inside peak of the deck sits directly on the peak at the front of the cabin, as shown in Figure 16.81. You can temporarily switch to the 3D Wireframe visual style if this makes the task easier.

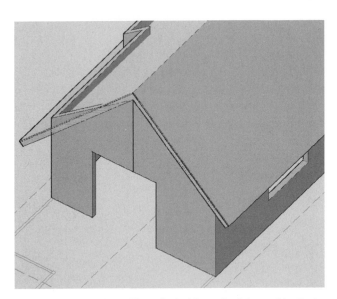

FIGURE 16.81: Move the inside peak of the roof to the top of the front wall peak.

11. Next, move the cabin roof forward 9′-6″ (3000 mm) (see Figure 16.82). Check the cabin from above to make sure the 3D roof is aligned with the 2D rooflines.

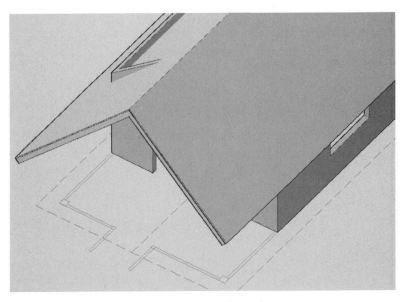

FIGURE 16.82: Move the roof objects forward.

Tweaking the Roof and Walls

As you can see, the walls poke through the roof on the south side of the cabin and you still need to modify the roof so that it only projects out over the pop-out. You'll do these tasks using the subobject grips and Boolean tools.

1. Use the ViewCube to rotate the view so that you can see the roof that covers the pop-out.

2. Make sure Dynamic UCS is turned on and Endpoint osnaps are running; then start the Box command.

3. Create a box, starting at the southeast corner of the roof with a footprint that is 3'-4" wide and extends to a point 1'-6" (457 mm) from the pop-out. Give the box some height and then repeat the process on the opposite side of the pop-out as shown in Figure 16.83. The Dynamic UCS tool creates the boxes aligned to the roof.

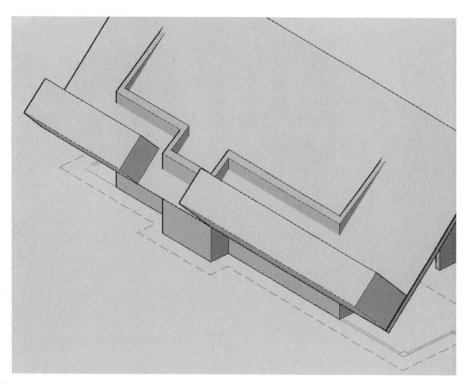

FIGURE 16.83: The boxes to be used to subtract the roof

4. Use the grips to extend the outside edges of the boxes beyond the edges of the roof (see Figure 16.84).

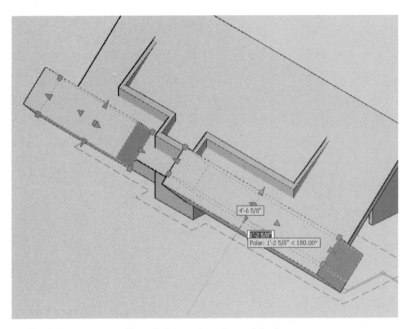

FIGURE 16.84: Extend the outside edges of the boxes.

5. Move the boxes so that they protrude through the roof using the endpoint of one edge as the first point of displacement and the midpoint of the same edge as the second. When you're finished, the model should look similar to the one shown in Figure 16.85.

6. If you subtract both roof objects at the same time, the resultant roof object will be a single entity. Use this procedure to cut the boxes out of the roof.

    a. Copy the boxes in-place using the same point as the base point and the displacement.

    b. Select the roof surface and subtract one set of boxes from it.

    c. Select the roof deck and subtract the second set of boxes from it.

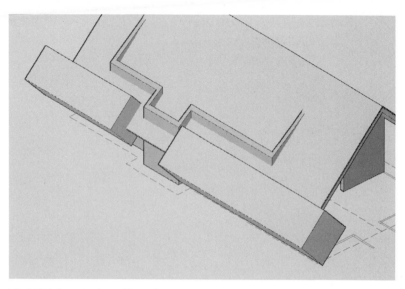

FIGURE 16.85: Move the boxes so they protrude through the roof.

When you are done, the roof should look like Figure 16.86.

7. Hold the Ctrl key down and click the middle of the outer wall of the pop-out. You may have trouble selecting the proper edge when both of the adjacent faces are visible. If you encounter a problem, try selecting the edge from a northeastern viewpoint.

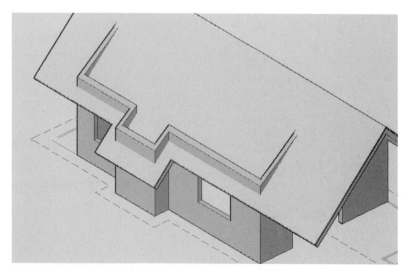

FIGURE 16.86: The roof after subtracting the boxes

8. Turn on ortho mode; then move the edge downward, below the surface of the roof. Figure 16.87 shows the edge being moved from a northeastern viewpoint.

9. Freeze and unlock all the 2D layers and thaw the 3D layers.

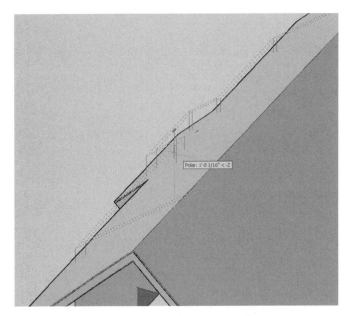

FIGURE 16.87: Adjusting the pop-out walls

10. Drag the ViewCube to change to an isometric view, and then adjust the height of the roof support posts so that they extend into the roof deck but not through the roof surface (see Figure 16.88).

FIGURE 16.88: Adjusting the height of the roof support posts

11. Your completed cabin should look like Figure 16.89.

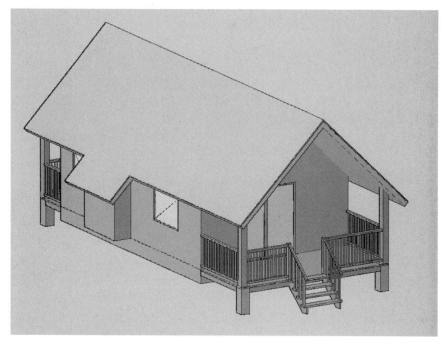

FIGURE 16.89: The completed cabin

12. Save your file as `cabin16e.dwg`.

Getting Further Directions in 3D

Covering 3D in real depth is beyond the scope of this book, but I can mention a few other tools and features that you might enjoy investigating. Here I'll summarize a few of the solids and surface-modeling tools that I didn't cover in the tutorial on the cabin. In the next chapter, we'll look at the rendering process as it's approached in AutoCAD.

Using Other Solids Modeling Tools

You used the Box primitive to build the block-outs for the cabin walls and the Cylinder primitive for the railing posts. There are several other primitive shapes, all found on the fly-out menu list on the right edge of the Modeling panel. Six of them are shown and described here, and you can also see a cue card describing the creation procedure, as shown in Figure 16.90, by pausing the cursor over any primitive option.

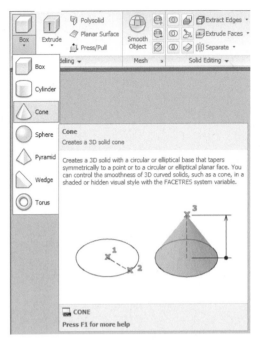

FIGURE 16.90: The other 3D primitives and the cue card for the cone

Cone You specify the center point of the base, the radius of the base, and the height of the pointed tip. The base is parallel to the XY plane, and the height is perpendicular to it. You can choose for the cone to be elliptical and for the top to be flat instead of pointed.

Sphere You specify the center point and radius or diameter.

Pyramid The pyramid primitive is similar to the cone primitive, but it can have up to 32 flat sides, rather than a curved side.

Wedge The wedge has a rectangular base and a lid that slopes up from one edge of the base. You specify the base as you do with the Box primitive and then enter the height.

Torus This is a donut shape. You specify a center point for the hole, the radius of the circular path that the donut makes, and the radius of the tube that follows the circular path around the center point.

The other tools on the Modeling panel are for creating additional 3D solids, for manipulating existing 3D shapes, or for using 2D shapes as components for making 3D shapes. You've already used some of these tools, and I'll cover the others here:

Planar Surface Creates a flat, rectangular surface that is segmented in both directions. The segments are only visible when the object is selected or in a wireframe visual style (see Figure 16.91).

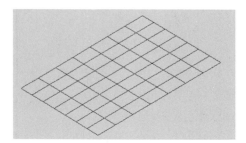

FIGURE 16.91: A Planar surface

Revolve Select a closed 2D shape, and then define the axis and the angle of rotation. A revolve object is shown on the left in Figure 16.92.

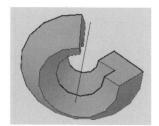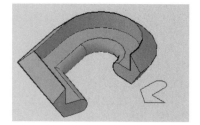

FIGURE 16.92: A Revolve object (left); a Sweep object (right)

Sweep Similar to the Extrude tool, the Sweep tool extrudes a 2D shape along a path to create a 3D shape. A sweep object is shown on the right in Figure 16.92.

Loft Similar to the Extrude and Sweep tools, the Loft tool extrudes a 2D shape along a path, but allows you to change cross sections along the path.

Press/Pull The Press/Pull tool creates a 3D object by extruding the perimeter of an area surrounded by a closed boundary. The left image in Figure 16.93 shows the closed area and the right image shows the resultant object. The boundary does not have to be a polyline; it can simply be a conglomeration of any objects that combine to define an open area.

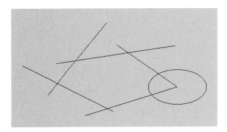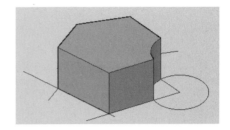

FIGURE 16.93: An enclosed area (left); the result of using the Press/Pull tool (right)

Helix A Helix object is a 2D or 3D spiral (see Figure 16.94). When you use it in conjunction with the Sweep tool, you can create springs, corkscrews, coils, and so forth.

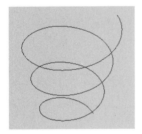

FIGURE 16.94: A helix extending in the Z direction

There are two other Boolean tools for modifying solids. When you formed the cabin walls, you used the Subtract tool as well as Slice. Two other solids-editing tools, Union and Intersect, create an object based on two overlapping objects. Union joins the two objects and eliminates any internal edges. Intersect finds the volume that two solids have in common and retains that volume while deleting the other portions of the objects.

This was only a brief introduction to the tools for creating and modifying solids, but it should be enough to get you started.

Using Surface-Modeling Tools

In addition to the solid objects available in AutoCAD, a set of tools is available to create surfaces or surface models. Unlike solids, surfaces can't be easily manipulated and do not have a true volume, just faces that surround an empty area. For example, imagine this book next to a cellophane wrapper having the same dimensions. The book would be a solid and the wrapper would be a surface.

Here is a brief description of a few of the surface tools on this menu (see Figure 16.95):

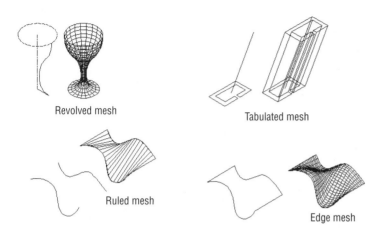

Revolved mesh

Tabulated mesh

Ruled mesh

Edge mesh

FIGURE 16.95: AutoCAD's surface modeling tools

Revolved Mesh Creates a 3D surface mesh by rotating a 2D curved line around an axis of revolution.

Tabulated Mesh Creates a 3D surface mesh by extruding a 2D object in a direction determined by the endpoints of a line, an arc, or a polyline.

Ruled Mesh Creates a 3D surface mesh between two selected shapes.

Edge Mesh Creates a 3D surface mesh among four lines that are connected at their endpoints. Each line can be in 2D or 3D, and the original shape must be a boundary of a shape that doesn't cross or conflict with itself.

Most 3D models today utilize the solid-modeling tools for their basic shapes because the tools for adding, subtracting, slicing, and so forth are easy to use and allow complex shapes to be fabricated quickly. Still, surface modeling, legacy tools retained from AutoCAD's initial foray into 3D, have their uses. Any serious 3D modeler will be familiar with both sets of tools.

Are You Experienced?

Now you can...

- ☑ change visual styles
- ☑ create linear 3D objects with the Polysolid tool
- ☑ extrude 2D shapes into 3D geometry
- ☑ cut holes in objects using the Subtract Boolean tool
- ☑ resize 3D objects using grips
- ☑ create 3D surfaces
- ☑ navigate in a 3D scene

CHAPTER 17

Rendering and Materials

- ▶ Using the Loft tool
- ▶ Creating cameras to reproduce views
- ▶ Creating a lighting scheme
- ▶ Enabling and controlling shadow effects
- ▶ Choosing the background
- ▶ Assigning materials to surfaces
- ▶ Adjust mapping and tiling
- ▶ Saving setup views and lights as restorable scenes
- ▶ Rendering and outputting to a file

A fter developing a 3D model, you'll usually want to apply materials and render it to get a better feel for the substance of the project and for a clearer presentation tool for the clients.

In this chapter, I'll give you a quick tour of some of these rendering steps as you set up a view of the cabin and render it. Developing a full rendering takes time and patience, but touching on a few of the many steps involved will give you a feel for the process. You've put in a lot of time working your way through this book, and you deserve to have a rendered 3D view of your cabin to complete the process. Be aware, however, that rendering is computationally intensive and can task your computer pretty heavily. It's a good rule to save your file prior to each rendering attempt.

Creating Cameras to Reproduce Views

Similar to the named views you saved in Chapter 10, a camera is a method for returning to a saved viewpoint. The most significant advantage of cameras is the ability to select the camera object and change its position or orientation rather than panning or zooming in the drawing area. Cameras can also be animated to show your model from a variety of locations. Before you place the cameras, however, you'll create some land for your cabin to sit on so that it no longer appears to be floating in the air.

Using the Loft Tool

The Loft tool builds 3D geometry in one of three ways: by connecting a series of 2D shapes, called *contour lines*, with 3D surfaces, by extruding a cross section along a path, or by controlling the transition between two cross sections with 2D guide curves. You'll use the first method to create a loft object to serve as the land by drawing concentric 3D polylines, converting them to splines, changing their elevations, and then lofting them. Follow these steps:

1. With Cabin16e.dwg as the current drawing, change to the 3D Wireframe visual style and zoom into the cabin.

2. Make a new layer named **3D-Land**, assign it color 94, and set it as the current layer. Freeze all the other layers except 3D-Foundation and 3D-Steps, and then thaw the Site and Site13a|Prop_Line layers. Switch to the 3D Wireframe visual style.

3. Start the 3D Polyline command and draw a closed polyline around the perimeter of the base of the foundation, as shown in Figure 17.1. Use the Endpoint osnap to draw the vertices of the polyline at the bottom corners of the foundation.

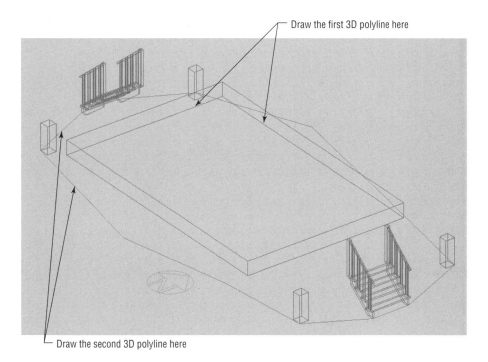

Draw the first 3D polyline here

Draw the second 3D polyline here

FIGURE 17.1: Draw the first two 3D polylines around the cabin.

4. Draw another closed 3D polyline around the concrete support posts, snapping the outside corner of each, and the outside corners of the stringers. You can pick an interim point between each of the long sides of the cabin to break up the perimeter. These are the first two contour lines.

5. Turn off Ortho Mode or Object Tracking if they are on; then click the TOP face of the ViewCube to switch to a top view. Draw two more oddly shaped closed 3D polylines between the cabin and the property line, and then trace the property line itself (see Figure 17.2).

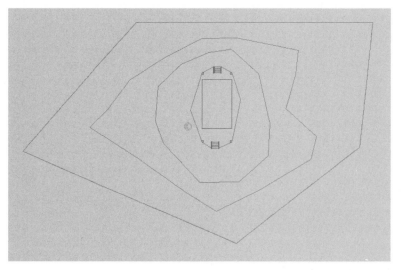

FIGURE 17.2: Draw three more 3D polylines around the cabin and property line.

6. Click the Edit Polyline button from the extended Modify panel or enter **pedit**↵. Enter **m**↵ to choose the Multiple option and select the two polylines between the cabin and the property line.

7. Click the Spline option in the context menu, as shown in Figure 17.3, to change the polylines into curved splines and then click ↵.

FIGURE 17.3: Select Spline from the context menu.

T I P   A spline is a curved line with control points for adjusting the curvature.

The last three contour lines you drew are at the same level as the top of the foundation. You need to move them downward to define the slope of the property away from the cabin.

1. Switch to an isometric view by holding down the Shift key and dragging with the left mouse button.

2. Turn on Polar Tracking, and then move the spline closest to the cabin foundation down 3′-6″ (1070 mm) in the negative Z direction. Move the spline closest to the property line down 4′-4″ (1320 mm), and then move the polyline that follows the property line down 5′-4″ (1625 mm). This should provide a gentle slope for the land.

3. Verify in a front or side view that each of the splines is lower than the previous (see Figure 17.4).

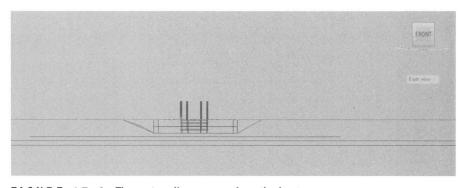

FIGURE 17.4: The contour lines as seen from the front

As you can see in the figure, the vertices of the polyline that follows the foundation and steps are at the proper elevation where they were snapped to an end point, but not where you simply clicked in the drawing area. This is because when you did not use a snap, the vertex defaulted to an elevation of 0. To fix this, you'll need to move the vertices down.

4. Turn off Object Snap, and then select the polyline.

5. Click one of the grips at a mislocated vertex and move it down until it is approximately at the same elevation as the bottom of the support posts, as shown in Figure 17.5. Repeat this step for any other vertices of this polyline that are at the incorrect elevation.

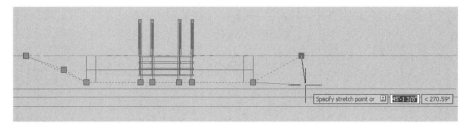

FIGURE 17.5: Changing the elevation of a vertex

6. Switch back to the current view, adjust the location of the vertices if necessary, and then freeze all layers except 3D-Land.

7. Click the Loft button in the Modeling panel. It may be hidden under the Extrude button.

8. At the Select cross sections in lofting order: prompt, first click the outermost polyline and then each subsequent spline or polyline in order from outside to inside.

9. At the Enter an option: prompt, enter c↵ for the Cross Sections Only option.

10. In the Loft Settings dialog, shown in Figure 17.6, click the Smooth Fit option. Smooth Fit creates a soft transition from one contour to the next.

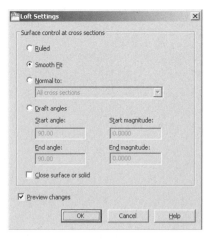

FIGURE 17.6: The Loft Settings dialog box

11. Click OK, then change to the Conceptual visual style. Your cabin land parcel should look similar to Figure 17.7.

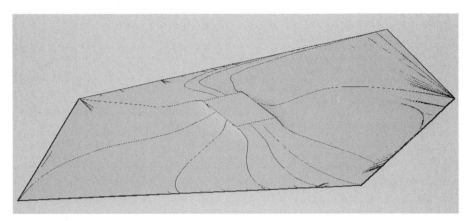

FIGURE 1 7 . 7 : The completed cabin land

12. Thaw all the 3D layers.

Creating the Cameras

AutoCAD uses a camera analogy to define reproducible views. The cameras and their respective targets are placed in model space and, using several available grips, are adjusted to capture the desired view.

1. Click the Render tab; then, on the Camera panel, click the Create Camera button and move the cursor into the drawing area. A camera icon appears at the cursor location.

T I P   If you don't see the Camera panel, right-click on the title bar of any panel and choose Panels ➢ Camera from the context menu.

2. Click near the edge of the land at a point southeast of the cabin, using the ViewCube as a guide, and then move the cursor again. Now the camera stays in place, as shown in Figure 17.8, and the target is moved with the cursor. The location of the target determines the orientation of the camera, and the visible cone emitting from the camera shows the camera's *field of view* (FOV), or the angle visible through the camera's lens.

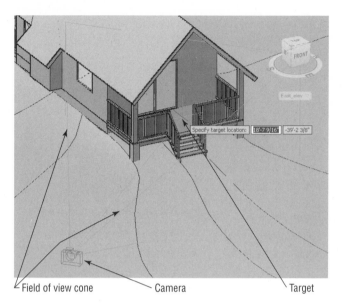

Field of view cone   Camera   Target

FIGURE 17.8: Placing a camera into the drawing

3. Turn off any running osnaps, and then click on the middle of the deck to place the target. The camera disappears temporarily while Auto-CAD waits for input at the cursor and the command line.

4. Enter n↵, or click Name, to activate the Name option. At the prompt, enter **Cam Southeast↵↵**. The camera reappears in the drawing area.

 T I P **You should always give your cameras descriptive names to make it easier to find the correct view when multiple cameras exist in a drawing. You can change the camera name in the Properties palette.**

5. Create another camera that views the cabin from the northwest corner of the property, place the target at the middle of the cabin, and name this camera **Cam Northwest**.

6. Use the ViewCube to change the current view to a viewpoint from the southeast and slightly above the cabin (see Figure 17.9).

7. Select the Cam Southeast camera. The Field of View cone and grips are displayed, and the Camera Preview dialog box opens. This dialog box displays the view from the camera in one of the available visual styles (see Figure 17.10). The 3D Wireframe visual style is the default and the one you will use here.

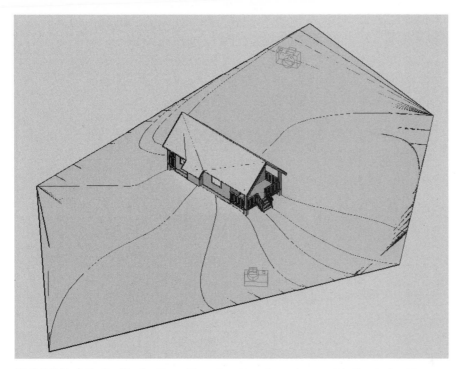

FIGURE 17.9: Viewing the cabin and cameras from above and to the southeast

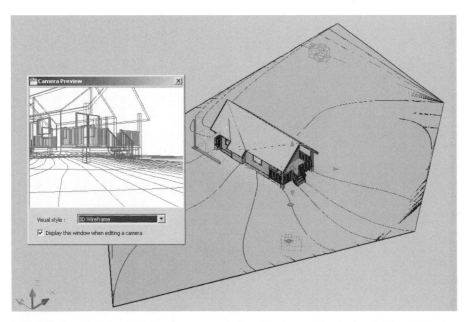

FIGURE 17.10: Selecting the camera displays its grips and the Camera Preview dialog box.

8. Place your cursor over the grip at the center of the camera, and you will see a tooltip that says Camera Location. Click the grip, and then move the camera 5′ (1524 mm) up in the Z direction to about eye level. You may need to click the grip again for the Camera Preview dialog box to refresh.

9. Select the Camera Target grip and move it 7′ (1880 mm) in the Z direction. Raising the target brings the cabin more into the preview window.

10. Press Esc to deselect the camera, and then select the Cam Northwest camera. Move it 30′ (9150 mm) in the Z direction to get a higher view of the structure. Next, adjust its view however you like by moving the square Target Location or triangular Lens Length/FOV grips.

 11. Click the View tab, then click the Named Views button to open the View Manager. Expand the Model Views entry in the Views window, and notice that the two cameras now appear in the list, as shown in Figure 17.11.

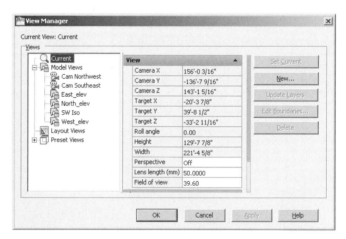

FIGURE 17.11: The View Manager dialog box showing the two new cameras listed

12. Select Cam Southeast from the list, click the Set Current button, and then click OK; your drawing area changes to view the scene from the selected camera, as shown in Figure 17.12.

13. Save your drawing as Cabin17A.dwg.

FIGURE 17.12: The cabin as seen through the Cam Southeast camera

Creating a Lighting Scheme

Without a well-thought-out lighting scheme, the scene can look flat and unappealing. In the following sections, you will add a light to represent the sun and then an additional light to add ambient illumination to the scene.

Creating a Light Source

AutoCAD has three kinds of lighting, each with a distinct method for distributing light rays into the scene. They are as follows:

Point Light All light rays are emitted from a single location and diverge as they get farther away. An incandescent light bulb is a real-world example of a point light, even though the light does not travel in the direction of the light's fixture.

Distant Light With this type of light, all light rays are parallel. Although the sun is technically a point light, at the enormous distance the light rays travel to Earth, they are nearly parallel.

Spotlight With this type of light, rays are emitted from a single point, but they are restricted to a conical portion of the amount of light that a similar point light would emit. Flashlights and headlights are examples of spotlights.

Each light type has a unique set of parameters. The sun is a special distant light and has its own settings, including determining the light's position based on the geographic location of the scene and the date and time and the ability to add ambient light to the drawing.

To do this, you'll use tools in the Visualize tab of the Ribbon:

1. Click the Ribbon's Render tab.

2. In the expanded Lights panel, make sure the Default Lighting option is turned off. When it is off, the button will not have a blue background as the cursor pauses over it and there will be no default illumination in the scene.

3. In the Sun & Location panel, the Sun Status button turns on the effect of sunlight in the scene. Be sure it's toggled on by verifying that the button has a blue background.

4. Click the Sun Properties button, at the right end of the Sun & Location panel to open the Sun Properties dialog box, as shown in Figure 17.13. (The dialog box may be docked on the side of the AutoCAD window.) In the Sun Angle Calculator rollout, set Date to 9/25/2009 and Time to 3:00 PM. The date is set by clicking the button at the right end of the date field and choosing the date from a calendar.

FIGURE 17.13: Set the date in the Sun Properties dialog box.

5. In the Sun & Location panel, click the Set Location button. When the Geographic Location – Define Geographic Location dialog box

appears, select Enter The Location Values as the method to define the location of the cabin drawing (see Figure 17.14).

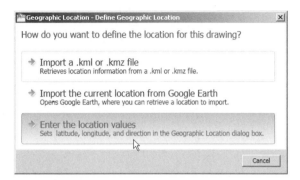

FIGURE 17.14: The Geographic Location – Define Geographic Location dialog box

The dialog closes and the Geographic Location dialog box opens (see Figure 17.15). If you have Google Earth installed, you can choose to import a .kml or .kmz file (Google Earth placemark files) or to import the location directly from Google Earth.

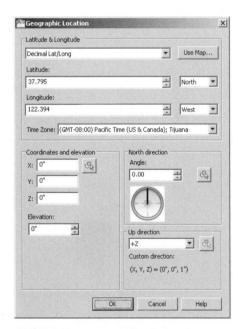

FIGURE 17.15: The Geographic Location dialog box

6. You can define nearly any location in the world as the location for the current drawing by entering the latitude and longitude in this dialog box. For your cabin, you'll select the city in which it's located from a map.

7. Click the Use Map button in the top-right corner of the dialog box to open the Location Picker dialog box, as shown in Figure 17.16.

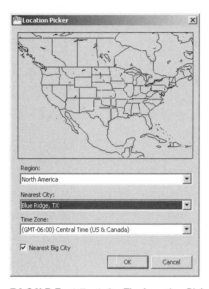

F I G U R E   1 7 . 1 6 : The Location Picker dialog box

8. In the Region drop-down list below the map, select the region that you prefer. Below that, in the Nearest City drop-down list, select a city within that region. The example here uses North America and Blue Ridge, Texas. A red cross appears over Blue Ridge (or wherever you've chosen) in the map. The Time Zone drop-down list displays the accurate time zone based on the location you selected.

9. Click OK to close this dialog box. If a dialog box appears asking if the time zone should be updated, click the Accept Updated Time Zone option. Click OK to close the Geographic Location dialog box.

T I P   If a particular city is not listed, you can uncheck the Nearest Big City option and then click directly on the map to set the location or enter the longitudinal and latitudinal coordinates in the left side of the Geographic Location dialog box.

Enabling Shadows

Shadows add depth and realism to a scene and tie the objects to the surfaces that they rest on or near. You have significant control over the types of shadows cast by the lights in the drawing and whether those shadows appear in the viewports. You adjust how the shadows appear in the viewport and how they render in the Render tab.

Shadows can be soft- or hard-edged, and you can calculate them using a couple of methods. Soft-edged shadows represent scenes where the light is diffused and appear to be originated from an area that is spread out. Hard-edged shadows are used to display a scene where the light is intense and unobstructed before it illuminates the object. This part of the rendering process is too technical to go into in this book, but you can follow along and end up with at least one setup for shadows that will enhance the rendering of the cabin:

1. In the Lights panel, click the down arrow under the No Shadows icon and choose Full Shadows from the fly-out menu, as shown in Figure 17.17. This displays an approximation of the shadows in the viewport.

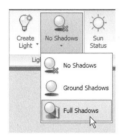

FIGURE 17.17: Choosing the Full Shadows option

 WARNING The Full Shadows option requires that your video card utilize hardware acceleration. See the Display Backgrounds and Shadows page of the AutoCAD 2010 help file for information on determining whether your system is equipped with hardware acceleration.

 2. Click the Advanced Render Settings button on the right end of the Render panel's title bar.

3. In the Advanced Render Settings palette that appears, scroll down to the Shadows rollout, and make sure Mode is set to Simple and Shadow Map is set to On (see Figure 17.18).

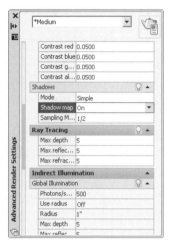

FIGURE 17.18: The Shadows settings in the Advanced Render Settings palette

4. Close the Advanced Render Settings palette.

The First Render

A rendering is the visual result of the program calculating the effects of the lights and materials on the surfaces in the drawing. Let's make a preliminary render now. Later, you'll add materials and a background and then render the drawing again.

1. Click the Render button on the Render panel. The Render window opens and after a few moments, the rendering fills in the graphic area (see Figure 17.19).

2. As you can see, the right side of the cabin is unlit and in total darkness. Click the Point button in the Lights panel (it may be hidden under another light button), and then click to place the light on the ground about 20′ (6100 mm) northeast of the front deck.

3. Click the Name option in the context menu that appears at the cursor and give the light the name **Northeast Ambient**. As with cameras, you should give your lights descriptive names.

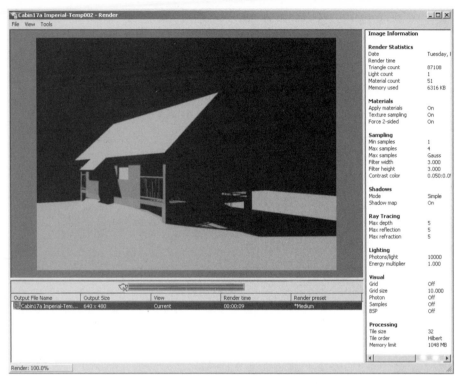

The first cabin rendering in the Render window

4. Double-click the light to open its Properties palette, and make the following changes:

   ▶ Position Z: 30′(9150)

   ▶ Shadows: Off

   ▶ Intensity Factor: 60.000

   ▶ Lamp Intensity: 15,000 Cd

5. Click the down arrow in the Filter Color field, and then choose Select Color. In the Select Color dialog box that appears, enter 252, 250, 212 in the Color field, as shown in Figure 17.20. This gives the light a pale yellow hue.

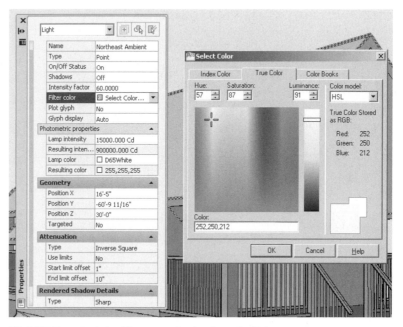

FIGURE 17.20: The properties for the point light

6. Click OK to close the Select Color dialog box and close the Properties palette.

7. Switch back to the Cam Southeast view if necessary and render the scene again.

As you can see in Figure 17.21, this time the shadows on the right side of the cabin are not as stark as they were previously, but the overall appearance is still pretty dark. We need to add some ambient light.

8. Open the Advanced Render Settings palette again, and then click the lightbulb icon next to Global Illumination in the Indirect Illumination rollout (see Figure 17.22). This will add a measure of ambient light into your scene without washing it out.

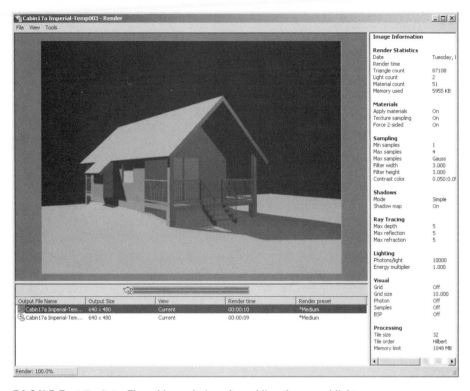

FIGURE 17.21: The cabin rendering after adding the second light

FIGURE 17.22: Turning on Global Illumination

9. This rendering looks a bit better than the last (see Figure 17.23). The Render window maintains a history of the recent renderings, and you can compare them by clicking on any of the renderings listed in the pane at the bottom of the Render window. To delete a rendering, select it, right-click, and then choose Remove From The List.

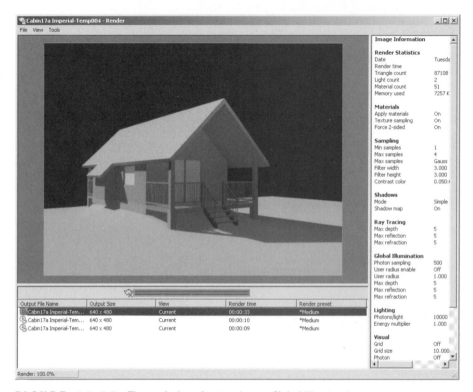

FIGURE 17.23: The rendering after turning on Global Illumination

You can continue to tweak the lighting as you want. For indoor projects that require rendering, a good rule of thumb is to expect to dedicate 15 to 25 percent of the total project time to creating an excellent lighting scheme. For outdoor scenes, dedicating 5 to 10 percent should be sufficient.

The building looks fine, but it would be nice to have something in the background other than the blank screen and the lights need to be tweaked.

Controlling the Background of the Rendering

The following are some of the options you can set when choosing a background for the rendering:

The AutoCAD Background This is what you used for the preliminary rendering.

Another Solid Color Use the slider bars to choose another solid color.

Gradient You can use varying colors (usually light to dark) blended together.

Image You can supply or choose a bitmap image.

Sun & Sky Background You can use a computer-generated sky. This background has the option of introducing additional ambient illumination into the scene.

You'll use the Sun & Sky Background option with the Illumination option here:

1. Click the View tab, and then click the Named Views button in the View panel to open the View Manager dialog box.

2. Expand the Model Views entry, and then select Cam Southeast.

3. Expand the drop-down list for the Background Override entry in the General rollout, and then choose Sun & Sky, as shown in Figure 17.24.

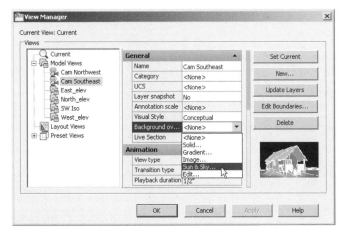

FIGURE 17.24: The Cam Southeast camera selected in the View Manager dialog box

Doing so opens the Adjust Sun & Sky Background dialog box, as shown in Figure 17.25.

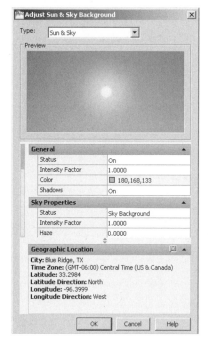

FIGURE 17.25: The Adjust Sun & Sky Background dialog box

N O T E   The sky background options are only available when the lighting units are not set to generic. This is controlled by the `lightingunits` system variable. Enter **lightingunits⏎ 2⏎** to set the lighting units to International. A setting of 1 sets the lighting units to American, and 0 sets them to generic units.

4. In the Sky Properties rollout, change the Intensity Factor value to 3; then expand the Status drop-down list, and choose Sky Background and Illumination.

5. Click OK to close the Adjust Sun & Sky Background dialog box.

6. Click Set Current in the View Manager dialog box, and then click OK to close it.

7. Open the Advanced Render Settings palette from the Render tab's Render panel. Scroll down to the Final Gather rollout, and make sure the Mode is set to Auto or On. Background Illumination will not work if Final Gather Mode is set to Off.

8. Save your drawing as `Cabin17b.dwg`.

9. Render the scene. It will take a little longer to process this image, and you'll notice the image in the Render window is replaced twice; the first time with a very rough-looking representation of the cabin and then again with a sharper result. When it is done, your Render dialog box should look similar to Figure 17.26. The background image not only appears behind the cabin and ground, but it also contributes light to the scene.

FIGURE 17.26: The cabin rendered with the Sun & Sky background and additional illumination

NOTE Rendering is a processor-intensive function. It's not uncommon to experience a lag in computer performance or to hear increased cooling fan activity while a rendering is in progress.

Adding Materials

Adding the proper materials to a scene can greatly increase the realism of the drawing and convey a better sense of size and texture to the person viewing the image. This chapter assumes that you installed the material library that ships with AutoCAD 2010, along with the rest of the package.

You can assign materials to your drawing objects from several premade libraries, you can create materials from scratch, or you can edit materials that originate from the libraries. In the next exercise, you will apply materials from AutoCAD's libraries.

1. Click the View tab, and then click the Tool Palettes button in the Palettes panel to open the tool palettes.

2. Click near the bottom edge of the tool palette tabs where it looks as if all the tabs are bunched together. This expands a large list of the available tool palettes. Choose Doors and Windows – Materials Sample from the list (see Figure 17.27). The palette now displays the seven materials available in the palette.

N O T E   If all the palettes are not displayed, right-click on the palette title bar and choose **All Palettes** from the context menu.

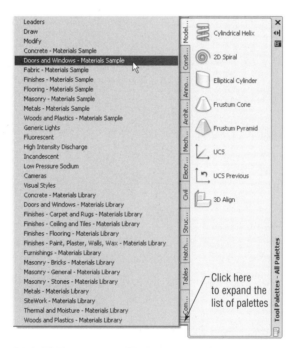

FIGURE 17.27: The list of available tool palettes, including the material libraries

3. Make the 3D- Pivot-Doors layer current, and then freeze the other 3D layers, except 3D-Win-Frame.

4. Click the Doors – Windows.Wood Doors.Ash sample sphere in the palette. You can see the entire material name by pausing the cursor

over the sample sphere. The cursor changes shape to resemble a paintbrush.

5. Place the cursor over each of the doors and window frames; then click or drag a selection window around all of them, and press ↵ to assign the ash wood material to the objects. Render the drawing to see the effect. The doors and frames are rendered with the light wood material.

6. Thaw the 3D-Glazing layer, make it current, and freeze the other two layers. Click the Doors – Windows.Glazing.Glass.Clear sample sphere in the palette, and then drag a selection window around the glazing objects in the drawing area. Don't worry about including a camera or light in the selection—they aren't affected by materials.

7. Thaw the 3D-Foundation and 3D-Land layers, make one of them current, and then freeze the 3D-Glazing layer.

8. Display the list of palettes, and then choose Concrete Materials Library from the list. In the palette, click Concrete.Cast-In-Place.Flat.Grey.1, and then click the four concrete support posts and the foundation. Click ↵.

9. Switch to the Sitework Materials – Library palette and scroll down until you see the Sitework.Planting.Grass.Thick material shown in Figure 17.28. Click the sample sphere and drag the material onto the 3D-Land object. Dragging and dropping is another way to assign material to objects.

F I G U R E   1 7 . 2 8 : The list of available tool palettes, including the material libraries

Material names must be unique within any one drawing. When you select a material and that same material, or a material with the same name, has already been assigned to an object in the drawing, a Material Exists warning dialog box appears. Because you are using only materials from the AutoCAD libraries, choose Overwrite The Material.

10. Assign materials to the objects on the remaining layers as follows:

Layer	Library	Material
3D-Deck and 3D-Steps	Woods and Plastics Woods - Plastics.	Finish Carpentry.Wood.Boards
3D-Floor	Finishes - Flooring	Finishes.Flooring.Wood.Hardwood.1
3D-Roof-Deck and 3D -Wall-Int	Finishes - Paint, Plaster, Walls, Wax	Finishes Painting.Paint.White
3D-Roof-Surface	Thermal and Moisture	Thermal-Moisture. Shingles. Asphalt.Shingles. 3-Tab.Black.
3D-Wall-Ext	Thermal and Moisture	Thermal-Moisture. Shakes. Weathered
3D-Thresh	Metals	Ornamental Metals. Aluminum. Brushed. Satin.

11. Thaw all of the 3D layers, and then save your drawing as Cabin17c.dwg.

12. Render it one more time; it should look like Figure 17.29. Notice how the roof is reflected in the living room window.

N O T E   During the rendering process, I'm sure you noticed the small black squares being replaced one at a time by small areas of the rendered drawing. This indicates that AutoCAD is using bucket rendering. Before the rendering process begins, AutoCAD determines the sequence to process the squares, called *buckets*, in order to maximize the memory usage and thus increase the efficiency of the rendering.

FIGURE 17.29: The cabin rendered with materials applied to the remaining 3D objects

Adjusting the Material Mapping

Image maps are the components of a material that consist of image files, such as a JPEG or TIFF. When a material uses an image file, it can be to change the color of an object (diffuse maps), to give the illusion of texture (bump maps), or to define the transparency of a surface (opacity maps).

Each map consists of an image file, measured in pixels, that is applied to the surfaces of an object. By default, the image is stretched across each surface and repeated only once. There are several parameters that you can control that determine how each map is applied to each object, including how many times the image is repeated, called *tiling*; the rotation of the map; and the method used to project the map onto the surface, called *mapping*.

1. Zoom into the front corner of the cabin and render the scene. As you can see in Figure 17.30, the brick appears rotated.

2. Select the two exterior wall objects, then click the down arrow to expand the Material Mapping fly-out menu in the Materials panel, and choose the Box option. Box mapping projects the map evenly in all six directions; Top, Bottom, Right, Left, Front, and Back.

FIGURE 17.30: A close-up rendering of the cabin shows problems with the materials.

3. Zoom out and you'll see the yellow mapping gripper tool surrounding the selected objects, as shown in Figure 17.31. As you can see, it's rotated and this is what caused the odd orientation of the brick shown in Figure 17.30.

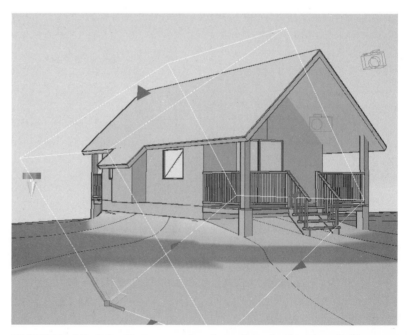

FIGURE 17.31: The box mapping gizmo shown for the selected objects

4. At the Accept the mapping or [Move/Rotate/reseT/sWitch mapping mode: prompt, enter r⏎ to display the 3D rotate gizmo.

5. Rotate the mapping until it matches the orientation of the cabin and then press ⏎.

6. Zoom in to the front corner of the cabin again, and then render the drawing. Figure 17.32 shows the cabin with the orientation of the bricks fixed.

FIGURE 17.32: The new brick orientation

Adjusting the Map Size

The individual properties of all materials are controlled in the Materials palette. Here you'll find the controls for setting the parameters for the size of the map, which map to use, and several other features for the selected material.

1. In the View tab, click the Materials icon in the 3D Palettes panel.

2. In the Available Materials in Drawing rollout, at the top of the Materials palette that opens, select Thermal – Moisture.Shakes.Weathered material (see Figure 17.33). The material's parameters are reflected in the other rollouts in the palette.

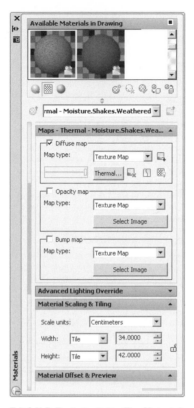

FIGURE 17.33: The Materials palette with the Shake material selected

3. Click the Visual Styles button in the 3D Palettes panel, and change the visual style to Realistic. The Realistic style displays the materials and maps and the changes that you make to them, all at the expense of system performance. You should only use this visual style when necessary.

4. In the Material Scaling & Tiling rollout, change Scale Units to Inches (Millimeters), set the Width value to 30 (762), and set the Height value to 36 (915). After a brief pause, the new settings are reflected in the material seen in the viewport (see Figure 17.34).

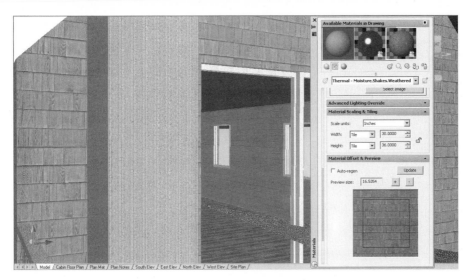

FIGURE 17.34: The modified material in the Materials palette and the cabin in the Realistic visual style

Adding Texture

The exterior walls of the cabin consist of flat surfaces, and there are no features that would cause shadows to be cast. The Bump Map option adds apparent texture by adding shadows where they would appear, if the surfaces had texture. In the Maps rollout, you can see that only the Diffuse Map option is checked, meaning that there is no map used to define the opacity and bump features of the material. Opacity maps and bump maps don't use any of the color information from an image map, but this doesn't mean that color maps can't be used—only that the grayscale equivalent of the colors will be interpreted by AutoCAD.

1. In the Maps rollout, check the Bump Map option.

2. In the Bump Map area, click the Select Image button to open the Select Image File dialog box. It should open to the Documents and Settings\All Users\Application Data\Autodesk\AutoCAD 2010\R18.0\enu\Textures folder; if not, navigate there.

3. Select the Thermal - Moisture.Shakes.Weathered.jpg file, the same file used as the diffuse map, and then click Open.

4. Move the Bump Map Slider to approximately 550 (see Figure 17.35) to reduce the amount of bump applied to the map.

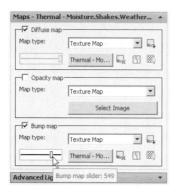

FIGURE 17.35: Changing the amount of bump applied to a map

Figure 17.36 shows the cabin rendered with the new material parameters.

FIGURE 17.36: The cabin with the new material parameters

5. Adjust the mapping and materials for the remaining objects, and then save your file as Cabin 17d.dwg.

There are enough tools and features relating to AutoCAD materials to fill several chapters, and this was just an introduction. Some of the features not covered are copying mapping between objects, applying different maps to different surfaces of the same object, and using opacity maps. I strongly encourage you to investigate the full capabilities of the AutoCAD materials.

Rendering to a File

By default, the Render feature creates a rendering in the Render dialog box only. The picture is not saved unless you explicitly tell AutoCAD to save it. You can also instruct the program as to the quality level of the rendering and the size, in pixels, of the image created. Follow these steps:

1. Switch back to the Conceptual visual style and the Cam Southeast view.

2. From the Render tab's Render panel, click the Render Output File button and then the Browse For File button to open the Render Output File dialog box.

3. Navigate to the folder where you want to place the new image file, and then select a supported image file type in the Files Of Type drop-down list. For this exercise, choose TIF as the file type, and name the file Cabin Rendering Small.tif (see Figure 17.37). Click the Save button.

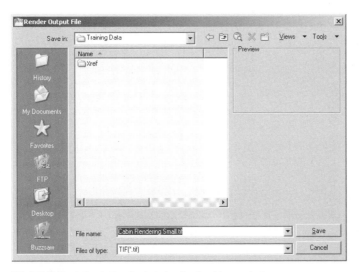

FIGURE 17.37: Saving the final cabin rendering

4. Depending on the file type you choose in the future, an Options dialog box, similar to the one shown in Figure 17.38, will appear. In the TIFF Image Options dialog box, select 24 Bits (16.7 Million Colors), make sure the Compressed option is checked, and then click OK.

FIGURE 17.38: The TIFF Image Options dialog box

The next time you render the drawing, the rendering is saved as an image file on your hard drive, and the filename appears in the Output File Name column of the Render window, with a folder and check mark next to it (see Figure 17.39). The files with clocks and teapots are unsaved, but you can open them in the Render window by clicking the appropriate filename.

FIGURE 17.39: The saved file shown at the bottom of the Render window

5. In the AutoCAD window, expand the Render Presets drop-down list, and select Presentation, as shown in Figure 17.40.

FIGURE 17.40: Choose the Presentation rendering preset.

6. Expand the Render panel, expand the Render Output Size drop-down list, and then choose Specify Image Size (see Figure 17.41) to open the Output Size dialog box.

FIGURE 17.41: Set the output size.

7. In the Output size dialog box (see Figure 17.42), set Width to 2000 and Height to 1600, and then click OK. This is the resolution required to print a 10″×8″ image at 200 dots per inch (dpi).

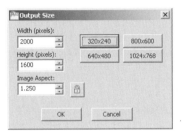

FIGURE 17.42: The Output Size dialog box

8. Click the Browse For File button to open the Render Output File dialog box. Name this file Cabin Rendering Large.tif, and make it a 24-bit TIF file at 200 dpi. Click OK.

9. Save your drawing and then click the Render button again and wait a while as the new image renders. With the higher quality and larger image size, this may take considerably longer to process.

10. When the rendering is completed, look at the file size in Windows Explorer, and then compare the two images in your image-viewing software. The larger file is much crisper than the smaller image at the expense of increased rendering time.

This has been a brief introduction to the world of 3D and rendering in Auto-CAD, but you should now be oriented to the general way of doing things and have enough tools to experiment further. For a more in-depth discussion of the process, including rendering, see *Mastering AutoCAD 2010 and AutoCAD LT 2010* (Wiley, 2009) by George Omura.

Are You Experienced?

Now you can...

- ☑ **create a loft object using contour lines**
- ☑ **create and manipulate cameras**
- ☑ **add sunlight to a scene**
- ☑ **place a point light**
- ☑ **specify a scene's real-world location**
- ☑ **assign materials to the objects in a drawing**
- ☑ **adjust mapping and tiling**
- ☑ **render a drawing and save the result as an image file**

NUMBERS AND SYMBOLS

3D face

A triangular or four-sided flat surface that is the basic unit of a 3D surface.

3D mesh

A set of adjacent flat surfaces that together form a geometrical depiction of a three-dimensional surface.

3D model

An AutoCAD object that occupies 3D space and represents building components or geometrical objects in the real world. See also *object*.

3ds Max

A complementary product to AutoCAD, also produced by Autodesk. With 3ds Max, you can create and animate 3D scenes.

A

absolute coordinates

Values for locating a point in space that describe its displacement from the *origin* (0,0,0) point of the drawing.

alias

A shortcut for starting commands. It's a set of one or two letters that you can enter at the *command line* instead of the full command.

aligned dimension

A linear dimension measuring the distance between two points. The dimension line for an aligned dimension is parallel to a line between the two points.

angular dimension

A dimension that measures the angle between two lines or the angle inscribed by an arc.

angular unit

The unit in which angle values are displayed. The choices are Decimal Degrees, Degrees-Minutes-Seconds, Grads, Radians, and Surveyor's units.

associative dimension

A dimension that updates automatically when the object being dimensioned changes size.

associative hatch pattern

A hatch pattern that updates automatically when the shape of the hatched area is modified. See also *hatch pattern*.

AutoCAD object

See *object*.

AutoSnap

A feature of AutoCAD that works with the Object Snap tools by displaying a symbol on the places that can be snapped to within the drawing. Each of these Object Snap modes has a different AutoSnap symbol. The symbol appears when the *cursor* is near a location where the active object snap can be used. See also *Object Snap mode*.

B

baseline dimension

A dimensioning option that allows you to do multiple measurements from a designated origin.

base point

1. The initial point of reference for a number of modify commands including Copy, Move, Rotate, Stretch, and Scale. 2. The insertion point for a drawing as designated by the Base command.

batch plot

See *publish*.

bearings

See *Surveyor's units*.

bind

To transform an external reference file into a permanent part of the host file as a block. See also *external reference*.

block

See *block reference*.

block definition

The description of a grouping of AutoCAD objects that is stored with the drawing file and includes a name, an *insertion point*, and a listing of objects in the grouping.

block reference

An instance of a grouping of objects that is inserted into a drawing and is based on the block definition for that grouping. Informally called a *block*.

Boolean function

The procedure that uses the volumes of two or more objects to create a single object by combining or subtracting the volumes.

ByLayer

A value that can be assigned to colors and linetypes so that objects receive their color and linetype properties according to the layer they are on.

C

Cartesian coordinate system

A 2D system of locating points on a plane. It uses a horizontal (X) and a vertical (Y) component to locate a point relative to the 0,0 point or origin.

cascading menu

A submenu that appears adjacent to the current menu when an option with an arrow next to it is clicked.

coordinate filters

See *point filters*.

command line

The information in the text window at the bottom of the screen that displays `Command:` prompts. This is where you see what you're entering through the keyboard. When Dynamic Input is active, the command line input appears at the cursor as well. See also *Command window* and *dynamic input*.

Command: prompt

The prompt shown at the *command line* when no commands are currently running.

Command window

The window at the bottom of the user interface where command prompts and user input are shown. See also *command line*.

context menu

A menu that appears on the drawing area, usually as the result of a right-click, and contains options relevant to what the user is doing at that moment.

continued dimension

A dimensioning option that allows you to place sequential dimensions that are adjacent to each other so that the dimension lines are aligned.

crosshair cursor

A form of the *cursor* that consists of a horizontal line and a vertical line intersecting at their midpoints, resembling the crosshair in a sighting device.

crossing selection window

A selection tool that selects an area defined by two points acting as opposite corners of a rectangle, which is made from left to right. All objects within or crossing the rectangle are selected. See also *regular selection window*.

current UCS

The *User Coordinate System* that is active in a drawing. It determines the positive X, Y, and Z directions.

cursor

The pointing symbol on the computer monitor that is moved using the mouse. It can appear as, among other things, an arrow, a *pickbox*, and a crosshair. See also *crosshair cursor*.

custom workspace

See *workspace*.

cutting edge

The role certain objects can be temporarily assigned to play in a trimming operation. If an object is designated as a cutting edge, lines or other objects being trimmed are trimmed back to the point where they intersect the cutting edge.

cycling

A procedure for selecting a particular object when it coincides with one or more other objects. To cycle, hold down the Shift key and the spacebar, and then click on the line until the particular line you want ghosts. When that happens, release the Shift key and spacebar and press ↵.

D

default

A value or option in a command that will be used unless you designate otherwise. In Auto-CAD, default values and options are enclosed in angle brackets (< >).

dimension style

A collection of settings for *dimension variables* that is saved in a drawing under a specified name. Dimensions placed in the drawing follow the settings of the current dimension style.

dimension text

The text in a dimension. It expresses the measurement that the dimension is displaying.

dimension variables

A group of settings and values that control the appearance of dimensions in AutoCAD.

direct entry

An option for specifying the next point in a series of points by using the *cursor* to indicate direction and the keyboard to enter the distance from the last point.

docking

Relocating a toolbar or a palette to a place outside the *drawing area* so it won't interfere with the AutoCAD drawing or other items on the screen.

donut

A closed, circular polyline created with the Donut command.

drawing area

The portion of the monitor screen where you draw objects and view your drawing.

drawing extents

The minimum rectangular area with the same proportions as your *drawing area* that will enclose nonfrozen objects in your drawing. When you *Zoom* to Extents, the rectangular area fills the drawing area.

drawing limits

The area in a drawing that is covered by the *grid*. It can be defined by the user. It's stored as the coordinates of the lower-left and upper-right corners of the rectangular area covered by the grid. If on the Snap and Grid tab of the Drafting Settings dialog box the Display Grid Beyond Limits check box is selected, AutoCAD displays the grid on the entire screen regardless of the limits.

drawing units

The intervals of linear and angular measurements chosen for use in a drawing.

.dwg

The file extension and format for the standard AutoCAD drawing.

dynamic block

A block that, after insertion, can be edited to take on a preset range of shapes and sizes to fulfill a variety of conditions in the drawing, such as windows with a multiplicity of widths and heights. It also can be set up to align automatically with geometry in the drawing.

dynamic input

A feature that, when turned on, displays coordinate, distance, angle, and command prompt information near the *crosshair cursor* in the drawing area. The information displayed varies with the execution of the command. The Dynamic Input button on the status bar controls whether this feature is on or off.

E

edge

1. The side of a 3D face or a *3D mesh*. 2. When capitalized, a command for controlling the visibility of the edges of 3D faces.

elevation

A view of a building that viewers get when they look at it horizontally, perpendicular to an interior or exterior wall.

entity

See *object*.

explode

A command to undo a grouping of objects. It can be used on *blocks*, *multiline text*, *polylines*, and dimensions. Exploded multiline text becomes single-line text. Exploded polylines become lines. Exploded blocks become the individual objects that make up the block.

external reference

A drawing file that has been temporarily attached to another drawing for read-only purposes. Also called an *xref*.

external reference host file

The drawing file to which external references have been attached.

extrusion

1. A 2D object that has been given *thickness*. 2. A 3D solid object created with the Extrude command, by sliding a closed 2D shape along a path that is usually perpendicular to the 2D shape. If you use the Path option of the Extrude command, the extrusion need not be perpendicular to the 2D shape.

F

field of view

The angle, from a camera's location, visible through its lens.

fill

A display mode that can be set to on or off. When it's set to on, it displays a solid color for shapes made with wide *polylines*, 2D solids, and *hatch patterns* using the Solid pattern. When it's set to off, the solid color area is invisible and only the boundary of the fill is displayed.

floating toolbar

A toolbar that is located in the drawing area. You can move it around by dragging its title bar.

floating viewports

Openings created in the *paper space* of a drawing that allow you to view a drawing in *model space*.

font

A group of letters, numbers, and other typographic characters all sharing common features of design and appearance.

freeze

The option of the layer property called Freeze/Thaw that turns off the visibility of objects on layers and restricts AutoCAD from considering the geometry of these objects during a selection or *regeneration*. See also *layer*.

G

geometric tolerancing

A type of dimensioning where several acceptable variances in the manufacture of a part are displayed, including perpendicularity, concentricity, and cylindricity.

ghosting

The fuzzy or hazy appearance that a line or another object takes on when it's selected.

graphical user interface

See *graphics window*.

graphics window

The appearance of your screen when Auto-CAD is running. It consists of the *drawing area* and surrounding toolbars, menu bars, the *Command window*, and the status bar. Also called the graphical user interface, GUI, or UI. See also *menu bar*.

grid

1. A drawing aid that consists of a set of regularly spaced dots in the *drawing area*. 2. A series of horizontal and vertical lines in a floor plan or section that locate the main structural elements of a building, such as columns and walls. Also called a column grid or a structural grid.

grips

An editing tool that allows you to perform five modify commands on selected objects without having to start the commands themselves. When grips are enabled, small squares appear on selected objects. By clicking a square, you activate the first of the available commands. To access the five commands, press the spacebar to *cycle* through the commands or right-click and choose from the context menu.

H

hatch

See *hatch pattern*.

hatch pattern

A pattern of lines, dots, and other shapes that fill in a closed area.

hatch pattern origin

A point in the drawing on which the geometry of the applied *hatch pattern* is based.

header

A horizontal support member that spans the top of a doorway or window opening.

host file

See *external reference host file*.

hyperlink

An electronic connection between an Auto-CAD object and any of several places, including another drawing, a Word document, a website, and so on.

I

icon

One of a set of small pictures on a toolbar or the Ribbon. When the *cursor* rolls across an icon, it takes on the appearance of being a picture on a button.

implied windowing

Starting a *selection set* by selecting a blank area in the drawing and creating a regular or crossing selection window.

insertion point

A reference point that is part of a block and is used to locate the block when it's inserted into a drawing. It's attached to the *cursor* while a block is being inserted. Once a block has been inserted, use the Insertion *osnap* to snap to the insertion point of the block.

Isometric view

A pictorial view of a 3D object in which all lines that are parallel on the object appear parallel in the view. See also *Perspective view*.

J

jamb

A surface that forms the side or top of an opening for a door or window in a wall.

justification point

A reference point on a line of single-line text or a body of multiline text that acts like the *insertion point* for blocks.

L

lateral tolerance

An acceptable deviation from the stated dimension and a plus and/or minus value.

layer

An organizing tool that operates like an electronic version of transparent overlays on a drawing board. Layers can be assigned color and *linetypes*, and their visibility can be controlled. All *objects* in an AutoCAD drawing are assigned to a layer.

layout

An optional interface that serves as an aid to the user in setting up a drawing for printing. It rests "on top of" the *model space* in which the drawing of the building resides. It contains the title block, notes, scale, and other information. Users view a drawing through openings in the layout called *viewports*. A single drawing file can have multiple layouts, one for each print to be made from the file. The layout interface is sometimes referred to as *paper space*.

leader

A dimensional note that contains descriptive or instructional text and an arrow pointing at the subject of the text.

limits

See *drawing limits*.

linetype

The style of appearance of a line. AutoCAD styles include continuous, dashed, dash-dot, and so on.

linetype scale

A numeric value for noncontinuous linetypes that controls the size of dashes and spaces between dashes and dots. In an AutoCAD drawing, a global linetype scale controls all noncontinuous linetypes in the drawing, and an individual linetype scale can be applied to one or more selected lines.

lineweight

The value of a line's width. AutoCAD offers 24 lineweights in a range from 0.00″ to 0.083″.

M

mapping

The method used to project an image map onto the surfaces of an object.

menu bar

The set of drop-down menus at the top of the AutoCAD graphics window. These menus are not shown by default. See also *Ribbon*.

Mirror

A command that makes a copy of selected objects and flips the copy around a specified line to produce a mirror image of those objects.

mirror line

An imaginary or existing line about which an object is flipped by the Mirror command.

model space

The portion of an AutoCAD drawing that contains the lines representing the building or object being designed, as opposed to the notes and title block information, which are kept on a *layout*.

Mtext

See *multiline text*.

multileader

Similar to leader, a multileader has additional options for controlling the leader text and combining the leader lines. See *leader*.

multiline text

A type of text in which an entire body of text is grouped together as one object. Informally called Mtext, it can be edited with word processing techniques. Individual characters or words in the Mtext can have different heights, fonts, and colors from the main body of Mtext. *Dimension text* is Mtext. When exploded, Mtext becomes *single-line text*.

N

named view

A view of your drawing that is saved and given a name so that it can be restored later.

O

object

A basic AutoCAD graphical element that is created and manipulated as part of the drawing, such as a line, an arc, a dimension, a block, or text. Also called an *entity*.

Object Snap mode

Any one of a set of tools for precisely picking strategic points on an *object*, including Endpoint, Midpoint, Center, and so on. It's informally called *Osnap*.

Object Snap Tracking

The process by which the user sets up temporary points or angles as guides for the *cursor*, used to locate desired points in the process of drawing. *Object Snap Tracking* (or Otrack) creates the temporary points, and *Polar Tracking* sets the angles. See also *Object Snap mode*.

operand

One of the objects selected whose volume is used in a *Boolean function*.

origin

The point with the coordinates 0,0,0, where the x-, y-, and z-axes intersect.

orthogonal drawing

A system of creating views in which each view shows a different side of a building or an object, such as the top, front, left side, right side, and so on.

Ortho mode

An on/off setting that, when on, forces lines to be drawn and objects to be moved in a horizontal or vertical direction only.

Osnap

See *Object Snap mode*.

P

Pan

A command that slides the current drawing around on the drawing area without changing the magnification of the view.

panel

Any of the subdivisions of the *Ribbon* that house related commands and tools.

paper space

A term sometimes used to refer to the interface for a drawing that contains layouts. See also *layout*.

path

The hierarchy of drive, folder, and subfolders where a file is stored, along with the file's name, such as `C:\Program Files\AutoCAD2010\Training Data\Cabin8a.dwg`.

Perspective view

A pictorial view of a 3D object in which parallel lines that aren't parallel to the plane of the screen appear to converge as they move farther from the viewer, similar to the way objects appear in the real world (such as railroad tracks in the distance). See also *Isometric view*.

pickbox

A form of the *cursor* as a small square that occurs when AutoCAD is in *selection mode*.

pick button

The button on the mouse (usually the left one) that is used to pick points, buttons, or menu items, and select objects in the drawing area.

Plan

The command used to display the *Plan view* per the current *UCS*.

Plan view

A view of a drawing in which the viewer is looking straight at the *XY plane* in a direction parallel to the z-axis.

plot style

A group of settings assigned to a layer, a color, or an object. These settings determine how that layer, color, or object is printed.

plot style table

A set of plot styles that controls the way in which a layout or drawing is printed.

point filters

A set of tools that allow you to specify a point in the drawing by using some of the x-, y-, and z-coordinates from another point or points to generate the coordinates for the point you're specifying.

polar coordinates

Values for locating a point in space that describe the location relative to the last point picked as defined by an angle and a distance.

Polar Tracking

A tool for temporarily aligning the *cursor* movement to preset angles while drawing.

polyline

A special type of line that (a) treats multiple segments as one object, (b) can include arcs, (c) can be smoothed into a curved line, and (d) can have width in 2D applications.

polysolid

A 3D object, drawn as a series of interconnected panels.

precision of units

The degree of accuracy in which linear and angular units are displayed in dialog boxes, at the *command line*, or in dimensions.

prompt

The text at the command line that asks questions or tells you what action is necessary to continue the execution of a command. The `Command:` *prompt* tells you that no command is currently running.

purge

The practice of removing unwanted and unused objects from a drawing, usually by using the Purge dialog box.

publish

The procedure and command used to plot more than one drawing or drawing layout at a time.

R

Redraw

A command to refresh the *drawing area* or a particular *viewport*, thereby ridding it of any graphic distortions that show up on the monitor while you're drawing.

regeneration

A process in which the geometry for the objects in the current drawing file is recalculated.

registration points

In traditional board drafting, marks used to align transparent sheets with the base drawing below.

regular selection window

A selection tool that selects an area defined by two points acting as opposite corners of a rectangle. All objects completely within the rectangle are selected. See also *crossing window*.

relative coordinates

Values for locating a point in space that describe its displacement from the last point picked in the drawing rather than from the *origin*.

rendering

The practice of calculating the surfaces, lights, materials, and environment used to create an image file. The command to do so is called Render.

rise

The vertical distance from one step tread to the next.

Ribbon

The user interface element at the top of the drawing area where most of the AutoCAD 2010 tools can be found. The Ribbon is subdivided into tabs and panels.

rubberbanding

The effect of a line extending between the last point picked and the *crosshair cursor*, stretching like a rubber band as the cursor is moved.

run

The distance from the front of a step tread to the back.

Running Object Snap

An *Object Snap mode* that has been set to be activated continually until turned off.

S

scale factor

The number that expresses the *true ratio* of a scale. For example, 48 is the scale factor for quarter-inch scale ($\frac{1}{4}'' = 1'-0''$).

selection cycling

A procedure for selecting a particular object when it coincides with one or more other objects. To cycle, hold down the Shift key and the spacebar and then click the object until the particular object you want becomes dashed. When that happens, release the Shift key and spacebar and press .

selection mode

The phase of a command that requires the user to select objects, and thereby build up a *selection set* of objects to be modified by or otherwise used in the function of the command.

selection set

Any object or group of objects that have been selected for modification or have been selected to be used in a modification process.

selection window

A tool for selecting objects whereby the user creates a rectangular window in the *drawing area*. Objects are selected in two ways, depending on whether the selection window is a *crossing window* or a *regular window*.

single-line text

A type of text *object* in AutoCAD in which each line of text is treated as a single object with its own *justification point*, whether it be a sentence, word, or letter.

Snapbase

A command (and setting) used to reset the origin of a *hatch pattern*. By default, Snapbase is set to 0,0,0.

Snap mode

An on/off setting that locks the *cursor* onto a spatial grid, which is usually aligned with the *grid*, allowing you to draw to distances that are multiples of the grid spacing. When the grid spacing is set to 0, the grid aligns with the snap spacing.

soffit

The underside of the roof overhang that extends from the outside edge of the roof, back to the wall.

solid

1. The name of a hatch pattern that fills a defined boundary with a solid color. 2. A three-dimensional object in AutoCAD that has properties similar to those of a solid block of material, such as mass, center of gravity, density, and so on.

stud

A vertical piece of lumber or metal used in framing walls. It's usually 2″×4″ or 2″×6″ in cross dimension and extends the height of the wall.

Surveyor's units

An angular unit of direction in which the value is the angle that the direction deviates away (or *bears*) from true north or south, toward the east or west.

T

table

A matrix of information arranged like a spreadsheet, usually included in construction or mechanical drawings that contains data presented in rows and columns separated by lines.

template drawing

A drawing that has been set up to serve as a format for a new drawing. This allows the user to begin a new drawing with certain parameters already set up, because various settings have been predetermined.

temporary tracking points

The temporary points that are set up for use in *Object Snap Tracking*.

text style

A collection of settings that controls the appearance of text and is saved in a drawing under a specified name. Text placed in the drawing will follow the settings of the current text style.

thaw

The option of the layer property called Freeze/Thaw that turns on the visibility of objects on layers and allows AutoCAD to consider the geometry of these objects during a selection or *regeneration*. See also *layer*.

thickness

The property of a 2D object that defines how far it is extruded in a direction perpendicular to the plane in which it was originally drawn. This is not a true 3D object, just a 2D object that is projecting into the z-axis. See also *extrusion*.

tiling

The repeating of an image map over the surface of an object.

toolbar locking

A feature whereby a toolbar can be semi-permanently fixed in a position on the screen and can't be accidentally moved.

tracking

See *Object Snap Tracking*.

transparent command

A command that can be executed while another command is running, without interfering with the running command. Display commands, such as *Zoom* and *Pan*, are transparent.

true ratio

An expression of two numbers that defines the actual size differentiation in a scale; that is, the number of units represented by a single unit. See also *scale factor*.

U

UCS

See *User Coordinate System*.

UCS icon

The double-arrow icon in the lower-left corner of the *drawing area* that indicates the positive directions of the x- and y-axes for the current *User Coordinate System*. In 3D views, the z-axis is also represented in the icon.

User Coordinate System (UCS)

A definition for the orientation of the x-, y-, and z-axes in space relative to 3D objects in the drawing or to the *World Coordinate System*. UCSs can be named, saved, and restored.

V

view

A picture of the current drawing from a particular user-defined perspective that is displayed on the screen or in a *viewport*. Views can be named, saved, and restored.

ViewCube

A navigation device used to switch between standard, isometric, and freeform views in a 3D environment.

viewport

An opening, usually rectangular but not always, through which the user can view a drawing or a portion of it. There are two kinds of viewports: tiled viewports (used in *model space*) and *floating viewports* (used in layouts). See also *layout*.

visual style

Any of five variations of settings that control the appearance of 3D objects to a viewer: 2D Wireframe, 3D Hidden, 3D Wireframe, Conceptual, or Realistic. Found on the View panel of the *Ribbon* when using the 3D Modeling workspace.

W

wireframe

A view of a 3D object that uses lines to represent the intersections of planes. The planes defined by these lines represent surfaces of building components, machine parts, and so on.

workspace

A customizable arrangement of dockable palettes, menus, and toolbars for the graphics window that can be named, saved, and made current by using the Tools ➢ Workspaces menu.

World Coordinate System

The default *User Coordinate System* for all new drawing files, in which the positive directions for the x- and y-axes are to the right and upward respectively, and the positive direction for the z-axis is toward the user and perpendicular to the plane of the screen.

WYSIWYG

An acronym for "what you see is what you get." It's a description applied to preview features that show you exactly what a screen will look like when printed.

X

xref

See *external reference*.

XY plane

The 2D flat surface, defined by the x- and y-axes, which is parallel to the monitor screen in a new AutoCAD drawing file.

Z

Zoom

The name of a command with several options, all of which allow the user to increase or decrease the magnification of the *view* of the current drawing in the *drawing area* or in a *viewport*.

INDEX

Note to Reader: **Bolded** page numbers refer to definitions and main discussion of a topic. *Italicized* page numbers refer to illustrations.